AFRO-AMERICAN HISTORY

AFRO-AMERICAN HISTORY PAST TO PRESENT

Edited by Henry N. Drewry
and Cecelia H. Drewry
Princeton University

Charles Scribner's Sons
New York

To
Leonard and Bessie

George and Olive
Our parents

Table of Contents

Introduction   xi

Part 1 · **African Background**

Travels in Asia and Africa—*Ibn Battuta*   5
My Early Life in Eboe—*Olaudah Equiano*   7
The African Past—*Lerone Bennett, Jr.*   12
Lost Cities of Africa—*Basil Davidson*   20

Part 2 · **Slavery**

To Make Them Stand in Fear—*Kenneth Stampp*   27
Slavery and Personality—*Stanley Elkins*   36
Slavery and Racism—*Henry N. Drewry*   42
Abolition's New Breed—*Benjamin Quarles*   50

Part 3 · **The Civil War and Reconstruction**

Slave Conduct During the War—*Bell Irvin Wiley*   63
Negro Soldiers in the Union Army—*James M. McPherson*   72
The Propaganda of History—*William E. B. Du Bois*   85
Reconstruction—Black and White—*John Hope Franklin*   100

Part 4 · In Search of Direction

POLITICS:

The Negro Problem Always Ye Have With You—
  Paul H. Buck   119
Southern Suffrage Restrictions—*V. O. Key*   128
Tom Watson—*C. Vann Woodward*   136
Progressivism—For Whites Only—*C. Vann Woodward*   145
Instruments of Wrong—*Loren Miller*   152

EDUCATION:

The Uses of Adversity—*Louis Harlan*   162
Teaching School in a Stable and a Hen-House—
  Booker T. Washington   178
What Is the Matter With the Atlanta Schools?   184

LEADERSHIP:

The Atlanta Exposition Address—*Booker T. Washington*   187
The Beginnings of Organized Negro Protest, 1901–1916—
  Constance McLaughlin Green   196
Of Mr. Booker T. Washington and Others—
  William E. B. Du Bois   213
Accommodating Leadership—*Gunnar Myrdal*   222

THE MOVE TO THE CITIES:

Black Metropolis—*St. Clair Drake and Horace R. Cayton*   237
Organized Labor and the Negro—*Charles H. Wesley*   253
Negro City Life—*George G. Bradford, Rosa Morehead
  Bass, W. B. Matthews*   268
Alienation: New York and the Negro—*Gilbert Osofsky*   275

Part 5 · World War I and After

Black Manhattan—*James Weldon Johnson*   297
The Participation of Negroes in World War I—
  Emmett J. Scott   308
Documents of the War—*William E. B. Du Bois*   318
Back to Africa—*Harold R. Isaacs*   326
Du Bois versus Garvey: Race Propagandists at War—
  Elliott Rudwick   337

THE HARLEM RENAISSANCE:

Infants of the Spring—*Wallace Thurman* 347
Harlem: The Culture Capital—*James Weldon Johnson* 358
The City—*LeRoi Jones* 365
American Negro Art—*Cedric Dover* 379

Part 6 · Prelude to Protest

The Negro and the Republican Party, 1932–1940—
   Elbert Lee Tatum 389
The Roosevelt Coalition—*Arthur M. Schlesinger, Jr.* 395
The Negro on Relief—*Richard Sterner* 407
The NAACP and the Communist Party—*Wilson Record* 410
Negro Labor and the Government—*Robert C. Weaver* 428
A Man Called White—*Walter White* 439
The Negro GI in Korea—*Thurgood Marshall* 455
The Bid for Desegregation—*Henry A. Bullock* 461

Part 7 · Protest

Lawlessness and Violence in America—*Allen D. Grimshaw* 475
Civil Disorders—*The National Advisory Commission* 479
Letter from Birmingham Jail—*Martin Luther King, Jr.* 493
The Fire Next Time—*James Baldwin* 505
Mission Accomplished—*Ben Caldwell* 513
A Black at the Gridiron Dinner—*Roger Wilkins* 516
Black Power and Black History—*John Henrik Clarke* 520
Black Muslims—*Malcolm X* 529
Domestic Law and International Order—*Eldridge Cleaver* 540

Introduction

Collections of essays, documents, and readings in Afro-American history are appearing almost daily. They deal with a wide range of topics and time periods including among them slavery, black protest thought, the twentieth century, and black views of America. For the person with considerable background or for those who wish to dwell on some one aspect of the Afro-American experience, these can be of real assistance. They do not, however, serve the needs of a number of students and general readers who approach the subject of Afro-American history without the background of knowledge which they do have for dealing with topics related to the political history of the United States. Our experiences suggest that those who are without this framework might be well served by having access to a brief collection of readings covering the history of Americans of African descent. This book is the result of our efforts to provide such a collection. The attempt here is to serve the needs of the reader in several ways: (1) to trace the history from the period of slavery to the present with attention called to the African background of black Americans; (2) to nudge and motivate the reader toward further exploration and study in the sources from which the readings are taken and in other sources; (3) to raise enough questions for general discussion that this further study will result in expanded insight and, perhaps, knowledgeable action based on that insight; (4) to introduce readers to a range of authors and approaches which individually provide important ideas and information and which collectively suggest certain clear patterns with regard to the black experience in the United States; (5) to demonstrate the importance of materials from several disciplines in the study of Afro-American history.

In putting together this collection we have drawn upon the fields of history, sociology, economics, literature, and drama. The major emphasis is on historical works, however, and all materials were selected so as to focus on a general understanding of the topic. Both primary and secondary sources are used. Primary materials include all the selections in the last chapter, the writings of Equiano, Battuta, and several others. Although some errors in grammar and spelling have been corrected throughout, we have attempted to keep the excerpts as consistent as possible with the sources. When passages have been omitted, we have still retained the original footnote numbering as an aid to those who wish to read further in the various works. A review of the readings chosen for use shows the secondary sources to be about evenly divided between black and white authors. Overall, two-thirds of the writers included are black. Whatever nuances occur because of this fact are evident.

These selections are intended to fit together to cover the sweep of Afro-American history. Efforts were made to select excerpts which complement each other. For example, Johnson's *Black Manhattan* reviews the temper and the "flavor" of Harlem in the twenties; when it is coupled with the research of *Black Metropolis* by Drake and Cayton, however, these companion pieces make important though sardonic comments on the lives of black people in American cities. It goes without saying that additional selections would result in an improved product. The problem of what to include and what to omit, while maintaining balance between various sections, is ever present in collections of readings. This one is no exception. In making the kind of decisions demanded by space and balance we have sometimes omitted traditional points of view either because they are so widely published and well known as to have little claim on the limited space of a one-volume collection or because they are more useful as sources on white racial attitudes or historiography, topics that are too specialized for this work.

As to how one might use this collection, our recommendation is simple. Plunge in! Each of the seven sections is sufficiently self-contained for the reader to begin at any point. Of course, moving chronologically from "African Background" to "Protest" insures the most complete picture of the editors' approach and may be the wisest course for those with slim knowledge of the field. For others who wish to investigate a certain period or topic, the readings offer a number of possibilities. The introduction to each section serves to comment on the selections therein and to bridge the informational gap between the readings. It might be refreshing to read the excerpts *before* the introductions, thereby setting the stage for preliminary discussion of each, unencumbered by the editors' comments.

The titles of the first three sections are self-explanatory. Section one aims to emphasize the importance of a look at the African background of black Americans and to suggest that the failure of many American historians to deal realistically with the cultural background of Africa was not due entirely to lack of material. The second section is concerned with the nature of the slave institution which developed in the "democratic," Christian United States. No attempt is made to provide descriptions of the plantation system, the daily life of the slave, or the political debate which arose over slavery. The third section presents information on the active part played by Afro-Americans during the Civil War and the Reconstruction period. In doing so it introduces a theme characteristic of the sections which follow, that being the active role of blacks in seeking to chart their future in American society. In section four the readings concern the efforts of blacks to seek upward mobility through the traditional American methods: politics, education, leadership, and the opportunities for advancement in the growing urban areas. When the realities of life demonstrated that faith and hope in such approaches were misplaced, and with the impetus given by events of the period of World War I through World War II, blacks turned to yet another traditional American approach as old as the nation itself and used by a wide variety of groups, that of organized protests. Sections five and six focus on those aspects of the period of the wars which set the stage for protest, the subject of section seven.

The student of history searches the past for the long view that helps to illuminate the present. His concern is with rigorous exploration of all the material available for an understanding of the topic under consideration, in this case, the phenomenon of the brutalizing, dehumanizing effects of slavery and discrimination on blacks and their efforts to make a life for themselves within the American system. This premise undergirds our work. For the student of black history, however, two other directives are imperative. The material has been so poorly covered in general histories of the United States that efforts must be made to view it in relation to concurrent events and movements. This is a responsibility of the reader of these selections. Then, and most important, because of the critical and continuing battering of black people in America, the student of black history must urge more than any other academic activist that new insights be utilized to gain justice in a hitherto unjust society.

Cecelia H. Drewry
Henry N. Drewry

AFRO-AMERICAN HISTORY

Part 1

⊕

AFRICAN BACKGROUND

No work concerning the history of Afro-Americans should begin without a look at the geographic areas from which the ancestors of American blacks came. Traditional approaches to United States history have included such introductory topics as "Europe Before the Age of Discovery," and "European Background of Americans." Africa is first mentioned as the coast along which the Portuguese seamen sailed in search of a route to the east, and it is next mentioned as the source of black servants sold to English colonists at Jamestown by the master of a Dutch ship in the year 1619. The absence of any mention of the background of the Africans who appeared in North America contributed to the myth which has long dominated American thinking about Africa and the black men from that land. This myth holds that Africans came from a land whose history offered nothing worthy of study and thus they were less deserving of humane treatment and scholarly study than those persons coming to the New World from Europe. This omission and misrepresentation has influenced the way blacks in the United States have viewed themselves and the way they have been viewed by whites. From this myth developed the traditional view of Africa as uncivilized, a land of jungle and savages. Nothing was to be found in this background of which blacks could be proud or which blacks or whites should or could respect. One of the best expressions of this view of Africans is found in the writing of the historian Ulrich B. Phillips. In *Life and Labor in the Old South,* published in 1929, he wrote of persons brought from Africa to North America, "They were heathens who by transportation to some Christian land might attain eternal bliss at the mere price of lifetime labor." Phillips' approach dominated American historical opinion during much of the first half of the twentieth century.

While much of the history of Africa is yet to be known, recent discoveries have caused us to take a new look at that land. In addition, much more information was available than found its way into the traditional accounts. The readings in this section include some which have long been available as well as the reflections of a black American writer and an Africanist. H. A. R. Gibb's translation of Ibn Battuta's *Travels in Asia and Africa,* 1929, draws together writings of that fourteenth-century Arab traveler in West Africa. Battuta pictures well-organized political and social systems, and his descriptions differ markedly from the myth which dominated American thinking centuries later. Similarly, Olaudah Equiano's description of his homeland in the early 19th century given in *Equiano's Travels* edited by Paul Williams, bears little resemblance to what Americans believed at the time.

Writers Lerone Bennett and Basil Davidson suggest what new discoveries and reconsideration of the old evidence tell us of Africa before and during the active period of slave trading. The selections here are from *Before the Mayflower; A History of the Negro in America,* Bennett, and *The Lost Cities of Africa,* Davidson.

Travels in Asia and Africa*

Ibn Battuta

I was at Mállí during the two festivals of the sacrifice and the fast-breaking. On these days the sultan takes his seat on the *pempi* after the midafternoon prayer. The armour-bearers bring in magnificent arms—quivers of gold and silver, swords ornamented with gold and with golden scabbards, gold and silver lances, and crystal maces. At his head stand four amírs driving off the flies, having in their hands silver ornaments resembling saddle-stirrups. The commanders, qádí, and preacher sit in their usual places. The interpreter Dúghá comes with his four wives and his slave-girls, who are about a hundred in number. They are wearing beautiful robes, and on their heads they have gold and silver fillets, with gold and silver balls attached. A chair is placed for Dúghá to sit on. He plays on an instrument made of reeds, with some small calabashes at its lower end, and chants a poem in praise of the sultan, recalling his battles and deeds of valour. The women and girls sing along with him and play with bows. Accompanying them are about thirty youths, wearing red woollen tunics and white skull-caps; each of them has his drum slung from his shoulder and beats it. Afterwards come his boy pupils who play and turn wheels in the air, like the natives of Sind. They show a marvellous nimbleness and agility in these exercises and play most cleverly with swords. Dúghá also makes a fine play with the sword. Thereupon the sultan orders a gift to be presented to Dúghá and he is given a purse containing two hundred *mithqáls* of gold dust, and is informed of the contents of the purse before all the people. The commanders rise and twang their bows in thanks to the sultan. The next day each one of them gives Dúghá a gift, every man according to his rank. Every Friday after the *'asr* prayer, Dúghá carries out a similar ceremony to this that we have described.

On feast-days, after Dúghá has finished his display, the poets come in. Each of them is inside a figure resembling a thrush, made of feathers, and provided with a

* From Ibn Battuta, *Travels in Asia and Africa, 1325–1354*, trans. H. A. R. Gibb (New York: Robert M. McBride & Company, 1929), pp. 328–30. Reprinted by permission of A. M. Kelly, Publishers.

wooden head with a red beak, to look like a thrush's head. They stand in front of the sultan in this ridiculous make-up and recite their poems. I was told that their poetry is a kind of sermonizing in which they say to the sultan: "This *pempi* which you occupy was that whereon sat this king and that king, and such and such were this one's noble actions and such and such the other's. So do you too do good deeds whose memory will outlive you." After that, the chief of the poets mounts the steps of the *pempi* and lays his head on the sultan's lap, then climbs to the top of the *pempi* and lays his head first on the sultan's right shoulder and then on his left, speaking all the while in their tongue, and finally he comes down again. I was told that this practice is a very old custom amongst them, prior to the introduction of Islám, and that they have kept it up.[26]

The negroes disliked Mansá Sulaymán because of his avarice. His predecessor was Mansá Maghá, and before him reigned Mansá Músá, a generous and virtuous prince, who loved the whites and made gifts to them. It was he who gave Abú Isháq as-Sáhilí four thousand *mithqáls* in the course of a single day. I heard from a trustworthy source that he gave three thousand *mithqáls* on one day to Mudrik ibn Faqqús, by whose grandfather his own grandfather, Sáraq Játa, had been converted to Islám.

The negroes possess some admirable qualities. They are seldom unjust, and have a greater abhorrence of injustice than any other people. Their sultan shows no mercy to anyone who is guilty of the least act of it. There is complete security in their country. Neither traveller nor inhabitant in it has anything to fear from robbers or men of violence. They do not confiscate the property of any white man who dies in their country, even if it be uncounted wealth. On the contrary, they give it into the charge of some trustworthy person among the whites, until the rightful heir takes possession of it. They are careful to observe the hours of prayer, and assiduous in attending them in congregations, and in bringing up their children to them. On Fridays, if a man does not go early to the mosque, he cannot find a corner to pray in, on account of the crowd. It is a custom of theirs to send each man his boy [to the mosque] with his prayer-mat; the boy spreads it out for his master in a place befitting him [and remains on it] until he comes to the mosque. Their prayer-mats are made of the leaves of a tree resembling a date-palm, but without fruit.

Another of their good qualities is their habit of wearing clean white garments on Fridays. Even if a man has nothing but an old worn shirt, he washes it and cleans it, and wears it to the Friday service. Yet another is their zeal for learning the Koran by heart. . . .

---

[26] Delafosse remarks that this custom, like almost all those described by Ibn Battuta, has been retained down to the present day in most of the countries of the Sudan.

My Early Life in Eboe[*]

Olaudah Equiano

That part of Africa known by the name of Guinea to which the trade for slaves is carried on extends along the coast above 3,400 miles, from the Senegal to Angola, and includes a variety of kingdoms. Of these the most considerable is the kingdom of Benin, both as to extent and wealth, the richness and cultivation of the soil, the power of its king, and the number and warlike disposition of the inhabitants. It is situated nearly under the line and extends along the coast about 170 miles, but runs back into the interior part of Africa to a distance hitherto I believe unexplored by any traveller, and seems only terminated at length by the empire of Abyssinia, near 1,500 miles from its beginning. This kingdom is divided into many provinces or districts, in one of the most remote and fertile of which, called Eboe, I was born in the year 1745, situated in a charming fruitful vale, named Essaka. The distance of this province from the capital of Benin and the sea coast must be very considerable, for I had never heard of white men or Europeans, nor of the sea, and our subjection to the king of Benin was little more than nominal; for every transaction of the government, as far as my slender observation extended, was conducted by the chiefs or elders of the place. The manners and government of a people who have little commerce with other countries are generally very simple, and the history of what passes in one family or village may serve as a specimen of a nation. My father was one of those elders or chiefs I have spoken of and was styled Embrenché, a term as I remember importing the highest distinction, and signifying in our language a *mark* of grandeur. This mark is conferred on the person entitled to it by cutting the skin across at the top of the forehead and drawing it down to the eyebrows, and while it is in this situation applying a warm hand and rubbing it until it shrinks up into a thick *weal* across the lower part of the forehead. Most of the judges and senators were thus marked; my father had long borne it. I had seen it conferred on one of my brothers, and I was also *destined* to receive it by my parents. . . .

* From Paul Edwards, ed., *Equiano's Travels* (New York: Frederick A. Praeger, Inc., 1967), pp. 1–2, 3–9. Reprinted by permission.

•   •   •

We are almost a nation of dancers, musicians, and poets. Thus every great event such as a triumphant return from battle or other cause of public rejoicing is celebrated in public dances, which are accompanied with songs and music suited to the occasion. The assembly is separated into four divisions, which dance either apart or in succession, and each with a character peculiar to itself. The first division contains the married men, who in their dances frequently exhibit feats of arms and the representation of a battle. To these succeed the married women, who dance in the second division. The young men occupy the third and the maidens the fourth. Each represents some interesting scene of real life, such as a great achievement, domestic employment, a pathetic story, or some rural sport, and as the subject is generally founded on some recent event it is therefore ever new. This gives our dances a spirit and variety which I have scarcely seen elsewhere. We have many musical instruments, particularly drums of different kinds, a piece of music which resembles a guitar, and another much like a stickado. These last are chiefly used by betrothed virgins who play on them on all grand festivals.

As our manners are simple, our luxuries are few. The dress of both sexes is nearly the same. It generally consists of a long piece of calico or muslin, wrapped loosely round the body somewhat in the form of a highland plaid. This is usually dyed blue, which is our favourite colour. It is extracted from a berry and is brighter and richer than any I have seen in Europe. Besides this our women of distinction wear golden ornaments, which they dispose with some profusion on their arms and legs. When our women are not employed with the men in tillage, their usual occupation is spinning and weaving cotton, which they afterwards dye and make into garments. They also manufacture earthen vessels, of which we have many kinds. Among the rest tobacco pipes, made after the same fashion and used in the same manner, as those in Turkey.

Our manner of living is entirely plain, for as yet the natives are unacquainted with those refinements in cookery which debauch the taste: bullocks, goats, and poultry, supply the greatest part of their food. These constitute likewise the principal wealth of the country and the chief articles of its commerce. The flesh is usually stewed in a pan; to make it savoury we sometimes use also pepper and other spices, and we have salt made of wood ashes. Our vegetables are mostly plantains, eadas, yams, beans, and Indian corn. The head of the family usually eats alone; his wives and slaves have also their separate tables. Before we taste food we always wash our hands: indeed our cleanliness on all occasions is extreme, but on this it is an indispensable ceremony. After washing, libation is made by pouring out a small portion of the drink on the floor, and tossing a small quantity of the food in a certain place for the spirits of departed relations, which the natives suppose to preside over their conduct and guard them from evil. They are totally unacquainted with strong or spirituous liquors, and their principal beverage is palm wine. This is got from a tree of that name by tapping it at the top and fastening a large gourd to it, and sometimes one tree will yield three or four gallons in a night. When just drawn it is of a most delicious sweetness, but in a few days it acquires a tartish and more spirituous flavour, though I never saw anyone intoxicated by it. The same tree also produces nuts and oil. Our principal luxury is in perfumes; one sort of these is an odoriferous wood of delicious fragrance, the other a kind of earth, a small portion of which thrown into the fire diffuses a more powerful odour. We beat this wood into powder and mix it with palm oil, with which both men and women perfume themselves.

In our buildings we study convenience rather than ornament. Each master of a family has a large square piece of ground, surrounded with a moat or fence or enclosed with a wall made of red earth tempered, which when dry is as hard as brick. Within this are his houses to accommodate his family and slaves which if numerous frequently present the appearance of a village. In the middle stands the principal building, appropriated to the sole use of the master and consisting of two apartments, in one of which he sits in the day with his family. The other is left apart for the reception of his friends. He has besides these a distinct apartment in which he sleeps, together with his male children. On each side are the apartments of his wives, who have also their separate day and night houses. The habitations of the slaves and their families are distributed throughout the rest of the enclosure. These houses never exceed one story in height: they are always built of wood or stakes driven into the ground, crossed with wattles, and neatly plastered within and without. The roof is thatched with reeds. Our day-houses are left open at the sides, but those in which we sleep are always covered, and plastered in the inside with a composition mixed with cow-dung to keep off the different insects which annoy us during the night. The walls and floors also of these are generally covered with mats. Our beds consist of a platform raised three or four feet from the ground, on which are laid skins and different parts of a spungy tree called plantain. Our covering is calico or muslin, the same as our dress. The usual seats are a few logs of wood, but we have benches, which are generally perfumed to accommodate strangers: these compose the greater part of our household furniture. Houses so constructed and furnished require but little skill to erect them. Every man is a sufficient architect for the purpose. The whole neighborhood afford their unanimous assistance in building them and in return receive and expect no other recompense than a feast.

As we live in a country where nature is prodigal of her favours, our wants are few and easily supplied; of course we have few manufactures. They consist for the most part of calicoes, earthenware, ornaments, and instruments of war and husbandry. But these make no part of our commerce, the principal articles of which, as I have observed, are provisions. In such a state money is of little use; however we have some small pieces of coin, if I may call them such. They are made something like an anchor, but I do not remember either their value or denomination. We have also markets, at which I have been frequently with my mother. These are sometimes visited by stout mahogany-coloured men from the south-west of us: we call them *Oye-Eboe,* which term signifies red men living at a distance. They generally bring us fire-arms, gunpowder, hats, beads, and dried fish. The last we esteemed a great rarity as our waters were only brooks and springs. These articles they barter with us for odoriferous woods and earth, and our salt of wood ashes. They always carry slaves through our land, but the strictest account is exacted of their manner of procuring them before they are suffered to pass. Some times indeed we sold slaves to them, but they were only prisoners of war, or such among us as had been convicted of kidnapping, or adultery, and some other crimes which we esteemed heinous. This practice of kidnapping induces me to think that, notwithstanding all our strictness, their principal business among us was to trepan our people. I remember too they carried great sacks along with them, which not long after I had an opportunity of fatally seeing applied to that infamous purpose.

Our land is uncommonly rich and fruitful, and produces all kinds of vegetables in great abundance. We have plenty of Indian corn, and vast quantities of cotton and tobacco. Our pineapples grow without culture; they are about the size of the largest sugar-loaf and finely flavoured. We have also spices of different kinds, particularly pepper, and a variety of delicious fruits which I have never seen in Europe, together with gums of various kinds and honey in abundance. All our industry is exerted to improve those blessings of nature. Agriculture is our chief employment, and everyone, even the children and women, are engaged in it. Thus we are all habituated to labour from our earliest years. Everyone contributes something to the common stock, and as we are unacquainted with idleness we have no beggars. The benefits of such a mode of living are obvious. The West India planters prefer the slaves of Benin or Eboe to those of any other part of Guinea for their hardiness, intelligence, integrity, and zeal. Those benefits are felt by us in the general healthiness of the people, and in their vigour and activity; I might have added too in their comeliness. Deformity is indeed unknown amongst us, I mean that of shape. Numbers of the natives of Eboe now in London might be brought in support of this assertion, for in regard to complexion, ideas of beauty are wholly relative. I remember while in Africa to have seen three negro children who were tawny, and another quite white, who were universally regarded by myself and the natives in general, as far as related to their complexions, as deformed. Our women too were in my eyes at least uncommonly graceful, alert, and modest to a degree of bashfulness; nor do I remember to have ever heard of an instance of incontinence amongst them before marriage. They are also remarkably cheerful. Indeed cheerfulness and affability are two of the leading characteristics of our nation.

Our tillage is exercised in a large plain or common, some hours walk from our dwellings, and all the neighbours resort thither in a body. They use no beasts of husbandry, and their only instruments are hoes, axes, shovels, and beaks, or pointed iron to dig with. Sometimes we are visited by locusts, which come in large clouds so as to darken the air and destroy our harvest. This however happens rarely, but when it does a famine is produced by it. I remember an instance or two wherein this happened. This common is often the theatre of war, and therefore when our people go out to till their land they not only go in a body but generally take their arms with them for fear of a surprise, and when they apprehend an invasion they guard the avenues to their dwellings by driving sticks into the ground, which are so sharp at one end as to pierce the foot and are generally dipped in poison. From what I can recollect of these battles, they appear to have been irruptions of one little state or district on the other to obtain prisoners or booty. Perhaps they were incited to this by those traders who brought the European goods I mentioned amongst us. Such a mode of obtaining slaves in Africa is common, and I believe more are procured this way and by kidnapping than any other. When a trader wants slaves he applies to a chief for them and tempts him with his wares. It is not extraordinary if on this occasion he yields to the temptation with as little firmness, and accepts the price of his fellow creatures liberty with as little reluctance as the enlightened merchant. Accordingly he falls on his neighbours and a desperate battle ensues. If he prevails and takes prisoners, he gratifies his avarice by selling them; but if his party be vanquished and he falls into the hands of the enemy, he is put to death: for as he has been known to foment their quarrels it is thought dangerous to let him survive, and no ransom can save him, though all other prisoners may be redeemed. . . .

The African Past*

Lerone Bennett, Jr.

A series of revolutionary discoveries has spurred a radical re-evaluation of the strong bronzed men and regal black women from whose loins sprang one out of every ten Americans.

This re-evaluation has yielded a new perspective on African and human history. Africa, long considered the Dark Continent, is now regarded as the place where man first received light. Ancient Africans, long considered primitive and ignorant, are now revealed as creative contributors to Egyptian civilization and builders of powerful states in the Sudan.

From Olduvai Gorge in East Africa, from caves in the Sahara and excavations in the Nile Valley have come bits of bone and husks of grain which speak more eloquently than words of the trials and triumphs of the African ancestors of the American Negro. Consider the following items:

Olduvai Gorge: A series of startling discoveries in this area suggests that the most important and fascinating developments in human history took place in the Dark Continent. Discoveries by Dr. L. S. B. Leakey and other scholars indicate that man was born in Africa, that he began to use tools there and that this seminal invention spread to Europe and Asia.

The Nile Valley: Important finds in the Sudan and Nile Valley prove that peoples of a Negro type were influential contributors to that cradle of civilization—Egypt. Discoveries at excavations near Khartoum in the Sudan and at El Badari on the Nile indicate that Stone Age Negroes laid the foundation for much of the civilization of the Nile Valley and manufactured pottery before pottery was made in the world's earliest known city.

The Congo: Archeologists unearth remains of Ishongo people who lived some 8,000 years ago and used a primitive abacus or multiplication table, possibly the oldest in the world.

* From Lerone Bennett, Jr., *Before the Mayflower: A History of Black America* (Chicago: Johnson Publishing Co., Inc., 1962), pp. 3–7, 12–17, 24–28. Copyright 1961, 1969 by Johnson Publishing Company, Inc., Chicago. Reprinted by permission.

The Sahara: Henri Lhote, French explorer, discovers rock paintings which suggest to Author Basil Davidson that "peoples of a Negro type were painting men and women with a beautiful and sensitive realism before 3,000 B.C. and were, perhaps, the originators of naturalistic human portraiture."

"Later discoveries," W. M. Whitelaw writes, "all the way from Kenya to Transvaal not only of early human remains but also of advanced anthropoid types have brought the historical anthropologists to a state of confused expectancy. Considerably more evidence will have to be brought to light, however, before even the main outlines of man's early history in Africa can be drawn. It is already reasonable, however, to believe that such evidence may be forthcoming as will require a radical change of perspective on African history, if not on history itself."

When the human drama opened, Africans were on the scene and acting. For a long time, in fact, the only people on the scene were Africans. For some 600,000 years, Africa and Africans led the world. Were these people who gave the world fire and tools and cultivated grain—were they Negroes? The ancient bones are silent. It is possible, indeed, probable that they were dark-skinned. More than that cannot be said at this time.

Civilization started in the great river valleys of Africa and Asia, in the Fertile Crescent in the Near East and along the narrow ribbon of the Nile in Africa. In the Nile Valley, that beginning was an African as well as an Asian achievement. Negroes, or people who would be considered Negroes today, were among the first people to use tools, paint pictures, plant seeds and worship gods.

Back there, in the beginning, blackness was not an occasion for obloquy. In fact, the reverse seems to have been true. White men were sometimes ridiculed for the "unnatural whiteness of their skin."

Black people were known and honored throughout the ancient world. Ancient Ethiopia, a vaguely defined territory somewhere to the south of Egypt, was hailed as a place fit for the vacation of the gods. Homer praised Memnon, king of Ethiopia, and black Eurybates:

> *Of visage solemn, sad, but sable hue,*
> *Short, wooly curls, o'erfleeced his bending head, . . .*
> *Eurybates, in whose large soul alone,*
> *Ulysses viewed an image of his own.*

Homer, Herodotus, Pliny, Diodorus, and other classical writers repeatedly praised the Ethiopians. "The annals of all the great early nations of Asia Minor are full of them," Lady Flora Louisa Lugard writes. "The Mosaic records allude to them frequently; but while they are described as the most powerful, the most just, and the most beautiful of the human race, they are constantly spoken of as black, and there seems to be no other conclusion to be drawn, than that at that remote period of history the leading race of the Western World was a black race."

The Ethiopians claimed to be the spiritual fathers of Egyptian civilization. Diodorus Siculus, the Greek historian who wrote in the first century B.C., said: "The Ethiopians conceived themselves to be of greater antiquity than any other nation; and it is probable that, born under the sun's path, its warmth may have ripened them earlier than other men. They supposed themselves to be the inventors of worship, of festivals, of solemn assemblies, of sacrifices, and every religious practice."

However that may be, it is well established that black people *from somewhere* were an important element among the peoples who fathered Egyptian civilization. Badarian culture proves that black men camped on the banks of the Nile thousands of years before the Egypt of the Pharaohs. Bodies were excavated at El Badari amid artifacts suggesting a date of about 8,000 B.C. In the intestines of these bodies were husks of barley which indicated that the Badarians, a people of a Negro type, had learned how to cultivate cereals. The beautifully fashioned pottery the Badarians made was never surpassed, not even in Egypt's days of greatest glory.

A study of skulls provides additional evidence. Scholars who examined some 800 skulls of the predynastic Egyptians found that at least one-third of them were definitely Negroid.

"The more we learn of Nubia and the Sudan," Dr. David Randall-MacIver said, "the more evident does it appear that what was most characteristic in the predynastic culture of Egypt is due to intercourse with the interior of Africa and the immediate influence of that permanent Negro element which has been present in the population of Southern Egypt from the remotest times to our own day."

If Negroes were an important element among the peoples who fathered Egyptian civilization, what were the Egyptians? The question bristles with thorns. The only thing that can be said with assurance is that they probably were not Caucasians. The evidence suggests that they were a black-, brown-, and yellow-skinned people who sprang from a mixture of Negro, Semitic, and Caucasian stocks.

How did the Egyptians see themselves?

They painted themselves in three colors: black, reddish-brown, yellow. The color white was available to them, but they used it to portray blue-eyed, white-skinned foreigners. One of the great murals of Egyptian art is the procession from a tomb of Thebes in the time of Thotmes III. The Egyptians and Ethiopians in the procession are painted in the usual brown and black colors. Thirty-seven whites in the procession are rendered in white tones. Who were they? G. A. Hoskins said they were probably "white slaves of the king of Ethiopia sent to the Egyptian king as the most acceptable present."

Great Negro scholars (W. E. B. Du Bois, Carter G. Woodson, William Leo Hansberry) have insisted that the ancient Egyptians, from Menes to Cleopatra, were a mixed race which presented the same physical types and color ranges as American Negroes—a people, in short, who would have been forced to sit on the back seats of the busses in Mississippi. "If the Egyptians and the majority of the tribes of Northern Africa were not Negroes," Carter Woodson said, "then there are no Negroes in the United States."

Most scholars deny that the Egyptians were Negroes, despite the testimony of an eyewitness. Herodotus, the Greek historian, visited the country some 500 years before Bethlehem. The Egyptians, he said, were "black and curly-haired."

Group identity aside, it is clear from the record that a large proportion of the ancient Egyptians—at least one-third—were undoubted Negroes. Many, perhaps most, of the soldiers were Negroes. Black people toiled on the pyramids, offered prayers to the sun-god and served with distinction in the state bureaucracy. "Ancient Egypt knew him [the Negro]," Alexander Chamberlain said, "both bond and free, and his blood flowed in the veins of not a few of the mighty Pharaohs."

• • •

When the Arabs exploded and carried Islam across North Africa and into Spain, Negroes went with them. As a religious ethic, Islam was unusually effective in cutting across racial lines. All Moslems, whatever their color, were brothers in the faith. "If a Negro slave is appointed to rule you," Mohammed said, "hear and obey him, though his head be like a dried grape."

In this climate, a man could be a slave today and a prime minister tomorrow. An extraordinarily large number of Negroes played heroic roles in the rise and spread of Islam—men like Mohammed Ahmad, the Sudanese Negro who claimed to be the Messiah; Abu'l Hasan Ali, the black sultan of Morocco and Bilal, the friend of Mohammed. There were also numerous black generals, administrators, and poets. The abundant and detailed descriptions of interracial relations in the *Arabian Nights* and other Oriental literature prove that race was not a crucial factor in the Islamic world.

Negroes went with crusading Islam into southern Europe, where a "learned and celebrated poet, a black of the Sudan, Abu Ishak Ibrahamin Al Kenemi" was a favorite at the court of Almansur in Seville, Spain.

In the Islamic Era, three powerful states—Ghana, Mali, and Songhay—emerged in the western Sudan, a broad belt of open country, sandwiched between the Sahara in the north and the rain forests of the Guinea Coast on the south. At one time, the peoples and rulers of these countries were classified out of the Negro race. It is now known that they were Negroes, some of whom were converted to Islam in the eleventh century. The extent of Moslem influence is debatable. But it seems probable that the upper classes and leaders, especially in the large cities, were black Moslems.

As political entities, Ghana, Mali, and Songhay do not suffer in comparison with their European contemporaries. In several areas, the Sudanese empires were clearly superior. "It would be interesting to know," Basil Davidson wrote, "what the Normans might have thought of Ghana. Anglo-Saxon England could easily have seemed a poor and lowly place beside it."

The economic life of these states revolved around agriculture, manufacturing, and international trade. Rulers wielded power through provincial governors and viceroys and maintained large standing armies. Chain-mailed cavalrymen, who carried shields and fought with swords and lances, formed the shock troops of the armies.

Ibn Batuta, an Arab traveler who visited Mali in the fourteenth century, was impressed by the orderly flow of life. "Of all people," he said, "the blacks are those who most detest injustice. Their Sultan never forgives anyone who has been guilty of it."

Proud, a little haughty perhaps, the Sudanese were a formidable people. When the monarch of one state was overthrown, the women committed suicide because "they were too proud to allow themselves to fall into the hands of white men." Batuta was flabbergasted by the servile behavior of the whites in Mali. The black viceroy who received the merchants of the caravan with which Batuta was traveling remained seated while the whites stood before him. He spoke to the whites through an interpreter, although he understood their language. He did this, Batuta said, "solely to indicate his disdain for them."

Trade and commerce flourished in the great cities that sprang up in the Sudanese savannah. And the intellectual life was brisk and stimulating. Jenné and Timbuktu were known throughout the Moslem world as centers of culture and learning. The citizens were sophisticated and knowledgeable. Batuta said the black women were "of surpassing beauty." They were neither downtrodden nor meek, these women. Batuta said they were "shown more respect than the men." He added: "Their men show no signs of jealousy whatever . . . [the women] show no bashfulness before men and do not veil themselves."

The power and wealth of Ghana, Mali, and Songhay stemmed from the trans-Saharan trade, which exerted a profound influence on Sudanese civilization. The basis of this trade was gold. From the north came caravans of 12,000 or more camels, laden with wheat, sugar, fruit, textiles and salt which were exchanged in the Sudan for gold and other products. In the power politics of that day, the country which controlled this trade controlled the Sudan.

Ghana, which was old when the Arabs first mentioned it in A.D. 800, dominated the Sudan for almost 300 years. It flourished in the ninth and tenth centuries and reached the peak of its power in the early part of the eleventh century. The rulers of Ghana, which was one of the main suppliers of gold for North Africa and Europe, were fabulously wealthy. El Bekri, an Arab geographer who wrote in 1067, said the king owned a nugget of gold so large that he could tether his horse to it.

●   ●   ●

The core of West African society was the family which was organized among many tribes on a matrilineal basis—that is, descent was traced through the mother. Polygamy was common, though, in practice, the poor, like poor people everywhere, contented themselves with monogamy. Some tribes, incidentally, were acquainted with the allegedly modern practice of birth control. Bantu tribes said it was not good for a woman to give birth to more than one child in a three-year period.

Social life was well organized. The old, the sick, the infirm were cared for. Spinsters were rare; prostitution was unknown. The villages and the surrounding gardens and fields were as safe as the streets of some American cities. Some tribes, as fantastic as it may seem, vaccinated for smallpox. Other Africans insisted that there was a cause and effect relationship between the mosquito and malaria. A European traveler in Abyssinia noted: "The Natives hereabouts say that Malaria is caused by the bite of the mosquito, but, of course, we know better—it is caused by the miasmas of the swamps!"

The West Africans were a bewildering mixture of various stocks. Centuries of contact and interbreeding had already produced different types. Some of the West Africans were short and broad-nosed. Some were tall, with straight hair and aquiline noses. They were of all colors: chocolate, asphalt, café au lait, persimmon, cream.

Although they spoke many tongues, there was a common substratum. Only four

African languages were reduced to writing before the coming of the white man: Egyptian, Ethiopian, a variety of Berber and an invention of the Vai people of Liberia. Though not reduced to writing, African languages were far from simple. Mario Pei has given a classic description of one African language, Swahili. "Swahili," he wrote, "is a complete refutation of the rather general belief that languages of 'primitive' peoples are necessarily primitive, and consist largely of grunts, groans and mixed-up ideas. Swahili has a euphony that is comparable to Italian, with clear, distinct sounds, vowel endings, and a most pleasing arrangement of syllables that consist for the most part of consonant-plus-vowel. It is capable of such absolute precision that the Swahili version of the Pentateuch contains fewer words than the Hebrew original, without the slightest loss or distortion of meaning. Its grammatical and syntactical structure is logical, almost to the point of being philosophical. . . . Using Swahili roots, prefixes and suffixes, it would be as easy to construct the vocabulary of nuclear fission (or of any other science or philosophy) as it is in languages like the modernized Irish of Eire or the modernized Hebrew of Israel. . . ."

Of whatever tongue, of whatever color, Africans were a deeply religious people. For a long time, African religion was written off as a form of animism. We know now that it was a great deal more complicated than that. Like advanced peoples everywhere, the Africans wrestled with the big questions. What is man? What happens to him after death? Is life a gigantic hoax or has it purpose and meaning?

The answers Africans gave to these questions determined the form of their religion. There was, to begin with, a supreme God who created the earth. There was also a pantheon of lesser gods identified sometimes with terrestrial objects. Intertwined with these concepts were the cults of fate and ancestor worship. Undergirdling all was the basic concept of "life forces." The life force of the Creator was thought to be present in all things, animate and inanimate. This force, "a kind of individualized fragment of the Supreme Being itself," continued to exist, even after the death of the individual. It continued, the African said, in a pure and perfect state which could influence the lives of living things.

This sophisticated concept bears a striking resemblance to Henri Bergson's *elan vital.* Bernard Fagg has found some parallels between African philosophy and modern subatomic physics. "African thought," he said, "is conditioned by their ontology, that is, their theory of the nature of being; for them being is a process and not a mere state, and the nature of things is thought of in terms of force or energy rather than matter; the forces of the spirit, human, animal, vegetable and mineral worlds are all constantly influencing each other, and by a proper knowledge and use of them a man may influence his own life and that of others."

Religion, to the African, was life. Every event was suffused with religious significance; and the climax of life was death. The African's attitude toward death, anthropologists say, survived the Atlantic crossing and took root in the soil of Negro life. Another religious root, spirit possession, thrives, they say, in the shouting and ecstasy complex of some American Negro churches.

Art, like religion, was a life expression. There were no art museums or opera houses in pre-white man Africa. Art and aesthetic expression were collective experiences in which all the people participated. Art, in short, was not for art's sake, but for life's sake.

The different faces of beauty—line, color, sound, rhythm—fascinated the African ancestors of the American Negro. And their art—embodied in cubistic masks, terra cotta pieces, gold figurines, three dimensional objects and naturalistic representations of the human body—is one of the great flights of the human spirit. Fascinated by the non-human geometry of African art, Picasso and other modernists turned their backs on the Greco-Roman and Renaissance visions and immersed themselves in the vocabulary of Benin, Ife and other West African art centers. In 1907, Picasso altered the faces of his huge canvas, *Les Demoiselles d'Avignon,* to resemble African masks. This was the beginning of cubism, a turning point in Western art.

Before the coming of the white man, music and rhythm were everyday things in Africa. Music was everywhere and it was grounded in two techniques which survived in the New World: polyrhythmic percussive technique and the call-and-response pattern (leader and chorus alternating). The poetry of tom-toms, the symphonies of synchronized bodies: these ebbed and flowed with the rhythm of life. Men and women danced because dancing had a social and religious meaning. And more—because dancing *was* meaning, was life itself. This attitude came to America, too. The Afro-American dances from Afro-Cuba and the Afro-American dances from Afro-Harlem are rooted in an African *mystique.* It is of more than casual significance that films made in an African village contained a perfect example of the Charleston.

There was much, to be sure, that was mean and base in African life: slavery, for example, although it was a thousand times more moderate than American slavery; human sacrifice and, of course, the use of man by man. Men used other men in Africa, as they did in Greece and Rome. The only thing that can be said for human exploitation in Africa is that it was as well organized as it was in "more advanced" cultures.

The man who emerged from this African chrysalis was a courageous, warlike individual. He was not soft; he was hard. He had fought the tsetse fly, the mosquito and hundreds of nameless insects and he had survived. He had wrested from the hungry jungle gaps of land and he had found time to think beautiful thoughts and to make beautiful things. He was used to hard work and he was accustomed to an elaborate social code. If he were a nobleman or a rich merchant or a priest, if, in short, he belonged to the upper classes, as did many who came to America in chains, he was used to political responsibility, to giving orders and taking them, to making and altering rules, to governing. In fine, as Stanley M. Elkins has said, "he was the product of . . . cultural traditions essentially heroic in nature."

Was this rich cultural heritage transplanted and preserved in the American environment?

Some scholars find little in American Negro life that can be traced to the African past. Others, like Melville J. Herskovits, find Africanisms (survivals of African cultural patterns) in the family life, motor habits, religious practices and music of American Negroes. Lorenzo Turner has found a large number of survivals in the syntax, word-formations and intonations of American Negroes. Among the words he found "in fairly general use . . . especially in the South" were goober (peanut), gumbo (okra), ninny (female breast), tote (to carry), yam (sweet potato). Turner also found "several hundred" African names among Negroes on the South Side of Chicago. Among the names and their African derivation are:

Bobo, one who cannot talk (Vai)
Geeji, a language and tribe in Liberia
Agona, a country in Ghana (Twi)
Ola, that which saves (Yoruba)
Sambo, name given the second son (Hausa)
Zola, to love (Congo)

John Hope Franklin, the eminent modern-day scholar, says: "The survival of varying degrees of African culture in America does not suggest that there has been only a limited adjustment of the Negro to the New World situation. To the contrary, it merely points up the fact that he came out of an experience that was sufficiently entrenched to make possible the persistence of some customs and traditions. . . . After all, perhaps the survival of Africanisms in the New World was as great as it was because of the refusal of the members of the dominant group in America to extend, without reservations, their own culture to the Negroes whom they brought over."

Franklin's summation underlines the great numbers of answers which are available to students who echo the poet:

One three centuries removed
From the scenes his fathers loved,
Spicy grove, cinnamon tree,
What is Africa to me?

Lost Cities of Africa[*]

Basil Davidson

MALI

Timbuktu and Djenné, both to become famous throughout the Islamic world for their commerce and learning, seem to have grown into cities by the twelfth century. But their eminence dates from Mandingo supremacy and its empire of Mali. Then it was, in 1307, that the most renowned of all the monarchs of the old Sudan, *Mansa* (sultan or emperor) Kankan Musa, inherited power over Mali and began to extend its dominion. After much success in conquest and diplomacy, this remarkable man followed others from the Western Sudan on pilgrimage to Mecca, and gave the world a proof of the widespread loyalties of Islam as well as a chance of measuring the wealth of Sudanese civilization.

His going through Cairo in 1324, his camel trains and servants and his wives and gifts and arrogant horsemen, all the trappings of a king whose realm would soon comprise a land as large as western Europe and as civilized as most of its kind in Europe, still lingered as familiar gossip in North Africa a hundred years later; for Kankan Musa went with a pleasantly memorable supply of gold as well as pomp and circumstance. An interesting contemporary estimate of Cairo's opinion was later recorded by a senior official of that city. Although El Omari's *Africa without Egypt* was written some time later, the writer was in a position to found his chapter on Mali from information gathered by men who had seen the Mandingo monarch on his way to Mecca.

He quotes a jurist of Cairo, who had talked with Kankan Musa, as having heard from the emperor that the length of his realm was "about one year." El Omari adds that he heard the same from another source, "but Ed Dukkali considers that it is four months long and as much wide; and this opinion of Ed Dukkali is preferable, since Kankan Musa may very well have swollen the real size of his realm." We know in fact that Mali at the time of Kankan Musa's journey, or soon after, had enclosed within its

---

[*] From Basil Davidson, *The Lost Cities of Africa* (Boston: Little, Brown and Company, Inc., 1959), pp. 90–93, 94–98. Copyright © 1959 by Basil Davidson. Reprinted by permission of Atlantic-Little, Brown and Co.

governing system the approaches to the salt deposits of Taghaza on the northern fringes of the Sahara, as well as the approaches to the gold country in the far south on the southern fringes of the savannah; while to the west it reached as far as the Atlantic, and eastward held the copper mines and caravan center of Takedda and probably the lands beyond.

This realm had grown during Kankan Musa's pilgrimage. In 1325 his army commander, Sagaman-dir, took the Songhay capital of Gao on the middle Niger; and with Gao there fell to the dominion of Mali the whole wide trading area which the Songhay had already captured to the north of them. Thus for size and wealth if not for the number of its people, who were comparatively few when compared with the empires of the East, Mali was one of the greatest states in the world of its time. Kankan Musa returned home by way of Gao, enjoying his general's conquest and receiving the submission of the Songhay king and notables, and went on upstream to Timbuktu.

There in Timbuktu he caused new mosques to be raised, mosques that would long be famous in the whole Sudan. They are said to have followed the design of a poet of Granada in southern Spain, Abu Ishaq es Saheli, whom the emperor had come to know in Mecca and persuaded to return with him. Ibn Battuta, visiting Timbuktu some twenty years later, says that he saw the grave of this "meritorious poet," while the Sankuré mosque of Timbuktu, attached to Abu Ishaq's name, would long be famous. And soon after Kankan Musa's visit, according to tradition, the earliest flat-roofed houses were built in Gao and Timbuktu. In any case the wealth of these cities must greatly have expanded from this time, for Mali had succeeded better than Ghana and now controlled the country to the north as well as the country to the south—many sources of copper, salt, and gold, as well as the caravan trails between.

Centers of commerce and religion, these cities became centers of learning. Scholars sheltered in their relative ease and security. The literate culture of the Western Sudan, already in existence for several hundred years, flowered in Timbuktu during years that saw, in Europe, the ravage of the Hundred Years' War. No one now can say how much it flowered, nor what fruits it bore, for the books that men read or wrote there are lost or not yet found; but Leo Africanus, two centuries later, gives some measure of the city's intellectual life. "In Timbuktu," he says, "there are numerous judges, doctors and clerics, all receiving good salaries from the king. He pays great respect to men of learning. There is a big demand for books in manuscript, imported from Barbary. More profit is made from the book trade than from any other line of business." The king in question was Mohammed Askia of Songhay; but conditions would not have greatly differed in the years of plenitude that came in the wake of Kankan Musa's conquest.

This was a civilization in its own right, standing to North Africa in much the same relationship of influence as Kush had stood to Egypt, and achieving, as Kush had achieved, its own original and independent growth. Peace reigned over the long caravan trails. Men were free to travel and trade and prosper as they could. There would be interruptions in this security, true enough—Mossi raiders would pillage Timbuktu only eight years after Kankan Musa's visit—but they would remain interruptions, disturbing rarely the everyday peace that Ibn Battuta found. And they must have disturbed even less the peasants and pastoralists who dwelt and throve on the banks of the Niger and out across the plains beyond. Many of these remained pagan even at the height of Islamic fame in the cities and gave, with their stolid clinging to the ancient ways, another native and authentic accent to this Sudanese civilization.

•   •   •

With the conquests of Kankan Musa the rulers grew wealthier; and the cities, profiting from their control of the caravan terminals and their increasing monopoly of the more important products, followed suit. Perhaps Djenné was the greatest of them. "It is because of this hallowed town," the author of the *Tarikh es Sudan* would write some three hundred years later, but the comment will apply to the dominion of Mali as well as to the later dominion of Songhay, "that caravans come to Timbuktu from all points of the horizon." Crossing southward over the Sahara in the mid-nineteenth century, Heinrich Barth could still find potent evidence of the extent and wealth of this far-flung trading system. Though reduced by then to proportions that might be insignificant when compared with the carrying trade of nineteenth century Europe, it made a still convincing witness to the commercial machinery which had helped to build and maintain states and long-enduring dynasties in this savannah country of the Middle Ages.

Even through the eyes of this late observer, the scene grows wonderfully clear and vivid. Precise and intelligent, Barth was never content with general observations; he had the good reporter's attachment to fact. He always went to the heart of the matter and wanted to know the scale of trading profit, not only for his own day, but also for the past. "The importance of the trade of Agadès, and the wealth of the place in general," he comments in one of his typically factual observations, "appear very clearly from the large tribute, of 150,000 ducats, which the king of Agadès was able to pay to that of Songhay"—some 250 years, that is, before Barth himself would visit the place.

In the same thoughtful probing manner he looked into the value and the nature of the salt trade, a trans-Saharan staple whose handling would not have greatly changed over the centuries, and has left an admirably detailed account of the means whereby bold and enterprising men could profit from it. During the dominion of Songhay, he found, the second-in-authority at Agadès—one of the south Saharan caravan stations—had had to levy tax on all merchandise imported into the town. (It would not have been much different under the earlier dominion of Mali; and the king of Ghana, long before that, had done the same on his narrower frontiers.) This office had been of great importance in providing royal revenue, but also in the means of individual enrichment.

For the chief duty of this official, Barth found, was "to accompany annually the salt caravan of the Kel-Gerès, which supplies the western part of the Middle Sudan with the salt of Bilma, from Agadès or Sokoto; and to protect it on the road as well as to secure it against exorbitant exactions on the part of the Fulbe [Fulani] of Sokoto. For this trouble he receives one *kantu*, that is to say the eighth part of a middle-sized camel load . . . a contribution which forms a considerable income in this country, probably of from eight to ten thousand Spanish dollars; the caravan consisting generally of some thousand camels, not all equally laden, and the *kantu* of salt fetching in Sudan from five thousand to seven or eight thousand *kurdi,* or shells, which are worth from two to three dollars. Under such circumstances those officers, who at the same time trade on their own account, cannot but amass considerable wealth."

Tales of fabulous kingly wealth had always been common. El Bekri had long before reported the king of Ghana as having a nugget of gold so large and heavy that he could safely tether his horse to it. But with the growth of Mali and its trading network the fables acquired a more statistical shape, and ceased perhaps to be fables after all. Kankan Musa was said to have taken five hundred slaves on the Mecca pilgrimage, each carrying a staff of gold that weighed about six pounds. On his baggage camels there were said to be eighty to one hundred loads of gold, each weighing about three hundred pounds. And anyone who has chanced to see a modern durbar of chiefs and traditional rulers in West Africa, a parade flashing with scores and hundreds of golden staffs— wooden staffs, no doubt, yet covered with beaten gold—will not find this so hard to credit.

Accumulation of wealth promoted trade, but it also promoted industry. "The great advantage of Kano," Barth wrote of that north Nigerian town, but medieval Timbuktu and Gao and Djenné would have reproduced something of the same pattern, "is that commerce and manufactures go hand in hand, and almost every family has its share in them. There is really something grand in this kind of industry, which spreads to the north as far as Murzuk, Ghat, and even Tripoli; to the west, not only to Timbuktu, but in some degree as far as the shores of the Atlantic, the very inhabitants of Arguin [on the Atlantic coast] dressing in the cloth woven and dyed in Kano; to the east, all over Bornu, although there it comes into contact with the native industry of the country; while to the south it maintains a rivalry with the native industry . . ."

Trading links multiplied. By 1400, according to Ibn Khaldun, annual caravans across the Sahara by way of the Hoggar Mountains counted no fewer than twelve thousand camels; and this was only one of half a dozen well-used routes. But the caravans went in many directions as well as to and from the northward and the Mediterranean; the whole Sudan was crisscrossed by their patient profit-seeking trails. Thus Bornu—in what is now northeastern Nigeria—bought copper from Wadai, its neighbor to the eastward; and Wadai had this copper in turn from Darfur, again to the eastward. Mali imported vastly from the Mediterranean as well as from Egypt, whether by way of the eastern or the northern routes—silks and damascened blades and horses in quantity. Schoolmen of the Muslim seats of learning traveled back and forth. Pilgrims walked to Mecca. Currencies evolved in gold or copper or shells or weight of stuffs, or in salt or metal pieces. Only to the southward could these savannah kingdoms seldom penetrate, but even there, beyond the forest barrier, they had their trading interest; and cola nuts from southern Nigeria were much in demand.

Against this restless enterprising background of conquest and centralizing government and continental trade, the kingdoms and empires rose and fell across a thousand years and more; yet only now perhaps, while the Western Sudan stands on the threshold of a regained independence, can their achievement win its full perspective and importance. This achievement was large and memorable, and is relevant to the re-emergence of an independent Sudan. When Kankan Musa died in 1352 he left behind him, in Bovill's words, "an empire which in the history of purely African states was as remarkable for its size as for its wealth; and which provided a striking example of the capacity of the Negro for political organisation."

Part 2

SLAVERY

The source material on slavery is abundant and varied. It includes official documents, religious tracts, slave narratives, plantation records, accounts of slave owners, writings of those opposed to slavery, and a wide range of biographies and novels. Based on these sources, vast amounts of materials have been written. In spite of the quantity, much is yet to be said on many aspects of the topic. Widespread agreement exists on the nature of the institution of slavery, but there are serious gaps in our understanding of its evolution and the reasons it developed as it did. This is not surprising since it is only in recent years that writers have begun to address themselves to the important questions which can help in understanding these issues.

Materials written on slavery before World War II tended to be confined to examination of questions relating to the legality and morality of the institution. It was not until the 1940s that major changes in the scholarship began to appear. Beginning with *An American Dilemma,* Gunnar Myrdal, 1944, writers expressed concern with the influence of slavery on black and white Americans and on the social and political institutions they created. Comparative studies of slavery also appeared as a fertile field for inquiry.

The writings included herein are a part of the approach to this topic introduced by the sociologist Myrdal. For much of the twentieth century before the 1940s, the historical approach to slavery was dominated by the writings of Ulrich B. Phillips. He was the first historian to draw systematically on documentary evidence in an effort to describe slavery. However, his selection of the evidence to be used and the degree to which his personal bias colored his history, exposed *American Negro Slavery* and other of his writings to serious criticism. Phillips saw slavery as a benign institution beneficial to Africans as a civilizing and Christianizing influence. He was cited as the leading authority throughout the Progressive period, World War I, and much of the New Deal.

Historians writing since World War II have established the faults in Phillips's research design and in his thesis. In the selection from *The Peculiar Institution,* Kenneth Stampp challenges Phillips on his own ground. Drawing on a greater range of source material, Stampp established the oppressive nature of slavery as reflected in the selection included here.

Various interpretations have been advanced to explain why American Negro slavery developed as it did. A selection herein from *Slavery: A Problem in American Institutional and Intellectual Life* suggests the approach of Stanley Elkins. Elkins compares North American and Latin American slavery, and he examines the psychological reactions of inmates in World War II German concentration camps in support of his position.

Two other works are represented here. "The U. S. Rationalized Slavery and Produced Racism," Henry N. Drewry, suggests that one must examine those political and social ideals which white Americans claimed to believe in and sought to develop side by side with slavery in seeking to understand why so peculiar a system developed. *Black Abolitionists,* Benjamin Quarles, provides a glimpse of free blacks in the North before the Civil War. Quarles sees their actions as a major influence in the abolitionist movement in the country.

To Make Them Stand in Fear*

Kenneth Stampp

A wise master did not take seriously the belief that Negroes were natural-born slaves. He knew better. He knew that Negroes freshly imported from Africa had to be broken into bondage; that each succeeding generation had to be carefully trained. This was no easy task, for the bondsman rarely submitted willingly. Moreover, he rarely submitted completely. In most cases there was no end to the need for control—at least not until old age reduced the slave to a condition of helplessness.

Masters revealed the qualities they sought to develop in slaves when they singled out certain ones for special commendation. A small Mississippi planter mourned the death of his "faithful and dearly beloved servant" Jack: "Since I have owned him he has been true to me in all respects. He was an obedient trusty servant. . . . I never knew him to steal nor lie and he ever set a moral and industrous example to those around him. . . . I shall ever cherish his memory." A Louisiana sugar planter lost a "very valuable Boy" through an accident: "His life was a very great one. I have always found him willing and obedient and never knew him to fail to do anything he was put to do." [7] These were "ideal" slaves, the models slaveholders had in mind as they trained and governed their workers.

How might this ideal be approached? The first step, advised those who wrote discourses on the management of slaves, was to establish and maintain strict discipline. An Arkansas master suggested the adoption of the "Army Regulations as to the discipline in Forts." "They must obey at all times, and under all circumstances, cheerfully and with alacrity," affirmed a Virginia slaveholder. "It greatly impairs the happiness of a negro, to be allowed to cultivate an insubordinate temper. Unconditional submission

* From Kenneth M. Stampp, *The Peculiar Institution* (New York: Alfred A. Knopf, Inc., 1956), pp. 144–51, 185–91. Copyright © 1958 by Kenneth M. Stampp. Reprinted by permission of Alfred A. Knopf, Inc.

[7] Baker Diary, entry for July 1, 1854; Alexander Franklin Pugh Ms. Plantation Diary, entry for June 21, 1860.

is the only footing upon which slavery should be placed. It is precisely similar to the attitude of a minor to his parent, or a soldier to his general." A South Carolinian limned a perfect relationship between a slave and his master: "that the slave should know that his master is to govern absolutely, and he is to obey implicitly. That he is never for a moment to exercise either his will or judgment in opposition to a positive order." [8]

The second step was to implant in the bondsmen themselves a consciousness of personal inferiority. They had "to know and keep their places," to "feel the difference between master and slave," to understand that bondage was their natural status. They had to feel that African ancestry tainted them, that their color was a badge of degradation. In the country they were to show respect for even their master's nonslaveholding neighbors; in the towns they were to give way on the streets to the most wretched white man. The line between the races must never be crossed, for familiarity caused slaves to forget their lowly station and to become "impudent." [9]

Frederick Douglass explained that a slave might commit the offense of impudence in various ways: "in the tone of an answer; in answering at all; in not answering; in the expression of countenance; in the motion of the head; in the gait, manner and bearing of the slave." Any of these acts, in some subtle way, might indicate the absence of proper subordination. "In a well regulated community," wrote a Texan, "a negro takes off his hat in addressing a white man. . . . Where this is not enforced, we may always look for impudent and rebellious negroes." [1]

The third step in the training of slaves was to awe them with a sense of their master's enormous power. The only principle upon which slavery could be maintained, reported a group of Charlestonians, was the "principle of fear." In his defense of slavery James H. Hammond admitted that this, unfortunately, was true but put the responsibility upon the abolitionists. Antislavery agitation had forced masters to strengthen their authority: "We have to rely more and more on the power of fear. . . . We are determined to continue masters, and to do so we have to draw the reign tighter and tighter day by day to be assured that we hold them in complete check." A North Carolina mistress, after subduing a troublesome domestic, realized that it was essential "to make them stand in fear"! [2]

In this the slaveholders had considerable success. Frederick Douglass believed that most slaves stood "in awe" of white men; few could free themselves altogether from the notion that their masters were "invested with a sort of sacredness." Olmsted saw a small white girl stop a slave on the road and boldly order him to return to his plantation. The slave fearfully obeyed her command. A visitor in Mississippi claimed that a master, armed only with a whip or cane, could throw himself among a score of

[8] *Southern Cultivator,* IV (1846), pp. 43–44; XVIII (1860), pp. 304–305; *Farmers' Register,* V (1837), p. 32.

[9] *Southern Planter,* XII (1852), pp. 376–79; *Southern Cultivator,* VIII (1850), p. 163; *Farmers' Register,* I (1834), pp. 564–65.

[1] Douglass, *My Bondage,* p. 92; Austin *Texas State Gazette,* October 10, 1857.

[2] Phillips (ed.), *Plantation and Frontier,* II, pp. 108–11; *De Bow's Review,* VII (1849), p. 498; Mary W. Bryan to Ebenezer Pettigrew, October 20, 1835, Pettigrew Family Papers.

bondsmen and cause them to "flee with terror." He accomplished this by the "peculiar tone of authority" with which he spoke. "Fear, awe, and obedience . . . are interwoven into the very nature of the slave." [3]

The fourth step was to persuade the bondsmen to take an interest in the master's enterprise and to accept his standards of good conduct. A South Carolina planter explained: "The master should make it his business to show his slaves, that the advancement of his individual interest, is at the same time an advancement of theirs. Once they feel this, it will require but little compulsion to make them act as it becomes them." [4] Though slaveholders induced only a few chattels to respond to this appeal, these few were useful examples for others.

The final step was to impress Negroes with their helplessness, to create in them "a habit of perfect dependence" upon their masters. [5] Many believed it dangerous to train slaves to be skilled artisans in the towns, because they tended to become self-reliant. Some thought it equally dangerous to hire them to factory owners. In the Richmond tobacco factories they were alarmingly independent and "insolent." A Virginian was dismayed to find that his bondsmen, while working at an iron furnace, "got a habit of roaming about and *taking care of themselves.*" Permitting them to hire their own time produced even worse results. "No higher evidence can be furnished of its baneful effects," wrote a Charlestonian, "than the unwillingness it produces in the slave, to return to the regular life and domestic control of the master." [6]

A spirit of independence was less likely to develop among slaves kept on the land, where most of them became accustomed to having their master provide their basic needs, and where they might be taught that they were unfit to look out for themselves. Slaves then directed their energies to the attainment of mere "temporary ease and enjoyment." "Their masters," Olmsted believed, "calculated on it in them—do not wish to cure it—and by constant practice encourage it." [7]

Here, then, was the way to produce the perfect slave: accustom him to rigid discipline, demand from him unconditional submission, impress upon him his innate inferiority, develop in him a paralyzing fear of white men, train him to adopt the master's code of good behavior, and instill in him a sense of complete dependence. This, at least, was the goal.

But the goal was seldom reached. Every master knew that the average slave was only an imperfect copy of the model. He knew that some bondsmen yielded only to superior power—and yielded reluctantly. This complicated his problem of control.

"Never be induced by a course of good behavior on the part of the negroes, to relax the

---

[3] Douglass, *My Bondage,* pp. 250–51; Olmsted, *Back Country,* pp. 444–45; [Ingraham], *South West,* II, pp. 260–61.

[4] *Farmers' Register,* IV (1837), p. 574.

[5] *Southern Cultivator,* IV (1846), p. 44.

[6] *Southern Planter,* XII (1852), pp. 376–79; Olmsted, *Seaboard,* pp. 58–59; Charleston *Courier,* September 12, 1850.

[7] Olmsted, *Seaboard,* pp. 128–29.

strictness of your discipline. . . . The only way to keep a negro honest is not to trust him. This seems a harsh assertion; but it is unfortunately, too true." So wrote a Southerner who was giving advice to overseers. To a former slave it sometimes appeared that masters, "with skilled and practiced eyes," probed into the chattel's mind and heart to detect his changing moods. A slave, Olmsted observed, "is trusted as little as possible to use his own discretion, and it is taken for granted that he will never do anything desired of him that he dares avoid." [8]

Because most Negroes were imperfect slaves, because they needed to be watched constantly, each master devised a set of rules for the efficient day-by-day operation of his enterprise. Slaveholders were not always in accord about the value of specific rules, but there were large areas of agreement nevertheless. They recorded the rules they considered most important in their private journals, in their instructions to overseers, and in essays published in agricultural periodicals. Here are the ones they generally accepted:

1. An overseer was not to be absent from the estate without his employer's consent. He was to stay constantly in the fields while the hands were at work, to search the cabins periodically for weapons or stolen goods, and to guard the keys to the corn crib, smoke house, and stable. If there were no overseer, the master (even on small establishments) assumed responsibility for these police measures.

2. A slave was not to be out of his cabin after "horn-blow," usually at eight o'clock in winter and nine o'clock in summer. The master or overseer was to tour the cabins at night to see that none were missing. Some masters established a system of regular night watches.

3. A slave was not to leave the estate without a pass which gave his destination and the time he was to return. Some owners issued passes generously when slaves were not at work; others issued them sparingly. Many agreed that bondsmen should not visit neighboring estates, or associate with "mean white men" who might be disposed to make them dissatisfied. By keeping them at home "they do not know what is going on beyond the limits of the plantation, and feel satisfied that they could not . . . accomplish anything that would change their condition." Strangers, white and black, were to be "run off" the plantations.[9]

4. Free Negroes or whites were not to work with slaves. One planter, for example, discharged a white mechanic for "talking with the negroes." Another believed that the value of a slave was "always impaired by contact with white labor," because the whites worked less, received "more consideration," and enjoyed "higher privileges." [1] Whites who associated with slaves became objects of suspicion. According to a Texan, "no white men will ever be found on familiar terms with negroes, who are not either of an abandoned or worthless character or are abolitionists." [2]

---

[8] Printed instructions in Affleck, *Cotton Plantation Record and Account Book*; Douglass, *My Bondage,* pp. 276–77; Olmsted, *Seaboard,* pp. 478–79.

[9] *Southern Cultivator,* XVIII (1860), p. 305; St. John R. Liddell Ms. Diary, entry for October 18, 1841.

[1] *Southern Planter,* XIII (1853), p. 23.

[2] Austin *Texas State Gazette,* June 16, 1855; J. Benwell, *An Englishman's Travels in America* (London, n.d.), pp. 165–66.

5. Slaves were not to marry free Negroes, though some were permitted to marry slaves living on other estates. Often they were required to select their spouses only among the master's own chattels. Men who married away from home were frequently absent and thus exposed "to temptations from meeting and associating with negroes . . . with various habits and views." Women with husbands abroad brought to the home estate slaves accustomed to different treatment and thus created a rendezvous for a "medley of characters." It was better for a master to buy husbands or wives for his bondsmen when necessary. Otherwise, "if they cannot be suited at home," it should be a settled principle that "they must live single." [3]

6. A slave was not to sell anything without a permit, have whiskey in his cabin, quarrel or fight, or use abusive language.

These rules were to be enforced consistently, and no violations were to pass unnoticed. Master and overseer must make it clear that they were in perfect agreement, for slaves soon discovered "any little jarring" between them and were "sure to take advantage of it." Moreover, each neighborhood of slaveholders needed to be harmonious; when all enforced similar rules and maintained effective discipline, the government of slaves was easier . . .

•   •   •

Although cruelty was endemic in all slaveholding communities, it was always most common in newly settled regions. Along the rough southern frontier thousands of ambitious men were trying swiftly to make their fortunes. They operated in a frantically competitive society which provided few rewards for the virtues of gentility and almost put a premium upon ruthlessness. In the eastern tobacco and rice districts brutality was unquestionably less prevalent in the nineteenth century than it had been during the colonial period. But in the Southwest only limited areas had developed a mellowed gentry as late as 1860. In the Alabama-Mississippi Black Belt, in the cotton and sugar parishes of Louisiana, along the Arkansas River, and in eastern Texas the master class included the "parvenus," the "cotton snobs," and the "Southern Yankees." If these planters failed to observe the code of the patrician, they apparently thought none the less of each other for it.

The hired slave stood the greatest chance of subjection to cruel punishments as well as to overwork. His employer, a Kentucky judge confessed, had no incentive to treat him kindly "except the mere feelings of humanity, which we have too much reason to believe in many instances . . . are too weak to stimulate the active virtue." [6] This was no exaggeration.

Southerners who were concerned about the welfare of slaves found it difficult to draw a sharp line between acts of cruelty and such measures of physical force as were an inextricable part of slavery. Since the line was necessarily arbitrary, slaveholders themselves disagreed about where it should be drawn. Was it barbarous to "correct" a slave by putting him in the stocks, or by forcing him to wear chains or an iron collar? How

---

[3] *Southern Cultivator,* IV (1846), p. 44; VIII (1850), p. 164.
[6] Catterall (ed.), *Judicial Cases,* I, p. 284.

severely might a slave be flogged before the punishment became brutal? These were matters of personal taste.

But no master denied the propriety of giving a moderate whipping to a disobedient bondsman. During the seventeenth and eighteenth centuries the lash was used to punish free men as well as slaves. By mid-nineteenth century, however, it was seldom used upon any but slaves, because public opinion now considered it to be cruel. Why it was less cruel to whip a bondsman was a problem that troubled many sensitive masters. That they often had no choice as long as they owned slaves made their problem no easier to resolve.

Bennet H. Barrow, a Louisiana planter, kept an unusually full record of punishments—a record which illustrates the difficulty of distinguishing between cruelty and reasonable "correction." A substantial and respected man in his community, Barrow inherited lands and slaves from his father; he was in no sense a crude parvenu. Yet he flogged his chattels freely, sometimes severely. On various occasions he had a "general whipping frollick," whipped "every hand in the field . . . comencing with the driver," or gave "a number of them a good flogging." He broke his sword cane on the head of one offending slave, "beat" another "very much" and "cut him with a club in 3 places verry bad." Barrow was one of the few large planters who refused to employ overseers, because of their bad reputation.[7]

If it was cruel to flog slaves so frequently and severely that their backs were permanently scarred, southern newspapers provided evidence of an abundance of this variety of inhumanity. The following illustrations are from ante-bellum fugitive-slave advertisements and from sheriffs' committal notices: Charles, "an old sinner" who escaped from a Louisiana plantation, had "many stripes of the lash"; a Mississippi slave had "large raised scars or whelks in the small of his back and on his abdomen nearly as large as a person's finger"; Nancy, a Georgia slave, was "considerably marked by the whip"; Esther, an Alabama slave, was "marked about the shoulders from whipping"; a Missouri fugitive had "many scars on his back"; Gid, according to his North Carolina master, had a "remarkably bad temper" and had in consequence "marks of the lash upon his back"; Tom, who was held by the jailer of Augusta County, Virginia, had "the appearance of frequent and severe flogging"; Anaca, who escaped from her Kentucky master, had "a large scar immediately on her chest from the cut of a whip."

After northern abolitionists began scanning the southern press for atrocities, specific references to slaves who were "marked by the whip" declined. The number of slaves identified more vaguely as having "scars" or "burns" increased.

Beyond this were cases of pure brutality—cases of flogging that resulted in the crippling, maiming, or killing of slaves. An early nineteenth-century Charleston grand jury presented "as a serious evil the many instances of Negro Homicide" and condemned those who indulged their passions "in the barbarous treatment of slaves."[8] "Salting"—washing the cuts received from the whip with brine—was a harsh punishment inflicted upon the most obstinate bondsmen. Though all but a few deplored such

---

[7] Davis (ed.), *Diary of Bennet H. Barrow, passim.*
[8] Henry, *Police Control,* pp. 67–68.

brutality, slaveholders found themselves in a dilemma when nothing else could subdue a rebel.

If a master was too squeamish to undertake the rugged task of humbling a refractory bondsman, he might send him to a more calloused nieghbor or to a professional "slave breaker." John Nevitt, a Mississippi planter not averse to the application of heroic remedies, received from another master a young chattel "for the purpose of punishing him for bad conduct." Frederick Douglass remembered a ruthless man in Maryland who had a reputation for being "a first rate hand at breaking young negroes"; some slaveholders found it beneficial to send their beginning hands to him for training.[9]

The branding of slaves was a widespread custom in colonial days; it was less common in the nineteenth century. But as late as 1838, a North Carolinian advertised that Betty, a fugitive, was recently "burnt . . . with a hot iron on the left side of her face; I tried to make the letter M." In 1848, a Kentuckian identified his runaway Jane by a brand mark "on the breast something like L blotched." [1] Mutilation as a form of punishment also declined without disappearing entirely. A Louisiana jailer, in 1831, gave notice that he had a runaway in his custody: "He has been lately gelded, and is not yet well." Another Louisianian recorded his disgust for a neighbor who had "castrated 3 men of his." [2]

Some masters who were otherwise as humane as the peculiar institution would permit tolerated almost anything that might "cure" habitual runaways. Andrew Jackson once offered fifty dollars reward for the capture of a fugitive, "and ten dollars extra for every hundred lashes any person will give him to the amount of three hundred." A Georgian punished his runaways by pulling out one of their toenails with a pair of pincers. Others hunted them with shotguns. A North Carolinian advertised for an escaped slave who had "some marks of shot about his hips, thighs, neck and face." Bennet H. Barrow caught Jerry "in the Bayou behind the Quarter, [and] shot him in the thigh"; when Jerry absconded again, Barrow vowed he would this time "shoot to kill." A Mississippian, apparently wishing to give his slaves a stern warning, promised to compensate whoever captured his fugitive "dead or alive." [3]

The tracking of runaways with dogs was no figment of abolitionist imaginations; it was a common practice in all slave states, defended and justified in the courts. Groups of slaveholders sometimes rode through the swamps with their dogs and made the search for fugitives a sport comparable to fox hunting. Others preferred to hire professional slave catchers who provided their own "Negro dogs." A Mississippi master described the talents of a slave catcher he employed: "He follows a negro with his dogs 36 hours after he has passed and never fails to overtake him. It is his profession and he

[9] Nevitt Plantation Journal, entry for June 5, 1828; Douglass, *My Bondage,* p. 203; Sydnor, *Slavery in Mississippi,* pp. 69–70.

[1] Johnson, *Ante-Bellum North Carolina,* pp. 493–94; Coleman, *Slavery Times in Kentucky,* pp. 248–49.

[2] Taylor, "Slavery in Louisiana," p. 236; Davis (ed.), *Diary of Bennet H. Barrow,* pp. 173–74.

[3] Phillips (ed.), *Plantation and Frontier,* II, pp. 85–88; Olmsted, *Texas,* pp. 104–105; Davis (ed.), *Diary of Bennet H. Barrow,* pp. 239, 242; Jackson *Mississippian,* July 11, 1834.

makes some $600 per annum by it." [4] Southern newspapers carried the advertisements of professionals who solicited the patronage of slaveholders, and of those who trained "Negro dogs" for sale.

The dogs could give a fugitive a severe mauling if the owner was willing to permit it. After a Mississippi master caught an escaped slave he allowed his dogs to "bite him very severely." A Louisiana planter "treed" a runaway and then "made the dogs pull him out of the tree, Bit him very badly, think he will stay home a while." On another occasion his dogs tore a slave naked; he then "took him Home Before the other negro[es] . . . and made the dogs give him another over hauling." [5]

The angry mobs who dealt extra-legal justice to slaves accused of serious crimes committed barbarities seldom matched by the most brutal masters. "They call it Lintch's Law," wrote a frightened Louisiana plantation mistress during a local insurrection panic. "If they continue hanging, as they have done for some time past, we should be careful of the children, otherwise the World might be left without people." [6] Fear turned groups of decent white men into ferocious mobs—fear and the knowledge that the law was not strong enough to touch them.

After the Nat Turner rebellion a Richmond newspaper declared that the reprisals of the whites were "hardly inferior in barbarity to the atrocities of the insurgents." During the insurrection panic of 1856, a Texas editor affirmed that at such a time "the popular vengeance may be meted out to the criminal with as much necessity as we would strike down an enemy in self-defence, or shoot a mad dog in our path." A Mississippian was ready for the "fagot and the flame" and to "let every tree in the country bend with negro meat." Four years later a Georgia editor urged the oldest and best citizens in each community to examine persons suspected of encouraging slave rebellions; if they were adjudged guilty, "swing the vagabonds from the nearest tree, and say nothing about it." [7]

Mobs all too frequently dealt with slaves accused of murder or rape. They conducted their own trials or broke into jails or court rooms to seize prisoners for summary execution. Their more fortunate victims were hanged; the others were burned to death, sometimes in the presence of hundreds of bondsmen who were forced to attend the ceremony. Thus, wrote a Mississippian after one such incident, "justice was satisfied; the law of retaliation was inflicted . . . while the example made of this wretch had, no doubt, a salutary effect upon the two thousand slaves who witnessed his execution." An Alabama editor justified the burning of a slave at the stake by "the law of self-protection, which abrogates all other law. . . . There was no passionate conduct here. The

[4] Gustavus A. Henry to his wife, November 23, 1849, Henry Papers; Coleman, *Slavery Times in Kentucky,* pp. 61–62; Olmsted, *Back Country,* pp. 214–15.
[5] William Read to Samuel S. Downey, August 8, 1848, Downey Papers; Davis (ed.), *Diary of Bennet H. Barrow,* pp. 369–70, 376.
[6] Rachel O'Conner to Frances S. Weeks, September 7, 1835, Weeks Collection.
[7] Richmond *Whig,* quoted in Alexandria (Va.) *Phenix Gazette,* September 1, 1831; Austin *Texas State Gazette,* November 15, 1856; Jackson *Mississippian,* December 19, 1856; *Augusta Daily Chronicle and Sentinel,* September 9, 1860.

whole subject was disposed of with the coolest deliberation and with regard only to the interest of the public." [8]

   The abolition of slavery, of course, did not bring to a close the record of brutality in the South any more than it did elsewhere. But it did make less tenable the argument that brutality was sometimes in the public interest. And it did rescue many a master from the dilemma he faced when his desire to be humane was compromised by the demands of proper discipline.

●   ●   ●

[8] Vicksburg *Weekly Sentinel,* June 13, 1855; Huntsville *Democrat,* quoted in Sellers, *Slavery in Alabama,* pp. 262–63.

Slavery and Personality[*]

Stanley Elkins

PERSONALITY TYPES AND STEREOTYPES

An examination of American slavery, checked at certain critical points against a very different slave system, that of Latin America, reveals that a major key to many of the contrasts between them was an institutional key: The presence or absence of other powerful institutions in society made an immense difference in the character of slavery itself. In Latin America, the very tension and balance among three kinds of organizational concerns—church, crown, and plantation agriculture—prevented slavery from being carried by the planting class to its ultimate logic. For the slave, in terms of the space thus allowed for the development of men and women as moral beings, the result was an "open system": a system of contacts with free society through which ultimate absorption into that society could and did occur with great frequency. The rights of personality implicit in the ancient traditions of slavery and in the church's most venerable assumptions on the nature of the human soul were thus in a vital sense conserved, whereas to a staggering extent the very opposite was true in North American slavery. The latter system had developed virtually unchecked by institutions having anything like the power of their Latin counterparts; the legal structure which supported it, shaped only by the demands of a staple-raising capitalism, had defined with such nicety the slave's character as chattel that his character as a moral individual was left in the vaguest of legal obscurity. In this sense American slavery operated as a "closed" system—one in which, for the generality of slaves in their nature as men and women, *sub specie aeternitatis,* contacts with free society could occur only on the most narrowly circumscribed of terms. The next question is whether living within such a "closed system" might not have produced noticeable effects upon the slave's very personality.

The name "Sambo" has come to be synonymous with "race stereotype." Here is an automatic danger signal, warning that the analytical difficulties of asking questions

* From Stanley Elkins, *Slavery: A Problem in American Institutional and Intellectual Life* (Chicago: The University of Chicago Press, 1959), pp. 81–89. © 1959 by the University of Chicago. Reprinted by permission of author and publisher.

about slave personality may not be nearly so great as the moral difficulties. The one in-
hibits the other; the morality of the matter has had a clogging effect on its theoretical
development that may not be to the best interests of either. And yet theory on group
personality is still in a stage rudimentary enough that this particular body of material—
potentially illuminating—ought not to remain morally impounded any longer.

Is it possible to deal with "Sambo" as a type? The characteristics that have been
claimed for the type come principally from Southern lore. Sambo, the typical plantation
slave, was docile but irresponsible, loyal but lazy, humble but chronically given to lying
and stealing; his behavior was full of infantile silliness and his talk inflated with child-
ish exaggeration. His relationship with his master was one of utter dependence and
childlike attachment: it was indeed this childlike quality that was the very key to his
being. Although the merest hint of Sambo's "manhood" might fill the Southern breast
with scorn, the child, "in his place," could be both exasperating and lovable.

Was he real or unreal? What order of existence, what rank of legitimacy, should
be accorded him? Is there a "scientific" way to talk about this problem? For most Southerners in 1860 it went without saying not only that Sambo was real—that he was a dominant plantation type—but also that his characteristics were the clear product of racial
inheritance. That was one way to deal with Sambo, a way that persisted a good many
years after 1860. But in recent times, the discrediting, as unscientific, of racial explanations for any feature of plantation slavery has tended in the case of Sambo to discredit
not simply the explanation itself but also the thing it was supposed to explain. Sambo
is a mere stereotype—"stereotype" is itself a bad word, insinuating racial inferiority and
invidious discrimination.[1] This modern approach to Sambo had a strong counterpart in
the way Northern reformers thought about slavery in ante-bellum times: they thought
that nothing could actually be said about the Negro's "true" nature because that nature
was veiled by the institution of slavery. It could only be revealed by tearing away the

---

[1] The historian Samuel Eliot Morison was taken to task a few years ago by students of Queens College,
Long Island, for his use of the name "Sambo" (in Volume I of his and H. S. Commager's text, *The Growth of
the American Republic*) and for referring to the pre-Civil War Negroes as "a race with exasperating habits" and
to the typical slave as "childlike, improvident, humorous, prevaricating, and superstitious." As a result, the
use of the text at Queens was discontinued. See *Time,* February 26, 1951, pp. 48–49.

The following is from the "Concluding Summary" of one of the series of studies begun in the late
1930's under the inspiration of Gunnar Myrdal: "The description of the stereotypes held concerning the
American Negro indicates the widespread tendency to look upon the Negro as inferior, and to ascribe to him
qualities of intellect and personality which mark him off with some definiteness from the surrounding white
American population . . . [;] not all these alleged characteristics of the Negro are uncomplimentary, but
even those which may be regarded as favorable have the flavor of inferiority about them. When the Negro is
praised, he is praised for his childlike qualities of happiness and good nature or for his artistic and musical
gifts. . . . Negro writers do express much more frequently, as one would expect, the belief that whites and
Negroes have essentially equal potentialities, and that it is only the accidents of training and economic opportunity which have produced temporary differences; even among Negro writers, however, some have accepted
the prevailing stereotype." Otto Klineberg (ed.), *Characteristics of the American Negro* (New York: Harper,
1944). Instead of proposing an actual program of inquiry, the intentions of this line of thought appear to be
primarily moral and its objectives to be of a normative sort: desistance from the use of stereotypes.

veil.[2] In short, no order of reality could be given to assertions about slave character, because those assertions were illegitimately grounded on race, whereas their only basis was a corrupt and "unreal" institution. "To be sure," a recent writer concedes, "there were plenty of opportunists among the Negroes who played the role assigned to them, acted the clown, and curried the favor of their masters in order to win the maximum rewards within the system. . . ."[3] To impeach Sambo's legitimacy in this way is the next thing to talking him out of existence.

There ought, however, to be still a third way of dealing with the Sambo picture, some formula for taking it seriously. The picture has far too many circumstantial details, its hues have been stroked in by too many different brushes, for it to be denounced as counterfeit. Too much folk-knowledge, too much plantation literature, too much of the Negro's own lore, have gone into its making to entitle one in good conscience to condemn it as "conspiracy." One searches in vain through the literature of the Latin-American slave systems for the "Sambo" of our tradition—the perpetual child incapable of maturity. How is this to be explained?[4] If Sambo is not a product of race (that "explanation" can be consigned to oblivion) and not simply a product of "slavery" in the abstract (other societies have had slavery),[5] then he must be related to our own peculiar

[2] See below, Part IV, pp. 190–91.

[3] Kenneth Stampp, "The Historian and Southern Negro Slavery," *American Historical Review*, LVII (April, 1952), 617.

[4] There is such a word as "Zambo" in Latin America, but its meaning has no relation to our "Sambo." "A Zambo or Sambo (Spanish, *Zambo*, 'bandy-legged') is a cross between a *Negro* and an Amerindian (sometimes this name is given to the cross between a pure Negro and a mulatto, which the French called 'griffe')." Sir Harry Johnston, *The Negro in the New World* (London: Methuen, 1910), p. 3. I am not implying that racial stigma of some kind did not exist in South America (see above, pp. 77–78, n. 113); indeed, anthropological research has shown that the Latin-Americans were, and are, a good deal more conscious of "race" than such writers as Gilberto Freyre have been willing to admit. Even in Brazil, derogatory Negro stereotypes are common, and are apparently of long standing. On this point see Charles Wagley, *Race and Class in Rural Brazil* (Paris: UNESCO, 1952). On the other hand, it would be very difficult to find evidence in the literature of Brazil, or anywhere else in Latin America, of responsible men seriously maintaining that the Negro slave was constitutionally incapable of freedom. The views of a man like James H. Hammond, or for that matter the views of any average Southerner during the ante-bellum period, would have had little meaning in nineteenth-century Latin America. One is even inclined to think that these Latin-American stereotypes would compare more closely with the stereotypes of eastern and southern European immigrants that were held by certain classes in this country early in the twentieth century. See, e.g., Madison Grant's *Passing of the Great Race* (New York: Scribner, 1916). There are stereotypes and stereotypes: it would be quite safe to say that our "Sambo" far exceeds in tenacity and pervasiveness anything comparable in Latin America.

[5] It is, however, one thing to say that no longer are there any responsible men of science to be found advancing the racial argument, and quite another to assert that the argument is closed. In an odd sense we still find any number of statements indicating that the *other* side of the controversy is still being carried on, long after the bones of the enemy lie bleaching on the sands. For example, in the preface to a recent study on the American Negro by two distinguished psychologists, the authors define their "scientific position" by announcing that their book was "conceived and written on the premise that group characteristics are adaptive in nature and therefore not inborn, but acquired" and that "anyone who wishes to quote from [its] conclusions . . . to uphold any other thesis risks doing injustice to the material in the book, to the intentions of the authors, and to the Negro people." They then quote a kind of manifesto, signed by a group of prominent psy-

variety of it. And if Sambo is uniquely an American product, then his existence, and the reasons for his character, must be recognized in order to appreciate the very scope of our slave problem and its aftermath. The absoluteness with which such a personality ("real" or "unreal") had been stamped upon the plantation slave does much to make plausible the ante-bellum Southerner's difficulty in imagining that blacks anywhere could be anything but a degraded race—and it goes far to explain his failure to see any sense at all in abolitionism. It even casts light on the peculiar quality of abolitionism itself; it was so all-enveloping a problem in human personality that our abolitionists could literally not afford to recognize it. Virtually without exception, they met this dilemma either by sidetracking it altogether (they explicitly refused to advance plans for solving it, arguing that this would rob their message of its moral force) or by countering it with theories of infinite human perfectibility. The question of personality, therefore, becomes a crucial phase of the entire problem of slavery in the United States, having conceivably something to do with the difference—already alluded to—between an "open" and a "closed" system of slavery.

If it were taken for granted that a special type existed in significant numbers on American plantations, closer connections might be made with a growing literature on personality and character types, the investigation of which has become a widespread, respectable, and productive enterprise among our psychologists and social scientists.[6] Realizing that, it might then seem not quite so dangerous to add that the type corresponded in its major outlines to "Sambo."

Let the above, then, be a preface to the argument of the present essay. It will be assumed that there were elements in the very structure of the plantation system—its "closed" character—that could sustain infantilism as a normal feature of behavior. These

---

chologists and social scientists, attesting that "as social scientists we know of no evidence that any ethnic group is inherently inferior." This is followed by a portion of the 1950 UNESCO "Statement on Race" which declares that "biological studies lend support to the ethic of universal brotherhood." From Abram Kardiner and Lionel Ovesey, *The Mark of Oppression: A Psychosocial Study of the American Negro* (New York: Norton, 1951), pp. v–vi. While these are sentiments which may (and must) be pronounced on any number of occasions among men of good will (the President regularly conceives it his duty to do this), their *scientific* content (which is the level at which they are here being offered) has long since ceased to be a matter of controversy.

[6] Among such studies are Robert K. Merton, "Bureaucratic Structure and Personality," *Social Forces,* XVIII (May, 1940), 560–68; Erich Fromm, *Man for Himself* (New York: Rinehart, 1947); David Riesman, *The Lonely Crowd* (New Haven: Yale University Press, 1950); and Theodore Adorno and Others, *The Authoritarian Personality* (New York: Harper, 1950)—a work which is itself subjected to examination in Richard Christie and Marie Jahoda (eds.), *Studies in the Scope and Method of "The Authoritarian Personality"* (Glencoe, Ill.: Free Press, 1954); and H. H. Gerth and C. Wright Mills, *Character and Social Structure: The Psychology of Social Institutions* (New York: Harcourt, Brace, 1953). For a consideration of this field in the broadest terms, see Alex Inkeles and Daniel J. Levinson, "National Character: The Study of Modal Personality and Sociocultural Systems," *Handbook of Social Psychology,* ed. Gardner Lindzey (Cambridge, Mass.: Addison-Wesley, 1954), II, 977–1020.

elements, having less to do with "cruelty" per se than simply with the sanctions of authority, were effective and pervasive enough to require that such infantilism be characterized as something much more basic than mere "accommodation." It will be assumed that the sanctions of the system were in themselves sufficient to produce a recognizable personality type.[7]

It should be understood that to identify a social type in this sense is still to generalize on a fairly crude level—and to insist for a limited purpose on the legitimacy of such generalizing is by no means to deny that, on more refined levels, a great profusion of individual types might have been observed in slave society. Nor need it be claimed that the "Sambo" type, even in the relatively crude sense employed here, was a universal type. It was, however, a plantation type, and a plantation existence embraced well over half the slave population.[8] Two kinds of material will be used in the effort to picture the mechanisms whereby this adjustment to absolute power—an adjustment whose end product included infantile features of behavior—may have been effected. One is drawn from the theoretical knowledge presently available in social psychology, and the other, in the form of an analogy, is derived from some of the data that have come out of the German concentration camps. It is recognized in most theory that social behavior is regulated in some general way by adjustment to symbols of authority—however diversely "authority" may be defined either in theory or in culture itself—and that such adjustment is closely related to the very formation of personality. A corollary would be, of course, that the more diverse those symbols of authority may be, the greater is the permissible variety of adjustment to them—and the wider the margin of individuality, consequently, in the development of the self. The question here has to do with the wideness or narrowness of that margin on the ante-bellum plantation.

The other body of material, involving an experience undergone by several million men and women in the concentration camps of our own time, contains certain items of relevance to the problem here being considered. The experience was analogous to that of slavery and was one in which wide-scale instances of infantilization were observed. The material is sufficiently detailed, and sufficiently documented by men who not only took part in the experience itself but who were versed in the use of psychological theory for analyzing it, that the advantages of drawing upon such data for purposes of analogy seem to outweigh the possible risks.

The introduction of this second body of material must to a certain extent govern

---

[7] The line between "accommodation" (as conscious hypocrisy) and behavior inextricable from basic personality, though the line certainly exists, is anything but a clear and simple matter of choice. There is reason to think that the one grades into the other, and vice versa, with considerable subtlety. In this connection, the most satisfactory theoretical mediating term between deliberate role-playing and "natural" role-playing might be found in role-psychology. See below, pp. 131–33.

[8] Although the majority of Southern slaveholders were not planters, the majority of slaves were owned by a planter minority. "Considerably more than half of them lived on plantation units of more than twenty slaves, and one-fourth lived on units of more than fifty. That the majority of slaves belonged to members of the planter class, and not to those who operated small farms with a single slave family, is a fact of crucial importance concerning the nature of bondage in the ante-bellum South." Stampp, *Peculiar Institution*, p. 31.

the theoretical strategy itself. It has been recognized both implicitly and explicitly that the psychic impact and effects of the concentration-camp experience were not anticipated in existing theory and that consequently such theory would require some major supplementation.[9] It might be added, parenthetically, that almost any published discussion of this modern Inferno, no matter how learned, demonstrates how "theory," operating at such a level of shared human experience, tends to shed much of its technical trappings and to take on an almost literary quality. The experience showed, in any event, that infantile personality features could be induced in a relatively short time among large numbers of adult human beings coming from very diverse backgrounds. The particular strain which was thus placed upon prior theory consisted in the need to make room not only for the cultural and environmental sanctions that sustain personality (which in a sense Freudian theory already had) but also for a virtually unanticipated problem: actual change in the personality of masses of adults. It forced a reappraisal and new appreciation of how completely and effectively prior cultural sanctions for behavior and personality could be detached to make way for new and different sanctions, and of how adjustments could be made by individuals to a species of authority vastly different from any previously known. The revelation for theory was the process of detachment.

These cues, accordingly, will guide the argument on Negro slavery. Several million people were detached with a peculiar effectiveness from a great variety of cultural backgrounds in Africa—a detachment operating with infinitely more effectiveness upon those brought to North America than upon those who came to Latin America. It was achieved partly by the shock experience inherent in the very mode of procurement but more specifically by the type of authority-system to which they were introduced and to which they had to adjust for physical and psychic survival. The new adjustment, to absolute power in a closed system, involved infantilization, and the detachment was so complete that little trace of prior (and thus alternative) cultural sanctions for behavior and personality remained for the descendants of the first generation. For them, adjustment to clear and omnipresent authority could be more or less automatic—as much so, or as little, as it is for anyone whose adjustment to a social system begins at birth and to whom that system represents normality. We do not know how generally a full adjustment was made by the first generation of fresh slaves from Africa. But we do know— from a modern experience—that such an adjustment is possible, not only within the same generation but within two or three years. This proved possible for people in a full state of complex civilization, for men and women who were not black and not savages.

[9] See esp. below, p. 118 and n. 83

Slavery and Racism*
Henry N. Drewry

To understand the complex roots of racism in America, one must realize that slavery did not begin with the coming of Europeans to the Americas. Its history reaches back to ancient times. It was prevalent in Europe until replaced by serfdom in the Middle Ages, and it continued to exist long after that in parts of Asia and Africa. But for the most part, those slaves were prisoners of war or persons convicted of major crimes. The general attitude was that they were unfortunate, but no widely accepted idea existed connecting the condition of slavery with ethnic, racial, or individual inferiority. Slaves once freed disappeared into the society of those old world cultures. Why did this not happen here? Why was slavery's impact on the personalities of blacks and whites in the U.S. so severe and so long lasting? Why did slavery become what historians have called "the peculiar institution"?

Slavery in the English North American colonies came about because of the great need on the part of the colonists, once their settlements were established, for labor. There were never enough new colonists or indentured servants arriving, and the availability of free land meant that free men sought their own property and were difficult to keep as laborers.

In 1619 when the first Africans arrived in the English colonies they were sold as indentured servants and, as such, were able to obtain their freedom after working out their indenture. But beginning in the 1640s most Africans arriving in the colonies had no indenture and therefore could not look forward, ever, to receiving their freedom. Clearly the "freedom-loving" colonists—who had at first regarded Africans as merely different and not inferior—needed to rationalize this act of holding men in bondage permanently; had to adopt a philosophy and attitude that would allow them to live with a slave system which existed in all colonies but which proved most profitable in the plantation economy of the South. And that philosophy was that *black slaves were not human*

* From Henry N. Drewry, "U. S. Rationalized Slavery and Produced Racism," *University: A Princeton Quarterly,* no. 41 (Summer, 1969), 4–7. Reprinted by permission.

beings and thus not entitled to the considerations due humans. I will return to this. But first some additional background.

Slaves were brought out of Africa in increasingly large numbers. It has been estimated that that continent's loss of population because of slavery was as high as 50 million persons. Numbers died resisting capture, or traveling to the slave factories along the African coast, or in the crowded ships that transported them to the New World. Probably most of those who survived landed in the West Indies and South America. Horrors of the crossing and the experiences among hostile people undoubtedly had a major effect on the men and women who were brought here. Descriptions of these are available to us. One such is provided by Olavdah Equiano, a kidnaped member of the Ibo tribe of the kingdom of Benin (present-day Nigeria), who later wrote about his experiences:

> I was immediately handled and tossed up to see if I was sound, by some of the crew; and I was now persuaded that I had got into a world of bad spirits, and that they were going to kill me. Their complexions, too, differing so much from ours, their long hair, and the language they spoke, which was very different from any I had ever heard, united to confirm me in this belief. . . . When I looked around the ship too, and saw a large furnace or copper boiling, and a multitude of black people, of every description, chained together, every one of their countenances expressing dejection and sorrow, I no longer doubted of my fate. . . . I asked . . . if we were not to be eaten by those white men with horrible looks, red faces, and long hair. . . .
>
> I was soon put down under the decks, and there I received such a salutation to my nostrils as I had never experienced in my life: so that, with the loathsomeness of the stench, and with my crying together, I became so sick and low that I was not able to eat. . . . Two of the white men offered me eatables; and, on my refusing to eat, one of them held me fast by the hands, and laid me across, I think, the windlass, and tied my feet, while the other flogged me severely. . . .
>
> The closeness of the place, and the heat of the climate, added to the number in the ship, being so crowded that each had scarcely room to turn himself, almost suffocated us. . . . This deplorable situation was again aggravated by the galling of the chains. . . . The shrieks of the women, and the groans of the dying, rendered it a scene of horror almost inconceivable. Happily, perhaps, for myself, I was soon reduced so low here that it was thought necessary to keep me almost continually on deck; and from my extreme youth, I was not put in fetters.

By the time of the American Revolution the slave population was over 300,000. After independence it grew rapidly, as the following figures show.

Year	No. of slaves	Year	No. of slaves
1790	750,000	1830	2,328,000
1800	1,002,000	1840	2,873,000
1810	1,380,000	1850	3,638,000
1820	1,777,000	1860	4,441,000

The total population of the country had risen from 4,000,000 in 1790 to 31,443,000 in 1860. In 1860 the white population of the 15 slave states was 8,000,000.

The large percentage of the slaves in the Southern population is often used to explain the fear of a slave uprising, the consequent harshness of the system, and the hatred of blacks which developed from these. (It is generally acknowledged that rationalizing whites hated blacks because they mistreated them—and needed an excuse for doing so—rather than that they mistreated them because they hated them.) As the system became harsher the need on the part of slaveholders to justify it became greater—as did the difficulty of doing so logically. Stanley Elkins writes of the South's philosophical contortions:

> . . . [The] body of thought was governed by the fact that the South was talking no longer to the world, or even to the North, but to itself. It is this fact—the fact of internal consensus and the peculiar lack of true challenge-points at any level of Southern society—that gives the proslavery polemic its special distinction. . . . The mind could now conceive the enemy in any size or shape it chose; specters were utterly free to range, thrive, and proliferate.
>
> Only in such a setting of nightmare does it seem plausible, for example, that one of the most non-intellectual of paradoxes should have developed in men's writing and talk regarding the Negro slave and his present and hypothetical behavior. On the one hand, the ideal picture of Southern life was one of contentment, of plantations teeming with faithful and happy black children—young and old—helpless, purposeless children incapable of sustained and unsupervised initiative. On the other hand was the picture of doom; the hint of freedom, whispered by designing abolitionists would galvanize the sleeping monster in every slave, arouse bloody revolt, and bring hordes of black primitives bent on murder and destruction.

Southerners, while often irrational in their fears, could cite the slave revolts that *did* take place as evidence that their fears were well founded. Gabriel, a blacksmith who lived outside Richmond, Va., led a revolt in 1800; Denmark Vessey was the leading spirit in the 1822 plot at Charleston, S.C.; and Nat Turner struck fear into the hearts of all slaveholders in 1831 when he led an uprising in Virginia that took the lives of 60 whites and fought a pitched battle with state and federal troops before being crushed.

So shaken was the South by Turner's rebellion that several state legislatures, in emergency sessions, passed new laws to restrict the actions of slaves and even of free blacks. These laws deprived slaves of whatever freedom of movement they had had, and steps were taken to end the freeing of individual blacks. Severe reprisals and stricter codes were everywhere enforced.

But the number of blacks and the fear of insurrections fail to explain fully the lasting influence of slavery on our institutional life. Major slave revolts in ancient Rome had no such effect. To take an example closer to home, in Brazil, where the proportion of slaves to free men was greater than in the U.S., and where slave revolts were more common than in the U.S.—and where, as in the U.S., slaves were black and owners white—patterns of racism similar to those in this country did not develop. So for an explanation of U.S. racism one must dig deeper into the American character—strangely enough, into those experiences, ideas, and institutions which Americans set forth as their brightest contributions: For the paradoxical fact is that *the peculiar institution of American Negro slavery developed side-by-side with institutions which spoke of the dignity of man, government with the consent of the governed, majority rule, and protection of the rights of the individual.* Indeed, it may have been *because* these ideas and institutions were so strongly held and respected that strong feelings had to be marshalled against those persons who were not allowed to share them.

Rationalizing slavery in strictly religious terms was no problem for most God-fearing American slavery supporters, in the beginning. The concept of man's finding salvation through direct contact with God was a widely accepted doctrine of the majority of people in the English colonies, and bringing "heathens" to the "true religion" was an acceptable explanation for holding one's brother in bondage. At least it seemed to suffice during the 17th and much of the 18th centuries when many, if not most, of the slaves in America were Africa-born.

In 1693 English courts found common law support for the detaining of Negroes as slaves on the ground that they were heathens. The effect of this in Virginia, where Africans were for the first time legally designated as slaves in 1670, was to sanction slavery for servants imported from other than Christian lands.

But in the late 18th and 19th centuries, this justification could no longer be cited —because by then most American slaves were the offspring of Christian parents. It became necessary to provide another rationalization for subjugation and now it was the concept of the natural inferiority of blacks. The stage for this was set in many of the colonies by legislation similar to that of the Virginia Assembly which decided in 1667 that "Baptisme doth not alter the condition of the person as to his bondage or freedom; in order that diverse masters freed from this doubt may more carefully endeavor the propagation of Christianity."

Naturally, Biblical arguments in support of slavery were far more numerous when most Negroes were Christian than in the days before most had been converted. The publisher's preface to Rev. Josiah Priest's 1852 pamphlet entitled *Bible Defense of Slavery* states:

> In the book of Mr. Priest, on the subject of 'Slavery as it relates to the Negro, or African Race, Examined in the Light of Circumstances, History, and the Holy Scripture; with an Account of the Black Man's Color, Causes of his State of Servitude, and Traces of his Character; as well in Ancient as in Modern Times, with Strictures on Abolitionism,' the reader may confidently expect to find a work of great research and ability—one of deep interest, and well worthy his candid perusal. The author has sought, in the oracles of God, in authentic history, and in

the analogies of nature, the key to the mystery of the degradation, through the unchronicled ages of the past, of the negro race. The fact of the inferiority and consequent subordination of the black race to the white, being in accordance with the will of the Supreme Ruler of the universe, is not like a mathematical problem, susceptible of absolute demonstration; yet we think the reader of this work will acknowledge that the author has let in a flood of light upon this deeply interesting subject, through the mist in which ignorance and misguided sympathy has enveloped it.

In the text of the material Mr. Priest comments:

. . . if the spirit and tendencies of religion, can not, as yet, remove these disabilities or obstacles to man's happiness in this world, how, therefore, can it be expected that it can alter the doom of the negro race, which, as the Bible establishes, is founded on the same foundation, that of the decree of God, and raises a barrier which is impassable and insurmountable to all earthly power: even the famous words of our Lord called the Golden Rule, cannot apply here.

James A. Sloan spoke to the same issue in a pamphlet published in Memphis in 1857. *The Great Question Answered Or Is Slavery a Sin in Itself* contains the following:

We are considering the question of slavery in the light of the Bible, not by the theories of men; we, therefore, join issue with the doctrine that 'all men are created equal.' That such was the case at the beginning, before the entrance of sin, no one disputes. That man, and woman too, were equal, we do not deny; but we contend that that equality has been destroyed, or taken away by the express doing of the Creator himself, and that it was taken away as a punishment for sin. . . . 'Wives submit yourselves unto your own husbands, as it is fit, in the Lord.' [Col.III,18] Why then, is it fit that wives should submit themselves to their own husbands, when they were both created equal as to the right to rule? Simply because sin has deranged the relations of men; simply because God has inflicted this subjection on women as a punishment for sin. Whatever, then may have been the original equality of men and the freedom of their persons, God has taken away this freedom as a punishment of sin, and subjected the race of Ham to the will of the other two great divisions of the human family. 'Cursed be Canaan: a servant of servants shall he be unto his brethren.' [Gen. ix, 25–27.]

Amos Patriae takes a similar position in *The Blasphemy of Abolitionism Exposed: Servitude and the Rights of the South Vindicated: A Bible Argument,* published shortly before the Civil War:

Now, Hon. Sirs, I have cited, I believe, all the passages of scripture in both Old and New Testament, of any importance, that touch directly upon the subject under consideration—enough, at any rate, one would think, to satisfy the most sceptical, that slavery is a DEVINE INSTITUTION, *recognized and established by God's own order.* He says, *ye shall buy*—our brother abolitionists says, *ye shall not!* He commands slaves to be *obedient to their masters;* to serve with *fear and trembling; not purloin;* and to serve the *froward* as well as the good. But our abolition brethren teach *to disobey.* . . .

Had it not been for the institution of *slavery,* all the negroes in this country, both bond and free, civilized and christianized, if alive, would this day be slaves in their own native country, their bodies to black tyrannical masters, and their souls to the devil, through the worship of cats and alligators; and the colony of Liberia, which is destined in the providence of God, to civilize and christianize all Africa, never heard of. . . .

God never would have authorized slavery, had it not been intended as a *blessing to mankind.* And if it does not so result, it is the fault of man, not the institution. . . .

Religious attempts to justify slavery were still under way as the Civil War moved toward its conclusion. In *Southern Slavery and the Bible, A Scriptural Refutation of the Principal Arguments Upon Which the Abolitionists Rely,* published in Macon, Ga., in 1864, Rev. E. W. Warren speaks through his leading character Nellie Norton, a Northern girl visiting her uncle, Mr. T., in Georgia, to make his point:

. . . Mr. T., turning to Nellie, . . . said 'As we will not have another opportunity for several evenings, to converse on this subject again, I wish to mention a few of the points contained in the quotation you have just read, that you may consider them at your leisure.

'1st. It establishes the domestic slave trade: 'ye shall buy bondmen and bondmaids.' 2d. They were permitted to buy children from their parents: 'Of the children of the strangers that do sojourn among you, of them shall ye buy.' 3d. They were the property, or chattel, of the owner: 'And they shall be your possession.' 4th. There was no limit to their servitude, it was to be made perpetual: 'And inheritance for your children, your *bondmen forever.*' Here you have divine proof that a holy and just God did perpetuate slavery.'

Equal attention must be given to political developments. The colony of Maryland which passed the Toleration Act in 1649, passed in its Assembly in 1664 an act declaring

. . . all Negroes and other slaves already within the province, and all Negroes and other slaves to be hereafter imported into the province, shall serve *durante vita.* And all children born of any Negro or other slave shall be slaves as their fathers were, for the term of their lives. And forasmuch as divers freeborn English women, forgetful of their free condition and to the disgrace of our nation, marry Negro slaves . . . such freeborn women . . . shall serve the master of such slave during the life of her husband. And that all the issue of such freeborn women so married shall be slaves as their fathers were.

Georgia, which in 1734 had passed "an act for rendering the Colony of Georgia more Defensible by Prohibiting the Importation and use of Black Slaves or Negroes into the same," repealed that law in 1750 because "it may be a benefit to the said colony and a convenience and encouragement to the inhabitants thereof to permit the importation and use of them into the said colony."

This American society, which by 1776 had fixed a badge of inferiority to the Negro, produced that famous document which reads:

> We hold these truths to be self evident, that all men are created equal, that they are endowed by their creator with certain inalienable rights, that among these are life, liberty and the pursuit of happiness. That to secure these rights, governments are instituted among men, deriving their just powers from the consent of the governed, that whenever any form of government becomes destructive of these ends it is the right of the people to alter or abolish it.

The Constitution and the Bill of Rights became the law of the land while new Southern states wrote protective clauses for slavery into their constitutions. Jeffersonian and Jacksonian Democracy were concerned with rights for whites, not for blacks. Defense of slavery in the halls of Congress was common, as in the case of the Calhoun resolution in 1838 which stated:

> Resolved, That domestic slavery, as it exists in the Southern and Western States of this Union, composes an important part of their domestic institutions, inherited from their ancestors, and existing at the adoption of the Constitution, by which it is recognized as constituting an important element in the apportionment of powers among the States, and that no change of opinion or feeling, on the part of the other States of the Union in relation to it, can justify them or their citizens in open and systematic attacks thereon, with the view to its overthrow; and that all such attacks are in manifest violation of the mutual and solemn pledge to prote and defend each other, given by the States respectively, on entering into the constitutional compact which formed the Union, and such are a manifest breach of faith, and a violation of the most solemn obligations.

Thus did the philosophical conflicts which the colonists and early Americans faced concerning slavery give birth to rationalizations which the South, and to an unmeasurable extent the rest of the country, came to accept and to treat as eternal truths. These rationalizations of the righteousness of slavery and the inferiority of blacks caused problems for many of those who considered themselves sensitive and just. The framer of the Declaration of Independence had included in his draft the following reference to the King of England:

> He has waged cruel war against human nature itself, violating its most sacred rights of life and liberty in the person of a distant people who never offended him, captivating and carrying them into slavery in another hemisphere, or to incur miserable deaths in the transportation thither.

But this passage was stricken from the document before it was signed as a result of the opposition of slave interest represented by South Carolina and merchant interest represented by Rhode Island, both of which profited from the slave trade.

"I wonder if it be a sin to think slavery a curse to any land," wrote Mary Boykin Chestnut from Montgomery, Ala., in March of 1861. "Men and women are punished when their masters and mistresses are brutes, not when they do wrong. . . . God forgive us but ours is a monstrous system, a wrong and an iniquity!"

But for a country that believed in democratic principles and at the same time wanted the advantages it saw in slavery, the more questions were raised, the more firmly it must declare the righteousness of its position.

What I am suggesting is that it was *not in spite of but because of* America's moral and political principles that racism grew out of the peculiar institution of slavery. Conflict between high ideals on the one hand, and the desire for slave labor on the other, led to the tortured rationalizations which produced for white America the concept of the black as not entitled to judgment under the same morality and not entitled to the benefits of the political system because he was, by his very nature, inferior.

The Civil War put an end to the legal existence of the peculiar institution without erasing its effects upon the institutional, intellectual and emotional lives of blacks, of whites, and of their joint life in the United States.

Abolition's New Breed*

Benjamin Quarles

Fortunately the weather was not warm, for Bethel Church, Philadelphia, was crowded almost to suffocation on an evening in late January 1817. Never before had such a large number of Negro Americans assembled, not fewer than three thousand persons sitting and standing in the main floor and the U-shaped balcony. On the platform stood James Forten, a wealthy sail-maker who owned a country residence and kept a carriage. At a table behind him sat the secretary for the occasion, Russell Parrott, a public speaker who was prominent in Negro circles as the assistant to Absalom Jones, pastor of St. Thomas Episcopal Church. Jones himself was likewise a platform participant, along with his friend and early associate Richard Allen, Bethel's pastor and bishop in the African Methodist Episcopal Church. Conspicuously present was another pioneer Negro clergyman, John Gloucester of the African Presbyterian Church.

There was only one issue that could bring together a Negro gathering so numerous, of such diverse sponsorship, and of a mixture of the well-to-do and literate with the poor and unschooled. This binding issue was that of colonization, of sending Negroes to the west coast of Africa. Such a program had been proclaimed a month earlier by the newly formed American Colonization Society from its headquarters at the nation's capital. Any ambiguity in its official title, "American Society for Colonizing the Free People of Color in the United States," was removed by its avowed intent of sending the Negroes across the Atlantic.

Standing before the single-minded audience, Forten called for the "ayes" of those favoring colonization. A complete hush was the only response, as if his listeners were taking a deep breath for a full-throated response in the negative. Forten then called for those who opposed colonization. One long, loud, tremendous "No" went up which, wrote Forten, "seemed as it would bring down the walls of the building." [1]

In more formal fashion the assembly condemned the colonization scheme as an unmerited stigma upon the free Negro, and they vowed that they never would voluntar-

---

* From Benjamin Quarles, *Black Abolitionists* (New York: Oxford University Press Paperback, 1970), pp. 3–12, 14–19, 22. Copyright © 1969 by Oxford University Press, Inc. Reprinted by permission of author and publisher.
[1] *The Emancipator* (New York), June 30, 1835.

ily separate themselves from their brethren in slavery. They also empowered a commit-tee of twelve, including Forten, Jones, Allen, and Gloucester, to call another general meeting if the need developed.

Within a few days this committee found itself pressed into a most unexpected service—to meet the key figure in the founding of the American Colonization Society, Robert Finley. A clergyman, Finley viewed colonization as a means of uplifting the free Negro and of extending Christian missions to far-off lands. One of those whose advice Finley had sought was Paul Cuffe, a Negro merchant and shipbuilder. In 1814 Cuffe, a Quaker, had petitioned Congress to permit him to transport cargoes to and from Sierra Leone, and to carry a number of families thereto. The bill passed the Senate but was de-feated in the House by a close vote after a long debate. But as soon as the War of 1812 was over, Cuffe had transplanted thirty-eight Negroes to Sierra Leone, bearing most of the $4000 cost of the voyage. In response to Finley's request, Cuffe reported his impres-sions of west-coast Africa.[2]

Finley had sought other advice and support in the founding of the colonization society. His success had been marred only by the disturbing news of the meeting at Bethel Church. Hence as he left Washington to return to his New Jersey home he ar-ranged to stop over at Philadelphia. Calling upon a fellow Presbyterian minister, John Gloucester, Finley learned of the existence of the committee of twelve and requested an interview.

Finley spent the first hour trying to convince the Negro delegation that the colo-nization society was benevolently motivated and bent on working for the best interest of the colored people. Convinced of Finley's own goodwill, the Negro committeemen made no embarrassing comment on the motives of some of his fellow workers. Instead they went into a discussion of the most suitable place for colonization. Africa had some-thing to recommend it, said Gloucester, it being so far away as not to invite settlement by restless whites. Richard Allen said that Sierra Leone had attractions of its own, and he praised the work of Paul Cuffe.[3]

Although Finley came out of the meeting with a feeling of optimism, he had not changed any minds. This became evident a few months later when the colonization so-ciety selected Philadelphia as one of the five spots to establish its first auxiliaries. The city's black population responded as before. Gathering at the Green Court schoolhouse on August 10, they listened to a succession of speakers, reserving their most thoughtful attention for the statement entitled, "An Address to the Humane and Benevolent In-habitants of the City and County of Philadelphia." Written by Forten, the statement, which explained their hostility toward colonization, was adopted by unanimous vote.[4]

---

[2] *Annals of Congress*, Thirteenth Congress, first and second sessions, May 24, 1813, to Apr. 18, 1814, 569–72, 601, 861–63. *Biography of the Rev. Robert Finley, D.D.* (2nd ed., Phila., 1875), 126; hereafter cited as *Bi-ography of Finley*. For Negro removal sentiment in post-Revolutionary America, see Winthrop D. Jordan, *White over Black* (Chapel Hill, 1968), 546–69.

[3] *Biography of Finley*, 123.

[4] *Niles' Register* (Baltimore), Nov. 27, 1819. Edward Needles, *An Historical Memoir of the Pennsylvania Society for the Abolition of Slavery; the Relief of Free Negroes Unlawfully Held in Bondage and for Improving the Con-dition of the African Race* (Phila., 1848), 66; hereafter cited as *Memoir of Pennsylvania Society*.

As initially voiced by the Philadelphia Negroes, and adopted quickly by those elsewhere, the opposition to African colonization resulted from the evil effects it would have on all Negroes, slave and free. Colonization would cause a rise in the price of slaves, thus making it less likely that they would be freed. Colonization would make slavery more secure by removing the free Negro, a source of discontent to the slave and his possible ally in a rebellion. Moreover, free Negroes who went to Africa would be turning their backs on the slave, "our brethren by the ties of consanguinity, suffering, and wrong," as a resolution of the January 1817 meeting phrased it, adding that "we feel there is more virtue in suffering privations with them, than fancied advantages for a season."

Negroes charged that the colonization society threatened them with exile. One of the strongest arguments of the colonization group was that of Negro inferiority, his innate inability to make good in America as a free man. Left to his own devices, ran this line of reasoning, he tended to be corrupt and depraved, a predestined failure. Such baleful predictions provoked Negroes, who knew only too well how much more difficult it is to succeed when no one believes you can. Moreover, as typical Americans, Negroes were suspicious of schemes proposed for them by other people. This attitude on the part of Negroes was intensified in the case of the American Colonization Society, since its officers had never bothered to solicit their viewpoint, with the exception of Finley, who died within a year after its founding.

The Negro protest against African expatriation was recorded by Philadelphia Negroes in 1818 for the third time and once again in 1819. In subsequent years other voices took up the refrain. "Abide in the ship, or you cannot be saved," advised the New York weekly, *Freedom's Journal*. To Lewis Woodson of Chilicothe, Ohio, it was pointless to speak of Africa since "we never asked for it—we never wanted it; neither will we ever go to it." Samuel Cornish, editor of *Rights of All*, the successor to *Freedom's Journal*, said that the best way of repaying Africa the debt we owe her was not to return her sons to her coasts but to do them justice wherever we found them.[5]

Peter Williams, pastor of St. Philips Episcopal Church in New York, in a Fourth of July philippic against the colonization society, forcefully stated the case as the Negro saw it: "We are *natives* of this country; we only ask that we be treated as well as *foreigners*. Not a few of our fathers suffered and bled to purchase its independence; we ask only to be treated as well as those who fought against it."[6]

In a speech at the African Masonic Hall in Boston, the deeply religious Maria W. Stewart, the first native-born American woman to speak in public and leave extant texts of her addresses, strongly rebuked the colonization society, vowing that before she would be driven to a strange land, "the bayonet shall pierce me through." Another young woman, a Washington, D.C., domestic with a "yellowish tint," had a more subdued reaction—to her it "was not fair to send the Negro back after they had disfigured the colour."[7]

---

[5] *Freedom's Journal* (New York), June 8, 1827, Jan. 31, 1829; *Rights of All* (New York), June 12, 1829.
[6] Carter G. Woodson, *Negro Orators and Their Orations* (Washington, D.C., 1925), 80, hereafter cited as *Negro Orators*.
[7] *The Liberator* (Boston), Feb. 27, 1833. For Mrs. Stewart, see Lillian O'Connor, *Pioneer Woman Orators* (New York, 1954), 53–55, and Eleanor Flexner, *Century of Struggle: The Woman's Rights Movement in the United States* (Cambridge, Mass., 1959), 44–45. Jesse Torrey, *The American Slave Trade* (London, 1822), 118.

Those few Negroes who favored colonization risked obloquy and burning in effigy. In December 1826 when a group of Baltimore Negroes expressed a somewhat mild approval of the colonization society, a mass meeting of Philadelphia protesters, headed this time by John Bowers and Jeremiah Gloucester, drafted a formal "Remonstrance" charging that the Baltimoreans were grossly misleading the public. John B. Russwurm, Bowdoin graduate and the only influential Negro to come out for colonization during the first two decades of the society's existence, was forced as a consequence to resign from the editorship of the newspaper he had established. In letters marked "private" to R. R. Gurley, secretary of the American Colonization Society, Russwurm spoke of the "violent persecution" to which he had been subject by "the most influential of our people." [8]

The colonization scheme had a unifying effect on Negroes in the North, bringing them together in a common bond of opposition. Within a two-year span in the early 1830's Negroes in twenty-two cities held formal meetings of protest.[9] Their resolutions might vary in form—one group might declare themselves the legitimate sons of America, with no desire to leave their native land, and another group might report that they regarded the colonization society in the same light that lambs regarded wolves. But there was no mistaking their common attitude. Indeed, this hostility to the American Colonization Society led the delegates to a national Negro convention meeting in Philadelphia in 1835, to adopt unanimously a resolution "to remove the title of African from their institutions." [10]

The free Negro opposition to African colonization was not chronicled by contemporary observers and as a consequence the credit went elsewhere—to the new abolitionists.

In her work, *The Martyr Age of the United States of America,* the English writer and social critic, Harriet Martineau, credited the American Colonization Society with having "originated abolitionism" by arousing the free blacks and the opponents of slavery.[11] Miss Martineau sensed the interrelatedness of colonization and abolition, but it might be more clarifying to characterize the colonization issue as one of the salient points of difference between two schools of abolitionism—the pioneers who began their work in Revolutionary War times and those who succeeded them half a century later.

---

[8] *The Genius of Universal Emancipation* (Baltimore), Feb. 24, 1827. Russwurm to Gurley, Feb. 24, 1829, May 7, 1829, American Colonization Society Manuscripts, Library of Congress.

[9] Columbia, Harrisburg, Lewiston, Philadelphia, Pittsburgh and York in Pennsylvania; Hartford, Lyme, Middletown, and New Haven, Connecticut; Boston, Nantucket, and New Bedford, Massachusetts; Brooklyn, Catskill, and New York, New York; Newport and Providence, Rhode Island; Trenton and Wilmington, Delaware and Baltimore and Washington.

[10] *Minutes of the Fifth Annual Convention for the Improvement of the Free People of Colour in the United States, Held by Adjournments in the Wesley Church, Philadelphia, from the First to the Fifth of June, Inclusive, 1835* (Phila., 1835), 15.

[11] Harriet Martineau, *The Martyr Age of the United States of America, with an Appeal in Behalf of Oberlin Institute* (Newcastle-upon-Tyne, 1840), 2; hereafter cited as *Martyr Age.*

Abolitionists of whatever time or place believed slavery to be a wrong and were prepared to act upon their convictions. But a common dislike for slavery and a willingness to work for its downfall did not ensure a common pulling together. Abolitionists differed in their approach; nowhere could this be better illustrated than in the contrast between the old-school, pre-1830 reformers and their more strident successors. A descriptive glance at the earlier school will provide a sharpening of focus.

American antislavery sentiment can be traced back to such colonial figures as Judge Samuel Sewall in Calvinist Massachusetts and the tailor-scrivener John Woolman among the Quakers. The first formally organized society against slavery was founded in Philadelphia in 1775, and it was incorporated fourteen years later under the kind of long title that became characteristic of the early groups, The Pennsylvania Society for Promoting the Abolition of Slavery, the Relief of Free Negroes Unlawfully Held in Bondage, and for Improving the Condition of the African Race. An antislavery society was organized in New York in 1785, and soon after in New Jersey, Delaware, Maryland, Connecticut, Rhode Island, and Virginia. Early in 1794 delegates from five of these groups met in Philadelphia to form a national organization, The American Convention for Promoting the Abolition of Slavery and Improving the Condition of the African Race, a loose federation of state societies.

These earlier abolitionists had a religious orientation, a moderate and conciliatory tone, and, as previously noted, a colonizationist outlook. With branches in the slaveholding South, these reformers counted in their ranks an imposing roster of men of means and high public position. No Negroes or women held membership in their societies, and no attempt was made to form children's auxiliary chapters.

The religious impulse that guided these early reformers was the belief that slavery was a sin for which God would eventually exact retribution. The Friends were prominent in the movement.[12] In Pennsylvania they were its backbone; indeed, only Quakers were admitted to the first two conventions of the Pennsylvania abolitionists. Quakers had good precedents for the work; out of their number had come John Woolman and his close friend and successor, Anthony Benezet, the leading antislavery propagandist in late-eighteenth-century America. Quaker reformers were active in Maryland and Virginia before the 1700's drew to a close. Other religious groups adopted official resolutions condemning slavery, Virginia Baptists taking such a step in 1789, the Presbyterian General Assembly in 1795, and the Methodists during a series of four conferences from 1780 to 1796.

Early abolitionism had a certain Southern flavor. In 1827 the free states had 24 societies with a membership of 1500, but this hardly compared with the 130 societies in the slave states with a membership of 6625.[13] One of the more zealous of the Southern organizers was a Quaker, Charles Osborne, who in 1814 organized the Tennessee Society for Promoting the Manumission of Slaves, thus advancing a reformist outlook in East Tennessee.

[12] For antislavery sentiment among the early Quakers, see David Brion Davis, *The Problem of Slavery in Western Culture* (Ithaca, 1966), 291–332.

[13] *Genius of Universal Emancipation,* Oct. 13, 1827.

With rare exceptions, like that of Osborne, these early abolitionists were gradu-
alists, trusting to what they conceived as the slow but inevitable operation of religious
and equalitarian principles. They felt that slavery was not to be abolished overnight but
that it would certainly disappear in the fulness of time. They believed "that an abhorrence of slavery would gradually work its way, and that it was the duty of the society patiently to wait the event," wrote William Rawle, onetime president of the Pennsylvania
Society. James G. Birney, a slaveholder turned abolitionist, attributed the "declension"
of the early societies to their failure to press for immediate emancipation.[14]

Because they expected slavery to die out by slow degrees at some distant, un-
specified date, the early abolitionists counseled Negroes to bear and forbear. They advised free Negroes to live within their income so that they would have something to
give to the unfortunate, and "to cultivate feelings of piety and gratitude to your Heav-
enly Father for the many blessings you enjoy." Free Negroes who somehow might be in
communication with slaves were advised "to impress them with the necessity of con-
tentment with their situations" to the end that their masters would respond with humanity and gentleness.[15]

In their addresses to the slaveholders, the earlier abolitionists used calm and temperate language, in line with their belief that a harsher tone would seem provocative.
They avoided passionate denunciations or the reciting of atrocity stories. They avowed
that their plans were of a pacific nature and that any opposition to slaveholders was opposition to a brother rather than to an enemy.

Conciliatory to the core, the earlier generation of abolitionists seemed to go out
of their way to win the love and esteem of the South. William Ellery Channing, whose
fame as a scholar and a Unitarian clergyman extended far beyond his Boston parishioners, typified this olive-branch approach. In a letter to Daniel Webster in May 1828,
Channing suggested that Northerners should allay the fears of Southerners by saying to
them, "We consider slavery as your calamity, not your crime, and we will share with
you the burden of putting an end to it." [16]

The early abolitionists gave constant and positive assurance to Southerners that
they had no intention of interfering with the rights of property. Hence slave emancipation was not to be achieved without compensation to the owners. In part this attitude
stemmed from the elite composition of the membership. The founders of the New
York Manumission Society, for example, included such distinguished names as Philip
Schuyler, James Duane, and Chancellor Livingston, and its first president was John Jay,
who was succeeded in that office by Alexander Hamilton. Such men of wealth or high

[14] Edward R. Turner, *The Negro in Pennsylvania* (Washington, D.C., 1911), 220. *Correspondence Between
the Hon. F. H. Elmore . . . and James G. Birney* (New York, 1838), 8.

[15] *The American Convention for Promoting the Abolition of Slavery to the Free People of Colour in the United
States, Philadelphia, 1829* (Phila., 1829), 5. *Minutes of the Proceedings of the Ninth American Convention for Promoting the Abolition of Slavery and Improving the Condition of the African Race, January 9–13, 1804* (Phila., 1804),
33.

[16] Channing to Webster, May 14, 1828, in *The Works of Daniel Webster* (ninth ed., 6 vols., Boston,
1856), V, 367.

station were highly sensitive to the sanctity of capital investments, however deplorable its form. Not through the purse strings would they strike.

As a national organization the earlier abolitionists were hesitant at first in supporting colonization. Before giving an official opinion, the American Convention for Promoting the Abolition of Slavery invited James Forten to appear at its meeting in December 1818. After receiving his views the convention issued a report opposing colonization on the grounds that Negroes were averse to it and that they were determined not to be transported to Africa unless by force. Again in 1821 the parent organization expressed official disapproval of colonization. But such action had little influence on the subsidiary societies, the Manumission Society of North Carolina having pledged its support to the American Colonization Society before the latter had celebrated its first anniversary.[17]

After 1821 the American Convention quietly abandoned its opposition to colonization, breaking its silence in 1829 to come out in flat endorsement of the voluntary emigration of free Negroes and of Congressional assistance in effecting it. The school conducted by the New York Manumission Society, the African Free School, worked out an agreement with the colonization society in 1828 and 1829 to educate two young Negroes, Washington Davis and Cecil Ashman, for teaching in Liberia. When one of the students of the school, Isaac H. Moore, expressed an interest in Liberia, he was encouraged by principal Charles C. Andrews to write to the colonization society, and when John B. Russwurm was preparing to go to Liberia as a principal in the summer of 1829, Andrews offered to brief him on school administration.[18]

The early abolitionist movement was by no means barren of accomplishment. It had rescued hundreds of Negroes illegally held in bondage, the Delaware Society alone having liberated twelve in the span of a year. True, the organizations did not admit Negroes to membership; the constitution of a Southern auxiliary was likely to be restricted to free, white males, and the Pennsylvania Society for Promoting the Abolition of Slavery admitted only one Negro from 1775 to 1859, the lightskinned Robert Purvis.[19]

●   ●   ●

Obviously the abolitionist approach of brotherly reconciliation found itself progressively weakened in a period in which sectional hostilities were sharpening. The parent organization held no regular meetings after 1832 and formally dissolved in 1838,

[17] *Minutes of the Proceedings of a Special Meeting of the Fifteenth American Convention for Promoting the Abolition of Slavery, and Improving the Condition of the African Race, Assembled at Philadelphia, December 10–15, 1818* (Phila., 1818), 39. Minutes of the Proceedings of a Convention of Delegates from the Abolition Societies, 1798, in "Documents: The Appeal of the American Convention of Abolition Societies, *The Journal of Negro History,* April 1921 (VI), 213. Early Lee Fox, *The American Colonization Society, 1817–1840* (Baltimore, 1919), 181.

[18] Andrews to Gurley, June 28, 1828, Nov. 6, 1828, Jan. 9, 1829, American Colonization Society Manuscripts. Moore to Gurley, Apr. 9, 1829. Ibid. Russwurm to Gurley, July 24, 1829. Ibid.

[19] *Minutes of the American Convention for Promoting the Abolition of Slavery and Improving the Condition of the African Race, January 9, 1804* (Phila., 1804), 13. The list of members from 1775 to 1859 may be found in *Act of Incorporation of the Pennsylvania Society for Promoting the Abolition of Slavery* (Phila., 1860), 13–36.

after forty-four years of existence. These early abolitionists were men of good intention, and their work had not been without its good fruit. But new occasions teach new duties and time makes ancient good uncouth, in the words of one of the new breed, James Russell Lowell.

"We shall spare no exertions nor means to bring the whole nation to speedy repentance," ran one of the resolutions marking the first meeting of the American Anti-Slavery Society in December 1833 at Philadelphia.[23] Thus did abolitionism take on a new character, a direct confrontation—not a flank attack—on slavery. Impelled by a sense of urgency hitherto missing, these new spokesmen insisted that the nation face up to the question. Believing that they best served their countrymen by rebuking them for their faults, they were determined to rivet public attention on an issue most people would have preferred to ignore.

The new school stood for uncompensated emancipation, holding that if anybody deserved payment it was the slave. When a bondman became free by purchase, even by self purchase, these abolitionists deplored it as a violation of principle, however much they may have shared the elation of the ransomed. Men of limited patience, they called for immediate and unconditional emancipation. To them gradualism was wrong in theory, weak in practice, and fatally quieting to the conscience of the slaveholder. The doctrine of immediatism had not originated with the new abolitionists,[24] but it had little influence before their arrival. At first the immediatist doctrine was interpreted by some of the new abolitionists to mean gradual emancipation beginning at once, but by 1840 this modification had all but disappeared.

To their radical approach the new breed brought a vocabulary that was equally unsettling. They held that social revolutionaries may have to overstate their case to make their point. "The pleas of crying soft and sparing never answered the purpose of a reform, and never will," wrote the Negro reformer David Ruggles. Thomas Wentworth Higginson held that loud language was needed for those whose ears were stopped with Southern cotton. Hence many of these reformers abandoned the restraints of polite discourse and went in for shock-effect statements. With a fondness for epithet, they might label a slaveholder as a man-thief, a child-seller, and a woman-whipper. At one of their meetings a typical resolution, such as the following by former slave William Wells Brown, might brand the United States as a wilful liar, a shameless hypocrite, and the deadliest enemy of the human race. Wendell Phillips could characterize the South as "one great brothel, where half a million of women are flogged to prostitution, or worse still, are degraded to believe it honorable." Death brought no surcease from their attack; they hailed the "removal" of Webster, Clay, and Calhoun, "those great obstacles of freedom." [25]

[23] *Proceedings of the Anti-Slavery Convention Assembled at Philadelphia, December 4, 5, 6, 1833* (New York, 1833), 15.

[24] George W. Julian, "The Genesis of Modern Abolitionism," *The International Review* (New York), June 1882 (XII), 533–54.

[25] *Emancipator,* Feb. 3, 1835. Thomas Wentworth Higginson, *Contemporaries* (Boston, 1899), 69. *Six-*

However uncharitable their language, most of these reformers were religious men, many of whom felt a personal guilt for the sin of slavery. Abolitionism was to some an outlet for religious anxiety, a seeking for self-purification. The abolition crusade, however, was not church-centered; it was by and large an extra-church movement, in part because the far-reaching whip of the reformers did not spare the clergy.

A broad employment base characterized the post-1830 reformers. Their leaders tended to be college-trained, and they ran the gamut of the professions, including law, medicine, religion, and education. A handful of businessmen joined the cause, among them Arthur and Lewis Tappan, former members of the New York Society for Promoting the Manumission of Slaves. But if the leaders came from an elite class, the movement was essentially grass-roots, its monies coming from thousands of small donors, women as well as men.

By 1833 when the new national society was organized, the abolition movement had become largely concentrated in one section of the country. The numerous societies in the South had all but disappeared in less than a decade. In part this was due to a document which issued from Boston followed by an act which took place at Southampton County, Virginia, both of which alarmed and angered the Southerners,[26] causing them to close ranks.

The disquieting document bore a lengthy title, generally shortened to *David Walker's Appeal.*[27] Its self-taught author was a tall, slender, dark-skinned dealer in clothes, new and secondhand, who had left Wilmington, North Carolina, to settle in Boston. Here he had become a rising figure in the Negro community; he was the local agent for the *Rights of All;* he had been second marshal at a public dinner, held at the African Masonic Hall, for Prince Abdul Rahaman of Footah Jallo; and he had subscribed to the fund to purchase the freedom of George Horton of North Carolina,[28] the most celebrated slave poet since Phillis Wheatley. Walker was a member of the Massachusetts General Colored Association, founded in 1826 for racial betterment and slave abolition. *Walker's Appeal,* a seventy-six-page pamphlet that ran into three editions in 1829 and 1830, was a call to militant action. It bore the marks of careful reflection, and its phrasing was often eloquent, although not free of faulty sentence structure and punctuation. Above all, Walker minced no words: "Remember Americans, that we must and shall be free and enlightened as you are, will you wait until we shall, under God, obtain our liberty by the crushing arm of power? Will it not be dreadful for you? I speak Americans for your own good." [29]

teenth Annual Report of the Massachusetts Anti-Slavery Society, January 26–27 1848 (Boston, 1848), 89. The Phillips quotation and the reference to Webster, Clay, and Calhoun are in *Twenty-First Annual Report of the Massachusetts Anti-Slavery Society, January 26–27, 1853* (Boston, 1853), 107, 92.

[26] On this whole point, see Gordon Esley Finney, "The Anti-slavery Movement in the South, 1787–1836: Its Rise and Decline and Contribution to Abolitionism in the West," Ph.D. dissertation, Duke University, 1962.

[27] For this document and an analysis of its setting and its meaning, see Herbert Aptheker, *One Continual Cry* (New York, 1965).

[28] *Freedom's Journal,* Oct. 3, 1828; Oct. 24, 1828.

[29] Aptheker, *One Continual Cry,* 137.

Walker's pamphlet "alarmed society not a little," wrote Harriet Martineau. The greatest of the turn-of-the-century anti-slavery workers, the Quaker, Benjamin Lundy, called it the most inflammatory publication in history, disavowing it as an injury to the cause. *Walker's Appeal* led Georgia and North Carolina to enact laws against incendiary publications and prompted the mayor of Savannah, William T. Williams, and the governor of Georgia, George R. Gilmer, to send letters of protest to the mayor of Boston, Harrison Gray Otis. In February 1830 four Negroes were arrested in New Orleans on the charge of circulating it. Walker's death in 1830 did not diminish the influence of his *Appeal,* Negroes regarding it as "an inspired work" and Southern whites viewing it as "the diabolical Boston Pamphlet." Both would have agreed with their contemporary, Samuel J. May, that "the excitement which had become so general and so furious against the Abolitionists throughout the slaveholding States was owing in no small measure to . . . David Walker." [30]

A much profounder traumatic experience was in store for the South in the Nat Turner insurrection in tidewater Virginia, in the late summer of 1831. The revolt was conceived and planned by a slave preacher, Nat Turner, a dedicated revolutionary but also something of a mystic torn between a New Testament affirmation of love and an even more consuming Old Testament passion for massive warfare against the Satanic hosts, in this instance, slavery. After receiving what he considered a sign from heaven, Turner and his followers set about their grim business, killing some sixty whites.

Turner's rebellion, Walker's pamphlet, and the appearance of the new abolitionists did not completely crush antislavery sentiment in the South.[31] But they combined to give it a blow from which it could never recover, and they were all but fatal to the organized expressions of antislavery sentiment, the hitherto numerous manumission societies. Southern abolitionists could not cope with the massive assault by slavery's supporters, who could now put them in a class with Walker, Turner, and the new militants—the South's new symbols of outrage, detestation, and fear.

The loss of the South as a recruiting ground for abolitionists coincided with the acquisition of a new element, greater in ardor than the lost component if somewhat below it in formal education and social rank. This new element was the Negro. "The grand abolition movement of the day, which is now agitating the Northern states, is of a mixed complexion, with a slice of black and a slice of white, in somewhat unequal proportions," observed the New York *Herald* with a typical touch of derision.[32] This new black element made its debut at the same time as and in close conjunction with that of the Boston reformer destined to become the movement's best known name— William Lloyd Garrison.

---

[30] Martineau, *Martyr Age,* 11. *Genius of Universal Emancipation,* Apr. 1830. *Niles' Register,* Mar. 27, 1830, and see Clement Eaton, "A Dangerous Pamphlet in the Old South," *The Journal of Southern History,* 1936 (II), 323–34. *The African Repository* (Washington, D.C.), Mar. 1830 (VI), 29. Samuel J. May, *Some Recollections of our Anti-slavery Conflict* (Boston, 1869), 133; hereafter cited as *Some Recollections.*

[31] See, for example, Kenneth Stampp, "The Fate of the Southern Anti-Slavery Movement," *Journal of Negro History,* Jan. 1943 (XXVIII), 10–22.

[32] In *The North Star* (Rochester), Nov. 10, 1848.

Looking back in 1855 from a vantage of twenty-five years, J. McCune Smith, the Negro physician and abolitionist, observed that it was hard to tell which loved the other most —Mr. Garrison the colored people, or the colored people Mr. Garrison.[33] This reciprocal sentiment first emerged in Baltimore where Garrison spent some eight months during 1829–30 assisting Benjamin Lundy in editing *The Genius of Universal Emancipation.* The Garrison-Negro bond of affection was sealed upon Garrison's return to Boston to launch *The Liberator.* Its first issue, dated January 1, 1831, struck the militant note so typical of the new school. He was in earnest and he would be heard, wrote Garrison; moreover, he would be "as harsh as truth, and as uncompromising as justice." The twenty-five-year-old editor had a special message "to our free colored brethren," seeking their support and promising them his, inasmuch as "we know that you are now struggling against wind and tide." [34]

•   •   •

Meeting in mid-July 1831 in the African School Room of the two-story brick meetinghouse in Belknap Street, a group of Boston Negroes took note of Garrison's unstinted exertions on their behalf, viewing him as greatly commanding their thanks and gratitude. The man they so honored hardly seemed of hall-of-fame calibre. Certainly in appearance he was not impressive. Prematurely bald and wearing steel-rimmed glasses, he looked mild and benign, with a touch of the funereal in his dress, customarily a black suit and a black cravat. As a speaker he tended to become monotonous. He had a penchant for strong epithets, which his associate, Lydia Maria Child, attributed to "his being very thoroughly imbued with the phraseology of the Bible," [43] and he was overly quick to charge an opponent with moral blindness or a lack of integrity. He was untidy in his ideas and his grasp of history, law, and politics was slight.

But whatever the catalogue of his shortcomings, his unswerving championship of human rights marked him as a providential figure in an age when the forces of slavery and antislavery met head-on in America. This confrontation was welcomed by the latter-day abolitionist, with young leadership, some of it Garrison's, and with new blood, some of it the Negro's.

[33] *Frederick Douglass' Paper* (Rochester), Jan. 26, 1854.

[34] *Liberator,* Jan. 1, 1831.

[43] *Liberator,* July 16, 1831. Lydia Maria Child, "William Lloyd Garrison," *The Atlantic Monthly* (Boston), Aug. 1879 (XLIV), 234.

Part 3

THE CIVIL WAR
AND
RECONSTRUCTION

The Civil War and Reconstruction periods are unmatched in American History in the wide variety of explanations and interpretations given to them. Historian Thomas J. Pressly has suggested that "the farther the Civil War receded into the past the greater the disagreement among twentieth century historians over its causes, and the greater the strength of the emotions with which these divergent viewpoints were upheld." [1] Similarly, the editor's preface to *Reconstruction After the Civil War* states, "The Reconstruction era has properly been called the bloody battleground of American History." [2] Not the least obvious and subtle issue with which historians have dealt is the role played by and the influence of events on the black American.

Materials in this section are part of this historical conflict. None of them fall within what might be called the traditional school which assigns to blacks a passive role during the Civil War and a negative role during Reconstruction. Instead, these selections see blacks as active, on their own behalf, in and out of the military service during the war, and they view the reality of Reconstruction as less tragic than the traditional legend would have us believe. Two of the books from which selections are taken were

[1] Thomas J. Pressly, *Americans Interpret Their Civil War,* New York, 1962, Collier Books, p. 9.
[2] John Hope Franklin, *Reconstruction After the Civil War,* Chicago, University of Chicago Press, 1961, p. vii.

written in the 1930s, the others in the 1960s. The student of history will immediately recognize these as periods with little kinship as far as historical interpretations are concerned. William E. B. Du Bois, writing in 1935, was, because of race, experience, and personality, not in line with most American historians of his day on issues involving race. Recent scholarship, however, has given much support to some positions which he staked out. As for Bell I. Wiley, who wrote in 1938, the importance of his work was overlooked as a result of the conventional historical wisdom of the day. Consequently, these two selections do not reflect the dominant opinions of the 1930s on black Americans.

The activities of black Americans during the war are the concerns of *Southern Negroes, 1861–1865,* Bell I. Wiley, and *The Negro's Civil War,* James M. McPherson. Wiley's 1938 work takes issue with the traditional emphasis on almost uniform loyalty of slaves to masters during the war and wholesale return of freedmen to their former plantations at the end of the fighting. Through careful examination of diaries, plantation records, newspapers, and the writings of many southerners he appraises the conduct of slaves during the five-year struggle. McPherson examines the sources for actions and feelings of those blacks involved in the armed forces. In the selection from *The Negro's Civil War* he draws heavily on the comments of the soldiers themselves in looking at the Negro soldier in the Union army in 1863 and 1864.

Black Reconstruction, William E. B. Du Bois, and *Reconstruction After the Civil War,* John Hope Franklin, take issue with the traditional interpretation of the period. The pattern for this interpretation had been set by Professor William A. Dunning of Columbia University and developed by some of his graduate students, outstanding among them the historian James G. Randall who wrote in the 1930s. As a lonely voice of dissent from this group, Du Bois concludes his *Black Reconstruction* with the selection included here, "The Propaganda of History." He views a sense of national shame growing out of the events of the war and Reconstruction as leading to a falsification of history which distorts the true role of black Americans.

Like Du Bois, John Hope Franklin sees black Americans playing an important and productive part in Reconstruction governments. The selection included from *Reconstruction After the Civil War* discusses this participation and some of the lasting benefits for southern states resulting from this period.

Slave Conduct During the War[*]

Bell Irvin Wiley

An appraisal of the behavior of the slaves during the struggle which involved their freedom is made difficult by the conflicting nature of much of the evidence on the subject. The tenor of statements made during the war is generally in marked contrast with those made afterwards. Contemporary commendations of the slaves' conduct do not harmonize with the steps which were taken to insure a more rigid control.[1] There also is a pronounced difference between the testimony of North and South, both during and after the conflict. This is attributable in part to the close association of the conduct of the slaves with the issues of the war. For the Negroes to show a disposition to resist the authority of their owners, to "throw off the yoke of bondage," and to give secret aid and joyful reception to the Federal armies, supported the claim of the North that the "institution" was irksome, oppressive, and cruel; for them to perform positive acts of loyalty to their masters, to resist the allurements of the "Yankees," or simply to go about their work in a quiet way with evident unconcern, bolstered the Southern contention that the general influences of slavery were wholesome and benevolent, and that the Negroes were content with a servile position in society. This situation tended to make Confederates suppress and minimize reports of misconduct and insubordination—at least to reserve them for "home consumption"; their circulation in the North gave the "Yankees" too much satisfaction. Federals, on the other hand, showed a disposition to make the most of instances of the slaves' desertion of their master and their support of the Union cause, as indications of the weakness of the South's system of social and political in-

[*] From Bell Irvin Wiley, *Southern Negroes, 1861–1865* (New Haven: Yale University Press Paperback, 1965), pp. 63–69, 72–77, 83–84. Copyright © 1938 by Yale University Press, 1965 by Bell I. Wiley. Reprinted by permission.

[1] See Chapter II. There was a general tightening of the state patrol laws throughout the Confederacy at the beginning of the war. At various later times, this action was repeated in the different states. W. H. Russell, correspondent of the London *Times,* noticed and commented on this divergence of expression and action. Charleston *Mercury,* June 26, 1861.

equality. The persistence of the tendency of North and South to use the war-time conduct of the Negroes as a justification of their respective positions on the slave question,
coupled with the proneness to idealize that part of the past which is pleasant and to forget that which is unpleasant, continued to prejudice thought on the question long after
the clash of arms had ended.

There were a number of factors which influenced the slaves' conduct during the
war, one of the most pertinent of which was that of personal attachment. Those Negroes who were closely associated with their owners were usually the most loyal under
trying circumstances. The body servants of the Confederate soldiers were more intimately associated with their masters than any of the others. In many cases, soldiers and
servants had been childhood playmates. Each had a genuine affection for the other,
which was cemented by common exposure and hardship in the army. No class of slaves
had as good opportunities for desertion and disloyalty as the body servants but none was
more faithful. Next in the rank of close association with the whites were the house
servants; they were also next in the degree of loyalty. When the young masters left for
the war, they sometimes received the embrace as well as the parting blessing of the old
kitchen "mammy." [2] When the home was saddened by the news of death, the tears of
the black members of the household were often more profuse and just as sincere as
those of the whites.[3] When the "Yankees" made their dreaded raids, the uneasiness of
the whites was often shared by the black domestics; together they watched through
hours of uncertainty until the danger passed.[4] Next to the domestic servants in the degree of intimacy and frequency of association with the whites were the drivers or fore-
men, and, as a general rule, their conduct was much more loyal than that of the rank
and file. They were often entrusted with the keys when the approach of the enemy necessitated the masters' flight.

Just as the understanding and affection engendered by close association tended to
keep slaves loyal and well-behaved in times of distress, so did remoteness and lack of association make them more susceptible to disorder and disloyalty. On the large plantations the field hands were the first to give trouble. On plantations in the charge of overseers, rarely visited by the owners, there was often very little affection felt by the
Negroes for their masters; and they were usually disloyal when the "Yankees" came.
On small farms where the master and his Negroes were accustomed to work side by
side, instances of unfaithfulness were less common.

The influence of close association on the conduct of the slave was much greater
when it was supported by a specific commitment of trust. The body servant was
strengthened in his determination to render faithful service by the explicit charge of the
mistress to stay with "Mas' Henry" under all circumstances and not to come home
without him. The domestic to whom valuables were unreservedly entrusted for safe-
keeping rarely failed to return them, even though several years might elapse before safe

[2] John Allen Wyeth, *With Sabre and Scalpel,* p. 54.
[3] Mrs. Irby Morgan, *How It Was,* p. 90.
[4] Dolly Sumner Lunt, *A Woman's War-Time Journal,* p. 32.

delivery was possible. The calling together of the slaves by the master on his departure for the war and the commitment of his family to them for safe-keeping seemed to have a salutary effect on their later conduct;[5] but this charge, involving more persons, was less definite and consequently tended to be less effective than the individual commitments mentioned above. Booker T. Washington's statement that a Negro rarely betrays a specific trust has much support in the history of the war between North and South.[6]

Negroes who had been well treated before the outbreak of the war were generally more faithful during the trying days which followed.[7] Slaves of kind and considerate masters who were induced to leave them, or were forced away, sometimes came back after the passing of the Federals, and resumed the discharge of their plantation duties.[8] In cases where the Negroes had been driven and cruelly treated, they were inclined to use the discomfiture of the owners to their own advantage. This is reflected in the action of the slaves at Magnolia after the coming of the Federals to the vicinity gave them an opportunity to assert their wishes. Contrary to general practices, the Negroes on this plantation were not given a Christmas holiday. On December 25, 1862, they went to work as usual, but shortly after breakfast they returned to the "quarter" saying, according to the record of the overseer, "that never having had a chance to keep it [Christmas Day] before, they would avail themselves of the privilege now, they thought." [9] So averse were some Negroes to their masters, on account of treatment accorded them in slavery days, that they refused to work for them after the adoption of the wage basis for labor.[10]

The amount of outside interference was also a very important element in the behavior of the slaves. The mere proximity of Federal soldiers had disquieting effects, but their entry into a town or community, bringing to the Negroes exaggerated ideas of freedom and encouraging them to seize property, and sometimes to commit acts of violence against their masters, was invariably the occasion of disturbance. That the slaves were orderly before the "Yankees" came and that they were disorderly after they came is a general rule that might be applied to almost any invaded portion of the Confederacy.

However, all of the disorder among the Negroes attendant upon Federal invasion cannot be attributed directly to the invaders. Their coming was immediately preceded by the exodus of most of the resident whites capable of exercising any effective discipline. Considerable disturbance would have resulted from this withdrawal of accustomed authority had the "Yankees" not come at all.[11] A resident of Port Gibson, Missis-

---

[5] W. W. Malet, *An Errand to the South in the Summer of 1862,* p. 46.

[6] *Up from Slavery,* p. 13.

[7] R. H. Williams, *With the Border Ruffians,* p. 441.

[8] De Saussure, *Old Plantation Days,* p. 82.

[9] Magnolia Plantation Records, entry of Dec. 25, 1862.

[10] Williams, *With the Border Ruffians,* p. 440.

[11] A. E. Burnside wrote to Secretary Stanton from New Berne, N. C., in March, 1862, "Nine-tenths of the depredations on the 14th after the enemy and citizens fled from the town were committed by the Negroes before our troops reached the city. They seemed to be wild with excitement and delight. . . . The city is being overrun with fugitives from the surrounding towns and plantations." *O. R.,* Ser. I, IX, 199.

sippi, wrote to Governor Pettus in February, 1863, that "the Negroes are under no restraint at night . . . nightly depredations are committed on my place. No care and forethought can prevent this unless we have a white man on the place." [12] Another Mississippian wrote from Bolivar County in August, 1864, stating that the recent withdrawal of the military patrol from the vicinity had been followed by manifestations of insubordination and rebellion among the Negroes, and protesting against the removal of any more of the adult males from the county.[13] Communications from other areas tell the same story; where control was lacking disturbances were common.[14]

The infrequency of serious disorders in the interior regions was due, to a considerable extent, to the general adoption of the policy of overlooking minor infractions and administering swift and severe punishment for offenses of an insurrectionary nature. This practice made it possible for a few civilians, aided in some areas by military detachments, to keep the slaves in subjection. The procedure in cases of plots to rebel is illustrated by an instance in Brooks County, Georgia, in August, 1864. On the same day that evidences of the plot were discovered a public meeting was called, an examining committee of twelve appointed, and at six o'clock in the afternoon three Negroes were hanged.[15] In September, 1864, a group of about thirty Amite County, Mississippi, Negroes who had armed themselves with their masters' guns and ridden off toward the river cheering and shouting were overtaken within a few miles of their destination by a group of Confederate scouts and most of them killed.[16]

Severe punishments were administered for other offenses which threatened to subvert authority. Scouts in South Carolina disguised themselves as "Yankees," went to a cabin of a Negro whom they suspected, and offered him a bribe if he would show them to the camp of the "Rebel" troops who were hid in the swamp. The unsuspecting Negro complied with alacrity. When the party came to the hiding place, the Negro was seized by the *pseudo* "Yankees" and "strung up" to a limb.[17] A slave arrested on a suspicion that he had designed "to commit a great crime against the peace of a family" in Blakely, Alabama, was killed when he tried to break away from the patrollers. The man arraigned for firing the fatal shot was acquitted with the explanation that the community was in a state of great uneasiness and alarm at the time.[18]

The effectiveness of stringent measures was increased by giving them a wide publicity. Newspapers gave their ready coöperation by carrying exchanges in order that

---

[12] E. C. Patterson to Governor Pettus, Feb. 23, 1863, Miss. Archives, Ser. E, no. 59.

[13] A. B. Bradford to Governor Clark, Aug. 27, 1864, *ibid.,* no. 66.

[14] For example see: Emily Hewitt to Governor Shorter, Aug. 13, 1862; citizens of Lowndes County to Governor Shorter, Sept. 10, 1862; Mrs. S. A. Parsons to Governor Shorter, Nov. 4, 1862; Jane Moore to Governor Shorter, Dec. 21, 1862, Ala. Archives; H. Hines to Governor Pettus, May 14, 1861; J. W. Boyd to Governor Pettus, Aug. 1, 1862, Miss. Archives, Ser. E, no. 57; *Two Diaries* (Misses Susan R. Jervey and Charlotte St. J. Ravenal), *passim; O. R.,* Ser. I, II, 1010; VI, 78 ff.; XV, 534; Neblett Papers, *passim.*

[15] *Southern Recorder,* Aug. 30, 1864. For a similar case in Mississippi early in 1861, see J. D. L. Davenport to Governor Pettus, May 14, 1861, Miss. Archives, Ser. E, no. 52.

[16] H. Clessedy to Governor Clark, Sept. 12, 1864, Miss. Archives, Ser. E, no. 66.

[17] *Two Diaries,* p. 18 (Diary of Miss Susan R. Jervey).

[18] Mobile *Daily Advertiser and Register,* Nov. 15, 1863.

planters everywhere might be able to inform their slaves what happened to "bad niggers" in other sections and to let them draw their own conclusions.

•   •   •

Disloyalty of slaves to their masters has been a neglected phase of Confederate history. Yet in the invaded areas insubordination seems to have been more common than submission; and the latter was not a rule without exception in the interior regions. A common type of misconduct was insolence toward the whites. A Fredericksburg lady, just a few days after the Federals camped on the opposite side of the Rappahannock River and began to play patriotic airs, wrote in her diary: "The Negroes are going off in great numbers and are beginning to be very independent and impudent." [32] A North Carolinian wrote to his governor in August, 1864: "Our Negroes are beginning to show that they understand the state of affairs, and insolence and insubordination are quite common." [33] Even the little Negroes became impudent with the change of conditions. A Savannah, Georgia, woman was awakened one morning early in 1865 by a dusky urchin jumping up and down beneath her window and singing with great gusto,

> All de rebel gone to h———,
> Now Par Sherman come. [34]

That domestic servants, though generally not susceptible to "Yankee" suggestions, were sometimes guilty of impudence is indicated by the action of a Culpeper, Virginia, coachman who, after the Federals told him that he was free, "went straightly to his master's chamber, dressed himself in his best clothes, put on his best watch and chain, took his stick, and returning to the parlor where his master was, insolently informed him that he might for the future drive his own coach." [35]

All cases of insolence are not traceable directly to "Yankee" influence, however. An editorial in the Selma (Alabama) *Morning Reporter,* August 27, 1863, expressed regret at the lack of order resulting from the diminution of the police force, and stated that "the Negroes . . . are becoming so saucy and abusive that a police force has become positively necessary as a check to this continued insolence." A bill was introduced in the Georgia House of Representatives in November, 1862, "to punish slaves and free persons of color for abusive and insulting language to white persons." [36]

---

[32] Diary of Betty Herndon Maury, entry of April 25, 1862. Isaac Applewhite wrote to Governor Pettus from Columbia, Mississippi, on June 6, 1862: "There is greatly needed in this county a company of mounted rangers . . . to keep the Negroes in awe, who are getting quite impudent. Our proximity to the enemy has had a perceptible influence on them." Miss. Archives, Ser. E, no. 57.

[33] E. R. Tiles to Governor Vance, Aug. 7, 1864, Vance Papers.

[34] Francis Thomas Howard, *In and Out of the Lines,* p. 204.

[35] Richmond *Enquirer,* Aug. 6, 1862.

[36] *Southern Recorder,* Nov. 25, 1862. Available records do not permit the tracing of this bill. It seems never to have become a law, however. For other evidences on the insolence of slaves, see: J. Belflowers to Mrs. R. F. W. Allston, Oct. 19, 1864, Allston Papers; *O. R.,* Ser. 1, XVII, pt. 2, 201, Sherman to Rawlins; Magnolia Plantation Records, entry of Oct. 2, 1862; Pringle, *Chronicles of Chicora Wood,* pp. 269 ff.; Richmond *Daily Examiner,* Dec. 2, 1864; Elizabeth F. Andrews, *War-Time Journal of a Georgia Girl,* pp. 70, 122.

Impudence of the slaves was frequently associated with a refusal to work. The owner of Greenwood Plantation in South Carolina wrote in August, 1862: "We have had hard work to get along this season, the Negroes are unwilling to do any work, no matter what it is." [37] Mrs. C. C. Clay, Sr., complained that she had to beg the slaves to do "what little is done" on the Clay Plantation; that the ones who milked the cows "grumbled and threatened if someone else did not go get the calves; that the one who built the fire in the plantation house objected to being ordered to make fires elsewhere." [38] Negroes on the Crain Plantation in Louisiana began to refuse to work on Saturday in 1862, after Farragut's fleet passed up the river. All during the years 1863 and 1864, the Negroes on this place seem to have worked or loafed, very much according to their own inclinations. [39] Shortly after the Federals came into the vicinity of Magnolia Plantation in 1862, the slaves began to manifest a more leisurely attitude toward their duties. The overseer complained in August, 1862, that "the Negros was very slow getting out and some Two or three did not get out a tall [sic]." [40] Three weeks later he wrote: "negros are moving very slowly. The ring of the Bell no longer a delightful sound. . . . Many negros continually going along the road back and fro to the forts . . . great demoralization among the negros." [41] The continued refusal of the slaves to work with any degree of regularity provoked the overseer to say in October: "*I wish every negro would leave the place* as they will do only what pleases them, go out in the morning when it suits them, come in when they please, etc." [42]

The refusal to work was sometimes a "strike for wages." The slaves on Woodland Plantation in Louisiana presented themselves before the overseer one morning in August, 1862, and said that "they would not work eny moore unless they got pay for their work." After a parley they agreed to go on without pay for another week. [43] Within the next few weeks this owner and those of all surrounding plantations had to go over to the wage basis, due largely to Federal influences. Magnolia Plantation was the only exception; here, though work was irregular and demands for pay reiterated, the owner succeeded in holding his Negroes through the season of 1862 by promising them a "handsome present" when the crops were "taken off." [44] A refusal to grant wages often resulted in a wholesale flight of the blacks to the Federal camp. [45]

Another form of irregularity of conduct was the refusal of slaves to submit to punishment for their misdoings. An aged Texas planter tried to whip a recalcitrant hand

[37] Greenwood Plantation Records, entry of Aug. 8, 1862.

[38] Mrs. C. C. Clay, Sr., to C. C. Clay, Jr., Sept 5, 1863, Clay Papers.

[39] Univ. of Texas Archives, A. E. Crain Plantation Account Book, 1861–1867.

[40] Magnolia Plantation Records, entry of Aug. 25, 1862.

[41] *Ibid.,* entry of Sept. 12, 1862. J. Belflowers wrote to Mrs. R. F. W. Allston on March 20, 1865: "the People the way that they work will not make them Bread. go out at 10 Oclock come in at 12 O'clock." Allston Papers.

[42] Magnolia Plantation Records, entry of Oct. 18, 1862.

[43] *Ibid.,* entry of Aug. 11, 1862.

[44] *Ibid.,* entries of Aug. 25, 1862, and Jan. 25, 1863. The owner's promise was kept; $2,500 was distributed among the slaves.

[45] Diary of Betty Herndon Maury, entry of May 13, 1862.

in the summer of 1863. The Negro, according to the statement of a neighbor, "cursed the old man all to pieces," walked off into the wood, and then sent back word that he would return to his work if a pledge were given that he would not be whipped. The terms were accepted and he came back.[46] Other slaves in this Texas community seem to have been under very little control. They rode their masters' horses at night, took hogs and beeves for their own use, and worked or loafed much as they chose. One of the overseers on the Neblett Plantation, named Myers, attempted to whip a Negro who was reported to have said that "Myers or no white man" would flog him. The Negro walked off saying that he had done nothing deserving punishment. Myers was openly resisted by two other Negroes on the place, one of them holding the overseer off with a stick. The mistress of the plantation finally advised Myers to refrain from the use of severe methods with the slaves as long as they went about their work. On one occasion she wrote to her husband who was absent in the army that it would make matters no better to have the Negroes whipped, "so I shall say nothing and if they stop work entirely I will try to feel thankful if they let me alone." [47] Planters in this and other communities actually became afraid to punish their slaves. A Tennessee woman wrote to her husband in 1863 that "overseers generally are doing very little good and they complain of the negroes getting so free and idle, but I think it is because most every one is afraid to correct them. I tried to correct our negroes for a thing last summer; it would frighten Mr. Ashford [the overseer] out of his wits almost." [48] Senator Clay's mother wrote him from Alabama, September 5, 1863, that one of her men had told her of the threat of three of the other slaves to kill the overseer if he attempted to punish them. She advised a neighbor who had hired one of her slave women not to punish her because the Negroes had threatened to burn the neighbor's house when the "Yankees" came if he did. Mrs. Clay even went to the colored woman and "begged her to think of the sin" of her proposed crime.[49]

Unfaithfulness of slaves was also demonstrated by the fact that wherever the Federal armies penetrated they received abundant aid from the Negroes in the way of information and guidance.[50] This was given secretly until the actual appearance of the soldiers and then it was often given openly and unreservedly. The prevalence of the practice of Negroes acting as guides to the Federals is indicated by the letter of a Confederate States district attorney to General Winder in 1864 urging severe punishment for a Negro, Heath, who had been found guilty of that offense, on the ground that "the crime with which he is charged is one of such frequent occurrence that an example should be made of Heath. It is a matter of notoriety in the sections of the Confederacy where raids are frequent that the guides of the enemy are nearly always free Negroes and slaves." [51]

[46] Mrs. W. H. Neblett to her husband, Aug. 13, 1863, Neblett Papers.

[47] Mrs. W. H. Neblett to her husband, Aug. 13, Nov. 23, Nov. 29, 1863, and March 7, March 12, March 18, April 6, 1864, Neblett Papers.

[48] Mrs. James Abernethy to her husband, Jan. 11, 1863, Abernethy Papers (MSS. in private possession).

[49] Mrs. C. C. Clay, Sr., to C. C. Clay, Jr., Sept. 5, 1863, Clay Papers.

[50] *O. R.,* Ser. 1, X, pt. 2, 162; Charleston *Mercury,* Jan. 11, 1862; Cumming, *Hospital Life in the Confederate Army of Tennessee,* p. 159; *New Englander,* LI (1889), 355.

[51] *O. R.,* Ser. 2, VI, 1053.

Slaves, more particularly field hands, often aided the Federal soldiers in their search for valuables. Shortly after a "Yankee" raid, a South Carolinian wrote that "the people about here would not have suffered near as much if it had not been for these Negroes; in every case they have told where things have been hidden and they did most of the stealing." [52] A soldier who marched with the Union Army through Louisiana in 1863 said that all along the road the Negroes stood at the gates ready to tell the whereabouts of their masters' saddles and horses. "Many a man," he added, "who has boasted that all his slaves could be trusted . . . had his eyes opened on those days of our advance." He ventured the conjecture that "nearly half our cavalry horses were changed in the Teche country, and in the vast majority of cases, it was the favorite servants who pointed out the hiding place and said, 'you gives us free, and we helps you all we can.' " Such cases, he said, were "innumerable." [53]

•   •   •

A survey of the evidence of the period makes inescapable the conclusion that disorder and unfaithfulness on the part of the Negroes were far more common than postwar commentators have usually admitted. A correspondent of Senator Clay's wife wrote in 1863 from Selma, Alabama, where he had been in a position to observe the doings of Negroes in an exposed locality, that "the 'faithful slave' is about played out. They are the most treacherous, brutal, and ungrateful race on the globe." [77] This statement is doubtless extreme, but it is no farther from the truth than the encomiums of the slaves' loyalty and devotion which have been so universally circulated and accepted in the South.

The majority of Negroes in the Confederacy, however, were neither loyal nor disloyal in a positive way. They simply waited to see what would happen. Their situation is reflected, though not with entire correctness, in the answer which one of them is said to have given when asked by a fellow slave if he thought that the issuance of the Emancipation Proclamation meant a general arming of the Negroes: "Yo' talkin' fool talk nigger! Ain' yo' nebber seen two dogs fighten ober bone 'fo' now . . . well den, yo' ain nebber seen de bone fight none is you?" [78]

When the Federals came, the Negroes usually welcomed them. But if a change in the fortune of war restored the control of their masters, they made the best of the situation. A Negro soldier captured by "Rebel" cavalrymen in 1864 was brought to Libby Prison in Richmond. Like most of the ex-slave prisoners, he said that he had been forced into the Union army against his will. When asked if he was willing to take the oath of allegiance to the Confederacy, he replied, "Yes, Massa, I takes anything I can get my hands on." [79]

As a general rule, unfaithfulness and disorder were common in the invaded areas

---

[52] *Two Diaries*, p. 35 (Diary of Charlotte St. J. Ravenel).
[53] George H. Hepworth, *The Whip, Hoe, and Sword*, pp. 142–144.
[77] John F. Andrews to Mrs. C. C. Clay, Jr., July 10, 1863, Clay Papers.
[78] Allen C. Redwood, "The Cook of the Confederate Army," *Scribner's Monthly*, XVIII (1879), 560.
[79] Richmond *Enquirer*, March 10, 1864.

and rare in the interior. Most of the serious disturbances were attributable to Federal influences, but some of them were due as much to the withdrawal of accustomed authority as to outside suggestion. That the slaves in the interior did not "rise up" against their masters is not surprising when one takes into consideration their lack of facilities for rapid communication and concerted action, the affection which the most intelligent ones had for their master's families, the fear inspired by the summary execution of those whose plots to rebel were detected, and the tremendous advantage which the whites had over them in every respect, save that of numbers.

Negro Soldiers in the Union Army, 1863–64*

James M. McPherson

Fully convinced of the utility of a large Negro army, the Union government extended its recruiting activities to the border slave states in 1863–64. Although the brutality of impressment characterized the operations of some recruiters in these areas as it had elsewhere, most of the freedmen who joined the army in the border states did so voluntarily. The Negroes of Nashville held a meeting on October 20, 1863, where a colored leader declared:

Then let every able bodied descendant of Africa rally to arms, for arms alone will achieve our rights. God will rule over our destinies. He will guide us, for He is the friend of the oppressed and down-trodden. The God of battles will watch over us and lead us. We have nothing to lose, but everything to gain. (Applause.) Then why not enter upon the work with holy zeal, and throw ourselves with might and main into the breach? The decision of the great questions of the day rests with us. . . . Slavery can never be what it has been, but let us not sit supinely by, but rather take a share in the great events transpiring. Let us make a name for ourselves and race, bright as the noonday sun. Let us show, as Greece has done, a people bursting their bonds and rallying for freedom. . . . Present to the world a picture of manhood; show yourselves lion-hearted; be not afraid to die. (Cheering and applause.)

Jerry Sullivan, another colored man, said:

God is in this war. He will lead us on to victory. Folks talk about the fighting being nearly over, but I believe there is a heap yet to come. Let the colored men accept the offer of the President and Cabinet, take arms, join the army, and then we will whip the rebels, even if Longstreet and all the Streets of the South, concentrate at Chattanooga. (Laughter and applause.) Why, don't you remember how afraid they used to be that we would rise? And you know we would, too, if we could. (Cries of "that's so.") I

* From James McPherson, *The Negro's Civil War* (New York: Pantheon Books, 1965), pp. 205–22. Copyright © 1965 by James McPherson. Reprinted by permission of Pantheon Books, Inc. a Division of Random House, Inc.

ran away two years ago. . . . I got to Cincinnati, and from there I went straight to General Rosecrans' headquarters. And now I am going to be Corporal. (Shouts of laughter.)

Come, boys, let's get some guns from Uncle Sam, and go coon hunting; shooting those gray back coons [Confederates] that go poking about the country now a days. (Laughter.) Tomorrow morning, don't eat too much breakfast, but as soon as you get back from market, start the first thing for our camp. Don't ask your wife, for if she is a wife worth having she will call you a coward for asking her. (Applause, and waving of handkerchiefs by the ladies.) I've got a wife and she says to me, the other day, "Jerry, if you don't go to the war mighty soon, I'll go off and leave you, as some of the Northern gentlemen want me to go home and cook for them." (Laughter.) . . . The ladies are now busy making us a flag, and let us prove ourselves men worthy to bear it.[1]

In September 1863, Elijah Marrs, a Kentucky slave, escaped with some of his fellow slaves and went to Louisville, where they joined the army. Marrs, who had been born in 1840, became a teacher and a minister to his people in Kentucky after the war. In his memoirs he described his escape from slavery in 1863:

I remember the morning I made up my mind to join the United States Army. I started to Simpsonville, and walking along I met many of my old comrades on the Shelbyville Pike. I told them of my determination, and asked all who desired to join my company to roll his coat sleeves above his elbows, and to let them remain so during the day. I marshaled my forces that day and night. I had twenty-seven men, all told, and I was elected their captain to lead them to Louisville. Our headquarters were at the colored church. During the day some one brought the news that the rebels were in Simpsonville, and that they were preparing to make a raid upon the church. For a time this news created a panic—women screamed, jumped out the windows, crying "Murder!"—strong men ran pell-mell over the women and took to the woods. I, myself, crowded into the corner of the church, and Captain Marrs was about, for the time being, to throw up the sponge. But I did not despair. I picked up courage and rallied my men, and news soon came that the report was false. . . .

Our arms consisted of twenty-six war clubs and one old rusty pistol, the property of the captain. There was one place on our route we dreaded, and that was in Middletown, through which the colored people seldom passed with safety. When we got within two miles of the place I ordered my men to circle to the left until we got past the town, when we returned to the Pike, striking it in front of Womack's big woods. At this place we heard the rumbling of vehicles coming at full speed, as we supposed, towards us. I at once ordered the men to lie down in a ditch by the roadside, where we remained some twenty-five minutes, but hearing nothing further I ordered my men to arise and we took up our line of march.

Day was now breaking, and in one half hour we were within the lines of the Union Army, and by eight o'clock we were at the recruiting office in the city of Louisville. Here we found Mr. George Womack, the Provost Marshal, in whose dark woods we had taken shelter the night before. By twelve o'clock the owner of every man of us

[1] *The Colored Citizen,* November 7, 1863.

was in the city hunting his slaves, but we had all enlisted save one boy, who was considered too young.[2]

A drummer boy in one of the Kentucky Negro regiments composed a delightful piece of doggerel in 1864:

> Captain Fidler's come to town,
>   With his abolition papers;
> He swears he's one of Lincoln's men,
>   He's cutting almighty capers.
>
> Captain Fidler's come to town,
>   With his abolition triggers;
> He swears he's one of Lincoln's men,
>   "Enlisting all the niggers." . . .
>
> You'll see the rebels on the street,
>   Their noses like a bee gum;
> I don't care what in thunder they say,
>   I'm fighting for my freedom! . . .
>
> My old massa's come to town,
>   Cutting a Southern figure;
> What's the matter with the man?
>   Lincoln's got his niggers.
>
> Some folks say this "almighty fuss
>   Is getting worse and bigger";
> Some folks say "it's worse and worse,"
>   Because I am a "nigger."
>
> We'll get our colored regiments strung
>   Out in a line of battle;
> I'll bet my money agin the South
>   The rebels will skedaddle.[3]

New York was one of the last Northern states to become active in the enlistment of Negro soldiers. Colored men of New York held a convention at Poughkeepsie in July 1863 and formed a committee to recruit soldiers in the state.[4] The Union League of New York City also formed a recruiting committee. But Governor Horatio Seymour was strongly opposed to the idea

[2] Elijah P. Marrs, *Life and History of the Rev. Elijah P. Marrs* (Louisville, 1885), pp. 17–20.
[3] Published in the *Anglo-African,* September 24, 1864.
[4] Poughkeepsie *Daily Eagle,* July 20, 1863.

of colored soldiers, and he refused to allow any to be enrolled under state authority. New York advocates of Negro troops finally obtained permission from the War Department to recruit colored regiments directly under national authority. The first New York regiment departed for the front in March 1864, and two more followed soon afterward.[5]

The parade of the Twentieth U.S. Colored Infantry down Broadway on March 5, 1864, was a mighty symbol of the revolution wrought in the Negro's status by the Civil War, and especially by the arming of colored men. Eight months previously, Negroes in New York had been lynched in the streets by a maddened and drunken mob. Now they marched proudly behind a military band while thousands of spectators cheered from the sidewalks. A correspondent of the Christian Recorder *described the occasion:*

I think that some of the same rabble, who were in the proslavery melee of July 13, 1863, were made to shed tears of repentance on beholding the 20th regiment of Colored Troops off Riker's Island, as they marched through the streets of this great city in glorious array, onward to the defence of their country, God, and the right, notwithstanding the outrages they suffered a few months past at the hands of the . . . copperheads. . . .

Saturday, then, was a great day; all seemed to be one grand jubilee. A new era has been ushered in, colored soldiers gloriously welcomed in the streets of New York City, and protected by the whole force of police; their columns headed, as they marched down to the steam-boat landing, en route to New Orleans, by some one hundred of the most influential merchants and business men of the city; also upwards of twelve hundred of the most prominent colored men of the country, in the wake, and with the two best brass bands of music the state could afford, next to them 1,000 strong of the brave 20th U.S. Colored Troops, S.N.Y., and as they passed along see the white and colored ladies wave their handkerchiefs—see the wealthy merchant leave his desk and perplexed accounts, to behold the scene; he claps his hands and smiles. The national ensign hung out at every window; on they go, cheer after cheer. Ain't that a victory? . . .

The colored people are getting along here very well; they will soon shake off this tyranny, and stand forth bold, clothed with courage. Go it Ethiopia, for when you get old you can't.[6]

There were the beginnings of a revolution in the South as well as in New York. The bottom rail was on top, at least temporarily, in several Southern communities. A member of the Fourteenth Regiment of Rhode Island Heavy Artillery (colored) wrote in May 1864:

In the city of New Orleans, we could see signs of smothered hate and prejudice to both our color and present character as Union soldiers. But, for once in his life, your humble correspondent walked fearlessly and boldly through the streets of a southern city! And he did this without being required to take off his cap at every step, or to give all the side-walks to those lordly princes of the sunny south, the planters' sons! Oh, chivalry! how has thou lost thy potent power and charms! By what means, pray tell me, hast thou so degenerated as to lose the respect and admiration even of the sable sons of

---

[5] John Jay, *The Union League Club of New York, Its Memories of the Past* (New York, 1868).
[6] *Christian Recorder,* March 12, 1864.

Africa? Methinks that the spirit of thy charms is clothed in a strange and unwonted garb! [7]

In February 1865 the First U.S. Colored Infantry occupied Smithville, North Carolina. The Rev. Henry M. Turner, chaplain of the regiment, went to visit one of the leading colored women of the town, and while he was there some white women came into the yard

and commenced a jabber about some wood, which the colored lady was appropriating to her use. She told them it was Yankee wood, and not theirs, and the tongue battle raged most furiously for some minutes, when one of the white women called her a liar, with another expression too vulgar to mention. To this the colored woman responded, "I am no more a liar than you are." This expression, from a negro wench, as they called her, was so intolerable, that the white women grabbed up several clubs, and leaped in the door, using the most filthy language in the vocabulary of indecency. They had not yet observed me as being on the premises. But at this juncture, I rose up, met them at the door, and cried out, "Halt!" Said they, "Who are you?" "A United States Officer," was my reply. "Well, are you going to allow that negro to give us impudence?" "You gave her impudence first," was my reply. "What, we give a negro impudence! We want you to know we are white, and are your superiors. You are our inferior, much less she." "Well," said I, "all of you put together would not make the equal of my wife, and I have yet to hear her claim superiority over me." After that, I don't know what was said, for that remark was received as such an aggravated insult, that I can only compare the noise that followed, to a gang of fierce dogs, holding at bay a large cur dog, with a bow-wow-wow-wow. Finally, becoming tired of their annoying music, I told them to leave or I would imprison the whole party. They then went off, and dispatched one of their party to Head Quarters, to Colonel Barney, to induce him to send a file of men, and have me arrested. But the Colonel, I believe, drove her off, and that was the end of it. I afterwards learned that they were some of the Southern aristocracy.[8]

One feature of the revolution was the way in which thousands of Negro soldiers used their spare time to learn to read and write. Frances Beecher, wife of Colonel James Beecher, commander of the Thirty-fifth U.S. Colored Infantry, taught many men of this regiment to read and write while they were stationed at Beaufort and Jacksonville. She later recalled:

My mornings were spent in teaching the men of our regiment to read and write, and it became my pleasing duty and habit, wherever our moving tents were pitched, there to set up our school. Sometimes the chaplain assisted, and sometimes the officers; and the result was that when the men came to be mustered out each one of them could proudly sign his name to the pay-roll in a good legible hand. When enlisted, all but two or three of them were obliged to put a mark to their names as written by the pay-master, thus:

>   his
> John   X   Jones
>   mark

[7] *Ibid.,* May 28, 1864.

[8] Turner to the editor of the *Christian Recorder,* February 4, 1865, in the *Christian Recorder,* February 25.

while their eagerness to learn and the difficulty that many found in learning were very touching. One bright mulatto man particularly worked at his letters for two years, and then could only write his own name; while others learned at once. Whenever they had a spare moment, out would come a spelling-book or a primer or Testament, and you would often see a group of heads around one book.[9]

Robert Cowden, colonel of the Fifty-ninth U.S. Colored Infantry, wrote that soon after his regiment went into winter quarters near Memphis in 1863,
a commodious schoolhouse was built where the men, when off duty, were taught by the faithful chaplain and his no less devoted wife, to read, spell, and write. . . .

In the schoolhouse, not only the enlisted men, but the colored women and children of the neighborhood were gathered for instruction every day. It also served the purpose of a chapel where on Sabbaths especially during inclement weather, they were gathered for Bible instruction or Sabbath-school in the morning, and preaching-service in the afternoon. It was astonishing to note the eagerness with which these poor, ignorant creatures entered into the work of study, and also the rapid progress they made in learning. Their enthusiasm knew no bounds as one or another came out first or second best in the contests that secured prizes for best spelling, etc. Such intense interest was created that men going on duty were generally seen carrying their spelling-books or Testaments under their belts to their posts of duty and spending their time when off post in learning their lessons. In this way about two hundred and fifty of the enlisted men of this regiment learned to read and write.[10]

Joseph T. Wilson, a colored trooper in the Fifty-fourth Massachusetts Regiment, later wrote in his history of Negro soldiers that "every camp had a teacher, in fact every company had some one to instruct the soldiers in reading, if nothing more. Since the war I have known of more than one who have taken up the profession of preaching and law making, whose first letter was learned in camp; and not a few who have entered college." [11] *And James Monroe Trotter, a Negro who rose to the rank of lieutenant before the war was over, wrote many years later that* scattered here and there over this broad country to-day are many veteran soldiers who are good readers and writers, some of them even fair scholars, who took their first lessons from some manly officer or no less manly fellow-soldier in the manner mentioned, during such camp intervals as were allowed by the dread arbitrament of war. . . . But let it not be supposed for a moment that only officers and men of another race were engaged in this noble work of school-teaching in our colored army. Not a few of the best workers were colored chaplains, who wisely divided their time between preaching, administering to the sick by reason of wounds or otherwise . . . while many noncommissioned officers and private soldiers cheerfully rendered effective service in the same direction.[12]

[9] Frances P. Beecher, "Two Years with a Colored Regiment, A Woman's Experience," *New England Magazine*, XVII (January, 1898), 536.

[10] Robert Cowden, *A Brief Sketch of the Organization and Services of the Fifty-Ninth Regiment of United States Colored Infantry* (Dayton, Ohio, 1883), pp. 60–61.

[11] Joseph T. Wilson, *The Black Phalanx* (Hartford, 1888), p. 504.

[12] Quoted from the New York *Age* in Wilson, *Black Phalanx*, pp. 506–7.

Most Negro soldiers, even the illiterate ones, knew what they were fighting for. Corporal Thomas Long of Higginson's regiment, acting as chaplain one Sunday, told his fellow soldiers:

If we hadn't become sojers, all might have gone back as it was before; our freedom might have slipped through de two houses of Congress & President Linkum's four years might have passed by & notin been done for we. But now tings can never go back, because we have showed our energy & our courage & our naturally manhood.

Anoder ting is, suppose you had kept your freedom widout enlisting in dis army; your chilen might have grown up free, & been *well cultivated* so as to be equal to any business; but it would have been always flung in dere faces—"Your fader never fought for he own freedom"—and what could dey answer? *Neber can say that to dis African race any more,* (bringing down his hand with the greatest emphasis on the table). Tanks to dis regiment, never can say dat any more, because we first showed dem we could fight by dere side.[13]

A young Tennessee Negro who had joined the army when he was nineteen recalled much later:

I was in the Battle of Nashville, when we whipped old Hood. I went to see my mistress on my furlough, and she was glad to see me. She said, "You remember when you were sick and I had to bring you to the house and nurse you?" and I told her, "Yes'm, I remember." And she said, "And now you are fighting me!" I said, "No'm, I ain't fighting you, I'm fighting to get free." [14]

But not all Negro soldiers were heroically dedicated to the cause for which they were fighting. One colored trooper related that he had spent much of his time on the battlefield just praying for survival:

I prayed on the battle field some of the best prayers I ever prayed in my life. Why? Sometimes it looked like the war was about to cut my ears off. I would lay stretched out on the ground and bullets would fly over my head. I would take a rock and place it on top of my head, thinking maybe it would keep the bullet from going through my brain, for I knew that would kill me. I'd just lay out, and I was just as thin and looked like one of these old spreading-adder snakes. After a while they would say, "Forward March." They never say, "Get up." So I'd get up myself and move off and then they would tell me to commence firing. . . . The Chaplain or some one of them would pray sometimes. . . . They would ask God to "give us the victory this day." Words of praise was not to the strong or to the swift, but to he who held out to the end. For my part, I said what I ever heard anybody else say. I wan't giving God no heart. I was just saying what I heard the other people say. But I made God some of the finest promises that ever were made.[15]

And Thomas Cole, a slave who ran away from his plantation in North Alabama in 1863, later recounted his subsequent experiences:

[13] Thomas Wentworth Higginson, Journal, entry of March 24, 1864, Higginson Papers, Houghton Library, Harvard University.

[14] Social Science Institute, Fisk University, "Unwritten History of Slavery: Autobiographical Account of Negro Ex-Slaves," Social Science Source Documents, No. 1 (Nashville, 1945), p. 253.

[15] *Ibid.,* pp. 150–51.

I eats all the nuts and kills a few swamp rabbits and cotches a fish. I builds the fire and goes off 'bout a half a mile and hides in the thicket till it burns down to the coals, then bakes me some fish and rabbit. I's shaking all the time, 'fraid I'd get cotched, but I's nearly starve to death. I puts the rest of the fish in my cap and travels on that night by the North Star and hides in a big thicket the next day, and along evening I hears guns shooting. I sure am scared this time, sure 'nough. I's scared to come in and scared to go out, and while I's standing there, I hears two men say, "Stick you hands up, boy. What you doing?" I says, "Uh-uh-uh, I dunno. You ain't gwine take me back to the plantation, is you?" They says, "No. Does you want to fight for the North?" I says I will, 'cause they talks like Northern men. Us walk night and day and gits in General Rosecrans' camp, and they thunk I's the spy from the South. They asks me all sorts of questions and says they'll whip me if I didn't tell them what I's spying 'bout. Finally they 'lieves me and puts me to work helping with the cannons. I feels 'portant then, but I didn't know what was in front of me, or I 'spects I'd run off 'gain.

I helps sot them cannons on this Chickamauga Mountain, in hiding places. I has to go with a man and wait on him and that cannon. First thing I knows—bang! bang! boom!—things has started, and guns am shooting faster than you can think, and I looks round for the way to run. But them guns am shooting down the hill in front of me and shooting at me, and over me and on both sides of me. I tries to dig me a hole and git in it. All this happen right now, and first thing I knows, the man am kicking me and wanting me to holp him keep that cannon loaded. Man, I didn't want no cannon, but I has to help anyway. We fit till dark, and the Rebels got more men than us, so General Rosecrans sends the message to General Woods to come help us out. When the messenger slips off, I sure wish it am me slipping off, but I didn't want to see no General Woods. I just wants to git back to that old plantation and pick more cotton. . . .

There was men laying wanting help, wanting water, with blood running out them and the top or sides their heads gone, great big holes in them. I just promises the good Lord if He just let me git out that mess, I wouldn't run off no more, but I didn't know then He wasn't gwine let me out with just that battle. He gwine give me plenty more, but that battle ain't over yet, for next morning the Rebels 'gins shooting and killing lots of our men, and General Woods ain't come, so General Rosecrans orders us to 'treat and didn't have to tell me what he said, neither. The Rebels comes after us, shooting, and we runs off and leaves that cannon what I was with setting on the hill, and I didn't want that thing nohow.

We kept hotfooting till we gits to Chattanooga, and there is where we stops. . . . There a long range of hills leading 'way from Lookout Mountain, nearly to Missionary Ridge. . . . They fights the Rebels on Orchard Knob Hill, and I wasn't in that, but I's in the Missionary Ridge battle. We has to come out the timber and run 'cross a strip or opening up the hill. They sure kilt lots our men when we runs 'cross that opening. We runs for all we's worth and uses guns or anything we could. The Rebels turns and runs off, and our soldiers turns the cannons round what we's capture and kilt some the Rebels with their own guns.

I never did git to where I wasn't scared when we goes into the battle. This the last one I's in, and I's sure glad, for I never seed the like of dead and wounded men. We picks them up, the Rebels like the Unions, and doctors them the best we could. . . .

I sure wished lots of times I never run off from the plantation. I begs the General not to send me on any more battles, and he says I's the coward and sympathizes with the South. But I tells him I just couldn't stand to see all them men laying there dying and hollering and begging for help and a drink of water and blood everywhere you looks. . . .

Finally, the General tells me I can go back to Chattanooga and guard the supplies in camp there and take the wounded soldiers and prisoners. A bunch of men is with me, and we has all we can do. We gits the orders to send supplies to some general, and it my job to help load the wagons or boxcars or boats. A train of wagons leaves sometimes. We gits all them supplies by boat, and Chattanooga am the 'stributing center. When winter comes, everybody rests awhile and waits for spring to open. The Union general sends in some more colored soldiers. There ain't been many colored men, but the last year the war there am lots. The North and the South am taking anything they can get to win the war.[16]

Most Negro soldiers, however, had some comprehension of why they were fighting and as much willingness as any other race of men to die for their cause. In fact, it required more courage for Negroes than for whites to become soldiers, because the Confederacy had not revoked its stated intention to punish captured Negroes as insurrectionists. The Richmond government never officially enforced this policy, but in some cases rebel officers or soldiers refused to take colored prisoners, or murdered such prisoners in cold blood after capture. The so-called "Fort Pillow Massacre" was the most notable instance of the murder of Negro prisoners after capture. Fort Pillow was a Union outpost on the Mississippi River, garrisoned by approximately 570 troops, of whom slightly less than half were colored. On April 12, 1864, General Nathan Bedford Forrest led a rebel attack on the fort and captured it. An undetermined number of Union soldiers, mostly Negroes, were murdered in cold blood after they had surrendered. A Congressional committee charged that "at least 300" of the Union troops were massacred. Some historians have denied that the alleged "massacre" took place at all, and have claimed that the Unionists were killed during the course of the battle. The most recent and objective studies, however, have concluded that while the Congressional committee's report was distorted and exaggerated, nevertheless several score Negro soldiers and some white troopers were indeed murdered after they had surrendered.[17]

The Congressional committee interrogated twenty-one Negro survivors of the Fort Pillow affair. The testimony of four of these soldiers is excerpted below:

Sergeant Benjamin Robinson, (colored) company D, 6th United States heavy artillery, sworn and examined. . . .

    QUESTION. Were you at Fort Pillow in the fight there?

    ANSWER. Yes, sir.

---

[16] B. A. Botkin, ed., *Lay My Burden Down: A Folk History of Slavery* (Chicago, 1945), pp. 199–201.

[17] Dudley T. Cornish, *The Sable Arm: Negro Troops in the Union Army, 1861–1865* (New York, 1956), pp. 173–75; Albert Castel, "The Fort Pillow Massacre: A Fresh Examination of the Evidence," *Civil War History,* IV (March, 1958), 37–50.

QUESTION. What did you see there?

ANSWER. I saw them shoot two white men right by the side of me after they had laid their guns down. They shot a black man clear over into the river. Then they hallooed to me to come up the hill, and I came up. They said, "Give me your money, you damned nigger." I told him I did not have any. "Give me your money, or I will blow your brains out." Then they told me to lie down, and I laid down, and they stripped everything off me.

QUESTION. This was the day of the fight?

ANSWER. Yes, sir.

QUESTION. Go on. Did they shoot you?

ANSWER. Yes, sir. After they stripped me and took my money away from me they dragged me up the hill a little piece, and laid me down flat on my stomach; I laid there till night, and they took me down to an old house, and said they would kill me the next morning. I got up and commenced crawling down the hill; I could not walk.

QUESTION. When were you shot?

ANSWER. About 3 o'clock.

QUESTION. Before they stripped you?

ANSWER. Yes, sir. They shot me before they said, "come up."

QUESTION. After you had surrendered?

ANSWER. Yes sir; they shot pretty nearly all of them after they surrendered. . . .

Major Williams, (colored) private, company B, 6th United States heavy artillery, sworn and examined.

By the chairman:

QUESTION. Where were you raised?

ANSWER. In Tennessee and North Mississippi.

QUESTION. Where did you enlist?

ANSWER. In Memphis. . . .

QUESTION. Were you in the fight at Fort Pillow?

ANSWER. Yes, sir. . . .

QUESTION. What did you see done there?

ANSWER. We fought them right hard during the battle, and killed some of them. After a time they sent in a flag of truce. . . .

QUESTION. When did you surrender?

ANSWER. I did not surrender until they all run.

QUESTION. Were you wounded then?

ANSWER. Yes, sir; after the surrender. . . .

QUESTION. Did you have any arms in your hands when they shot you?

ANSWER. No, sir; I was an artillery man, and had no arms. . . .

Eli Carlton, (colored) private, company B, 6th United States heavy artillery, sworn and examined.

By the chairman:

QUESTION. Where were you raised?

ANSWER. In East Tennessee.

QUESTION. Have you been a slave?

ANSWER. Yes, sir. . . .

QUESTION. Where did you join the army?

ANSWER. At Corinth, Mississippi, about a year ago.

QUESTION. Were you at Fort Pillow at the time it was taken?

ANSWER. Yes, sir.

QUESTION. State what happened there.

ANSWER. I saw 23 men shot after they surrendered; I made 24; 17 of them laid right around me dead, and 6 below me.

QUESTION. Who shot them?

ANSWER. The rebels; some white men were killed.

QUESTION. How many white men were killed?

ANSWER. Three or four.

QUESTION. Killed by the privates?

ANSWER. Yes, sir; I did not see any officers kill any. . . .

QUESTION. Were you shot with a musket or a pistol?

ANSWER. With a musket. I was hit once on the battle-field before we surrendered. They took me down to a little hospital under the hill. I was in the hospital when they shot me a second time. Some of our privates commenced talking. They said, "Do you fight with these God damned niggers?" they said, "Yes." Then they said, "God damn you, then, we will shoot you," and they shot one of them right down. They said, "I would not kill you, but, God damn you, you fight with these damned niggers, and we will kill you;" and they blew his brains out of his head. . . .

George Shaw, (colored) private, company B, 6th United States heavy artillery, sworn and examined.

By Mr. Gooch:

QUESTION. Where were you raised?

ANSWER. In Tennessee.

QUESTION. Where did you enlist?

ANSWER. At Fort Pillow.

QUESTION. Were you there at the fight?

ANSWER. Yes, sir.

QUESTION. When were you shot?

ANSWER. About four o'clock in the evening.

QUESTION. After you had surrendered?

ANSWER. Yes, sir.

QUESTION. Where were you at the time?

ANSWER. About ten feet from the river bank.

QUESTION. Who shot you?

ANSWER. A rebel soldier.

QUESTION. How near did he come to you?

ANSWER. About ten feet.

QUESTION. What did he say to you?

ANSWER. He said, "Damn you, what are you doing here?" I said, "Please don't shoot me." He said, "Damn you, you are fighting against your master." He raised his gun and fired, and the bullet went into my mouth and out the back part of my head. They threw me into the river, and I swam around and hung on there in the water until night.

QUESTION. Did you see anybody else shot?

ANSWER. Yes, sir; three young boys, lying in the water, with their heads out; they could not swim. They begged them as long as they could, but they shot them right in the forehead. . . .

QUESTION. How old were the boys?

ANSWER. Not more than fifteen or sixteen years old. They were not soldiers, but contraband boys, helping us on the breastworks.

QUESTION. Did you see any white men shot?

ANSWER. No, sir. I saw them shoot three men the next day.

QUESTION. How far from the fort?

ANSWER. About a mile and a half; after they had taken them back as prisoners.

QUESTION. Who shot them?

ANSWER. Private soldiers. One officer said, "Boys, I will have you arrested, if you don't quit killing them boys." Another officer said, "Damn it, let them go on; it isn't our law to take any niggers prisoners; kill every one of them." Then . . . two others came up, and said, "Damn you, we will kill you, and not be fooling about any longer." I said, "Don't shoot me." One of them said, "Go out and hold my horse." I made a step or two, and he said, "Turn around; I will hold my horse, and shoot you, too." I no sooner turned around than he shot me in the face. I fell down as if I was dead. He shot me again, and hit my arm, not my head. I laid there until I could hear him no more, and then I started back. I got back into Fort Pillow about sun up, and wandered about there until a gunboat came along, and I came up on that with about ten others.[18]

The Christian Recorder *commented editorially on "The Capture of Fort Pillow":*

It is needless, perhaps, for us to repeat to our readers, the butchery of black soldiers at Fort Pillow, for its sickening details have already been spread before them by the daily papers. We had hoped, however, that the first report might have been exaggerated; but, in this we have been doomed to disappointment. Every additional report only goes to confirm the first. We say, emphatically, that the massacre, at Fort Pillow, has been invited by the tardiness of the government, and the action of Congress. While they have professed to regard every man wearing the U.S. uniform, as being equal in theory, they have acted towards the black soldiers, in such a way, as to convince the Confederate government that they, themselves, do not regard the black soldiers as equal to the white. The rebels have taken advantage of this equivocation, to commit just such horrible butchery as that at Fort Pillow.[19]

    [18] *Reports of the Committee on the Conduct of the War,* "Fort Pillow Massacre" (House of Representatives, 38th Cong., 1 Sess., Report #65, Washington, 1864), pp. 17, 25–28.
    [19] *Christian Recorder,* April 23, 1864.

We now call on our noble brethren in the army, to swear anew never to cease fighting, until they shall have made a rebel to bite the dust for every hair of those three hundred of our black brethren massacred in Fort Pillow; and, whenever you may be called upon to measure arms or bayonets, with the rebel horde, give no quarter; take no prisoners; make it dangerous to take the life of a black soldier by these barbarians; then, they will respect your manhood, and you will be treated as you deserve at the hands of those who have made you outlaws. . . . Warriors! remember that you fight for liberty! Remember the wives and children you have left behind! Remember, you from New York, the *July riots!* You from the South, who are soldiers of the Republic, remember your old gray-headed mothers, who are yet within the lines of rebeldom; remember your daughters, dishonored by those red-handed murderers of your race! Remember, that for two hundred and fifty years, your people have been sold and bartered like so many beasts, and then bow down before God, and swear anew to uphold your country's cause, and the cause of universal liberty.[20]

The Fort Pillow Massacre did indeed have the effect of making Negro troops fight more desperately, for they feared the consequences of capture. Negro troops at Memphis were reported to have taken an oath "on their knees" to avenge Fort Pillow and to show rebel troops no quarter.[21] An officer of one of the colored regiments in the Army of the Potomac wrote from a Virginia battlefield in May 1864:

The real fact is, the rebels will not stand against our colored soldiers when there is any chance of their being taken prisoners, for they are conscious of what they justly deserve. Our men went into these works after they were taken, yelling, "Fort Pillow!" The enemy well knows what this means, and I will venture the assertion that that piece of infernal brutality enforced by them there has cost the enemy already two men for every one they so inhumanly murdered.[22]

*A white soldier in one of the Pennsylvania regiments fighting before Petersburg wrote home that "the Johnnies are not as much afraid of us as they are of the Mokes [colored troops]. When they charge they will not take any prisoners, if they can help it. Their cry is, 'Remember Fort Pillow!' Sometimes, in their excitement, they forget what to say, when they catch a man they say: 'Remember what you done to us, way back, down dar!' "[23]

---

[20] "R.H.C.," in *Christian Recorder*, April 30, 1864.

[21] *O.R.,* Ser. 1, Vol. XXXII, Pt. i, p. 588.

[22] *Liberator*, July 22, 1864.

[23] Letter printed in the Philadelphia *Press*, July 12, 1864.

The Propaganda of History*

William E. B. Du Bois

> How the facts of American history have in the last half century been fal-
> sified because the nation was ashamed. The South was ashamed because it fought
> to perpetuate human slavery. The North was ashamed because it had to call in
> the black men to save the Union, abolish slavery and establish democracy.

What are American children taught today about Reconstruction? Helen Boardman has
made a study of current textbooks and notes these three dominant theses:

1. *All Negroes were ignorant.*

"All were ignorant of public business." (Woodburn and Moran, "Elementary
American History and Government," p. 397.)

"Although the Negroes were now free, they were also ignorant and unfit to govern themselves." (Everett Barnes, "American History for Grammar Grades," p. 334.)

"The Negroes got control of these states. They had been slaves all their lives,
and were so ignorant they did not even know the letters of the alphabet. Yet they now
sat in the state legislatures and made the laws." (D. H. Montgomery, "The Leading
Facts of American History," p. 332.)

"In the South, the Negroes who had so suddenly gained their freedom did not
know what to do with it." (Hubert Cornish and Thomas Hughes, "History of the
United States for Schools," p. 345.)

"In the legislatures, the Negroes were so ignorant that they could only watch
their white leaders—carpetbaggers, and vote aye or no as they were told." (S. E. Forman, "Advanced American History," Revised Edition, p. 452.)

"Some legislatures were made up of a few dishonest white men and several Ne-

* From William Edward Burghardt Du Bois, *Black Reconstruction in America, 1860–1880* (New York:
Russell & Russell, 1956), pp. 711–23. © 1935. Reprinted by permission.

groes, many too ignorant to know anything about law-making." (Hubert Cornish and Thomas Hughes, "History of the United States for Schools," p. 349.)

2. *All Negroes were lazy, dishonest and extravagant.*

"These men knew not only nothing about the government, but also cared for nothing except what they could gain for themselves." (Helen F. Giles, "How the United States Became a World Power," p. 7.)

"Legislatures were often at the mercy of Negroes, childishly ignorant, who sold their votes openly, and whose 'loyalty' was gained by allowing them to eat, drink and clothe themselves at the state's expense." (William J. Long, "America—A History of Our Country," p. 392.)

"Some Negroes spent their money foolishly, and were worse off than they had been before." (Carl Russell Fish, "History of America," p. 385.)

"This assistance led many freed men to believe that they need no longer work. They also ignorantly believed that the lands of their former masters were to be turned over by Congress to them, and that every Negro was to have as his allotment 'forty acres and a mule.' " (W. F. Gordy, "History of the United States," Part II, p. 336.)

"Thinking that slavery meant toil and that freedom meant only idleness, the slave after he was set free was disposed to try out his freedom by refusing to work." (S. E. Forman, "Advanced American History," Revised Edition.)

"They began to wander about, stealing and plundering. In one week, in a Georgia town, 150 Negroes were arrested for thieving." (Helen F. Giles, "How the United States Became a World Power," p. 6.)

3. *Negroes were responsible for bad government during Reconstruction:*

"Foolish laws were passed by the black law-makers, the public money was wasted terribly and thousands of dollars were stolen straight. Self-respecting Southerners chafed under the horrible regime." (Emerson David Fite, "These United States," p. 37.)

"In the exhausted states already amply 'punished' by the desolation of war, the rule of the Negro and his unscrupulous carpetbagger and scalawag patrons, was an orgy of extravagance, fraud and disgusting incompetency." (David Saville Muzzey, "History of the American People," p. 408.)

"The picture of Reconstruction which the average pupil in these sixteen States receives is limited to the South. The South found it necessary to pass Black Codes for the control of the shiftless and sometimes vicious freedmen. The Freedmen's Bureau caused the Negroes to look to the North rather than to the South for support and by giving them a false sense of equality did more harm than good. With the scalawags, the ignorant and non-propertyholding Negroes under the leadership of the carpetbaggers, engaged in a wild orgy of spending in the legislatures. The humiliation and distress of the Southern whites was in part relieved by the Ku Klux Klan, a secret organization which frightened the superstitious blacks." [1]

Grounded in such elementary and high school teaching, an American youth attending college today would learn from current textbooks of history that the Constitu-

---

[1] "Racial Attitudes in American History Textbooks," *Journal of Negro History*, XIX, p. 257.

tion recognized slavery; that the chance of getting rid of slavery by peaceful methods was ruined by the Abolitionists; that after the period of Andrew Jackson, the two sections of the United States "had become fully conscious of their conflicting interests. Two irreconcilable forms of civilization . . . in the North, the democratic . . . in the South, a more stationary and aristocratic civilization." He would read that Harriet Beecher Stowe brought on the Civil War; that the assault on Charles Sumner was due to his "coarse invective" against a South Carolina Senator; and that Negroes were the only people to achieve emancipation with no effort on their part. That Reconstruction was a disgraceful attempt to subject white people to ignorant Negro rule; and that, according to a Harvard professor of history (the italics are ours), "Legislative expenses were grotesquely extravagant; the *colored members in some states engaging in a saturnalia of corrupt expenditure*" (Encyclopaedia Britannica, 14th Edition, Volume 22, p. 815, by Frederick Jackson Turner).

In other words, he would in all probability complete his education without any idea of the part which the black race has played in America; of the tremendous moral problem of abolition; of the cause and meaning of the Civil War and the relation which Reconstruction had to democratic government and the labor movement today.

Herein lies more than mere omission and difference of emphasis. The treatment of the period of Reconstruction reflects small credit upon American historians as scientists. We have too often a deliberate attempt so to change the facts of history that the story will make pleasant reading for Americans. The editors of the fourteenth edition of the Encyclopaedia Britannica asked me for an article on the history of the American Negro. From my manuscript they cut out all my references to Reconstruction. I insisted on including the following statement:

"White historians have ascribed the faults and failures of Reconstruction to Negro ignorance and corruption. But the Negro insists that it was Negro loyalty and the Negro vote alone that restored the South to the Union, established the new democracy, both for white and black, and instituted the public schools."

This the editor refused to print, although he said that the article otherwise was "in my judgment, and in the judgment of others in the office, an excellent one, and one with which it seems to me we may all be well satisfied." I was not satisfied and refused to allow the article to appear.

War and especially civil strife leave terrible wounds. It is the duty of humanity to heal them. It was therefore soon conceived as neither wise nor patriotic to speak of all the causes of strife and the terrible results to which sectional differences in the United States had led. And so, first of all, we minimized the slavery controversy which convulsed the nation from the Missouri Compromise down to the Civil War. On top of that, we passed by Reconstruction with a phrase of regret or disgust.

But are these reasons of courtesy and philanthropy sufficient for denying Truth? If history is going to be scientific, if the record of human action is going to be set down with that accuracy and faithfulness of detail which will allow its use as a measuring rod and guidepost for the future of nations, there must be set some standards of ethics in research and interpretation.

If, on the other hand, we are going to use history for our pleasure and amusement, for inflating our national ego, and giving us a false but pleasurable sense of accomplishment, then we must give up the idea of history either as a science or as an art using the results of science, and admit frankly that we are using a version of historic fact in order to influence and educate the new generation along the way we wish.

It is propaganda like this that has led men in the past to insist that history is "lies agreed upon"; and to point out the danger in such misinformation. It is indeed extremely doubtful if any permanent benefit comes to the world through such action. Nations reel and stagger on their way; they make hideous mistakes; they commit frightful wrongs; they do great and beautiful things. And shall we not best guide humanity by telling the truth about all this, so far as the truth is ascertainable?

Here in the United States we have a clear example. It was morally wrong and economically retrogressive to build human slavery in the United States in the eighteenth century. We know that now, perfectly well; and there were many Americans North and South who knew this and said it in the eighteenth century. Today, in the face of new slavery established elsewhere in the world under other names and guises, we ought to emphasize this lesson of the past. Moreover, it is not well to be reticent in describing that past. Our histories tend to discuss American slavery so impartially, that in the end nobody seems to have done wrong and everybody was right. Slavery appears to have been thrust upon unwilling helpless America, while the South was blameless in becoming its center. The difference of development, North and South, is explained as a sort of working out of cosmic social and economic law.

One reads, for instance, Charles and Mary Beard's "Rise of American Civilization," with a comfortable feeling that nothing right or wrong is involved. Manufacturing and industry develop in the North; agrarian feudalism develops in the South. They clash, as winds and waters strive, and the stronger forces develop the tremendous industrial machine that governs us so magnificently and selfishly today.

Yet in this sweeping mechanistic interpretation, there is no room for the real plot of the story, for the clear mistake and guilt of rebuilding a new slavery of the working class in the midst of a fateful experiment in democracy; for the triumph of sheer moral courage and sacrifice in the abolition crusade; and for the hurt and struggle of degraded black millions in their fight for freedom and their attempt to enter democracy. Can all this be omitted or half suppressed in a treatise that calls itself scientific?

Or, to come nearer the center and climax of this fascinating history: What was slavery in the United States? Just what did it mean to the owner and the owned? Shall we accept the conventional story of the old slave plantation and its owner's fine, aristocratic life of cultured leisure? Or shall we note slave biographies, like those of Charles Ball, Sojourner Truth, Harriet Tubman and Frederick Douglass; the careful observations of Olmsted and the indictment of Hinton Helper?

No one can read that first thin autobiography of Frederick Douglass and have left many illusions about slavery. And if truth is our object, no amount of flowery romance and the personal reminiscences of its protected beneficiaries can keep the world from knowing that slavery was a cruel, dirty, costly and inexcusable anachronism, which nearly ruined the world's greatest experiment in democracy. No serious and unbiased student can be deceived by the fairy tale of a beautiful Southern slave civilization. If those who really had opportunity to know the South before the war wrote the truth, it was a center of widespread ignorance, undeveloped resources, suppressed humanity and unrestrained passions, with whatever veneer of manners and culture that could lie above these depths.

Coming now to the Civil War, how for a moment can anyone who reads the *Congressional Globe* from 1850 to 1860, the lives of contemporary statesmen and public characters, North and South, the discourses in the newspapers and accounts of meetings and speeches, doubt that Negro slavery was the cause of the Civil War? What do we gain by evading this clear fact, and talking in vague ways about "Union" and "State Rights" and differences in civilization as the cause of that catastrophe?

Of all historic facts there can be none clearer than that for four long and fearful years the South fought to perpetuate human slavery; and that the nation which "rose so bright and fair and died so pure of stain" was one that had a perfect right to be ashamed of its birth and glad of its death. Yet one monument in North Carolina achieves the impossible by recording of Confederate soldiers: "They died fighting for liberty!"

On the other hand, consider the North and the Civil War. Why should we be deliberately false, like Woodward, in "Meet General Grant," and represent the North as magnanimously freeing the slave without any effort on his part?

"The American Negroes are the only people in the history of the world, so far as I know, that ever became free without any effort of their own. . . .

"They had not started the war nor ended it. They twanged banjos around the railroad stations, sang melodious spirituals, and believed that some Yankee would soon come along and give each of them forty acres of land and a mule." [1a]

The North went to war without the slightest idea of freeing the slave. The great majority of Northerners from Lincoln down pledged themselves to protect slavery, and they hated and harried Abolitionists. But on the other hand, the thesis which Beale tends to support that the whole North during and after the war was chiefly interested in making money, is only half true; it was abolition and belief in democracy that gained for a time the upper hand after the war and led the North in Reconstruction; business followed abolition in order to maintain the tariff, pay the bonds and defend the banks. To call this business program "the program of the North" and ignore abolition is unhistorical. In growing ascendancy for a calculable time was a great moral movement which turned the North from its economic defense of slavery and led it to Emancipation. Abolitionists attacked slavery because it was wrong and their moral battle cannot be truthfully minimized or forgotten. Nor does this fact deny that the majority of Northerners before the war were not abolitionists, that they attacked slavery only in order to win the war and enfranchised the Negro to secure this result.

One has but to read the debates in Congress and state papers from Abraham Lincoln down to know that the decisive action which ended the Civil War was the emancipation and arming of the black slave; that, as Lincoln said: "Without the military help of black freedmen, the war against the South could not have been won." The freedmen,

[1a] W. E. Woodward, *Meet General Grant,* p. 372.

far from being the inert recipients of freedom at the hands of philanthropists, furnished 200,000 soldiers in the Civil War who took part in nearly 200 battles and skirmishes, and in addition perhaps 300,000 others as effective laborers and helpers. In proportion to population, more Negroes than whites fought in the Civil War. These people, withdrawn from the support of the Confederacy, with threat of the withdrawal of millions more, made the opposition of the slaveholder useless, unless they themselves freed and armed their own slaves. This was exactly what they started to do; they were only restrained by realizing that such action removed the very cause for which they began fighting. Yet one would search current American histories almost in vain to find a clear statement or even faint recognition of these perfectly well-authenticated facts.

All this is but preliminary to the kernel of the historic problem with which this book deals, and that is Reconstruction. The chorus of agreement concerning the attempt to reconstruct and organize the South after the Civil War and emancipation is overwhelming. There is scarce a child in the street that cannot tell you that the whole effort was a hideous mistake and an unfortunate incident, based on ignorance, revenge and the perverse determination to attempt the impossible; that the history of the United States from 1866 to 1876 is something of which the nation ought to be ashamed and which did more to retard and set back the American Negro than anything that has happened to him; while at the same time it grievously and wantonly wounded again a part of the nation already hurt to death.

True it is that the Northern historians writing just after the war had scant sympathy for the South, and wrote ruthlessly of "rebels" and "slave-drivers." They had at least the excuse of a war psychosis.

As a young labor leader, Will Herberg, writes: "The great traditions of this period and especially of Reconstruction are shamelessly repudiated by the official heirs of Stevens and Sumner. In the last quarter of a century hardly a single book has appeared consistently championing or sympathetically interpreting the great ideals of the crusade against slavery, whereas scores and hundreds have dropped from the presses in ignoble 'extenuation' of the North, in open apology for the Confederacy, in measureless abuse of the Radical figures of Reconstruction. The Reconstruction period as the logical culmination of decades of previous development, has borne the brunt of the reaction." [2]

First of all, we have James Ford Rhodes' history of the United States. Rhodes was trained not as an historian but as an Ohio business man. He had no broad formal education. When he had accumulated a fortune, he surrounded himself with a retinue of clerks and proceeded to manufacture a history of the United States by mass production. His method was simple. He gathered a vast number of authorities; he selected from these authorities those whose testimony supported his thesis, and he discarded the others. The majority report of the great Ku Klux investigation, for instance, he laid aside in favor of the minority report, simply because the latter supported his sincere belief. In the report and testimony of the Reconstruction Committee of Fifteen, he did practically the same thing.

[2] Will Herberg, *The Heritage of the Civil War*, p. 3.

Above all, he begins his inquiry convinced, without admitting any necessity of investigation, that Negroes are an inferior race:

"No large policy in our country has ever been so conspicuous a failure as that of forcing universal Negro suffrage upon the South. The Negroes who simply acted out their nature, were not to blame. How indeed could they acquire political honesty? What idea could barbarism thrust into slavery obtain of the rights of property? . . .

"From the Republican policy came no real good to the Negroes. Most of them developed no political capacity, and the few who raised themselves above the mass, did not reach a high order of intelligence." [3]

Rhodes was primarily the historian of property; of economic history and the labor movement, he knew nothing; of democratic government, he was contemptuous. He was trained to make profits. He used his profits to write history. He speaks again and again of the rulership of "intelligence and property" and he makes a plea that intelligent use of the ballot for the benefit of property is the only real foundation of democracy.

The real frontal attack on Reconstruction, as interpreted by the leaders of national thought in 1870 and for some time thereafter, came from the universities and particularly from Columbia and Johns Hopkins.

The movement began with Columbia University and with the advent of John W. Burgess of Tennessee and William A. Dunning of New Jersey as professors of political science and history.

Burgess was an ex-Confederate soldier who started to a little Southern college with a box of books, a box of tallow candles and a Negro boy; and his attitude toward the Negro race in after years was subtly colored by this early conception of Negroes as essentially property like books and candles. Dunning was a kindly and impressive professor who was deeply influenced by a growing group of young Southern students and began with them to re-write the history of the nation from 1860 to 1880, in more or less conscious opposition to the classic interpretations of New England.

Burgess was frank and determined in his anti-Negro thought. He expounded his theory of Nordic supremacy which colored all his political theories:

"The claim that there is nothing in the color of the skin from the point of view of political ethics is a great sophism. A black skin means membership in a race of men which has never of itself succeeded in subjecting passion to reason, has never, therefore, created any civilization of any kind. To put such a race of men in possession of a 'state' government in a system of federal government is to trust them with the development of political and legal civilization upon the most important subjects of human life, and to do this in communities with a large white population is simply to establish barbarism in power over civilization."

Burgess is a Tory and open apostle of reaction. He tells us that the nation now believes "that it is the white man's mission, his duty and his right, to hold the reins of political power in his own hands for the civilization of the world and the welfare of mankind." [4]

[3] Rhodes, *History of the United States,* VII, pp. 232–233.
[4] Burgess, *Reconstruction and the Constitution,* pp. viii, ix.

For this reason America is following "the European idea of the duty of civilized races to impose their political sovereignty upon civilized, or half civilized, or not fully civilized, races anywhere and everywhere in the world." [5]

He complacently believes that "There is something natural in the subordination of an inferior race to a superior race, even to the point of the enslavement of the inferior race, but there is nothing natural in the opposite." [6] He therefore denominates Reconstruction as the rule "of the uncivilized Negroes over the whites of the South." [7] This has been the teaching of one of our greatest universities for nearly fifty years.

Dunning was less dogmatic as a writer, and his own statements are often judicious. But even Dunning can declare that "all the forces [in the South] that made for civilization were dominated by a mass of barbarous freedmen"; and that "the antithesis and antipathy of race and color were crucial and ineradicable." [7a] The work of most of the students whom he taught and encouraged has been one-sided and partisan to the last degree. Johns Hopkins University has issued a series of studies similar to Columbia's; Southern teachers have been welcomed to many Northern universities, where often Negro students have been systematically discouraged, and thus a nation-wide university attitude has arisen by which propaganda against the Negro has been carried on unquestioned.

The Columbia school of historians and social investigators have issued between 1895 and the present time sixteen studies of Reconstruction in the Southern States, all based on the same thesis and all done according to the same method: first, endless sympathy with the white South; second, ridicule, contempt or silence for the Negro; third, a judicial attitude towards the North, which concludes that the North under great misapprehension did a grievous wrong, but eventually saw its mistake and retreated.

These studies vary, of course, in their methods. Dunning's own work is usually silent so far as the Negro is concerned. Burgess is more than fair in law but reactionary in matters of race and property, regarding the treatment of a Negro as a man as nothing less than a crime, and admitting that "the mainstay of property is the courts."

In the books on Reconstruction written by graduates of these universities and others, the studies of Texas, North Carolina, Florida, Virginia and Louisiana are thoroughly bad, giving no complete picture of what happened during Reconstruction, written for the most part by men and women without broad historical or social background, and all designed not to seek the truth but to prove a thesis. Hamilton reaches the climax of this school when he characterizes the black codes, which even Burgess condemned, as "not only . . . on the whole reasonable, temperate and kindly, but, in the main, necessary." [8]

Thompson's "Georgia" is another case in point. It seeks to be fair, but silly stories about Negroes indicating utter lack of even common sense are included, and

---

[5] Burgess, *Reconstruction and the Constitution*, p. 218.

[6] Burgess, *Reconstruction and the Constitution*, pp. 244–245.

[7] Burgess, *Reconstruction and the Constitution*, p. 218.

[7a] Dunning, *Reconstruction, Political and Economic*, pp. 212, 213.

[8] Hamilton, "Southern Legislation in Respect to Freedmen," in *Studies in Southern History and Politics*, p. 156.

every noble sentiment from white people. When two Negro workers, William and Jim, put a straightforward advertisement in a local paper, the author says that it was "evidently written by a white friend." There is not the slightest historical evidence to prove this, and there were plenty of educated Negroes in Augusta at the time who might have written this. Lonn's "Louisiana" puts Sheridan's words in Sherman's mouth to prove a petty point.

There are certain of these studies which, though influenced by the same general attitude, nevertheless have more of scientific poise and cultural background. Garner's "Reconstruction in Mississippi" conceives the Negro as an integral part of the scene and treats him as a human being. With this should be bracketed the recent study of "Reconstruction in South Carolina" by Simkins and Woody. This is not as fair as Garner's, but in the midst of conventional judgment and conclusion, and reproductions of all available caricatures of Negroes, it does not hesitate to give a fair account of the Negroes and of some of their work. It gives the impression of combining in one book two antagonistic points of view, but in the clash much truth emerges.

Ficklen's "Louisiana" and the works of Fleming are anti-Negro in spirit, but, nevertheless, they have a certain fairness and sense of historic honesty. Fleming's "Documentary History of Reconstruction" is done by a man who has a thesis to support, and his selection of documents supports the thesis. His study of Alabama is pure propaganda.

Next come a number of books which are openly and blatantly propaganda, like Herbert's "Solid South," and the books by Pike and Reynolds on South Carolina, the works by Pollard and Carpenter, and especially those by Ulrich Phillips. One of the latest and most popular of this series is "The Tragic Era" by Claude Bowers, which is an excellent and readable piece of current newspaper reporting, absolutely devoid of historical judgment or sociological knowledge. It is a classic example of historical propaganda of the cheaper sort.

We have books like Milton's "Age of Hate" and Winston's "Andrew Johnson" which attempt to re-write the character of Andrew Johnson. They certainly add to our knowledge of the man and our sympathy for his weakness. But they cannot, for students, change the calm testimony of unshaken historical facts. Fuess' "Carl Schurz" paints the picture of this fine liberal, and yet goes out of its way to show that he was quite wrong in what he said he saw in the South.

The chief witness in Reconstruction, the emancipated slave himself, has been almost barred from court. His written Reconstruction record has been largely destroyed and nearly always neglected. Only three or four states have preserved the debates in the Reconstruction conventions; there are few biographies of black leaders. The Negro is refused a hearing because he was poor and ignorant. It is therefore assumed that all Negroes in Reconstruction were ignorant and silly and that therefore a history of Reconstruction in any state can quite ignore him. The result is that most unfair caricatures of Negroes have been carefully preserved; but serious speeches, successful administration and upright character are almost universally ignored and forgotten. Wherever a black head rises to historic view, it is promptly slain by an adjective—"shrewd," "notorious," "cunning"—or pilloried by a sneer; or put out of view by some quite unproven charge of bad moral character. In other words, every effort has been made to treat the Negro's part in Reconstruction with silence and contempt.

When recently a student tried to write on education in Florida, he found that the official records of the excellent administration of the colored Superintendent of Education, Gibbs, who virtually established the Florida public school, had been destroyed. Alabama has tried to obliterate all printed records of Reconstruction.

Especially noticeable is the fact that little attempt has been made to trace carefully the rise and economic development of the poor whites and their relation to the planters and to Negro labor after the war. There were five million or more non-slaveholding whites in the South in 1860 and less than two million in the families of all slaveholders. Yet one might almost gather from contemporary history that the five million left no history and had no descendants. The extraordinary history of the rise and triumph of the poor whites has been largely neglected, even by Southern white students.[9]

The whole development of Reconstruction was primarily an economic development, but no economic history or proper material for it has been written. It has been regarded as a purely political matter, and of politics most naturally divorced from industry.[10]

All this is reflected in the textbooks of the day and in the encyclopedias, until we have got to the place where we cannot use our experiences during and after the Civil War for the uplift and enlightenment of mankind. We have spoiled and misconceived the position of the historian. If we are going, in the future, not simply with regard to this one question, but with regard to all social problems, to be able to use human experience for the guidance of mankind, we have got clearly to distinguish between fact and desire.

In the first place, somebody in each era must make clear the facts with utter disregard to his own wish and desire and belief. What we have got to know, so far as possible, are the things that actually happened in the world. Then with that much clear and open to every reader, the philosopher and prophet has a chance to interpret these facts; but the historian has no right, posing as scientist, to conceal or distort facts; and until we distinguish between these two functions of the chronicler of human action, we are going to render it easy for a muddled world out of sheer ignorance to make the same mistake ten times over.

One is astonished in the study of history at the recurrence of the idea that evil must be forgotten, distorted, skimmed over. We must not remember that Daniel Webster got drunk but only remember that he was a splendid constitutional lawyer. We must forget that George Washington was a slave owner, or that Thomas Jefferson had mulatto children, or that Alexander Hamilton had Negro blood, and simply remember the things we regard as creditable and inspiring. The difficulty, of course, with this phi-

[9] Interesting exceptions are Moore's and Ambler's monographs.
[10] *The Economic History of the South* by E. Q. Hawk is merely a compilation of census reports and conventionalities.

losophy is that history loses its value as an incentive and example; it paints perfect men and noble nations, but it does not tell the truth.

No one reading the history of the United States during 1850–1860 can have the slightest doubt left in his mind that Negro slavery was the cause of the Civil War, and yet during and since we learn that a great nation murdered thousands and destroyed millions on account of abstract doctrines concerning the nature of the Federal Union. Since the attitude of the nation concerning state rights has been revolutionized by the development of the central government since the war, the whole argument becomes an astonishing *reductio ad absurdum,* leaving us apparently with no cause for the Civil War except the recent reiteration of statements which make the great public men on one side narrow, hypocritical fanatics and liars, while the leaders on the other side were extraordinary and unexampled for their beauty, unselfishness and fairness.

Not a single great leader of the nation during the Civil War and Reconstruction has escaped attack and libel. The magnificent figures of Charles Sumner and Thaddeus Stevens have been besmirched almost beyond recognition. We have been cajoling and flattering the South and slurring the North, because the South is determined to re-write the history of slavery and the North is not interested in history but in wealth.

This, then, is the book basis upon which today we judge Reconstruction. In order to paint the South as a martyr to inescapable fate, to make the North the magnanimous emancipator, and to ridicule the Negro as the impossible joke in the whole development, we have in fifty years, by libel, innuendo and silence, so completely misstated and obliterated the history of the Negro in America and his relation to its work and government that today it is almost unknown. This may be fine romance, but it is not science. It may be inspiring, but it is certainly not the truth. And beyond this it is dangerous. It is not only part foundation of our present lawlessness and loss of democratic ideals; it has, more than that, led the world to embrace and worship the color bar as social salvation and it is helping to range mankind in ranks of mutual hatred and contempt, at the summons of a cheap and false myth.

Nearly all recent books on Reconstruction agree with each other in discarding the government reports and substituting selected diaries, letters, and gossip. Yet it happens that the government records are an historic source of wide and unrivaled authenticity. There is the report of the select Committee of Fifteen, which delved painstakingly into the situation all over the South and called all kinds and conditions of men to testify; there are the report of Carl Schurz and the twelve volumes of reports made on the Ku Klux conspiracy; and above all, the *Congressional Globe.* None who has not read page by page the *Congressional Globe,* especially the sessions of the 39th Congress, can possibly have any idea of what the problems of Reconstruction facing the United States were in 1865–1866. Then there were the reports of the Freedmen's Bureau and the executive and other documentary reports of government officials, especially in the war and treasury departments, which give the historian the only groundwork upon which he can build a real and truthful picture. There are certain historians who have not tried deliberately to falsify the picture: Southern whites like Frances Butler Leigh and Susan Smedes; Northern historians, like McPherson, Oberholtzer, and Nicolay and Hay. There are foreign travelers like Sir George Campbell, Georges Clemenceau and Robert

Somers. There are the personal reminiscences of Augustus Beard, George Julian, George F. Hoar, Carl Schurz and John Sherman. There are the invaluable work of Edward McPherson and the more recent studies by Paul Haworth, A. A. Taylor, and Charles Wesley. Beale simply does not take Negroes into account in the critical year of 1866.

Certain monographs deserve all praise, like those of Hendricks and Pierce. The work of Flack is prejudiced but built on study. The defense of the carpetbag régime by Tourgée and Allen, Powell Clayton, Holden and Warmoth are worthy antidotes to the certain writers.

The lives of Stevens and Sumner are revealing even when slightly apologetic because of the Negro; while Andrew Johnson is beginning to suffer from writers who are trying to prove how seldom he got drunk, and think that important.

It will be noted that for my authority in this work I have depended very largely upon secondary material; upon state histories of Reconstruction, written in the main by those who were convinced before they began to write that the Negro was incapable of government, or of becoming a constituent part of a civilized state. The fairest of these histories have not tried to conceal facts; in other cases, the black man has been largely ignored; while in still others, he has been traduced and ridiculed. If I had had time and money and opportunity to go back to the original sources in all cases, there can be no doubt that the weight of this work would have been vastly strengthened, and as I firmly believe, the case of the Negro more convincingly set forth.

Various volumes of papers in the great libraries like the Johnson papers in the Library of Congress, the Sumner manuscripts at Harvard, the Schurz correspondence, the Wells papers, the Chase papers, the Fessenden and Greeley collections, the McCulloch, McPherson, Sherman, Stevens and Trumbull papers, all must have much of great interest to the historians of the American Negro. I have not had time nor opportunity to examine these, and most of those who have examined them had little interest in black folk.

Negroes have done some excellent work on their own history and defense. It suffers of course from natural partisanship and a desire to prove a case in the face of a chorus of unfair attacks. Its best work also suffers from the fact that Negroes with difficulty reach an audience. But this is also true of such white writers as Skaggs and Bancroft who could not get first-class publishers because they were saying something that the nation did not like.

The Negro historians began with autobiographies and reminiscences. The older historians were George W. Williams and Joseph T. Wilson; the new school of historians is led by Carter G. Woodson; and I have been greatly helped by the unpublished theses of four of the youngest Negro students. It is most unfortunate that while many young white Southerners can get funds to attack and ridicule the Negro and his friends, it is almost impossible for first-class Negro students to get a chance for research or to get finished work in print.

I write then in a field devastated by passion and belief. Naturally, as a Negro, I cannot do this writing without believing in the essential humanity of Negroes, in their ability to be educated, to do the work of the modern world, to take their place as equal citizens with others. I cannot for a moment subscribe to that bizarre doctrine of race that makes most men inferior to the few. But, too, as a student of science, I want to be fair, objective and judicial; to let no searing of the memory by intolerable insult and cruelty make me fail to sympathize with human frailties and contradiction, in the eternal paradox of good and evil. But armed and warned by all this, and fortified by long study of the facts, I stand at the end of this writing, literally aghast at what American historians have done to this field.

What is the object of writing the history of Reconstruction? Is it to wipe out the disgrace of a people which fought to make slaves of Negroes? Is it to show that the North had higher motives than freeing black men? Is it to prove that Negroes were black angels? No, it is simply to establish the Truth, on which Right in the future may be built. We shall never have a science of history until we have in our colleges men who regard the truth as more important than the defense of the white race, and who will not deliberately encourage students to gather thesis material in order to support a prejudice or buttress a lie.

Three-fourths of the testimony against the Negro in Reconstruction is on the unsupported evidence of men who hated and despised Negroes and regarded it as loyalty to blood, patriotism to country, and filial tribute to the fathers to lie, steal or kill in order to discredit these black folk. This may be a natural result when a people have been humbled and impoverished and degraded in their own life; but what is inconceivable is that another generation and another group should regard this testimony as scientific truth, when it is contradicted by logic and by fact. This chapter, therefore, which in logic should be a survey of books and sources, becomes of sheer necessity an arraignment of American historians and an indictment of their ideals. With a determination unparalleled in science, the mass of American writers have started out so to distort the facts of the greatest critical period of American history as to prove right wrong and wrong right. I am not familiar enough with the vast field of human history to pronounce on the relative guilt of these and historians of other times and fields; but I do say that if the history of the past has been written in the same fashion, it is useless as science and misleading as ethics. It simply shows that with sufficient general agreement and determination among the dominant classes, the truth of history may be utterly distorted and contradicted and changed to any convenient fairy tale that the masters of men wish.

I cannot believe that any unbiased mind, with an ideal of truth and of scientific judgment, can read the plain, authentic facts of our history, during 1860–1880, and come to conclusions essentially different from mine; and yet I stand virtually alone in this interpretation. So much so that the very cogency of my facts would make me hesitate, did I not seem to see plain reasons. Subtract from Burgess his belief that only white people can rule, and he is in essential agreement with me. Remember that Rhodes was an uneducated money-maker who hired clerks to find the facts which he needed to support his thesis, and one is convinced that the same labor and expense could easily produce quite opposite results.

One fact and one alone explains the attitude of most recent writers toward Reconstruction; they cannot conceive Negroes as men; in their minds the word "Negro" connotes "inferiority" and "stupidity" lightened only by unreasoning gayety and humor. Suppose the slaves of 1860 had been white folk. Stevens would have been a great statesman, Sumner a great democrat, and Schurz a keen prophet, in a mighty revolution of rising humanity. Ignorance and poverty would easily have been explained by history, and the demand for land and the franchise would have been justified as the birthright of natural freemen.

But Burgess was a slaveholder, Dunning a Copperhead and Rhodes an exploiter of wage labor. Not one of them apparently ever met an educated Negro of force and ability. Around such impressive thinkers gathered the young post-war students from the South. They had been born and reared in the bitterest period of Southern race hatred, fear and contempt. Their instinctive reactions were confirmed and encouraged in the best of American universities. Their scholarship, when it regarded black men, became deaf, dumb and blind. The clearest evidence of Negro ability, work, honesty, patience, learning and efficiency became distorted into cunning, brute toil, shrewd evasion, cowardice and imitation—a stupid effort to transcend nature's law.

For those seven mystic years between Johnson's "swing 'round the circle" and the panic of 1873, a majority of thinking Americans in the North believed in the equal manhood of black folk. They acted accordingly with a clear-cut decisiveness and thorough logic, utterly incomprehensible to a day like ours which does not share this human faith; and to Southern whites this period can only be explained by deliberate vengeance and hate.

The panic of 1873 brought sudden disillusion in business enterprise, economic organization, religious belief and political standards. A flood of appeal from the white South reënforced this reaction—appeal with no longer the arrogant bluster of slave oligarchy, but the simple moving annals of the plight of a conquered people. The resulting emotional and intellectual rebound of the nation made it nearly inconceivable in 1876 that ten years earlier most men had believed in human equality.

Assuming, therefore, as axiomatic the endless inferiority of the Negro race, these newer historians, mostly Southerners, some Northerners who deeply sympathized with the South, misinterpreted, distorted, even deliberately ignored any fact that challenged or contradicted this assumption. If the Negro was admittedly sub-human, what need to waste time delving into his Reconstruction history? Consequently historians of Reconstruction with a few exceptions ignore the Negro as completely as possible, leaving the reader wondering why an element apparently so insignificant filled the whole Southern picture at the time. The only real excuse for this attitude is loyalty to a lost cause, reverence for brave fathers and suffering mothers and sisters, and fidelity to the ideals of a clan and class. But in propaganda against the Negro since emancipation in this land, we face one of the most stupendous efforts the world ever saw to discredit human beings, an effort involving universities, history, science, social life and religion.

The most magnificent drama in the last thousand years of human history is the transportation of ten million human beings out of the dark beauty of their mother continent into the new-found Eldorado of the West. They descended into Hell; and in the third century they arose from the dead, in the finest effort to achieve democracy for the working millions which this world had ever seen. It was a tragedy that beggared the Greek; it was an upheaval of humanity like the Reformation and the French Revolution. Yet we are blind and led by the blind. We discern in it no part of our labor movement; no part of our industrial triumph; no part of our religious experience. Before the dumb eyes of ten generations of ten million children, it is made mockery of and spit upon; a degradation of the eternal mother; a sneer at human effort; with aspiration and art deliberately and elaborately distorted. And why? Because in a day when the human mind aspired to a science of human action, a history and psychology of the mighty effort of the mightiest century, we fell under the leadership of those who would compromise with truth in the past in order to make peace in the present and guide policy in the future.

Reconstruction— Black and White*

John Hope Franklin

The elections held in the former Confederate states following the writing of the new constitutions were preceded by strenuous campaigns. Conservatives, already gathering strength from new amnesties and individual pardons and from defections in the ranks of the loyal native Southerners, were making a last-ditch stand to defeat Radical Reconstruction. One of the first efforts to defeat Radical Reconstruction was an appeal to Negroes to join the Democratic party. In many communities they were invited to Democratic party conventions and rallies. "Let every white man and honest black man in the State fall into the Democratic ranks and make a crushing charge upon the shattered cohorts of scalawags and carpetbaggers," counseled the Montgomery *Advertiser*. The appeal won few converts. Failing to entice Negroes into their ranks, they took a stand against Negro suffrage. In Virginia, Colonel R. E. Withers, late of the Confederate army and an unsuccessful Conservative candidate for governor, said that he was the standard-bearer of the white man's party. "I do not ask the support of the Negroes, nor do I expect it, for I consider them unfit to exercise the right of suffrage." The Conservatives were determined never to accept Radical Reconstruction, and every move they made in the ensuing months and years proved this. Although unable to place one of their number in any of the gubernatorial chairs in these first elections, they sent representatives to the legislatures in practically every state. In 1868 they had a majority in both houses of the Georgia legislature. In Florida they were a respectable minority of almost one-third.

But the strength of the Conservative opponents of Radical Reconstruction is not to be measured merely by the numbers of those who regarded themselves as Conservatives. At times they supported Northerners or loyal Southerners, when they had assur-

* From John Hope Franklin, *Reconstruction After the Civil War* (Chicago: The University of Chicago Press, 1961), pp. 127–51. © 1961 by the University of Chicago. Reprinted by permission of author and publisher.

ances that such persons would adhere to policies and programs that were essentially conservative. For governor of Virginia they turned from Colonel Withers to the Northerner Gilbert Walker, who had long been a resident of Norfolk and who was about as conservative as any Virginian. Walker was elected. In Georgia many Conservatives supported the successful gubernatorial candidate, Rufus B. Bullock. Although he was born in the North, he had come South before the war and had served in the Confederate army. In time, however, even while Radical Reconstruction continued, the Conservatives succeeded in electing their own members governors and leaders in the legislatures. Witness, for example, the accession in 1870 of Robert B. Lindsay, a Democrat, to the Alabama governor's chair. Lindsay's counterparts were rising all over the South within a very few years after the beginning of Radical Reconstruction.

It is in the context of a vigorous, threatening opposition that the new reconstruction in the South must be observed. The opposition was versatile, at times throwing its own candidates into the field, at other times coalescing with loyal Southerners for some common goal or co-operating with Northerners when that tactic served its ends. It generally opposed Negro suffrage but at times supported this radical measure where control of the Negro vote seemed likely. Likewise, it supported certain economic measures sponsored by the Radicals but clearly benefiting the Conservatives. Indeed, it is somewhat inaccurate to call this group the opposition. With its extensive resources, enormous prestige, and ample experience in the field of public affairs it was a formidable force in the South in the postwar years. Even while laboring under political disabilities these men could easily make themselves felt all over the South. And as their disabilities were removed, the Radicals found them ever more difficult to cope with.

As each new government was established in the South, the Conservatives usually observed the occasion by making dire predictions of the evils that would flow from it. In Alabama they set aside the day for fasting and prayer to Almighty God for the deliverance of the state "from the horrors of Negro domination." They seemed not to be consoled by the fact that the attorney general and the president of the new Board of Education were Conservatives and former officers in the Confederate army. One editor exclaimed, "We must render this either a white man's government, or convert the land into a Negro man's cemetery." But since Conservatives were as anxious as everyone else to have their states readmitted to the Union, they held their heavy fire until admission had been achieved.

The first task of the new governments was to secure the ratification of the Fourteenth Amendment, one of the conditions for readmission laid down by the Reconstruction Acts. By midsummer, 1868, seven states—Alabama, Arkansas, Florida, Georgia, Louisiana, North Carolina, and South Carolina—had organized their governments and ratified the Fourteenth Amendment. Congress, therefore, readmitted them to the Union on the condition that Negro suffrage forever remain a part of their fundamental laws. Problems related to the suffrage provisions of their constitutions and other details delayed the readmission of Virginia, Texas, and Mississippi, all of which came back into the Union in 1870.

Immediately upon the readmission of their states the Conservatives, calling themselves variously the Democratic party, Conservative Union party, or the Democratic and Conservative party, began their running attack on the new administrations. Overthrow would come soon, they felt, if they worked hard enough at it. When federal authority was withdrawn from Georgia after it was readmitted, the Conservative Democrats opened fire on the three Negro senators and twenty-nine Negro representatives in the state legislature. After the failure of a move to expel the Negro senators as a group, the legislature began to attack the Negro members individually. It began with the most vulnerable Negro member, Aaron Alpeoria Bradley. This colorful figure had moved from New York to Savannah at the close of the war. Soon he became a leader among the Negroes of his adopted home and was elected to the constitutional convention of 1868. He was expelled after a majority of the members cited him for "gross insults" to them. He then organized the Negroes in Savannah and won a seat in the legislature, but the senate moved his expulsion on the grounds of an alleged criminal conviction in New York. When Bradley was not permitted to defend himself, he resigned.

The senate then challenged the eligibility of its other two Negro members. For one hour they sought to establish their claim to their seats, but they were unsuccessful and were forthwith expelled by a vote of 24 to 11. The twenty-nine Negro members in the house were not safe from the attack; and in August, 1868, resolutions to expel them were passed by a vote of 83 to 23, with the Negro members abstaining. Only four Negroes remained, and this was because their fair complexion made it impossible to prove that they were Negroes.

In September, 1868, the Georgia legislature formally declared all Negro members ineligible to sit in that body. But Negroes were prepared to fight. Henry McNeal Turner, the most articulate—and most disliked—Negro member, published and circulated throughout the state his impassioned defense, which the legislature did not print in its minutes, of the Negroes' right to their seats. "It is very strange," he said, "if a white man can occupy on this floor a seat created by colored votes, and a black man cannot do it. . . . It is extraordinary that a race such as yours, professing gallantry, chivalry, education, and superiority, living in a land where ringing chimes call child and sire to the Church of God—a land where Bibles are read and Gospel truths are spoken, and where courts of justice are presumed to exist . . . that with all these advantages on your side, you can make war upon the poor defenseless black man."

The Republicans appealed to the state supreme court for relief. The court in a 2 to 1 decision declared the Negroes eligible, but there was serious doubt that the legislature would respect the decision. In October 136 Negroes from eighty-two counties met in Macon to protest the action of the legislature. They described their condition as intolerable and pleaded for federal relief. Governor Bullock transmitted their appeal to Congress together with his own view that the legislature was illegally constituted. The Committee on Reconstruction of the United States House of Representatives investigated the matter and heard Negroes tell of numerous outrages against them. The United States Senate, meanwhile, refused to seat Joshua Hill, who had been elected by the Georgia legislature in July. The case against Georgia lawlessness was building up.

Congress, reconvening from the heated elections in November, was in a state of indecision over what to do about Georgia. Finally, when the state legislature rejected the Fifteenth Amendment in March, 1869, Congress went into action. Georgia was immediately put under military rule once more, and the ratification of the Fifteenth Amendment was made a condition for readmission. General Terry expelled twenty-four Democrats from the legislature on the ground that they were disfranchised by the Fourteenth Amendment. He then filled their places with Republicans and restored the Negro members to their places. The legislature ratified the Fifteenth Amendment, recognized the Negro members, and voted back pay for them. In a remarkable display of magnanimity a Negro member introduced and secured the passage of a resolution providing for the compensation of the displaced white representatives. On January 10, Georgia was admitted to the Union for the second time under Radical Reconstruction. No other former Confederate state put on such a display of incorrigibility.

No group has attracted more attention or has had its role more misrepresented by contemporaries and by posterity than Southern Negroes during Radical Reconstruction. The period has been described as one of Negro rule, as one of gross perfidy with the Negro as the central figure, since the reins of misgovernment were supposedly held by black militiamen. Negroes were not in control of the state governments at any time anywhere in the South. They held public office and, at times, played important parts in the public life of their respective states. But it would be stretching a point to say that their roles were dominant, and it would be hopelessly distorting the picture to suggest that they ruled the South. It was in South Carolina that they had the greatest numerical strength. In the first legislature there were eighty-seven Negroes and forty whites. From the outset, however, whites controlled the state senate and in 1874 the lower house as well. At all times the governor was white. There were two Negro lieutenant governors, Alonzo J. Ransier in 1870 and Richard H. Gleaves in 1872. There were other Negro leaders. Samuel J. Lee was speaker of the House in 1872 and Robert B. Elliot in 1874. From 1868 to 1872 Francis L. Cardozo was secretary of state, and from 1872 to 1876 he was state treasurer. Jonathan J. Wright, a member of the Pennsylvania bar before coming to South Carolina, sat on the state supreme court for seven years, but he was the only Negro to achieve a judicial position of that level in any state.

Despite their large numbers, 437,400 compared to 353,800 whites in 1860, Negroes in Mississippi did not approximate a numerical domination of the state government. In the first reconstruction legislature there were 40 Negro members out of a total of 115. According to John R. Lynch, Negro speaker of the house in 1872, "Of seven state officers, only one, that of Secretary of State, was filled by a colored man, until 1873 when colored men were elected to three of the seven offices." They were A. K. Davis, lieutenant governor, James Hill, secretary of state, and Thomas W. Cardozo, superintendent of education. Of the situation in 1873 Lynch declared, "Out of seventy-two counties in the State . . . electing on an average twenty-eight officers to a county, it is safe to assert that not five out of one hundred of such officers were colored men." Vernon Wharton, after a careful study of the problem, concludes that "although Negroes formed a majority of the population in thirty counties in Mississippi, they almost never took advantage of their opportunity to place any large number of their race in local offices."

Several Louisiana Negroes were prominent and influential, but they never approached a dominant position in public affairs. The forty-two Negroes in the first legislature were in the minority, as were the Negroes in succeeding legislatures. Three Negroes served as lieutenant governor: Oscar J. Dunn, 1868–71; P. B. S. Pinchback, 1871–72, who acted as governor for forty-three days in 1872 when Governor Warmoth was ousted; and C. C. Antoine, 1872–76. Other Negroes held important offices, including P. G. Deslonde, secretary of state, 1872–76; Antoine Dubuclet, state treasurer, 1868–69; and W. G. Brown, superintendent of public education, 1872–76. Most of the Louisiana Negro leaders had been free before the war and had enjoyed some educational opportunities. Of the seven Negroes in the state senate in 1868 only one, Oscar J. Dunn, had been a slave; and before the war he had purchased his own freedom. Pinchback, a well-to-do former captain in the Union army, had been educated in Cincinnati. He had the physical appearance of a white man but his white skin gave him little advantage in the hurly-burly of reconstruction politics in Louisiana.

In the other state governments the roles of Negroes were even less significant. In the North Carolina legislature they constituted barely one-seventh of the membership, and the only Negro official of any consequence was James Walker Hood, who served as assistant superintendent of public instruction for several years. The first Alabama legislature saw only twenty-six Negroes out of a total membership of eighty-four, and there were no important state offices in the hands of Negroes. The "horrors of Negro domination" from which Alabamans prayed deliverance simply did not exist. James T. Rapier is the only Negro who was at all prominent; after serving as assessor of internal revenue in Alabama he went on to Congress. What influence Negroes might have had in Georgia was nullified by their expulsion from the legislature. By the time they returned, Radical Reconstruction had been so effectively undermined that there was little chance for Negroes to exert any considerable influence.

Florida had only nineteen Negroes in its first legislature, which contained seventy-six members. Their influence was extremely limited. The only high-ranking Negro in the state government was Jonathan C. Gibbs, who was secretary of state from 1868 to 1872 and superintendent of public instruction from 1872 to 1874. Very few Negroes held other than minor offices in the new government in Virginia. Twenty-seven sat in the first legislature, and there were none among the policy-makers in the executive branch of the government. The influence of Negroes in Arkansas was meager. At the beginning of the period none held any important offices. In 1871 W. H. Grey was appointed commissioner of immigration, a position he held until 1873. J. C. Corbin, a graduate of Oberlin College, served as superintendent of education from January, 1873, to October, 1874. There were no important Negro officeholders in Texas, but G. T. Ruby of Galveston wielded considerable political influence, while Norris Wright Cuney, also of Galveston, held several offices, including membership on the county school board and state inspector of customs.

In a different but highly significant category were the sixteen Negroes who served in Congress between 1869 and 1880. Two of them, Hiram R. Revels and Blanche K. Bruce, represented Mississippi in the Senate. Revels was a North Carolina free Negro who had lived in several Northern states and had studied at Knox College in Illinois. By the time of the Civil War he had become an ordained minister in the African Methodist Episcopal Church and had taught school in several places. During the war he recruited Negroes for the Union army, founded a school for freedmen in St. Louis, and joined the army as chaplain of a Negro regiment in Mississippi. At the war's end he settled in Natchez, entered politics, and in 1870–71 filled the Senate seat previously held by Jefferson Davis. Bruce had been born a slave in Virginia. When war came he escaped to Missouri and soon was teaching Negroes in Hannibal. After the war he studied in the North for several years and went to Mississippi in 1869. Soon he got into politics and worked up from tax collector to sheriff to county superintendent of schools. In 1875 he went to the United States Senate, where he served a full term. His wide range of interests as a lawmaker is seen in his introduction of bills on the Geneva award for the Alabama claims, aid to education, railroad construction, and the reimbursement of depositors in the Freedmen's Savings Bank.

South Carolina sent six Negroes to the House of Representatives, the largest number from a single state. But they were not all in the House at one time. Alabama was second with three. Georgia, Florida, Mississippi, North Carolina, and Louisiana sent one each. Most of these men had some experience in public service before going to Congress. Alonzo Ransier of South Carolina had been a member of the constitutional convention, auditor of Charleston County, and lieutenant governor. John R. Lynch of Mississippi and James T. Rapier of Alabama had served their states in similar fashion. Some were war heroes, like Robert Smalls of South Carolina who had seized the Confederate ship "Planter" in 1862 and delivered it to Union authorities. In addition to representing their constituents in the usual ways, Negro members of Congress showed considerable interest in a wide range of national questions. Joseph Rainey of South Carolina and Josiah T. Walls of Florida were strong advocates of federal aid to education. John A. Hyman of North Carolina championed relief for the Cherokee Indians, while all were outspoken in their vigorous support of civil rights legislation. Their responsible conduct moved James G. Blaine, their contemporary, to observe, "The colored men who took their seats in both Senate and House did not appear ignorant or helpless. They were as a rule studious, earnest, ambitious men, whose public conduct . . . would be honorable to any race."

When the new governments were launched, the Negro legislators and state officers joined the others in developing and carrying forward programs for the rebuilding and improvement of their states. The legislatures implemented the constitutional provisions for welfare and educational institutions, and the governors appointed officials to fill the posts. Six of the ten governors were labeled carpetbaggers, but one of them, Rufus Bullock of Georgia, had adopted that state in 1859 and had served as an officer in the Confederate army. Another, H. C. Warmoth of Louisiana, was born in Illinois but he had "not a drop of any other than Southern blood" in his veins. Mississippi's Northern governor, Adelbert Ames, was shortly elected to the Senate and was succeeded by a native of the state, J. L. Alcorn. Thus, whether Southern legislators and governors were transplanted Northerners or native Southerners depended on the personnel available, and there was constant shifting from one group to the other.

Appointments to public office also depended on available personnel, as well as on the inclinations of the chief executive. Governor Bullock of Georgia was close to many former Confederates and appointed a number of them to office. Indeed, the "Augusta ring" that received so many favors from Bullock was largely ex-Confederate. On the other hand, Governor W. W. Holden of North Carolina was intimate with carpetbaggers and relied on them to carry out his policies. He appointed Milton Littlefield, a native of New York, as state printer, and he saw to it that when he became governor this "Prince of Carpetbaggers" succeeded him as president of the Union League. In Florida Governor Harrison Reed relied heavily on Jonathan Gibbs, the Negro leader who was the first secretary of state in the reconstruction government. Later, Reed's successor, Governor O. B. Hart, appointed him superintendent of public instruction.

All the new programs were expensive. Public buildings had to be repaired or rebuilt altogether. Not only did the damage from the war require public attention, but the general lag in public works had to be overcome. Many public roads were practically impassable, and numerous bridges had either been destroyed or had collapsed under constant use without maintenance. In some states departments of public works were established, in others the work of improving public roads and buildings was assigned to various state and county officials. There was much more excitement, however, in the area of railroad construction; and the legislators as well as others, in and out of the government, took a lively interest in such projects. The rebuilding of old roads was encouraged by state aid, usually in the form of bonds or state indorsement of railroad bonds. Charters were granted for the construction of new roads. The activity was feverish, as if railroad building symbolized the emergence of a modern South equal to the North, behind which it had lagged for a generation before the Civil War. But it was feverish for another, more practical, reason. It was a non-controversial, bipartisan activity in which Northerners, Negroes, and every group of Southerners could participate with profit— honestly if possible, dishonestly if necessary.

Every conceivable kind of economic activity was encouraged. Some states, like South Carolina, had land commissioners to facilitate the purchase of land by persons without private financial resources. Some states, like Alabama, had commissioners of industries to encourage the establishment of new industrial and commercial activities. Several states set up bureaus of immigration under a commissioner whose duty was to collect and publish information on matters of interest to prospective investors and settlers. Arkansas placed under the control of its commissioner of immigration all lands in which the state had an interest. He was to make assignments of land to actual settlers and perform other duties that would have the effect of attracting "northern capital and labor to the state." If such projects were not always successful, it was because prospective settlers found more attractive places elsewhere or because of political and social instability in the South or both. But the new governments were attempting to strengthen economic life. And despite the fact that they were denounced for their efforts, settlers and capital flowed into the South in the fifteen years following the war.

The new public school system, too, was expensive. After the states had re-entered the Union, the legislatures began to implement the provisions for free universal education that had been written into the constitutions. By 1870 a public school system was in operation all over the South. Except for South Carolina and Louisiana no serious attempt was made to put into operation a racially mixed school system. South Carolina's effort was wholly unsuccessful and Louisiana's only scarcely better. Two systems of education increased the expenses of a poverty-stricken and educationally backward region. In its first year of operating a school system, Mississippi spent more for education than for all other government activities combined. South Carolina went so far as to provide free textbooks to children who could not pay for them, but it found itself unable to raise sufficient funds to finance its expensive school program. Poverty, the inability of the states to collect taxes, and inefficiency and corruption in many places prevented the successful operation of the schools. The pattern was there, however, and in more instances than is usually admitted the system was operating successfully. In 1870 there were 30,448 children in South Carolina's 769 schools. Six years later there were 123,035 students attending 2,776 schools. Similar increases were to be found in other states and included Negro as well as white students.

The new governments took other steps, significant in one way or another. They raised salaries and expense allowances of officials and increased the number of officials—innovations that were expensive and sometimes needless. Where constitutional conventions had not done so, legislatures repealed the more objectionable features of the black codes. There were efforts to increase the efficiency of government through a reorganization of the judicial system, the redistribution of powers in towns and counties, and the modification of registration and election laws. The penal systems were modified, although not always improved. In Alabama and Georgia the practice of leasing convict labor for private use, which had actually been initiated by federal officials, became more deeply intrenched. Some states enacted homestead legislation or adapted existing legislation. Finally, there was some effort to enact at the state level the kind of civil rights legislation that Sumner and his friends were seeking in Congress. In 1873 the Arkansas legislature passed a law requiring hotels and places of public accommodation to admit Negroes and school districts to provide equal facilities in separate schools.

The mounting costs of government plagued the new administrations from the beginning. There is no point in making comparisons with the ante-bellum governments, for the role of government in the South had undergone a radical change, bringing with it new responsibilities and new costs. The school system, the ambitious public works and railroad building programs, and the many new services were problems with which Southern governments did not have to cope before 1860. The spiral of inflation mounted steadily, adding to the woes of those who attempted to finance the new programs. Extravagance and corruption played their part, too, as the winds of public immorality sweeping New York and Washington took their toll also in the South. Under the circumstances deficit spending was almost inevitable, and state indebtednesses rose to the danger point. Louisiana's public debt increased from $17,347,000 in 1868 to $29,619,000 in 1872. For the same period South Carolina's debt increased from $14,896,000 to $22,480,000. Alabama's debt in 1869 was $8,355,000; in 1874 it was $25,503,000, including railroad bonds. It was essentially the same in the other states, but even as the debt mounted, each state sought ways and means of paying the cost as far as possible. Taxation, of course, became the principal means of financing, although borrowing was a source that was not overlooked.

To finance their operations the Radicals of South Carolina instituted a "uniform rate of assessment of all property at its fair money value," in contrast to the ante-bellum system that was easy on land and slaves and hard on mercantile, professional, and banking interests. Between 1868 and 1872 the average rate was nine mills on the dollar, but because of the decreased valuation of property and the difficulty of collecting, it rose to more than eleven mills by 1876. For the same reasons the rate in Mississippi rose from one mill in 1869 to fourteen mills in 1874. In Louisiana the rate increased from 5.25 mills in 1869 to 21.5 mills in 1872. There were other taxes. Poll taxes, widely levied before the war, were continued and sometimes increased. In North Carolina the poll tax in 1867 was fifty cents. In 1870 it was one dollar. Seventy-five per cent of this tax was to be used to support the public schools, and similar use of it was made in Georgia, Arkansas, and several other states. From time to time there were special taxes, on luxury items such as furs and jewelry, on land and other properties to pay the interest on state bonds, and on businesses and professions to pay the costs of education and special services.

Some states supplemented their tax programs with schemes for borrowing capital, while others, like Georgia, relied largely on borrowing. In Georgia the rate of taxation during the brief so-called Radical regime remained about the same as that fixed by the Confederate reconstruction government in 1866. But the indebtedness of the state mounted steadily, largely as a result of the issuance of bonds. Between 1868 and 1872 the government issued $6,831,000 in bonds, as well as indorsing railroad bonds in the amount of $5,733,000. The most widely recognized purpose for the issuance of state bonds was to finance some phase of railroad development. The usual method was for the state to issue state bonds to the railroad in exchange for bonds of the company. Shortly after the congressional reconstruction of North Carolina began, the legislature undertook to finance the Chatham Railroad in this fashion, followed by similar moves supporting the Williamston and Tarboro Railroad, the Western North Carolina Railroad, and the Northwestern North Carolina Railroad.

In Alabama the state began to give indorsement of the bonds of certain railroads as early as February, 1867. Among the companies benefiting from state action were the Montgomery and Eufala, the South and North, and the Wills Valley railroads. The state permitted the reorganization and merger of old lines and issued charters to new companies. It supported construction of new lines to the extent of $12,000 to $16,000 per mile. Not infrequently, when the railroad defaulted in its payment of interest, Alabama, as well as other states, found it necessary to take over the railroads and operate them in the name of the state. Such activities almost invariably increased the indebtedness of the state from 50 to 75 per cent.

If the ex-Confederate whites scoffed at the very idea of Southern state governments operating without their leadership, they were outraged when the governments proceeded to impose the heaviest burdens on those who were disfranchised. They gave little attention to increasing expenses resulting from new functions assumed by the government or to the inflation that resulted from an expanding national economy and numerous shortages. Their sense of outrage was intensified by a traditional antipathy to high taxes, which they were determined to fight with every resource at their disposal. In some states taxpayers' conventions met to organize opposition to increases. Two such conventions in South Carolina, in 1871 and 1874, protested against the enormous rise in taxation—the result of "frauds the most flagrant, and corruption the most dangerous and demoralizing" ever perpetrated by state officials. The second convention, the Orangeburg *Times* said, should protest at Washington "against further taxation, under such a filthy, disgusting, loathsome State government and ask to be made a territorial dependency, or a conquered province, anything rather than the football of [Governor] Moses and his crew." While the convention formally sought a revision of the existing tax law, which was "cumbrous, obscure, and intricate," it was very busy strengthening the determination of many to refuse to pay their assessed taxes. This it did by forming tax unions in the several counties. These organizations were to see that taxes were fairly assessed, collected, and expended. But they became centers of resistance not only to taxes but to the entire Radical regime.

In other states resistance was even more pronounced. In Louisiana a strong Tax Resisting Association was organized in 1872 to co-ordinate the efforts of numerous parish groups that had been active since 1869. In Mississippi some citizens described their taxes as "awful, monstrous, and ruinous" and in various ways indicated their unwillingness to give financial support to the new regime. The result was, of course, a steady decline in revenue accompanied by the inability of the state and local governments to meet their obligations. Many farms and plantations were sold for taxes. In 1869 some twenty-three Wake County plantations in North Carolina containing 7,872 acres were sold for taxes and brought only $7,718. When tax sales brought insufficient revenues, states resorted to the issuance of scrip, which depreciated almost immediately, giving rise to more problems than it solved. In the end the fact remained that the reconstruction governments were unable to raise the funds required for their administration.

Most opponents argued that the troubles of the state and local governments arose from their extravagance and corruption that, in turn, resulted from the abnormalities inherent in "Negro-carpetbag-scalawag" rule. J. G. de Roulhac Hamilton, the historian of North Carolina reconstruction, has gone so far as to say that the presence of the Negro in politics was responsible for the "blunting of the moral sense of the white people." It would be remarkable if the very small fraction of Negroes in political life in North Carolina could destroy or even blunt the "highly developed political sense" or the "equally high standard of political morality" of the whites of North Carolina. The fact is that such assertions ignore certain very important considerations highly relevant to any understanding of the problems of extravagance and corruption during the reconstruction era.

The national forces conducive to the decline of public morality were powerful, and the South was not immune. Among them was the rapid wartime expansion of the economy that encouraged all sorts of ventures and attracted all sorts of people. Closely connected with this was an expanded role of government in facilitating and stimulating economic expansion. After the war those who had made huge profits were seeking still more, while those who had not were desperate in their determination to make a "killing." Anything was fair game, especially new areas to be exploited, new groups with potential political power, and new opportunities arising out of instability of one kind or another. These are the factors that made it possible for William M. Tweed to flourish as the corrupt boss of New York City during these years. Drawing his strength from his adept manipulation of the lower classes, he and his confederates, Mayor Oakey Hall,

Peter B. Sweeny, and Richard B. Connolly, took more than $100,000,000 from the city. The city spent $11,000,000 for the partial construction of a courthouse, $350,000 for carpets, and $179,929 for forty chairs and three tables. It seemed incredible that a large, politically mature city could have succumbed to such crude graft and corruption.

But the situation was essentially the same elsewhere. In 1869 Jim Fisk and Jay Gould conceived a plot to corner the gold on the New York market and to make millions by selling at the proper moment. Taking advantage of the President's innocence in such matters, they drove the price of gold steadily upward with assurances that the federal treasury would not enter the market. Many bribes passed and many honest men were driven into bankruptcy. Finally the federal government offered to sell $4,000,000 worth of gold to end the panic created by the Fisk-Gould machinations. Even closer to the federal government was the Credit Mobilier scandal. Several members of Congress and Vice-President Schuyler Colfax had accepted shares of stock and dividends from this railroad construction company, which in return had received handsome favors from the government. Then there was the scandal of the Whiskey Ring, which was exposed as having robbed the federal treasury of several million dollars in internal revenue and which included President Grant's private secretary. Meanwhile Grant's Secretary of War, W. W. Belknap, was discovered to have regularly sold the privilege of disbursing supplies to Indians to persons who made fortunes by furnishing substandard goods.

Such was the national climate in which graft and corruption flourished. In the Southern states much of the graft was petty. In North Carolina two members of the legislature charged mileage for 154 miles, although they lived in Raleigh, where the legislature met. In Arkansas a Negro was paid $9,000 for bridge repairs that reportedly cost only about $500. In South Carolina the legislature voted $1,000 extra compensation for the speaker after he allegedly had lost that amount on a horse race. In Louisiana large amounts of cash from the permanent school funds of the parishes regularly disappeared.

There was big graft also, especially in connection with the states' participation in railroad construction. In North Carolina General M. S. Littlefield headed a lobby of railroad interests that dispensed numerous favors to legislators. And his efforts to bring "railroad development" to the state were indorsed as enthusiastically by Conservatives as by Radicals. In Georgia Hannibal I. Kimball of New York sought and gained legislative favors by a variety of corrupt means. If he wielded influence among the Republicans during their brief tenure, his connections with the Conservatives seemed even closer. When he secured by questionable means the lease of the state-owned Western and Atlantic Railroad in 1870, he could list among his associates the Confederate governor Joseph E. Brown, the Confederate Vice-President Alexander H. Stephens, and respected Conservatives like Ben H. Hill, H. B. Plant, Richard Peters, and John P. King.

Alabama has provided some of the prime examples of big graft during reconstruction. Numerous railroads fed at the public trough by bribing legislators and other officials and through the use and misuse of state funds placed at their disposal. The state literally underwrote much of the construction of railroads during the period, sometimes by subsidizing each mile to be built, sometimes by indorsing the bonds issued by railroad companies. Carpetbaggers and scalawags were not alone in their efforts to advance "railroad development" with state aid. On the boards of the railroads sat many respectable, prominent, ex-Confederate Alabamans. Josiah Morris, the Montgomery banker, was on the board of several roads, including the Mobile and Montgomery and the South and North; and it was his money that John Milner used to bribe members of the Alabama assembly. Robert Patton, Johnson's provisional governor, became vice-president of the Alabama and Chattanooga Railroad, a company whose bonds he had helped indorse shortly before he left the governor's office. In the public financing of railroads, by fair means and foul, there was no marked difference in Alabama policy when the Republicans came into power in 1868 or when a Democratic governor was elected in 1870 or when the Republicans were finally driven from power in 1874. Corruption was bisectional, bipartisan, and biracial.

If no party or race had a monopoly on public immorality, none could boast that it was the sole keeper of the public conscience. In 1872 the Democrats were outraged by the revelations of corruption in high places. But there were some Republicans, like Carl Schurz, Horace Greeley, Charles Francis Adams, and B. Gratz Brown, whose sense of outrage was equally great. It was this group that organized the Liberal Republican party to crusade for clean honest government. The Democrats went so far as formally to support the Liberal Republican platform and its candidates, Greeley and Brown. This combination was no match for Grant, who was easily re-elected. But it frightened the Republicans into relaxing their control over the South. Even before the election many of the remaining disabilities under which former Confederates lived were removed, and President Grant adopted a policy of using federal troops less frequently in Southern elections. When Governor Adelbert Ames sent a desperate plea for federal troops to cope with the chaotic conditions in Mississippi in 1875, Grant, through his Attorney General, refused the request. It was on this occasion that he declared, "The whole public are tired of the annual autumnal outbreaks in the south."

In the South there were frequent tirades against the corruption of the Radical regime. Indeed, this became one of the principal arguments for its overthrow, even when Conservatives were among the beneficiaries of Radical policies. Former Confederate leader James H. Clanton, one of the receivers for the Alabama and Chattanooga Railroad, said that the effect of dishonesty in Alabama was "to drive the capital from the State, paralyze industry, demoralize labor, and force our best citizens to flee Alabama as a pestilence." But some Negroes and white Republicans were likewise distressed over dishonesty and corruption. As early as 1869 a group of Arkansas Republicans denounced those members of the party who seemed to be interested solely in the exploitation of the state. Later in the same year a group, including several Negroes, organized the Liberal Republican party of Arkansas and called on Democrats and former Whigs to assist them in their fight for good government. In 1872 a group of Negro members of the Florida legislature made a public declaration against corruption. One of them, John W. Wyatt, said, "We want no *Tom Scotts, Jim Fisks,* or *Vanderbilts* in this State to govern us. . . . The great curse of Florida has been dishonest corporations, rings, and cliques, with an eye single to their central interest. . . . The recent expose of the Tammany Ring in New York has satisfied all right thinking men that the power exercised by strong bodies, composed of many corporations, is the most dangerous to the public good and safety."

Thus, the tragedy of public immorality in the Southern states was only part of a national tragedy. The added misfortune of the South was that it could least afford it, not only because of poverty and political instability, but because already critics in and out of the South were anxious to find excuses to discredit any effort to reconstruct the South. The instances of corruption provided by the Radical regime, even if they were not general or typical, were sufficient excuses for those who needed no convincing that Radical Reconstruction was an unmitigated curse. If the opponents of reconstruction needed an issue on which to base their fight, those in power all too often handed it to them. The leaders of counter reconstruction used it for all it was worth.

Part 4

IN SEARCH
OF DIRECTION

During the Reconstruction Era black Americans sought to protect their interest through the traditional American pattern of involvement in politics. Lack of widespread political experience and the absence of an economic base placed them at a disadvantage in the contests with former Confederates. The position in which they found themselves became untenable when waning northern interest in the welfare of freedom led to the withdrawal of the last federal troops from the South. The Compromise of 1877, of which this withdrawal was a part, brought Reconstruction to an end and made possible the return to political power of anti-Negro whites in those areas where this had not already happened. Thus, while blacks legally retained suffrage (in some areas) and other civil rights, protection of these rights depended on actions by men who had fought to prevent blacks from being freed from slavery.

The forces in Congress supporting civil rights did not completely disappear in the late 1870s. However, this interest continued to weaken so that by the early twentieth century it was clear that the North, for the most part, had accepted the southern point of view toward the treatment of black Americans. The explanation of this shift is the focus of *The Road to Reunion* by Paul Buck. The author identifies the problems setting the two areas apart in the years following the Civil War, and he describes the approaches of the two sections in dealing with them. He sees economic and political problems giving way to the inspired desire for unity to the point that only the problem of the rights of blacks separated the two areas. In the selection from *The Road to Reunion* included here, "The Negro Problem Always Ye Have With You," the author sees the "inevitable race problem" as incapable of solution and pictures the North as accepting the southern *modus operandi* in relations between the races.

What then would be the direction taken by black Americans? That direction proved to be quite conservative as they sought to promote their interests through the accepted American channels of political action, education, development of leaders, and migration to the areas of greater economic opportunity. Seldom have more conservative approaches been tried.

Several selections herein deal with the political situation of blacks after Reconstruction. In the chapter on "Southern Suffrage Restrictions: Bourbon Coup d'état?" from *Southern Politics,* V. O. Key discusses the wresting from the Negro of the potential source of power represented by the ballot. Thus traditional politics could no longer be expected to protect the rights of the nation's largest minority. At the same time, however, traditional politics was itself under pressure. Two major reform movements swept the country, temporarily raising the hopes of blacks. One was the Populist Movement, the subject of *Tom Watson: Agrarian Rebel* and the other the Progressive Movement, described in *Origins of the New South.* Both books are by C. Vann Woodward. *Tom Watson* pictures a microcosm of the Populists as, under Watson, they offer new political direction to blacks, only to switch positions along with Watson when he became anti-black with a vehemence outdone by only a few other racist demagogues of his day. The selection from *Origins of the New South* identifies the many areas of reform with which Progressivism was concerned and focuses on the absence of attention to those things concerned with the rights of blacks. In relative terms and in some absolute ways these reform movements damaged rather than helped conditions.

Where should a citizen look when local and state governments pass laws detrimental to his welfare and when courts fail to protect his constitutional rights? *The Petitioners,* Loren Miller, suggests that it was not in the direction of the Supreme Court. The selection from the chapter, "Instrument of Wrong," sees in the *Plessy* vs. *Ferguson* decision the ultimate step of the federal judiciary in removing itself as an instrument for the protection of black rights. Traditional politics clearly did not offer direction for black Americans.

The tradition of public education is woven into the fabric of American history. In spite of periods of indifferent support and public apathy, the common school was well established in parts of the country by mid-nineteenth century. Its stimulus toward and benefits to a free society were well recognized—perhaps for that reason, it did not exist on any wide scale in the South prior to 1865. The common school had been an instrument of socialization and upward mobility for newcomers to the United States, and thus it is not surprising that the Reconstruction period witnessed a major movement by the freedmen for education, a movement which continued after 1877.

An examination of southern school reform after Reconstruction and the corruption of that reform by racism is the central concern of *Separate and Unequal* by Louis R. Harlan. The selection here outlines northern interest in aid to southern education and the manipulation of education along lines dictated by racism, one example being the misuse of state education funds by counties to the detriment of education for blacks.

The nature of higher education for blacks is the subject of material from Booker T. Washington's *Up From Slavery* and "What is the Matter with the Atlanta Schools?" from the November 1907 issue of *Colored Magazine*. Washington describes the creation of Tuskegee Institute for instruction in industrial education and justifies his approach by arguing that it serves the needs of the day for blacks. The article in *Colored Magazine*, which Washington controlled, attacks the liberal arts education being attempted by the colleges in Atlanta.

In the years after 1877 two clear trends can be seen in education for black Americans. One was accommodating to and supportive of the view of the "black man's place" in society as set forth in the Atlanta Compromise. The other, favored by a small number of private schools and colleges, was hostile to any assumed inferiority or any assumed moral inadequacies of blacks as a race. Efforts to implement both of the approaches suffered from the conscious and willful degrading of public education for blacks.

The success of blacks in working out their destinies in any area would depend, in part, on the leadership which evolved. The end of the Civil War had witnessed the rise of a group of black leaders, a surprising occurrence in light of their limited education and experiences. However, these men were removed from positions of influence with the end of Reconstruction. In the years that followed, the problems of black leadership became all too obvious.

In 1895 Booker T. Washington was catapulted into a position of leadership as a result of his address at the Atlanta Exposition: in *Up From Slavery* he provides that address and his description of the reactions to it. His "Atlanta Compromise" spoke to the concerns of hard work, education, and tolerance, but it took an accommodating stance on the matter of equality. Implicit in the address was Washington's acceptance of the concept of white superiority. This leadership position into which white Americans projected Booker T. Washington and the way in which he used his position cast him in a mold much like that of the black plantation drivers. They adapted to the existing system and depended on power and influence to maintain themselves.

The issue of leadership is a major concern in the selection, "The Beginnings of Organized Protest, 1901–1916" from *Washington, Capitol City 1879–1950* by Constance McLaughlin Green. The attitudes of Presidents of the period, the actions of the Congress, and the hesitancy of the upper-class blacks to expose themselves to the problems related to intensifying racism created difficulties for leadership which adherence to the philosophy of Booker T. Washington would not solve. The response of American blacks in the form of the Niagara Movement and the founding of the National Association for the Advancement of Colored People represents the birth of the slow upward movement for civil rights and of leadership dedicated to that end. In this connection the name of William E. Burghardt Du Bois stands out prominently.

The *Souls of Black Folk* is the best-known work by this prolific writer. While the author had flirted for a time with the approaches of Booker T. Washington, his publication of this collection of essays in 1903 was highly critical of the gentleman at Tuskegee. The essay, "Of Mr. Booker T. Washington and Others," asserts that Washington was asking black Americans to give up, at least for a time, their claim to political and social rights and higher education, the very things necessary to produce black leadership. Du Bois pictures the Washington approach as having dominated blacks and being in part responsible for the increased limitations on the rights of his fellowmen. Thus, he calls on blacks to oppose Booker T. Washington to the degree that his program interfered with education for talented blacks.

The conflict between supporters of Washington and Du Bois continued for some years. At the time, the Washington concept of accommodation predominated. Because of the influence Washington had among whites and the power resulting from this, he became the symbol and the model for numerous black leaders. The extent to which his approach influenced leadership is the subject of a chapter in Gunnar Myrdal's *An American Dilemma*. Written in 1944 this work describes the patterns developed in the years following the Civil War as "Accommodating Leadership."

One can conclude that, in spite of the conflicting points of view, black leadership between Reconstruction and World War I placed emphasis on adjustment and accommodation to the patterns of race relations decreed by whites. For the most part it offered no direction to manhood and civil rights for oppressed blacks. Du Bois, and a small but growing segment of leadership, was setting the ideological base for future leaders.

The northern city, spurred by industrial development during and after the Civil War, appeared to offer new opportunities for numbers of blacks living in the rural South. It was in this direction that many turned. The movement to cities and comparison of the experiences of the various migrant groups is the concern of *Black Metropolis*, St. Clair Drake and Horace R. Cayton. In the selection herein the authors trace the emergence of the "black belt" in Chicago and its promises and problems for those who settled in it. Attention is given to the implication of white Chicago in crime in the black belt and white resistance to efforts to relieve the population pressure.

Migration of rural blacks to urban areas represented a change in life style. Some migrants had lived in southern cities, but the majority moved from rural environments and an agricultural economy to the developing ghettos of northern cities. Important in this change of life style was the way of earning a living. People accustomed to farm work and the personal relationships of tenant and land owner found themselves in the impersonal labor pools of the industrial economies of Detroit, Chicago, New York, Pittsburgh and other large cities scattered across the country. The experiences of black workers in these urban areas is the concern of the selection from *Negro Labor in the United States 1850–1925*, Charles H. Wesley. Specifically, the selection pictures the attitude of organized labor toward blacks as a reflection of the national attitude. This view by labor was at odds with the concept of labor solidarity as the national view was at odds with the national ideals of equality and justice. Labor's response contained the same ambivalences and contradictions as the response of the country to the rights of blacks.

Problems related to unions and employment were only a few of the many complications of life in the "promised land" of the northern cities. The extent and the seriousness of some of these difficulties are reflected in *Mortality Among Negroes in the Cities*, a report from a Conference for Investigating City Problems, held at Atlanta University in 1896. The selections from this report set forth the conference purpose and its statements on poverty and ignorance as causes of mortality.

Not the least of the problems of the migrants to the cities and perhaps the most significant in terms of its long lasting influence is discussed in the chapter on "Alienation: New York and the Negro," from *Harlem: The Making of a Ghetto* by Gilbert Osofsky. Large-scale migration of blacks from the South intensified white opposition to blacks which in turn served to increase the disaffection on the part of many who had come North with high hopes. The author traces the growth of racial antagonisms in New York leading up to the race riot of 1900. The failure of the community to respond to legitimate black claims of police brutality served to intensify the alienation and set the stage for more serious problems at a later date.

In spite of its many problems, urbanization as a direction for blacks offered some benefits, and the sources from which these selections are drawn reflect these. Large black communities offered psychological supports and the basis for political influence. Clearly the direction for blacks in the late nineteenth and early twentieth centuries was toward the city.

The Negro Problem
Always Ye Have with You*
Paul H. Buck

No question connected with the South rested more heavily and, it must be said, more wearily upon the American mind during the eighties than the problem of the Negro. For half a century the black man had been a symbol of strife between the sections. The chasm dug by the intemperance of the abolition attack against slavery and the Reconstruction crusade to give equality of status to the freedman had fortunately closed. But a line of demarcation still divided the nation. On one side lived a people faced with the menace of Negro domination, on the other a people committed by their intervention in the past to securing justice for the inferior race. Final reconciliation waited upon an adjustment that would quiet the apprehensions of the South and still the conscience of the North.

Southern whites had fought stolidly and unyieldingly for control over a problem they insisted was domestic in nature. They continued to resist without compromise any suggestion of outside pressure. Their minds were strong in the conviction that orderly society could exist only when the Negro was rigidly disciplined. The people of the North after 1877 were for the most part in substantial agreement that the Negro was not prepared for equality and that the South should be allowed to deal with the problem in its own way, "Henceforth," as one Northern journal observed, "the nation as a nation, will have nothing more to do with him [the Negro]." [1] The South had won its major point. No longer would the black man figure as "a ward of the nation" to be singled out for special guardianship or peculiar treatment.

The discipline the South elaborated in the years following Reconstruction rested frankly upon the premise of the Negro's inferiority. Much was said about the South acting defensively to erect bulwarks against the threat of Negro domination. But actually

---

* From Paul H. Buck, *The Road to Reunion* (Boston: Little, Brown and Company, 1937), pp. 283–89, 292–97. Copyright 1937 by Paul H. Buck. Reprinted by permission of Atlantic-Little, Brown and Co.

[1] *Nation*, April 5, 1877.

the South moved aggressively to reduce the Negro's status to something comparable to serfdom. The intention openly averred was to give an inferior people an inferior rôle and to efface them as positive factors in the section's life. To this end the new discipline excluded the colored man from politics by disfranchising him, rendered him economically impotent by making him a peon, and isolated him socially by an extensive practice of segregation. The net result was to deprive the Negro of more privileges than was necessary to keep him from becoming a menace and to make the South a "white man's country."

The methods of suppressing the Negro vote softened after the whites gained control of the machinery of state and local government, but they continued to be a mixture of fraud, trickery, intimidation and violence. Polling places were set up at points remote from colored communities. Ferries between the black districts and the voting booths went "out of repair" on election day. Grim-visaged white men carrying arms sauntered through the streets or stood near the polling booths. In districts where the blacks greatly outnumbered the whites, election officials permitted members of the superior race to "stuff the ballot box," and manipulated the count without fear of censure. Fantastic gerrymanders were devised to nullify Negro strength. The payment of poll taxes, striking at the Negro's poverty and carelessness in preserving receipts, was made a requirement for voting. Some states confused the ignorant by enacting multiple ballot box laws which required the voter to place correctly his votes for various candidates in eight or more separate boxes. The bolder members of the colored race met threats of violence and, in a diminishing number of instances, physical punishment. When the black man succeeded in passing through this maze of restrictions and cast his vote there was no assurance that it would be counted. Highly centralized election codes vested arbitrary powers in the election boards, and these powers were used to complete the elimination of the Negro vote.[2]

These practices testified eloquently to the resourcefulness of the Southern whites, but they could not be considered as an adequate or permanent solution. So long as the South persisted by extra-legal and illegal methods to nullify the spirit of the Fifteenth amendment of the Federal constitution and to violate the letter of their own state constitutions framed in the Reconstruction era, there remained a potential danger of a Federal "force bill" or a refusal on the part of Congress to seat a congressman elected from a Southern district where the abuses seemed more than ordinarily flagrant. Furthermore the practices worked to the disadvantage of certain elements of the Southern whites. Fraud could not be used against the Negro without demoralizing the whole structure of politics. Walter Hines Page pointed to instances where a group in power used its control of the election machinery to "count out" white opponents who had polled a majority vote. The illiterate and impoverished white man frequently found himself enmeshed in the restrictions that had been framed to embarrass the Negro. But most serious was the fact that, so long as the constitutional provisions for universal suffrage remained unchanged, division among the whites might result in a recrudescence of Negro voting.

[2] The best monograph on Negro suffrage is P. Lewinson's, "Race, Class, and Party" (London, 1932).

When Benjamin F. Tillman led the dirt farmers of South Carolina in a common man's movement against the conservatives who had ruled the state since 1877 he found his opponents voting the Negroes of the Black Belt against him.[3] The rise of Populism in the nineties accentuated the evil. Wherever the whites divided as Democrats and Populists, the rival factions courted the colored vote and some of the turbulence of Reconstruction came back again.[4]

Obviously the time had arrived for the constitutional disfranchisement of the Negro. The negative language of the Fifteenth amendment[5] was easily surmounted. But it was not so easy to frame a measure without at the same time disfranchising the illiterate white. The Mississippi Constitutional Convention of 1890 found the solution in a cleverly devised literacy test. No person was permitted to vote who was unable to read any section of the national constitution when submitted to him, or to interpret its meaning when read to him. Significant discretionary powers permitted the registration officers to discriminate in accepting illiterate whites and rejecting illiterate blacks. South Carolina followed in 1895 with a literacy test based upon that of Mississippi. Louisiana in 1898 introduced a variant in the "grandfather clause" whereby any person was exempt from the literacy test who had voted before January 1, 1867, or who was the son or grandson of a person who had enjoyed that right. By this device her registration lists were purged of colored voters but included all classes of whites. Other variants in the form of literacy tests or educational requirements flatly designed to discriminate against the Negro were adopted in North Carolina in 1900 and Virginia in 1902. Before the twentieth century was a decade old the constitutional disfranchisement of the Negro was a fact throughout the South.

Southerners universally hailed this as an achievement of constructive statesmanship for which no apology was necessary. The Negro was branded as an alien whose ignorance, poverty, and racial inferiority were wholly incompatible with logical and orderly processes of government.[6] No difference of opinion separated Southern leaders on this point. A champion of the dirt farmers, Tillman, led the disfranchisement in South Carolina. A conservative, Aycock, waged his most significant campaign on the issue of "white supremacy" and dominated the North Carolina movement to eliminate the Negro from politics. Vardaman, of Mississippi, might express the sectional attitude with greater violence and less regard for consequences than Carter Glass, of Virginia, but it was the latter who asserted on the floor of the Virginia Constitutional Convention, "Discriminate! Why that is precisely what we propose; that, exactly, is what this convention was elected for—to discriminate to the very extremity of permissible action under the limitations of the Federal Constitution, with a view to the elimination of

[3] F. B. Simkins, "The Tillman Movement in South Carolina" (Durham, N. C., 1926).

[4] R. D. W. Connor and C. Poe, "The Life and Speeches of Charles Brantley Aycock" (Garden City, 1916), 64–72.

[5] "The right of citizens of the United States to vote shall not be denied or abridged by the United States or by any State on account of race, color, or previous condition of servitude."

[6] Cf. H. W. Grady's speech at Augusta, Ga., Nov. 1887, quoted in Harris, "Grady" 126; and C. H. Otken, "The Ills of the South" (New York, 1894), 8.

every negro voter who can be gotten rid of legally, without materially impairing the numerical strength of the white electorate." Thoughtful Southerners found consolation in the fact that the unworkable principle of universal suffrage had been frankly discarded and looked forward to an era of peace when political battles would not be fought in terms of race antagonism.

The conditions which placed the Negro in economic peonage have been discussed in an earlier chapter.[7] It was a prevalent notion among Southerners that the colored man was shiftless, prone to idleness, and unstable as a worker. But the fact remains that he continued to do most of the rough labor of the section. Sixty per cent. of the race were farmers, and of these the vast majority were tenants on the land of white men. Thirty per cent. found employment in domestic and menial service. Others worked as unskilled laborers in mining, industry and transportation. A diminishing proportion earned a livelihood as skilled artisans while some, especially in the cities, entered the middle class occupations of tradesmen, ministers, lawyers and doctors.

The dominant race universally believed that "darkies should work for white folks." But the lowly estate of the black man resulted from his poverty, ignorance, lack of opportunity and the evils of tenancy rather than from any conscious program of the white classes. Everywhere the Negro's right to work was recognized and his permanence in the South accepted. The spread of trade unions excluded him from certain occupations he formerly had held, but with this exception the Negro at work met with little race antagonism. Nevertheless he stood on the lowest rungs of the economic ladder with little chance to mount higher. The control of industry and agriculture rested firmly in the hands of white employers. This phase of the new discipline received little contemporary attention. But its significance was great in giving stability to the structure of Southern society.

The social segregation of the Negro, on the other hand, provoked almost as much discussion as the process of disfranchisement. Here the South had to move positively against the earlier program of social equality and racial association advocated and applied by the politicians and missionaries of the Reconstruction era. State legislatures, upon the expulsion of the Carpetbaggers, stringently prohibited interracial marriages. The educational system was revised to make obligatory separate schools and colleges. Separation extended into the churches where mixed congregations became a thing of the past. The South received encouragement in its stand on segregation when the Supreme Court in 1883 virtually nullified the restrictive features of the Civil Rights Act of 1875. "Jim Crow" cars became universal on Southern railways. Negroes were barred from admittance to hotels, inns, restaurants, and amusement places which catered to white people. Street cars had separate sections reserved for whites and blacks. Local ordinances and customs supplemented these general features of segregation, and everywhere throughout the South a color line separated the races.

Segregation did not proceed from or necessarily imply race antagonism. It was in harmony with a basic Southern assumption that "there is an instinct, ineradicable and

[7] *Supra,* 145–148.

positive, that will keep the races apart." [8] It recognized the biracial character of Southern society and greatly lessened the opportunities for friction. Yet it must be obvious
that it did little to separate the races where the Negro came into contact with the white
man as a menial. It affected mostly the black man's aspirations for equality. As such it
further accomplished the oft stated purpose of making the South a land where the white
man dominated.

The South paid heavily for its new discipline. The subordination of all other political issues to the one great principle of Negro disfranchisement suspended the natural
development and operation of a two-party system. Democratic solidarity remained after
the colored man was safely eliminated as a factor in politics. In fact its necessity was
preached as a creed to which all respectable Southerners must subscribe. In places this
descended to the mean device of "nigger baiting" by which the lower type of politicians
perpetuated their hold on office. Inasmuch as the one issue that justified party solidarity
had been settled, there remained little inducement for the ordinary citizen to participate
in politics or even to vote. Politics in the South became a game for professionals, and in
every state where constitutional disfranchisement occurred the number of white votes
diminished in alarming proportions. The social segregation of the races added burdens
equally as onerous. The meagre resources of the South proved insufficient to provide
adequately for the double system of schools made necessary by the color line. Most
costly of all the consequences of segregation was its retarding influence on new proposals for social and economic reform. The South could ill afford to espouse measures for
progressive change until those measures had been conservatively adjusted to the biracial
nature of its population. The fact that thoughtful Southerners fully appreciated the price
they were paying is proof, perhaps, that the new discipline grew out of necessity and
was not a reflection of an inhumane spirit.

The Negro, likewise, paid a heavy price. Disfranchisement, ruthlessly extended
even into the upper classes of the race, closed to him the practical school by which de-
mocracies have trained their citizens. Economic peonage was a dreary routine of work
and debt which tended to discourage ambition and enterprise and to encourage a shiftless adaptation to a bare subsistence standard of living. Segregation with its countless
distinctions beat endlessly against the black man's pride and self-respect. Early in life
the Negro child learned the hazards of the color line. It was the lot of every Negro to
accept, as most of his race did, the badge of inferiority or to carry hidden within his
inner soul an impotent yet agonizing spark of rebellion against the fateful injustice of
his position.

●   ●   ●

While the South shaped its new discipline and the Negro adjusted his life to the
new conditions, Northern opinion was subjected to a flood of propaganda which sought
to describe and to debate the Negro's place in American society. Congressmen discussed
the issues in the national legislature, newspapers sent special reporters on tours of investigation, publicists wrote books, periodicals undertook series of articles on all sides of

[8] Harris, "Grady," 289.

the question, scholars prepared what purported to be impartial and learned monographs, business men contributed their opinions, and clergymen preached sermons.[16]

The Southern point of view was forcibly presented. One line of approach was taken by Thomas Nelson Page and Basil L. Gildersleeve, the distinguished classicist. They pictured the beauties of race relationships and the mutual understanding that had existed under slavery, noted how extraneous forces had broken the entente during Reconstruction, and suggested that the reëstablishment of a discipline over the Negro would restore a spirit of friendship between whites and blacks. Henry Grady and Henry Watterson vigorously defended the disfranchisement of the Negro and attempted to explain how a Solid South was a matter of imperative necessity and constituted no menace to any national interest. P. A. Bruce was foremost among those whose scholarly approach won recognition. His "The Plantation Negro As a Freeman," published in 1889, was a careful delineation of the Negro's mental, moral and physical traits with the pessimistic conclusion that he was unfit for self-government, needed direction, and should confine himself to the lower occupations. Atticus G. Haygood explained to the North the need for separate schools, stressed the importance of patience and pleaded for Northern aid and coöperation. The Southern argument was effectively summarized by Page: "We have educated him [the Negro]; we have aided him; we have sustained him in all directions. We are ready to continue our aid; but we will not be dominated by him. When we shall be, it is our settled conviction that we shall deserve the degradation into which we shall have sunk." [17]

The close of the century gave Southerners two additional arguments. For a long time assertions had been made to the effect that in spite of their pretentions Northerners possessed as much race antipathy toward the colored man as did Southerners. It remained for a Negro historian and sociologist, W. E. B. Du Bois, to produce conclusive documentation of the fact. Du Bois's "The Philadelphia Negro, A Social Study," published in 1899, revealed a problem in the North not unlike that in the South, one that was handled in much the same way, and one that was equally as far from solution. The moral, if one needed to be drawn, was, as expressed in the *Nation*, "patience and sympathy toward the South whose difficulties have been far greater than those of the North." [18] The acquisition of the Philippine Islands under Republican auspices taught another lesson in consistency. The party refused to grant equality of rights to a "back-

[16] Contemporary books dealing with various aspects of this debate are: F. Bancroft, "The Negro in Politics" (New York, 1885); P. A. Bruce, "The Plantation Negro as a Freeman" (New York, 1889); G. W. Cable, "The Silent South" (New York, 1885), and "The Negro Question" (New York, 1888); W. H. Crogman, "Talks for the Times" (Atlanta, Ga., 1896); H. M. Field, "Bright Skies and Dark Shadows" (New York, 1890); T. T. Fortune, "Black and White" (New York, 1884); A. G. Haygood, "Our Brother in Black" (New York, 1881); T. N. Page, "The Old South" (New York, 1892); and A. W. Tourgée, "An Appeal to Caesar" (New York, 1884). Periodical articles appeared in great number. In one decade the *North American Review*, CXXV–CXLIII (1877–1886), published more than two-score articles on the Negro. Godkin's editorials continued to make the *Nation* valuable. The *Forum*, newly founded in 1886, sought provocative articles. The *Century, Atlantic, Harper's Monthly*, and *Lippincott's* all contain material of importance.

[17] T. N. Page, "Old South," 344.

[18] *Nation*, Oct. 26, 1899.

ward people" in the new possession. Could it continue the pretense of championing the right of a "backward people" at home to participate on equal terms in the affairs of government?

One important Southern voice was raised in protest against the treatment of the Negro. George Washington Cable refused to recognize a system built on discrimination, exclusion and subjugation. He charged his fellow-Southerners with deliberate and persistent evasion of the laws enacted to protect the freedmen. He charged them with cherishing and perpetuating prejudices born in slavery and building a false creed on the fiction of instinctive and ineradicable differences between the races. Cable wrote effectively and at length. He received a courteous hearing in the North but his influence was negligible. Even his unpopularity and voluntary exile from the South caused little comment. The drift of Northern opinion was distinctly set in channels other than Cable wished to direct it. Thomas Nast caught the essence of this fact in a cartoon captioned "A Dead Issue," in which the South is pictured as too busy at work to find time for mistreating Negroes, much to the chagrin of Northern doctrinaires who reluctantly see the Negro issue die.[19]

Among Northerners the attack on the Southern position was limited to politicians like Foraker and Blaine, die-hards like Judge Tourgée and General Sherman, and partisan editors like Murat Halstead and Whitelaw Reid. The ordinary citizen left no record of his views, but newspapers commented on his growing unconcern with the welfare of the Negro, an opinion which finds corroboration in the inefficacy of the "bloody shirt" in politics. Northern reporters of Southern conditions after the middle eighties followed the pattern of McClure, J. B. Harrison, and Schurz and sympathetically portrayed the Southern attitude. Meanwhile the intellectuals who controlled the Northern periodicals were exceedingly understanding. This was especially true of Gilder, in the *Century,* and Godkin, in the *Nation,* both of whom waged consistent campaigns to explain the conditions which made necessary in the South a discipline over the colored man. "The fact is, and the sooner the fact is recognized the sooner we shall be rid of many dangerous illusions," wrote Gilder in a typical passage, "that the negroes constitute a peasantry wholly untrained in, and ignorant of, those ideas of constitutional liberty and progress which are the birthright of every white voter; that they are gregarious and emotional rather than intelligent, and are easily led in any direction by white men of energy and determination." [20] The obvious conclusion is the one made by Godkin, "I do not see, in short, how the negro is ever to be worked into a system of government for which you and I would have much respect." [21]

It seems even more remarkable that the men in the North most interested in the welfare of the Negro should accept so largely the Southern defense. Thomas Wentworth Higginson, who will be remembered as an ardent abolitionist and an officer of Negro troops, revisited the South in 1878 and reported that he found the Negroes in-

[19] *Harper's Weekly,* Aug. 29, 1885.
[20] Editorial, *Century,* XXIII (1883), 945–946.
[21] Ogden, "Godkin," II, 114.

dustrious, prospering, and progressive, and noted a conspicuous absence of any strained relations between the races.[22] Six years later Higginson paid a glowing tribute to the South. "I know nothing more manly in this generation than the manner the Southern whites since the war have addressed themselves to the problem of educating the blacks." [23]

What was true of Higginson was true of A. D. Mayo whose great educational work in the South was a bright feature of sectional coöperation in the field of humanitarian endeavor. He too believed that the Negro was far below the standard of meriting full citizenship. He was as fulsome as Page in praising the personal attachment of Southerners to the colored folk and as meticulous as Harris in defending the necessity of white leadership. His conclusion was that "the logic of the new Southern life is all on the side of the final elevation of the Negro." [24]

Workers who canvassed the North for funds to aid the Negro in the South also spread a conciliatory message. Industrial training was the fancy of the day and the prestige of Tuskegee further popularized the tendency to ask for funds in terms of an acquiescing philosophy. In any case Northerners heard the voice of philanthropy saying that the blacks must be for some time servants, farm laborers, and mechanics, that they should be trained to do skillful work and thus be made good citizens, that they needed to be taught less about books and more about life and daily duties, that they must begin at the bottom and slowly move upward.

From the prolonged discussion of the Negro problem certain conventional attitudes gradually emerged to become fixed and basic formulæ in the American credo. It might be informative to list a number of these attitudes, associating with each the names of several Northerners who expressed it in print.

1. The mass of Negroes are unfit for the suffrage.—R. W. Gilder, A. D. Mayo, and the Englishman James Bryce.

2. The only hope for good government in the South rests upon the assured political supremacy of the white race.—Edward Atkinson, E. L. Godkin, Carl Schurz, Charles Eliot Norton, C. D. Warner.

3. The Negroes are the American peasantry.—N. S. Shaler, J. B. Harrison, H. M. Field.

4. One race or the other must rule; the true interests of both races require that the control should be in the hands of the whites.—Hugh McCulloch, A. K. McClure, G. F. Hoar.

5. If there be a race problem, time and education can alone supply its solution.— R. C. Winthrop, A. W. Tourgée, C. F. Adams.

6. Northerners when confronted with the race problem at home show the same

<hr>

[22] T. W. Higginson, "Some War Scenes Revisited," *Atlantic Monthly*, XLII (1878), 1–9.

[23] T. W. Higginson, "Young Men's Party" (pamphlet, New York, 1884).

[24] A. D. Mayo, "The Negro-American Citizen in the New American Life" (pamphlet, Lake Mohonk, N. Y., 1890).

prejudices Southerners do. In fact, the attitude of the Anglo-Saxons toward the Negro the world over is essentially the same.—E. L. Godkin, S. C. Armstrong, J. G. Holland, T. W. Higginson, H. M. Field.

7. The Negro is better off in Southern hands.—A. D. Mayo, T. W. Higginson, R. W. Gilder.

8. The history of the Negro in Africa and America "leads to the belief that he will remain inferior in race stamina and race achievement."—A. B. Hart.

Few Northerners could be found at the close of the century who did not subscribe to the greater part of this credo. A tremendous reversal of opinion had materialized. The unchanging elements of the race problem had become apparent to most observers and the old impatient yearning for an immediate and thorough solution had passed away. Once a people admits the fact that a major problem is basically insoluble they have taken the first step in learning how to live with it. The conflicting elements of the race problem had dropped into a working adjustment which was accepted and rationalized as a settlement. Imperfect as it was, it permitted a degree of peace between North and South hitherto unknown, gave to the South the stability of race relations necessary to reconcile her to the reunited nation, and gave to the Negro a chance to live and to take the first steps of progress.

Southern
Suffrage Restrictions

V. O. Key

The sharp drop in Texas electoral participation immediately following the 1896 campaign requires careful observation in the interpretation of the consequences of suffrage
restrictions. In that campaign the Democratic presidential candidate appropriated the
Populist policies, and over the nation the agrarian movement rapidly lost strength. In
Texas the disillusionment of the Populists and their desertion by many of their leaders
were accompanied by a drop in electoral interest. The race question, of course, had no
bearing on the subsidence of Populism nationally, but in Texas the Populists and Democrats had bid for Negro votes. The fear, fancied or real, that the Negroes would gain
and hold the balance of power if the whites continued to divide among themselves was
played upon. The slogan of white supremacy aided in closing the ranks of the whites,
and the burning issues, fought with religious fervor by the Populist leaders, disappeared
from campaigns. The turnout at the 1902 election was less than half that of the peak of
1896. The drop occurred *before* the effect of the poll tax was felt; that tax, adopted by
constitutional amendment in 1902, first influenced an election turnout in 1904.[1]

By the time the Texas poll tax became effective not only had Negroes been disfranchised but a substantial proportion of the white population had begun to stay away
from the polls. Party conflict had been repressed; Populists leaders had almost completely given up the battle. Conservative Democratic forces and whites of the black-belt
counties had joined forces to kill off dissent. Should the poll tax be held responsible for
low levels of voting interest consistently maintained since 1904? Apparently the poll tax
merely reflected a fait accompli; opposition had been discouraged and suppressed. The

---

* From V. O. Key, Jr., *Southern Politics in State and Nation* (New York: Alfred A. Knopf, Inc., 1949),
pp. 534–41. Copyright 1949 by Alfred A. Knopf, Inc. Reprinted by permission of the publisher.

[1] The total vote in the general election of 1896, 539,000, was not reached again until the Democratic primary of 1918 when 678,491 votes were polled. At that primary woman suffrage—for the primaries—became
effective and the state also had a heated gubernatorial campaign.

solidification of economic power, characteristic of the one-party system, had been accomplished and the electoral abdication of a substantial part of the white population signed and sealed.

In other southern states the process toward monopolization of political control by a small proportion of the white population did not precisely parallel the Texas pattern; nevertheless Texas experience points to the necessity of discriminating interpretation of disfranchisement systems in their bearing on citizen-interest in elections.[2]

1. LEGALIZATION OF FAIT ACCOMPLI: DISFRANCHISEMENT WITHIN THE LIMITS OF THE FIFTEENTH AMENDMENT, 1890–1908

Oddly enough those who urge an institutional change to enable them to gain power usually first win virtual control without benefit of the procedural or organizational advantage they seek. Law often merely records not what is to be but what is, and ensures that what is will continue to be. Before their formal disfranchisement Negroes had, in most states, ceased to be of much political significance and the whites had won control of state governments. If disfranchisement merely anchored in power those already in control, the crucial issue in the interpretation of the disfranchisement movement lies in the identification of the groups pushing it, for by no means were all whites united on the issue. To lay the ground work for such an analysis requires a record of the chronology of Negro disfranchisement.[3]

Triumph of Radical Republicans in Congress over the moderates led to Negro enfranchisement under the Reconstruction Act of 1867. That act, in effect, made the establishment of southern state governments conditional upon the formation of new constitutions by delegates elected by male citizens "of whatever race, color or previous condition." During Reconstruction Negroes were organized, led, and exploited by Radical Republican politicians who had facilities for electoral agitation in the Freedmen's Bureau, the Union League, and other types of official and semi-official agencies. A few white leaders annexed most of the Negro votes to the Republican party. In the 'seventies whites regained control of the state governments. The withdrawal of Federal troops knocked the props from under the Radical Republicans, but the fatal blow to the Negro-white combination ruling the South was struck by whites organized to capture control by force, if necessary. Presently, most Negroes realized that it was wiser not to attempt to vote. Moreover, their inclination to vote weakened when their white leaders found it safer to reside outside the South.

As whites regained control of the states in the 'seventies a first stage in disfran-

---

[2] For instance, voter-turnout in Georgia reached a peak of 221,750, in the gubernatorial race of 1894, a level not again equaled, it appears from available figures, until the Democratic primary of 1920 despite a steady population growth.

[3] The exclusion of the Negro from general elections preceded and underlay his exclusion from the Democratic primaries in the later period of unchallenged one-party dominance. For treatment of the white primary, see below, chap. 29.

chisement got into motion. Legislators contrived devious electoral procedures to nullify the efforts of blacks who still had the inclination to vote.[4] In addition, in all southern states during the 'seventies and 'eighties mild and unexceptionable electoral qualifications and procedural requirements were adopted to discourage Negro voting.[5] Virginia, for example, in its legislative session of 1875–76 made petit larceny a disqualification for voting.[6] All these disfranchising measures, of course, contributed nothing to the power of the whites. Force and threat of force had put the whites in power. Within 10 or 15 years after 1867 the premature enfranchisement of the Negro was largely undone, and undone by veritable revolution.[7]

In almost every state from time to time white factions competed for the remaining Negro vote. They rarely used fair methods of political competition: bribery and coercion served at times as instruments to enlist Negro support for one white faction; intimidation and fraud, as means by which one white faction might offset Negro support of the other.

In most states intense competition between white factions for Negro votes preceded the second stage of disfranchisement, viz., the contrivance after 1890 of methods of disfranchisement compatible with the Fifteenth Amendment of the Federal Constitution. Circumvention of that amendment demanded ingenious legal sophistry; it reads as follows:

> SECTION 1. The right of citizens of the United States to vote shall not be denied or abridged by the United States or by any State on account of race, color, or previous condition of servitude.
>
> SECTION 2. The Congress shall have power to enforce this article by appropriate legislation.

Mississippi, South Carolina, and Louisiana invented the principal techniques for voiding the Constitution by constitutional means, although not all states adopted such drastic limitations as these three. In 1890 Negroes made up more than 50 per cent of the population of each of these states. Mississippi's constitutional convention of 1890 first contrived ways to disfranchise the Negro without formal violation of the Fifteenth Amendment. The convention, however, moved with trepidation; it was breaking new ground. The possibility remained of Federal intervention to protect the Negro; the month before the convention gathered the national House of Representatives had passed Senator Lodge's "force bill" to provide Federal supervision of congressional elec-

[4] W. A. Dunning, "The Undoing of Reconstruction," *Atlantic Monthly,* 88 (1901), pp. 437–49.

[5] For a running summary of actions in the various states, see S. B. Weeks, "The History of Negro Suffrage in the South," *Political Science Quarterly,* 9 (1894), pp. 671–703.

[6] At a Negro convention in Richmond in 1875 a delegate remarked, "It is hard that a poor Negro cannot take a few chickens without losing his right to vote."

[7] The revolution interpretation is that of S. S. Calhoon, President of the Mississippi Constitutional Convention of 1890, "The Causes and Events that Led to the Calling of the Constitutional Convention of 1890," *Publications of the Mississippi Historical Society,* VI (1902), pp. 104–10.

tions. The convention's action had to bear all the earmarks of constitutionality. Moreover, it had to disfranchise Negroes and at the same time leave a loophole for all whites
to vote. The counties with few Negroes had been reluctant to concur in the calling of a
convention that might, by some such qualification as the educational test, take the ballot from many whites.

The solutions evolved by the Mississippi convention, which were widely imitated, can be summarized as follows:

> *Residence.* A residence requirement of two years in the state and one year in the
> election district or in the incorporated city or town. The lengthy residence re-
> quirement was expected to bear more heavily on Negroes because of their sup-
> posedly peripatetic habits.
>
> *Poll tax.* A cumulative poll tax as a prerequisite for voting. The rate was fixed
> at $2 per year for state purposes, and county authorities could levy up to $1 addi-
> tional. Persons offering to vote were required to produce satisfactory evidence
> that they had paid "all taxes" legally required of them "for the two preceding
> years." The poll tax in itself was calculated to discourage Negro voting; the re-
> quirement that evidence of payment be presented to election officials presumably
> discriminated by reason of the absence among Negroes of a predilection for the
> preservation of records.
>
> *Literacy and the alternative of "understanding."* The crowning achievement of
> the convention was the "understanding" clause. The new constitution required
> that every elector shall "be able to read any section of the Constitution of this
> State; or he shall be able to understand the same when read to him, or give a rea-
> sonable interpretation thereof." By this clause the fears of illiterate whites were
> to be quieted. If a white man could not read, he could certainly "understand" or
> give a "reasonable interpretation" of a section of the constitution to a white reg-
> istration official, whereas it was not expected that sophistication on constitutional
> matters would be general among Negroes.
>
> *Registration.* Registration four months before an election was made a necessary
> qualification to vote.
>
> *Disqualification.* Conviction for certain crimes operated as a disqualification.
> They were: bribery, burglary, theft, arson, obtaining money or goods under false
> pretenses, perjury, forgery, embezzlement or bigamy. The list was not so long as
> that adopted in other states, and this method undoubtedly occupied a relatively
> insignificant place in the calculations of the constitution framers.

All the suffrage provisions of the Mississippi constitution were phrased to exclude from the franchise not Negroes, as such, but persons with certain characteristics
most of whom would be Negroes. A Mississippian, writing in 1902, explained, presumably with a straight face, how the convention kept within the limitations of the Fifteenth Amendment:

> Every provision in the Mississippi Constitution applies equally, and without
> any discrimination whatever, to both the white and the negro races. Any assump-

tion, therefore, that the purpose of the framers of the Constitution was ulterior, and dishonest, is gratuitous and cannot be sustained.[8]

In 1895 a South Carolina constitutional convention promulgated a constitution whose suffrage provisions resembled in most respects those of Mississippi. The principal South Carolina contribution to the technique of disfranchisement was the contrivance of additional alternatives to literacy by which whites might qualify to vote. A person unable to read and write a section of the constitution might qualify by showing that he owned and had paid taxes during the previous year on property assessed at $300 or more. The new Louisiana constitution, put into effect without popular vote in 1898, was notable for the "grandfather clause," a device that had been rejected in South Carolina because of doubts about its constitutionality. The clause was not, of course, in itself a method of Negro disfranchisement. It was an exception to the literacy test which could be taken advantage of only by illiterate whites. The Louisiana clause provided that

> no male person who was on January 1st, 1867, or at any date prior thereto, entitled to vote under the Constitution or statutes of any State of the United States, wherein he then resided, and no son or grandson of any such person not less than twenty-one years of age at the date of the adoption of this Constitution, . . . shall be denied the right to register and vote in this State by reason of his failure to possess the educational or property qualifications. . . .

The right to register under the clause was temporary; it had to be exercised prior to September 1, 1898.

The Mississippi, South Carolina, and Louisiana constitutions contained the basic techniques that were incorporated in various combinations in other state constitutions.[9] In 1900 North Carolina established an educational qualification for all save those who could register under the grandfather clause. The usual poll-tax and extended-residence qualifications were added. In 1901 Alabama adopted a new constitution framed primarily with a view to disfranchising the Negro. Virginia followed in 1902. Georgia, which had long had a poll tax, in 1908 adopted a constitutional amendment prescribing a literacy test. In general, suffrage qualifications were most stringent in those states with the largest percentages of Negro population. States with fewest Negroes limited themselves, insofar as formal legal action was concerned, to the poll tax. These states, with the dates of action, were: Florida (1889), Tennessee (1890), Arkansas (1893), and Texas (1902).

Outside the formal modes of disfranchisement an extralegal method developed that was to prove more effective than the formal ones. This was the "white primary."

---

[8] Frank Johnston, "Suffrage and Reconstruction in Mississippi," *Publications of the Mississippi Historical Society,* VI (1902), p. 228.

[9] This is the conclusion of York Willbern, *The Adoption of Legal and Constitutional Devices for the Disfranchisement of the Negro in the South, 1870–1910* (M. A. Thesis, University of Texas, 1938).

As the Democratic party succeeded in liquidating Republican and Populist opposition it became possible by private party action—presumed not to be in violation of the Fifteenth Amendment since it was not state action—to limit participation in the Democratic primary to whites.

2. FORCES IN THE DRIVE FOR DISFRANCHISEMENT

Why, after white supremacy had been generally re-established, did southern states set to work to effect legally what had already been accomplished more or less outside the law? It was suggested earlier that the explanation might be found by the identification of forces driving for disfranchisement. While those elements and their avowed motives differed from state to state, several common features characterized the agitation in all states.

Most interpretations of disfranchisement movements give great weight to the American constitutional mores that place a high value on legality and regularity in government. Illegal, irregular, and informal practices, according to this argument, produced painful conflicts with inherited notions of propriety in government. The efficacy of the inner urge toward constitutionality can be debated, but undoubtedly pressures external to the South re-enforced whatever compulsion toward legality that existed. The House of Representatives, in seating Representatives from southern districts frequently examined the legality of elections. From 1874 to 1900, for example, in 16 of the 20 Virginia elections contested before the House, fraud was the basis for contest.[10] Furthermore, fear of Federal intervention to police elections remained. In 1889 President Harrison advocated such a measure in his message to Congress and the House passed the Lodge "force bill," around which centered a bitter debate that "served only to stir up past memories and to increase this solidarity of the South against the aggressiveness of Northern Republicans." [11]

Politicians, newspaper editors, and other leaders of opinion emphasized the demoralizing effects upon the whites of the methods used to disfranchise Negroes. Numerous practices, none of them quite cricket, were employed to dissuade the black man from voting and to nullify his ballot when he did vote. Gerrymandering, trickery in election administration, fraud in casting and counting ballots were tactics that pricked sensitive consciences. Moreover, these methods could be, and were, used against whites as well as blacks.

Although protestations of revulsion against corrupt electoral practices were frequent, the principal drive for Negro disfranchisement in most states came from those areas in which Negroes constituted a majority of the population. Negro disfranchise-

[10] R. C. McDanel, *The Virginia Constitutional Convention of 1901–1902* (Baltimore: Johns Hopkins Press, 1928), p. 11.

[11] R. L. Morton, *The Negro in Virginia Politics, 1865–1902* (Charlottesville: University of Virginia Press, 1918), p. 130.

ment was not a question of "the South" disfranchising "the Negro." The problem of interracial conflict for power occurred in its most acute form in connection with local government and legislative representation in those counties and cities with black majorities,
which areas were by no means the entire South.

The whites in the black counties occupied a most insecure position. It is the custom to speak of the Negro question as a minority problem. In these counties the whites
were the minority. Nor could the whites gain a balance-of-power position between com-
peting Negro factions, for the blacks did not split politically. In racial solidarity they
clung to their savior, the Republican party. Under these circumstances in black localities, "With universal negro suffrage, the logical alternatives were between negro government on the one hand and illegal election contrivances on the other." [12]

The whites in the black counties had to win support of the white counties. Only
by that means could the Negro be disfranchised to the end that white supremacy could
be assured in local governments of the black counties. In a sense the managers of the
disfranchisement agitation were up against the same problem as that of the ante-bellum
slaveowners. Nonslaveholding whites had no burning zeal for the South's peculiar institution; the slaveholding minority, territorially segregated in a small part of the South,
had sufficient political skill to rally southerners generally to their cause. Similarly, in the
disfranchising movement the generating force came fundamentally from whites in the
predominantly black counties, and one of their chief motives was the preservation of
white control of local government. To assure this end, like the slaveocracy, they had to
rally to their cause the white counties less immediately concerned about white supremacy.

After 1876, as an interim arrangement, the traditional practices of local self-government were radically subverted in many states to assure white control in black
counties. Instead of electing county and city officials, several states vested their appointment in the governor. With white control of the governorship assured, it could con-
fidently be expected that whites would be appointed to local offices.

Of great practical significance in some states in setting off the movement for disfranchisement was the fact that in the agrarian movement informal restraints on Negro
participation in politics had weakened. The Farmers Alliance and the Populist party
generated a dispute among whites whose outcome was of such deep concern that both
factions breached the consensus to keep the black from the polls. Both Democrats and
Populists were willing to bid for Negro support. According to southern tradition Negroes were in a position to hold the balance of power between white factions. The degree to which Negroes actually voted *en bloc* and participated in the elections of the
agrarian uprising has never been adequately investigated, and the difficulties of finding
the facts would be formidable. Nevertheless, the Populists, either alone or in combination with Republicans, threatened Democratic supremacy, and a situation emerged in
which the plea for white supremacy could be made effectively. The pattern of events
varied. In some states, the disfranchising constitutions came immediately on the heels of

[12] Johnston, "Suffrage and Reconstruction in Mississippi," p. 205.

"agrarian trouble"; in others, as in Texas, the Populist specter had been laid before suffrage limitations became effective.

The sequence of events in which disfranchisement usually followed divisions among the whites has spawned the legend that the whites, seeing the error of their ways, united to take the vote from the Negro lest he enjoy forever a pivotal position in southern affairs. In later days a contrary interpretation has been advanced, viz., that the conservative or, as they were known at the time, Bourbon Democrats, took the lead in disfranchisement, with the intent of depriving many agrarian radicals of the vote along with the Negro. An inkling of the validity of these conflicting hypotheses can be obtained from the record of agrarian revolt and disfranchisement.

Tom Watson[*]

C. Vann Woodward

What explained the bitterness and violence that characterized the Populist struggle in the South? To answer in a word—"race." And that is much too simple an answer. But if to race be added the complexities of the class economy growing out of race, the heritage of manumitted slave psychology, and the demagogic uses to which the politician was able to put race prejudice—then "race" may be said to be the core of the explanation.

In later life Watson once wrote a retrospective (and quite candid) comparison of his own career with that of William Jennings Bryan. In it he said: "Consider the advantage of position that Bryan had over me. His field of work was the plastic, restless, and growing, West: mine was the hide-bound, rock-ribbed Bourbon South. Besides, Bryan had *no everlasting and overshadowing Negro Question to hamper and handicap his progress:* I HAD." [10] There is no doubt that Watson thought of the Negro problem as the Nemesis of his career. He fled it all his days, and in flight sought every refuge—in attitudes as completely contradictory and extreme as possible. At this stage, however, he faced his problem courageously, honestly, and intelligently. As the official leader of the new party in the House, and its only Southern member in Congress, Watson was the logical man to formulate the Populist policy toward the Negro. This he did in a number of speeches and articles.

The Populist program called for a united front between Negro and white farmers. Watson framed his appeal this way:

> Now the People's Party says to these two men, "You are kept apart that you may be separately fleeced of your earnings. You are made to hate each other because upon that hatred is rested the keystone of the arch of financial despotism which enslaves you both. You are deceived and blinded that you may not see how this race antagonism perpetuates a monetary system which beggars both." [11]

[*] From C. Vann Woodward, *Tom Watson: Agrarian Rebel* (New York: Galaxy Books, 1968), pp. 219–23, 372–80. Reprinted by permission of the author.
[10] *Jeffersonian Weekly,* Jan. 20, 1910.
[11] T. E. W., "The Negro Question in the South," *Arena,* Vol. VI (1892), p. 548.

This bold program called for a reversal of deeply rooted racial prejudices and firmly fixed traditions as old as Southern history. In place of race hatred, political proscription, lynch law, and terrorism it was necessary to foster tolerance, friendly cooperation, justice and political rights for the Negro. This was no small task; yet Watson met each issue squarely.

It should be the object of the Populist party, he said, to "make lynch law odious to the people." [12] Georgia at that time led the world in lynchings. Watson nominated a Negro to a place on the state executive committee of his party, "as a man worthy to be on the executive committee of this or any other party." "Tell me the use of educating these people as citizens if they are never to exercise the rights of citizens." [13] He spoke repeatedly from the same platform with Negro speakers to mixed audiences of Negro and white farmers. He did not advocate "social equality" and said so emphatically, since that was "a thing each citizen decides for himself." But he insisted upon "political equality," holding that "the accident of color can make no difference in the interests of farmers, croppers, and laborers." In the same spirit of racial tolerance he was continually finding accomplishments of the Negro race at home and abroad to praise in articles and speeches.[14]

Tom Watson was perhaps the first native white Southern leader of importance to treat the Negro's aspirations with the seriousness that human strivings deserve. For the first time in his political history the Negro was regarded neither as the incompetent ward of White Supremacy, nor as the ward of military intervention, but as an integral part of Southern society with a place in its economy. The Negro was in the South to stay, insisted Watson, just as much so as the white man. "Why is not the colored tenant open to the conviction that he is in the same boat as the white tenant; the colored laborer with the white laborer?" he asked. With a third party it was now possible for the Negro to escape the dilemma of selling his vote to the Democrats or pledging it blindly to the Republican bosses. Under Watson's tutelage the Southern white masses were beginning to learn to regard the Negro as a political ally bound to them by economic ties and a common destiny, rather than as a slender prop to injured self-esteem in the shape of "White Supremacy." Here was a foundation of political realism upon which some more enduring structure of economic democracy might be constructed. Never before or since have the two races in the South come so close together as they did during the Populist struggles.

No one was more keenly aware of the overwhelming odds against his social program than Tom Watson. In an article in the *Arena*[15] he wrote:

> You might beseech a Southern white-tenant to listen to you upon questions of finance, taxation, and transportation; you might demonstrate with mathematical precision that herein lay his way out of poverty into comfort; you might have

[12] *P. P. P.,* Nov. 3, 1893.

[13] *Ibid.,* May 24, 1894.

[14] For example, the work of a Negro member of the Georgia Legislature (*P. P. P.,* Dec. 2, 1892) and a South African king's resistance to Cecil Rhodes (*P. P. P.* Dec. 29, 1893).

[15] T. E. W.,"The Negro Question in the South," *Arena,* Vol. VI (1892), p. 541.

him "almost persuaded" to the truth, but if the merchant who furnished his farm supplies (at tremendous usury) or the town politician (who never spoke to him excepting at election times) came along and cried "Negro rule!" the entire fabric of reason and common sense which you had patiently constructed would fall, and the poor tenant would joyously hug the chains of an actual wretchedness rather than do any experimenting on a question of mere sentiment. . . . The Negro has been as valuable a portion of the stock in trade of a Democrat as he was of a Republican.

Henry Grady's statement in 1889 that "The Negro as a political force had dropped out of serious consideration" sounded strange indeed in 1892. The Negro as a political force was the concern of everybody. The Democrats sought industriously to resurrect the scare of the Republican "Force Bill," introduced in the House and defeated in the Senate in 1890. "All agree," said the Augusta *Chronicle,* "that this is the overshadowing issue," and it was obvious that the Populists were "aiding the Republicans in their nefarious schemes." "The old issue of sectionalism is confronting the South," asserted the *Constitution,* and White Supremacy is more important than "all the financial reform in the world." [16]

●   ●   ●

Since 1898, when the Populists had last put forth a state ticket, a succession of staunchly conservative governors had ruled the state. They belonged to that wing of the party which, since the 'seventies, had been hospitable toward Northern capital, and friendly to corporate interests, especially the railroads. Resistance to the dominance of this wing had reached its lowest ebb in 1904, when the candidate had been reëlected without opposition. In the spring of 1905, more than a year before the next election, Clark Howell announced himself as a candidate for the gubernatorial nomination. A logical successor in the scheme of office rotation, Howell had back of him a long record of party service and the support of the conservative machine. His prospects could hardly have been fairer.

Early in 1905, Thomas W. Hardwick, congressman from Watson's district, and a representative of the opposition to the Howell faction, came to Watson to discuss the proposal concerning disfranchisement. Together they worked out a platform combining that issue with several reform demands for railroad regulation, and agreed upon Pope Brown as a suitable candidate. Then shortly after Watson's support of his candidacy became known, Pope Brown withdrew from the race in favor of Hoke Smith. It later developed that Brown took this step because he received from Hardwick the impression that Watson desired it.[5]

Watson was left in perplexity after this maneuver, and for several months he refused to commit himself. There had been political enmity between Watson and Hoke

[16] Augusta *Chronicle,* July 5, 1892; *Constitution,* quoted in *P. P. P.,* July 15, 1892; Macon *Telegraph,* July 27, 1892.
[5] Pope Brown to T. E. W., Feb. 22, 1908.

Smith ever since the 'nineties, when, as a member of Cleveland's cabinet, Smith had led the gold forces in Georgia. It had not been six months since Watson had written the editor of the Atlanta *Journal,* with which Smith had long been associated, asking that his name be removed from the circulation list. He explained: "In this campaign you have pursued me with such bitter vindictiveness that I can no longer accept any favor at your hands." [6] The editor was doubtless justified in denying the charge. Tom Watson was ever quick in perceiving injury and ever slow in forgiving.

On the other hand, there were certain forces at work to draw Smith and Watson together. Since the subsidence of the silver issue, Howell and Smith had reversed positions with respect to relative conservatism. The critical issue now was government control and ownership, and Hoke Smith, an anti-corporation lawyer, was far in advance of Howell upon this question. In 1902 he had joined Watson in speaking before the Georgia legislature in support of a bill prohibiting child labor.[7] For years he had been fighting the state machine in the columns of the Atlanta *Journal,* a rival of Howell's *Constitution.* He charged that the machine was owned by the railroads and that the state railway commission served the railroads. He pointed out rate discriminations, abuses, and corrupting influences. Smith's platform for 1906 might have been written by a Populist. It contained demands for primaries to nominate by popular vote all officers, including senators; for the abolition of poll-workers and the disfranchisement of vote-buyers; for a stringent corrupt practices act; for making pass-giving and lobbying a crime; for compulsory domestication of Georgia railroads and their submission to state courts and to heavier taxation; for an elective railway commission; and for state ownership of railroads.[8]

It was the heyday of the reform governor—La Follette of Wisconsin, Folk of Missouri, Colby of New Jersey—and Smith of Georgia was hailed by national reformers as one of that number. Herbert Quick said that Smith wrote "the most radical platform ever adopted, with perhaps one exception, by a state convention of either of the two great parties of these times." Smith "has no corporation collar. He is a successful party revolutionist." [9] There was one plank of Smith's platform that struck his Progressive admirers as a bit incongruous. Yet it was the one singled out to appear day after day in bold-faced capital letters on the editorial page of the *Journal:* he favored "THE ELIMINATION OF THE NEGRO FROM POLITICS . . . BY LEGAL AND CONSTITUTIONAL METHODS . . . WITHOUT DISFRANCHISING A SINGLE WHITE MAN."

While Watson hesitated over his decision, James K. Hines, Populist candidate for governor in 1894, urged him to come out for Smith. Hines would go even further. "Let us accept the invitation, often extended by both factions, to come home," he wrote.

---

[6] Quoted in the editor's reply: J. R. Gray to T. E. W., Nov. 14, 1904.

[7] T. E. W., *Life and Speeches of Thomas E. Watson,* pp. 184–189.

[8] Augusta *Herald,* June 29, 1905; Herbert Quick, "Hoke Smith and the Revolution in Georgia," *The Reader,* Vol. X (Aug., 1907), pp. 241–247.

[9] H. Quick, *op. cit.,* p. 241.

"Let us take charge of the Democratic Party in Georgia and make it the People's Party."
Again he wrote: "You are stronger than any man in Georgia. When Mr. Stephens quit
the whigs and joined the democrats he justified himself by saying that the democrats
had come to him. Much more true is it, that the democrats have come to you." [10] Hardwick served as a zealous intermediary between Hickory Hill and the Atlanta *Journal*. He
begged Watson to tell him "exactly what reparation you think Mr. Smith ought to
make" and he would "get Mr. Smith and the *Journal* to do the right thing." [11] It appeared that a number of "reparations" were required, as well as some changes in the
platform. They were all eagerly made, however: Smith's in public speeches, the *Journal's*
in an editorial actually written by Hardwick.[12]

On September 12 Watson wrote Smith promising his support, and in the October number of his magazine, widely circulated in Georgia at Smith's expense, made public his position. He first reminded his followers that Smith and Howell "were both
rock-ribbed, moss-backed, unterrified Democrats" and mortal enemies of Populism back
in the 'nineties. "But times have changed," he said. "If . . . [Smith] can do for Georgia
what La Follette has done for Wisconsin and Folk has done for Missouri, he will become a heroic figure in the eyes of reformers throughout the land. No matter how
faulty his record in the past may have been, he is hitting the bull's-eye *this* time." Cautious in his commitments at first, he refused to say he would vote for Smith. Later he
plunged in more wholeheartedly. He was still a Populist, and he refused to commit
himself two years in advance to the National Democratic ticket, but he pledged the
Populists not to put out a state ticket, and to abide by the result of the white primary. "I
am going to vote for Hoke Smith," he finally declared. "And I appeal to every Populist
of McDuffie and the surrounding counties, and every Populist throughout the state . . .
to follow me now; and if it turns out I am wrong then punish me hereafter by never listening to me with respect upon any issue." [13]

Smith was profuse in his expressions of gratitude. "I cannot tell you how much
I appreciate your coöperation," he wrote, and he told of how his campaign had undergone a rejuvenation the moment Watson's support was made public.[14] Continuous correspondence was kept up between the two throughout the campaign, and whole pages
of the *Journal* were given over to Watson's opinions. Was it reported that the farmers
of north Georgia suspected Negro disfranchisement of being a scheme to disfranchise illiterate whites? Off went Watson to reassure them. Were the Populists in the South rebellious at voting for a former gold bug? Watson was there to tell them that "Hoke
Smith is trying to do what we want done and cannot do ourselves."

The campaign was the hottest since the 'nineties, and judging from the nature of
Howell's attack, one might suppose Watson was the candidate instead of Smith. Smith

[10] James K. Hines to T. E. W., June 8 and Dec. 9, 1905, and July 12, 1906.
[11] Thomas W. Hardwick to T. E. W., June 26, 1905.
[12] *Ibid.*, Aug. 9, 1905.
[13] Atlanta *Journal*, Aug. 7, 1906.
[14] Hoke Smith to T. E. W., Sept. 16, 1905 and Dec. 19, 1905.

was declared to be a "demagogue" and a "Muckraker" who was "run by Tom Watson." He had "surrendered his convictions and his democratic allegiance to Tom Watson for the latter's support." In a surprisingly accurate prophecy, the *Constitution* predicted: "The spectacle of Tom Watson controlling the machinery of the Democratic party— and at the same time remaining an open and avowed populist—is one which the Democrats of this state may have to endure." [15] Some of the edge of this attack was taken off when Watson made public a letter from Clark Howell to him begging an interview before Watson had sided with Smith.[16]

As for Smith, he "wouldn't give Tom Watson for the whole crowd."

The executive committee of the Democratic party, under control of the Howell wing, attempted to rule Populists out of the party primary by requiring that all ballots bear the following inscription: "By voting this ticket, I hereby declare that I am an organized Democrat, and I hereby pledge myself to support the organized Democracy, both state and national." [17] The ruling was loudly denounced by Watson and Smith, however, and failed in its purpose.

The foremost issue of the campaign was the question of Negro disfranchisement. None of Howell's objections to the measure was aimed at the principle of disfranchisement, but merely at its effectiveness. It would disfranchise illiterate whites while allowing educated Negroes to vote; it had failed of its purpose in Alabama, and it encouraged Negroes to climb out of their "place" into the ranks of the literate.

The most serious tactical blunder made by Howell and his friends was their attempt to defend the corporations and railroads upon whom Watson and Smith made war. Charles R. Pendleton, editor of the Macon *Telegraph,* launched a bitter personal attack on Watson and undertook to answer his editorial onslaughts upon Samuel Spencer, president of the Southern Railroad, a Morgan subsidiary. The attack precipitated a cloudburst of railroad-denunciation from Watson. Wall Street's plundering of Southern railroads—the stock frauds, illegal combinations, extortionate rates, criminal negligence —were already a familiar story.[18] But no one could make these villainies quite so heinous, nor the villains quite so monstrous as Tom Watson. It was a specialty with him. Early in 1905 he had pronounced J. P. Morgan *"the absolute king of the railroads in Georgia."* "He makes the Governor," Watson charged, "controls the legislature, overrides the commission and tramples the Constitution of the State under his feet." Samuel Spencer's crime, moreover, was "unnatural as well as heinous." "He is the Sepoy, the hireling of a foreign master, trained, uniformed, armed and paid to conquer and plunder his own people. A Southern man, he has looted the South; a Georgian, he has robbed Georgia." When Watson read Spencer's report of a 525 per cent increase in net earnings in eleven years his indignation was "deep and hot," and he wrote:

> Those eleven years rose up in perspective before me, and the awful MEANS by which Sam Spencer had reached that END stalked by like a procession of

[15] *Constitution,* June 24 and Aug. 3 and 5, 1906; Macon *Telegraph,* Aug. 5, 1906.
[16] Clark Howell to T. E. W., Aug. 4, 1905; Atlanta *Journal,* Jan. 13, 1906.
[17] A. M. Arnett, *op. cit.,* p. 221; *Constitution,* Aug. 3, 1906
[18] Lewis Corey, *The House of Morgan,* pp. 381–382.

spectres. The frightful loss of human life; the bribing of politicians; the corrupting of men in power; the violation of state laws and Federal statutes; the disregard of the rights of shippers and passengers; the discriminations which have ruined whole communities; the extortionate charges which have beggared
individuals . . . the defiance of State Commissions and of public opinion; the
overwork and underpay of the men who bear the brunt of the toil. . . .

Watson declared that "we lost fewer lives to the invading host of Sherman's army than
we have lost to the railroads" during Spencer's regime. He demonstrated that the railroads owned considerable stock in the Macon *Telegraph,* and turned furiously upon the
editor: "you hypocrite, you sneak, you corporation slave . . ."[19]

Joel Chandler Harris's Populist character, "Mr. Billy Sanders," summed up the
old guard's response to Watson's campaign: "I'll tell you the honest truth: thar ain't
skacely a night passes that I ain't rid by some red-eyed trust or 'nother, an' ef 'tain't a
trust, then it's some villainous railroad corporation; an' that's lots wuss'n a trust, bekeze
the trains is allers late, an' they've got a habit of switchin' back'erds and forrerds on the
pit of my stomach—I reckon they think it's some new kind of a turn-table."[20]

The primary election resulted in an overwhelming victory for Hoke Smith. How
much of the credit was due Tom Watson is, of course, difficult to estimate. "To swing
90,000 populists to your candidate [Smith] required the hardest fighting I had done
since 1892," wrote Watson, and surely his efforts were not wasted. However the votes
were obtained, there is less doubt about the issues, for they were clearly Watson issues.
Some of the sweetness of victory was soured for Watson by his failure to carry his own
county, after he had made a special effort to do so. In general, however, he was much
elated by the turn events were taking. Pointing out that Smith was making "the same
fight we used to make," that President Roosevelt had put his hands to "the same work
we wanted to do," and that "the Bryan boom for 1908 lashes itself to the most radical
plank of the Populist platform," he concluded that "the skies do verily begin to redden
. . . for the glorious coming of the morning."[21]

There was a tragic sequel to the election—the Atlanta race riot of 1906. Its mention gains pertinence in view of the future history of Watson and of Watsonism. "Everybody knew that the Disfranchisement issue was the cause of our success," wrote
Watson. During the campaign the papers of Atlanta were almost daily filled with sensational stories of Negro atrocities. Lynching was openly advocated and frequently practiced. A concerted crusade of race bigotry and hatred was preached. Partly it was the result of newspaper rivalry, augmented by the recent intrusion of Hearst into Atlanta, but
the political significance was readily apparent. An editorial of the Atlanta *Journal,* one of
the milder papers, indicates the trend. It was printed in bold-face capitals:

[19] T. E. W., "Clark Howell's Defense of the Corporation," *Tom Watson's Magazine,* Vol. IV (March, 1906), pp. 1–8; "Sam Spencer," *ibid.,* Vol. IV (April, 1906), pp. 161–165; Atlanta *Journal,* July 13 and Aug. 11, 1906.
[20] Joel Chandler Harris, "Mr. Billy Sanders," *Uncle Remus Magazine,* Vol. I, No. 4 (Sept., 1907).
[21] Atlanta *Journal,* July 13, 1906.

Political equality being thus preached to the negro in the ring papers and on the stump, what wonder that he makes no distinction between political and social equality. He grows more bumptious on the street. More impudent in his dealings with white men; and then, when he cannot achieve social equality as he wishes, with the instinct of the barbarian to destroy what he cannot attain to, he lies in wait, as that dastardly brute did yesterday near this city, and assaults the fair young girlhood of the south. . . . It is time for those who know the perils of the negro problem to stand together with deep resolve that political power shall never give the negro encouragement in his foul dreams of a mixture of races.[22]

Watson employed the same appeal in his speeches for Smith.

A few days after the election the riot broke upon the streets of Atlanta. It raged for four days. Innocent men and women were hunted by packs and shot down in the streets of the city. Destruction, looting, robbery, murder, and unspeakable brutality went unrestrained. A committee of indignant citizens was shocked that "the small minority which constitutes the tough element was allowed to crucify this community in the eyes of the world . . ."[23] The "tough element" expressed no regrets. It wrote no editorials.

Between the rôle of national reformer and the rôle of defender of White Supremacy stretched an embarrassing hiatus. Faithful readers of *Tom Watson's Magazine* might now find wedged between a defense of the Russian revolutionists and an attack on Wall Street such editorials as one entitled "The Ungrateful Negro."[24] Watson closed an editorial attacking Booker T. Washington with the remark:

What does Civilization owe to the negro?
Nothing!
Nothing! !
NOTHING! ! ![25]

This editorial was more widely quoted in the South, especially in Georgia, than anything he wrote. The response of the reformers and progressives, on the other hand, ranged from bewilderment to dismay in tone. "It is all so disappointing," wrote a Southern woman. "I thought I'd struck the magazine, the writer, and the reformer after my own heart."[26] A Northern reformer wrote Watson: Your position on the Negro puts you in "the same category with the men you censure," very close, indeed, to "a pro-

[22] Atlanta *Journal,* Aug. 1, 1906.

[23] Glenn W. Rainey, "The Atlanta Race Riot of 1906" (Master's thesis, Emory University), *passim; Constitution,* Dec. 29, 1906.

[24] *Tom Watson's Magazine,* Vol. IV (April, 1906), pp. 165–174.

[25] *Ibid.,* Vol. I (June, 1905), p. 298.

[26] Mrs. Martin Singer to T. E. W., May 27, 1905.

fessed politician merely out for his own advantage." [27] Upton Sinclair wrote a long letter of remonstrance. Thomas H. Tibbles reported that "the Populists are all at sea over the negro question in the South and are writing to me about it." [28]

The tenuous lines that Watson had tied between National Progressivism and Southern Agrarianism—practically the only prospect of a bond between them—had snapped under the tension of the race issue.

[27] James F. Morton, Jr. to T. E. W., Jan. 6, 1905.
[28] Upton Sinclair to T. E. W., June 25, 1905; Thomas H. Tibbles to T. E. W., Oct. 8, 1906.

Progressivism— For Whites Only*

C. Vann Woodward

The Southern counterpart of a Northern progressivism developed nearly all traits familiar to the genus, but it was in no sense derivative. It was a pretty strictly indigenous growth, touched lightly here and there by cross-fertilization from the West. It sprouted in the soil that had nourished Populism, but it lacked the agrarian cast and the radical edge that had frightened the middle class away from the earlier movement. Southern progressivism was essentially urban and middle class in nature, and the typical leader was a city professional man or businessman, rather than a farmer. Under the growing pressure of monopoly, the small businessmen and urban middle class overcame their fear of reform and joined hands with the discontented farmers. They envisaged as a common enemy the plutocracy of the Northeast, together with its agents, banks, insurance companies, public utilities, oil companies, pipelines, and railroads. Southern progressivism often took a sectional character, identifying the popular enemy with "foreign" interests. These interests were defended by Southern apologists who were strongly entrenched within the old party and frequently controlled it through bosses and state machines. William E. Dodd, then a college professor in Virginia, described the situation in his state to Walter Clark, a critic of machine rule in North Carolina. "This state," wrote Dodd, "is no more self-governing to-day than the Catholic Church. Thomas F. Ryan is our master and he lives in New York. Thomas S. Martin is his henchman and we have powerful newspapers to defend both with none to oppose either." [10] The struggle for progressive democracy was directed against such bosses as Martin and was carried on within the old party between conservative and reform factions.

* From C. Vann Woodward, *Origins of the New South, 1877–1913* (Baton Rouge: Louisiana State University Press, 1951), pp. 371–74, 388–94. Reprinted by permission.

[10] William E. Dodd, Ashland, Va., to Walter Clark, September 7, 1906, in Hugh T. Lefler (ed.), "Selected William E. Dodd–Walter Clark Letters," in *North Carolina Historical Review*, XXV (1948), 91–92.

Several circumstances favored the reform factions in the first decade of the new century. The Populist party, bearing the odium attached to any threat to white solidarity, had in large measure constituted an obstruction to the spread of reform ideas in the South. The collapse of the third party not only removed a stigma from reformism, but it brought back into the old party its disaffected left wing. Returning, the Populists brought along with them their ideological baggage, for which room had to be found.

Whether as a cause or a result, the direct-primary system of nominating party candidates appeared with progressive movements all over the South. The direct primary was not invented in Wisconsin in 1903, as is sometimes said, for by that time a majority of the Southern states were already practicing the system, and by 1913 all the remaining ones had adopted it except North Carolina, which fell into line in 1915.[11] A part of the paraphernalia of progressivism in all sections, the primary was one of the first demands of the reformers. "In the South this demand was even stronger than at the North,"[12] because in the one-party system nomination meant election. The adoption of the primary was in part the fulfillment of the implied pledge of the disfranchisers that once the Negro was removed from political life the white men would be given more voice in the selection of their rulers. In part also it was a gesture of welcome to the returning Populist prodigals. The great hope of the progressives was that since the old convention system of nomination had facilitated boss and machine control, the substitution of the primary would restore popular control. In at least five states, Alabama, Arkansas, Florida, Mississippi, and Texas, the change to the primary was an immediate, or nearly immediate, antecedent of the victory of a reform administration. It is probable that in those cases the primary paved the way for reform.

The joker in the Southern primaries was the fact that they were *white* primaries. Southern progressivism generally was progressivism for white men only, and after the poll tax took its toll not all the white men were included.[13] The paradoxical combination of white supremacy and progressivism was not new to the region, but it never ceased to be a cause of puzzlement and confusion above the Potomac—and not a little, below. The paradox nevertheless had its counterpart in the North, where it was not uncommon for one man to champion both progressivism and imperialism. In such instances it was a matter of white supremacy over browns instead of blacks. Hiram Johnson was apparently no more troubled by his advocacy of proscription of Japanese in California than Hoke Smith by his treatment of Negroes in Georgia. The Southern leader who professed reactionary racial views and advanced political and economic reforms in the

[11] Local and county primaries appeared even earlier, but reference here is to Democratic state-wide primaries, whether mandatory or not. The system was adopted in South Carolina in 1896, Arkansas in 1897, Georgia in 1898, Florida and Tennessee in 1901, Alabama and Mississippi in 1902, Kentucky and Texas in 1905, Louisiana in 1906, Oklahoma in 1907, Virginia in 1913, and North Carolina in 1915. Link, "Progressive Movement in the South," *loc. cit.*, 188–90.

[12] Charles B. Spahr, "Method of Nomination to Public Office: An Historical Sketch," in *Proceedings of the Chicago Conference for Good City Government and the Tenth Annual Meeting of the National Municipal League* (Philadelphia, 1904), 324.

[13] The poll tax payment was not a prerequisite for voting in Tennessee primaries.

same breath was known as a "demagogue," unless he happened to be a political ally, in which case he was a "progressive."

Had La Follette and White undertaken the most casual survey of legislation and platforms in the South they would have discovered there all the progressive doctrines and experiments familiar to Wisconsin and Kansas and their latitudes. Southern reformers sought to "bust the trusts" and regulate them at the same time. They strengthened their railroad and public-utility commissions, hauled railroads and other malefactors into court, reduced rates, fought discrimination, and passed unfair-practice laws, safety and inspection laws for mines and factories, pure-food and drug bills, penitentiary reforms, and much humanitarian legislation. Progressives here and there experimented with all the political inventions associated with the movement. Besides the direct primary, these included the initiative, referendum, and recall; preferential primaries; and corrupt practices and antilobby acts.

• • •

In municipal reform progressives held up two innovations as the cures for the "shame of the cities." These were the commission plan and the city-manager plan of municipal government. Both of them originated in the South. The first city in the country to adopt the commission plan was Galveston, Texas. The devastating hurricane and tidal wave of September, 1900, not only swept away a large part of the city but the antiquated city-council form of government as well. In the crisis of reconstruction and relief that followed, the city commission proved its efficiency by rebuilding the city, restoring its credit, and constructing a mighty sea wall. Houston followed the example of her neighbor in 1903, and by 1907 Dallas, Denison, Fort Worth, El Paso, Greenville, and Sherman had adopted the commission plan. The movement spread eastward and was taken up by Memphis, New Orleans, Jackson, Birmingham, and Charlotte. By 1913 most of the larger cities in the South and many of the smaller ones were using the new type of government. Des Moines, Iowa, adopted it in 1907 and from there it spread over the North and West under the name of the "Des Moines Idea." [59] Likewise, the city-manager plan was first tried by Staunton, Virginia, in 1908, then by Sumter, South Carolina, in 1911, but it spread over the rest of the country under the name of the "Dayton Idea" after that city adopted it in 1914.[60]

Partly by chance the prohibition crusade made juncture with the progressive movement in the South, and the two forces marched together for a time. Occasionally they quarreled, but common enemies more often drew them together, and they fought many of their battles in close alliance.

Until 1907 no state-wide prohibition law existed in the South; only three survived in the country, and none had been passed since 1889. Then in August, 1907, Georgia passed a drastic state-wide law that touched off the third national prohibition wave, the first since the eighties. In rapid succession within the next nine months Okla-

[59] John J. Hamilton, *The Dethronement of the City Boss* (New York, 1910), 17–25.
[60] Leonard D. White, *The City Manager* (Chicago, 1927), 125–28.

homa, Alabama, Mississippi, and North Carolina followed Georgia's example, and Tennessee joined them in January, 1909. Four of the six states acted through their legislatures, two by popular vote. Florida and Texas came within a handful of popular votes of adopting prohibition, and the remaining states crowded the saloons into the cities and diminishing pockets of territory.[61] The suddenness with which the prohibitionists appeared to seize whole states was deceptive. For years they had besieged the demon rum in county campaigns by the local-option method. In Georgia 125 of the 145 counties were already dry before state-wide prohibition was adopted, and in Alabama, 90 per cent of the state. In Mississippi 69 of the 76 counties, and in North Carolina 62 of the 97 counties had banished the saloon before the states took action.

Even in Kentucky the cause of good bourbon whisky had been lost in 94 of the 119 counties by 1908. One computation at the beginning of 1907, before the prohibition "wave" was heard of found 825 of the 994 counties in the ex-Confederate states under prohibition laws.[62]

The remarkable success of the movement in the South was often attributed to the presence of the Negro, but a close study of the region concludes that "the negro has been an inconsiderable factor" and that "the saloon has been abolished and retained in the communities of the South without apparent reference to the presence of the negro."[63] There was, however, a pronounced correlation between the success of prohibition and a high percentage of native born, rural, Protestant elements in the population. In Georgia, Alabama, Mississippi, North Carolina, and Tennessee, which were among the strongest and earliest prohibition states, the native born constituted 99 per cent or more of the population, the rural element ranged from 88 to 79 per cent, and Protestants comprised from 99 to 92 per cent of the church population.[64] More specifically it was the nine tenths of the Protestants included in the Baptist and Methodist folds who filled the dry ranks, for their ministers carried the crusade into their pulpits and preached not temperance but teetotalism. Hand in hand with the Anti-Saloon League and the temperance organizations, the parsons gradually perfected their methods in local campaigns. They tapped the sources of reformism that sustained the contemporary education and child-labor crusades, but they also used revival tactics and stormed polls with mobs of singing and praying women and children. Their success earned for the South the name of being "the mainspring" and "the propagandic base of the national agitation." The region was "well-nigh puritanized" by the White Ribboners.[65]

[61] For a time it appeared that the Southern plan would be the state or local dispensary system, first introduced into the country by Georgia in 1891, and adopted more widely by South Carolina and on a limited basis by three other states. The plan was discredited by administrative scandals, in South Carolina, and it never satisfied the genuine prohibitionists.

[62] John E. White, "Prohibition: The New Task and Opportunity of the South" in *South Atlantic Quarterly,* VII (1908), 133; Frank Foxcroft, "Prohibition in the South," in *Atlantic Monthly,* CI (1908), 627–31; D. Leigh Colvin, *Prohibition in the United States* (New York, 1926), 333–34, 344.

[63] Blakey, *Sale of Liquor in the South,* 32.

[64] Peter H. Odegard, *Pressure Politics* (New York, 1928), 32.

[65] William Garrott Brown, "The South and the Saloon," in *Century Magazine,* LXXVI (1908), 463, 465; White, "Prohibition: The New Task," *loc. cit.,* 133.

Even though prohibition was primarily a countryman's cause, it won converts among the urban progressive leaders. Reform governors Glenn of North Carolina, Comer of Alabama, and Smith of Georgia took up the cause, and their reform legislatures enacted state prohibition. The farmer-labor coalition that wrote the most advanced shibboleths of progressivism into the Oklahoma constitution also wrote in prohibition. It was a simple matter to lump the rum demon with the railroad monster as enemies of the people. An identification of prohibition with progressivism was furthered by a tendency of the bosses and machines to join with the liquor interests and fight prohibition. This was not invariably true, for in Virginia, Boss Thomas S. Martin and his machine worked harmoniously with the Anti-Saloon League and its Methodist leader, James Cannon, against the progressives. Where the prohibitionists did infiltrate the progressive ranks they tended to subordinate all other reforms to a single-minded and sometimes reckless drive toward their goal. Governor Comer, after his limited railroad reforms were achieved, proclaimed the saloon to be the only remaining enemy worthy of his steel. Child-labor reformers could get no support for their bill from the millowning governor nor divert any attention of the electorate from the emotional prohibition crusade. Comer and prohibition both went down to defeat in the election of 1910, and the progressives were driven from office in Alabama by conservatives.[66] The prohibition issue completely disrupted the Democratic party in Tennessee and returned the Republicans to power. Malcolm R. Patterson, conservative, antiprohibitionist machine candidate, defeated Edward R. Carmack, prohibitionist candidate for governor, in a violently fought Democratic primary in 1908. In November of that year two close friends of Governor Patterson shot and killed Carmack in the streets of Nashville, and the Governor pardoned one of them. In the name of their martyred leader, the prohibition Democrats passed their bill over the Governor's veto. When the machine threatened to renominate Patterson on an antiprohibition platform in 1910, the prohibitionists bolted their party, organized the Independent Democrats, and endorsed Ben W. Hooper, the dry candidate of the Republican party. Hooper became the first Republican governor of Tennessee in thirty years.[67]

The ephemeral victories of the White Ribboners over the saloons, like those of the shippers over railroads, independent oilmen over pipelines, policyholders over insurance companies, and righteous amateurs over political bosses, constituted satisfactions of a tangible sort to a considerable class of Southerners. But there were other Southerners, many of them, who were relatively unmoved by these triumphs of the righteous and whose political urges were not fulfilled by progressivism. They had nothing to ship by classified freight rates, no oil wells to protect against pipelines, and no insurance policie to bother about. Perhaps they were also deficient in righteousness, for come Saturday night they wouldn't mind if they had a drink. But they did harbor deep and abiding grievances and powerful, if inarticulate, political urges. Those of them who had sought

---

[66] James B. Sellers, *The Prohibition Movement in Alabama, 1702–1943* (Chapel Hill, 1943), 129–48; Davidson, *Child Labor Legislation in the Southern Textile States*, 224–26.

[67] George A. Gates, "Democratic Insurgency in Tennessee," in *Independent*, LXIX (1910), 866–68; Hamer (ed.), *Tennessee: A History*, II, 704–706.

satisfaction in the independent rebellions and the Populist revolt came away frustrated and cheated. It is doubtful that many of them were later able to identify themselves completely with citified reformers like Comer the manufacturer, and Smith the publisher, nor with Glenn, Campbell, Goebel, and Broward. Jeff Davis they could claim as their very own, and Vardaman and Tillman could speak their idiom. But Tillman, harsh and ascetic as ever, drew away from them, and both he and Vardaman ascended unto Washington and left their flocks untended. In their absence, a new type of shepherd took charge of the fold.

By some obscure rule of succession, Bleases tended to follow Tillmans and Bilbos to succeed Vardamans. The new type of leader could hardly be said to have had a program or a party. Instead, he had prejudices and a following. Abuse by the city press was grist to his mill, and the more he was badgered and set upon by respectable politicians, reforming parsons, and Northern liberals, the more readily and joyfully did a slandered, misunderstood, and frustrated following uphold his cause and identify themselves with the persecuted leader. The leader often flouted sober conventions, sometimes consorted with lewd company, and in numerous ways proclaimed himself one of the boys. Cole Blease, Jeff Davis, and Tom Watson were periodically embroiled with parsons, missionaries, and prohibitionists. But they oftener tilted with foes more vulnerable and farther afield.

In one instance the transition from the old to the new type of leadership was accomplished by a single individual, though at tragic cost to his integrity and mental health. Tom Watson, who in his Populist days had stepped forth alone like a young David to battle the Goliath of his people's foe, spent his latter days rallying villainous mobs to bait and hound minorities. Turning against the progressive Hoke Smith, whom he had helped to elect, he defeated him in 1908 by combining with the reactionary Joseph M. Brown. Meanwhile, he diverted his following with a seven-year crusade against the Pope, forays upon the Socialists, and tirades against his onetime allies of the Negro race that were matchless in their malevolence. For two years he poured forth a flood of obscene and incendiary slander against the Jewish defenders of Leo Frank, who was eventually lynched and brutally mutilated by a mob that drove the Governor from the state. By such devices he recouped his lost political power and for sixteen years virtually bossed the Democratic party of Georgia while acknowledging no loyalty to it.

As an understudy of Tillman, Cole L. Blease imitated the master but improved his technique and expanded his appeal. For Blease embraced within his fold the people the master had described as "the damned factory class," and with them the large depressed rural element that had been entranced by the violence of Tillman's language but disappointed by the mildness of his performance. Agricultural colleges were very nice, but these people, when they were so much as literate, rarely aspired to more than grade school. Not that Blease gave them anything more tangible than Tillman, but he was more lavish with the intangibles—which were better than nothing. In vain his opponents pointed out that Blease had knifed labor bills, opposed child-labor laws, and repeatedly betrayed the classes he professed to love.[68] Those classes cherished him for

[68] Columbia State, September 3, 5, 8, 19, 1910. For an autobiographical sketch, see Cole Blease's mes-

voicing their bitter hatreds and frustrations and for his unabashed defiance of the self-righteous and respectable. They loved him when he humiliated the old state by praising lynchers before the Governors' Conference of 1912 and threatening to "wipe the inferior race from the face of the earth." [69] After two Blease administrations, Tillman had more than he could stand. "It makes me sad and angry," he said in a premature "farewell address" in 1914, "to be told that Tillmanism is the direct cause of Bleaseism," though he admitted that "there is just enough likeness to deceive the ignorant." To defeat Blease and save his own failing political fortunes, Tillman joined hands with his old conservative enemies, the very people he had taught the Bleaseites (and onetime Tillmanites) to hate. Blease's rise was temporarily scotched, but the future of Calhoun's onetime Greek Democracy lay in Cole Blease's hand as surely as it had once lain in Tillman's.[70]

---

sage, in *Reports and Resolutions of the General Assembly of the State of South Carolina, Regular Session Commencing January 12, 1915* (Columbia, 1915), III, 198–205.

[69] Richmond *Times-Dispatch,* December 6, 1912.
[70] Simkins, *Pitchfork Ben Tillman,* 485–503.

Instruments of Wrong*

Loren Miller

The law books don't tell us how the conductor knew that Homer A. Plessy, whose colored blood was not discernible, was violating Louisiana's Jim Crow law by taking a seat in the "white" railroad coach that was running between New Orleans and Covington, Louisiana, on June 7, 1892. All we know is that he ordered Mr. Plessy, who held a first-class ticket, to ride in the "colored" coach and that Mr. Plessy staged a nineteenth-century sit-down. He refused to budge. The conductor summoned police officers, who removed the obstinate passenger and filed a criminal complaint, as required by Louisiana's 1890 statute.

Judge John L. Ferguson was all set to hear the case, but the resourceful Mr. Plessy sought a writ from the state's higher courts—a writ of prohibition, as the lawyers call it. He alleged that Louisiana's segregation law was unconstitutional because it violated the Thirteenth Amendment and in particular because it denied him that equal protection of the laws guaranteed by the Fourteenth Amendment. He asked the higher courts to prohibit Judge Ferguson from holding the trial.

The case of *Plessy v. Ferguson* had been born.[1]

In due season, the Louisiana supreme court upheld the law on the ground that racial classification of citizens was reasonable under the circumstances and decided that a state law ordering racial separation of passengers on a railroad train did not offend the equal-protection clause of the Fourteenth Amendment, as long as equal facilities were provided for both whites and Negroes. The dissatisfied Mr. Plessy then asked the Supreme Court to intervene and save him from Judge Ferguson's judicial wrath. When the Court agreed to examine the issue, the stage was all set for a decision that would shape American race relations for a long time to come and, incidentally, rescue Mr. Plessy and Judge Ferguson from the obscurity that would otherwise have been theirs.

If opponents of Jim Crow laws wanted a Supreme Court decision that would settle the issue of constitutionality of state-imposed racial segregation, they chose the worst possible test case. The Supreme Court that decided the case was composed of six justices

* From Loren Miller, *The Petitioners: The Story of the Supreme Court of the United States and the Negro* (New York: Pantheon Books, 1966), pp. 165–77. Copyright © 1966 by Loren Miller. Reprinted by permission of Pantheon Books, Inc. a Division of Random House, Inc.
[1] *Plessy v. Ferguson,* 163 U.S. 537.

who had served as lawyers for railroads or corporations closely allied with railroads, of Justice Stephen Field who had had a long judicial love affair with the Southern Pacific Railroad and of Justice John M. Harlan. Justice David Brewer, the ninth justice, did not participate in the case. The seven justices who had old ties with railroads were all honorable men, but it is not remarkable that they should entertain some sympathy with public carriers which had troubles enough with state regulation without championing the cause of Negroes who were neither large shippers nor lucrative passengers.

There was also the very practical consideration that railroads could furnish equal accommodations—they could in fact provide identical facilities for whites and Negroes. Added to all that was the circumstance that the Court had come dangerously close to approving Jim Crow laws for railroads in prior decisions. Public carriers had been one of the first targets for Jim Crow laws, probably because they had traditionally provided two classes of service for passengers, and had almost universally assigned Negroes to their second-class facilities. It was easy to graft segregation laws onto the first- and second-class accommodations that were offered. Mr. Plessy's chances of success were not bright.

The Court had been shadowboxing with the issue of separate racial transportation accommodations for almost two decades. In 1877 it had decided *Hall v. De Cuir,*[2] which concerned the validity of an 1869 Louisiana law giving common carriers the power to make rules and regulations regarding passenger service within the state, "provided said rules make no discrimination on account of race or color." Mrs. De Cuir, a Negro woman, tried to buy a first-class ticket on an interstate boat operating between New Orleans and another Louisiana city. Refused first-class accommodations, she bought a second-class ticket and promptly took possession of a first-class cabin set apart for whites. She was ejected, and sued for damages. A Louisiana jury awarded her damages in the sum of $1000, and the Louisiana courts upheld the verdict. The very fact that Louisiana prohibited racial segregation in 1869 by public carrier and required it in 1890 is a thumbnail history of the rise and fall of equalitarian sentiment and of Negro political power in that state, a course matched throughout the South. Equally significant is the circumstance that segregation was accepted as "discrimination" in 1869 and touted as equality under the equal-and-separate doctrine in 1895 by the Louisiana courts.

The Supreme Court, speaking through Chief Justice Waite, reversed Mrs. De Cuir's state court victory, on the narrow ground that the law was a regulation of interstate commerce. "While [the statute] purports only to control the carrier when engaged within the state, it must necessarily influence his conduct to some extent . . . throughout his voyage," the Chief Justice said. "A passenger in the cabin set apart for the use of whites without the states must, when the boat comes within, share the accommodation . . . with" colored passengers. "If," he added, "the public good requires such legislation, it must come from Congress and not from the states."[3]

Mississippi took the opposite tack in 1888 and passed a law requiring railroads

[2] *Hall v. De Cuir,* 95 U.S. 485.
[3] In fact, such legislation had come from Congress. The 1875 Civil Rights Act did forbid discrimination by public carriers.

operating within the state to maintain separate accommodations for white and Negro passengers and to separate such passengers by race. The Louisville, New Orleans and Texas Railway was prosecuted and fined by Mississippi for refusal to obey that section of the law requiring it to provide separate accommodations.[4] Obviously, the legal situation was exactly the same as that presented in Mrs. De Cuir's case as far as interstate commerce was concerned: if the requirement of nonsegregation was a regulation of interstate commerce in her case, the requirement of segregation was also such a regulation in the Mississippi case. Nevertheless, the Court majority, in an opinion written by Justice Harlan dissented: "I am unable to perceive," he said, "how the [Louisiana law] is a regulation of interstate commerce and the [Mississippi law] is not." Justice Bradley agreed with him.

Justice Brewer professed to find the difference in the circumstance that the Mississippi courts had held that its law was applicable only to travel within the state, a distinction without a difference, in lawyers' language. In the course of his opinion, he was at some pains to point out that the issue of whether the use of the required Jim Crow accommodations "is to be a matter of choice or compulsion does not enter into the case. . . . All that we can consider is whether the state has power to require . . . separate accommodations for the two races." The states did have such power, he said. The decision meant that the Court had determined that a state could compel a railroad to maintain Jim Crow accommodations within a state, but that it had ducked the question of whether or not Negro passengers had to use the separate facilities and submit to segregation imposed by law or railroad regulations. Mr. Plessy's case would supply the answer as far as state law was concerned.

As almost any lawyer could have predicted upon a reading of its railroad decisions, the Supreme Court spent little time—and precious little law for that matter—in disposing of Mr. Plessy's complaint. There was a distinct air of impatience in Justice Brown's seven-to-one majority opinion. "A statute," he wrote, "which implies merely a legal distinction between the white and colored races—a distinction which is founded on the color of the races, and which must always exist so long as white men are distinguished from the other race—has no tendency to destroy the legal equality of the two races. . . ." This facile generalization entirely neglected the very obvious truth that Mr. Plessy, whose colored blood was not discernible, was not "distinguished from the other race" by color. More important and ominous, it was a throwback to Chief Justice Taney's dictum that the "unhappy black race were separated from the white by indelible marks."

Justice Brown remarked in passing that he did not "understand that the Thirteenth Amendment was strenuously relied on" and hurried on to a consideration of the Fourteenth Amendment. He agreed that the object of that amendment "was undoubtedly to enforce the absolute equality of the two races before the law," but he was sure that "in the nature of things it could not have been intended to abolish distinction based on color, or to enforce social, as distinguished from political equality, or a com-

[4] *L., N.O. & T. Rwy. v. Mississippi,* 133 U.S. 587.

mingling of the two races upon terms unsatisfactory to either." He added that "Laws permitting, and even requiring separation [of the races] in places where they are liable to be brought into contact do not necessarily imply the inferiority of either race to the other and have been generally, if not universally, recognized as within the competency of the state legislatures in the exercise of their police power." He bolstered that argument with a reference to eight state cases in which separate schools had been approved, the most important of which had been decided *before* the Fourteenth Amendment. Justice Brown was entirely mistaken, or worse, as to the purport and impact of the Fourteenth Amendment; it was entirely clear from debates and history and from prior decisions of the Court itself that the major purpose of that amendment was to abolish all legal distinctions based on race.

Having reduced the Fourteenth Amendment to little more than a pious goodwill resolution, Justice Brown decided that as far as a "conflict with the Fourteenth Amendment is concerned, the case reduces itself to the question of whether the statute of Louisiana is a reasonable regulation and with respect to it . . . the legislature . . . is at liberty to act with reference to the established usages, customs and traditions of the people and with a view to the promotion of their comfort, and the preservation of the public peace and good order." That test was in direct conflict with the Court's own rulings; even in the very limiting decision in the *Civil Rights Cases,* Justice Bradley had been very careful to say that the states could not sanction or support privately imposed discrimination. Congress had also proceeded on a diametrically opposite assumption in every instance from passage of the Civil Rights Act of 1866 to that of 1875. Where the Court had invalidated congressional laws, it had done so only because the legislation prohibited private discrimination not supported or sanctioned by a state. The vice in the Plessy case was the fact that the state had imposed the discrimination.

Finally, Justice Brown pounced on what he said was the fallacy in Mr. Plessy's complaint. "We consider the underlying fallacy of the plaintiff's argument to consist in the assumption that the enforced separation of the two races stamps the colored race with a badge of inferiority. If this be so, it is not by reason of anything found in the Act, but solely because the colored race chooses to put that assumption upon it." What he had said was that if the Negro would cheerfully accept his place, he would not find it degrading. Having advised the Negro to accept his place with equanimity, Justice Brown had a word of advice on the virtues of humility. He warned against the assumption that "social prejudices may be overcome by legislation" and charged Mr. Plessy with seeking an "enforced commingling of the two races." He had no difficulty in demolishing the strawman he had erected: "If the two races are to meet on the terms of social equality, it must be the result of natural affinities, a mutual appreciation of each other's merits, and a voluntary consent of individuals."

Justice Brown finally put the stamp of judicial approval on Professor William Graham Sumner's dogma that law ways cannot change folkways. "Legislation," he intoned, "is powerless to eradicate racial instincts based upon physical differences, and the attempt to do so can only result in accentuating the difficulties of the present situation. If the civil and political rights of both races be equal, one cannot be inferior to the other civilly or politically. If one race be inferior to the other socially, the Constitution of the

United States cannot put them upon the same plane." He had smuggled Social Darwinism into the Constitution and had armed future generations of segregationists with the cherished doctrine that they could protect racial discrimination *through law* while preserving it against change with the fiction that *law* could not function in that sphere of human affairs!

Justice Harlan was as eloquent and lonely—and as correct—in dissent as he had been in the *Civil Rights Cases.* He scorned the rationalization that the equal-and-separate law was passed with any concern for the rights of Negroes. "Everyone knows," he said, "that the statute . . . had its origin and purpose, not to exclude white persons from railroad cars occupied by blacks. . . . The thing to accomplish was, under the guise of equal accommodations for whites and blacks, to compel the latter to keep to themselves while traveling in railroad passenger coaches. No one would be so wanting in candor as to assert the contrary." The effect of the law, he said, was that "it interferes with the personal freedom of citizens." He reminded the Court of the essential purpose of the Civil War Amendments.

"These notable additions to the fundamental law were welcomed by friends of liberty throughout the world," Justice Harlan wrote. "They removed the race line from our governmental system. They had, as this Court has said, a common purpose . . . to secure to [Negroes] 'all the civil rights that the superior race enjoy.' They declared . . . 'that the law in the states shall be the same for the black as for the white; that all persons whether colored or white, shall stand equal before the laws of the states. . . .' " He called the Court's attention to the fact that it had declared that the "words of the Amendment . . . contain a necessary implication of a . . . right to exemption from unfriendly legislation against [Negroes] . . . exemption from legal discriminations, implying their inferiority in civil society. . . ." He could see clearly that in "the view of the Constitution, in the eye of the law, there is in this country no superior, dominant ruling class of citizens. There is no caste here. Our Constituion is colorblind, and neither knows nor tolerates classes among citizens."

Justice Harlan pursued the constitutional doctrine of equality before the law to its relentless conclusion. "The law," he said, "regards man as man, and takes no account of his . . . color when his civil rights as guaranteed by the supreme law of the land are involved. It is therefore to be regretted that this high tribunal, the final expositor of the fundamental law of the land, has reached the conclusion that it is competent for a state to regulate the enjoyment by citizens of their civil rights solely upon the basis of race. In my opinion, the judgment this day rendered will, in time, prove to be quite as pernicious as the decision made by this tribunal in *The Dred Scott Case.* . . ."

He reviewed the Dred Scott case and reminded his judicial brethren that the case had rested upon the proposition of racial inequality and the unbridled right of the white majority to deny Negroes all rights under the Constitution: "The recent amendments, it was supposed, had eradicated these principles from our institutions," he said. But, he said reproachfully, "it seems that we have yet in some of the states a dominant race—a superior class of citizens, which assumes to regulate the enjoyment of civil rights, common to all citizens, upon the basis of race."

Justice Harlan accurately foresaw that the separate-but-equal doctrine would not be confined to railroads, but he could not forecast the lengths to which it would be carried. "Why," he asked with obvious sarcasm, may not the legislature "punish whites and blacks who ride together in street cars . . . ? Why may it not require sheriffs to assign whites to one side of the court room and blacks to the other? And why may it not also prohibit the commingling of the two races in the galleries of legislative halls or in public assemblages convened for consideration of the political questions of the day?" The answer given to these inquiries "at the argument," he said, "was that regulations of the kind they suggest would be unreasonable, and could not, therefore, stand before the law."

Even Justice Harlan could not predict that the time would come when streetcar segregation would be the universal rule in the entire South, to be abandoned only after a sensational Negro boycott in Montgomery, Alabama—first capital of the Confederacy —had pricked the national conscience and prodded another Supreme Court to nullify such laws almost 65 years later.[5] Nor could he foresee that a vice-presidential candidate would be arrested in 1948 for violating a Jim Crow law requiring separation of the races "in public assemblages convened for consideration of the public questions of the day." [6] And it was a melancholy fact that his grandson would be sitting on the Supreme Court when that high tribunal invalidated court rules requiring sheriffs to assign "whites to one side of the court room and blacks to the other." [7]

What Justice Harlan did foresee with uncanny accuracy was that "the present decision . . . will not only stimulate aggressions, more or less brutal and irritating, upon the admitted rights of colored citizens, but will encourage the belief that it is possible, by means of state enactments, to defeat the beneficent purposes which the people . . . had in view when they adopted the recent Amendments of the Constitution. . . . The destinies of the two races in this country are indissolubly linked together, and the interests of both require that the common government of all shall not permit the seeds of race hate to be planted under sanction of law. What can more certainly arouse race hate . . . than state enactments which in fact proceed on the ground that colored citizens are so far inferior and degraded that they cannot be allowed to sit in public coaches occupied by white citizens? That, as all will admit, is the real meaning of such legislation as was enacted in Louisiana. . . ." History would bear out Justice Harlan's prognosis.

He had a final word for those who insisted that segregation statutes would assure racial harmony. The Negro, he said, "objects, and ought never to cease objecting, to the proposition that citizens of the white and black races can be adjudged criminals because they sit, or claim the right to sit, in the same public coach, on a public highway. . . . The thin disguise of 'equal' accommodations for passengers in railroad coaches will not mislead anyone, or atone for the wrong this day done."

But the wrong was done.

[5] *Gayles v. Browder,* 352 U.S. 903.

[6] Senator Glenn Taylor, vice-presidential candidate on the Henry Wallace ticket in 1948, was arrested, convicted, and fined for entering the "Negro entrance" of a Negro church to attend a political meeting!

[7] *Johnson v. Virginia,* 373 U.S. 61

It would be compounded many times over in the flood of Jim Crow statutes that would deluge the South in its wake.[8]

Although the immediate and intended effect of the Plessy decision was that it sanctioned Jim Crow laws, it cut far deeper than that. It grafted a color-caste system onto the amended Constitution, a result achieved by vesting the states, and presumably the national government, with power to classify their citizens and residents on the basis of race. The power to classify in law is exercised in order to differentiate in the treatment of citizens or persons. If a state has the power to classify a group, it can exercise power to pass special legislation affecting that classified group. Minors are classified in distinction to adults in order that the states or the national government may protect them against exploitation through passage of child labor laws and other protective legislation. Women workers are classified apart from other workers in order to validate laws prescribing hours and working conditions for their benefit. These and many other classifications are beneficent in design.

The other side of the coin is that classification may be undertaken to impose disabilities. Thus, persons convicted of crime are put in a special class and denied the right to vote or hold office; persons with communicable diseases are classified so that they may be quarantined or isolated. Southern states asserted the right to classify Negroes on a racial basis—to make them a distinct class—in order to exclude them from accommodations or facilities provided for white citizens. Negro railroad coaches, Negro schools, Negro parks, Negro playgrounds, Negro army units, Negro libraries—the whole paraphernalia of separate institutionalism—could be created and could exist only as long as the governmental unit which ordered them had power to classify persons on a racial basis. In the final analysis, all that a law, or judicial decision or executive order, does when it forbids racial segregation by a state is to deny the state the right to classify persons on a racial basis. Such a law or decision or order compels the state to be "color-blind" and to regard "man as man" in Justice Harlan's searching phrases.

The Court's discovery of constitutional recognition and approval of the color-caste system by the amended Constitution in its Plessy decision extended its dominion over the Negro's exercise of civil rights. As has been pointed out, that dominion was asserted in the *Slaughter House Cases,* with their ruling that there were two classes of citizenship rights—national and state—and that the Court had sole power to determine whether a particular right was dependent on national or state citizenships; in the Cruikshank and Harris cases, which decided that Congress could not legislate to protect Negroes against mob violence in the absence of state sanction; and in the *Civil Rights Cases,* where it was held that Congress could not interdict individual invasion of individual rights and that the Court must determine whether or not state action, sufficient to invoke protection of the Fourteenth Amendment, was involved when a Negro's rights were invaded or denied.

In the jury cases the Court held that arbitrary exclusion of Negroes from grand

[8] Formal Jim Crow laws never kept pace with informal segregation practices. See C. Vann Woodward, *The Strange Career of Jim Crow* (New York: Oxford University Press, 1957).

and trial jury panels by state jury commissioners in violation of the fourth section of the 1875 Civil Rights Act simply gave the Negro a right to challenge his own indictment or conviction, and saddled him with the burden of proving racial discrimination. The Supreme Court was the final arbiter of that claim.

The Negro's right to the exercise of the franchise was also dependent on the Supreme Court's adjudication. In the case where he was excluded from the polling place by a mob or his vote refused by arbitrary action of the election judge in state elections, he would have to prove to the Court's satisfaction that the interference or refusal was undertaken because of his race or color. Moreover, the Court held, Congress lacked power to legislate in his behalf against individual wrongdoing in state elections; it could move only when there was state action to deprive him of the vote because of his race or color. Where the state imposed restrictions on registration and consequent voting through laws that were fair on their face, the Negro would have to satisfy the Court that the law was an evasive attempt at disfranchisement because, the Court said, the Fifteenth Amendment did not confer the franchise but only prohibited discrimination in the exercise of the voting privilege. But, strangely enough, the Court held in the Giles case that it could not, or would not, intervene to protect the Negro against wholesale disfranchisement through an evasive scheme because the right was "political" in nature and its protection dependent on congressional protection. The Court had the final say-so as to when a right was political in the sense in which it used the term.

The Plessy case added another condition of Negro dependency on the Supreme Court. The right to common use of state facilities or public utility accommodations with white persons was denominated a "social right," and not a civil right. What was a "social right"? Only the Court could answer. What was equality within the purview of the separate-but-equal doctrine? Again, only the Court could answer.

This long and necessarily tedious recital may seem only a set of abstractions, but it had a very practical meaning when the everyday life of a white American was contrasted with that of his Negro neighbor, who belonged to the same economic category or social group, in the situation where both were residents of a southern state after the overthrow of Reconstruction governments and rendition of the Supreme Court decisions we have just considered.

With only his color as a touchstone, the white American could enjoy all rights and privileges afforded by federal and state constitutions and laws. It made no difference to him whether the right he wanted to exercise flowed from his national or his state citizenship. If it arose out of national citizenship, the federal government would protect him; if it came from state citizenship, the state would shield him.

With his color as a badge, the Negro faced all manner of difficulties. Assaulted and beaten by a Klan mob intent on keeping him in his place, he might seek redress through laws passed by Congress to put down Klan violence; if so, he would ultimately be told by the Supreme Court that the laws on which he depended were void, because the right he claimed was not an attribute of his national citizenship, but of his state citizenship. He would also be told that the Fourteenth Amendment did not empower Congress to protect rights flowing from state citizenship and that he must turn to his state for protection. In practice, the hostile state would not protect him; 231 Negroes were lynched in 1892—the yearly average between 1882 and 1901 was 150. Congress could do nothing under the Supreme Court ruling. The Negro would have to bow to the mob's dictates.

If the white American was charged with an act of aggression against his Negro neighbor, his case would be referred to a grand jury, more often than not composed of white citizens, from which all Negroes had been excluded in plain violation of the Civil Rights Act of 1875. The probabilities of indictment were slim, but if by some fortuitous circumstance an indictment was preferred, trial would be set before an all-white trial jury, also selected in violation of the Civil Rights Act. Conviction was improbable.

If the Negro was charged with an aggression against his white neighbor, that same all-white grand jury would be quick to indict and the all-white trial jury as quick to convict. True enough, the Negro could contest the issue of Negro exclusion from those juries and get the indictment thrown out or his almost certain conviction reversed, if he could prove that Negroes had been excluded from the juries on the basis of race and color. Proof was difficult indeed in hostile state trial and appeals courts. If the Negro persisted all the way to the Supreme Court of the United States, he would certainly get a resounding opinion inveighing against the evil of jury discrimination, but all too often he would learn that his proof of discrimination was not particular enough or that errors in procedure foreclosed relief in his case. Meanwhile, all-white juries chosen in violation of federal law would settle disputes on contracts or land boundaries or issues of debt that arose between the white American and his Negro neighbor. "The law belongs to the white man," the Negro would say with bitterness—and with truth.

When election rolled around and it was time to select state lawmakers, the judges, and sheriffs, and jury commissioners, the white American could vote without let or hindrance.

Barred from the polls by a mob or cheated out of his vote by the refusal of the election judge to receive or count his ballot, the Negro who appealed to the Supreme Court would learn that the Fifteenth Amendment had not conferred the right to vote on him but that it was only designed to protect him against racial discrimination in the casting or counting of his ballot. He would have to prove more than that the mob had barred him from the polling place or that the corrupt judge had refused to accept or count his ballot in state elections; he would have to *prove* that the wrong done him had been done because of his race or color.

The white American had easy and open access to hotels, inns, restaurants, and other places of public accommodation.

His Negro neighbor, assured the same right by the Civil Rights Act of 1875, would be told by the Supreme Court that the act was void and that he must suffer discrimination and exclusion—unless his state assured that right. The Fourteenth Amendment, the Court would say, did not empower Congress to proscribe individual invasion of individual rights, although it did prohibit state sanction or support of racial discrimination through legislative, executive, or judicial action. The white American did not need to be concerned about state action in furtherance of racial discrimination against him. There would be none. On the other hand, his Negro neighbor would have to engage in long, expensive, and tedious litigation in an effort to discover and prove that state action had been exerted against him, if he hoped to enjoy the protection of the Fourteenth Amendment in his attempt to use places of public accommodation. If the state stood aside and did nothing except let popular prejudices take their toll, the white man would continue to have easy and open access to hotels, inns, and restaurants. The Negro would be barred, branded as a pariah, solely because of his race.

The Plessy case validated segregation in schools, where it had existed even prior to the decision. And always the question would occur, what was equality? Ordinarily— almost always—the answer would be that equality consisted of the use of whatever accommodations were provided for the voteless by those who controlled the lawmaking power. Sometimes it meant a one-room, one-teacher school for the Negro's children, contrasted to a graded school for his white neighbor's children; sometimes it meant a park for the white American and the mere promise of a future park for his Negro neighbor. At other times it meant barring the Negro from swimming in the ocean, if only one beach was available. The Negro had his remedy in law—a hazardous and expensive suit to compel the state to provide a facility equal to that provided without question for his white neighbor. These disabilities, by fiat of the Supreme Court, satisfied that equal protection of the law guaranteed by the Fourteenth Amendment.

The short of the matter was that a white American, by the circumstance of color, could and did exercise the common garden variety of personal rights without question and without—indeed, with no thought of—resort to law. His Negro neighbor, citizen of the United States and of the state wherein he resided, was required to pay his way through the courts, often to the highest court in the land to beg the same boon.

The Uses of Adversity*

Louis R. Harlan

Introduction of the Northeastern public school into the South was an important war aim of the North in the Civil War and found its place in the postwar Reconstruction program. The public school was to have a dual purpose—to stand *in loco parentis* for the freed Negro and to act as an entering wedge of the New Order, a means of bringing the conquered white people into ideological harmony with the victors. At the end of the tragic internecine conflict, the humanitarians sought to justify the breakdown of democracy and the resort to violence by a radical reconstruction of Southern society on the ruins of the slave-plantation economy. At the same time, during the war and the Reconstruction period, men moved by considerations of political and economic power were interested in harnessing the Industrial Revolution to reward their section and themselves. The Schoolma'am and the Carpetbagger rode into the South together, Yankees both, one to uplift, the other to exploit. Though the Carpetbagger often spoke of developing the country, he was primarily concerned with the opportunities available in a colonial area. The Northern teacher in the South, on the other hand, modeled her program after that of the Massachusetts town public school, which had developed in an area of high population density and expanding industry. The Schoolma'am's ideal, though not impossible, was difficult of attainment in the South.

It was clear by 1900, thirty years after the state school systems were created in the South, that the Massachusetts school existed nowhere in the region, except for white children in a handful of cities. Not even the American school system, a Southern Negro teacher told a federal investigating commission in 1901, existed in his county. "What is the American school system?" he asked. "When you have no schoolhouse, and when you have no teacher, why call it a school system? If you must take a little old, tumble-down log hut, with no desks or blackboard or map or text-books, except a blue-back speller here and there, and the man who teaches can hardly count his cotton weights, and school only lasts three months a year, can you say that is an American school system? Even if exceptions for the better exist, this condition of things bears as heavily on

* From Louis R. Harlan, *Separate and Unequal* (Chapel Hill: The University of North Carolina Press, 1958), pp. 3–19, 27, 39–44. Reprinted by permission.

the poor whites as on the negro. We live in a land of one-room cabins, mere crop-mort-gaged cotton peasants." [1] This condition certainly did not bear as heavily on whites as on Negroes, but only that equivocation before a white gathering mars the candor of the description. Such a school had little relation to "the American system." By 1900 the Southern public school had proved a hardy perennial, surviving as a democratic institution in such incongruous places as poverty-stricken rural areas of states ruled by oligarchies. Anchored in the sod, in the needs and aspirations of common white and Negro, it was stunted and starved.

Though there were Southern schools before the Civil War, some supported by local taxation or by state Literary Funds, universal education was not accepted as a state obligation through state taxation until the Reconstruction era. [2] The Southern states led in the establishment of state universities, but on the eve of the war there was about one elementary school per forty square miles in South Carolina, and Draconic laws forbade the education of Southern Negroes. The typical ante-bellum educational institution was the pauper school, rather than the common or free school, and illiteracy was symbolic of an ethical failure of the Old Order, as it was in the same period a cardinal indictment of English aristocratic rule.

Southern state-supported common schools, then, were revolutionary institutions, cut by aliens from the alien pattern of New England education. In framing new school laws, Carpetbaggers were assisted by emancipated Negroes and, in Virginia and Georgia at least, by native whites. Between 1868 and 1870 the new plans were developed on paper in constitutional conventions and legislatures from Virginia to Georgia, as elsewhere in the South. Provision for Negro education in this region antedated that in some border states: Delaware, for instance, limited public schooling to whites until 1875. The schools themselves materialized more slowly, under special handicaps. In Georgia, for example, corrupt legislators diverted school funds into improper channels. Local resentment of the new institutions by some whites was aggravated by the bankruptcy which followed the Confederate collapse. Co-education of Negroes and whites does not seem to have been a major focus of the hostility of native whites; segregation was legalized in Virginia and Georgia from the start and was practiced in the other states.

Though the schools themselves were poorly maintained at the end of Reconstruction, the public school idea was successful in the long view. It was more than a mere fad among freedmen. The state system of public education in the "conquered terri-

---

[1] Rev. Pitt Dillingham, principal of Calhoun Colored School, Lowndes County, Alabama, in *Report of the Industrial Commission* (19 vols., Washington, 1900–02), X, 164–65. Though his school was outside of the Southern seaboard, his description fits the rural schools of that region.

[2] Edgar W. Knight (ed.), *A Documentary History of Education in the South Before 1860* (5 vols., Chapel Hill, 1949–53), contains abundant evidence of ante-bellum schools. *Idem,* "Education in the South," letter to the editor, in *Nation,* C (March 18, 1915), 304, and rejoinder by Samuel J. Fisher in *ibid.,* C (June 17, 1915), 682–83, are early evidence of sectional debate on the history of Southern education. Fletcher H. Swift, *A History of Public Permanent Common School Funds in the United States, 1795–1905* (New York, 1911), is a useful reference on its subject.

tories" ranks as one of the few constructive and permanently popular achievements of Radical Reconstruction.[3] Native white Redeemers who restored Home Rule in the South, politically if not economically, in the mid-seventies usually promised to retain the public schools. "Free men! Free ballots!! Free Schools!!!" was the title of a Wade Hampton pamphlet in 1876 in the campaign by which South Carolina's oligarchy returned to power. Such exclamations indicate, if they do not measure, a phase of reconstruction which had gone beyond sudden counter-revolution.

Attitudes in the dominant Northeast were also changing. In the Gilded Age educational philanthropy for the freedmen waned as industrial corporations expanded. With rare exceptions the humanitarian Radicals retreated from the South along with the political agencies of Reconstruction, and many of them also retreated from their earlier philanthropic position into a mood of cynicism. Considerations of power gained ascendancy over considerations of reform. Black Reconstruction had failed. Its economic measures were not sufficiently radical to give the freedmen land on which to defend their freedom, in an agrarian society in which land was the basis of security. Its educational measures were not so much too little as too brief. The wards of the nation, left to shift for themselves, were especially vulnerable, for it was as true as in Jefferson's day that to expect men to be ignorant and free in a state of civilization was to expect what never was and never would be.

There was a final effort at national responsibility in the eighties. Amid the ruminations of the Great Barbecue was heard the voice of Senator Henry W. Blair of New Hampshire urging the passage of his bill for federal aid to states for public common schools in amounts proportionate to the extent of illiteracy. This bill circumvented most of the objections raised against the earlier Hoar bill of 1870 and would disburse the embarrassing surplus built up by high-tariff collections. Southern opinion, though divided, was predominantly in favor of the bill, and it aroused enthusiasm among educators. But the Northern press, led by the New York *Evening Post* and the *Nation,* set upon Blair and his bill like snarling dogs. The Senator was a "crank." His "Humbug Bill" was "quixotic," "preposterous," and a "nuisance." Republicans and Alliancemen, for different reasons, opposed the measure, nor was Grover Cleveland's celebrated courage enlisted in its behalf.[4] The bill passed the Senate three times, each time failing in

[3] This view is strongly presented in W. E. Burghardt Du Bois, "Reconstruction and Its Benefits," in *American Historical Review,* XV (July, 1910), 781–99; and *idem, Black Reconstruction* (New York, 1935). Dissenting views are expressed by Henry L. Swint, *The Northern Teacher in the South, 1862–1870* (Nashville, 1941), and E. Merton Coulter, *The South During Reconstruction,* Vol. VIII of *A History of the South* (Baton Rouge, 1947), pp. 70–91, 315–30. A balance in favor of this phase of Reconstruction is struck by recent research, John and La Wanda Cox, "General O. O. Howard and the 'Misrepresented Bureau'," in *Journal of Southern History,* XIX (November, 1953), 427–56; George R. Bentley, *A History of the Freedmen's Bureau* (Philadelphia, 1955); Henderson H. Donald, *The Negro Freedman* (New York, 1952), pp. 93–109.

[4] Gordon C. Lee, *The Struggle for Federal Aid, First Phase: A History of the Attempts to Obtain Federal Aid for the Common Schools 1870–1890:* Teachers College, Columbia University, Contributions to Education, No. 957 (New York, 1949), fills the need for a careful monograph on the history of efforts for federal aid to public schools, and carefully reviews the public debate. Quotations are from Rayford W. Logan, *The Negro in Ameri-*

the House, until finally the Senate defeat of 1890 ended the movement. Southern whites and Negroes, their hopes dashed, blamed the failure on New England votes. Gordon C. Lee has concluded that "with a Godkin favoring the bill the results might have been quite different." Equally significant, as Lee notes, is the fact that Edwin L. Godkin of the *Evening Post* and the *Nation,* plumed knight of nineteenth-century liberalism, did oppose the bill.[5]

The residue of Northern interest in Southern education was some philanthropic foundations, notably the Peabody Education Fund for both races and the Slater Fund for Negroes, and a number of missionary organizations of diminished membership and scope of activity. "Ministering now and then, in obscure localities, to individuals and families, brings no permanent relief to the race," observed J. L. M. Curry on the basis of wide experience. Society could not be essentially "improved by tinkering at it in spots; and no uplift that amounts to anything" could be secured "except through the class, as a whole, that requires it." [6] The Peabody and Slater Funds appropriated money for Negro education only to schools which conformed to Southern white insistence on "industrial education" for the subject race. The missionary associations stood more firmly for Negro human rights. The curriculum in both industrial schools and missionary colleges was "antediluvian," as Myrdal has pointed out. The colleges, however, did maintain the ideal of aspiration, a *sine qua non* for the development of Negro leadership.[7]

In the Redeemed South, meanwhile, upper-class oligarchies honored the letter of their pledges to retain the state school systems, though freely expressing doubt and disinclination. The whites never quite brought themselves to complete repudiation of democracy or the destruction of Negro schools. Negroes never quite renounced citizen-

---

can Life and Thought: The Nadir 1877–1901 (New York, 1954), pp. 192–93. For an account based on the Jabez L. M. Curry Papers, see Merle Curti, *Social Ideas of American Educators* (New York, 1935), pp. 270–73. A sample of New-South opinion is Robert Bingham, *The New South: An Address in the Interest of National Aid to Education Delivered February 15, 1884* . . . (2nd ed., n.p., 1899); on Northern opinion, see [Carl Schurz], "National Aid to Common Schools," editorial in *Nation,* XXXVI (February 1, 1883), 96, and also editorials in *ibid.,* XLII (January 21, 1886), 51–52, XLII (February 18, 1886), 142–43, XLII (March 4, 1886), 184, XLVI (January 5, 1888), 5–6. Southern views are treated in detail in Allen J. Going, "The South and the Blair Education Bill," in *Mississippi Valley Historical Review,* XLIV (September, 1957), 267–90.

[5] Lee, *The Struggle for Federal Aid, First Phase,* p. 139. See Amory D. Mayo, *The Government of the South by the Plain People* . . . (Berea, Kentucky, 1905?), for a jeremiad against New England by a persistent humanitarian; in *Proceedings of the Department of Superintendence of the National Educational Association at Its Meeting in Washington, February 14–16, 1888:* Bureau of Education, Circular of Information No. 6, 1888 (Washington, 1888), pp. 146–65, cf. addresses by Superintendents Alexander Hogg of Fort Worth, Texas, and J. A. B. Lovett of Huntsville, Alabama, with that by Superintendent A. P. Marble of Worcester, Massachusetts. In fairness to Godkin and some Southern opponents, their opposition to the Blair bill stemmed from opposition to the protective tariff.

[6] Curry's report as agent and chairman of education committee, in *Proceedings of the Trustees of the John F. Slater Fund for the Education of Freedmen,* 1897 (Baltimore, 1897), p. 11.

[7] Gunnar Myrdal and assistants, *An American Dilemma: The Negro Problem and Modern Democracy* (2 vols., New York and London, 1944), II, 906; August Meier, "The Vogue of Industrial Education," in *Midwest Journal,* VII (Fall, 1955), 241–66.

ship and equality of rights. And the Negro schools occupied the zone between, being kept deliberately poor but not destroyed. All of the Southern schools, like the economy of the New South, remained in an unwholesome condition.[8]

Negro children were generally segregated during Reconstruction, and laws requiring the practice were passed as soon as native whites controlled the state governments. Besides the inequality inherent in the segregation of a lower-caste minority, there was also a widening discrepancy in financial support between Negro and white schools administered by whites. White schools were so poorly maintained that this gap was not as wide as it later became. The landlord and creditor cared little for the schools of the masses, regardless of race. The fact that the Negro schools were not completely abandoned may be explained by the Fifteenth Amendment, under which Negroes retained a potential suffrage, and by white fear of illiteracy among freedmen.[9] Though the schools of neglected men survived, they too were neglected by the conservative regimes of the seventies and eighties. Most of the school funds were county funds. The states did furnish some money from licenses and convict lease, for "the southern Bourbon Democrats saw no incongruity in taking convict blood money and earmarking it for public education." [10] In the nineties white small farmers who gained control of Southern seaboard state governments increased expenditures and built new schools, mostly for whites. In 1900 the schools were little better than in their infancy in the seventies, and in some ways they were worse.

There are limits to what statistics will reveal; the federal reports on education were based on inaccurate reports from the states. But the contrast is clear between Southern and other American school systems. The average term in the Southern seaboard was less than 100 days, about half that of New England.[11] Even for these short terms, only three-fifths of the children in the Southern seaboard were enrolled, and less than three-fifths of those enrolled were included in average daily attendance. Thus barely over one-third of the children of school age in these states were normally in

[8] Charles W. Dabney, *Universal Education in the South* (2 vols., Chapel Hill, 1936), I, 162–63; Edgar W. Knight, *Public Education in the South* (Boston, 1922), pp. 415–23. See the disenchanted view of George Washington Cable, "Education for the Common People of the South," *Cosmopolitan*, XIV (November, 1892), 65, quoted in Philip Butcher, "George W. Cable and Negro Education," in *Journal of Negro History*, XXXIV (April, 1949), 128; Arlin Turner, *George W. Cable: A Biography* (Durham, 1956), pp. 194–226.

[9] W. E. Burghardt Du Bois, *The Negro Common School:* Atlanta University Publications, No. 6 (Atlanta, 1901), p. 38.

[10] Fletcher M. Green, "Some Aspects of the Convict Lease System in the Southern States," in Green (ed.), *Essays in Southern History Presented to Joseph Gregoire de Roulhac Hamilton. . . :* The James Sprunt Studies in History and Political Science, XXXI (Chapel Hill, 1949), 122; Sidney M. Finger, in *North Carolina School Report, 1886–1888*, p. xxiv.

[11] The schools of Virginia were open in 1900 only 119 days, in Georgia 112 days, in South Carolina 88.4 days, and in North Carolina only 70.8 days out of 365, while in the North Atlantic states the school term was 177.1 and in Massachusetts 189 days. *Report of the Commissioner of Education for the Year 1899–1900* (2 vols., Washington, 1901), I, lxix. The Virginia figure is for the year 1898–99. Some state reports give different estimates of the school terms. The federal commissioner's method of determining length of term, however, as explained in his report for 1900, I, lxx-lxxi, seems the most accurate of several customary methods.

school.[12] The average North Carolina child attended school 21.9 days a year, or one-fifth as long as the Massachusetts child.[13]

In school finance the contrast was equally striking. The average daily expenditure per pupil in attendance in 1900 ranged from 8.2 cents in Virginia to 5 cents in South Carolina, while it was 20 cents in Massachusetts. The difference in school terms made annual expenditures more divergent, ranging in the Southern seaboard from $9.70 in Virginia to $4.34 in North Carolina, whereas the national average was $20.29 and the Massachusetts total was $37.76 per pupil. On a basis of school population regional discrepancies were wider yet. For each child of school age in South Carolina $1.80 was expended, and in North Carolina $1.65; the amount in Massachusetts was $21.55, over twelve times as large.[14]

There was far less to attract young Southerners to schools. The value of school property for every child of school age ranged from $5.33 in Virginia to $1.64 in North Carolina. In the nation as a whole it was $24.20 and in Massachusetts $60.92. Children of the Northern state were given nearly forty times better facilities than young North Carolinians. Of course the Southerners had the advantage of a milder winter—small comfort for broken panes or drafts through the cracks of a rough-hewn schoolhouse.[15]

Salaries of teachers in the Southern seaboard were also lower. As nearly as they can be computed, the average annual salary was $168.19 in Virginia, $82.87 in North Carolina. Such salaries hardly compared with the $566.09 average in Massachusetts, and the agricultural state of Kansas paid its teachers $236.26 a year.[16]

By any quantitative measurement, Southern seaboard schools were unlike non-Southern schools. They were not faithful replicas, even in miniature, of the Massachusetts pattern. Southern school facilities in fact represented one of the extremes of which the mean was a misleading national average. In view of their educational facilities, it is not surprising that in the four Southern seaboard states there were 1,517,450 illiterates ten years of age or over in 1900, of whom more than one-fourth were native whites.

[12] Over a million children of school age were not enrolled, and another half-million were absent on the average day. *Report of the Commissioner of Education, 1900,* I, lxvi–lxviii.

[13] *Ibid.,* I, lxix. The Massachusetts figure was 107.4 days per school-age child. "The teachers of public schools always make out averages above the actual," reported J. G. Fulton, Goodwill, Forsyth County, North Carolina, in *Tenth Annual Report of the North Carolina Bureau of Labor Statistics, 1896* (Winston, 1897), p. 193.

[14] *Report of the Commissioner of Education, 1900,* I, lxiii, lxviii, lxxvii, lxxix; *North Carolina School Report, 1898–1900,* pp. 154–56.

[15] *Report of the Commissioner of Education, 1900,* I, lxiii, lxxiii.

[16] The yearly salary was $122.98 in Georgia, $122.28 in South Carolina. *Georgia School Report, 1900,* pp. 32–33; *South Carolina School Report, 1899,* pp. 77, 117; *Report of the Commissioner of Education, 1900,* I, lxix, lxxii, lxxiii. South Carolina and Virginia figures are for the school year 1898–99. For convenience, titles of state school reports will be cited in shortened form as above, with appropriate calendar or school years. Figures above were computed by multiplying average monthly salary of male teachers by the number of male teachers, and the same for female teachers, adding these totals, then dividing by the total number of teachers, and multiplying by the number of months of the school term, the latter being on the basis of twenty days in each school month. The contrast with Northern states is more striking when it is considered that 42 per cent of the teachers in the Southern seaboard were men and therefore more often heads of families, whereas only 9 per cent in Massachusetts and 33 per cent in Kansas were men.

With less than one-tenth of the nation's population, these states were burdened with over one-fourth of the nation's illiterates.[17] A less formal measure, the number of library books, shows a similar disparity. Virginia had 20 books for every hundred inhabitants, North Carolina 13. It is true that Kansas, Nebraska, and the Dakotas were even more bookless, but rural Maine had 81 books and Massachusetts 204 for every 100 people.[18]

Besides these regional discrepancies which set Southern schools apart from the rest of the country, there were gaps within the region between the educational offerings of one school and another. An institutional fault line separated the Negro school from the white school in the same community. In South Carolina in 1915 the average white child of school age received twelve times as much from the school fund as the average Negro child.[19] Moreover, each community by maintaining two schools made districts too large, except in urban areas, and schools too small. A second discrepancy which baffled educational reformers was that between rural and urban areas.[20] Cities and small towns raised walls about their taxable property and maintained good schools, while rural children struggled along in one-room schools with rudimentary equipment. Rural Negroes under the dual system suffered not merely a double, but a compound handicap. And nearly all Negroes were rural.

By its sanction of "separate but equal" facilities for whites and Negroes in the *Plessy v. Ferguson* case in 1895, the federal Supreme Court not only recognized a Southern *fait accompli* as to separation, but also ignored the real condition of inequality of facilities.[21] The over-all extent of racial inequality in education can only be estimated, for the pertinent statistics are incomplete and inaccurate. The federal commissioner's guess in 1900 was that in sixteen former slave states and the District of Columbia the average Negro child received half as much school money as the average white child, that Negroes, with 32.8 per cent of the school population, received about 20 per cent of the school funds.[22] This proportion was only an estimate, and seems to be too high. By the

[17] United States Census Office, *Abstract of the Twelfth Census of the United States, 1900* (Washington, 1902), pp. 74–75. Illiteracy in South Carolina was 35.9 per cent, a proportion greater than in Hawaii and topped only by Louisiana. North Carolina had a larger proportion of white illiterates, 19.4 per cent, than any other state except New Mexico. In South Carolina and Georgia a majority of Negroes ten or over were illiterate, and for the four states 49.9 per cent were illiterate.

[18] *Report of the Commissioner of Education, 1900*, I, 944.

[19] See below, Chapter VI. On enrollment rather than school population, the discrimination was eight to one. *South Carolina School Report, 1915*, p. 20.

[20] The city of Richmond, for example, expended $29.98 per child of school age in 1914–15, and had $89.07 in school property per child, while rural Prince Edward County, Virginia, expended $9.22 per child and had $11.25 in school property per child, and mountainous Bland County, Virginia, expended $7.27 and had $8.44 in school property per child. *Virginia School Report, 1914–1916*, pp. 217, 233, 239, 258, 269, 275, 340, 353, 359. The balance at the end of the year has been subtracted from the figures for expenditures.

[21] The legal implications and effects of this decision are ably discussed in Harry E. Groves, "Separate But Equal—The Doctrine of *Plessy v. Ferguson*," in *Phylon*, XII (First Quarter, 1951), 66–72.

[22] *Report of the Commissioner of Education, 1900*, II, 2501. The estimate was based on records of North Carolina, Kentucky, Florida, Maryland, and the District of Columbia. These were not all typical Southern states.

commissioner's records for 1899–1900 in his next report, Negroes in North Carolina received 28.3 per cent of the school funds for 34.7 per cent of the school population. But
federal records for South Carolina indicate that Negroes, who were 61.0 per cent of the
school population, received only 22.6 per cent of the school fund.[23] And the South Carolina state report shows Negroes getting only 20.8 per cent, or barely one-sixth as much
per child.[24] In Georgia the average Negro child received at most one-fourth as much as
the average white child,[25] and in Virginia about one-third as much.[26]

Negro children suffered other disadvantages also. Terms were shorter, by as
much as thirty days in South Carolina. Negro attendance was less by about 40 per cent,
with about one-fourth of the Negro children attending. Their schools were fewer and
therefore more distant, an important factor in a rural region with poor roads and
bridges. There were fewer teachers in small schools. In Georgia there were 110 Negro
children per school and 108 per teacher, while the average white school had 68 and the
white teacher only 61. The average Georgia Negro teacher's salary was $95.83 a year,
about half that of whites; in North Carolina white teachers received less than $100 a
year, but Negro women only $64.42 a year.[27] Negro public school property in Georgia
amounted to $23.79 per school, less than 25 cents per Negro child, less than one-fifth as
much as for white children. In Virginia in 1908 there were seats for 50 per cent of
Negro children and for 83 per cent of white children.[28] Negro schools were open about
four months in the year.

Considerable evidence supports the charge of W. E. B. Du Bois that "enforced
ignorance" was "one of the inevitable expedients for fastening serfdom on the country
Negro." By "determined effort," he declared in 1907, Negro schools had been made less
efficient than twenty years earlier; "the nominal term is longer and the enrolment
larger, but the salaries are so small that only the poorest local talent can teach. There is
little supervision, there are few appliances, few schoolhouses and no inspiration." [29]

[23] *Reports of the Commissioner of Education, 1900,* II, 2503; *1901,* I, xcix–c. There was no accounting of
school funds for Negroes in Virginia and Georgia.
[24] *South Carolina School Report, 1900,* p. 253. According to the federal commissioner's estimate of Negro
school population in South Carolina, Negro children of school age in South Carolina received 55.13 cents
each, one-seventeenth of the national average, and one-thirty-ninth of the Massachusetts average.
[25] Georgia's Negro children, who were 44.32 per cent of the school-age population in 1899, received
21.55 per cent of payments to teachers. Since these payments were about 90 per cent of the school fund, and
Negroes certainly received less supervision and far less for school buildings and equipment, the estimate
above seems conservative. Du Bois, *The Negro Common School,* pp. 68–69.
[26] By the same measure as in Georgia, Virginia Negroes in 1899 were about 42 per cent of the school
population; their teachers received 21.16 per cent of salary payments, which represented about 90 per cent of
total school expenditure. *Ibid.,* p. 52; *Report of the Commissioner of Education, 1900,* II, 2503.
[27] *North Carolina School Report, 1898–1900,* pp. 155–56; Du Bois, *The Negro Common School,* pp. 68–69;
United States Census Office, *Abstract of the Twelfth Census of the United States, 1900,* p. 73; *Report of the Commissioner of Education, 1900,* I, lxiii, lxxii; Frank A. De Costa, "The Relative Enrollment of Negroes in the Common Schools in the United States," in *Journal of Negro Education,* XII (Summer, 1953), 420–22. Figures above
are computed on the basis of population of school age. Only 25.6 per cent of the Negro children of Georgia
and 25.2 per cent of those in South Carolina attended school daily.
[28] Du Bois, *The Negro Common School,* pp. 68–69; *Virginia School Report, 1907–1909,* pp. 152, 258.
[29] Du Bois, "The Economic Revolution," in Du Bois and Booker T. Washington, *The Negro in the*

Though Negro schools in Southern cities were generally better off because of their proximity to white wealth, some were like those of Augusta, whose superintendent reported in 1904 that 2,100 pupils of the 6,500 in the Negro school population were accommodated only by having two sessions a day in the lower grades, giving the teacher as many as 100 pupils to teach in the two sessions.[30] Jabez L. M. Curry, the elderly agent of the Peabody Fund and the John F. Slater Fund, found the Negro occupying "an incongruous position in our country," and all of the work in the Negro's behalf seemed hedged about with "discouragements and difficulties," "complications and limitations." [31]

Southerners never knew quite what to expect of federal investigations, nor quite what to say on the Negro question. Most witnesses before the Industrial Commission in 1901 swore that school funds were distributed "equally per capita, absolutely." Harry Hammond, cotton grower of Beach Island, South Carolina, was more frank:

"Q. Is that distribution fairly equitable?"

"A. I suppose it is; the money does the most good in the white schools. The wording of the law is that it shall be distributed according to the best uses that can be made of it." [32]

The differences between white and Negro schools continued to widen. In 1900 the South Carolina Negro child received about one-sixth as much as the white child for education. By 1915 the disparity had doubled and the Negro child received only one-twelfth as much. The system of segregation, far from being a burden, was a convenient means of economizing at the expense of Negro children.[33]

The schools of the Reconstruction period were largely in the towns, and as the urban schools advanced, a differential grew between them and rural schools. Yet the Southern people were overwhelmingly rural. "The thought of the North is of cities.

South: His Economic Progress in Relation to His Moral and Religious Development, Being the William Levi Bull Lectures for the Year 1907 (Philadelphia, 1907), pp. 102–03.

[30] Thomas Jesse Jones and associates, *Negro Education: A Study of the Private and Higher Schools for Colored People in the United States:* United States Bureau of Education, Bulletins, 1916, Nos. 38 and 39 (2 vols., Washington, 1917), I, 32.

[31] Jabez L. M. Curry, *Difficulties, Complications, and Limitations Connected with the Education of the Negro:* The Trustees of the John F. Slater Fund, Occasional Papers, No. 5 (Baltimore, 1895), 14–15, 20.

[32] Testimony in *Report of the Industrial Commission*, X, 826. Cf. Governor Allen D. Candler of Georgia in *ibid.*, VIII, 537.

[33] In 1915 Negro children represented 61.02 per cent of the school population and received 11.24 per cent of the school fund. This estimate is computed from *South Carolina School Report, 1915*, p. 310; *Report of the Commissioner of Education, 1917* (2 vols., Washington, 1917), II, 17, estimating school population in 1915. Valuable studies of racial inequalities of school opportunity in this period include Du Bois, *The Negro Common School*; Du Bois and Augustus G. Dill (eds.), *The Common School and the Negro American:* Atlanta University Publications, No. 16 (Atlanta, 1911); Charles L. Coon, "Public Taxation and Negro Schools," in *Twelfth Conference for Education in the South, Proceedings* (Atlanta, 1909), pp. 157–67. Indispensable to the study of the general problem are two works by Horace M. Bond, *Social and Economic Influences on the Public Education of Negroes in Alabama 1865–1930* (Washington, 1939), which also appeared under the title: *Negro Education in Alabama: A Study in Cotton and Steel*; and *The Education of the Negro in the American Social Order* (New York, 1934).

Ought it to be the same in the South?" asked George S. Dickerman in 1901. Crowded communities anywhere might copy the Massachusetts schools, but would they fit a people whose cabins and country homes were a mile apart? "New England has not yet answered in her own domain the question of education for her rural people. But in the South this is the main question. . . . The neglected few in Massachusetts or Maine multiply into millions." [34] And it was in the country districts that both the financial and social costs of the dual school system were heaviest. In the cities Negro and white school districts were coterminous with areas of residential segregation, whereas in rural areas children of the two races were scattered out side by side. "Usually we separate the races in our thought and discussion," Dickerman noticed. "It is not so easy to separate them actually."

In Virginia, which seems fairly typical of the Southern seaboard states in the matter of urban-rural disparity, there were nineteen independent city school systems, which in 1907–08 expended for education over twice as much per child as the rural schools, and had four times as much school property per child. Three-fourths of city school buildings and only one-fiftieth of rural school buildings were of brick; all of the 596 log schools were in rural districts. There was a school library book for every third white city child, one for every six white rural children, with few for any Negroes anywhere. Richmond, which may be compared with Charleston or Atlanta in other seaboard states, expended $14.19 per child of school age, nearly three times as much as in rural schools. It had about one-seventh of the state's school property, over five times as much in value per child as in rural areas. There was a book for almost every white child in the Richmond school libraries. [35]

Pitifully meager as it was, "the State 'average,' and even the County 'average,' charitably covers, as with a blanket, the nakedness of the backwoods country schools." [36] This was true of all of them, though not equally so. Within the rural areas the schools were operated at different levels. Weak support of Negro schools gave rise to a difference between white schools. School money derived from state taxation flowed from the state capitals to the counties in proportions based upon total enrollment, and, *mirabile dictu,* without regard to race or color. The "black counties," usually located on the coastal plain or lower Piedmont of each state and having a large Negro proportion of population, received money from the state for Negro children, gave Negro schools the usual pittance, and used the considerable remainder for the support of white schools. In "white counties," usually in the mountains and upper Piedmont and having few if any Negroes, school authorities received a negligible sum for Negro children, gave Negroes usually even less for their scattered little schools, but even so had but an infinitesimal residue to apply to white schools. The motive, method, and procedure were the same in white and black counties, but the results were not at all similar.

[34] George S. Dickerman, "The South Compared with the North in Educational Requirements," in *Fourth Conference for Education in the South, Proceedings* (Winston-Salem, North Carolina, 1901), pp. 15–16.

[35] Computed from *Virginia School Report, 1907–1909,* pp. 113, 152, 218, 244, 258.

[36] *South Carolina School Report, 1902,* p. 13.

There were variations of this practice in the several states, but only minor ones. An example from each state will perhaps illuminate the pattern. In five Virginia black counties in 1907–08, Negro children were 69.83 per cent of the school population, but salaries of Negro teachers were less than one-third of the counties' total salary payments. Assuming that other school payments were divided in the same proportion as salaries, though almost certainly they were lower, white schools in these five counties received as a bonus about $10,000. The White Man's Burden rested lightly indeed. In the same year in five populous white counties, the Negro 6.08 per cent of the school population received only 2.6 per cent of salary payments. But here little blood could be wrung from a stone. Only about $500 went to white schools by virtue of the presence of Negro children.[37]

Eight rural counties in North Carolina in which the Negro proportion of the school population was about 60 per cent or higher paid annual salaries to white teachers about twice as high as in the nineteen counties where 90 per cent were white.[38] In South Carolina nearly all counties had Negro majorities, and there nearly all of the school funds were derived from taxation within the counties. Within each county the white schools in districts with Negro majorities were especially favored by the system of apportionment, and had long terms, good houses, and high salaries. Georgia had so large a state school fund that counties with a large Negro population needed no local taxation to maintain comparatively good white schools. They simply gathered up and enrolled as many Negro children as possible. Thus the twenty-one Georgia counties with Negro names on two-thirds or more of their school rolls reported monthly expenditures per Negro pupil ranging from 25 cents to 79 cents and, with four exceptions, from $1.50 to $4.00 per white pupil. In thirteen counties less than one-tenth Negro, the monthly expenditures for whites ranged from 75 cents to $1.14, on the whole less than half of the amounts for whites in black counties.[39]

[37] The five black counties in Virginia—Amelia, Charles City, James City, King William, and New Kent—received from the state $26,617.50. Since Negro children were 69.83 per cent of their aggregate school population, the Negroes' share of the state fund was $18,587.00. Negro teachers in the five counties received salaries amounting to $10,867.88. The five white counties—Bath, Craig, Giles, Highland, and Shenandoah—received from the state $34,622.32, of which only $2,105.04 accrued to them by virtue of the Negro 6.08 per cent of the school population. Negro teachers received $1,655.59 in salaries. Computed from *Virginia School Report, 1907–1909*, pp. 67–79, 128–50, 194–214. Figures for school revenue do not include balance.

[38] The annual salaries of white teachers in black counties were: Edgecombe, $250.02; Halifax, $249.59; Vance, $248.48; Craven, $219.26; Robeson, $214.69; Warren, $165.53; Hertford, $148.39; Bertie, $136.26. In the white counties annual salaries of white teachers were: Ashe, $77.72; Alexander, $91.36; Alleghany, $93.62; Yancey, $97.18; Mitchell, $100.16; Yadkin, $104.84; Graham, $105.55; Clay, $106.15; Watauga, $107.87; Cherokee, $108.08; Swain, $113.42; Wilkes, $116.90; Madison, $118.30; Macon, $119.79; Stanly, $125.29; Surry, $128.88; Jackson, $149.04; McDowell, $163.01; Haywood, $203.51. Negro salaries in the black counties were also slightly higher, by about 30 per cent. And part of the differences in salary resulted from greater taxable wealth in the black counties. But there were few local taxes in either area, and consequently there was a great dependence on county taxation and state appropriations in both. *North Carolina School Report, 1906–1908*, Part II, pp. 184–91, 193–200. Figures are for the school year 1907–08.

[39] *Georgia School Report, 1906*, pp. 364–67. The black counties were Burke, Chattahoochee, Clay, Clinch, Columbia, Dougherty, Greene, Harris, Jasper, Jones, Macon, McIntosh, Putnam, Quitman, Stewart, Sumter,

Thus the white people of black counties—or black districts in South Carolina—received special advantages from state and county funds by virtue of their Negro children. Their educational and political leaders were the chief defenders of the existing system of apportionment, and sometimes even appeared to be paternalistic champions of a dependent race. A glance at the Negro schools of black counties would put that claim to rest. In Greene County, Georgia, for example, three-fourths of the Negro schools in 1910 convened in churches and private homes, and at least three Negro schoolhouses were built by closing down the schools for three months and using the teachers' salaries to buy materials.[40] W. E. B. Du Bois spent several months in 1898 taking his own census of Negroes in Dougherty County, Georgia, where whites were outnumbered by five to one. He found that only 27 per cent of the Negroes could read and write. Of the Negro schoolhouses there he reported: "I saw only one schoolhouse there that would compare in any way with the worst schoolhouses I ever saw in New England. . . . Most of the schoolhouses were either old log huts or were churches—colored churches —used as schoolhouses." [41]

The leading opponents of Negro education came from the mountains and Piedmont of every Southern seaboard state. Probably their primary motive was to hold down the Negroes, but they were not unaware of the use made of Negro school funds in the black counties.[42] Their redundant theme, louder in the wake of disfranchisement campaigns around the turn of the century, was that white men's taxes should not be used to educate Negro children. In a sense, the battle between hill and plain over Negro education was a sham battle. If indirect taxes be included, Negro schools under the existing system were receiving little, if any, more than the share of tax funds paid by Negroes.[43] This was pointed out when up-country legislators proposed to give Negroes only the receipts from their taxes, and usually sufficed to still the clamor. As George Washington Cable said in the nineties, "The Negro, so far from being the educational pauper he is commonly reputed to be, comes, in these states, nearer to paying entirely for his chil-

---

Talbot, Taliaferro, Terrell, Troup, and Warren, in the coastal plain and lower Piedmont. The white counties, all but one of which were in the northern corner of the state, were Catoosa, Dawson, Echols, Fannin, Forsyth, Habersham, Murray, Paulding, Pickens, Rabun, Towns, Union, and White.

[40] Arthur F. Raper, *Tenants of the Almighty* (New York, 1943), p. 138.

[41] Testimony of Du Bois in *Report of the Industrial Commission,* XV, Part II, 159–61; *Georgia School Report, 1896,* p. ccccxvii.

[42] Key points out that, in their actual voting, the whites of black counties, rather than those of the uplands, have been the most ardent supporters of White Supremacy. V. O. Key, *Southern Politics in State and Nation* (New York, 1949), pp. 5, 9.

[43] Du Bois, in *The Negro Common School,* pp. 90–91, concluded that in seven states in 1899 Negroes paid as much as they received, in four others whites paid less than 25 per cent of the cost of Negro schools, and in four others the whites paid between 25 and 50 per cent of the cost of Negro schools. Coon, in "Public Taxation and Negro Schools," *Twelfth Conference for Education in the South, Proceedings,* pp. 160–65, concluded after a careful analysis of taxation and educational expenditures in Virginia, North Carolina, and Georgia, that Negro schools in 1906–1907 were "not a burden on white taxpayers." Both argued that Negroes as legal residents were entitled to their share of corporation taxes, that they paid their share of liquor taxes and fines, and that in a unique way they contributed to Georgia's revenue from convict hire. See also Du Bois and Dill, *The Common School and the Negro American, passim.*

dren's schooling, such as it is, than any similarly poor man in any other part of the enlightened world." [44] But within each state there was a sectional impasse among whites about the direction of educational policy that, while it revolved about the Negro school, was really a question of which white schools got the available funds. One result was the retardation of all rural schools, while the relatively unvexed cities and towns, largely in the Piedmont, developed much more adequate schools for their own children. . . .

•   •   •

The "old law of supply and demand," [73] with the farm wage as a measurement, worked particular hardship on Negro teachers, though lack of other suitable jobs drove the better-educated Negroes into teaching. In Georgia in 1900, for example, five of the fifteen Negro teachers of Telfair County and seventeen of the thirty-seven in Newton County received monthly salaries of $10, while seven white teachers of Telfair County received $15 a month, each for a term of five months. Four white teachers in Milton County received $6.81 a month or $40.86 a year, and two Negroes in the same county $5.80 a month or $34.80 a year. "Teaching seems to be the meanest of trades," said William H. Hand of South Carolina.[74]

•   •   •

The Negro child's share in Southern education was related to the Southern economy, but is not entirely explained by it. He was a marginal child in school opportunities as his parent was the marginal man in agriculture. But the inferior opportunities were also part of the pattern of Southern racial customs. Education went deeper than dwellings, eating, riding, and spectator amusement in setting the races apart. It wove the tapestry of habit that was draped over the hard walls of caste. And where whites had all the power and controlled the Negro school funds, the Negro schools conformed within their cramped limits with values of the whites. The white landowner and employer of Negroes had little use for Negro literacy; the poorer white feared the power that literacy would give the Negro. Inferior education for Negroes seems to have been one of the few things upon which most whites agreed. Despite its poor facilities, there was magic in the Southern public school, which Southern whites were reluctant to share.[116]

Negro disfranchisement in the South near the turn of the century affected the

---

[44] Quoted in Richard R. Wright, Jr., *Self Help in Negro Education* (Cheyney, Pennsylvania, 1909?), p. 18.

[73] Marion L. Brittain, "The Work of the Normal Schools as the County Commissioner Sees It," in Southern Educational Association, *Proceedings, 1900* (Richmond, 1901), p. 309. "The main trouble with our rural school," said a low-country South Carolina superintendent, "is, that trustees and patrons are so slow in realizing the value of a high-priced teacher. It seems that as the only salaried people with whom they have to deal is [sic] the farm laborer, they, in all their comparisons, use this as a standard, and thereby form the opinion that teachers are paid too much salary already."—Joe P. Lane, Superintendent of Marion County, in *South Carolina School Report, 1909*, p. 61.

[74] *Georgia School Report, 1900*, pp. cclv, cclxxv, ccxiv, cccxlviii (Roman numerals were used in pagination throughout the report, apparently to train the teachers); William H. Hand, "Report of State High School Inspector, 1915–1916," *Bulletin* of the University of South Carolina, No. 51 (December, 1916), p. 8.

[116] On the role of the Negro school in the pattern of segregation, see Myrdal, *An American Dilemma*, I, 337–44, 632–33, II, 879–907; William E. Burghardt Du Bois, *The Souls of Black Folk* (Chicago, 1903, 13th ed., 1922), pp. 60–74.

school systems in several ways. In the first place, disfranchisement made the Negro vote negligible and stripped Negro school funds of what meager protection they had earlier enjoyed. In states where the change was made by constitutional convention, educational law was altered at the same time to make easier the diversion of Negro school funds to white schools at county or district levels. In the two states which disfranchised by constitutional amendments, North Carolina in 1900 and Georgia in 1908, racial prejudice was fanned to get whites to vote for measures they feared might disfranchise them too. Under the spell of White Supremacy orators, poor whites voted for poll taxes and illiterate whites for literacy tests. The social cost of this sort of propaganda is indicated by the rise in lynchings and the drop in voting participation.

Secondly, the literacy test for suffrage in several states, particularly North Carolina, created some demand among poor rural whites for enough education to qualify their children to vote, even though illiterate whites were often allowed to vote by arrangement with election judges and by other means. The South Carolina and Virginia constitutional conventions, on the other hand, were dominated by political leaders who did not stir the white electorate on education. By the time of the Georgia amendment, it was clear that literacy clauses could be evaded by whites, and besides there were alternatives such as "good character," "understanding," possession of forty acres or $500. But North Carolina educators, who capitalized on the momentary excitement to launch a public school crusade, eventually stimulated similar movements in other Southern states.[117]

Thirdly, while disfranchisement registered the ebb of Populism and hopes for political action, many agrarians, rather than surrender hope as their leaders were doing, hitched their hopes to other stars such as education. The educational orator offered a Promised Land not open to the adult farmer himself. But the very failure of his own high hopes in the agrarian movement inured the farm parent to this shortcoming of the educational movement. As for Negroes, they took to the same educational faith for very similar reasons. It was one of the few avenues of aspiration open to a frustrated and depressed people.

Disfranchisement, however, was only the legal aspect of the political phase of White Supremacy, which was itself the simplified propaganda slogan of a more complex movement. Whites had been supreme all along, of course. And the public attitudes of extreme racism and public policies of racial aggression beginning in the nineties simply intensified earlier trends. Woodward argues convincingly that extreme racism rose to dominate Southern affairs not by conversion, but by a weakening and discrediting of various forces which had earlier held it in check. The chief restraining forces he describes were Southern conservatism, Southern Populist radicalism, and Northern liberalism.[118]

---

[117] Key, *Southern Politics in State and Nation,* pp. 556–69. North Carolina disfranchisement and its effect on education are discussed in the next chapter.

[118] C. Vann Woodward, *The Strange Career of Jim Crow* (New York, 1955), pp. 51–52 *et passim.* This brief account and fresh interpretation of racial segregation will be used without further citation on the next few pages.

Southern conservatives, who found Negroes useful, regarded Negrophobia as a mark of lower-class status and protected some of the Negro's elemental rights until the nineties. As they lost popularity largely because of their economic policies and were challenged by Populism, conservatives themselves raised the cry of "Negro domination." At the same time they used controlled Negro ballots in the black counties to defeat Populist whites and achieve what they called White Supremacy. To say the least, this weakened their moral authority as opponents of extreme racism.

Radical Populism pursued a racial policy consistent with its equalitarian principles, but both policy and movement collapsed under the pressure of conservative White Supremacy tactics. Its heritage was frustration and bitterness, and many disappointed ex-Populists made the Negro the scapegoat of their disappointment. Turning from a hopelessly stronger foe to a helplessly weak one, they convinced themselves that the Negro was an author rather than a fellow victim of their defeat. This mood offered a stimulus rather than a check to racism.

Most Negroes were silent during the White Supremacy movement because of fear or apathy. Booker T. Washington of Tuskegee Institute, the universally recognized leader of the Negroes, sought for his people a "social adjustment," to borrow a term from recent sociologists, an adjustment based on accommodation to the demands of the dominant whites. He established rapport with the dwindling group of upper-class Southerners of paternalistic humor. Through lectures and fund-raising tours in the North he built alliances with philanthropic capitalists and won powerful friends for his conservative race leadership. To the businessman of the New South persuasion, busily humming the tune of progress in a period of depression and race conflict, Washington offered a Negro labor force which would avoid unions and radicalism. The Negro Moses was significantly an educator, taking the long road through the wilderness of Southern race relations. Even his protest against racial disfranchisement was qualified. "In the degree that you close the ballot box against the ignorant," he told the Louisiana disfranchisement convention, "you open the school house." [119] And even in education there had to be accommodation to the ideas of whites on school boards as to what was suitable for members of a subordinate race. These school board members, usually of the class which Washington sought as allies, provided a Negro education inferior in quantity and quality. Nor did endowed industrial schools for Negroes escape the racial handicap. Hampton and Tuskegee led many of their graduates up blind alleys of manual skill at a time when skills were being displaced by new machinery and techniques of mass production.

The failure of Northern emancipators and their sons to resist effectively the

[119] Quoted in Logan, *The Negro in American Life and Thought*, p. 210. On Washington's leadership, the best biographical study so far is Samuel R. Spencer, Jr., *Booker T. Washington and the Negro's Place in American Life* (Boston, 1955), pp. 87–143. Also see Oliver C. Cox, "The Leadership of Booker T. Washington," in *Social Forces*, XXX (October, 1951), 91–97; Bond, *Negro Education in Alabama*, pp. 195–225. But August Meier, "Toward a Reinterpretation of Booker T. Washington," in *Journal of Southern History*, XXIII (May, 1957), 220–27, presents impressive evidence of Washington's surreptitious but "direct attack upon disfranchisement and segregation."

Southern wave of racism may be explained by many changes in Northern attitudes since Reconstruction. The Northeast and West wooed the South politically. Northern liberals conciliated Southern whites in the hope of reciprocal support for reform measures. Others had long since laid down the burden of the freedmen to turn without restraint to the pursuit of economic gain, which proved more exciting and rewarding. A less direct, but pervasive influence on Northern attitudes was the climate of Social Darwinism in which the progressive movement flourished. One of its offshoots was racism, which applied the metaphor of the "struggle for existence" uncritically to racial groups. Used in Europe and America to condone imperialism, racism became a vogue in America in time to coincide with the Southern White Supremacy movement. The white North for a whole generation was ethically disarmed for the task of lecturing Southerners about aggression against American Negroes.[120] And some Northerners were ready to draw on Southern white experience for the management of "new-caught, sullen peoples" in American colonies.[121]

Around 1900 came "the end of the Negro's resistance to the determination on the part of the white South to reduce him to a subordinate status," [122] and a nation-wide "peculiar institution" for the freed Negro had been developed. The incidental violence began to taper off before the end of the nineties, as Negroes bowed in submission to the ten-to-one odds.[123] The new stratification was a Color Line, compounded of segregation, discrimination, and the imminent threat of violence.

[120] Robert Bingham, "Sectional Misunderstandings," in *North American Review,* CLXXIX (September, 1904), 363.

[121] Richard Hofstadter, *Social Darwinism in American Thought, 1860–1915* (Philadelphia, 1944), pp. 69–70, 154, 174–76. On Darwinism as a common element in reform movements and imperialism, see William E. Leuchtenburg, "Progressivism and Imperialism: The Progressive Movement and American Foreign Policy, 1898–1916," in *Mississippi Valley Historical Review,* XXXIX (December, 1952), 483–504.

[122] Frazier, *The Negro in the United States,* pp. 161–62. Rayford W. Logan suggests that "the nadir" was reached about 1901.

[123] See, for example, the diagram of lynchings from 1882 to 1936, in Frazier, *The Negro in the United States,* p. 160. The peak of lynchings was in 1892, when there were 163, and they tapered off as Negroes accepted, outwardly at least, the status accorded them by whites.

Teaching School in a Stable and a Hen-House*

Booker T. Washington

I confess that what I saw during my month of travel and investigation left me with a very heavy heart. The work to be done in order to lift these people up seemed almost beyond accomplishing. I was only one person, and it seemed to me that the little effort which I could put forth could go such a short distance toward bringing about results. I wondered if I could accomplish anything, and if it were worth while for me to try.

Of one thing I felt more strongly convinced than ever, after spending this month in seeing the actual life of the coloured people, and that was that, in order to lift them up, something must be done more than merely to imitate New England education as it then existed. I saw more clearly than ever the wisdom of the system which General Armstrong had inaugurated at Hampton. To take the children of such people as I had been among for a month, and each day give them a few hours of mere book education, I felt would be almost a waste of time.

After consultation with the citizens of Tuskegee, I set July 4, 1881, as the day for the opening of the school in the little shanty and church which had been secured for its accommodation. The white people, as well as the coloured, were greatly interested in the starting of the new school, and the opening day was looked forward to with much earnest discussion. There were not a few white people in the vicinity of Tuskegee who looked with some disfavour upon the project. They questioned its value to the coloured people, and had a fear that it might result in bringing about trouble between the races. Some had the feeling that in proportion as the Negro received education, in the same proportion would his value decrease as an economic factor in the state. These people feared the result of education would be that the Negroes would leave the farms, and that it would be difficult to secure them for domestic service.

The white people who questioned the wisdom of starting this new school had in

---

* From Booker T. Washington, *Up From Slavery: An Autobiography* (New York: Doubleday & Company, Inc., 1933), pp. 85–95. Reprinted by permission of Doubleday & Company, Inc.

their minds pictures of what was called an educated Negro, with a high hat, imitation gold eye-glasses, a showy walking-stick, kid gloves, fancy boots, and whatnot—in a word, a man who was determined to live by his wits. It was difficult for these people to see how education would produce any other kind of a coloured man.

In the midst of all the difficulties which I encountered in getting the little school started, and since then through a period of nineteen years, there are two men among all the many friends of the school in Tuskegee upon whom I have depended constantly for advice and guidance; and the success of the undertaking is largely due to these men, from whom I have never sought anything in vain. I mention them simply as types. One is a white man and an ex-slaveholder, Mr. George W. Campbell; the other is a black man and an ex-slave, Mr. Lewis Adams. These were the men who wrote to General Armstrong for a teacher.

Mr. Campbell is a merchant and banker, and had had little experience in dealing with matters pertaining to education. Mr. Adams was a mechanic, and had learned the trades of shoemaking, harness-making, and tinsmithing during the days of slavery. He had never been to school a day in his life, but in some way he had learned to read and write while a slave. From the first, these two men saw clearly what my plan of education was, sympathized with me, and supported me in every effort. In the days which were darkest financially for the school, Mr. Campbell was never appealed to when he was not willing to extend all the aid in his power. I do not know two men, one an ex-slaveholder, one an ex-slave, whose advice and judgment I would feel more like following in everything which concerns the life and development of the school at Tuskegee than those of these two men.

I have always felt that Mr. Adams, in a large degree, derived his unusual power of mind from the training given his hands in the process of mastering well three trades during the days of slavery. If one goes to-day into any Southern town, and asks for the leading and most reliable coloured man in the community, I believe that in five cases out of ten he will be directed to a Negro who learned a trade during the days of slavery.

On the morning that the school opened, thirty students reported for admission. I was the only teacher. The students were about equally divided between the sexes. Most of them lived in Macon County, the county in which Tuskegee is situated, and of which it is the county-seat. A great many more students wanted to enter the school, but it had been decided to receive only those who were above fifteen years of age, and who had previously received some education. The greater part of the thirty were public-school teachers, and some of them were nearly forty years of age. With the teachers came some of their former pupils, and when they were examined it was amusing to note that in several cases the pupil entered a higher class than did his former teacher. It was also interesting to note how many big books some of them had studied, and how many high-sounding subjects some of them claimed to have mastered. The bigger the book and the longer the name of the subject, the prouder they felt of their accomplishment. Some had studied Latin, and one or two Greek. This they thought entitled them to special distinction.

In fact, one of the saddest things I saw during the month of travel which I have described was a young man, who had attended some high school, sitting down in a one-room cabin, with grease on his clothing, filth all around him, and weeds in the yard and garden, engaged in studying a French grammar.

The students who came first seemed to be fond of memorizing long and complicated "rules" in grammar and mathematics, but had little thought or knowledge of applying these rules to the everyday affairs of their life. One subject which they liked to talk about, and tell me that they had mastered, in arithmetic, was "banking and discount," but I soon found out that neither they nor almost any one in the neighbourhood in which they lived had ever had a bank account. In registering the names of the students, I found that almost every one of them had one or more middle initials. When I asked what the "J" stood for, in the name of John J. Jones, it was explained to me that this was a part of his "entitles." Most of the students wanted to get an education because they thought it would enable them to earn more money as school-teachers.

Notwithstanding what I have said about them in these respects, I have never seen a more earnest and willing company of young men and women than these students were. They were all willing to learn the right thing as soon as it was shown them what was right. I was determined to start them off on a solid and thorough foundation, so far as their books were concerned. I soon learned that most of them had the merest smattering of the high-sounding things that they had studied. While they could locate the Desert of Sahara or the capital of China on an artificial globe, I found out that the girls could not locate the proper places for the knives and forks on an actual dinner-table, or the places on which the bread and meat should be set.

I had to summon a good deal of courage to take a student who had been studying cube root and "banking and discount," and explain to him that the wisest thing for him to do first was thoroughly to master the multiplication table.

The number of pupils increased each week, until by the end of the first month there were nearly fifty. Many of them, however, said that, as they could remain only for two or three months, they wanted to enter a high class and get a diploma the first year if possible.

At the end of the first six weeks a new and rare face entered the school as a co-teacher. This was Miss Olivia A. Davidson, who later became my wife. Miss Davidson was born in Ohio, and received her preparatory education in the public schools of that state. When little more than a girl, she heard of the need of teachers in the South. She went to the state of Mississippi and began teaching there. Later she taught in the city of Memphis. While teaching in Mississippi, one of her pupils became ill with smallpox. Every one in the community was so frightened that no one would nurse the boy. Miss Davidson closed her school and remained by the bedside of the boy night and day until he recovered. While she was at her Ohio home on her vacation, the worst epidemic of yellow fever broke out in Memphis, Tenn., that perhaps has ever occurred in the South. When she heard of this, she at once telegraphed the Mayor of Memphis, offering her services as a yellow-fever nurse, although she had never had the disease.

Miss Davidson's experience in the South showed her that the people needed something more than mere book-learning. She heard of the Hampton system of education, and decided that this was what she wanted in order to prepare herself for better work in the South. The attention of Mrs. Mary Hemenway, of Boston, was attracted to her rare ability. Through Mrs. Hemenway's kindness and generosity, Miss Davidson, after graduating at Hampton, received an opportunity to complete a two years' course of training at the Massachusetts State Normal School at Framingham.

Before she went to Framingham, some one suggested to Miss Davidson that, since she was so very light in colour, she might find it more comfortable not to be known as a coloured woman in this school in Massachusetts. She at once replied that under no circumstances and for no considerations would she consent to deceive any one in regard to her racial identity.

Soon after her graduation from the Framingham institution, Miss Davidson came to Tuskegee, bringing into the school many valuable and fresh ideas as to the best methods of teaching, as well as a rare moral character and a life of unselfishness that I think has seldom been equalled. No single individual did more toward laying the foundations of the Tuskegee Institute so as to insure the successful work that has been done there than Olivia A. Davidson.

Miss Davidson and I began consulting as to the future of the school from the first. The students were making progress in learning books and in developing their minds; but it became apparent at once that, if we were to make any permanent impression upon those who had come to us for training, we must do something besides teach them mere books. The students had come from homes where they had had no opportunities for lessons which would teach them how to care for their bodies. With few exceptions, the homes in Tuskegee in which the students boarded were but little improvement upon those from which they had come. We wanted to teach the students how to bathe; how to care for their teeth and clothing. We wanted to teach them what to eat, and how to eat it properly, and how to care for their rooms. Aside from this, we wanted to give them such a practical knowledge of some one industry, together with the spirit of industry, thrift, and economy, that they would be sure of knowing how to make a living after they had left us. We wanted to teach them to study actual things instead of mere books alone.

We found that the most of our students came from the country districts, where agriculture in some form or other was the main dependence of the people. We learned that about eighty-five per cent of the coloured people in the Gulf states depended upon agriculture for their living. Since this was true, we wanted to be careful not to educate our students out of sympathy with agricultural life, so that they would be attracted from the country to the cities, and yield to the temptation of trying to live by their wits. We wanted to give them such an education as would fit a large proportion of them to be teachers, and at the same time cause them to return to the plantation districts and show the people there how to put new energy and new ideas into farming, as well as into the intellectual and moral and religious life of the people.

All these ideas and needs crowded themselves upon us with a seriousness that seemed well-nigh overwhelming. What were we to do? We had only the little old shanty and the abandoned church which the good coloured people of the town of Tuskegee had kindly loaned us for the accommodation of the classes. The number of students was increasing daily. The more we saw of them and the more we travelled through the country districts, the more we saw that our efforts were reaching, to only a partial degree, the actual needs of the people whom we wanted to lift up through the medium of the students whom we should educate and send out as leaders.

The more we talked with the students, who were then coming to us from several parts of the state, the more we found that the chief ambition among a large proportion of them was to get an education so that they would not have to work any longer with their hands.

This is illustrated by a story told of a coloured man in Alabama, who, one hot day in July, while he was at work in a cotton-field, suddenly stopped, and, looking toward the skies, said: "O Lawd, de cotton am so grassy, de work am so hard, and the sun am so hot dat I b'lieve dis darky am called to preach!"

About three months after the opening of the school, and at the time when we were in the greatest anxiety about our work, there came into the market for sale an old and abandoned plantation which was situated about a mile from the town of Tuskegee. The mansion house—or "big house," as it would have been called—which had been occupied by the owners during slavery, had been burned. After making a careful examination of this place, it seemed to be just the location that we wanted in order to make our work effective and permanent.

But how were we to get it? The price asked for it was very little—only five hundred dollars—but we had no money, and we were strangers in the town and had no credit. The owner of the land agreed to let us occupy the place if we could make a payment of two hundred and fifty dollars down, with the understanding that the remaining two hundred and fifty dollars must be paid within a year. Although five hundred dollars was cheap for the land, it was a large sum when one did not have any part of it.

In the midst of the difficulty I summoned a great deal of courage and wrote to my friend General J. F. B. Marshall, the Treasurer of the Hampton Institute, putting the situation before him and beseeching him to lend me the two hundred and fifty dollars on my own personal responsibility. Within a few days a reply came to the effect that he had no authority to lend me money belonging to the Hampton Institute, but that he would gladly lend me the amount needed from his own personal funds.

I confess that the securing of this money in this way was a great surprise to me, as well as a source of gratification. Up to that time I never had had in my possession so much money as one hundred dollars at a time, and the loan which I had asked General Marshall for seemed a tremendously large sum to me. The fact of my being responsible for the repaying of such a large amount of money weighed very heavily upon me.

I lost no time in getting ready to move the school on to the new farm. At the time we occupied the place there were standing upon it a cabin, formerly used as the dining room, an old kitchen, a stable, and an old hen-house. Within a few weeks we had all of these structures in use. The stable was repaired and used as a recitation-room, and very presently the hen-house was utilized for the same purpose.

I recall that one morning, when I told an old coloured man who lived near, and who sometimes helped me, that our school had grown so large that it would be necessary for us to use the hen-house for school purposes, and that I wanted him to help me give it a thorough cleaning out the next day, he replied, in the most earnest manner:

"What you mean, boss? You sholy ain't gwine clean out de hen-house in de *day*-time?"

Nearly all the work of getting the new location ready for school purposes was done by the students after school was over in the afternoon. As soon as we got the cabins in condition to be used, I determined to clear up some land so that we could plant a crop. When I explained my plan to the young men, I noticed that they did not seem to take to it very kindly. It was hard for them to see the connection between clearing land and an education. Besides, many of them had been school-teachers, and they questioned whether or not clearing land would be in keeping with their dignity. In order to relieve them from any embarrassment, each afternoon after school I took my axe and led the way to the woods. When they saw that I was not afraid or ashamed to work, they began to assist with more enthusiasm. We kept at the work each afternoon, until we had cleared about twenty acres and had planted a crop.

In the meantime Miss Davidson was devising plans to repay the loan. Her first effort was made by holding festivals, or "suppers." She made a personal canvass among the white and coloured families in the town of Tuskegee, and got them to agree to give something, like a cake, a chicken, bread, or pies, that could be sold at the festival. Of course the coloured people were glad to give anything that they could spare, but I want to add that Miss Davidson did not apply to a single white family, so far as I now remember, that failed to donate something; and in many ways the white families showed their interest in the school.

Several of these festivals were held, and quite a little sum of money was raised. A canvass was also made among the people of both races for direct gifts of money, and most of those applied to gave small sums. It was often pathetic to note the gifts of the older coloured people, most of whom had spent their best days in slavery. Sometimes they would give five cents, sometimes twenty-five cents. Sometimes the contribution was a quilt, or a quantity of sugarcane. I recall one old coloured woman, who was about seventy years of age, who came to see me when we were raising money to pay for the farm. She hobbled into the room where I was, leaning on a cane. She was clad in rags; but they were clean. She said: "Mr. Washin'ton, God knows I spent de bes' days of my life in slavery. God knows I's ignorant an' poor; but," she added, "I knows what you an' Miss Davidson is tryin' to do. I knows you is tryin' to make better men an' better women for de coloured race. I ain't got no money, but I wants you to take dese six eggs, what I's been savin' up, an' I wants you to put dese six eggs into de eddication of dese boys an' gals."

Since the work at Tuskegee started, it has been my privilege to receive many gifts for the benefit of the institution, but never any, I think, that touched me so deeply as this one.

What Is the Matter with the Atlanta Schools?*

The Atlanta Independent in its issue of September 28, has an editorial which we commend to the heads of educational institutions throughout the country. We scarcely recall any statement more informing, pointed and forceful than that which Editor Davis sends out through his valued publication. No institution can long deserve the respect of those whom it is designed to help unless its activities are brought in close contact with the direct needs of the people. An institution to succeed, as Mr. Davis points out, has got to helpfully come in touch with the community life of the people. The great fault of most of our schools is, that they do not touch the people in this particular direction. Mr. Davis' editorial follows:

As we understand our system of education, the college or university is of no more service in educating the people than it makes itself helpful in the education and uplift of the masses. The college that shuts itself out from the masses, and fails to be felt in the community life where it is located, falls far short of the purpose of higher education, and its influence contributes more to the destructive than to the creative.

Each and every college or university should enter so fully into the community life where it is located, that all the people would rightfully look to the university as the centre from which the life, conscience and character of the community issue. The chief work of the college is character-building, and in its construction of character, primarily, the college is no respecter of persons. Its field is mankind, and it is the duty of the institution to throw its influence into the struggle wherever there is a man that needs assistance. We fear that the tendency of our colleges is to drift into exclusiveness, and are not only removing themselves from the most helpful relations they might bear to the people they were instituted to serve, but are destroying their own influence and stunting the real growth of the men they are contributing to the national growth.

* From "What is the Matter With the Atlanta Schools?" *Colored American Magazine,* XIII (Nov. 1907), 333–35.

In this community we have five Negro colleges—Atlanta University, Atlanta Baptist College, Clark University, Spellman Seminary and Morris Brown College. These institutions rank in the public estimation about in order as named. To all intents and purposes these colleges are of no more service to Atlanta, where they are located and receive the greatest quota of their student body, than they are to Montgomery, New Orleans and Little Rock, a thousand miles away. Now, this condition of affairs ought not to exist. These institutions ought to be the most potent factors in the economic, industrial and social life of the community. It is no less true than deplorable that these institutions are not felt in the community in either the economic, industrial or political equation of the community where they are located.

The colleges, like the Chinese Empire, seem to have walled themselves in from the world, and know nothing and care less about what is going on outside of the wall.

The character of the college should be such that every citizen in the community would feel a common interest in its welfare, and would contribute both directly and indirectly to the sustenance of the college life. The boys and girls from the colleges who go out in the city, teach Sunday School and attend Church can not and will not accomplish much if the faculty does not throw its life and character into effort to generally uplift the people and make the college a potent factor in the solution of the every-day problems of life. The college can not reach its highest usefulness until it establishes itself among those who look into its doors every day. This can only be done by taking the community into its confidence and making a determined pull to permeate the entire community with the "college spirit."

At Tuskegee, Ala., the Negroes have only one school, and it is not a college. Mr. Washington is not even called president, only referred to as principal. Yet, in the community and throughout eastern Alabama, the Tuskegee spirit is the most potent factor in the social equation of the community. Tuskegee's influence is felt in Macon County, Ala., in every shop, on every farm, at every trade, and is the greatest developer of the economic and industrial life of the county. The student body of itself did not bring about these helpful results in Alabama, but the weight and character of Mr. Washington and his assistants are the motor which propels and constructs the community life in the neighborhood of the institute.

We have at the heads of our institutions here Drs. Crogman, Flipper, Hope, Ware and Misses Upton and Giles. All of these executives are able and conscientious men and women: yet they do not come helpfully in touch with the community life. Fulton County does not tellingly feel the influence of these colleges. These schools do not enter into the industrial, economic or political life of the community. With the exception of the president of Morris Brown College, the heads of Atlanta colleges are not seen out at any time elbowing among the people. The general impression entertained among the people is, the colleges were instituted for the favored few, and the university has no influence outside of the class-room. This defect in our college life has done more to relegate higher education among the Negroes and to paramount industrial education for all the black folk than any other one agency. The college does not tell most in the scholarship of the individual commissioned to go out, but in the influence for good reflected in the lives and characters of the men and women who leave the school.

With the exception of President Flipper, not a single college president in the community is identified with a single movement for the interest of the masses. The economic, industrial or civic welfare of the masses does not materially concern our local college men. Economic independence nor manhood rights challenges the attention of those who should figure largely in directing sentiment and thought in the defence of our rights.

It is not enough to attend the chapel service on the campus, Sunday. It is not enough to send a boy or two out each Sunday in a prosperous church where the student is not needed. But the social, industrial, domestic and economic condition of the masses in the community should be investigated, and the whole influence of the college and student body should be brought helpfully into play to better conditions and to bring the college and the community into helpful proximity. Don't wall yourselves in, but go out among your neighbors and interest them in your work by manifesting an abiding interest in them, and what concerns them. Considered in the light of the services our colleges are rendering this community, with a bare exception, seventy-five per cent of the people in the community would not know that we have college presidents here if it was not for the mere fact that certain men are at the head of our colleges. It is up to our college faculties to throw their influence into the community life and impress their individuality helpfully upon their neighbors.

The Atlanta Exposition Address*
Booker T. Washington

The Atlanta Exposition, at which I had been asked to make an address as a representative of the Negro race, as stated in the last chapter, was opened with a short address from Governor Bullock. After other interesting exercises, including an invocation from Bishop Nelson, of Georgia, a dedicatory ode by Albert Howell, Jr., and addresses by the President of the Exposition and Mrs. Joseph Thompson, the President of the Woman's Board, Governor Bullock introduced me with the words, "We have with us to-day a representative of Negro enterprise and Negro civilization."

When I arose to speak, there was considerable cheering, especially from the coloured people. As I remember it now, the thing that was uppermost in my mind was the desire to say something that would cement the friendship of the races and bring about hearty coöperation between them. So far as my outward surroundings were concerned, the only thing that I recall distinctly now is that when I got up, I saw thousands of eyes looking intently into my face. The following is the address which I delivered:—

MR. PRESIDENT AND GENTLEMEN OF THE BOARD
OF DIRECTORS AND CITIZENS.

One-third of the population of the South is of the Negro race. No enterprise seeking the material, civil, or moral welfare of this section can disregard this element of our population and reach the highest success. I but convey to you, Mr. President and Directors, the sentiment of the masses of my race when I say that in no way have the value and manhood of the American Negro been more fittingly and generously recognized than by the managers of this magnificent Exposition at every stage of its progress. It is a recognition that will do more to cement the friendship of the two races than any occurrence since the dawn of our freedom.

* From Booker T. Washington, *Up From Slavery: An Autobiography* (New York: Doubleday & Company, Inc., 1933), pp. 157–71. Reprinted by permission of Doubleday & Company, Inc.

Not only this, but the opportunity here afforded will awaken among us a new era of industrial progress. Ignorant and inexperienced, it is not strange that in the first years of our new life we began at the top instead of at the bottom; that a seat in Congress or the state legislature was more sought than real estate or industrial skill; that the political convention of stump speaking had more attractions than starting a dairy farm or truck garden.

A ship lost at sea for many days suddenly sighted a friendly vessel. From the mast of the unfortunate vessel was seen a signal, "Water, water; we die of thirst!" The answer from the friendly vessel at once came back, "Cast down your bucket where you are." A second time the signal, "Water, water; send us water!" ran up from the distressed vessel, and was answered, "Cast down your bucket where you are." And a third and fourth signal for water was answered, "Cast down your bucket where you are." The captain of the distressed vessel, at last heeding the injunction, cast down his bucket, and it came up full of fresh, sparkling water from the mouth of the Amazon River. To those of my race who depend on bettering their condition in a foreign land or who underestimate the importance of cultivating friendly relations with the Southern white man, who is their next-door neighbour, I would say: "Cast down your bucket where you are" —cast it down in making friends in every manly way of the people of all races by whom we are surrounded.

Cast it down in agriculture, mechanics, in commerce, in domestic service, and in the professions. And in this connection it is well to bear in mind that whatever other sins the South may be called to bear, when it comes to business, pure and simple, it is in the South that the Negro is given a man's chance in the commercial world, and in nothing is this Exposition more eloquent than in emphasizing this chance. Our greatest danger is that in the great leap from slavery to freedom we may overlook the fact that the masses of us are to live by the productions of our hands, and fail to keep in mind that we shall prosper in proportion as we learn to dignify and glorify common labour and put brains and skill into the common occupations of life; shall prosper in proportion as we learn to draw the line between the superficial and the substantial, the ornamental gewgaws of life and the useful. No race can prosper till it learns that there is as much dignity in tilling a field as in writing a poem. It is at the bottom of life we must begin, and not at the top. Nor should we permit our grievances to overshadow our opportunities.

To those of the white race who look to the incoming of those of foreign birth and strange tongue and habits for the prosperity of the South, were I permitted I would repeat what I say to my own race, "Cast down your bucket where you are." Cast it down among the eight millions of Negroes whose habits you know, whose fidelity and love you have tested in days when to have proved treacherous meant the ruin of your firesides. Cast down your bucket among these people who have, without strikes and labour wars, tilled your fields, cleared your forests, builded your railroads and cities, and brought forth treasures from the bowels of the earth, and helped make possible this magnificent representation of the progress of the South. Casting down your bucket among my people, helping and encouraging them as you are doing on these grounds, and to education of head, hand, and heart, you will find that they will buy your surplus land, make blossom the waste places in your fields, and run your factories. While doing this, you can be sure in the future, as in the past, that you and your families will be surrounded by the most patient, faithful, law-abiding, and unresentful people that the world has seen. As we have proved our loyalty to you in the past, in nursing your children, watching by the sick-bed of your mothers and fathers, and often following them with tear-dimmed eyes to their graves, so in the future, in our humble way, we shall stand by you with a devotion that no foreigner can approach, ready to lay down our lives, if need be, in defence of yours, interlacing our industrial, commercial, civil, and religious life with yours in a way that shall make the interests of both races one. In all things that are purely social we can be as separate as the fingers, yet one as the hand in all things essential to mutual progress.

There is no defence or security for any of us except in the highest intelligence and development of all. If anywhere there are efforts tending to curtail the fullest growth of the Negro, let these efforts be turned into stimulating, encouraging, and making him the most useful and intelligent citizen. Effort or means so invested will pay a thousand per cent. interest. These efforts will be twice blessed—"blessing him that gives and him that takes."

There is no escape through law of man or God from the inevitable:—

> *The laws of changeless justice bind*
> *Oppressor with oppressed;*
> *And close as sin and suffering joined*
> *We march to fate abreast.*

Nearly sixteen millions of hands will aid you in pulling the load upward, or they will pull against you the load downward. We shall constitute one-third and more of the ignorance and crime of the South, or one-third its intelligence and progress; we shall contribute one-third to the business and industrial prosperity of the South, or we shall prove a veritable body of death, stagnating, depressing, retarding every effort to advance the body politic.

Gentlemen of the Exposition, as we present to you our humble effort at an exhibition of our progress, you must not expect overmuch. Starting thirty years ago with ownership here and there in a few quilts and pumpkins and chickens (gathered from miscellaneous sources), remember the path that has led from these to the inventions and production of agricultural implements, buggies, steam-engines, newspapers, books, statuary, carving, paintings, the management of drugstores and banks, has not been trodden without contact with thorns and thistles. While we take pride in what we exhibit as a result of our independent efforts, we do not for a moment forget that our part in this exhibition would fall far short of your expectations but for the constant help that has come to our educational life, not only from the Southern states, but especially from Northern philanthropists, who have made their gifts a constant stream of blessing and encouragement.

The wisest among my race understand that the agitation of questions of social equality is the extremest folly, and that progress in the enjoyment of all the privileges that will come to us must be the result of severe and constant struggle rather than of artificial forcing. No race that has anything to contribute to the markets of the world is long in any degree ostracized. It is important and right that all privileges of the law be ours, but it is vastly more important that we be prepared for the exercises of these privileges. The opportunity to earn a dollar in a factory just now is worth infinitely more than the opportunity to spend a dollar in an opera-house.

In conclusion, may I repeat that nothing in thirty years has given us more hope and encouragement, and drawn us so near to you of the white race, as this opportunity offered by the Exposition; and here bending, as it were, over the altar that represents the results of the struggles of your race and mine, both starting practically empty-handed three decades ago, I pledge that in your effort to work out the great and intricate problem which God has laid at the doors of the South, you shall have at all times the patient, sympathetic help of my race; only let this be constantly in mind, that, while from representations in these buildings of the product of field, of forest, of mine, of factory, letters, and art, much good will come, yet far above and beyond material benefits will be that higher good, that, let us pray God, will come, in a blotting out of sectional differences and racial animosities and suspicions, in a determination to administer absolute justice, in a willing obedience among all classes to the mandates of law. This, this, coupled with our material prosperity, will bring into our beloved South a new heaven and a new earth.

The first thing that I remember, after I had finished speaking, was that Governor Bullock rushed across the platform and took me by the hand, and that others did the same. I received so many and such hearty congratulations that I found it difficult to get out of the building. I did not appreciate to any degree, however, the impression which my address seemed to have made, until the next morning, when I went into the business part of the city. As soon as I was recognized, I was surprised to find myself pointed out and surrounded by a crowd of men who wished to shake hands with me. This was kept up on every street on to which I went, to an extent which embarrassed me so much that I went back to my boarding-place. The next morning I returned to Tuskegee. At the station in Atlanta, and at almost all of the stations at which the train stopped between that city and Tuskegee, I found a crowd of people anxious to shake hands with me.

The papers in all parts of the United States published the address in full, and for months afterward there were complimentary editorial references to it. Mr. Clark Howell, the editor of the Atlanta *Constitution,* telegraphed to a New York paper, among other words, the following, "I do not exaggerate when I say that Professor Booker T. Washington's address yesterday was one of the most notable speeches, both as to character and as to the warmth of its reception, ever delivered to a Southern audience. The address was a revelation. The whole speech is a platform upon which blacks and whites can stand with full justice to each other."

The Boston *Transcript* said editorially: "The speech of Booker T. Washington at the Atlanta Exposition, this week, seems to have dwarfed all the other proceedings and the Exposition itself. The sensation that it has caused in the press has never been equalled."

I very soon began receiving all kinds of propositions from lecture bureaus, and editors of magazines and papers, to take the lecture platform, and to write articles. One lecture bureau offered me fifty thousand dollars, or two hundred dollars a night and expenses, if I would place my services at its disposal for a given period. To all these communications I replied that my life-work was at Tuskegee; and that whenever I spoke it must be in the interests of the Tuskegee school and my race, and that I would enter into no arrangements that seemed to place a mere commercial value upon my services.

Some days after its delivery I sent a copy of my address to the President of the United States, the Hon. Grover Cleveland. I received from him the following autographed reply:—

GRAY GABLES, BUZZARD'S BAY, MASS.,
October 6, 1895.

BOOKER T. WASHINGTON, ESQ.

MY DEAR SIR:

I thank you for sending me a copy of your address delivered at the Atlanta Exposition.

I thank you with much enthusiasm for making the address. I have read it with intense interest, and I think the Exposition would be fully justified if it did not do more than furnish the opportunity for its delivery. Your words cannot fail to delight and encourage all who wish well for your race; and if our coloured fellow-citizens do not from your utterances gather new hope and form new determinations to gain every valuable advantage offered them by their citizenship, it will be strange indeed.

Yours very truly,
GROVER CLEVELAND.

Later I met Mr. Cleveland, for the first time, when, as President, he visited the Atlanta Exposition. At the request of myself and others he consented to spend an hour in the Negro Building, for the purpose of inspecting the Negro exhibit and of giving the coloured people in attendance an opportunity to shake hands with him. As soon as I met Mr. Cleveland I became impressed with his simplicity, greatness, and rugged honesty. I have met him many times since then, both at public functions and at his private residence in Princeton, and the more I see of him the more I admire him. When he visited the Negro Building in Atlanta he seemed to give himself up wholly, for that hour, to the coloured people. He seemed to be as careful to shake hands with some old coloured "auntie" clad partially in rags, and to take as much pleasure in doing so, as if he were greeting some millionaire. Many of the coloured people took advantage of the occasion to get him to write his name in a book or on a slip of paper. He was as careful and patient in doing this as if he were putting his signature to some great state document.

Mr. Cleveland has not only shown his friendship for me in many personal ways, but has always consented to do anything I have asked of him for our school. This he has done, whether it was to make a personal donation or to use his influence in securing the donations of others. Judging from my personal acquaintance with Mr. Cleveland, I do not believe that he is conscious of possessing any colour prejudice. He is too great for that. In my contact with people I find that, as a rule, it is only the little, narrow people who live for themselves, who never read good books, who do not travel, who never open up their souls in a way to permit them to come into contact with other souls—with the great outside world. No man whose vision is bounded by colour can come into contact with what is highest and best in the world. In meeting men, in many places, I have found that the happiest people are those who do the most for others; the most miserable are those who do the least. I have also found that few things, if any, are capable of making one so blind and narrow as race prejudice. I often say to our students, in the course of my talks to them on Sunday evenings in the chapel, that the longer I live and the more experience I have of the world, the more I am convinced that, after all, the one thing that is most worth living for—and dying for, if need be—is the opportunity of making some one else more happy and more useful.

The coloured people and the coloured newspapers at first seemed to be greatly pleased with the character of my Atlanta address, as well as with its reception. But after the first burst of enthusiasm began to die away, and the coloured people began reading the speech in cold type, some of them seemed to feel that they had been hypnotized. They seemed to feel that I had been too liberal in my remarks toward the Southern whites, and that I had not spoken out strongly enough for what they termed the "rights" of the race. For a while there was a reaction, so far as a certain element of my own race was concerned, but later these reactionary ones seemed to have been won over to my way of believing and acting.

While speaking of changes in public sentiment, I recall that about ten years after the school at Tuskegee was established, I had an experience that I shall never forget. Dr. Lyman Abbott, then the pastor of Plymouth Church, and also editor of the *Outlook* (then the *Christian Union*), asked me to write a letter for his paper giving my opinion of the exact condition, mental and moral, of the coloured ministers in the South, as based upon my observations. I wrote the letter, giving the exact facts as I conceived them to be. The picture painted was a rather black one—or, since I am black, shall I say "white"? It could not be otherwise with a race but a few years out of slavery, a race which had not had time or opportunity to produce a competent ministry.

What I said soon reached every Negro minister in the country, I think, and the letters of condemnation which I received from them were not few. I think that for a year after the publication of this article every association and every conference or religious body of any kind, of my race, that met, did not fail before adjourning to pass a resolution condemning me, or calling upon me to retract or modify what I had said. Many of these organizations went so far in their resolutions as to advise parents to cease sending their children to Tuskegee. One association even appointed a "missionary" whose duty it was to warn the people against sending their children to Tuskegee. This missionary had a son in the school, and I noticed that, whatever the "missionary" might have said or done with regard to others, he was careful not to take his son away from the institution. Many of the coloured papers, especially those that were the organs of religious bodies, joined in the general chorus of condemnation or demands for retraction.

During the whole time of the excitement, and through all the criticism, I did not utter a word of explanation or retraction. I knew that I was right, and that time and the sober second thought of the people would vindicate me. It was not long before the bishops and other church leaders began to make a careful investigation of the conditions of the ministry, and they found out that I was right. In fact, the oldest and most influential bishop in one branch of the Methodist Church said that my words were far too mild. Very soon public sentiment began making itself felt, in demanding a purifying of the ministry. While this is not yet complete by any means, I think I may say, without egotism, and I have been told by many of our most influential ministers, that my words had much to do with starting a demand for the placing of a higher type of men in the pulpit. I have had the satisfaction of having many who once condemned me thank me heartily for my frank words.

The change of the attitude of the Negro ministry, so far as regards myself, is so complete that at the present time I have no warmer friends among any class than I have among the clergymen. The improvement in the character and life of the Negro ministers is one of the most gratifying evidences of the progress of the race. My experience with them, as well as other events in my life, convince me that the thing to do, when one feels sure that he has said or done the right thing, and is condemned, is to stand still and keep quiet. If he is right, time will show it.

In the midst of the discussion which was going on concerning my Atlanta speech, I received the letter which I give below, from Dr. Gilman, the President of Johns Hopkins University, who had been made chairman of the judges of award in connection with the Atlanta Exposition:—

JOHNS HOPKINS UNIVERSITY, BALTIMORE,
President's Office, September 30, 1895.

DEAR MR. WASHINGTON:

Would it be agreeable to you to be one of the Judges of Award in the Department of Education at Atlanta? If so, I shall be glad to place your name upon the list. A line by telegraph will be welcomed.

Yours very truly,
D. C. GILMAN.

I think I was even more surprised to receive this invitation than I had been to receive the invitation to speak at the opening of the Exposition. It was to be a part of my duty, as one of the jurors, to pass not only upon the exhibits of the coloured schools, but also upon those of the white schools. I accepted the position, and spent a month in Atlanta in performance of the duties which it entailed. The board of jurors was a large one, consisting in all of sixty members. It was about equally divided between Southern white people and Northern white people. Among them were college presidents, leading scientists and men of letters, and specialists in many subjects. When the group of jurors to which I was assigned met for organization, Mr. Thomas Nelson Page, who was one of the number, moved that I be made secretary of that division, and the motion was unanimously adopted. Nearly half of our division were Southern people. In performing my duties in the inspection of the exhibits of white schools I was in every case treated with respect, and at the close of our labours I parted from my associates with regret.

I am often asked to express myself more freely than I do upon the political condition and the political future of my race. These recollections of my experience in Atlanta give me the opportunity to do so briefly. My own belief is, although I have never before said so in so many words, that the time will come when the Negro in the South will be accorded all the political rights which his ability, character, and material possessions entitle him to. I think, though, that the opportunity to freely exercise such political rights will not come in any large degree through outside or artificial forcing, but will be accorded to the Negro by the Southern white people themselves, and that they will protect him in the exercise of those rights. Just as soon as the South gets over the old feeling that it is being forced by "foreigners," or "aliens," to do something which it does not want to do, I believe that the change in the direction that I have indicated is going to begin. In fact, there are indications that it is already beginning in a slight degree.

Let me illustrate my meaning. Suppose that some months before the opening of the Atlanta Exposition there had been a general demand from the press and public platform outside the South that a Negro be given a place on the opening programme, and that a Negro be placed upon the board of jurors of award. Would any such recognition of the race have taken place? I do not think so. The Atlanta officials went as far as they did because they felt it to be a pleasure, as well as a duty, to reward what they considered merit in the Negro race. Say what we will, there is something in human nature which we cannot blot out, which makes one man, in the end, recognize and reward merit in another, regardless of colour or race.

I believe it is the duty of the Negro—as the greater part of the race is already doing—to deport himself modestly in regard to political claims, depending upon the slow but sure influences that proceed from the possession of property, intelligence, and high character for the full recognition of his political rights. I think that the according of the full exercise of political rights is going to be a matter of natural, slow growth, not an over-night, gourd-vine affair. I do not believe that the Negro should cease voting, for a man cannot learn the exercise of self-government by ceasing to vote any more than a boy can learn to swim by keeping out of the water, but I do believe that in his voting he should more and more be influenced by those of intelligence and character who are his next-door neighbours.

I know coloured men who, through the encouragement, help, and advice of Southern white people, have accumulated thousands of dollars' worth of property, but who, at the same time, would never think of going to those same persons for advice concerning the casting of their ballots. This, it seems to me, is unwise and unreasonable, and should cease. In saying this I do not mean that the Negro should truckle, or not vote from principle, for the instant he ceases to vote from principle he loses the confidence and respect of the Southern white man even.

I do not believe that any state should make a law that permits an ignorant and poverty-stricken white man to vote, and prevents a black man in the same condition from voting. Such a law is not only unjust, but it will react, as all unjust laws do, in time; for the effect of such a law is to encourage the Negro to secure education and property, and at the same time it encourages the white man to remain in ignorance and poverty. I believe that in time, through the operation of intelligence and friendly race relations, all cheating at the ballot box in the South will cease. It will become apparent that the white man who begins by cheating a Negro out of his ballot soon learns to cheat a white man out of his, and that the man who does this ends his career of dishonesty by the theft of property or by some equally serious crime. In my opinion, the time will come when the South will encourage all of its citizens to vote. It will see that it pays better, from every standpoint, to have healthy, vigorous life than to have that political stagnation which always results when one-half of the population has no share and no interest in the Government.

As a rule, I believe in universal, free suffrage, but I believe that in the South we are confronted with peculiar conditions that justify the protection of the ballot in many of the states, for a while at least, either by an educational test, a property test, or by both combined; but whatever tests are required, they should be made to apply with equal and exact justice to both races.

196

The Beginnings of Organized Negro Protest, 1901–1916*

Constance McLaughlin Green

The optimism that warmed white Washington rarely penetrated the clouds hanging over the colored community. In the Deep South the exclusion of Negro voters from the polls in state after state had progressed inexorably, beginning with South Carolina in 1889 and, by 1901, extending to nine others. Determination to establish white supremacy on an immutable basis had multiplied Jim Crow laws and confined Negro education largely to the vocational and manual training deemed suited to a servile labor force. From Texas through the Gulf states and up into North Carolina, lynchings of Negroes had grown in frequency during the 1890's. Washington Negroes had not faced lynchings or overt intimidation. Here the black masses at the bottom of the heap were little worse off in 1901 than in the early eighties; in fact, with luck on jobs, consistent good health, and three or four years of schooling, hard workers might rise a peg into the ranks of the Negro lower middle class. It was the upper middle class and the aristocrats whose status and pride had suffered and from whom either courageous leadership or corrosive despair must emanate. During the preceding twenty years their role had become increasingly negative. Yet colored Americans throughout the country still looked to the privileged members of that group to act as standard bearers for them all.

Contrary to later, often quoted Republican claims, the position of Negroes continued to worsen during the Roosevelt and Taft administrations, although subtle changes rather than admitted shifts in official policy marked the decline. As President Cleveland's first Civil Service Commissioner, Theodore Roosevelt had exercised scrupu-

* From Constance McLaughlin Green, *Washington: Capital City 1879–1950*, Vol. II (Princeton: Princeton University Press, 1963), pp. 207–33. Copyright © 1963 by Princeton University. Reprinted by permission of Princeton University Press.

lous fairness in putting the merit system into effect in government, but the Colonel of the Rough Riders had deeply offended colored men by belittling the heroic services of the Black Cavalry at San Juan hill during the Spanish-American War. As President, the vigorous "Teddy" for a time seemed to colored Washington to be a staunch friend: one of his first acts was to invite Booker T. Washington to dine at the White House to discuss Negro appointments to office. Hopes built on that unusual gesture quickly shrivelled under the hot blast of arch-conservative Republican wrath. Within six months the Washington *Bee* was speaking of "the Negro political decapitation dinner." [1] The President stuck by his guns to the point of winning Senate concurrence in several Negro appointments, and he retained a number of colored men McKinley had put into office, but thereafter he made no further overtures. On the contrary, in 1906, when Negro troops in Brownsville, Texas, were involved in a brawl in which a white man was shot, presidential severity in approving the dishonorable discharge of the entire battalion for refusing to identify the guilty person alienated Roosevelt's colored supporters. His appointment of two Negroes to the Homes Commission in 1908 won him no applause since all members of the commission gave their services.

President Taft stirred up fewer animosities than his predecessor. Avowing belief in the Tuskegee philosophy of Negro economic advancement before enlargement of Negro political power, Taft declared himself unwilling to appoint colored men to posts in the South, where white resentment would create friction. But he selected colored men for several "offices of essential dignity at Washington," on the principle that it was better to give "large offices to well-equipped Negroes of the higher class" than to scatter "a lot of petty ones among the mass of their race." Rather apologetically he wrote to Robert Terrell: "I have not done all I ought to do or all I hope to do in the matter of the recognition of colored men, but positions are hard to find. Nobody resigns and nobody dies." However sound his reasons, Taft's policies offered the city's colored people meagre encouragement.[2]

Up to a point colored Washingtonians rejoiced at any Negro's receiving a responsible federal post, but they were dismayed at the President's consistently passing over well-qualified local Negroes even for the office of Recorder of Deeds for which local taxes paid half. The profound respect in which all colored Americans held Washington's upper-class colored community heightened the grievance. Upon Booker T. Washington's recommendation, President Roosevelt appointed Robert H. Terrell to a municipal judgeship, but colored Republicans from the states won the other six major federal assignments in the capital, namely the posts of Register and Deputy Register of the Treasury, Assistant District Attorney for the District of Columbia, Auditor of the

[1] E.g., Republican National Committee, *Republican Campaign Textbook, 1912,* p. 278; *Bee,* 15 Oct 1898, 19 Oct 1901, 8, 22 Feb 1902, 5 Aug 1905; Hayes, *Negro Govt Worker,* p. 22; Monroe N. Work, ed., *Negro Year Book, An Annual Encyclopedia of the Negro, 1912,* pp. 75–76.
[2] As in chapter VI, citations of the *Bee* are reduced in this chapter to a small sample, since relevant comments appear in almost every issue. *Bee,* 17, 24 Sep, 31 Dec 1904, 17 Mar, 21 Apr, 1, 8 Dec 1906, 4 May 1907; William F. Nowlin, *The Negro in American National Politics,* pp. 114–15; *Negro Year Book, 1912,* pp. 30–31; *Star,* 20 Jun 1909; President Taft to Judge Robert Terrell, 2 Mar 1910, Mary Church Terrell Mss (L.C.).

Navy Department, the District Recorder of Deeds, and Chief Surgeon at the Freed-men's Hospital. President Taft added two more, the office of Collector of Customs at Georgetown and, still more gratifying, the position of Assistant Attorney General of the United States, a plum which fell to a prominent colored lawyer from Boston. At those nine, Negro preferment stood till 1913.

The significance all Negroes attached to those nine offices seems at first out of proportion to their number or their intrinsic importance. But between 1901 and 1913 they represented far more to colored people than sops to racial ambition. For, during the first dozen years of the twentieth century when no colored man sat in Congress, Negro civil service employees came to depend upon the President's Negro appointees to serve as their bulwark against injustice. In the 1880's and 1890's Negro congressmen had filled that role, or at least so colored departmental clerks believed. Now they must look elsewhere for help in getting merited assignments when civil service rules swayed precariously in the winds of a stiffening racism. In 1910 a Negro journalist jokingly called Taft's nine principal Negro appointees "the Black Cabinet." The name stuck, and with some reason: although their intervention was not always successful, it sometimes had the desired effect.[3]

Nevertheless the civil service held fewer opportunities for intelligent Negroes than in the 1880's and 1890's. The commission's rules had always allowed a department or division chief a choice among the three top candidates whose examinations qualified them for a vacancy, but after the turn of the century that latitude, Negroes believed, increasingly came to be a weapon of racial subjugation. Certainly promotions became fewer and fewer for Negroes; more often white associates of lesser education and experience and therefore presumably of lesser competence were pushed ahead of them. By 1908 not more than three or four colored men had advanced into supervisory positions and all colored federal employees in Washington had dwindled from the 1,537 of 1892 to 1,450, about 300 of them clerks, the rest messengers or common laborers. Until 1909 the State Department had no colored employee ranking above a messenger, and the lone Negro who then attained a clerk's rating achieved it, he later explained, because his personal friend, the incoming Secretary of State, insisted that the merit system recognize merit. While Republican campaign literature of 1912 claimed that the federal government then had more than 4,100 colored employees in Washington earning over $4,000,000 a year, those figures were manifestly exaggerated and in any case made little impression upon educated Negroes, who knew that the color of their skins would keep them in the bottom grades of government service.

In the District government civil service rules did not apply at all. The wishes of members of the House or Senate District committees might determine who was hired or promoted and, when congressional patronage did not interfere, the preferences of individual commissioners or their immediate subordinates were the deciding factor. The

[3] *Bee,* 19 Apr 1909, 23 Feb, 25 Mar, 11 Sep 1911, 29 Mar, 12 Apr 1913; William McKinley Clayton to Woodrow Wilson, 19 Mar 1915, Wilson Mss; *Negro Year Book 1912,* pp. 70–71; Hayes, *Negro Govt Worker,* pp. 26–27, 32–35.

Bee insisted that the engineer commissioners never approved of Negroes in any but menial jobs, and of the civilian commissioners only Henry West displayed no "colorphobia." In 1908 out of a clerical force of 450 in the District Building, only 9 were Negroes; among 731 policemen and 498 firemen 39 and 9 respectively were colored; 79
clerks and 55 mail carriers were colored out of 881 city Post Office employees; 460 colored school teachers selected chiefly by the Assistant Superintendent completed the list
of the District's Negro employees in white collar jobs. The pay scale put the yearly income of all but a very few at less than $1,000. Four years later a city containing some
94,000 colored inhabitants and 20,000 colored taxpayers had about 900 Negroes on the
payroll, nearly half of them rated as unskilled laborers at wages of $500 or less a year.[4]

At the same time jobs open to Negroes in other fields, especially domestic service, shrank in number. Judge Terrell put the blame for householders' shift to white
servants upon his own people; for too often, he said, they skimped their work while
making unwarranted demands upon their employers. He viewed the refusal of Negroes
to work for other Negroes as particularly serious in a city where he estimated a tenth to
a fifth of the colored people were jobless; he told the National Negro Business League
in New York of a colored woman who, having advertised for a washwoman, was informed by a colored applicant: "Lady, I can't work for you; I'm in society myself." The
overcrowding of the professions in colored Washington, pronounced in the late nineteenth century, now intensified. In spite of the efforts of the local branch of the newly
organized Negro Business League, and in spite of a few isolated examples of modest
success—an insurance company, a shoe store, and several drug stores—Negro business
enterprises made no progress. In 1903 Washington's one Negro Savings Bank failed; attempts to organize another came to nothing. While the *Bee* improved its appearance,
gave better news coverage, and adopted a more dignified tone, the *Colored American,*
which Booker T. Washington had largely financed, ceased publication in 1904 after a
losing six-year struggle for existence. The *Bee,* in turn, ran into financial difficulties in
1908 when a rival, the Washington *American,* appeared. Calvin Chase's repeated attacks
upon Mr. Washington's "Uncle Tomism" notwithstanding, the educator came to the
Bee's rescue, for he considered a vigorous Negro press an important weapon in the fight
for advancement, and the national capital above all must have Negro newspapers.[5]

Accompanying the growing economic pinch was a gradual tightening of the cordon excluding Negroes from any slight share in a common social life in the city. The

[4] Hayes, *Negro Govt Worker,* pp. 125–30; *Republican Campaign Textbook, 1912,* pp. 71–72; Osceola Madden, "A Color Phase of Washington," *The World Today,* xiv, 549–52; *Bee,* 22 Jul 1905, 11 May, 16 Nov 1907,
2 Oct 1909, 4 May 1912, 20 Feb 1915; Kathleen Dudley Long, "Woodrow Wilson and the Negro, 1912–
1916 " (M.A. Thesis, Bryn Mawr College, 1956), pp. 14–17; H Committee on Reform in the Civil Service,
63C, 2S, "Hearings on Segregation of Clerks and Employees in the Civil Service," pp. 4–5; Sherman's *Directory and Ready Reference of the Colored Population of the District of Columbia, 1913,* pp. 388–417.

[5] *Star,* 20 Aug 1905; *Bee,* 26 Aug, 25 Nov 1905, 27 Mar 1909, 15 Feb 1913; *Rpt B/Ed,* 1910, pp. 207–08;
Booker T. Washington to Judge Robert Terrell, 19 Feb 1906, B. T. Washington Mss; *Negro Year Book, 1912,*
pp. 170, 175; August Meier, "Booker T. Washington and the Negro Press," *Journal of Negro History,* xxxviii,
68, 88–89.

one exception was the children's annual Easter Monday egg-rolling contest on the White House lawn when for a few hours white and colored children intermingled, "all beaten up as it were in a social omelette. Eggs of every color are rolled back and forth . . . and there are just as many shades, if not as many colors, of skin as of egg shell." The rest of the year race prejudice seeping down from parents poisoned the relations between white and colored youngsters. As Joe Gans, the Negro prize fighter, won fame in the ring, whenever a championship bout was scheduled, a boy of either race who ventured alone into Washington's streets beyond his own immediate neighborhood risked a beating up from a gang of the enemy intent upon upholding the honor of Gans or his white rival. One very light-colored, red-haired Negro boy faced double jeopardy, since colored contemporaries outside the Negro section of Foggy Bottom took him for a white, while white boys pounced on him as a Negro. Jack Johnson's victories over Jim Jeffries later made matters worse. Athletic prowess, which in post-World War II years would begin to bridge racial cleavages, merely widened the gulf.

The rapidity with which the breach developed in the first decade of the century is astonishing. In 1902 the Washington *Post,* with an unusual display of interest, devoted a half column to praise of the city's upper-class Negro society, "the Negro scholar in silk hat and frock coat," the well-to-do Negro lawyer, the half-dozen colored members of the Washington Board of Trade, the colored women graduates of Wellesley, Smith, Oberlin, and Russell Sage, the Treble Clef Club, "organized for the study of classical music," the Samuel Coleridge-Taylor Oratorio Society with its 225 voices, and the church choirs which "won golden opinions." Two years later the *Post* was deploring the unseemly ambition of Washington's colored leaders to get "the ballot, recognition, admission to theatres and restaurants, monopoly of the public parks and other like prerogatives," instead of pouring their efforts into establishing colored vocational and manual training schools as Negroes in the Deep South were doing. White residents overlooked the steady decline of illiteracy among Washington's adult Negroes; in 1910 it stood at less than 17 percent. The *Star* suggested that white people should not draw the color line in giving Christmas charity; but otherwise, save for an occasional friendly notice in the Washington *Times,* after 1903 the city's white press confined its favorable comments on Negro activities to applauding Booker T. Washington's Tuskegee program with its implied acknowledgment of Negroes' inherent racial inferiority. By 1908 a dispassionate appraisal of race relations in the capital led a magazine writer to conclude that in Washington "the separation of the races is more nearly complete than in any other city of the Union. The better class of white and colored people know absolutely nothing of each other."

Intelligent Negroes were painfully aware of what was happening. An anonymous article entitled "What It Means to be Colored in the Capital of the United States" listed for readers of the *Independent* some of the new manifestations of racism: in January 1906 the Columbian Debating Society at George Washington University debated the question: "Resolved that a Jim Crow law should be adopted and enforced in the District of Columbia"; the affirmative won; a few months later a bill for Jim Crow street cars was introduced into Congress with a citizens' association endorsement; until 1900 the colored schools had had colored directors of music, art, cooking, sewing, manual training, and physical culture; now all were white. "For fifteen years," wrote the author, "I have resided in Washington, and while it was far from being a 'paradise for colored people' when I first touched these shores, it has been doing its level best ever since to make conditions for us intolerable." [6]

Mounting white antagonism had its effect: from 31 percent of the total population in 1900, colored Washington dropped to 28½ percent in 1910 and would be only 25 percent by 1920. Knowing themselves unwelcome, the colored members of the Board of Trade resigned. At the request of the local chapter of the Women's Christian Temperance Union, Negro women withdrew in 1908 to form a Jim Crow unit. While the severity of sentences imposed on colored misdemeanants increased, white supremacists talked openly of reestablishing the whipping post to check Negro crime or of forcing all "niggers" out of the District. Even generously disposed northerners fell easily into the habit of using only the Christian name in speaking of or to a Negro, no matter how distinguished he might be. In her published *Recollections,* so kindly a person as Mrs. William Howard Taft alluded to her indebtedness to Arthur Brooks, a major in the colored unit of the District militia; but, perhaps because he was also a messenger in the War Department, she wrote of him as "Arthur," never "Major" or "Mr. Brooks"; every white person mentioned, except the Taft children and the uneducated Irish coachman, was dignified by his surname and title. Such minor slights were unimportant save as never-ending reminders to colored people that they had won scant respect from whites.

Probably a better gauge of the strengthening of the caste barrier lay in the attitude of white churchmen. At the Congregational Church, which had welcomed Negro members in the 1870's, a congressman from Maine received an ovation when he stated that colored men should never have been enfranchised *en masse,* but rather one by one as each proved himself ready. Episcopal Bishop Henry Satterlee went further. Giving Negroes equality through suffrage when they were not in fact equal, combined with the growth of the Negro population, he said, had promoted racial hostilities. Although he supported Christian missions for colored people, he thought Negroes "morally and intellectually a weaker race, and . . . even if they should become great landowners, men of wealth and of education, race antagonism would only become stronger and more sharply defined." Washington's Negro intelligentsia no doubt saw some truth in these pronouncements, but the Bishop's repudiation of education, wealth, and political power as means of closing the gap between the races and his statement that a solution must depend upon every Negro's winning for himself "a strong, robust Christ-like character" were profoundly discouraging. Seemingly, white men could remain devils, but colored must become saints. Told by white men year after year of the virtues of Booker T. Washington's subservient philosophy, Negro aristocrats listened without enthusiasm to the sage of Tuskegee when he informed them at the colored YMCA that the eyes of the world were upon them and they must set an example by ridding the city of loafers, drunkards, and gamblers.

---

[6] Mrs. R. Kent Beattie, "Easter Egg-Rolling," *Crisis,* XI, 313–14; *Bee,* 19 Feb 1916; *Post,* 3 Aug 1902, 9 Jan 1904; *Star,* 14 Dec 1903; Madden, "A Color Phase," p. 549; "What It Means to be Colored in the Capital of the United States," and "Our Washington Letter," *Independent,* LXII, 181–86, 1012.

Perhaps the most deadly blow the city's white churches dealt their dark-skinned Christian brethren came in 1910 with the assembling in Washington of the sixth World Sunday School Convention. The local committee on arrangements refused to seat local colored delegates or permit them to march in the parade because they were not members of the District Sunday School Association although they belonged to the World Association and had taken part in earlier conventions. The *Star* reported all "wrinkles . . . smoothed out" by a vote of the organization to make Booker T. Washington a life member, but as Mr. Washington represented "Uncle Tomism" to many local Negroes, the *Star*'s account smacked of belittling the issue.[7]

More alarming to colored Washingtonians were the multiplying instances of racial segregation in government offices. A "Jim Crow corner" first appeared in 1904 in the Bureau of Engraving and Printing. The *Bee* noted in 1905 "a systematic effort inaugurated to Jim Crow the Negro. The fever is spreading. . . . The Negro is afraid to complain." Race prejudice, having once gained a foothold under a Republican regime, quickly widened its reach. Before 1909 separate locker and washrooms and separate lunchroom accommodations had become the rule in several sections of the Treasury and the Department of the Interior, and, although the scheme did not spread far during the next four years, the administration made no move to check or forbid it.

What Republican officials saw fit to allow set the pattern for private concerns. In 1910, at the invitation of the Federation of Citizens' Association, ten recently organized Negro neighborhood groups attended a meeting, only to have their hosts then vote to exclude them from federation membership; the Negroes thereupon took the name Civic Associations and formed their own federation. The local civil rights acts still stood unrepealed, but restaurants, barber shops, and hotels now barred Negroes as a matter of course, theatres admitted them only to "nigger heavens," and railroads and buses carrying passengers into the District from Virginia and Maryland enforced Jim Crow seating. As a suit, if won in court, meant at most token damages for the plaintiff, Negroes ceased to invoke the law.[8] Indeed a good many of them obviously shrank from public complaint lest it feed fuel to the campaign to repeal the laws. White extremists might persuade Congress not only to destroy the last flimsy legal safeguards against racial discrimination in the District of Columbia but to make segregation mandatory.

From 1907 on, bills for Jim Crow cars in the District came up in the House of Representatives at intervals. While a new congressman from Georgia announced his determination to force all Negroes out of government service, agitation for a District anti-miscegenation law made headway. In February 1913 the House passed the bill in less than five minutes; only Senate inaction stopped it. When the Negro Register of the Treasury and a colored guest lunched in the House Office Building restaurant, five congressmen threatened a boycott that would close it down if such an affront to white man-

[7] *Rpt B/Ch*, 1901, p. 269; *Bee*, 11 Feb, 10 Dec 1905, 8 Feb 1908; *Post*, 18 Apr 1904, 7 Nov 1910; *Star*, 11 Jan 1905, 10 May, 20 Jun 1909, 20, 24 May 1910; Mrs. William Howard Taft, *Recollections*, pp. 279–80; *Times*, 14 Jul 1907; *Rpt B/Educ*, 1905, pp. 105–15.

[8] *Bee*, 3 Sep 1904, 11 Feb 1905, 7 May 1910, 4 May 1912.

hood ever recurred; the manager assured them it would not. With lynch law rampant in the Deep South, Negroes in Washington had some reason to think the moment inopportune to protest the curtailment of their own civil rights. Possibly only a few men understood the seriousness of the trend in the capital; before the summer of 1913 perhaps the rank and file were not apprehensive for themselves. But over a ten-year span the evidence the *Bee* assembled and published periodically indicated clearly that Washington Negroes, although spared lynchings, were already subject to most of the discriminations imposed upon colored people elsewhere in America.

The city's upper-class Negroes, however, reacted with growing militance to the accelerating racism of white Washington. Booker T. Washington kept many close friends in the capital, but educated colored people who accepted his program of "racial solidarity, self-help and economic chauvinism" increasingly rejected his methods and his disregard of political action. His conciliatory policies, his anxiety to avoid friction with whites, and his stress upon patience led to a break between him and a group of Negro radicals in 1906 when some twenty-nine "rebels" headed by the brilliant, young W. E. B. DuBois of Atlanta University and William Monroe Trotter, editor of the Boston *Guardian,* launched the so-called "Niagara Movement" with a manifesto of Negro rights and aims. Four Washington Negroes took part in the first Niagara conference. Inspired by that example, leadership long dormant in colored Washington began to reassert itself.

Kelly Miller, professor of sociology and later dean at Howard University, George W. Cook, Treasurer of Howard, the Reverend Samuel Carruthers of the Galbraith AME Church, Francis J. Grimké of the 15th Street Presbyterian Church, three or four other local pastors, Mary Church Terrell, the first president of the National Association of Colored Women, Calvin Chase of the *Bee,* and a score of other men and women who commanded prestige now abandoned the tactics of suffering indignities in silence and began a campaign of outspoken protest against social injustice. Few of them openly criticized Booker T. Washington, and Mrs. Terrell, while serving on the Board of Education, rebuked a Negro newspaperman for objecting to the "Tuskegee idea" of Negro education, although she herself advocated giving the colored child in the District the same schooling as the white. But irrespective of their feelings about Mr. Washington, all of the group joined in publicizing the fact that colored people were not content to be hewers of wood and drawers of water and that whites were deluded if, like the New York *Times,* they thought "the Negroes of the United States are doing very well." [9]

Although Washington's Negro militants constantly gained adherents, the city was not initially in the front of the fight, perhaps because the District's voteless status gave political leadership to New York, Boston, and Chicago, perhaps also because col-

[9] H Rpt 8072, 59C, 2S, Ser 5065; *Star,* 14 May 1909; *Herald,* 21 May 1907; *Post,* 11 Feb 1913; *Crisis,* v, 270–71; Hayes, *Negro Govt Worker,* p. 33; W. E. B. DuBois, *Dusk of Dawn,* pp. 88–89, 92–95; August Meier, "Booker T. Washington and the Negro Press," pp. 75, 79, 80–81; *Bee,* 25 Nov 1905, 25 Apr 1906, 26 Nov 1910, 29 Jul 1911; Mary Church Terrell to H. G. Pinkett, 9 Sep 1906, Terrell Mss; New York *Times,* 18 Apr 1913.

ored people in the largest Negro city in the country, having escaped the excesses of "lily-white" agitation that the Deep South was experiencing, were wary about forcing an issue locally lest it boomerang violently. If, as one scholar avers, Booker T. Washington's greatest ascendency, which spanned the first decade of the century, "coincided with the period of greatest oppression Negroes have faced since the Civil War," the birth of the National Association for the Advancement of Colored People in New York City in 1909 must be recognized as marking the beginning of the slow march upward. Started by a handful of earnest white people, the association from the first was intended to be bi-racial. But of its national officers and staff only W. E. B. DuBois was a Negro, and radicals such as William Trotter of Boston distrusted it too deeply to join or work with it. In Washington, caution and inertia apparently combined to delay until the spring of 1912 the organization of a local branch of the NAACP. Within a few months, it was one of the largest in the country and counted 143 dues-paying members, among them so distinguished a white man as Chief Justice Stafford. But, unlike the New York group, white members were few. Here the most able of the upper-class Negro community took charge, bending their first efforts to providing legal aid for Negro victims of discrimination.[10]

Grim as things looked for all American Negroes in 1912, gleams of hope were visible in Washington. They derived principally from the changing point of view of the city's professional social workers and the volunteers they trained as visitors in the slums. First-hand exposure to the conditions under which honest hard-working colored families had to live taught fair-minded investigators a good deal about the obstacles confronting the city's Negroes. The report of the President's Homes Commission and the United States Labor Department's eye-opening study had presented evidence that starvation wages and destitution were directly related. Businessmen occasionally talked as if lowering the Negro death rate was important only because high mortality interfered with favorable advertising for the city, but few men sounded as sure as once they had that Negro "shiftlessness" lay at the root of the problem. Furthermore, white assumptions that upper-class Negroes lacked civic-mindedness received a jolt when a compilation of scattered data revealed that Negroes had initiated and carried on several projects for their people, notably a day nursery for infants of working mothers. Of the $50,000 collected in Washington for a colored YMCA, colored people contributed $27,000. Conferences between Negro workers at the colored Southwest Settlement House and white philanthropists came to be "remarkably free from race consciousness, the one thought on both sides being the common welfare." Negroes thus brought into touch with whites active in Washington charities could feel the lightening of the atmosphere of censoriousness.[11]

[10] Meier, "Booker T. Washington," p. 88; *Negro Year Book, 1912*, p. 134; *Third Annual Report National Association for the Advancement of Colored People*, p. 23 (hereafter cited as *Anl Rpt NAACP*); Flint Kellogg, "Villard and the NAACP," *Nation*, CLVIII, 137–40; *Crisis*, VI, 190.

[11] A. C. *Rpt, 1903*, p. 23; *Crisis*, III, 51; *Rpt B/Tr*, 1910, p. 8; *Times*, 5 May 1911; Sarah C. Fernandis, "In the Making," *Charities*, XVI, 703–05; *Bee*, 13 Apr 1907, 17, 24 May, 5 Jul 1913; Washington *Sun*, 12 Feb, 14 May 1915.

Inasmuch as white men's respect, not their charity, was the goal of Negro leaders, any sign that a segment of white Washington was ready to work with them for the common good assumed importance. Reform was in the air throughout the United States as the presidential election of 1912 approached, and, noting the fervor with which white muckrakers and Progressives talked of the far-reaching social and political changes that must come, thoughtful colored men dared think reform might extend to race relations. None of the candidates made explicit promises, but while Republicans pointed to President Taft's record of Negro appointments and Theodore Roosevelt denounced "brutal" Democratic and "hypocritical" Republican racial policies, Woodrow Wilson preached the "New Freedom" with its guarantees of "fair and just treatment" for all. The *Bee,* wary of trusting any Democrat, urged its readers when the election was over to have faith in the assurances of Wilson's influential colored supporters that the incoming President would not countenance continued discrimination and segregation.[12]

Negroes in the capital waited eagerly for word of new appointments and measures that would wipe out the Jim Crow sections in government offices. March and most of April 1913 came and went. Confidence in the "New Freedom" gave way to uneasiness. Then piece by piece the world of colored Washington fell apart. Within the next few months the President dismissed all but two of the Negroes whom Taft had appointed "to offices of essential dignity at Washington" and replaced them with white men. He nominated a colored lawyer from Oklahoma for Register of the Treasury with the intention of making the Register's section an all-Negro unit, but when the nominee, intimidated by fierce opposition in the Senate, withdrew his name, Wilson appointed an American Indian. The District Recordship of Deeds, a colored preserve since 1881, went to a white man in 1916. By then the only Negro to hold an appointive position in Washington was Robert Terrell, confirmed in April 1914 for another term as a municipal judge. Disillusioning though these snubs were, they were pin-pricks compared to the segregationist policies officially sanctioned in government departments in the summer of 1913.

"Segregation," reported a white officer of the NAACP, "is no new thing in Washington, and the present administration cannot be said to have inaugurated it. The past few months of Democratic Party control, however, have given segregation impetus and have been marked by more than a beginning of systematic enforcement." As soon as the Virginia-born President was installed in the White House, a group of Negro baiters calling themselves the National Democratic Fair Play Association had undertaken to stir up trouble in order to get Negroes out of the civil service, to restrict them to menial jobs, or at the very least to keep white and colored workers separate. A Fair Play committee busily poking about in various offices had elicited complaints from "Democratic clerks and other white employees of the government who are inimical to the Negro," and had obtained the backing of office-seekers who declared it intolerable for white peo-

[12] Long, "Woodrow Wilson and the Negro," pp. 14–32; *Republican Campaign Text Book, 1912,* p. 238; Theodore Roosevelt, "The Progressives and the Colored Man," *Outlook,* CI, 909–12; *Journal of Negro History,* XXXII, 90; *Bee,* 12 Dec 1912.

ple to work in proximity to Negroes, let alone under their supervision.[13] The President, apparently convinced that racial friction was rife in the executive departments, was anxious to check it if only because it might imperil his legislative programs.

In view of the southern background of Postmaster General Albert Burleson, Secretary of the Treasury William McAdoo, and Secretary of the Navy Josephus Daniels, perhaps segregation would have become standard throughout their departments without the impetus supplied by outside agitation and the shocked disapproval of Mrs. Woodrow Wilson at seeing colored men and white women working in the same room in the Post Office Department. There the change, by whomever inspired, had gone into effect before the end of July 1913, and by autumn the Treasury, after cautiously watching public reaction, had consigned the colored employees of most divisions to separate rooms and forbidden all Negro employees to use the lunch tables and the toilet facilities that for years past they had shared with their white fellows. Similar rules applied in the Navy Department as well as in all federal offices where segregation had obtained under Republican rule.

"The effect is startling," the NAACP report noted. "Those segregated are regarded as a people apart, almost as lepers." White clerks, seemingly without personal convictions, now said they approved. To endorse the new arrangement had become "the thing to do." Yet ever since President Cleveland had quashed every proposal of segregation, the *Bee* pointed out, "Afro-American clerks" had worked side by side with white in "peace and harmony." In the summer of 1913 Booker T. Washington wrote a friend: "I have never seen the colored people [of Washington] so discouraged and so bitter as they are at the present time." Many of them refused at first to believe that the author of "The New Freedom" knew what was afoot, but in late October when a delegation led by William Monroe Trotter of Boston begged him to intervene, the President's evasive answer dissipated doubts: Jim Crowism in the federal government had his approval. A mass meeting to protest "the officializing of race prejudice" overflowed the Metropolitan AME Church, but for the moment Negroes in the government service dared go no further lest they precipitate a drastic change in the civil service law which would extend segregation into every federal department and be far harder to rescind than the word-of-mouth orders of departmental chiefs.[14]

Local leaders of the NAACP realized that "almost every man employed by the government and by the schools risks his position when he stands on our militant platform," but they believed that only a united front could stop the spread of racial discrimination. In November they organized a speakers' bureau to go from church to church,

[13] *Bee*, 29 Mar, 26 Jul, 25 Oct, 15 Nov, 6 Dec 1913; *Nation*, XCVII, 114; *Crisis*, VI, 9, 60–63, XII, 198; New York *Times*, 19 Feb, 25 Apr 1914; L. H. Pickford to Joseph Tumulty, 12 Jun 1916, Wilson Mss; *NAACP Report*, 13 Aug 1913, and "Segregation in Government Departments," *NAACP Report of an Investigation*, 1 Nov 1913, Wilson Mss (hereafter cited as *NAACP Rpt*, 1 Nov 1913); *Post*, 30 Apr 1913.

[14] *Post*, 2, 20 May 1913; Ralph Tyler to President Wilson, 12 May, Booker T. Washington to Oswald Garrison Villard, 10 Aug, enclosed in ltr, Villard to Wilson, 18 Aug 1913, and Villard to Wilson, 29 Sep 1913, Wilson Mss; *Bee*, 10, 17 May, 26 Jul, 6 Sep, 15 Nov 1913; Arthur Link, *The New Freedom*, pp. 245–54; *Crisis*, VI, 220, 289–99, VII, 89; *NAACP Report*, 1 Nov 1913.

society to society, and lodge to lodge, "to arouse the colored people themselves to their danger, to make them feel it through and through, and at the same time to make them willing to make sacrifices for the cause." The response was "nothing short of a miracle." In a city notoriously rent by "all sorts of factions," Archibald Grimké, president of the Washington NAACP branch, almost disbelievingly saw "school teachers whom you would not believe cared for anything but pleasure, society women, young men," join in the campaign. At the M Street High School a group of exceptionally inspiring teachers passed on the torch to their students; for them W. E. B. DuBois became a symbol of liberty. By the early months of 1914 the Washington NAACP had over seven hundred dues-paying members and had sent nearly $4,000 to national headquarters.[15]

Personal letters from influential white men pleading with the President to alter his course and indignant articles in the liberal magazines and newspapers failed to persuade Mr. Wilson to reverse his position. On the contrary, his resistance stiffened. When a second Negro delegation, again led by William Monroe Trotter, reminded him of his earlier promise to see justice done, Wilson lost his temper and told the delegation he was not to be high-pressured. The remonstrances, however, were almost certainly instrumental in preventing the wholesale adoption of segregation throughout the government. In March 1914 when the House Committee on Civil Service Reform held hearings on two bills calling for mandatory racial separation of government employees, a Louisiana sponsor of the bills argued that to put a member of "this inferior race" in a position of authority over Caucasians was unrighteous. By the stamp of color the Lord had decreed a lowly place for Negroes. When Congressman Martin Madden of Illinois asked: "Who can say the Almighty decreed it?" the Louisianan replied: "History, experience, and first-hand knowledge." Northern representatives killed both bills in committee.[16]

In the meantime a Supreme Court ruling that the federal Civil Rights Act of 1875, which had long ago been declared unconstitutional in the states, was invalid also in federal territory opened the door to new discriminatory laws in the District of Columbia. But fresh attempts to exclude Negroes from government service, District anti-miscegenation and Jim Crow street-car bills, and a segregated residential bill patterned on a Baltimore ordinance of 1913 all met with defeat. Pressures in fact eased slightly in 1915 when the Supreme Court in an unforeseen reversal of earlier opinions refused to allow nearby Maryland to write a "grandfather clause" into her constitution.

"More than seventy-five per cent of the present segregation," the *Bee* reminded its readers in 1915, "was transmitted to President Wilson by the Republicans," and the editor noted more Negro promotions in the civil service than in years past. But although the transit companies were not allowed to introduce Jim Crow cars, other District cor-

[15] *Crisis,* VII, 192–93, VIII, 32–33; Dr. Rayford Logan to the author, 9 Mar 1960.

[16] O. G. Villard, "The President and the Negro," *Nation,* XCVII, 114; Villard, "The President and the Segregation at Washington," *North American Review,* CXCVIII, 800–07; "Race Segregation at Washington," *Independent,* LXXX, p. 275; Washington *Herald,* 16 Nov 1914; *Times,* 13 Nov 1914; *Crisis,* IX, 119–27; *Negro Year Book, 1914–15,* pp. 34–36; H Comee on Reform in the Civil Service, 63C, 2S, *Segregation of Clerks and Employees in the Civil Service,* 6 Mar 1914, pp. 3, 7.

porations and individual white citizens interpreted the administration policy to mean that short of open violence they could carry discrimination virtually as far as they chose. Informal agreements between sellers and buyers effectively strengthened the residential color line. In 1914 an eminent Boston lawyer persuaded the American Bar Association to rescind its recent ruling that no Negro could be elected to membership, but the substitute provision that applicants must state their race served the same purpose. While not all white Washingtonians shared the prevailing colorphobia and Chief Justice Wendell Stafford fought it in the District Supreme Court, most of the white community took it for granted that colored teachers should be excluded from a teachers' lecture series held in the Congregational Church and that Negro civic organizations should not be invited to join with the fifty-six white groups in planning better correlation of the city's recreational activities.[17]

The attacks and the disheartening indifference of white people, however, had the effect of maintaining the new solidarity in the Negro world. In Washington's triple-tiered colored community a sense of cohesiveness, lacking for thirty years, had begun to emerge before 1911; it strengthened extraordinarily during the crisis of 1913 and 1914. Although, as the struggle against race prejudice dragged on, the failure to make headway might well have dissolved the new bonds, they endured. In northern cities also, upper-class Negroes, the "talented tenth" upon whom W. E. B. DuBois pinned hopes for the race, saw they could not remain detached from the lower-class black, no matter how superior they knew themselves to be and no matter how uncongenial they found his society. But the growth of "group-identification" among all classes of Washington Negroes had special significance, both because elaborate class distinctions were older here than in most of the United States and because all colored people recognized Washington as the center of Negro culture in America.

The new attitude of the *Bee* supplies an index to this change. Where the paper had once carried scathing accounts of Negro discrimination against Negro and had sneered at any colored man who achieved distinction, the editorials and news articles gradually took on a constructive character. The addition to the editorial staff of the wise, public-spirited George H. Richardson gave the *Bee* new dignity; his opinions carried weight. Calvin Chase, whose attacks on Booker T. Washington had stopped in 1908, lashed out periodically at W. E. B. DuBois, arch opponent of Mr. Washington's subservient teachings, but after the death of the Tuskegee leader in November 1915, those explosions ended. Chase and Richardson saw fit to needle colored men who sought their own advantage at the sacrifice of principle. Editorials called attention to the destructive selfishness of Negro candidates for office under the proscriptive Democratic regime. "Woody," one article declared, "believed his segregation policy was approved by the black gentry because so many of them were anxious to serve under him, segregation or

---

[17] *Crisis*, VII, 117, 142, 169, 252–53; *Negro Year Book, 1914–15,* pp. 30, 34–35, 39; *Times,* 3 Dec 1914; *Bee,* 4 Oct 1914, 27 Feb, 5 Mar, 15 May 1915; *Sun,* 26 Mar, 30 Apr, 25 Jun 1915; H Rpt 1340, 63C, 3S, Ser 6766; H Dis Comee, 64C, 1S, Hrgs, "Intermarriage of Whites and Negroes in the District of Columbia, and Separate Accommodations in Street Cars for White and Negroes in the District of Columbia."

no segregation." Sarcastically the *Bee* observed that no local colored men had had the courage to ask the President in person to define his position on race questions as William Monroe Trotter of Boston had twice obliged him to do, first in November 1913 and again a year later. Yet in taking cowards and the mean-minded to task, the *Bee* also accorded praise to colored men of firm convictions and larger vision. Scoldings at Negro short-comings became progressively fewer and turned instead into exhortations to push on with the noble work of establishing a self-respecting, self-sufficient Negro Washington within the larger community.[18]

Four other Negro publications were appearing regularly in Washington in 1914 and 1915—the short-lived *Sun,* put out by a talented but erratic protégé of Booker T. Washington, the *American,* the *Odd Fellows Journal,* and the *National Union,* organ of a Negro insurance company. In 1915 the *Journal of Negro History* began its long and useful career. The *American,* an uninspired, rather shabby sheet, and the ably edited *Sun* pursued the same line as the *Bee* in less bellicose language: buy colored, support colored charities and colored civic enterprises, take pride in Negro achievements, and don't be "Jim Crowed" by patronizing places where Negroes are segregated. The fourfold program, already familiar, put novel emphasis on Negro successes won by Negro cooperation. Gradually business firms and non-profit groups began to advertise what Negro solidarity had accomplished. They pointed out that the Howard Theatre, upon reverting to colored management after two or three years of white, provided good entertainment—some plays, more minstrel shows, and musical hits like those of the "Black Patti Troubadours"—and by renting the premises for amateur performances now and again served as a kind of community cultural center; at the *Majestic* vaudeville theatre and two new Negro movie houses colored audiences never had to face Jim Crowism. Le Droit Park's 5,000 colored residents could enjoy a similar freedom by giving their custom to the Negro-owned grocery store.

The *Sun,* remarking that the local Negro Business League had gone "to sleep" in 1913, began in 1915 to carry a directory of reliable Negro business firms in the city. A colored department store in a building on 14th Street employed only colored help and met a long-felt want. U Street in northwest Washington was becoming the colored Connecticut Avenue. In southwest Washington the new Douglass Hotel offered colored tourists and conventions comfortable accommodations. The Negro press now insisted on use of the capital *N,* and after 1914 frequently capitalized "colored" also; doubtless in the interest of racial harmony, colored newspapers practically dropped the term "black." Despite the militance of the new propaganda, it was refreshingly free of the braggadocio that had formerly accompanied attempts to encourage Negro enterprise.

Indeed, there was more in which to take pride, as the social disorganization that had long characterized colored Washington began to yield to community effort. Prog-

[18] *Negro Year Book, 1914-15,* pp. 43–45; Arnold M. Rose, *The Negro's Morale, Group Identification and Protest,* pp. 57–95; *Bee,* 21 Nov 1914, 27 Feb, 5 Mar 1915; Colonel Campbell C. Johnson to the author, 9 Jun 1960.

ress, begun even before the disasters of the Wilson era added impetus, was particularly noticeable in the realm of charities and civic undertakings. By the spring of 1913 the recently opened colored YMCA, built brick by brick by Negro workmen, was able to meet its first year's operating costs of $8,200 and show a 56-cent balance. "The fraternal spirit existing between the Y and the local ministry is happily shown in the use by a number of the churches of the great swimming pool for baptismal purposes." As a true community center, the Y became the meeting place of the local branch of the NAACP, the Public School Athletic League, the Christian Endeavor Union, the Federation of Civic Associations, the Negro Medical Society, and other organizations. The colored YWCA expanded its program and paid off all but a small indebtedness during 1913. While public-spirited Negroes admitted that too few well-to-do families contributed to charity, a new determination to carry on without white philanthropy went far toward obliterating their earlier attitude: let the whites shoulder the burden, since they are responsible for the colored man's plight. Roscoe Conkling Bruce, Assistant Superintendent for the colored schools, reminded the audience at the annual meeting of the Colored Social Settlement in December 1913 that Dr. John R. Francis, Washington's leading colored physician, had launched the center "about which many and various efforts for social uplift are organized." In appealing for generous support of this primarily Negro-sponsored charity, Bruce pleaded also for teaching colored children about the great men of their own race; only thus would the younger generation escape being overwhelmed by white prestige and avoid impairment of colored initiative. In much the same vein the newly organized Oldest Inhabitants Association (Colored) of Washington announced its purpose to be the fostering of Negro civic pride.[19]

It would be untruthful to picture colored Washington in 1915 and 1916 as a unified community free of the old divisive jealousies and destructive backbiting, its individual members now single-mindedly working all for one and one for all. Leaders faltered, quarrels persisted—particularly over teaching appointments and promotions in the school system—and self-contempt, shown in the sheer meanness of Negro to Negro, continued to interfere with the important task of raising the economic level of all classes. The *Sun* argued that the cost of racial disunity was as high for the light-colored Caucasian-featured person as for the black-skinned Negroid-looking, but few of the former were willing to discard class distinctions based largely upon degree of color. Moreover, the tightening of the net drawn by strengthened white hostility, while binding courageous colored people together in a common purpose, strangled the will of the weak and timid; circumstances that awakened a fighting spirit in some of the race stripped others of the capacity to hold up their heads at all. Nevertheless the energy with which Washington's Negro leaders fought lynching in the South and racial discrimination everywhere was impressive.[20]

[19] *Bee*, 17 May, 6 Dec 1913, 2 Oct 1915, 25 May 1916; *Sun*, 8 Jan, 12 Mar, 23 Apr 1915; *Crisis*, XI, 90–94; John H. Paynter, *A Souvenir of the Anniversary and Banquet of the Oldest Inhabitants Association (Colored) of the District of Columbia, April 16, 1914.*

[20] *Sun*, 12, 26 Feb 1915; M. C. Terrell to Robert Terrell, n.d., Terrell Mss. Practically every issue of the *Bee* carried some complaint about Negro school administrators' injustices.

W. E. B. DuBois later wrote of the early years of the Wilson administration: "Quite suddenly the program for the NAACP, which up to this time had been more or less indefinite, was made clear and intensive." The Washington branch forestalled adverse legislation, got a few Negroes reinstated in government jobs, and induced Congress to continue appropriations for Howard University and its 300 college students. Besides a vigorous separate University chapter, by 1916 the Washington branch of the NAACP, with 1,164 members, was the largest in the United States, and, according to national headquarters, constituted "really a national vigilance committee to watch legislation in Congress and lead the fight for Negro manhood rights at the capital of the nation." [21]

Differences of opinion inescapably arose over both long-term strategy and more immediate local tactics. For example, in which direction should Washington Negroes lean when the discussion of District Home Rule revived in 1916? At one time the colored press had argued that voting in municipal elections was essential to the progress of the city's Negro community. But as Henry West and Frederick Siddons had always treated Negroes with exemplary fairness and Oliver Newman and Louis Brownlow showed no racial prejudice, might not colored people be better off under the rule of commissioners like those than under officials chosen by a two-thirds white electorate? Most colored men side-stepped the question; if white citizens persuaded Congress to restore the franchise, then would be time enough for their colored neighbors to seek their share of local political power. Again, what was the wise course to pursue when "The Birth of a Nation" began its long run in Washington movie houses? Some men, seeing it as an incitement to race hatred, wanted to demand that the commissioners ban the picture, just as they had barred the prize fight film of Jack Johnson beating Jim Jeffries; other colored people believed that a petition for censorship would merely advertise the offensive DeMille film more widely.

While in the national arena Negro leaders examined alternatives as the presidential campaign of 1916 opened, in the voteless capital the question about working with whites for "national preparedness" caused uncertainty. In June 1916 the colored men who marched in a big preparedness parade were "Jim Crowed with a vengeance" and two days later were greeted with a formal segregation order from the War Department. At the request of a New Jersey congressman whose reelection hung in the balance, the order was later rescinded, but before the end of October the all-Negro battalion of the District National Guard was on the Mexican border. Six months later the United States' declaration of war upon the Central Powers would force upon all American Negroes a decision of whether to be Americans first and Negroes second or to let white Americans carry on without voluntary help from the people they treated as second-class citizens. [22]

[21] W. E. B. DuBois, *Dusk of Dawn*, pp. 235–36; *Sun*, 15 Jan, 12 Mar 1915; *Crisis*, IX, 217, XI, 35, 256, XII, 197; see also list of Washington members at the 1916 conference at Amenia, New York, *Programme*, Terrell Mss.

[22] *Bee*, 14 Nov 1908, 1 Apr 1916, 17, 19 Jun, 9 Sep, 21 Oct 1916; *Sun*, 9 Apr 1915; Rose, *The Negro's Morale*, pp. 38–39; *Seventh Anl Rpt NAACP*, 1917; *Crisis*, XII, 194, 268; W. E. B. DuBois to Woodrow Wilson, 10 Oct 1916, and Memorial, Boston Branch Negro Equal Political Rights League, 20 Apr 1917, Wilson Mss.

Still, every Washingtonian daily rubbed elbows with or at least was aware of the presence of people not of his own race. Scores of Negroes were as acutely concerned with municipal taxation, civic betterment, and artistic growth as were their white-skinned neighbors. Whether they would or no, some give-and-take resulted. An experiment of 1913 in publishing a Negro city directory was not repeated. Colored Washington, largely separate and wholly unequal in status, was still part of the over-all community.

Of Mr. Booker T. Washington and Others*

William E. B. Du Bois

From birth till death enslaved; in word, in deed, unmanned!

.　　.　　.　　.　　.　　.　　.

Hereditary bondsmen! Know ye not
Who would be free themselves must strike the blow?

BYRON.

Easily the most striking thing in the history of the American Negro since 1876 is the ascendancy of Mr. Booker T. Washington. It began at the time when war memories and ideals were rapidly passing; a day of astonishing commercial development was dawning; a sense of doubt and hesitation overtook the freedmen's sons,—then it was that his leading began. Mr. Washington came, with a single definite programme, at the psychological moment when the nation was a little ashamed of having bestowed so much sentiment on Negroes, and was concentrating its energies on Dollars. His programme of industrial education, conciliation of the South, and submission and silence as to civil and political rights, was not wholly original; the Free Negroes from 1830 up to wartime had striven to build industrial schools, and the American Missionary Association had from the first taught various trades; and Price and others had sought a way of honorable alliance with the best of the Southerners. But Mr. Washington first indissolubly linked these things; he put enthusiasm, unlimited energy, and perfect faith into this programme, and changed it from a by-path into a veritable Way of Life. And the tale of the methods by which he did this is a fascinating study of human life.

* From William Edward Burghardt Du Bois, *Souls of Black Folk* (New York: Fawcett Premier Books, 1916), pp. 42–54. Reprinted by permission of Shirley Graham Du Bois.

It startled the nation to hear a Negro advocating such a programme after many decades of bitter complaint; it startled and won the applause of the South, it interested and won the admiration of the North; and after a confused murmur of protest, it silenced if it did not convert the Negroes themselves.

To gain the sympathy and coöperation of the various elements comprising the white South was Mr. Washington's first task; and this, at the time Tuskegee was founded, seemed, for a black man, well-nigh impossible. And yet ten years later it was done in the word spoken at Atlanta: "In all things purely social we can be as separate as the five fingers, and yet one as the hand in all things essential to mutual progress." This "Atlanta Compromise" is by all odds the most notable thing in Mr. Washington's career. The South interpreted it in different ways: the radicals received it as a complete surrender of the demand for civil and political equality; the conservatives, as a generously conceived working basis for mutual understanding. So both approved it, and to-day its author is certainly the most distinguished Southerner since Jefferson Davis, and the one with the largest personal following.

Next to this achievement comes Mr. Washington's work in gaining place and consideration in the North. Others less shrewd and tactful had formerly essayed to sit on these two stools and had fallen between them; but as Mr. Washington knew the heart of the South from birth and training, so by singular insight he intuitively grasped the spirit of the age which was dominating the North. And so thoroughly did he learn the speech and thought of triumphant commercialism, and the ideals of material prosperity, that the picture of a lone black boy poring over a French grammar amid the weeds and dirt of a neglected home soon seemed to him the acme of absurdities. One wonders what Socrates and St. Francis of Assisi would say to this.

And yet this very singleness of vision and thorough oneness with his age is a mark of the successful man. It is as though Nature must needs make men narrow in order to give them force. So Mr. Washington's cult has gained unquestioning followers, his work has wonderfully prospered, his friends are legion, and his enemies are confounded. To-day he stands as the one recognized spokesman of his ten million fellows, and one of the most notable figures in a nation of seventy millions. One hesitates, therefore, to criticise a life which, beginning with so little, has done so much. And yet the time is come when one may speak in all sincerity and utter courtesy of the mistakes and shortcomings of Mr. Washington's career, as well as of his triumphs, without being thought captious or envious, and without forgetting that it is easier to do ill than well in the world.

The criticism that has hitherto met Mr. Washington has not always been of this broad character. In the South especially has he had to walk warily to avoid the harshest judgments,—and naturally so, for he is dealing with the one subject of deepest sensitiveness to that section. Twice—once when at the Chicago celebration of the Spanish-American War he alluded to the color-prejudice that is "eating away the vitals of the South," and once when he dined with President Roosevelt—has the resulting Southern criticism been violent enough to threaten seriously his popularity. In the North the feeling has several times forced itself into words, that Mr. Washington's counsels of submission overlooked certain elements of true manhood, and that his educational programme was unnecessarily narrow. Usually, however, such criticism has not found open expression, although, too, the spiritual sons of the Abolitionists have not been prepared to acknowledge that the schools founded before Tuskegee, by men of broad ideals and self-sacrificing spirit, were wholly failures or worthy of ridicule. While, then, criticism has not failed to follow Mr. Washington, yet the prevailing public opinion of the land has been but too willing to deliver the solution of a wearisome problem into his hands, and say, "If that is all you and your race ask, take it."

Among his own people, however, Mr. Washington has encountered the strongest and most lasting opposition, amounting at times to bitterness, and even to-day continuing strong and insistent even though largely silenced in outward expression by the public opinion of the nation. Some of this opposition is, of course, mere envy; the disappointment of displaced demagogues and the spite of narrow minds. But aside from this, there is among educated and thoughtful colored men in all parts of the land a feeling of deep regret, sorrow, and apprehension at the wide currency and ascendancy which some of Mr. Washington's theories have gained. These same men admire his sincerity of purpose, and are willing to forgive much to honest endeavor which is doing something worth the doing. They coöperate with Mr. Washington as far as they conscientiously can; and, indeed, it is no ordinary tribute to this man's tact and power that, steering as he must between so many diverse interests and opinions, he so largely retains the respect of all.

But the hushing of the criticism of honest opponents is a dangerous thing. It leads some of the best of the critics to unfortunate silence and paralysis of effort, and others to burst into speech so passionately and intemperately as to lose listeners. Honest and earnest criticism from those whose interests are most nearly touched,—criticism of writers by readers, of government by those governed, of leaders by those led,—this is the soul of democracy and the safeguard of modern society. If the best of the American Negroes receive by outer pressure a leader whom they had not recognized before, manifestly there is here a certain palpable gain. Yet there is also irreparable loss,—a loss of that peculiarly valuable education which a group receives when by search and criticism it finds and commissions its own leaders. The way in which this is done is at once the most elementary and the nicest problem of social growth. History is but the record of such group-leadership; and yet how infinitely changeful is its type and character! And of all types and kinds, what can be more instructive than the leadership of a group within a group?—that curious double movement where real progress may be negative and actual advance be relative retrogression. All this is the social student's inspiration and despair.

Now in the past the American Negro has had instructive experience in the choosing of group leaders, founding thus a peculiar dynasty which in the light of present conditions is worth while studying. When sticks and stones and beasts form the sole environment of a people, their attitude is largely one of determined opposition to and conquest of natural forces. But when to earth and brute is added an environment of men and ideas, then the attitude of the imprisoned group may take three main forms,— a feeling of revolt and revenge; an attempt to adjust all thought and action to the will of the greater group; or, finally, a determined effort at self-realization and self-development despite environing opinion. The influence of all of these attitudes at various times can be traced in the history of the American Negro, and in the evolution of his successive leaders.

Before 1750, while the fire of African freedom still burned in the veins of the slaves, there was in all leadership or attempted leadership but the one motive of revolt and revenge,—typified in the terrible Maroons, the Danish blacks, and Cato of Stono, and veiling all the Americas in fear of insurrection. The liberalizing tendencies of the latter half of the eighteenth century brought, along with kindlier relations between black and white, thoughts of ultimate adjustment and assimilation. Such aspiration was especially voiced in the earnest songs of Phyllis, in the martyrdom of Attucks, the fighting of Salem and Poor, the intellectual accomplishments of Banneker and Derham, and the political demands of the Cuffes.

Stern financial and social stress after the war cooled much of the previous humanitarian ardor. The disappointment and impatience of the Negroes at the persistence of slavery and serfdom voiced itself in two movements. The slaves in the South, aroused undoubtedly by vague rumors of the Haytian revolt, made three fierce attempts at insurrection,—in 1800 under Gabriel in Virginia, in 1822 under Vesey in Carolina, and in 1831 again in Virginia under the terrible Nat Turner. In the Free States, on the other hand, a new and curious attempt at self-development was made. In Philadelphia and New York color-prescription led to a withdrawal of Negro communicants from white churches and the formation of a peculiar socio-religious institution among the Negroes known as the African Church,—an organization still living and controlling in its various branches over a million of men.

Walker's wild appeal against the trend of the times showed how the world was changing after the coming of the cotton-gin. By 1830 slavery seemed hopelessly fastened on the South, and the slaves thoroughly cowed into submission. The free Negroes of the North, inspired by the mulatto immigrants from the West Indies, began to change the basis of their demands; they recognized the slavery of slaves, but insisted that they themselves were freemen, and sought assimilation and amalgamation with the nation on the same terms with other men. Thus, Forten and Purvis of Philadelphia, Shad of Wilmington, Du Bois of New Haven, Barbadoes of Boston, and others strove singly and together as men, they said, not as slaves; as "people of color," not as "Negroes." The trend of the times, however, refused them recognition save in individual and exceptional cases, considered them as one with all the despised blacks, and they soon found themselves striving to keep even the rights they formerly had of voting and working and moving as freemen. Schemes of migration and colonization arose among them; but these they refused to entertain, and they eventually turned to the Abolition movement as a final refuge.

Here, led by Remond, Nell, Wells-Brown, and Douglass, a new period of self-assertion and self-development dawned. To be sure, ultimate freedom and assimilation was the ideal before the leaders, but the assertion of the manhood rights of the Negro by himself was the main reliance, and John Brown's raid was the extreme of its logic. After the war and emancipation, the great form of Frederick Douglass, the greatest of American Negro leaders, still led the host. Self-assertion, especially in political lines, was the main programme, and behind Douglass came Elliot, Bruce, and Langston, and the Reconstruction politicians, and, less conspicuous but of greater social significance Alexander Crummell and Bishop Daniel Payne.

Then came the Revolution of 1876, the suppression of the Negro votes, the changing and shifting of ideals, and the seeking of new lights in the great night. Douglass, in his old age, still bravely stood for the ideals of his early manhood,—ultimate assimilation *through* self-assertion, and on no other terms. For a time Price arose as a new leader, destined, it seemed, not to give up, but to re-state the old ideals in a form less repugnant to the white South. But he passed away in his prime. Then came the new leader. Nearly all the former ones had become leaders by the silent suffrage of their fellows, had sought to lead their own people alone, and were usually, save Douglass, little known outside their race. But Booker T. Washington arose as essentially the leader not of one race but of two,—a compromiser between the South, the North, and the Negro. Naturally the Negroes resented, at first bitterly, signs of compromise which surrendered their civil and political rights, even though this was to be exchanged for larger chances of economic development. The rich and dominating North, however, was not only weary of the race problem, but was investing largely in Southern enterprises, and welcomed any method of peaceful coöperation. Thus, by national opinion, the Negroes began to recognize Mr. Washington's leadership; and the voice of criticism was hushed.

Mr. Washington represents in Negro thought the old attitude of adjustment and submission; but adjustment at such a peculiar time as to make his programme unique. This is an age of unusual economic development, and Mr. Washington's programme naturally takes an economic cast, becoming a gospel of Work and Money to such an extent as apparently almost completely to overshadow the higher aims of life. Moreover, this is an age when the more advanced races are coming in closer contact with the less developed races, and the race-feeling is therefore intensified; and Mr. Washington's programme practically accepts the alleged inferiority of the Negro races. Again, in our own land, the reaction from the sentiment of war time has given impetus to race-prejudice against Negroes, and Mr. Washington withdraws many of the high demands of Negroes as men and American citizens. In other periods of intensified prejudice all the Negro's tendency to self-assertion has been called forth; at this period a policy of submission is advocated. In the history of nearly all other races and peoples the doctrine preached at such crises has been that manly self-respect is worth more than lands and houses, and that a people who voluntarily surrender such respect, or cease striving for it, are not worth civilizing.

In answer to this, it has been claimed that the Negro can survive only through submission. Mr. Washington distinctly asks that black people give up, at least for the present, three things,—

First, political power,

Second, insistence on civil rights,

Third, higher education of Negro youth,—

and concentrate all their energies on industrial education, the accumulation of wealth, and the conciliation of the South. This policy has been courageously and insistently advocated for over fifteen years, and has been triumphant for perhaps ten years. As a result of this tender of the palm-branch, what has been the return? In these years there have occurred:

1. The disfranchisement of the Negro.
2. The legal creation of a distinct status of civil inferiority for the Negro.
3. The steady withdrawal of aid from institutions for the higher training of the Negro.

These movements are not, to be sure, direct results of Mr. Washington's teachings; but his propaganda has, without a shadow of doubt, helped their speedier accomplishment. The question then comes: Is it possible, and probable, that nine millions of men can make effective progress in economic lines if they are deprived of political rights, made a servile caste, and allowed only the most meagre chance for developing their exceptional men? If history and reason give any distinct answer to these questions, it is an emphatic *No.* And Mr. Washington thus faces the triple paradox of his career:

1. He is striving nobly to make Negro artisans business men and property-owners; but it is utterly impossible, under modern competitive methods, for workingmen and property-owners to defend their rights and exist without the right of suffrage.
2. He insists on thrift and self-respect, but at the same time counsels a silent submission to civic inferiority such as is bound to sap the manhood of any race in the long run.
3. He advocates common-school and industrial training, and depreciates institutions of higher learning; but neither the Negro common-schools, nor Tuskegee itself, could remain open a day were it not for teachers trained in Negro colleges, or trained by their graduates.

This triple paradox in Mr. Washington's position is the object of criticism by two classes of colored Americans. One class is spiritually descended from Toussaint the Savior, through Gabriel, Vesey, and Turner, and they represent the attitude of revolt and revenge; they hate the white South blindly and distrust the white race generally, and so far as they agree on definite action, think that the Negro's only hope lies in emigration beyond the borders of the United States. And yet, by the irony of fate, nothing has more effectually made this programme seem hopeless than the recent course of the United States toward weaker and darker peoples in the West Indies, Hawaii, and the Philippines,—for where in the world may we go and be safe from lying and brute force?

The other class of Negroes who cannot agree with Mr. Washington has hitherto said little aloud. They deprecate the sight of scattered counsels, of internal disagreement; and especially they dislike making their just criticism of a useful and earnest man an excuse for a general discharge of venom from small-minded opponents. Nevertheless, the questions involved are so fundamental and serious that it is difficult to see how men like the Grimkes, Kelly Miller, J. W. E. Bowen, and other representatives of this group, can much longer be silent. Such men feel in conscience bound to ask of this nation three things:

1. The right to vote.
2. Civic equality.
3. The education of youth according to ability.

They acknowledge Mr. Washington's invaluable service in counselling patience and courtesy in such demands; they do not ask that ignorant black men vote when ignorant whites are debarred, or that any reasonable restrictions in the suffrage should not be applied; they know that the low social level of the mass of the race is responsible for much discrimination against it, but they also know, and the nation knows, that relentless color-prejudice is more often a cause than a result of the Negro's degradation; they seek the abatement of this relic of barbarism, and not its systematic encouragement and pampering by all agencies of social power from the Associated Press to the Church of Christ. They advocate, with Mr. Washington, a broad system of Negro common schools supplemented by thorough industrial training; but they are surprised that a man of Mr. Washington's insight cannot see that no such educational system ever has rested or can rest on any other basis than that of the well-equipped college and university, and they insist that there is a demand for a few such institutions throughout the South to train the best of the Negro youth as teachers, professional men, and leaders.

This group of men honor Mr. Washington for his attitude of conciliation toward the white South; they accept the "Atlanta Compromise" in its broadest interpretation; they recognize, with him, many signs of promise, many men of high purpose and fair judgment, in this section; they know that no easy task has been laid upon a region already tottering under heavy burdens. But, nevertheless, they insist that the way to truth and right lies in straightforward honesty, not in indiscriminate flattery; in praising those of the South who do well and criticising uncompromisingly those who do ill; in taking advantage of the opportunities at hand and urging their fellows to do the same, but at the same time in remembering that only a firm adherence to their higher ideals and aspirations will ever keep those ideals within the realm of possibility. They do not expect that the free right to vote, to enjoy civic rights, and to be educated, will come in a moment; they do not expect to see the bias and prejudices of years disappear at the blast of a trumpet; but they are absolutely certain that the way for a people to gain their reasonable rights is not by voluntarily throwing them away and insisting that they do not want them; that the way for a people to gain respect is not by continually belittling and ridiculing themselves; that, on the contrary, Negroes must insist continually, in season and out of season, that voting is necessary to modern manhood, that color discrimination is barbarism, and that black boys need education as well as white boys.

In failing thus to state plainly and unequivocally the legitimate demands of their people, even at the cost of opposing an honored leader, the thinking classes of American Negroes would shirk a heavy responsibility,—a responsibility to themselves, a responsibility to the struggling masses, a responsibility to the darker races of men whose future depends so largely on this American experiment, but especially a responsibility to this nation,—this common Fatherland. It is wrong to encourage a man or a people in evil-doing; it is wrong to aid and abet a national crime simply because it is unpopular not to do so. The growing spirit of kindliness and reconciliation between the North and South after the frightful difference of a generation ago ought to be a source of deep congratulation to all, and especially to those whose mistreatment caused the war; but if that reconciliation is to be marked by the industrial slavery and civic death of those same black men, with permanent legislation into a position of inferiority, then those black men, if they are really men, are called upon by every consideration of patriotism and loyalty to oppose such a course by all civilized methods, even though such opposition involves disagreement with Mr. Booker T. Washington. We have no right to sit silently by while the inevitable seeds are sown for a harvest of disaster to our children, black and white.

First, it is the duty of black men to judge the South discriminatingly. The present generation of Southerners are not responsible for the past, and they should not be blindly hated or blamed for it. Furthermore, to no class is the indiscriminate endorsement of the recent course of the South toward Negroes more nauseating than to the best thought of the South. The South is not "solid"; it is a land in the ferment of social change, wherein forces of all kinds are fighting for supremacy; and to praise the ill the South is to-day perpetrating is just as wrong as to condemn the good. Discriminating and broad-minded criticism is what the South needs,—needs it for the sake of her own white sons and daughters, and for the insurance of robust, healthy mental and moral development.

To-day even the attitude of the Southern whites toward the blacks is not, as so many assume, in all cases the same; the ignorant Southerner hates the Negro, the workingmen fear his competition, the money-makers wish to use him as a laborer, some of the educated see a menace in his upward development, while others—usually the sons of the masters—wish to help him to rise. National opinion has enabled this last class to maintain the Negro common schools, and to protect the Negro partially in property, life, and limb. Through the pressure of the money-makers, the Negro is in danger of being reduced to semi-slavery, especially in the country districts; the workingmen, and those of the educated who fear the Negro, have united to disfranchise him, and some have urged his deportation; while the passions of the ignorant are easily aroused to lynch and abuse any black man. To praise this intricate whirl of thought and prejudice is nonsense; to inveigh indiscriminately against "the South" is unjust; but to use the same breath in praising Governor Aycock, exposing Senator Morgan, arguing with Mr. Thomas Nelson Page, and denouncing Senator Ben Tillman, is not only sane, but the imperative duty of thinking black men.

It would be unjust to Mr. Washington not to acknowledge that in several instances he has opposed movements in the South which were unjust to the Negro; he sent memorials to the Louisiana and Alabama constitutional conventions, he has spoken against lynching, and in other ways has openly or silently set his influence against sinister schemes and unfortunate happenings. Notwithstanding this, it is equally true to assert that on the whole the distinct impression left by Mr. Washington's propaganda is, first, that the South is justified in its present attitude toward the Negro because of the Negro's degradation; secondly, that the prime cause of the Negro's failure to rise more quickly is his wrong education in the past; and, thirdly, that his future rise depends primarily on his own efforts. Each of these propositions is a dangerous half-truth. The supplementary truths must never be lost sight of: first, slavery and race-prejudice are potent if not sufficient causes of the Negro's position; second, industrial and common-school training were necessarily slow in planting because they had to await the black teachers trained by higher institutions,—it being extremely doubtful if any essentially different development was possible, and certainly a Tuskegee was unthinkable before 1880; and, third, while it is a great truth to say that the Negro must strive and strive mightily to help himself, it is equally true that unless his striving be not simply seconded, but rather aroused and encouraged, by the initiative of the richer and wiser environing group, he cannot hope for great success.

In his failure to realize and impress this last point, Mr. Washington is especially to be criticised. His doctrine has tended to make the whites, North and South, shift the burden of the Negro problem to the Negro's shoulders and stand aside as critical and rather pessimistic spectators; when in fact the burden belongs to the nation, and the hands of none of us are clean if we bend not our energies to righting these great wrongs.

The South ought to be led, by candid and honest criticism, to assert her better self and do her full duty to the race she has cruelly wronged and is still wronging. The North—her co-partner in guilt—cannot salve her conscience by plastering it with gold. We cannot settle this problem by diplomacy and suaveness, by "policy" alone. If worse come to worst, can the moral fibre of this country survive the slow throttling and murder of nine millions of men?

The black men of America have a duty to perform, a duty stern and delicate,—a forward movement to oppose a part of the work of their greatest leader. So far as Mr. Washington preaches Thrift, Patience, and Industrial Training for the masses, we must hold up his hands and strive with him, rejoicing in his honors and glorying in the strength of this Joshua called of God and of man to lead the headless host. But so far as Mr. Washington apologizes for injustice, North or South, does not rightly value the privilege and duty of voting, belittles the emasculating effects of caste distinctions, and opposes the higher training and ambition of our brighter minds,—so far as he, the South, or the Nation, does this,—we must unceasingly and firmly oppose them. By every civilized and peaceful method we must strive for the rights which the world accords to men, clinging unwaveringly to those great words which the sons of the Fathers would fain forget: "We hold these truths to be self-evident: That all men are created equal; that they are endowed by their Creator with certain unalienable rights; that among these are life, liberty, and the pursuit of happiness."

Accommodating Leadership*

Gunnar Myrdal

1. LEADERSHIP AND CASTE

The Negro world conforms closely to the general American pattern just described. In fact, the caste situation—by holding down participation and integration of Negroes—has the effect of exaggerating the pattern.

We base our typology of Negro leadership upon the two extreme policies of behavior on behalf of the Negro as a subordinated caste: *accommodation* and *protest*. The first attitude is mainly static; the second is mainly dynamic. In this chapter we shall ignore almost entirely the dynamic attitude of protest and discuss the intercaste relation in terms of social statics. The object of study here is thus the role of the accommodating Negro leader. Our analysis will approach fuller realism only when we, in later chapters, bring in also the protest motive. This reservation should be held in mind when reading this chapter.

Accommodation is undoubtedly stronger than protest, particularly in the South where the structure of caste is most pervasive and unyielding. In a sense, accommodation is historically the "natural" or the "normal" behavior of Negroes and, even at present, the most "realistic" one. But it is practically never wholehearted in any American Negro, however well adjusted to his situation he seems to be. Every Negro has some feeling of protest against caste, and every Negro has some sort of conflict with the white world. Some Negroes are primarily driven by the protest motive. Social changes which affect Negro attitudes—for example, the development of Negro education, caste isolation, class stratification, and the northward migration—are all giving the protest motive increasing weight, at the same time as the economic, political, judicial, and ideological changes in American society tend to give an ever wider scope for Negro protest. Both main motives—or any intermediate one composed of a blend of these two—have their main origin in, and take their specific character from, the caste situation.

* From Gunnar Myrdal, *An American Dilemma* (New York: Harper & Bros., 1944). pp. 720–35. Copyright 1944, 1962 by Harper & Row, Publishers, Inc. Reprinted by permission of the publishers.

2. THE INTEREST OF SOUTHERN WHITES
AND NEGROES WITH RESPECT TO NEGRO
LEADERSHIP

The white caste has an obvious interest in trying to have accommodating Negro leaders to help them control the Negro group. Under no circumstances, in any community where the Negro forms a substantial portion of the total population, are the attitudes and behavior of the Negroes a matter of no concern to the whites. Negroes may be robbed of suffrage and subdued by partiality in justice, by strict segregation rules, by economic dependence, and by other caste sanctions; but it makes a great deal of difference to the whites how the Negroes—within the narrow margin of their freedom— feel, think and act.

The whites have a material interest in keeping the Negroes in a mood of wanting to be faithful and fairly efficient workers. They have an interest in seeing to it that the Negroes preserve as decent standards of homemaking, education, health, and law observance as possible, so that at least contagious diseases and crime will not react back upon the whites too much. In this particular respect, whites formerly under-estimated the community of interest which follows from being neighbors, but they are increasingly becoming aware of it.

Further, as we have seen, the whites in the South have a strong interest that Negroes be willing, and not only forced, to observe the complicated system of racial etiquette. Southern whites also see a danger in that Negroes are becoming influenced by certain social ideas prevalent in the wider society. They want to keep them away from "red agitators" and "outside meddlers." In most Southern communities the ruling classes of whites want to keep Negroes from joining labor unions. Some are quite frank in wanting to keep Negroes from reading the Constitution or studying social subjects. Besides these and other interests of a clearly selfish type, many whites feel an altruistic interest in influencing Negroes to gain improved standards of knowledge, morals and conduct.

As the contacts between the two groups are becoming increasingly restricted and formalized, whites are more and more compelled to attempt to influence the Negro masses indirectly. For this they need liaison agents in the persons of Negro "leaders." This need was considerably smaller in earlier times when numerous personal and, in a sense, friendly master-servant relations were in existence. These personal relations of old times are now almost gone. This means that the whites have seen their possibilities of controlling the Negro masses directly—that is, by acting themselves as "Negro leaders" —much diminished. The whites have increasingly to resort to leaders in the Negro group. They have, therefore, an interest in helping those leaders obtain as much prestige and influence in the Negro community as possible—as long as they cooperate with the whites faithfully.

On the other side of the caste gulf, the Negroes need persons to establish contact with the influential people in the white group. They need Negro leaders who can talk to, and get things from, the whites. The Negroes in the South are dependent upon the whites not only for a share in the public services, but individually for small favors and personal protection in a social order determined nearly exclusively by the whites, usually in an arbitrary fashion. The importance of Negro leaders to the masses of Negroes —as to the whites—is also increasing as it is becoming more rare for Negroes to have individual white friends to appeal to when they are in danger or in need of assistance.*

Under these circumstances it is understandable that the individual Negro who becomes known to have contact with substantial white people gains prestige and influence among Negroes for this very reason. Correspondingly, an accommodating Negro who is known to be influential in the Negro community becomes, because of this, the more useful to the whites. The Negro leader in this setting serves a "function" to both castes and his influence in both groups is cumulative—prestige in the Negro community being an effect as well as a cause of prestige among the whites. Out of this peculiar power system, a situation develops where Negro leaders play an even more important role than is usual, according to the common American pattern.

3. IN THE NORTH AND ON THE NATIONAL SCENE

In the North fewer white people are in a position where they have to care much about how the Negroes fare, or what they think and do. The Negroes, on their side, have the protection of fairly impartial justice and of the anonymity of large cities. They also have the vote and can press their needs in the regular fashion of American minority politics. They are, therefore, decidedly less dependent on accommodating leaders to court the whites. For neither of the two castes does the Negro leader fill such important functions as in the South.

But the pattern of pleading to the whites through their own leaders, who are trusted by the whites, is firmly rooted in the traditions of Southern-born Negroes who make up the great majority of adult Negroes in the North. Northern Negroes, also, are a poor group and are frequently in need of public assistance and private charity. They are discriminated against in various ways, particularly with respect to employment opportunities. They live in segregated districts and have few contacts with white people in most spheres of life. Though they have the vote, they are everywhere in a small minority. For all these reasons many of the Southern attitudes and policies in regard to Negro leadership can be observed to continue in the North.

Isolation breeds suspicion among Negroes against the majority group. And suspicion is, in fact, justified. For isolation bars the growth of feelings of mutual identification and of solidarity of interests and ideals in both groups. A white man's purposes when stepping down to lead Negroes must be scrutinized carefully before he can be trusted. This is a pragmatic truth obvious even to the most unsophisticated Negroes,

---

* Factors which are decreasing the importance of accommodating Negro leaders to the Negro masses in the South are, on the other hand: the raised standards of legal culture in the region, the increasing professionalism and independence in state and local government administration, and particularly the growth of federal assistance and control.

and it has a basis in the Negro people's history through centuries. Northern Negroes will thus be reluctant to listen to white people with a thorough trustfulness and an entirely open mind. Indeed, they are able to give freer play to their suspicion than Southern Negroes as they are less controlled and dependent. Too, the growing race pride exerts its influence in this direction. Northern Negroes, therefore, also seek the intermediation of leaders from their own group.

On the white side, those politicians, public officials, philanthropists, educators, union leaders, and all other white persons in the North who have to maintain contact with and exert influence upon the Negro group must sense this suspicion. They usually also find the Negroes strange in many ways. Negroes seldom constitute the main interest in their various pursuits. They welcome the Negro leader as a great convenience, therefore, as a means of dealing with the Negroes indirectly.[1]

The Northern situation, however, is different from the Southern situation in two closely coordinated respects: (1) that the white majority is not motivated by an interest solidarity against Negroes, reaching practically every white individual, and (2) that the Negro minority is not cramped by anything like the formidable, all pervasive, Southern system of political, judicial and social caste controls. One effect of this difference is that the Northern situation gives greater opportunity for the protest motive to come out in the open and not only, as in the South, to contribute its queer, subdued undertones to the pretended harmony of accommodation.

A number of circumstances make the Negro look to the North in his national political interest. National power is centered in the North. In national politics the South is quite like a minority group itself—a "problem" to the nation and to itself—politically, economically and culturally. Negroes have the vote in the North. For these reasons the relations between whites and Negroes in national affairs tend to conform more to Northern than to Southern local patterns. But Negro leaders are needed. The Negro people are set apart; they have distinctive problems; and they are hardly represented at all in the policy-forming and policy-deciding private or public organs. The federal government and its various agencies, the political parties, and the philanthropic organizations have difficulty in reaching Negroes through their normal means of public contact. They must seek to open up special channels to the Negro people by engaging trusted Negroes as observers, advisers and directors of Negro opinion. The Negroes feel the same need for "contact" persons of their own.

The individual Negroes who are appealed to in the national power field immediately win great prestige in the Negro world. To deal with Negro leaders who have great influence among the masses of Negroes is, on the other hand, a great asset to the white-dominated national organizations, including the federal government. Fundamentally the same causal mechanism, therefore, operates in the national realm of intercaste relations as in the Southern or Northern local community.

---

[1] An interesting parallel, which cannot be followed up here, would be with similar problems and tendencies in the relations between the wider society and other distinct minority groups such as the other color castes—Japanese, Chinese, Filipinos, Mexicans—and immigrant groups—Jewish, Czech, Polish, Italian.

4. THE "GLASS PLATE"

In the sphere of power and influence—in politics proper and outside of it, locally and nationally, in the South and in the North—the population thus becomes split into a white majority and a Negro minority, and the power relations running between these two blocs are concentrated and canalized in special liaison agents in the minority bloc. Whites who want to deal with the Negro masses do not have to go among them directly as they have to go among, say, Episcopalians. But it is, of course, just as difficult, and, in fact, more difficult, for Negroes to have direct contacts with the white population. Corresponding to the Negro leaders, there are white leaders.

The isolation implied in caste means thus, in the realm of power and influence, that *intercaste relations become indirect from both sides. Direct contacts are established only between the two groups of leaders, acting on behalf of the two blocs.* Except for those individuals, the invisible glass plate, of which Du Bois spoke,* is in operation. Common whites and blacks see each other, though usually only as strange stereotypes. But they cannot hear each other, except dimly. And they do not understand what they dimly hear from the other side of the glass plate. They do not trust and believe what they perhaps understand. Like two foreign nations, *Negroes and whites in America deal with each other through the medium of plenipotentiaries.*†

In a sense the white leaders have, from the Negroes' point of view, a similar "function" of acting as liaison agents to the Negro bloc. But there is this difference between the two groups of leaders: the white leaders are not "accommodating." They are not acting as "protest" leaders, either. The entire axis between the two extreme poles of accommodation and protest, which sets the orbit of Negro attitudes and behavior, exists only on the Negro side. The white leaders' "function" to serve as liaison agents with Negroes is only incidental to their power in white society. Unlike the Negro leaders they have, in addition, to run the whole society. This is a consequence of all the power being held on the white side. The Negroes do not, therefore, pick their white agents in the same manner as the whites choose their Negro ones. The Negroes cannot confer much power upon whites of their choice. In the South they do not partake in the selection of even political leaders. The Negroes—through their leaders—have to accept the white leadership as it exists, determined exclusively by the whites. They have to try to "get in" with the ones who are already on top in white society.**

---

* *Dusk of Dawn* (1940), pp. 130–131. Quoted in our Chapter 31, Section 2, p. 680.

† There are, of course, the exceptions of master-servant relations, but they are decreasing, and they have always been treated as exceptions. There are also the exceptions in the academic and artistic worlds, but they are few.

** It is true that, according to Southern aristocratic traditions, to have Negro dependents—who, in servant fashion, display gratitude and attachment—gives status in white society. Negroes are, therefore, in the position to deliver something to the white leader which has social significance. But in the Southern caste situation, the Negroes will have to be prepared to pay this price to practically any possessor of white power and influence who asks for it.

To this a few qualifications must be made. First, in some Southern communities white persons, distinguished by birth, education, or wealth, who have prestige but do not care to exert active leadership generally, may occasionally be induced to step in and use their potential power in favor of the Negroes or one individual Negro. When Negroes turn to such a person they might be said to pick him as a white leader for their purposes. The assumption is, however, that he already has latent power. The Negroes do not award him influence by selecting him, as whites do when they pick a Negro leader. He has, rather, to be careful not to assist the Negroes too often and too much, as this might wear out his prestige. He might even become known as a "nigger lover," which would be the end of his usefulness to the Negroes.

Second, some white persons actually specialize in becoming the fixers and pleaders for Negroes while they are not active as white leaders generally. They are the white interracialists of the South. In order to have protracted influence they require moral and financial backing from Northern philanthropists or, lately, from the federal government. They should, in addition, preferably have upper class status because of birth, education or occupation. Even when they have both Northern backing and Southern status their influence in matters affecting Negroes is likely to be uncertain and narrow in scope. Acclaim from the Negroes is usually more a result of their activity than a basis for the assumption of it.

In the North, the fact of Negro suffrage means that in the sphere of politics proper Negroes participate in selecting the white officeholders (and occasionally add some Negro representatives). Support from Negroes, therefore, means something in the North. Their opposition might occasionally turn an election against a candidate. The actual and the still greater potential significance of the Negroes' sharing in the political power in the North has been discussed in Chapters 22 and 23. Negroes are, however, only a tiny minority everywhere in the North. Even if the difference from the South is enormous, Negroes are, most of the time and in most respects, dependent on white leaders who do not feel dependent on Negro opinion.

This is, generally speaking, still more true in other power spheres than in politics proper; for example, in philanthropy, in educational institutions, in professional associations. Poverty and cultural backwardness generally prevent Negroes from having practically any primary power over the selection of white leaders in these fields. An exception is the labor movement. In so far as unions are kept open to Negroes, and where unions are democratic, Negroes have their due portion of power much according to the rules in politics. National power relations are much like those in Northern communities.

The following discussion will deal only with Negro leaders. It must never be forgotten, however, that Negro leaders ordinarily do not deal with the white people but only with white leaders. Negro leaders are, in fact, even more isolated from the whites in general than are the white leaders from the Negroes. We shall find, however, that some of the protest leaders actually do try to reach white public opinion. Walter White, and the whole set-up of the N.A.A.C.P., is steadily hammering at the glass plate, as did James Weldon Johnson and W. E. B. Du Bois before him and Frederick Douglass still earlier. Such an effort is effective practically only on the national scene. The carefully worded "letters to the editor" by Negroes to liberal Southern newspapers, which are sometimes printed—reminding the whites of their Constitution, their democratic faith and their Christian religion, and respectfully drawing their attention to some form of discrimination—represent local attempts in the same direction.

The direct approach by Negroes to the white world stems almost entirely from the protest motive. The accommodating Negro leaders generally do not even attempt to reach white public opinion directly. On the national scene, Booker T. Washington and, after him, Robert R. Moton were exceptions. But Moton's errand, when disclosing to the general public "what the Negro thinks," was to give vent to a protest, modified by acceptable and soothing words, and, in a degree, the same can be said of Washington. Washington's main motive, however, was accommodation *for a price*. This was his message in the Atlanta speech of 1895 and in countless other addresses to white audiences in the North and in the South, where he promised Negro patience, boosted Negro efforts, begged for money for his school and indulgence generally for his poor people. He had become a personality with prestige whose voice could pierce the caste wall. And he was freely allowed audience since he toned down the Negro protest. On the local scene the accommodation motive by itself does not usually encourage Negro leaders to such adventures of trying to reach behind the white leaders to the white people, and there is generally no white public which wants to listen to them.

5. ACCOMMODATING LEADERSHIP AND CLASS

Negro leadership—as determined by caste in the way we have sketched—stands in an even closer relation to class than does white leadership. In a previous part of this book, we saw that Negro classes generally were mainly a function of caste. One ramification of this thesis was touched upon only lightly and spared for the present discussion of Negro leadership: namely, that an individual Negro's relation to white society is of utmost importance for his class status in the Negro community.

It always gives a Negro scientist, physician, or lawyer prestige if he is esteemed by his white colleagues. Prestige will bring him not only deference but also clients and increased earnings. The Negro press eagerly records and plays up the slightest recognition shown a Negro by whites. A professional position outside the segregated Negro world, even if unpretentious, also carries high prestige. Being consulted by whites concerning Negro welfare, taking part in mixed conferences or having any personal relation to individual whites confers status.[2] This common view in the Negro community is, of

---

[2] This pattern has sunk deep into the entire class structure of the Negro community. It is commonly known that Negro domestics often consider it a degradation of their social status to work in a Negro family. An upper class Negro friend of mine testifies:

"I know of a good many instances, especially in Washington, and one or two of them are personal, where Negro domestics flatly refuse to work for Negroes, for fear that they will lose caste by doing so. My wife, who happens to fall in the category of the 'voluntary' or 'sociological' Negro, once hired a domestic at a wage admittedly higher than this girl had ever gotten before, when I chanced into the room. The young lady, a dark brown skin, promptly arose, exclaimed: 'Oh, I didn't know you were *colored*—I don't work for colored,'

course, realistic. White standards are, on the average, higher, and an indication that whites recognize a Negro as having approached or reached those standards means most of the time that he is exceptionally good in his line. More important still, the whites have the power, and friendly consideration from whites confers power upon the individual Negro participating in such a relation. The belief that whites have power has been exaggerated in the Negro community, so that friendly relations with certain individual whites confer status upon a Negro even when these whites actually have no power.

The import of this is that *leadership conferred upon a Negro by whites raises his class status in the Negro community.*[3] Correspondingly, it can be stated that an upper class position in the Negro community nearly automatically, with certain exceptions that we shall note later, gives a Negro the role of Negro leader.[4] He is expected to act according

---

and left without further ado. On another occasion we had employed a nice, inefficient but highly religious old lady in the same capacity. She had to attend church each Sunday morning, and would cook the dinner early and depart. After a few Sundays, she explained to us the reason for the generous portions of our larder with which she sallied out these Sunday mornings. She had a long tram ride to her home, she said, and on her car she would always encounter a number of her friends who were employed as domestics in white families. These friends were always well laden with tidbits, it seems, and she solemnly declared that this was the first time she had ever worked for colored; none of her friends ever had, though they knew she was so engaged, and that she wanted to show her friends that 'colored folks are just as good to work for as white folk.' Thus we sacrificed half of each Sunday dinner to maintain the prestige of the race."

[3] It should be noted that Negro leadership does not *per se* raise an individual's status in the eyes of white people in general. Only a few white people know about the leadership function he performs; to others he is just another Negro. His class status, on the other hand—which might be a function of his leadership—is easier to observe from his dress, manners, occupation, and so on, and may more generally command white respect. (See Chapter 30, Section 2, and Chapter 32, Section 4.) Whites will, however, regularly show respect if they come to know about an individual Negro's accomplishments or even if they come to know quite *in abstracto* that he is a "distinguished Negro."

[4] In this analysis of the relation between social class and leadership, color will be left out of account. It is true that most Negro leaders, particularly on the national plane, have been mulattoes and sometimes near-white or passable. (Compare E. B. Reuter, *The Mulatto in the United States* [1918].) This fact is, however, the less astonishing when we remember (1) how greatly mixed the entire Negro population is (Chapter 5), and (2) how color is an important factor in determining social class in the Negro community (Chapter 32). It is plausible that a light color is often an asset to a Negro leader in his dealings with both whites and Negroes, but it is also certain that a dark color is sometimes advantageous for a Negro leader. The two tendencies do not cancel each other since they occur in different types of leadership.

But color, independent of its relevance for class, is probably a minor factor for Negro leadership. Reuter's assertion that the mulatto is "the most vital point" in the race problem (*ibid.,* p. 87, *passim*) seems, for the reasons given, much exaggerated. An analysis directed to this particular relationship could only be warranted in a study which proceeded to distinguish between *all* the different factors determining leadership in the Negro community, that is, besides color: education, occupation, wealth, family background, and so forth. This we cannot undertake in the present abstract overview.

A story related to us by E. Franklin Frazier (conversation, July 11, 1942) might be repeated, however, to illustrate that dark color is sometimes an asset for a Negro leader. At a convention called to elect a bishop of one of the major Negro denominations, two candidates presented their qualifications. The first was very dark in color, and his keynote speech was that a dark man should lead the Negro people. The electors were predominantly dark and their applause indicated that his election was practically clinched. The other candito this role by both whites and Negroes. Because most upper class Negroes are leaders, there is an extraordinarily close correlation between leadership and class position in the Negro community. On the other hand, there are more lower class leaders among Negroes than among whites—partly because a much greater proportion of Negroes are lower class and partly because of the tradition of a strong lower class preacher and lodge leader among Negroes. Still, we believe that practically all upper class Negroes are leaders, something that is not true among whites. In order to understand this, several other things must be considered.

For one thing, the Negro upper class is—because of caste—such a small proportion of the total Negro population that the scarcity value of upper class status becomes relatively high. In smaller communities only a handful of persons have upper class status; in all communities they are few enough to be in close contact with each other.

The upper class Negro is, furthermore, culturally most like the group of whites who have social power. Under a long-range view, the social classes represent various degrees of acculturation to dominant American culture patterns or gradations of lag in the assimilation process.* During this process standards of living have been raised, illiteracy and mortality rates have declined, the patriarchal type of family organization has made its influence felt, and, generally, white American middle class norms and standards have been filtering downward in the Negro people. The upper class represents the most assimilated group of Negroes. In part, they have status in the Negro community for the very reason that they are culturally most like upper class whites. It is natural also that upper and middle class whites feel most closely akin to this group of Negroes.

The attitude of whites in the Old South was, on the contrary, that the lowly "darky" was the favored and trusted Negro, while the educated, socially rising "Negro gentleman" was to be suspected and disliked. When a social stratification in the Negro people first appeared during slavery, the whole complex of legislation to suppress the free Negroes, to hinder the education of slaves, and to check the meetings of Negroes was expressly intended to prevent Negro individuals of a higher status from leading the Negro masses, and, indeed, to prevent the formation of a Negro upper class. The inclinations of white people remained much the same after the Civil War. The Jim Crow legislation followed a similar tendency. The white masses even today are usually most bitter and distrustful toward upper class Negroes. This is still often the expressed opin-

---

date, a light man, met a hostile audience. He agreed that dark Negroes needed dark leaders, but said that sometimes admiration for dark skin was more important than dark skin itself. He then pointed to his opponent's wife and to his own wife in the audience. The opponent's wife had light skin, but his own wife had dark skin. He won the election.

Marcus Garvey's dark skin was an asset, but so may be Walter White's extremely light skin, since there may be a feeling that this man who could pass is making a personal sacrifice by being a "voluntary" Negro.

* We are referring to assimilation away from patterns in slavery, not patterns in Africa. See Hortense Powdermaker, *After Freedom* (1939), pp. 354, *passim*. See also Chapter 43, Section 1, of this book.

ion also of the upper class whites who are in control of the political and social power in Southern communities.

But even in the South it has become more and more unfeasible to trust the Negro leadership to the lower class "Uncle Toms" of the old type. One reason has already been mentioned: the paternalistic personal relations in which they developed have decreased in frequency. There are fewer "good old darkies" available. Also, as wealth and education have become somewhat more attainable to Negroes, those who were favored with these things—the slowly growing upper class, who thus came to symbolize Negro advancement and race pride—supplanted the "darkies" in prestige in the Negro community. Even white backing could not entirely shield the "darkies" from ridicule and contempt on the part of the Negroes of superior wealth and education.

In this situation, the upholding of the old-time "darkies" as white-appointed Negro leaders would have implied an unyielding refusal to recognize the entire rising Negro class structure and the Negro's respect for education. It soon became apparent that such a policy would be ineffective and unrealistic. The development of a Negro upper class could not be checked: as we have pointed out, this class grew partly because of segregation itself. A protracted resistance to recognizing the growth of class stratification in the Negro community would also have run contrary to the dominant class pattern within American white society. By analogy a Negro class structure seemed the more natural as personal ties to white society became broken, and as the Negro group was more definitely set apart.

Finally, a large portion of the Negro upper class is actually appointed by the whites or is dependent for status upon the influential local whites. The whites soon learned that they could find as many "Uncle Toms" among Negroes of upper class status as among the old-time "darkies," and that educated persons often were much more capable of carrying out their tasks as white-appointed Negro leaders.

6. SEVERAL QUALIFICATIONS

Thus the whites accepted and strengthened the ever closer correlation between leadership and upper class status. But the correlation is still not perfect. Part of the explanation is the carry-over of old slavery attitudes among whites. I have observed communities, particularly in the Old South, where the leading whites have insisted on giving their ear even in public affairs to some old, practically illiterate ex-servant, while cold-shouldering the upper class Negroes. In the dependent situation of Southern Negroes, the Negro community is then willy-nilly compelled to use those old "darkies" as pleaders whenever the influential whites have to be appealed to.

Under such circumstances, a tremendous internal friction in the Negro community is likely to develop. The contempt of the upper class Negroes for the uneducated white-appointed "leaders" becomes increased by resentment born of a feeling of extreme humiliation. The "leaders," on their part, feeling the contempt and resentment of the "uppity" Negroes, often turn into thorough sycophants toward the whites and into "stuck-up" petty tyrants toward the Negro community.[5]

For reasons already touched upon, this arrangement is not the kind of leadership control of the Negroes which is most effective from the point of view of white interests. In the cases of this type I have observed, it has been apparent that the influential whites are motivated not only by their pride in adhering to traditional paternalistic patterns of the Old South, by their fear of ambitious capable Negroes, and by their personal liking for their favored "darkies," but also that they actually enjoy putting the Negro community in this situation. The humiliation of the "uppity" Negroes is, in other words, intentional.*

Such situations are becoming rare. I have observed, however, that another custom is still widespread everywhere in the South: to use servants, ex-servants, and other lower class Negroes as reporters and stool pigeons in the Negro community. Even if those spotters are usually not used in attempts to influence the Negroes positively, their spy activity and their being known "to be in with" white people give them a sort of power among their own people. Often they are utilized by the whites to "let it be known" in an informal way what the whites want and expect. This is a remnant of the old direct caste control. It is declining as employment relations are becoming more impersonal and as race solidarity in the Negro group is increasing.

More important reasons for an imperfect correlation in the South between leadership and upper class position are, however, certain facts within the Negro community itself. Many upper class Negroes do not care for the leadership role. It is true that they have superior status only in relation to the masses of other Negroes, and that they often depend economically on lower class Negroes as clients and customers. But they also may have a desire to isolate themselves from the Negro lower classes. Many also do not have the easy manners, the engaging and spirited personality, and the ability to speak the language of "the people" necessary to approach and influence the Negro masses. Some have made themselves so personally unpopular with Negroes or whites that they cannot act as leaders.[6] Many are so filled by the protest motive that they feel a personal humiliation when this has to be put under cover in taking the role of accommodating Negro leaders. They retreat rather into the role of sullen, but personally watchful, individualists, nourishing hatred against the whites above them, contempt for the Negro

---

[5] A field interview by Ralph Bunche and myself with a local Negro leader of the type characterized in the text, and with some other people in the Southeastern coast city where he lives, is presented in excerpts in: Ralph Bunche, "A Brief and Tentative Analysis of Negro Leadership," unpublished manuscript prepared for this study (1940), pp. 94–111.

[6] A word might also be said about the "shady" upper class—the big-time gamblers and lords of vice and crime. In spite of the fact that they have, in a sense, upper class status and may be personally popular, they cannot be used as regular leaders because they do not fit the American idea of what a leader should be. They do act as "behind the scenes" political leaders, especially in the North.

* This is an example of the element of sadism generally so visible in the white Southerners' paternalism. It is also reflected in the standard stories told and retold about Negro stupidity and immorality, always with an intense display of pleasure which the outsider does not feel.

masses below them, and disgust—sometimes mixed with envy—for the accommodating Negro leaders beside them. Their "adjustment" is to "mind their own business."

In practically every Southern Negro community, there is this partial voluntary retreat of the Negro upper class from active leadership. Thus the common assumption among whites that upper class Negroes in general are leaders of their people is not quite true. Upper class Negroes pretend that it is true in order to gain prestige. It is also an expectation on the part of white community leaders who happen to know about them, observe their superiority in education, manners, standards, and wealth, and take their influence among the common Negroes for granted. It must always be remembered that the whites' actual knowledge about the Negroes in their own community nowadays is usually rudimentary. It is not unusual to find that a certain Negro has succeeded in impressing the local whites with an exaggerated belief in his actual influence among his own people.

More important than unwillingness or inability on the part of Negro upper class persons to play the leadership role is a more or less conscious repugnance on the part of the Negro lower classes against following them. "Too much" education often meets suspicion among lower class Negroes. Many Negro preachers, who usually do not suffer from over-education, have nourished this prejudice as they saw education draw people from religious faith and, particularly, from respect for themselves. The usual class envy between upper and lower class individuals in the Negro community is an ever present element in the situation, and is strengthened when, as in the case of the accommodating Negro leaders, the Negro protest against the whites cannot be invoked as a bond of race loyalty.

The extreme result of this class conflict is that the Negro masses in the South— as well as large parts of the white masses in the same region—often become, not only as inactive as is necessary for accepting readily the leadership imposed upon them from the outside, but, indeed, so utterly passive that they simply do not care very much for anything except their animal demands and their personal security. Their economic, social, and cultural situation, as we have described it in previous chapters, makes this understandable. It is difficult indeed to reach the amorphous Negro masses at all, especially in rural districts.

It is often said that the Negro church and the fraternal and burial lodges are the only media by which those masses can be reached. The present observer is inclined to consider this statement as exaggerated in two directions: first, even the church and the lodges do not have a steady and strong influence on the lowest Negro classes; second, the Negro school, the Negro press, and the Negro professions are becoming vehicles which have considerable influence with the lower strata.

But there is enough truth in the statement to raise it above doubt that the Negro preacher—and, to a lesser extent, the lodge official—has more influence with the Negro masses than a white lower class preacher or lodge leader has with the white masses. The majority of Negro preachers and many local lodge leaders are not highly educated and do not belong to the upper classes. Particularly is this true of the ministers in the lower class churches and of the "jack-leg preachers," who are the ones who really reach down to the masses. Their uncouth manners, language, and standards in general are assets in retaining a grip over lower class congregations. Negro ministers who are educated and who have upper class status actually often have to affect bad grammar and an accent and to use figures of speech taken from the cotton field and the corn patch in order to catch the attention of the masses and to exert some real leadership.[7] The great influence of the Negro preacher is exceptionally well known by the whites, and he is usually considered as a force for "good race relations," that is, for shepherding his flock into respect and obedience. Such are the barriers to and inhibitions of the Negroes of upper class status in becoming effective mass leaders in the Negro community. But with these reservations—and keeping in mind that a large portion of the Negro masses is amorphous, utterly apathetic, and not "led" much at all, but more like Thomas Nelson Page's vision of a "vast sluggish mass of uncooled lava" [8]—it remains true that leadership and upper class status are strongly correlated in the South and that the tendency is toward an even closer correlation.

The author also has the impression that Negro leaders, more often than whites (among their own people), take on a rather dictatorial and paternalistic attitude toward their Negro followers. They seem to mimic, in a small degree, the role of the upper class white Southerner in his relation to his Negro dependents. There is often a considerable amount of bossing and ordering around in a Negro group assembled for any purpose. The Negro upper class person in a leadership position will often entertain the observer with much the same generalized derogatory statements about the common run of Negroes as white people use. When the Negro preacher in church starts out to elaborate the shortcomings of "the race," the implication of his being a Negro leader is most of the time apparent. The teacher's cadence when addressing children in the Negro school sounds more condescending than in white schools. The organization of life in Negro colleges seems to be definitely less democratic than in white colleges in America, even, and not least, when the staff of teachers is mainly Negro. The president in his relations to the professors and they in their relations to the students act more dictatorially and more arbitrarily.

7. ACCOMMODATING LEADERS IN THE NORTH

In the North, there has never been much love for the lowly "darkies" on the part of the whites. They have never felt much of an interest or inclination to lift poor, uneducated servants as leaders over the Negro community. There has been more acclaim of social climbing generally than in the South. Almost from the beginning the Negro upper class was accepted by the whites, without resistance, as the source of Negro leaders.

On the other hand, probably a somewhat greater proportion of upper class Negroes in the North do not care for the responsibilities and rewards of being active

---

[7] J. G. St. Claire Drake, "The Negro Church and Associations in Chicago," unpublished manuscript prepared for this study (1940), p. 402; and Allison Davis, Burleigh B. Gardner, and Mary R. Gardner, *Deep South* (1941), pp. 236–239. This theme appears in literature, too. See Walter White, *The Fire in the Flint* (1924).

[8] *The Negro: The Southerner's Problem* (1904), p. 64.

Negro leaders. On the whole, the Negro masses are less passive. The preachers have, perhaps, rather less prominence as leaders and are, on the average, somewhat better educated and have a higher social status.

Negro suffrage in the North, however, creates space for a political leadership which, in order to be able to deliver the Negro vote to the party machines, must be chosen from people who really meet the common lower class Negroes. A good many of the petty politicians in Northern cities are lower class Negroes. Negroes who enjoy a sort of "upper class" status outside the respectable society—big-time gamblers, criminals, and so on—are often the machine lieutenants, precinct captains and bosses, or the "insiders" in the political game.

The odor of corruption and the connection with crime and vice which often surrounds American city politics, particularly in the slums, deter, of course, many upper class Negroes, as well as many upper class whites, from taking any active part in political leadership. This does not mean, however, that there is not a good deal of honest and devoted political leadership among Northern Negroes. It comes often from upper class Negroes. But proportionately the upper classes monopolize less of the actual leadership in local politics than in other fields. And the labor unions, which are stronger in the North, are training a new type of lower or middle class Negro leader of particular importance in politics. They can there often compete successfully with the upper class leaders. They are just as often as honest and as devoted to the Negro cause as are the upper class leaders.[9]

On the national scene, upper class status and, particularly, considerable education and personal ability are necessary for Negro leaders.

8. THE GLAMOUR PERSONALITIES

One peculiar angle of the relation between Negro leadership and social class is highlighted in the popular glamour and potential power of a Negro who has accomplished or achieved something extraordinary, particularly in competition with whites.

Attainments are apparently given a relatively higher rating in the Negro than in the white community. The Negro press eagerly publicizes "the first" Negro to win this or that degree, to be appointed to one position or another, or to succeed in a business or profession formerly monopolized by whites. This tendency among a subordinated group living in a society dominated by strong competitive motives is entirely natural; it has a close parallel in the women's world. In fact, the entire Negro upper class gets peculiar symbolic significance and power in the Negro community for the very reason that it consists of persons who have acquired white people's education and wealth and who are engaged in doing things which are above the traditional "Negro jobs." They have broken through the barriers, and their achievements offer every Negro a gloating consolation in his lowly status and a ray of hope.

---

[9] The best published study of Northern Negro political leaders is Harold F. Gosnell's *Negro Politicians* (1935).

Under this principle every Negro who rises to national prominence and acclaim is a race hero: he has symbolically fought the Negro struggle and won. Great singers like Roland Hayes, Marian Anderson, and Paul Robeson have their prestige augmented by the eager vibrations of pride and hope from the whole Negro people acting as a huge sounding board. So have successful Negro authors like Richard Wright and Langston Hughes; scientists like George Washington Carver and Ernest E. Just; athletes like Joe Louis and Henry Armstrong; entertainers like Bill "Bojangles" Robinson, the king of tap-dancing, and Duke Ellington, the famous jazz band leader.

Any one of them could, if he chose, exert a considerable power as an active Negro leader in a technical sense. Jesse Owens, who at the 1936 Olympics established himself as the world's fastest runner and one of the greatest track athletes in history, was young and inexperienced, in fact not yet out of college. But on the basis of his specialized mastery of running and the acclaim accorded him in the white and Negro press, Owens was considered a valuable political asset and employed by the Republican party to attract the Negro vote.

The situation of the Negro glamour personality is, however—and this must be noted if we want to observe true proportions—not different from what is ordinary in white America. The popularity of the "first" or the "oldest," the "biggest" or the "smallest," the "best" or the "worst," the "only" or the "most ordinary" specimen of a type has always given its particular color to American conceptions of things and persons. It is characteristic of a young culture. Negroes are only following a common American pattern, which, as usual, their caste status leads them to exaggerate somewhat. The early history of Charles Lindbergh is a case in point. The white public also influences Negroes to expect too much from a Negro who achieves something in a particular field. All Negroes look alike to many whites, and whoever, by whatever means, comes before the public eye becomes regarded as an outstanding Negro and is expected to hold a position of unwarranted importance in Negro affairs.

It must also be noted that Negro celebrities—actually perhaps even more carefully than white ones in America—generally show great restraint in avoiding the temptation of stepping outside their narrow field of competence. Marian Anderson is a good example of scrupulous adherence to this rule. When Paul Robeson and Richard Wright sometimes discuss general aspects of the Negro problem, they do so only after study and consideration. These two have deliberately taken up politics as a major interest. They act then in the same spirit and the same capacity as, for instance, Pearl Buck when she steps out of her role as a writer of novels and writes a social and philosophical essay on the women's problem. Although the possibilities and the temptations have been so great, glamour personalities have usually not exploited Negroes or the Negro problem.

It may be suggested that in the Negro world, and specifically in Northern Negro communities, women have a somewhat greater opportunity to reach active leadership than in white society. Negro women are not so often put aside into "women's auxiliaries" as are white women. If this hypothesis is correct, it corresponds well with the fact of Negro women's relatively greater economic and social independence.

Black Metropolis[*]

St. Clair Drake
and Horace R. Cayton

LAND OF PROMISE

EMERGENCE OF THE BLACK BELT (1865–1874)

At the outbreak of the Civil War a hundred thousand people lived in Chicago. Fifty years later, when the First World War began, the city boasted more than two million inhabitants. The material base for this rapid growth was laid between 1860 and 1890. The city's expanding stockyards and packing plants, farm-implement factories and railroad yards, warehouses and grain elevators attracted the hungry, the ambitious, and the foot-loose from all over the world. Fortunes sprouted in the grain pit. Millionaires were sired in the cattle pens. Reapers, made in Chicago and distributed in the wheat fields, brought prosperity to both countryside and city. George Pullman's sleeping cars, fabricated in its outskirts, carried the city's fame over America's ever-widening web of railroads. There was a magic in the names of Swift and Armour, Marshall Field and Levi Z. Leiter, Potter Palmer and Cyrus McCormick, that turned many a fortune-seeker's steps toward Chicago. Young, boisterous, and busy, the city became a symbol of the vast opportunities which the entire Middle West held for peoples of the eastern seaboard and Europe who were seeking a land of promise.

---

* From St. Clair Drake and Horace R. Cayton, *Black Metropolis: A Study of Negro Life in a Modern Community* (New York: Harcourt, Brace & World, Inc. 1945), pp. 46–54, 55–64. Copyright 1945 by St. Clair Drake and Horace R. Cayton. Reprinted by permission of Harcourt Brace Jovanovich, Inc.

The Chicago of 1870 was a boom town, its buildings and its people new and rough. Of its sixty thousand structures, forty thousand were made of wood. It was, as one contemporary newspaper said, "a city of everlasting pine, shingles, shams, veneers, stucco and putty." [1] Fires were frequent. In 1871 the Great Chicago Fire destroyed seventeen thousand buildings and left a hundred thousand people homeless—the damage amounted to $200,000,000. The story of Mrs. O'Leary's cow that kicked over a lamp that set a fire that burned a city became an international legend. Local ministers saw the holocaust as an expression of God's judgment upon a wicked city. Southerners and former Copperheads were sure that "God had stricken the Northern city to avenge the 'wanton' destruction which the Union armies had visited upon the South during the Civil War." [2] To most Chicagoans, however, the fire was an unlucky but exciting accident—an unfortunate, but in no sense fatal, catastrophe.

The great Chicago fire did not destroy the Negro community, although it consumed the contiguous central business area and the world-famous Red-light District. Since the fire also spared the rows of stately mansions near Lake Michigan, many burned-out businesses were temporarily housed in their owners' fashionable residences. The bulk of the gamblers and prostitutes took refuge in the Negro neighborhood—an area three blocks long and fifteen blocks wide, with some twenty-five hundred residents. When the city was rebuilt, the former Red-light District was taken over by the wholesale trade. The gay underworld remained among the Negroes.

Chicago clergymen again professed to see the handiwork of a persistent and vigilant Deity when in 1874 another conflagration burned out gamblers, prostitutes, *and* Negroes. As a result of this second fire, almost half of the colored families were dispersed among the white residents, but a new Negro community also arose from the ashes of the old. Here, in a long, thin sliver of land, sandwiched between a well-to-do white neighborhood and that of the so-called "shanty Irish," most of Chicago's colored residents and their major institutions were concentrated during the next forty years. The "Black Belt" had emerged.

BETWEEN THE FIRE AND THE FAIR
(1875–1893)

In the twenty years between the Great Fire and the first World's Fair (1893), the Negro population increased from five thousand to fifteen thousand. The Black Belt gradually expanded as Negroes took over the homes of white persons who were moving to the more desirable lake-front or to the suburbs. Most of the colored residents were employed as coachmen, butlers, cooks, and maids in the homes of the wealthy; as servants in stores, hotels, and restaurants; as porters on the increasingly popular Pullman coaches; and as maids and handymen in white houses of prostitution. A small Negro business and professional class developed, and by 1878 it had found a mouthpiece in a

---

[1] Chicago *Daily Tribune*, Sept. 10, 1871, quoted in Lewis and Smith, *op. cit.*, p. 119.
[2] Rushville (Ind.) *Democrat*, quoted in Lewis and Smith, *op. cit.*, p. 135.

weekly newspaper, the *Conservator,* whose editor, reminiscing years later, described the general status of Negroes in the Seventies and early Eighties as follows:[3]

> . . . There were about five thousand Negroes in Chicago. The *Conservator* was started as a means of expression for Negroes and to aid in the promotion of the welfare of the Negro group.
>
> When the paper was started the behavior of many of the Negroes was characterized by loose living and a lack of proper standards. There were few Negroes of culture and refinement, and only a few jobs of any consequence were held by Negroes. The paper was devoted to the idea of stressing the importance of education, social uplift and correct living. Conflict between the races was not very great at the time the paper was started, consequently there was little space given to the discussion of race relations in the local community. There were, however, occasional clashes between the Irish and the Negroes. When these . . . occurred they were discussed in the paper.

The picture gleaned from the pages of this paper is that of a small, compact, but rapidly growing community divided into three broad social groups. The "respectables" —church-going, poor or moderately prosperous, and often unrestrained in their worship—were looked down upon somewhat by the "refined" people, who, because of their education or breeding, could not sanction the less decorous behavior of their racial brothers. Both of these groups were censorious of the "riffraff," the "sinners"—unchurched and undisciplined. The "refined" set conceived themselves as examples of the Negro's progress since slavery. They believed that their less disciplined fellows should be prodded with ridicule and sarcasm, and restrained by legal force when necessary. They had an almost religious faith that education would, in the long run, transform even the "riffraff" into people like themselves.

The pages of the *Conservator* expressed these attitudes by colorful words of denunciation and applause. One editorial, for instance,[4] inveighed against the seamy side of life with rhetoric and pious sentiments typical of the period:

GOING TO RUIN

> We are calling attention to the fact that a number of our girls and boys are on the road to ruin. The boys rioting in the Clark and 4th Avenue dives, laying the foundations for lives of thieves, thugs and murderers, and the girls walking the streets in gaudy attire—attracting notice—exciting comment and rapidly linking their lives, with those whose "house is the gate of Hell, going down to the chambers of death."
>
> How sad it is to see the girls we have known in their innocent childhood,

---

[3] Quoted in Ralph Davis, "The Negro Newspaper in Chicago," unpublished manuscript, Parkway Community House, Chicago, 1939, p. 30.

[4] Davis, *op. cit.,* p. 34.

change their lives, just when life's days should be the brightest; change from piety, virtue and happiness to vice, dissipation and woe. Mothers are you blind? Fathers are you deaf? Christians are you asleep? For the sake of God and Humanity, let someone rescue these young lives from dissipation's perpetual gloom.

As opposed to this pattern of life, the paper held up[5] as pioneering models those young people who were "improving themselves," thereby "advancing the race":

> Four colored students graduated last week from the University of Michigan. Two in law and two in medicine. In conversation with colored students during the past year, we were glad to hear that scarcely a vestige of the "caste" spirit is ever seen. They attend, or are free to attend, all meetings, educational and social, and are never made to feel out of place. There has never yet been a colored graduate from the collegiate course.
>
> Miss Mary H. Graham whose matriculation in '76 caused such a stir in Michigan circles will be the first to achieve this distinction. . . . Mr. C. Williams, a Sophomore and a young man of rare moral worth, is winning a golden name at the University. . . . He is held in high degree of respect by the citizens and the Faculty. . . . Would there were more such men as he—Ethiopia might well rejoice.

The "young men of rare moral worth," the "girls walking the streets in gaudy attire," as well as plain, ordinary Negroes, continued to come to Chicago throughout the Eighties. By 1890 there were enough of them to sustain twenty churches, a dozen or so lodges, three weekly newspapers, and several social and cultural clubs. Certain individuals had managed to attain some prominence and wealth, and a few possessed well-established businesses catering to a white clientele. John Jones, abolitionist leader, was still tailoring for the city's elite in a building of his own in the heart of the city. Another Negro had invested $60,000 in a downtown office building. Smiley, a caterer, was laying up a small fortune from the lavish affairs he engineered for the Gold Coast—a fortune the remnants of which he was to leave to the University of Chicago.

For these men, the land of promise had been no mirage. None of them had amassed great fortunes or secured key positions of economic control, but they had been financially successful in a modest fashion. A few Negroes of the business and professional classes had also been active in politics since the early Seventies, thus setting the precedent for Negro political representation which subsequently became a part of the city's tradition. The first colored county commissioner, state legislator, policeman, and fireman all appeared before 1875.[6]

[5] Davis, *op. cit.,* p. 62.

[6] Harold F. Gosnell, *Negro Politicians* (University of Chicago, 1935, pp. 198 and 247), mentions the following persons: J. W. E. Thomas, state representative, 1876; John Jones, elected county commissioner in 1871 and 1872. The first colored police officer was appointed in the same year by the Republican mayor.

The twenty years between the Fire and Fair were the turbulent ones for Chicago.[7] On the heels of the post-fire boom, a six-year stretch of "hard times" ensued, during which there were serious labor troubles. The political antagonisms of the foreign-born and the native-whites (evenly divided as to numbers) were organized throughout this period around such issues as the passage of the Blue Sunday Laws and the struggle for control of the City Hall. Then came eight years of continuing prosperity and renewed European immigration, culminating in the panic of 1884–86, which brought in its wake a violent streetcar strike. In 1884, the Illinois State Federation of Labor passed a resolution against the "further importation of pauper labor from Europe." [8] The Haymarket riot in 1886 resulted in considerable antiforeigner hysteria.

The small Negro community was barely touched by these political and economic upheavals. Having adjusted themselves to the economic competition of the foreign-born by securing employment primarily in the service occupations, the masses of the Negroes had little reason to listen to the impassioned oratory of labor leaders who excoriated local capitalists and eastern bankers. Agitation for the eight-hour day carried no appeal for a colored working population over half of which was employed in servant capacities. It is significant that the one Negro preacher in the Eighties who publicly espoused the cause of Socialism quickly lost his pulpit.[9]

Although unconcerned with the violent struggles of the white workers, Negroes were persistently seeking to widen the areas of political and economic opportunity for themselves. They found allies among Republican politicians, civic-minded liberals, and the wealthy for whom many of them worked. Fighters for equal rights since the days of slavery, Chicago's Negro leaders resented any attempts to deny political and economic opportunity to themselves or their fellows. The Illinois Black Code was repealed in 1865. By 1870 Negroes had been guaranteed the right to vote. By 1874 segregation in the school system had been abolished. In 1885 the leaders climaxed their efforts by securing the passage of a state civil rights bill designed to protect the liberties of Negroes in the less advanced counties of southern Illinois. They insisted that every evidence of subordinate status should be eliminated. They were taking the promises of democracy seriously.

Ostensibly trivial matters sometimes assumed great importance in this struggle for recognition and respect. The *Conservator* on one occasion devoted an entire editorial, humorous in tone but serious in intent, to the use of the lower-case "n" for spelling the word Negro. The editor called the practice "a mark of disrespect," "a stigma," and "a badge of inferiority," and remarked that "the French, German, Irish, Dutch, Japenese [*sic*], and other nationalities are honored with a capital letter, but the poor sons of Ham must bear the burden of a small n." [10]

---

[7] For a colorful description of this period, see Lewis and Smith, *op. cit.,* pp. 138–67.

[8] Staley, *op. cit.,* pp. 159–60.

[9] A newspaper account of this minister's difficulties appeared in the Chicago *Daily Tribune,* Sept. 16, 1887.

[10] Quoted in Davis, *op. cit.,* p. 13.

Colored Chicagoans, like their foreign-born neighbors, cultivated a dual loyalty and pride—allegiance to an ethnic group as well as to America. But they did not feel that race pride should isolate them from the main streams of civic life. The editor of the *Conservator* expressed the dominant philosophy of the Negro community when he wrote in the late Eighties: "As a race let us forget the past so far as we can, and unite with other men upon issues, liberal, essential, and not dependent upon color of skin or texture of hair for its [*sic*] gravamen." [11]

The successful Negroes of the era, many of them former slaves, interpreted their own careers as proof that some day black men would be accepted as individuals and Americans. They visualized the progress of their race in terms of education, personal economic success, judicious political action, and co-operation with powerful and influential white people.

RETROSPECT AND PROSPECT (1894–1914)

In 1893 Chicago decided to show the world how it had survived panic, fire, and class war to become the second largest city in the nation—Midwest Metropolis. Its civic leaders ballyhooed, pressured, and begged until they won from Congress the privilege of playing host to the World's Columbian Exposition—the first World's Fair. For Negroes, too, this was a significant occasion. In 1891 a prominent European historian and traveler had remarked of Chicago that "the severity of the climate repels the Africans." [12] Yet, in 1893, there were fifteen thousand Negroes living in the city. It was only natural that they should wish to display what they and their co-racialists throughout the country had accomplished in the twenty-eight years since slavery. In 1892 a committee met in Quinn Chapel, once a station of the Underground Railroad, and formulated an appeal to Congress for representation at the Fair. A large Negro exhibit was eventually prepared, and colored speakers and singers appeared on various Exposition programs.

For the Negroes, the occasion was a sort of silver jubilee celebrating a generation of freedom. The Prudence Crandall Club, representing the "cultured" elements, entertained the aging but still eloquent Frederick Douglass, famous Negro orator and venerable symbol of the abolition struggle. Commemoration services "in honor of the leaders in the cause of freedom and political equality" were held in historic Quinn Chapel. Frederick Douglass spoke, and when he referred to the stormy Forties and Fifties, he urged the younger generation of Negroes not to forget that "forty years ago there were always here a roof, table, and house for the most abject abolitionist." [13] The night before he left the city, he was, as one daily newspaper reported, HONORED BY BOTH RACES AT HIS LEAVE TAKING. [14]

[11] *Ibid.,* p. 46.

[12] J. C. Ridpath, cited in Lewis and Smith, *op. cit.,* p. 172.

[13] Chicago *Daily Tribune,* Jan. 2, 1894, as quoted in St. Clair Drake, *Churches and Voluntary Associations in the Chicago Negro Community,* WPA (mimeographed), 1940, p. 89.

[14] *Ibid.*

"The church was filled with an audience of white and colored people. . . . In speaking of the prejudices against men of his race in the South, he said the people of the South had better beware as to how they aroused the strength in the black man's arm. When he made this reference he was cheered."

Before the echoes of Douglass's speech had died away a Negro was burned in effigy in the streets of Chicago. Colored laborers had been imported to break a strike in the stockyards, and the white workers had responded in a style suggestive of the South. But, significantly enough, in Chicago, the victim was burned *in effigy* rather than in person.[15]

There was nothing in the South to lend substance to Douglass's heroic warning. Booker T. Washington's philosophy of compromise was soon to become the holy scripture of southern leaders, white and black. Do not antagonize the white majority. Do not ask for the right to vote. Do not fight for civil liberties or against segregation. Go to school. Work hard. Save money. Buy property. Some day the other things may come.

For ten years after the Civil War, the Republican North had buttressed the southern Negro's franchise with federal power. By 1875, however, Republican ardor had cooled. The Party could now exist without the southern Negro vote, and northern businessmen needed the goodwill of the white South. The ex-slaves had never secured an economic base. Forty acres and a mule might have given them a sort of sturdy peasant independence. As it was, a system of sharecropping replaced slavery, and debt peonage was substituted for legal bondage. It was Booker T. Washington's hope that by hard work and thrift the Negro masses could ultimately establish their freedom by buying the land. But southern landlords, selling their cotton in a world market, had no intention of relinquishing the very source of their power. They used terror and intimidation to keep the former slaves in their place. A rigorous etiquette of race relations was enforced, in which the Negro's role was that of serf, sycophant, and buffoon, bowing and scraping at the throne of white supremacy. An effort was made to strait-jacket Negroes into an American version of the caste system. The promises of freedom were harmlessly enshrined in the Emancipation Proclamation and embalmed in the Thirteenth, Fourteenth, and Fifteenth Amendments.[16]

Many ex-slaves who had tasted complete freedom during the few short years of Reconstruction could not adjust to this southern New Order. So throughout the Eighties and Nineties a constant stream of Negro migrants trickled northward to join the larger stream of immigrants from Europe. Chicago attracted a large proportion of those who left the South between 1890 and 1910 in what has been called "the Migration of the Talented Tenth." [17] Among them were prominent preachers and politicians who,

[15] For a detailed account of this strike, see Alma Herbst, *The Negro in the Slaughtering and Meat Packing Industry in Chicago,* Houghton Mifflin, 1932, pp. 12–27.

[16] The literature on this period is voluminous, but one of the best studies of the mechanisms by which Negroes were "put in their place" is W. E. B. Du Bois, *Black Reconstruction,* Harcourt, Brace, 1935.

[17] C. G. Woodson, *A Century of Negro Migration,* Association for the Study of Negro Life and History, 1918, Chapter VIII, "The Migration of the Talented Tenth."

for a brief spell after the Civil War, sat in southern state legislatures and in Congress; less distinguished individuals who occupied minor political posts in county and town; and all the restless educated and half-educated, who were not content to live life on southern terms. Many visitors to the first World's Fair who came to look stayed to work. By 1910 there were 40,000 Negroes among the heterogeneous two million inhabitants of Midwest Metropolis. Almost imperceptibly the Black Belt had expanded and absorbed more than 10,000 people within a period of seventeen years.

Upon the narrow economic base of domestic and personal service, Negroes in Chicago had evolved a community life gathering primarily around lodge and church. A few business and professional men, politicians, and ambitious personal and domestic servants constituted a social élite. In the years between the Fair and the First World War, these were the civic leaders, and their wives the social arbiters. A diversified institutional life taking form between 1890 and 1914 included a hospital and training school for nurses, a YMCA, branches of national organizations such as the National Negro Business League, the National Association for the Advancement of Colored People (NAACP), and the Federated Women's Clubs.

● ● ●

W. T. Stead's sensational exposé already mentioned, *If Christ Came to Chicago,* started a battle between the segregationists, who believed in a legal Red-light District, and the non-segregationists who wished to abolish it. The struggle went on throughout this period, and engaged the attention of the entire Negro community. The Chicago Vice Commission reported in 1909 that the growing Negro population had never managed to keep even one jump ahead of the continuously expanding Red-light District. It also revealed that the great majority of the employees in the "resorts" were colored men, women, and children. In fact, some of the most exclusive "houses" were in the Black Belt. Inevitably the Black Belt became associated in the popular mind with "vice," and the reformers exhorted the Negro community to clean house. Some of the conservative Negro leaders accepted the assignment, but the more militant refused to admit complete blame for vice in the Black Belt.

One of the most prominent colored ministers declared himself "a firm believer in the segregation of vice," but accused a prominent white pastor of trying to widen the boundaries of the Red-light District at the expense of the Negro community. The white minister was charged with a desire to push "the boundary lines of vice beyond his own bailiwick" in order to prevent "a large exodus of his parishioners to a locality less honeycombed with dance halls, brothels and saloons." "So like Ajax of old," the Negro minister continued, "all through the long and bitter night, the prayer of this learned divine was for light to see his foemen's fall. And when he did, he gave them no quarter until he succeeded in driving these unfortunates to the very doors of Quinn Chapel, the Olivet Baptist and Bethel churches [colored congregations]. It will be only a matter of time before the churches mentioned will be forced to abandon their present fields. . . . The Negro, like the whites, does not care for his wife and daughter to elbow the Red-light denizens."

Chicago's "vice problem" was not solved by gerrymander, however. In 1912 the reform forces succeeded in abolishing the Red-light District, and the prostitutes were temporarily scattered from one end of the city to the other. The business finally went underground in various parts of the city, including the Black Belt. But the break-up of the segregated vice area did not remove either the reality or the stigma of vice from the Negro community.

Upon one occasion in 1912 when Booker T. Washington publicly urged Negroes in Chicago and other urban areas to wipe out vice from their communities, a colored civic leader retorted: "A good deal of the vice in the 'colored belt' is the white man's vice, thrust there by the authorities against the protest of the colored people. But the thing runs deeper than that. Vice and crime are in large measure the result of idleness, of irregular employment, and even of regular employment that is underpaid and exhausting. It would be fatuous for the white community to deny its responsibility, in very large measure, for the economic conditions under which thousands of Negro men and women struggle right here in Chicago."

The Chicago *Evening Post* supported this position, saying: "While it is a very useful thing to have Mr. Washington preaching free will and full responsibility to the colored people, it would be a very great mistake for the white community to regard this as the last word on the subject. For it is not true in any sense whatever that the colored community is wholly and entirely responsible for the vice and crime which appear now and then in its midst. . . . But these are disagreeable truths and we all shirk them when we can. . . . The colored problem cannot be solved by the colored man alone."

This emphasis upon the interrelatedness of white Chicago and the Negro community had become traditional by 1900. With the passing of the abolitionists, Chicago's wealthy merchants and industrialists had assumed a somewhat paternalistic interest in the Negro community as a part of their general pattern of philanthropy and civic responsibility. Between 1897 and 1906, five of Chicago's most prominent men died—George Pullman, P. D. Armour, Gustavus Swift, Potter Palmer, and Marshall Field I. All except the last were considered "friends of the Negro"—liberal in their contributions to Black Belt institutions and willing to employ them in servant capacities. It is reported that when Potter Palmer died a dozen Negro employees from the famous Palmer House Hotel wept at his bier.

Even after the deaths of these men, Negro leaders maintained their contact with wealthy and powerful whites, but from 1905 through to the First World War, they began to place increasing emphasis upon "racial self-reliance"—the development of political power and a strong business and professional class. They began to urge, too, a diversification of employment and assailed the bars which some labor unions had erected against colored artisans. On the eve of the First World War the pattern of Negro-white relations was one of stable equilibrium. But Negroes conceived of it as a moving equilibrium whose motive force must be "race pride" and unified political action.

Midwest Metropolis was busy absorbing immigrants from Europe between 1890 and 1910—a major "social problem." Because it was American and small, the Negro community was far less of a "problem" to native-white Chicagoans of the Nineties than were neighborhoods inhabited by the foreign-born. For their part, Negroes viewed the influx of European immigrants with mixed emotions. The foreign-born constituted a potential threat to their jobs as butlers and maids, janitors and waiters. They monopolized the skilled and semi-skilled trades. They did most of the city's common labor. Negroes feared them as economic competitors. Yet in the West Side Ghetto and among the Italians of the North Side, these recent immigrants often lived side by side with Negroes, sometimes in the same buildings with them, and fraternized freely.

On the whole, Negroes regarded foreigners with a certain amount of understandable condescension. The foreign-born, in turn, were not slow to adopt the prevailing stereotypes about Negroes. "Foreigners learn how to cuss, count and say 'nigger' as soon as they get here," grumbled the Negroes. Not until the First World War, however, were masses of Negroes thrown into direct competition with the foreign-born in industry.

THE GREAT MIGRATION

BLACK DIASPORA (1914–1918)

In 1914 the tide of European migration was suddenly reversed.[1] As country after country was drawn into the First World War, foreign-born men streamed home from Pittsburgh and Cleveland, Detroit and Toledo, from mills and mines, to shoulder arms. Immigration virtually ceased. Chicago, too, lost thousands of workmen.

As the war dragged on, the United States gradually transformed itself into an arsenal and granary for Europe. Farmers laid more land to the plow while industrial plants expanded production. A city whose economic life depended upon the foreign-born to handle its meat, wheat, and steel now experienced a manpower crisis at the very moment when profits were highest and production demands greatest.

Then the great mass of caste-bound Negroes in the South stirred. For several years the cotton kingdom had been ravaged by the boll weevil sweeping up from Mexico. Flood and famine, too, had continually harassed the cotton farmers of the Mississippi Valley. Prior to 1915, however, there had been little to encourage plantation laborers to risk life in the city streets. Now there were jobs to attract them. Recruiting agents traveled south, begging Negroes to come north. They sometimes carried free tickets in their pockets, and always glowing promises on their tongues. For the first time, southern Negroes were actually being invited, even urged, to come to Chicago. They came in droves—50,000 of them between 1910 and 1920. And as each wave arrived, the migrants wrote the folks back home about the wonderful North. A flood of relatives and friends followed in their wake.

A bewildered South had visions of a land left desolate for lack of labor. From every southern state the Negroes came, despite desperate attempts to halt the exodus:[2]

[1] Chicago Commission on Race Relations, *The Negro in Chicago,* University of Chicago, 1922, Chap. III (hereafter referred to as *The Negro in Chicago.*)

[2] E. J. Scott, *Negro Migration During the War,* Oxford, 1920, pp. 72–85.

Up from Florida—where the city fathers in Jacksonville passed an ordinance requiring labor recruiters from the North to buy a $1,000 license or take the alternative of sixty days in jail and a $600 fine.

Up from Georgia—where the Macon city council exacted a recruiting license fee of $25,000 and demanded that the labor agent be recommended by ten local ministers, ten manufacturers, and twenty-five businessmen.

Up from Alabama—where fines and jail sentences were imposed upon any "person, firm, or corporation" guilty of "enticing, persuading, or influencing" labor to leave Montgomery.

Up from Mississippi—where agents were arrested, trains stopped, ticket agents intimidated. And at Brookhaven, a chartered car carrying fifty men and women was deliberately sidetracked for three days.

Still they came!

As coercion failed, worried businessmen and planters resorted to conciliation and persuasion in an effort to stem the tide. Leading southern white newspapers began to condemn lynching and the inequitable treatment of Negroes in the courts. Conferences were held in large cities and out-of-the-way southern towns at which Negro leaders were implored to use their good offices with the field hands. The more astute Negro negotiators began to wring promises of more schools, better treatment, higher wages, and other reforms from men who a year before would have scorned to confer with "niggers." Idealistic southern friends of the Negro found their tasks suddenly eased by these economic imperatives. The southern caste system was in the process of profound modification.[3]

The Chicago *Defender,* a Negro weekly edited by Robert S. Abbott, a native of Georgia who had come north in the Nineties and made good, played a leading role in stimulating the migration. It coaxed and challenged, denounced and applauded. It organized a "Great Northern Drive" and succeeded in getting itself banned from many a southern community. It scoffed at the Southerners' reforms under duress:[4]

> Turn a deaf ear to everybody. . . . You see they are not lifting their laws to help you. Are they? Have they stopped their Jim Crow cars? Can you buy a Pullman sleeper where you wish? Will they give you a square deal in court yet? Once upon a time we permitted other people to think for us—today we are thinking and acting for ourselves with the result that our "friends" are getting alarmed at our progress. We'd like to oblige these unselfish (?) souls and remain slaves in the South, but to their section of the country we have said, as the song goes, "I hear you calling me," and have boarded the train singing, "Good-bye, Dixie Land."

[3] Allison Davis, B. R. Gardner, and Mary R. Gardner, *Deep South,* University of Chicago, 1941, pp. 422–82.

[4] Chicago *Defender,* editorial, Oct. 7, 1916.

Eventually America entered the war. More southern Negroes came to replace the men who were drafted. For four years the tug of war between northern industry and southern planters, northern Negro leaders and southern leaders, continued. The migrants kept streaming up the Mississippi Valley, riding the real trains of the Illinois Central over the same route their forefathers had traveled on the Underground Railroad. When the tide slackened in 1920, Chicago had over a hundred thousand Negroes among her population—an increase of 148 per cent in ten years.

Most Negroes visualized the migration as a step toward the economic emancipation of a people who had been tied to the southern soil and confined to common labor and personal service in the North. The Chicago *Defender* expressed this philosophy in an editorial shortly before the United States entered the war. Declaring that "it is an ill wind that blows no one good," Editor Abbott saw the European war not only as "bloody, tragic and deplorable" but also as "opportunity." Coldly realistic, he developed his apologia for encouraging the migration. The European war, he said,[5]

> . . . has caused the people of this and other neutral countries to prosper greatly in a financial way. It has meant that the thousands who a year ago were dependent upon charity are today employed and making a comfortable living for themselves and their families. The colored man and woman are, and must be for some years to come, laborers. There is no line of endeavor that we cannot fit ourselves for. These same factories, mills and workshops that have been closed to us, through necessity are being opened to us. We are to be given a chance, not through choice but because it is expedient. Prejudice vanishes when the almighty dollar is on the wrong side of the balance sheet. . . .
>
> Give the best that is in us when we answer the call. It is significant that the great west is calling to the southern black man to leave his old home and come out here where the prospects are bright for the future. Slowly but surely all over this country we are gradually edging in first this and then that place, getting a foothold before making a place for our brother. By this only can the so-called race problem be solved. It is merely a question of a better and a closer understanding between the races. We are Americans and must live together, so why not live in peace?

Negroes were getting the foothold, but the peace and understanding did not follow. White Chicagoans viewed the migrants with mixed feelings. As laborers they were indispensable. As neighbors they would have to be tolerated. Union men were apprehensive. Only "Big Bill" Thompson, the Republican Mayor, and his coterie of politicians truly welcomed them, as they pondered the traditional political loyalties of the Negro people and watched the First and Second Ward Black Belt precincts swell amazingly.

The attitudes of the general public were undoubtedly shaped to some extent by

[5] Chicago *Defender*, January 9, 1915.

Chicago's newspaper headlines and stories which, day after day, commented in a none too friendly vein:[6]

HALF A MILLION DARKIES FROM DIXIE SWARM TO THE NORTH TO BETTER THEMSELVES

NEGROES INCITED BY GERMAN SPIES
Federal Agents Confirm Reports of New Conspiracy in South;
Accuse Germans for Exodus from South

2,000 SOUTHERN NEGROES ARRIVE IN LAST TWO DAYS
Stockyards Demand for Labor Cause of Influx

COMMITTEE TO DEAL WITH NEGRO INFLUX
Body Formed to Solve Problem Due to Migration to Chicago
from South

WORK OUT PLANS FOR MIGRATING NEGROES
Influx from the South Cared For by the Urban League
and Other Societies

Negroes were rapidly replacing foreigners as Chicago's "problem."

BLACK LEBENSRAUM

The sudden influx of Negroes into Chicago immediately resolved itself into a struggle for living space. Between 1900 and 1914, the Black Belt and its satellite areas had absorbed over ten thousand Negroes without any serious difficulty. Now the saturation point was reached, and although the migrants had jobs, there were literally no houses to accommodate them. Building construction had virtually ceased with the outbreak of the war. Doubling-up and overcrowding became inevitable. The Black Belt had to expand, and this situation aroused exaggerated fears throughout the city. Where would the black masses, still bearing the mark of the plantation upon them, find a place to live?

As in the case of immigrants, the bulk of the southern migrants during the First World War gravitated first to those areas of their "colony" where rents were cheapest and housing poorest. They took over the old, dilapidated shacks near the railroad tracks and close to the vice area. These neighborhoods had been abandoned in the previous decade by Negroes who became more prosperous and were able to move away. Now their less affluent brothers replaced them.

This tremendous demand for houses resulted in an immediate skyrocketing of rents for all available accommodations and in the opening of new residential areas to Negroes. There were tremendous profits to be made by both colored and white realtors

---

[6] *The Negro in Chicago*, pp. 529–30.

who could provide houses. And so the spread of the Negro areas of residence began, with the whites fleeing before them. Artificial panics were sometimes created in white areas by enterprising realtors who raised the cry, "The Negroes are coming," and then proceeded to double the rents after the whites had fled.[7]

By 1920 a pincers movement of the Negro population had begun along the two boundaries of the Black Belt, a mile apart, and the pocket in between had begun to close up. (Figure 6.) As Negroes moved in, they bought the synagogues and churches, often at highly inflated prices, took over the parks and playgrounds, and transformed white and mixed communities into solidly Negro areas.

To the west of the Black Belt were the Irish, traditional enemies of the Negroes in Chicago; to the east were native-Americans and the more prosperous Jews, guarding jealously the approaches to the desirable lake front where they had made investments in residential property. The Negroes pressed against both communities, and as they swept southward, the whites in their path moved east and to the outlying areas of the city—but homes were scarce.

The impact of the expanding Black Belt on institutions in white middle-class communities has been vividly described by the pastor of Chicago's oldest white Baptist church, which was eventually sold to Negroes:[8]

> . . . In 1915 the cry was heard, "The Negroes are coming." . . . The church reported . . . in 1918, "Our church has been greatly handicapped during the past year by the great influx of colored people and the removal of many whites." . . . The Negroes coming from the South by tens of thousands, lured by the promise of high wages in the packing houses, mills, and railroad yards of Chicago, swarmed to the blocks surrounding the church building. Beautiful homes occupied by families belonging to the church for generations were sold for whatever price they could obtain. The membership declined to 403 and only 10 persons united with the church in that year. The church was face to face with catastrophe. No eloquent preaching, no social service, could save a church in a community that was nearly 100 per cent Negro. . . . Meanwhile the Negroes are steadily pushing down the alleys southward with their carts of furniture, but Forty-seventh Street running east and west still stands as a breakwater against the oncoming tide. If it crumbles there will be some new history for the First Church.

But the "breakwater" finally burst. Forty-seventh Street is now in the center of the Black Belt.

The expansion of the Black Belt developed so much friction that in the invaded neighborhoods bombs were occasionally thrown at Negro homes and those of real-estate men, white and colored, who sold or rented property to the newcomers. From July

[7] *Ibid.*, Chap. IV.

[8] P. J. Stackhouse, *Chicago and the Baptists,* University of Chicago, 1933, pp. 200–207.

EXPANSION OF THE BLACK BELT

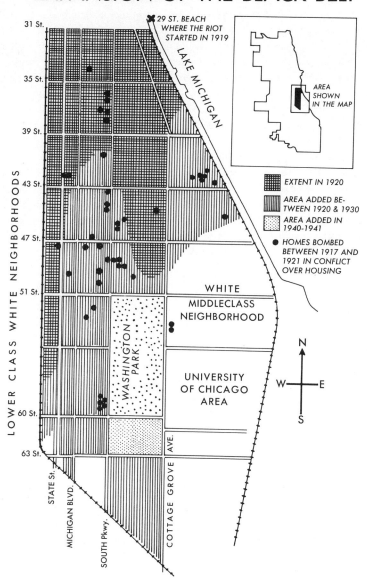

FIGURE 6
Adapted from map in *The Negro in Chicago,* Chicago Commission on Race Relations, University of Chicago Press, 1922.

1, 1917, to March 1, 1921, fifty-eight such bombs were hurled.[9] (Figure 6.)

This conflict over space often came to a head where Negroes and whites met in public places—at the beaches and playgrounds and in the public schools. Particular resentment was manifested against Negroes who frequented beaches that white people had come to think of as their own. Playground fights between Negro and white children were epidemic. Policemen, social workers, and teachers, even when they were not themselves antagonistic to Negroes, often resorted to segregation as a convenient method of keeping the peace.[10] Yet throughout this period, despite tension in the areas peripheral to the Black Belt, there were also adjusted neighborhoods in other sections of the city where Negroes and whites maintained their neighborly relations and where no hostility was evident.[11]

During the war period, civic leaders viewed the situation with some foreboding. The Chicago Urban League was founded in 1917 to deal specifically with the problem of adjusting the migrants to city life. The churches, the newspapers, the YMCA, and the YWCA had deliberately set themselves the task of training the peasant folk in the city ways and of trying to interpret them to the Negro Old Settlers and to those sections of the white community which resented their presence. Incident after incident, however, augured an eventual crisis. In 1919 it came.

---

[9] *The Negro in Chicago*, pp. 122–33.
[10] *Ibid.*, Chap. VI, "Racial Contacts."
[11] *Ibid.*, pp. 108–13.

Organized Labor and the Negro[*]

Charles H. Wesley

The American Labor Movement of earlier years had failed to secure any large success for the laboring groups. There were two consequences of this failure. One was renewed interest in the Knights of Labor, an organization which survived the disruptive tendencies of the labor movement after the Civil War, and the other was a new organization, the American Federation of Labor. The Noble Order of the Knights of Labor was organized in 1869, and its first large National Convention was held in 1876. It was supposed, according to its constitution, to make no distinction of race. It was organized to uphold the dignity of labor and to affirm the nobility of all who earn their bread by the sweat of their brow.[1] Mr. Powderly, one of its most influential leaders, declared that its purpose was to banish "that curse of modern civilization—wage slavery." [2]

The Negroes were to be organized with the encouragement of the National Organization. By 1885, it was reported that the Negroes were enthusiastically joining the organization, especially in Virginia, where there were seven assemblies in the city of Richmond, and a very large one in Manchester.[3] Because of the lack of discrimination, the Negroes joined the order in many other places. The decline of the organization was as rapid as its rise. After 1886, two factions appeared. One expected to secure labor reform through political action and the other planned to attain it by direct methods. The Knights of Labor exerted much influence on the treatment and organizations of Negro

[*] From Charles H. Wesley, *Negro Labor in the United States, 1850–1925* (New York: Vanguard Press, Inc., 1927), pp. 254–67, 269–80. Reprinted by permission of the publishers.
[1] C. D. Wright, *Historical Sketch of the Knights of Labor, Quarterly Journal of Economics,* January, 1887, pp. 142–143.
[2] Speech before the Annual Convention, 1880.
[3] Ely, *The Labor Movement,* p. 161.

workers. Their declarations rang true, and their associations and practice of brotherhood had its effects upon local organizations, some of which were not affiliated with it.

At New Orleans in 1883, the Central Trades and Labor Assembly, which was made up of the labor organizations of the city, was making efforts to organize the Negro workers. Parades were held in 1883, 1884 and 1885 in which Negroes took part. It was declared that this action on the part of the assembly did much in breaking up the antagonism between white workers and Negro workers, and that conditions were as fraternal there as in any part of the country. In 1886, the Brotherhood of Carpenters and Joiners reported that there were 14 unions of Negro carpenters affiliated with them in the South, and that they attended the conventions of the Brotherhood.[4] In this year it was stated that the "color line" in labor had been broken and all were working in a common cause.[5]

This statement was not true in all details, for at Richmond in this year an incident occurred which revealed an opposite sentiment among white workingmen. The Knights of Labor met at Richmond at their annual meeting. District Assembly No. 49, of New York, had in its representation a Negro, Mr. F. J. Ferrell. He was received at the meetings, but at the theatres and hotels he received continued rebuffs. When it became known that he occupied one of the best seats in the theatre, many persons left the building, and on the next evening the attendance was small, it was said, for the same reason. At the hotel, when the New York delegation appeared, they were told that Mr. Ferrell would not be admitted. A singular expression of loyalty to their comrade was shown by the delegates who left the place as a group and went to another hotel where no such objections were raised.

Later, in preparation of the program for the exercises in which the Governor of the State was to have part, it was suggested that Mr. Ferrell should be permitted to introduce the Governor. Mr. Powderly, then General Master Workman of the Knights of Labor, stated that this would be a violation of the recognized rule of the community, but that he would consider it an honor to have himself introduced to the assembly by Mr. Ferrell, and he in turn would introduce the Governor. In presenting Mr. Powderly, Mr. Ferrell said that one of the objects of the order was the extinction of the color line and he believed that he was presenting a man who was above this superstition.[6] This was true in part, for Mr. Powderly had championed the cause of Mr. Ferrell in a letter to *The Richmond Dispatch*, stating that the organization recognized "no line of race, creed, politics or color." This sentiment was in the thought of labor leaders in this decade. McNeill also wrote that "no Mason and Dixon's line, no color tests divide North, South, East and West. Whenever laborers congregate, whether in the factories of New England or the sunless mines of Pennsylvania, one chord of sympathy unites them all. No demagogue's cant of race or creed will hold them from their purpose to be free." [7]

[4] McNeill, *The Labor Movement*, pp. 168, 171, 360.
[5] Ibid.
[6] T. V. Powderly, *Thirty Years of Labor*, pp. 643–651–654.
[7] McNeill, *The Labor Movement*, p. 461. See quotations from many newspapers concerning this event in Public Opinion, Vol. II, pp. 1–5.

At the same period the American Federation of Labor was started. This organization was formed in 1881 from among the dissatisfied members of the Knights of Labor. The Federation was founded on the principle of self-determination for the local bodies. Its declaration on matters of race was therefore in the nature of advice to the unions. In 1920, the American Federation of Labor was composed of 110 National and International Unions, 1,286 Local and Federal Unions, 46 State Federations and 926 City Central bodies. The national and international unions have self-government, but the local unions are more circumscribed. At the outset it was declared that associations which refused admission to Negroes were excluded from membership in the Federation. The International Association of Machinists, as we shall note later, was not admitted to membership until the word "white" was removed from its constitution.[8] Such was the early attitude of the American Federation of Labor. There was to be no division on creed, color, sex or nationality. However, subsequent events were to reveal modifications in the practice of this policy.

Strikes by American workingmen began on a large scale and continued in the decade 1880–1890. The places of the strikers were taken by foreigners and by American Negroes. These substitutions often occasioned bitterness, and only the wisdom of organization leaders prevented bloodshed and violence.[9] Business failures, unemployment, wage quarrels and racial antipathy gave much discredit to the labor movement in this decade. A declaration by the International Labor Union of America in 1878 stated that race was being arrayed against race in the labor struggle, and that this competition was retarding the progress of all workingmen.

In the early days of the labor movement fostered by the American Federation of Labor, the democratic sentiment was so great that there were few evidences on the part of the National organization of any feeling of color. At Birmingham, Alabama, in 1885, the delegates refused to take part in a banquet because there were three Negro delegates who had not been invited. Local unions and national trade organizations often manifested a like liberal spirit. In the same year the Cigarmaker's International Union left a hotel because the Treasurer, who was a Negro, was given a place for the service of his meals outside of the regular dining room. The Cigarmakers had a large number of Negroes who were members and it appeared that they made no race distinction in their membership.[10] In New Orleans the Negro draymen had formed a Union and they sought to make a wage agreement with their employers. The employers refused to treat with the draymen as Unionmen, whereupon organized labor in New Orleans went on a sympathetic strike and recognition was finally secured.[11]

The Negro hod-carriers of Wheeling, West Virginia, had formed an organization known as Labor's Progress Assembly. This organization was affiliated with the Knights of Labor. Another assembly, known as Prosperity Assembly, was formed. It

[8] Report of the Industrial Commission, Vol. XVII, p. 36.
[9] McNeill, *The Labor Movement,* p. 260.
[10] Report of the Industrial Commission, Vol. VII, pp. 648–649.
[11] Ibid., p. 647.

was composed of workmen of both races in all trades which were not strong enough in numbers to have separate trade unions formed. The laws of the Knights of Labor allowed the formation of these two unions. It thus happened that most of the Negroes belonged to Labor's Progress Assembly and that there were both white and Negro hod-carriers in the Prosperity Assembly. These workmen often were at work on the same locations and at the same tasks. With the organization of the American Federation of Labor, both groups applied for admission, after withdrawing from the Knights of Labor. One of the rules of the Federation was that all men working at one kind of employment must belong to the same local union. According to this ruling the Negroes and the whites must belong to one Hod-Carriers' Union. Arbitration by the District officers of the Federation was necessary in order to prevent the disruption of both organizations.[12]

In 1899 the same difficulty arose among the longshoremen of Newport News, Virginia. The local unions were composed of Negroes and the whites refused to join them. The question was settled by the issuance of a separate charter to the white workers.[13] Thus the policy of the American Federation was being trimmed to suit local conditions. Its democratic welcome was changed to the policy of separation along racial lines of white and Negro workmen. Foreigners of all types might be received into the regular old-line organizations but Negroes were placed in separate locals.

The Federation Convention of 1897 passed a resolution condemning the statement reported to have been made that the trades unions were placing obstacles in the path of the economic advance of the Negro worker. The convention reaffirmed its welcome to all ranks of labor, "without regard to creed, color, sex, race or nationality." During this session it was said that an affiliated union had no right to limit its membership so as to debar the Negroes.[14]

In spite of these declarations of policy, practical exclusion and separation were in operation, and this action seriously affected the economic status of Negro labor in many localities. In 1900, President Gompers suggested that local unions composed of Negroes should be encouraged and that separate central bodies composed of Negro workers should be established where it was deemed advisable. The convention of 1902 provided that separate charters might be issued to Central Labor Unions, Local Unions and Federal Labor Unions which were composed exclusively of Negro laborers.[15] Thus another step was taken in the separation of the races in their labor organizations.

An investigation concerning the number of Negroes who were in the trades unions was made by Atlanta University in 1902. The list and the tabulations are incomplete and they therefore can be only suggestive of the facts. The following results were reported through correspondence with the trades unions which had a considerable num-

[12] *The Tradesman*, March 15, 1890, p. 58.

[13] *Proceedings of the Convention of the American Federation of Labor*, 1900, p. 11. *Report of the Industrial Commission*, Vol. XVII, p. 264.

[14] *Proceedings of the Convention of the American Federation of Labor*, 1897, pp. 82–83.

[15] *Convention Proceedings*, 1900, 1902, 1910; *Annals of the American Academy of Political and Social Science*, Vol. XLIX, p. 114.

ber of Negro members.[16] There were 200 Negro members of the Journeymen Barbers' International Union in 1890 and 800 Negro members in 1900. In 1890 there were only 50 Negro members of the International Brick, Tile and Terra-cotta Workers' Alliance and 200 in 1900. There were 1,000 Negroes who belonged to the United Brotherhood of Carpenters and Joiners in 1900. The Carriage and Wagon Workers' International Union reported 240 Negro members in 1890 and 500 in 1900. The Coopers International Union had 200 Negro members and the International Brotherhood of Stationary Firemen had 2,700 Negro members in a total membership of 3,600 as reported in 1901. The International Longshoremen's Association had increased its Negro membership from 1,500 in 1890 to 6,000 in 1900. The United Mine Workers of America reported a Negro membership of 20,000 in a total membership of 224,000 in 1901. The Tobacco Workers' International Union reported a decrease. There were 1,500 Negro members in 1890 and 1,000 in 1900. The membership of the Knights of Labor, as would be expected, showed a decrease from 8,000 in 1890 to 6,000 in 1900.

At this period Negroes were not actively encouraged to become members of the trades unions, and it is not surprising that the increases were small, and that in some cases decreases were recorded. The labor unions had not realized the value of organizing Negro workingmen. The Negro labor leaders in these organizations continued to urge the recognition of Negro labor. The American Federation of Labor had adopted an indifferent attitude. It would not force its views "upon individual or affiliated unions without their consent." Apparently the fight had to be waged from within the local unions. This was difficult because of the barriers against the admission of Negro workers, in the constitutions, the governing regulations, and the social restrictions of the local labor organizations. The line of approach which was followed by Negro labor leaders was the continuance of their efforts in both the national and the local fields with the hope that the national organization would decide in the future to take high ground in the organization of Negro labor.

In 1880 a strike among the Miners in the Tuscarawas Valley, Pennsylvania, led to the importation of Negro workers. Similar strikes in other places led to the same results.[17] Such conditions caused greater activity in the organization of Negro labor. It was thought by labor leaders that it was better to have the cooperation of Negro workingmen than to have their competition, and therefore efforts were made to perfect their organization. The local labor unions as a rule would not accept Negroes, and with organizations refusing membership to them and the members refusing to work with them, the Negro's way to skilled labor was effectively barred. In a few instances Negro applications were accepted, but as rapidly as possible separate unions composed exclusively of Negroes were formed. This sentiment was encouraged by the social tradition through which permanent mixed racial unions were regarded as impossible in the South.[18]

The railroad brotherhoods began to exclude Negroes by constitutional clauses.

[16] Atlanta University Publications, No. VII, p. 158 (1902).
[17] McNeill, *The Labor Movement,* p. 260.
[18] *Report of the Industrial Commission on Capital and Labor,* Vol. VII, pp. 554–555.

The International Association of Machinists, which was organized in 1888, inserted a clause in its constitution excluding Negro workers. The American Federation of Labor refused to admit unions which made distinctions based upon color, and thus the Machinists were excluded. The Federation continued to refuse admission to the Association of Machinists because the organization would not remove the color line. Finally in 1891 the Executive Council of the Federation issued a call for a conference of the unions of the trade, and to this meeting the members of the old organization would send no delegates. The delegates who assembled organized the International Machinists Union. In the report of President Gompers to the Convention of 1890, it was stated that as soon as the old organization had removed the color line, the new organization would pledge itself to amalgamate with the old organization.[19]

At the convention of 1892, a committee of the Federation was appointed to receive the President of the Machinists. He expressed satisfaction at the action of the Executive Council, and said that it was his belief that the Machinists would abolish the barrier against Negroes at their next convention.[20] It was not until 1895 that this action was secured and the convention of the Federation of this year withdrew the charter of the new organization, the International Machinists Union.

There were unions which made no distinction of race. The Hotel Employees did not exclude Negroes but they insisted that they should be organized in separate local organizations. The Tobacco Workers made no racial differences in their membership. Their constitution stated that they "will draw no line of distinction between creed, color or nationality." However, in the majority of the trades, separate locals have been demanded from the first, although there were unions in which the two workers met.[21]

In the first annual session of the American Federation of Labor, in 1881, the color question came to the front. The Federation was started from a meeting of the disaffected members of the Knights of Labor. This session was termed the Federation of Organized Trades and Labor Unions of the United States and Canada. It met at Pittsburgh, September 15–18, 1881. A Negro delegate, Jeremiah Grandison, of the Labor Assembly, Knights of Labor of Pittsburgh, was present. Concerning the purposes of the organization, Mr. Grandison said: "Our object, as I understand it, is to federate the whole laboring element of America. I speak more particularly with a knowledge of my own people and declare to you that it would be dangerous to skilled mechanics to exclude from this organization the common laborers, who might, in an emergency, be employed in positions they could readily qualify themselves to fill." He was urging that the Negroes, who in the main were common laborers, should be organized, but he admitted in his discussion that occasions would arise in which Negroes would be used in higher grades of labor and thereby come in conflict with white workers.[22]

---

[19] *Proceedings of the Convention of the American Federation of Labor,* 1891, pp. 12, 37, 38.

[20] Ibid., 1892, p. 38. Ibid., 1895, p. 92. *Report of the Industrial Commission on Capital and Labor,* Vol. XVII, p. 217.

[21] Ibid., Vol. XVII, pp. 24, 36, 37.

[22] *Report of The First Annual Session of the Federation of Organized Trades and Labor Unions of The United States and Canada, at Pittsburgh, Pa., September 15–18, 1881,* p. 16.

Referring to the admission of the various laboring elements to the Federation at the same session, Mr. Pollner, one of the convention secretaries, representing the Trades Assembly of Cleveland, said: "We recognize neither creed, color nor nationality, but want to take into the folds of this federation the whole labor element of the country, no matter what calling." Mr. Gompers said that it should be the purpose not to exclude "Any working man who believes in and belongs to organized labor." [23] No mention was made of Negro labor in the constitution of the American Federation of Labor, but the declaration of its first sessions appear to lead to the conclusion that it was opposed to any racial distinction.

One of the causes for the weakness of the Negro Labor Movement was its lack of organization. No organized efforts had succeeded in creating strong unions among the Negroes. White workmen said that they objected to working with Negroes on this account. Employers said that they could not employ non-union men or their union men would leave. Finally, when there were employers who were bold enough to employ Negroes in spite of the union objections, and when the Negroes became strong competitors with white workmen, the national labor organizations began to take action. As we have noticed, the American Federation of Labor, at the annual meeting of its National Council in 1910, voted to invite the Negro laborers to enter its ranks along with all races.[24] In 1913 this action was reaffirmed. The Federation reported a little later that it had maintained organizers who worked among the Negroes for the purpose of organizing and protecting the interests of labor. There were soon formed unions of exclusive Negro membership, which were affiliated with the Federation, and there were unions composed of whites and blacks who seemed to work together without great friction.[25]

It is interesting to note, however, that while there were 51 national organizations out of 60 which reported in 1913 that there was no constitutional objections to Negro membership, there were nine which barred Negroes from their organizations. These organizations were: The International Brotherhood of Maintenance of Way Employees, The Switchmen's Union, The Brotherhood of Railway Trainmen, The Brotherhood of Locomotive Firemen and Enginemen, The Brotherhood of Locomotive Engineers, The Order of Railway Conductors of America, The Order of Railway Telegraphers, The American Wire Weavers Protective Association, The International Brotherhood of Boilermakers, and the Iron Shipbuilders and Helpers of America.[26]

The apathy of the majority of the members of the labor unions toward the unionization of Negro workers, and the opposition which Negro workers encountered in many places, caused some of them to cooperate with radical labor leaders and radical labor organizations. Militant industrialism therefore found supporters in the Negro group. It was not until 1905 that labor militancy seriously challenged the influence of

[23] Ibid.

[24] Convention Proceedings, 1910.

[25] *The American Federationist,* Vol. VIII, p. 118. Interview with officials of the Federation confirmed this opinion.

[26] *The Negro Year Book,* 1921–1922, pp. 316–317. Southern Workman, September, 1914, p. 505.

the normal labor movement. A convention was held in Chicago in this year. The result was the formation of the Industrial Workers of the World. From 1909 to 1917 the I. W. W. enjoyed an increasing numerical strength and influence. Its opposition to the war and the activity of the government in prosecuting its search for internal enemies caused a loss of public favor. When members of the I. W. W. were arrested for breaches of the law in war-time, Negroes were discovered in their number. The presence of Negroes among the radical labor groups is another evidence of their dissatisfaction with the efforts of Organized Labor in their behalf.

Negro thinkers also interested themselves in creating a sentiment among the Negro population which would lead to a more serious consideration of the economic basis of life. Several magazines carried this message to all groups. *The Messenger,* a monthly magazine, published in New York under able editorial direction, sent forth a call for aggressive and organized activity. *Opportunity,* another New York monthly, published under the direction of the National Urban League, assumed a more conservative attitude, but in no less clear and certain terms clamored for a larger opportunity for Negro labor and encouraged labor organization. *The Crisis,* the organ of the National Association for the Advancement of Colored People, for years had voiced to the Negro world the need of organized effort in all phases of life. Negro newspapers, such as *The Chicago Defender, The Afro-American, The New York Age* and others considered the interests of labor fundamental to other interests. In the course of events the results of these activities were the more serious consideration of the needs of Negro labor and a more aggressive assault upon the stronghold of American organized labor.

At the conventions of the American Federation in 1916, 1917 and 1918, the problem created by the appearance of Negro labor was discussed and it was decided that the Negroes ought to be organized. But no effective machinery was created to put this decision into operation. A resolution was also presented at this convention by the San Francisco Labor Council favoring the return to Africa of those Negroes who so desired, deploring the treatment of Negroes in the South and requesting the grant of citizenship rights. The resolution had originally been presented to the San Francisco Labor Council by the International Negro League with the request that it be presented to the convention of the American Federation of Labor. There were objections to this resolution when it was presented and it was amended by the statement that the convention was not responsible for these declarations, and in fact rejected them, but as much of the resolution as concerned the organization of Negro Labor was referred to the Executive Council. In this amended form the resolution was passed.[27]

The National League on Urban Conditions among Negroes at its meeting in New York City, January 29–31, 1918, passed resolutions urging the organization of

---

[27] *Report of the Proceedings of the 37th Annual Convention of the American Federation of Labor at Buffalo, New York, 1917,* pp. 350–351. It is not altogether true, as some authors have stated, that the Federation recommended that portions of the African Continent be turned over to persons of African descent. This resolution was presented to the Convention through the plan of a group of Negroes. The statements were rejected and the resolution passed only in the amended form noted above.

Negro labor and protesting against the past attitude of the American Federation of Labor. *The Labor News* of Detroit asserted that the time had come for "the American Labor Movement to face squarely the fact that the Negro is a big factor in our industrial life and that he must be taken into account in the adjustment of our economic differences; never again can the Negro be ignored. Unionism must welcome the Negro to its ranks." [28]

At the annual meeting of the American Federation in 1918 a letter was read from a committee which represented a number of Negro Organizations. This letter quoted the remarks of President Gompers that Negro workers were welcomed by the Federation and the following suggestions were made: (1) that a published statement of this welcome to Negroes should be given to the public press, (2) that qualified Negro organizers should be employed by the Federation, (3) that the cooperation of Negro organizations should be encouraged, and (4) that the American Federation of Labor should assume a more advanced position in the matter of Negro workers. The statement was signed by E. K. Jones of the National League on Urban Conditions among Negroes; Fred R. Moore, of *The New York Age;* R. R. Morten, of Tuskegee Institute; J. R. Shilladay, of the National Association for the Advancement of Colored People; A. H. Grimke, of the Washington branch of this association; Thomas J. Jones, Educational Director of the Phelps-Stokes Fund; J. H. Dillard, of the Jeannes Fund; G. C. Hall, of the Chicago Urban League. When the letter was presented, it was referred to the committee on organization, which reported a few days later that the Federation viewed with pleasure that the leaders of the race were realizing the necessity of the organization of Negro labor, and a meaningless declaration was offered by the committee urging that the President of the American Federation of Labor should give special attention to the organization of Negro workers. The report of the committee was unanimously adopted.[29]

• • •

The most significant action of organized labor in recent times was taken at the Fortieth Convention of the American Federation of Labor in Montreal, June 7–19, 1920. It resulted from the strong presentation of the case for Negro Labor by Negro delegates themselves. Resolutions were presented urging that since the World War was ended, and since the American Negro had fought for the freedom due to all, he himself should not be barred from participation in the freedom for which he had fought, and that therefore American Labor should recognize him. This set of resolutions was signed by delegates of the Freight Handlers' Union of Jonesboro, Arkansas; the Freight Handlers' Union of Cleveland, Ohio; the Railroad Freight Handlers' Union of Wichita Falls, Texas; the Railroad Coach and Station Cleaners' and Porters' Union of Cleveland, Ohio; the Baggage Handlers', Freight Handlers, and the Stationmen's Union, of Philadelphia; the Federal Labor Union, of Knoxville, Tennessee; and the Coach and Car Cleaners' Union, of Philadelphia.

[28] *The Labor News,* August, 1918.
[29] *Report of the Proceedings of the 38th Annual Convention of the American Federation of Labor, St. Paul, Minnesota, June 10–20, 1918,* pp. 198, 199, 205.

A second resolution was presented, signed by some of the organizations which are listed above and by several Boilermaker and Blacksmith organizations. It reviewed the fair stand of the American Federation of Labor regarding Negro labor, but it deplored the fact that results had not followed. In order to secure a more successful operation of the Federation among Negroes, it was suggested that (1) a campaign of education among both white and colored workingmen should be conducted in order to convince all persons of "the necessity of bringing into the ranks of labor all men who work, regardless of race, creed or color," that (2) there should be periodic conferences of white and colored leaders with the Executive Council of the American Federation of Labor on questions affecting Negro labor, (3) that there should be employed a competent agent as Executive Secretary of a Special Committee on Negro workers at the Washington headquarters and (4) that there should be, in all states, Negro organizers in all crafts whose duty it would be to build up the Negro membership. These resolutions were submitted to the Committee on Organization which reported a few days later its recommendation to strike out sections two and three of the resolution and that section four should be amended to read that Negro organizers be appointed, where necessary, to organize Negro workers. This last recommendation was referred to the Executive Council for action if the funds of the American Federation of Labor should permit.

The committee to which the first resolution was referred reported a strong statement of the attitude of the Federation toward Negro labor. It read, "The American Federation of Labor has never countenanced the drawing of a color line or discrimination against individuals because of race, creed or color. It recognizes that human freedom is a gift from the Creator to all mankind and is not to be denied to any because of social position or the limitations of caste or class, and that any cause which depends for its success on the denial of this fundamental principle of liberty cannot stand. We, therefore, concur in the resolution and recommend its adoption." The report of the Committee was adopted.

A third group of resolutions was submitted to this convention by representatives of the Railroad Machinists, the Boilermakers, the Blacksmiths, the Sheet Metal Workers, the Carmen, the Painters, and Trade Wagoners. These resolutions accompanied a petition requesting that the American Federation of Labor exercise its influence to have the Internationals accord recognition to the local Negro organizations which should come properly under their jurisdiction. This action was requested since there were a few of the larger organizations which refused admittance to Negroes. There were 110 national and international unions affiliated with the American Federation of Labor, and it was said that more than 100 of these admitted Negroes to membership.[32] There are eleven national and international unions which refuse by specific ruling to grant the privilege of membership to Negroes. Many other unions discourage Negro membership.[33]

---

[32] Ibid., p. 309. *Proceedings of the Fourth Annual Meeting of the National Conference on Social Work, 1921,* p. 324.

[33] Two studies are being made of the recent relations of the Negro in Organized Labor, one by the Social Science Research Council and the other by the National Urban League.

It was reported also that four of the six nationals and internationals which were not affiliated with the American Federation of Labor had provisions excluding Negroes. These included the Railroad Brotherhoods. Through a meeting of representatives of 27 different states in 1921, the result of this action was the creation of a Colored National Railroad Organization with Chicago as the headquarters. There were, however, two organizations, not affiliated with the American Federation of Labor which admitted Negroes—the Amalgamated Clothing Workers of America and the Industrial Workers of the World.[34]

The autonomy of the international unions has been respected absolutely by the American Federation of Labor, and their independent government has been conceded. It was therefore an unusual procedure which led this convention to request an affiliated organization to remove an excluding provision from its constitution. The Brotherhood of Railway Clerks had a clause expressly admitting white workers to membership. The constitution of the American Federation of Labor did not contain such a clause. Moreover, at the previous annual convention at Atlantic City, the President of the Brotherhood of Railway Clerks had promised to arrange the question of Negro membership in a satisfactory manner. When the Executive Committee to which the matter was referred met in Cincinnati, the question was passed over without action.

At the Montreal Convention, a resolution was presented requesting that the Federation use every means in its power either to have the words "only white" stricken from the constitution of the Brotherhood of Railway Clerks, or to have this Brotherhood relinquish its jurisdiction over the Negro workers and grant them the privilege of establishing a Brotherhood of their own. The committee on organization to which the resolution was referred, reported that it could not concur in the resolution since the American Federation of Labor could not interfere with the autonomy of the affiliated nationals and internationals. In addition, the report stated that the Negroes had the opportunity to join the Federation, for the Convention of 1919 had authorized the granting of charters to colored workers in cases where the nationals and internationals had refused to accept them.

A debate followed this report. One delegate asked if it was not contrary to the principles of the American Federation of Labor to draw the color line. Vice-President Duncan replied that the Federation since its organization had stood for federation without reference to color and that this was the position which it still assumed. He stated that the organization could not be expected to favor a charter of an affiliated union which discriminated against a worker because of his color. After some discussion, an amendment to the report was carried requesting the Railway Clerks to remove the words "only white" from their constitution.[35] Although this action was contrary to the accepted principle of complete governmental freedom for the internationals, the convention carried the amendment over the recommendation of the committee. It was also

[34] *Proceedings of the Fourth Annual Meeting of the National Conference on Social Work, 1921,* p. 324. American Labor Year Book, 1921–1922, p. 150.
[35] *Federation Proceedings, 1920,* pp. 309–310. See also the *American Labor Year Book, Vol. IV, 1921–1922,* p. 125.

voted later that the Brotherhood of Railroad Carmen should eliminate from their constitution all reference to colored workmen.[36]

At the next annual session of the American Federation of Labor at Denver, Colorado, it was stated that there were still some internationals which excluded Negroes. Jordan W. Chambers, a Negro delegate, said that the convention had ordered the word "white" stricken out, and also that conferences should be held between the officers of the internationals and the Negroes who sought membership, but that in a few cases only had action been taken. He advocated effective action on the part of the Federation. Specific complaints were presented against the Brotherhood of Railway Carmen, the International Brotherhood of Boilermakers, the Iron Ship Builders and Helpers of America, the Brotherhood of Railway and Steamship Clerks, the Freight Handlers, Express and Station Employees, calling attention to either exclusion or discrimination. A motion that there should be no discriminating laws in organized labor failed of adoption. In response to one resolution, President Gompers said that "The American Federation of Labor, almost from its inception, has declared that it is the duty of all workers to organize regardless of sex, nationality, race, religion or political affiliation. That declaration has been emphasized time and time again in the conventions of the American Federation of Labor; that declaration forms a part of the literature issued by the American Federation of Labor. That is the policy and principle of the American Federation of Labor, but it cannot enforce that declaration upon the affiliated international unions if those international unions decline or refuse to adopt them." However, conferences were ordered with the internationals within 90 days, with the object in view of having them change their attitude toward Negro labor.[37]

In July, August and September, 1921, as a result of conferences in Washington and at Toronto, organizations of Negro Freight Handlers and Station Employees were organized and Negroes were granted admission to other unions. The Brotherhood of Railroad Carmen agreed to admit separate lodges of Negroes under the jurisdiction of the nearest white local.[38] The American Federation of Labor has thus sanctioned the principle of race separation, although in words of declaration and policy it has proclaimed the necessity for all workers to organize. Racial barriers have made their way into the ranks of labor. There are some organizations where Negro and white workmen work and meet side by side. It is reported that this is the situation among the Longshoremen, the Garment Workers, the Candy Makers, the Stenographers and a few of the Building Trades. At the Biennial Session of the International Longshoremen's Convention at Buffalo, New York, in July, 1921, there were 80 Negro delegates who were present. Sixty-five of these delegates were from the North and 15 were from the South.

As a rule, however, the organization of Negro labor has not been encouraged as

    [36] *Report of the Proceedings of the 40th Annual Convention of the American Federation of Labor, 1920,* pp. 351–352.
    [37] *Report of the Proceedings of the 41st Annual Convention of the American Federation of Labor, Denver, 1921,* p. 433. *American Labor Year Book, 1921–1922,* p. 135.
    [38] *Report of the Proceedings of the 42nd Annual Convention of the American Federation of Labor, 1922,* pp. 118–119.

much as the organization of other groups. This is unfortunate, in view of the fact that Negroes form so large a part of the economic life of the United States. One of the significant results of the indifference of the American Federation of Labor has been the tendency for Negro Labor to organize itself independent of White Labor. The most important national organizations which have been organized on this basis are, The International Order of Colored Locomotive Firemen, The National Order of Locomotive Firemen, and The Shopmen's Craft of the Railway Men's International Benevolent Industrial Association. At Birmingham, Alabama, in January, 1921, a National Federation of Railway Men was organized. In May of that year a meeting of these groups was held in the same city, at which there were delegates from 15 states and railroad workers from 26 railroads. In addition to these persons there were representatives from 150 international trade organizations who were present. This type of independent organization may be expected to continue so long as Organized Labor does not give a ready welcome to Negro Workers.

This attitude of Organized Labor has led, on the one hand, to renewed agitation by Negroes themselves in the interest of the organization of Negro Labor and, on the other, to an increase in the possibility of radicalism among Negroes. At the 1924 Convention of the National Association for the Advancement of Colored People, the following statement in the form of an open letter was presented:

"AN OPEN LETTER TO THE AMERICAN FEDERATION OF
LABOR AND OTHER GROUPS OF ORGANIZED LABOR
Gentlemen:

For many years the American Negro has been demanding admittance to the ranks of union labor.

For many years your organizations have made public profession of your interest in Negro labor, of your desire to have it unionized, and of your hatred of the black 'scab.'

Notwithstanding this apparent surface agreement, Negro labor in the main is outside the ranks of organized labor, and the reason is, first, that white union labor does not want black labor, and, secondly, black labor has ceased to beg admittance to union ranks because of its increasing value and efficiency outside the unions.

We thus face a crisis in inter-racial labor conditions; the continued and determined race prejudice of white labor, together with the limitation of immigration, is giving black labor tremendous advantage. The Negro is entering the ranks of semi-skilled and skilled labor and he is entering mainly and necessarily as a 'scab.' He broke the great steel strike. He will soon be in a position to break any strike when he can gain economic advantage for himself.

On the other hand, intelligent Negroes know full well that a blow at organized labor is a blow at all labor; that black labor today profits by the blood and sweat of labor leaders in the past who have fought oppression and monopoly by organization. If there is built up in America a great black bloc of non-union laborers who have a right to hate unions, all laborers, black and white, eventually must suffer.

Is it not time, then, that black and white labor got together? Is it not time for white unions to stop bluffing and for black laborers to stop cutting off their noses to spite their faces?

We, therefore, propose that there be formed by the National Association for the Advancement of Colored People, the American Federation of Labor, the Railway Brotherhoods and any other bodies agreed upon, an Inter-racial Labor Commission.

We propose that this Commission undertake:

1. To find out the exact attitude and practice of national labor bodies and local unions toward Negroes, and of Negro labor toward unions.

2. To organize systematic propaganda against racial discrimination on the basis of these facts at the great labor meetings, in local assemblies, and in local unions.

The National Association for the Advancement of Colored People stands ready to take part in such a movement and hereby invites the cooperation of all organized labor. The association hereby solemnly warns American laborers that unless some such step as this is taken, and taken soon, the position gained by organized labor in this country is threatened with irreparable loss."

About the same time the National League on Urban Conditions among Negroes established a Department of Industrial Relations. Some of the purposes of this department were: to encourage friendly relations between white and black workingmen; to encourage technical education; "the organization and assistance of Negro mechanics; and the opening and finding of positions for Colored workers." The major part of the work of the Urban League in at least 29 cities is aid to Negro workmen. At its meeting in Detroit in 1919 the League adopted the following resolution concerning unionism—"We believe that Negroes should begin to think more and more in terms of labor-group movements, so as ultimately to reap the benefit of thinking in unison. To this end we advise Negroes to organize with white men whenever conditions are favorable. When this is not possible, they should band together to bargain with employers and with organized labor alike. With America and the whole world in labor turmoil, we urge white and black men, capital and labor, to be fair and patient with each other while a just solution is being worked out." The Inter-racial Committees in various parts of the country have taken great interest in improving the condition of Negro workingmen.

Radicalism has taken new developments among Negro laborers since the World War. Sympathy for Russia's new experiment was not unknown among Negro-Americans from the first. The declarations of the Russian labor congresses seemed to ring true on racial matters. The Fourth Congress of the Third Internationale in 1922 declared that its purpose was "not simply the organization of the enslaved white workers of Europe and America, but equally the organization of the oppressed colored peoples of the World." It was also agreed that it would "fight for race equality of the Negro with the white people, as well as for equal wages and political and social rights." The fact that radicalism among Negroes was being organized was demonstrated in the American Negro Labor Congress of 1925. This Congress met in Chicago, October 25–31. The addresses and resolutions attacked the policies of Organized Labor, in words which declared that "the failure of the American Federation of Labor officialdom, under pressure of race prejudice benefitting only the capitalists of the North and South, to stamp out race hatred in the unions, to organize Negro workers, and to build a solid front of the workers of both races against American Capitalism, is a crime against the whole working class. If the unions of the American Federation of Labor, through ignorance and prejudice, fail in this duty to the American workers and continue a policy of exclusion in the face of the influx of Negro workers into industry, we Negro workers must organize our own unions as a powerful weapon with which to fight our way into the existing labor movement on a basis of full equality." Thus the Negro asserts his own right to organize if neglected by others. The American Negro Labor Congress was sponsored by the Workers Party of America, and with its appeal on the basis of racial equality there is no doubt that the influences of this group will be predominant. If the conservative old-line labor organization will not accept the proffer of cooperation, Negro Labor will find its own way to organization. This is demonstrated in the recent organization of the Pullman Porters through the able leadership of Mr. A. Philip Randolph, Editor of *The Messenger.* At the present writing, in spite of the opposition of the Pullman Company and the apathy of some of the porters themselves, over one-half of these workers are organized.

If Negroes perform, as it has been asserted, one-seventh of the labor in the United States, the labor organizations of America can never be effective until the great mass of Negro workers are organized. The complaint cannot be made continuously that the Negro does not take to the unions and that he is not a "union-man." No workman who finds it to his interest to remain a non-union man will ever give up the privilege. Membership in a union should offer some advantage to the Negro. To every white workingman the union offers superior advantages. When union men strike, non-union men have large opportunity. These instances have been the occasions on which Negro labor has entered avenues which were hitherto closed to it.[39] In the Steel Strike of 1919–1920, Negroes were employed as strike-breakers, and in the coal strike of 1922 Negroes were introduced into the Pennsylvania coal fields. The result in each case was the realization among union workers that Negroes should be unionized. The United Mine Workers made strenuous efforts to bring Negroes into the local unions in the latter instance. Therefore, in the interest of itself, Organized Labor must organize the Negro workingmen. For this work Negro organizers should be appointed. In the present state of our race relations, it is exceedingly difficult for the average white organizer to sympathize fully with the special problems of Negro Labor and to encourage effectively its organization. The migration, with the resulting transfer of Negroes from agriculture to industry, has increased the necessity for *action* and not finely phrased declarations by Organized Labor.

[39] William Z. Foster, *The Great Steel Strike; an account of the Steel Strike of 1919–1920.*

Negro City Life*

OCCASION AND PURPOSE OF THE CONFERENCE, AND AN OUTLINE OF THE PLAN OF WORK:
Mr. George G. Bradford of Boston

The rapid growth of our great cities, within recent years, is one of the phases of modern life which brings with it problems whose solution calls for the best efforts of the leading men in the city communities, whether white or black. Special courses for the study of these problems have been established in the Northern colleges, and it is felt that the time has come when Atlanta University must take up the study of those problems of city life which its graduates are called upon to meet and solve. It is none too soon to begin this work, for each year a larger proportion of the colored race are concentrating in the cities.

In 1860, only 4.2 per cent of the colored population of the United States were living in the cities. By 1880, the number had increased to 8.4 per cent of the whole colored population, while by 1890, it had increased to 12 per cent. This process of concentration in the cities has been relatively much more rapid among the colored people than among the whites, the figures for whites during the same period being 10.9 per cent in 1860, and 15.7 per cent in 1890, or an increase of 4.8 per cent, as against 7.8 per cent for colored. How rapid this increase in the city population really is, may be illustrated by the growth of the colored population in the city of Atlanta, where the increase has been at a rate three times as great as for the country at large. For decade 1870–1880, the increase was 64 per cent; for 1880–1890, 72 per cent; while the average increase of colored population for the whole country during the same period was only 20 per cent in each decade.

In taking up the study of city problems, we feel that we cannot do better than begin by an inquiry into the physical and moral condition of the people. It is a line of inquiry which has not been previously pursued on any systematic or extensive scale. Up to the present time, students and investigators of the problems confronting the colored race have confined themselves principally to the study of problems of country life or di-

* From "Mortality Among Negroes In Cities," *Proceedings of the Conference for Investigation of City Problems Held at Atlanta University, May 26–27, 1896* (Atlanta: Atlanta University Press, 1896), pp. 7–11, 30–34.

rected their attention towards economic or educational questions. Of the physical condition of the Negro under the trying conditions of city life, we have little accurate information. Many of the Southern cities have not had, until within a few years, any city boards of health, and, as a result, there has not been hitherto sufficient official data from which any broad generalizations could be drawn, and such data as have been obtainable have not yet been brought together into available form. We have, however, some few data that are sufficient to prove the necessity of the inquiry upon which we have begun.

From the United States census for 1890, we have the mortality for the white and colored population of five of our largest cities—Washington, Baltimore, New Orleans, Louisville and St. Louis—as given in a paper published by the trustees of the Slater Fund:

RATES PER 1,000

	White	Colored
Washington	19	36
Baltimore	22	36
New Orleans	22	37
Louisville	18	32
St. Louis	17	35

The excess of colored over white is 100, 63.6, 68, 77 and 106 per cent.

By special report from Washington, these figures would appear to be for that city 19 whites, 34.7 colored; excess of colored over white, 83 per cent. The death-rate among the whites in these five cities ranged from 17 to 22 per thousand, and among the colored from 32 to 37 per thousand, or from 63 per cent to 106 per cent greater among the colored than among the whites. In the city of St. Louis, the death-rate among the colored was more than twice that among the whites.

The significance of this excessive mortality can be appreciated only when we come to study the causes of destitution in our great cities. There are some very valuable figures on this point in a comprehensive treatise by Amos G. Warner, Ph.D., entitled "American Charities." (See table annexed.) In his analysis of causes of destitution among the colored people of Baltimore, we find 38 per cent of all cases of destitution are due to sickness. We have no official figures on this point for Washington or any other Southern city. But a similar report for New York shows 37 per cent from sickness, and for Boston 45.6 per cent. These are among cases of destitution of which there is official record. The result might be different, could we obtain the facts for all cases. Among the whites, also, sickness is one of the chief causes of destitution, but the percentage is much smaller, averaging about 20 per cent, while the average among the colored people is 39 per cent, or nearly twice as great. We see, therefore, that one of the first things we must do in improving the condition of the masses of the poorer colored people crowded together in the great cities is to try to lighten the heavy burden of sickness now weighing them down. This will involve an inquiry not only into physical or economic conditions, but into moral conditions as well. We feel, therefore, that in beginning our study of city problems by an inquiry into the causes of the excessive mortality among the colored people, we are striking right at the root of many of the evils that we have been trying to reach.

Important as is the industrial education of a state, it is evident that no rapid economic advance can be made by a race physically or morally weak. It is evident that both physical and moral as well as the economic conditions should be carefully studied, and we shall see later that they should be studied together, as each one acts upon the other. The task, then, which we have undertaken is the inquiry into the exact conditions, physical, moral and economic, affecting life in city communities. Later, when we have gathered sufficient information, we may be able to point out how those conditions may be improved. But at present our chief aim must be to make a thorough and searching investigation.

The method which has been adopted for making this investigation is as follows: In order to gather the necessary data, uniform sets of blanks have been prepared and put in the hands of graduates of this University, and of educated colored men and women located in different cities. These sets consist of three different blanks, known as blanks Nos. 1, 2 and 3. Blank Nos. 1 and 2 are to serve the purpose of a permanent record by which to measure the progress of each city community from year to year. As in many cities the official records from which the data for these blanks must be gathered, have been in time past very incomplete, we shall be unable to review the past progress of those cities as we should like to, but these records are being made more complete each year, so that in the future we shall be able to measure progress made with some degree of accuracy. Blank No. 3, called the Family Budget blank, provides for a more intimate inquiry into the conditions of life existing in a particular community, and is intended to bring out the causes of results shown in blanks Nos. 1 and 2. The points of inquiry covered by this blank, No. 3 are:

First—General conditions of the home life, the size of the homes, their sanitary conditions, and the amount of sickness in the family.

Second—Economic conditions, occupations of family, the amount of income, etc.

Third—The expenditure of family for food, rent, intoxicants, etc., showing habits of life in the community.

The results of an investigation carried on along the above lines will be brought out in later papers.

In regard to the conferences: It is proposed each year to take up the discussion of certain phases of city life most deserving attention. Just what will be the subjects for these discussions will be determined by the results of investigations already begun, and announcements will be made later. The general plan of conference will be not unlike that of the National Conference of Charities and Corrections, and some of the subjects taken up will be similar to those discussed there, such as home life, child saving, district nursing, scientific study of social problems, municipal and county charities; or economic questions, such as diversity of employment, co-operation, loan associations, savings institutions, mutual insurance, etc. It will probably be found advisable to have at the conference next year section meetings where special topics can be discussed more freely and fully than in the general conference. This is, in general, an outline of the plan upon which the investigation and the conference will be conducted. As the work develops, and we gain more experience, the plan will be modified to meet the needs of the time.

The work of investigation will no doubt prove difficult, and will require not only patient and accurate work, but the willing co-operation of a large number of individuals. But we believe that there is no body of men and women so well able to do this important work for their communities as the graduates of Atlanta University and similar institutions. They are scattered through all the principal cities of Georgia and the neighboring States; they are all in positions where they have special facilities for the gathering of valuable data, and their zeal and industry will more than compensate for any lack of scientific statistical training. No one of these graduates can prosecute this work alone. His investigation would necessarily be too limited to produce any accurate results. It is only by comparing and compiling data from many different sources thaton - curacy can be insured. Co-operation, therefore, is essential. Though the results accomplished by each individual may seem to him incomplete and insignificant, the combined results of all will prove of the utmost value.

A word of caution: Some of the information brought out by this investigation may prove very unpleasant for us to contemplate. It may seem as if much of our work for the last twenty-five years had been of no avail. We may be tempted to shut our eyes to the real facts, or to doubt their existence. But if we are to make any progress, we must have the courage to look unpleasant facts in the face. We are not attempting to prove or disprove any theory, but we are trying to get at the most unfavorable conditions affecting our communities, in order that we may improve those conditions. . . .

POVERTY AS A CAUSE OF MORALITY:
Mrs. Rosa Morehead Bass ('80)

Slavery left the colored man the rich inheritance of a log cabin and patch of turnip greens. This log cabin is a piece of architecture that will soon be entirely relegated to the barbarous past. Peace be to its ashes! It has disappeared in the towns and cities, and is found only in the poverty-stricken rural districts. Cannot you recall the picture of that poor family who worked hard all day in the field while their little ones, almost nude, played around the door until the sun dropped behind that hill studded with beautiful trees? See the mother return and prepare her evening meal; the fire is lighted, the children, hungry and crying; behold the repast—fried bacon, poorly-cooked bread, and black molasses. A pine torch illumines the room that serves as a kitchen, dining-room, bed and bath-room. After supper the little ones are off to bed without being properly bathed and dressed, and after the usual chair-nap, the father and mother retire. There they are all in a row, and only one small window and door to let in nature's life-giving air that keeps them from suffocating. The out-door work, good water and a plenty of latitude curtail the rural death-rate, but the pine torch has ruined so many eyes. Now let us pass hastily the sparkling spring of cool water, the rosy-cheeked peach and apple, the browsing cow in meadows green and fair, the brawny-armed farmer, humming his mournful song, and visit an alley in our city whose church spires point heavenward, and whose inhabitants boast of being the most cultured people of the South. I say pause a moment and look down that alley, and near that branch of stagnant water, and see that long row of tenement houses, poorly built—out of old lumber, that has never been disinfected—and not even plastered. The inmates are poorly clad, poorly fed, and, strange to say, the poorer they are, the more filthy we find them. Disease and death are rivals. Whenever an epidemic of smallpox and fever visit us, they find these unfortunates their favored victims. Their poverty maddens their brain, and they strew disease and death in their pathway.

Summer is their favorite season, and the death-rate is somewhat diminished, but when the autumn days come, "the saddest of the year," the wailing winds their open houses invade and the majestic king of winter carpets the earth, and the poor shiver from want of clothes, food and fire, and the grim monster claims them as his favorite subjects. Their poverty rendered them unable to prepare like the wise ant, and when they become ill they have neither friends nor money, and actually die from the want of attention, medical, physical and spiritual.

We find great mortality among the children of the poor. Even before they can make their wants known, the mother is compelled to leave them daily, and a surprising number are burned to death. The older children are taught to go out and pick up trash to burn, rags, bones and iron to sell, thereby inviting disease and death. It is a strange fact, yet true, that all work that is obnoxious, dangerous and laborious is given the poor Negro at pay that would kill some people even to think of having it to do for a living. These people in buying food, etc., always seek *quantity* and not *quality;* hence the butcher, fisherman, fruiterer, dairyman and merchant are careful to anticipate their wants. (The health officer is occasionally heard of when the rich are imposed upon.) The manner in which they live breeds discontent, hatred and envy, and consequently they fight, kill each other, and rob and murder the more fortunate. Their misery is one of the devil's workshops, and they are his tools.

The coffers of the landlord are being filled with the blood of his neighbor, and not until the crowded alleys are consigned to the log-cabin era will health and life take an onward march, and as the X rays of the Atlanta University are turned on, will cleanliness, thrift, industry, happiness and hygienic living add their quota to the life-rate; and last, but not least, not until the whole Christian world plays her part in the Samaritan drama, will the life-rate in Heaven be increased, and the death-rate on earth diminished!

IGNORANCE AS A CAUSE OF MORALITY:
Prof. W. B. Matthews ('90)

Among the many causes which produce death in our large cities, it is by no means an easy matter to distinguish between ignorance, poverty and negligence. However, it is safe to assert that no few of the deaths which occur in our large cities are the result of ignorance, either directly or indirectly.

It will be seen from the outset that city life requires a more accurate observance of the laws of health than country or village life. With this fact in mind, all cities have established their boards of health to look after and remove any and all causes which in their minds might produce sickness or death. These boards are usually composed of the best informed physicians who, from time to time, make and publish rules which are to be observed and obeyed by all the citizens. These rules the ignorant classes do not obey, not because they are willfully disobedient, but because they are ignorant. They cannot read, they have no interest in public affairs; they know but little about the causes which bring sickness and disease among them, and hence are the easy prey of epidemics and contagions.

As to the laws of hygiene, they are generally ignored because they are unknown, but this does not excuse. The laws of nature and of health are as unvarying in the case of the ignorant as in the case of the intelligent. The violation of certain rules governing the health of our bodies brings the same results to all men alike. Our aim will be to show that the ignorant violate the rules of health, and are therefore more frequently the victims of disease and death.

Many suffer on account of improper ventilation, not knowing that impure air is the parent of every lung trouble known to the human family. Pure air is one of the freest and best gifts bestowed upon man by our beneficent Father; but alas! how many thousands in our large cities die every year from failing to use this gift! Men and women, through ignorance, shut the doors and windows to their houses, thus barring out God's life-giving atmosphere, and inviting consumption and death. Pure air gives life, foul air brings death.

Thousands of men, women and children are sick and dying in the slums of our large cities from liver and kidney troubles. These troubles have come to them because the proper care has not been taken of the skin. Would it be true to say that through ignorance of the true functions of the pores in our bodies, and their relation to good health, certain classes of people fail to keep their bodies clean and the pores of the skin open? Whoever closes these millions of doors, the inlets of life and outlets of death, will sooner or later succumb to the pangs of disease, for by so doing they shut out life and let in death.

But what of appetite, and what people are less liable to control their appetites? Are not the most ignorant? The glutton, through ignorance of the evil result of his intemperate habit, overloads his stomach and impairs its capacity to properly discharge its functions, thereby inducing many diseases which shorten life.

With the light that we have on the evil effects of alcohol upon the system, it would scarcely be permissible to say that men who take it are ignorant of its destructive elements. Yet I venture the assertion that there are many among the ignorant classes of our large cities who are entirely unconscious of the fact that the indulgence of the appetite for strong drink shortens life and cuts off the days of their posterity.

Thus we see, looking at the matter briefly from a hygienic point of view, that the body may be kept in a healthy state by obedience to the laws of health, but when they are neglected, the inevitable result is disease and death. Can men ignorant of such laws live in accordance therewith, or avoid the consequences of their disobedience?

Turning from the persons to the locality in which they live, we may find many things which will have the same effect upon health as the failure to obey hygienic laws. It must be admitted that a filthy home, unclean bedding and wearing apparel, not changed at proper intervals, are as productive of disease and death as any other cause. As a general rule, ignorant people live together in very thickly populated communities. Such communities are usually freighted with impure air, and the germs of disease are in the very water which they drink. Not knowing how much damage filth and impure water can do to health and life, the ignorant flock to these communities, sicken and die, and never inquire into the cause. In such places, water containing foreign matter from soiled clothes, slops, etc., is thrown indiscriminately at the back door, front door or under the bed-room window, and nothing more is thought of it. People who know the results of such acts of indiscretion do not often commit them. Disobedience to the laws of hygiene brings a curse with every broken law. The body is weakened, the human system impaired, and finally death seizes its victims. No person can live in accordance with laws of which he is ignorant. Knowing that many all around us are ignorant of the proper care and use of their bodies, is it a matter at which we should wonder when we note the daily deaths that are caused from impure air, unclean bodies, unwholesome food, excessive appetites and ungoverned passions? These are the fruits of ignorance which are to be found in our large cities, and they bring death to no small number. A filthy house, an unclean yard, a soiled bed, all invite disease; they are harbingers of death. Those persons who keep such homes cannot themselves keep well; their children cannot be well born, and all who accept such surroundings do so because they are ignorant of the effect upon themselves and their posterity. To learn and obey the laws of health, to understand and observe the rules of sanitation, men must be intelligent.

Alienation: New York and the Negro[*]

Gilbert Osofsky

I

For the Negroes of New York City the years after 1900 marked not only a new century but a breaking point in a way of life. As the Negro population of New York and other northern cities increased, so did racial antagonism, violence and patterns of social and residential segregation. "One of the striking developments of very recent years," one white northerner noted in 1906, "is the recrudescence of . . . prejudice against people of African descent. . . ." [1]

At no period in the history of New York City were Negroes accepted as full American citizens. Restrictions on Negro voting, equal access to public facilities and education were maintained even after emancipation was proclaimed in the early nineteenth century. Jim Crow street stages, with "For Colored People Only" signs hung over their sides, ran along Manhattan streets until the eve of the Civil War. Colored people sat in special Negro pews (whites called them "Nigger Pews") or in the balconies of white churches: "Negroes were not permitted to sit in any public assembly, court or church, except in the particular quarter set apart for them, [and] generally in the most remote and worst situation." In 1837, *The Colored American* denounced the "Negro Pew" as a technique which whites used to degrade Negroes.[2] The only minority group to suffer

* From Gilbert Osofsky, "Alienation: New York and the Negro," in *Harlem: The Making of a Ghetto* (New York: Harper Torchbook, 1968), pp. 35–52. Copyright © 1963, 1965, 1966 by Gilbert Osofsky. Reprinted by permission of Harper & Row, Publishers, Inc.

[1] Linton Satterthwait, "The Color-Line in New Jersey," *The Arena*, XXV (April 1906), 394.

[2] Joan Cohen, "The Social Conditions of the Negro in New York City, 1830–1865" (M.A. thesis, Columbia University, 1951), p. 38; Philmore L. Groisser, "The Free Negro in New York State, 1850–1860" (M.A. thesis, Columbia University, 1939), pp. 31–39; Dwight Lowell Dumond, *Antislavery: The Crusade for Freedom in America* (Ann Arbor, 1961), p. 300; Wilbur Young, "Plymouth Congregational Church" (WPA research paper, Schomburg Collection); *The Colored American,* June 3, 1837; Robert Ernst, *Immigrant Life in New York City, 1825–1863* (New York, 1949), p. 41; Charles Townsend Harris, *Memories of Manhattan in the Sixties and Seventies* (New York, 1928), p. 61.

franchise restrictions in the state was the Negro. Negroes were forced to meet property qualifications for voting after these had been abolished for all other New Yorkers in 1821, and they were further subject to longer residential requirements for voting than whites.[3] Although racial prejudice was never absent from city life, it was not always uniformly intense. The attitudes of New Yorkers toward Negroes—sometimes eased, at other times hardened—wavered with national trends of racial adjustment.

In the late nineteenth century, and especially in the 1870's and 1880's, most northern communities made significant progress in attacking *institutionalized* racial prejudice. Laws were passed in most state legislatures, including New York's, which attempted to guarantee equal rights for Negroes. The motivating force for this liberal attitude toward the Negro was undoubtedly a spirit for racial reform which came in the aftermath of the Civil War and Reconstruction. Serious restrictions on Negro rights that had existed in some form since colonial times were done away with. In New York State, Negroes were given the right to vote without impediment by the Civil Rights Act of 1873, and this was followed by two other civil rights acts before the end of the century. New legislation permitted Negroes to travel on transportation facilities, attend theaters, eat at restaurants, and be buried in all cemeteries which served the public. Acts which had previously outlawed intermarriage were repealed, and insurance companies were specifically prohibited from charging Negroes rates higher than those paid by white clients.[4] The first Negro to serve as a juryman in Manhattan did so in the 1880's.[5] In 1884, the last three Negro public schools in the city were made ward schools, thus ending the tradition of separate education which had existed in New York City since the eighteenth century. In 1895 the first permanent appointment of a Negro teacher to a predominantly white public school was made. Susan Elizabeth Frazier, a graduate of Hunter College, won an extended legal battle with the school board. After Miss Frazier's breakthrough other Negroes received similar appointments. Statewide, the *coup de grâce* to separate Negro education came through a general education act passed in 1900.[6]

Negro and white people in New York were aware of the change in racial status typified by these acts. Cases of discrimination in public places continued to occur,[7] but it

---

[3] Herman D. Bloch, "The New York Negro's Battle for Political Rights, 1777–1865," *International Review of Social History,* IX (1964), 65–80.

[4] "Health and Physique of the Negro American," *Atlanta University Studies,* No. 11 (Atlanta, 1906), p. 91; *The New York Age,* June 8, 1889, April 26, 1890, April 11, 1891; *The New York Globe,* February 9, 1884.

[5] *The New York Freeman,* July 2, 1887.

[6] The subject of Negro education in the North and in New York City is studied in great detail in Robert S. Dixon, "Education of the Negro in the City of New York, 1853–1900" (M.A. thesis, City College, 1935), and Leslie H. Fishel, Jr., "The North and the Negro, 1865–1900: A Study in Race Discrimination" (Ph.D. dissertation, Harvard University, 1954), pp. 183–248, 326–369, *passim.* The Fishel study is the most thorough history of race relations in the North in the late nineteenth century, and discusses all the specific points mentioned in this paragraph. It does not, however, emphasize the changing patterns of racial attitudes as I have attempted to do. Also see *The New York Age,* February 9, 1924, and June 27, 1925, for information on Miss Frazier.

[7] *The New York Globe,* December 29, 1883; *The New York Freeman,* June 19, 1886, July 9, 1887; *The New York Age,* June 7, 1890.

was generally recognized that significant progress was made in the area of race relations
subject to law since the end of the Civil War. Jacob A. Riis commented on the "wa-
vering color line" in New York City in 1890,[8] and Samuel R. Scottron later wrote of the
"decline of color prejudice" in these years.[9] When southern Negro politicians passed
through New York City in the 1880's they lived in the most exclusive hotels. P. B. S.
Pinchback regularly stayed at the Hoffman House, John Mercer Langston at the Fifth
Avenue Hotel, John R. Lynch at the Metropolitan Hotel.[10] The Negro *New York Freeman,* in an 1887 editorial, said that "Now in many of the best restaurants, hotels and
churches decent colored people receive courteous treatment." [11] "Respectable colored
men have little trouble in finding accommodations in the very best hotels," a Negro
New Yorker indicated in the 1880's.[12] It was the easing of racial tensions in the North
in these years that rekindled the traditional drive of the Negro middle class for total acceptance as Americans, not Negroes, within our society: "From the earliest times the attitude of the free negroes has been opposed to any organization or the segregation of the
negroes as such," W. E. B. DuBois wrote in 1901. "Men like Fortune, McCune Smith,
and Redmond [*sic*] insisted that they were American citizens, not negroes. . . ." [13]

II

In spite of the attack on institutionalized discrimination, however, there was very little
(if any) change in the stereotyped conception of the Negro that most white Americans
held. With rare exception, even in the North during the late nineteenth century, there
was general agreement on what contemporaries called the "peculiar genius" of the
Negro people.[14] The stereotyped image of the "sensuous," "lazy," "good-natured,"
"childlike," "faithful" Negro was presented by defenders as well as critics of the race—
both Negro and white. The literature of the time abounds with relevant examples of
this image. A New York rabbi, for example, in a sermon at Temple Emanu-El in 1906,
attacked the vicious racism embodied in the Reverend Thomas Dixon, Jr.'s, novel, *The
Clansman.* (Dixon's trilogy on race relations, of which *The Clansman* was a part, was the
basis for the successful movie *The Birth of a Nation,* a film which Negroes have protested against for five decades.)[15] The rabbi defended "the faithful, loyal Negro—his

[8] Jacob A. Riis, *How the Other Half Lives: Studies Among the Poor* (London, 1891), p. 148.

[9] *The New York Age,* January 4, 1900.

[10] *The New York Globe,* June 30, August 25, September 1, 1883; *The New York Freeman,* July 25, 1885,
July 16, September 3, 1887.

[11] *The New York Globe,* July 28, 1883.

[12] *The New York Freeman,* July 16, 1887.

[13] W. E. B. DuBois, "The Black North," *The New York Times,* December 15, 1901. For an analysis of
this attitude as a major theme in the Negro novel, 1890–1920, see Robert A. Bone, *The Negro Novel in America*
(New Haven, 1958).

[14] Benjamin Brawley, "The Negro Genius," *The Southern Workman,* XLIV (May 1915), 305–308.

[15] The success of *The Clansman* and other of Dixon's works in the first two decades of the twentieth century must be set against the rise of racial antagonism in the North in these years. See *The Crisis,* LXII (Janu-

humor, his pathos, his geniality, his shrewdness, his love of his master . . . his sympathy and charity, his even childlike patriotism, and love of freedom." [16] An Episcopal clergyman advocated the extension of church services to Negroes in the city in 1884: "The negro is exacting," he said, "therefore, let the Church . . . arouse him. If he is emotional, let the Church meet these emotions with a lively service, and thus subdue them. The negro is imitative," he concluded.[17] Train and hire Negro workers and they will always be loyal and never strike, a southern Negro educator told a group of northern businessmen in 1902: "Look at the great strikes you are having, and every time you have to make concessions," he said. "But if you educate this million and a half colored boys and girls and make skilled laborers of them they will take the place of these strikers." [18] "The negroes are . . . good-natured and happy under all circumstances," concluded a late-nineteenth-century writer.[19]

Negroes of prominence of New York City were often considered dark counterparts of white leaders. The Negro abolitionist Samuel Ringgold Ward was popularly known as a "Black Daniel Webster" prior to the Civil War.[20] After the war, a well-known Negro singer was called "Black Patti," and another "Colored Jenny Lind." [21] Three local colored politicians were respectively: "Black Depew," "Colored Croker," Negro "Mark Hanna." [22]

Popular images of the Negro were portrayed to New Yorkers in the numerous vaudeville and minstrel shows which regularly appeared in the city. New York City was the theater capital of America at the turn of the century and Negro vaudeville reached the height of its popularity then.[23] Many of the performances, including the Creole shows which specialized in presenting scantily clad and beautiful Negro women, were hits.[24] The hackneyed themes running almost without exception through all these plays were, in exaggerated form, a reflection of the generally accepted attitudes of white America toward Negro life. For the most part, they presented a comic and derisive caricature of an entire people: "The 'darky' to the white man is grotesquely amusing," Mary White Ovington wrote.[25]

The Negro of these plays was a ludicrous figure of a man—he was "darky," he

ary 1955), 37–38; Maxwell Bloomfield, "Dixon's *The Leopard's Spots:* A Study in Popular Racism," *American Quarterly,* XVI (Fall 1964), 387–401.

[16] *The New York Age,* January 4, 1906.
[17] *The Churchman,* L (September 20, 1884), 316.
[18] *The Worker,* May 18, 1902.
[19] Moses F. Sweester and Simeon Ford, *How to Know New York City* (New York, 1888), p. 11.
[20] Dumond, *Antislavery,* p. 330.
[21] *Harlem Local Reporter,* February 25, May 6, 1893; "Black Patti," in James Weldon Johnson Collection, Yale University.
[22] *The New York Times,* October 4, 1900.
[23] Diana N. Lockard, "The Negro on the Stage of the Nineteen Twenties" (M.A. thesis, Columbia University, 1960), chap. 1.
[24] "Emma Harris" (WPA research paper, Schomburg Collection).
[25] Mary White Ovington, *Half A Man: The Status of the Negro in New York* (New York, 1911), p. 135.

was "coon." Williams and Walker, for example, were billed as the "Two Real Coons." [26] Such plays as the *Gentlemen Coons' Parade* (Chorus: "You'll find no common second-class nigs/In the gentlemen coons' parade"), *The Coon at the Door, The Coon Musketeers, Dat Famous Chicken Debate* ("Resolved, That Stealing Chickens Ain't No Crime"), *Dat Watermillyon, The Coonville 'Ristocrat Club, The Coon and the Chink, Jes' Like White Folks, The Irishman and the Coon, The Policy Players, The Sons of Ham, In Bandanna Land, In Dahomey, In Abyssinia* and dozens of others were performed on the stage in New York City and cities throughout the country.[27] Songs such as "All Coons Look Alike to Me," "Coon, Coon, Coon," "I Wish My Color Would Fade," had "wide currency" in New York City in the 1890's. "It was no longer the 'darkey melody' [that was popular in the 1890's] but the 'coon song.' " New York historian Henry Collins Brown noted. These songs presented a "ribald school of 'babies,' 'honies,' mercenary wenches . . . and sundry 'no account niggers.' " [28] Characters like "Useless Peabody," "George Washington Jones," "Moses Abraham Highbrow," "John Jacob Astor House" (crushed silk hat, big bow tie, long white gloves, worn-out shoes), were always about to steal a chicken or a watermelon, or pretending to be something they were not. "Sam Lightfoot," the waiter in *Badly Sold,* changed his attitudes to suit the customer, or lied to get a bigger tip.[29] "Careless Cupid" applied for a job in a bakery and listed the following qualifications to his prospective employer: "I kin eat an' I kin sleep, and de res' ob de time jes' lay round. Say, boss, whar's yo lounge? I's gettin' tired standin' yere. . . . I'm a straight out nigger, I am, yessir." [30] Sam Caesar, Pompey Ducklegs, Julius Crow, Doolittle Black, were waiters, porters, servants, butlers, confidence men, who shuffled along in baggy pants, liberally used ungrammatical language, loved whiskey, shot dice, seemed eternally shiftless or carefree. The covers of *Denison's Black-Face Series* showed a broadly smiling, white-toothed Negro woman whose hair was always tied with white bows and curlers, or a white-haired old Negro man strumming on a banjo. James Weldon Johnson, who was personally involved in the production of some of these shows in New York City, summed up the themes that ran throughout them: "The Negro songs then the rage were known as 'coon songs,' " he wrote, "and were concerned with jamborees of various sorts and the play of razors, with the gastronomical delights of chicken, pork chops and watermelon, and with the experiences of red-hot 'mammas' and their never too faithful 'papas.' These songs were for the most part crude, raucous, bawdy, often obscene." [31]

[26] William L. Holler, "Bert Williams (Egbert Austin Williams), 1875–1922" (WPA research paper, Schomburg Collection), p. 3.

[27] These plays and many others are collected in a special box of Negro vaudeville and minstrel shows at the Schomburg Collection, and in the extensive and magnificent Atkinson Collection at the University of Chicago.

[28] Henry Collins Brown, *In the Golden Nineties* (New York, 1928), pp. 173–174; Howard W. Odum and Guy B. Johnson, *Negro Workaday Songs* (Chapel Hill, N.C., 1926), pp. 183–184.

[29] George H. Coes, *Badly Sold: A Negro Act in Two Scenes* (Chicago, 1893).

[30] F. E. Hiland, *Careless Cupid* (Boston, 1893), p. 5.

[31] James Weldon Johnson, *Along This Way* (New York, 1933), pp. 152–153.

Many Negroes seriously objected to these ludicrous characterizations of Negro life. "It is humiliating to be regarded as a curiosity," wrote one man in 1895. *The New York Age* angrily denounced "plays which burlesque the character of a people and tend to degrade them in the estimation of their fellow citizens." It proposed that they "be prohibited." [32] Negro performers attempted to gain recognition for themselves as true artists, not hacks, but they were unable to convince theater managers that anything but the standard fare was profitable: "Every show had to be studied carefully for anything that might offend white prejudices. . . ." [33] In speaking of his friend Bert Williams, the most famous Negro comic of the early twentieth century (whites called him "the darky comedian"), James Weldon Johnson later wrote that he expressed "only certain conceptions about Negro life that his audience was willing to accept and ready to enjoy." [34] "My job," said Bert Williams simply, "is to make them laugh." [35]

Why should the world be otherwise,
In counting all our tears and sighs?
Nay, let them only see us, while
We wear the mask.[36]

What was most striking about the Negro stereotype was the way it portrayed a people in an image so totally the reverse of what Americans considered worthy of emulation and recognition. The major and traditional American values were all absent from the Negro stereotype. The Negro was conceived of as lazy in an ambitious culture; improvident and sensuous in a moralistic society; happy in a sober world; poor in a nation that offered riches to all who cared to take them; childlike in a country of men. He seemed more fit to be a servant, a "half man," than anything else: "And the Nation echoed . . . : Be content to be servants, and nothing more; what need of higher culture for half-men." [37] "Let the Negro learn," said a *New York Times* editorial in 1900, "to clean stables, care for horses, feed and harness and drive them, run lawn mowers, make and keep gardens, and also keep engagements. . . ." [38] Negroes hoped for full acceptance in a culture which mocked their aspirations.[39]

[32] *The New York Age,* January 31, 1907; "Wealthy Negroes," *The New York Times,* July 14, 1895.

[33] Johnson, *Along This Way, passim;* Holler, "Bert Williams," p. 8.

[34] Johnson, *Along This Way,* p. 159. The game "Hit the Nigger" or "African Dodger"—in which vacationers threw baseballs at the head of a *real* person—was played in New York summer resorts until outlawed in 1917. *The Crisis,* X (July 1915), 114; *The New York Times,* October 2, 1916, May 3, 1917.

[35] Lawrence Gelbert, "Bert Williams: Philosophical Tidbits Gleaned from His Songs and Stories" (WPA research paper, Schomburg Collection).

[36] "We Wear the Mask," in *The Complete Poems of Paul Laurence Dunbar* (New York, 1921), p. 71.

[37] W. E. B. DuBois, *The Souls of Black Folk: Essays and Sketches* (New York, 1953), p. 10.

[38] "Raw Labor from the South," *The New York Times,* September 9, 1900.

[39] There was a constant mockery of the so-called Negro aristocracy and "400." See, for example, John Martin, "Dancing Through Two Centuries," Museum of the City of New York *Bulletin,* V (February 1942), 37.

III

With the increased migration of Negroes from the South, the brighter side of race relations in the city—the softening of institutionalized prejudices—came to an end. Among white people, Kelly Miller remarked in 1906, there was a "prevailing dread of an overwhelming influx from the South." [40] Even during the late nineteenth century Negroes argued that most white northerners knew little, and cared even less, about Negro life: "The Northern white man knows practically nothing of the Negro; he is looked upon more as a problem than as a factor in the general weal, with the same desires, passions, hopes, ambitions as other human creatures," a journalist concluded.[41] "Do we ever think of how such people live?" a reviewer of Dunbar's *The Sport of the Gods* wrote. "It is a . . . whole stratum of society of which all of us are densely ignorant and of whose very existence most of us are wholly unaware." [42] As the population increased, however, the city became more aware of its Negro residents, and responded by reversing the trend in formal race relations that had typified the 1870's and 1880's. The early twentieth century in New York City and in the North generally was a period of intensified racial alienation.

Racial antagonism was rekindled in a variety of ways. White churches, for example, which had formerly allowed small numbers of Negroes to participate in regular services, now attempted to ease their Negro members out: "In each of these churches when the number of Negro communicants was small the colored brother was accorded a hearty welcome, but as the Negro population steadily increased . . . from the white members would be heard generous suggestions that the Negro members get a place of worship of their own." [43] An Episcopal church in the area of San Juan Hill resolved its problem by holding separate services for Negroes.[44] Once the Negro population of Harlem expanded, the pastor of one white church told Negro members they were "Not Welcome," and then gave them an ultimatum to join one of the Negro institutions moving into the neighborhood: "When there were few black and colored communicants in the Harlem district the white . . . churches received them," a Negro New Yorker observed in 1913. "Of late years conditions have greatly changed. . . ." [45] "Trinity Vestry, in New York City, is making arrangements to provide a separate place of worship for the colored members," the NAACP journal *Crisis* recorded in 1914. "At present all worship at the same place." [46]

The separation that was evident in the churches was true of many other areas of racial contact in the city. When the "Colored Men's YMCA" was opened on West

[40] Kelly Miller, "The Industrial Condition of the Negro in the North," *The Annals,* XXVII (May 1906), 543.

[41] *The New York Freeman,* July 11, 1887.

[42] A clipping of this review which appeared in *The Bookman,* XXIII (April 1906), was pasted on the back of an obituary of Dunbar in the Gumby Collection, Columbia University.

[43] *The New York Age,* April 1, 1909.

[44] Clyde Griffen, "An Urban Church in Ferment: The Episcopal Church in New York City, 1880–1900" (Ph.D. dissertation, Columbia University, 1960), p. 32.

[45] *The New York Age,* April 17, 1913.

[46] *The Crisis,* VIII (May 1914), 12.

Fifty-third Street, it was taken for granted that Negroes would use these facilities exclusively rather than those Y's which catered to white people.[47] White fraternal organizations brought suit against Negro societies which used the same names.[48] The New York State Boxing Commission outlawed bouts between Negro and white fighters, and American society longed for a "White Hope" to defeat Negro heavyweight champion Jack Johnson.[49] There were innumerable legal suits brought by Negroes against white hotels, restaurants and theaters for refusing them service in the early twentieth century: "Northern Negroes believe this discrimination in public places against the black man [is] increasing in New York," Mary White Ovington noted.[50] Union restrictions and racial barriers in industry were so widespread that Negroes were largely excluded from "employment along lines other than those of beggarly paid menials." [51] As a result of these exclusions, the urban Negro continually represented a large group of unemployed workers readily available for strikebreaking: "In this matter of excluding colored men from unions, skilled mechanics must remember that they run the risk of building up in the United States a great body of justly indignant and always available STRIKE BREAKERS," a white journalist wrote in 1910. In 1895, 1904, 1907, 1910, 1911, 1912, 1916 and 1920 Negro strikebreakers were used to help break strikes of New York City longshoremen, laborers, street cleaners, baggage handlers, hod carriers, waiters, and garment workers.[52] There was even an unsuccessful attempt in 1910 to re-establish the state law barring intermarriage. The proposed "Act to Amend the Domestic Relations Law, in Relation to Miscegenation," proposed to void all marriages *"contracted between a person of white or Caucasian race and a person of the negro or black race."* [53] Negroes organized to oppose these new "Black Codes." [54] Assemblymen were urged to defeat the miscegenation

[47] *Ibid.,* IX (December 1914), 77–80.

[48] *The New York Age,* April 9, June 21, 1906.

[49] *Ibid.,* February 13, 1913. The depth of national racial hatred in the early twentieth century is clearly demonstrated in the longing and search for a "White Hope" to defeat Jack Johnson. Some of the anti-Negro legislation of these years, including those laws banning intermarriage, were partially stimulated by Johnson's second marriage to a white woman. See clippings under title "White Hope" in Gumby Collection, Columbia University. Florence Murray, editor, *The Negro Handbook, 1949* (New York, 1949), p. 350. The following, an article by Bill Corum in the *New York Journal American* at the time of Johnson's death in 1946, clearly demonstrates this racial antipathy: "Man alive, how I hated Jack Johnson in the Summer of 1910! Nor did I ever quite get over it. In recent years it became an aversion rather than a stronger feeling. But when he knocked out Jeffries at Reno I hated him. . . . I was 15 in a town of 4,000 people and until the Jeffries-Johnson fight . . . never heard of professional boxing." Clipping in Gumby Collection.

[50] Ovington, *Half A Man,* p. 210. *The New York Age* and *The Crisis* carried dozens of articles and comments on this subject.

[51] *The Crisis,* III (February 1912), 141.

[52] *The New York Evening Journal,* December 12, 1910. Also see *The New York Times,* December 1, 1901; Mary White Ovington, "The Negro in the Trades Unions in New York," *The Annals,* XXVII (May 1906), 551–558; R. R. Wright, Jr., "The Negro in Times of Industrial Unrest," *Charities,* XV (October 7, 1905), 69–73; Mrs. Paul Laurence Dunbar, "Hope Deferred," *The Crisis,* VIII (September 1914), 238–242; Alma Herbst, *The Negro in the Slaughtering and Meat-Packing Industry in Chicago* (Boston and New York, 1932), pp. xviii–xix, 14–32, *passim; The New York Age,* June 13, 1907, August 19, 1909, January 20, 1910, November 30, 1911, June 6, 1912, January 16, 1913.

[53] Italicized in the original. Copy of act in Bruce Manuscripts, Schomburg Collection.

[54] *The New York Age,* February 6, 1913.

bill. It was, a Negro New Yorker thought, but one part of a general "sentiment . . . that would 'Jim Crow' us at every turn, and that sentiment is growing in this State." [55] Negro Harlem was created in these years. It was a world that reflected the subtle and radical changes then taking place in many areas of life in major cities of the North.

Was there any solution to the problems created by the migration and the intensified racial hatreds? With almost no exception the only opinion that was publicly stated was that it was necessary to convince Negroes their proper place was in the South. Booker T. Washington made a tour of the tenement districts of New York City in 1904. One journalist said that his trip would be of great value because Washington could then return south and describe the poverty he saw. He would tell the "country negroes [to remain] on the farms in the South rather than [come] to an overcrowded city" where they certainly would die.[56] "Northern men visiting southern colored industrial schools advise[d] the pupils to remain where they [were]," a white reformer noted in 1910.[57]

IV

The migration of southern Negroes also created antagonisms which were intraracial in nature. Negroes who had lived in the city for generations, especially those who gloried in the easing of racial tensions during the late nineteenth century, blamed the southern migrant for reversing this trend. Similar antagonisms were evident among most immigrant groups—Jews, Italians, Greeks, and others—when earlier generations seemed overwhelmed by the problems of later arrivals from their countries. Negroes of "the old Knickerbocker stamp," "the old time aristocracy bearing Knickerbocker names" ("the best people," "aristocratic dark race circles"), some of whom were members of the Negro Society of the Sons of New York, railed against the lower-class southern Negro with the virulence of good white racists: "The taint of slavery was far removed from these people," Mary White Ovington remarked, and they "looked with scorn upon arrivals from the South." [58] "These people are thoroughly embarrassed by the raucousness, vulgarity, and violence with which they find themselves surrounded," a Negro clergyman concluded. "They do everything possible to disassociate themselves from it." Middle-class Negroes in Chicago, Philadelphia and Boston reacted in a similar manner.[59]

---

[55] Henry A. Spencer to John E. Bruce, March 22, 1910; Bruce to the Hon. Jesse S. Phillips, March 23, 1910. Bruce Manuscripts, Schomburg Collection.

[56] Clippings from the *New York American,* September 30, 1904, in Stokes Manuscripts, Columbia University, Box 75.

[57] Ovington, *Half A Man,* p. 76.

[58] *Ibid.,* p. 34; *The New York Freeman,* July 18, 1885, January 16, 1886; *The New York Age,* January 31, 1907; "Certificate of Incorporation of the Society of the Sons of New York," November 28, 1891, in New York City Hall of Records.

[59] See John H. Johnson, *A Place of Adventure: Essays and Sermons* (Greenwich, Conn., 1955), p. 10; "Boston, and Some Boston People," Bruce Manuscripts; W. E. B. DuBois, *The Philadelphia Negro: A Social Study* (Philadelphia, 1899), pp. 73n, 80; Roi Ottley, *The Lonely Warrior: The Life and Times of Robert S. Abbott* (Chicago, 1955), pp. 84–85; St. Clair Drake and Horace R. Cayton, *Black Metropolis: A Study of Negro Life in a Northern City* (New York, 1945), pp. 73–74, *passim.*

To many New York Negroes the migrants were "riff-raff," "illiterate," "thought-less," "lazy," "overdemonstrative," "boastful," "uncouth," "undesirable," "common." It was the southerner, they said, who created the "epidemic of negrophobia," the recent "spread of race antipathy in the North." [60] They listened too readily to "Tramp Preach-ers," and were too dirty—they were "the low element to our race . . . the class who own a lot of dirty rags and dogs and crowds of children," a correspondent of Booker T. Washington said.[61] The "Old Settlers" struck out against "the lower masses of their people" with an automatic, instinctive drive for "self-defense and self-preservation," Du-Bois wrote.[62] "We have too much unwarranted criticism to fight to be handicapped in this way," a Negro New Yorker complained in 1905.[63]

> God knows
> We have our troubles, too—
> One trouble is you:
> you talk too loud,
> look too black,
> don't get anywhere,
> and sometimes it seems
> you don't even care.[64]

The only solution that these people had to offer was basically the one that white New Yorkers proposed—keep the migrants in the South. In the 1880's, prior to any sig-nificant migration, *The New York Age* encouraged Negroes to flee the social and eco-nomic proscriptions of the South: "Why should they not seek in other sections to better their social, material and civil condition," it said. When migrants came in larger num-bers, however, the *Age* changed its tune: "It will well repay them to consider whether it will not be better to bear some of the ills they now do, than fly to others they know not of." "We believe the South is the best place for the great masses of the Afro-American people." [65] This same theme was emphasized and re-emphasized in a whole spate of arti-cles, editorials and speeches printed in Negro journals in the years preceding the First World War. The interracial Committee for the Industrial Improvement of the Condi-tion of the Negro in New York, established in 1906, sent circular letters to southern newspapers, churches and schools discouraging any thoughts of migration to New York City.[66] Kelly Miller and Booker T. Washington wrote numerous articles on "The Farm" as the "Negro's Best Chance," and on the evils and destructiveness of life in

[60] Charles Winslow Hall, "Racial Hatred," *The Colored American Magazine,* I (September 1900), 246; *The New York Age,* December 17, 1908, and *passim.*

[61] *The New York Age,* June 22, 1905; Letter to the editor from Melvin J. Chisum, *The New York Times,* June 10, 1900.

[62] DuBois, "The Black North," *The New York Times,* December 1, 1901.

[63] *The New York Age,* April 6, 1905.

[64] Langston Hughes, "High to Low," *The Midwest Journal,* I (Summer 1949), 26.

[65] *The New York Freeman,* January 16, 1886; *The New York Age,* January 5, 1889, January 25, 1890, July 6, 1905, July 27, 1908.

[66] *The New York Age,* May 14, 1908, July 7, 1910.

northern cities. Only "country life" and "working on the soil" would "uplift" the
Negro, it was argued. "There should be organized . . . a bureau of information which
should furnish the masses of the race . . . accurate knowledge of the evil of indiscriminate influx to the North," Miller thought.[67] But "even while they exclaimed," Paul Laurence Dunbar said, "they knew there was no way, and that the stream of young negro
life would continue to flow up from the South. . . ." ("I was born and raised in the
country/But Mamma I'm stayin' in town.")[68]

V

This negative view of the migration expressed by Negroes and whites was felt most intensely in the working-class districts of the city into which migrants moved. Interracial
conflicts became so common at the turn of the century, it will be remembered, that San
Juan Hill was named as a parody on them. Small but regular clashes ordinarily involving Negroes and the Irish were recorded in the New York press then. The antagonism
between these two peoples was undoubtedly one of the harshest intergroup hatreds in
American history. The deep strain of nativism that traditionally runs through American
Negro thought was especially evident during this period of overwhelming foreign immigration. The Negro, born in the United States, commonly expressed his antagonism
for foreigners in general and for the Irish immigrant in particular: "It is to be regretted," the Negro journalist John E. Bruce said, "that in this land of Bibles where the
outcasts—the scum of European society—can come and enjoy the fullest social and political privileges, the Native Born American with woolly hair and dark complexion is
made the Victim . . . of Social Ostracism." Such statements as "These low-foreheaded,
beetle-browed fellows . . . driven from Europe"; "tens of thousands of aliens are being
landed on these shores and freely given the employment which is denied Negro citizens"; "his brogue was so heavy it sounded like he had marbles in his mouth"; "the
time is upon us when some restriction will have to be placed upon the volume and
character of European immigration," were written by Negroes. A Negro journal spoke
of "the open dislike of the Irish and colored people. . . ." One man put it tersely.
Whatever the Negro is, he said, "he is no hyphenate." [69]

The Irish immigrant, in turn, was given full leeway by American society to look

---

[67] Miller, "Industrial Condition," 548; *The Boston Chronicle,* September 4, 1936. From 1900 to 1905 *The
Southern Workman* printed an entire series of Miller's articles on this subject, and he continued to advocate a
return to the farm until his death in 1939. See the excellent essay by Bernard Eisenberg, "Kelly Miller: The
Negro Leader as Marginal Man," *Journal of Negro History,* XLV (July 1960), 182–187.

[68] Paul Laurence Dunbar, *The Sport of the Gods* (New York, 1902), p. 213. The development of intraracial antagonism would be incomplete without mentioning the hostility that American Negroes, northern and
southern, showed toward Negro immigrants from the West Indies. New York City was the largest urban center for foreign-born Negroes in the early twentieth century (12,851 in 1910). As this antagonism did not become a major theme in city history until the 1920's, I have saved discussion of it for Chapter 9.

[69] John E. Bruce, "Practical Questions," Bruce Manuscripts, Schomburg Collection; *The Colored American Magazine,* XIII (July 1907), 68; "The Reminiscences of Samuel J. Battle" (Oral History Research Office,
Columbia University, 1960), pp. 16–17; *The Crisis,* XII (August 1916), 166–167; *The New York Freeman,* May
15, 1886; *The New York Age,* May 25, 1905, October 5, 1916.

with disdain upon the Negro. A European traveler to the city in the 1860's maintained that Irish immigrants considered Negroes "a soulless race." "I am satisfied that some of these people would shoot a black man . . . as they would a hog," he concluded. "Pat O'Flannagan does not have the least thing in the world against Jim from Dixie," a Negro educator remarked in 1909, "but it didn't take Pat long after passing the Statue of Liberty to learn that it is popular to give Jim a whack." "It is quite remarkable how easily . . . foreigners catch on to the notion . . . to treat Afro-Americans disdainfully and contemptuously," *The New York Age* noted.[70]

Throughout the nineteenth century this mutual antipathy erupted into violence many times. Since the Draft Riots of 1863, however, there were no major clashes between Negroes and Irish in New York City. Now, with increased racial tensions pervading the city, especially in the neighborhoods where the two groups had closest contact, there was a revival of bitterness. The Tenderloin was a common battleground.

A major race riot occurred in New York City in 1900. It was the first serious outbreak of racial violence since the Draft Riots. The riot of 1900 was a symbol of the entire new trend of increasing racial alienation and violence taking place throughout the city. The generally apathetic response of the white community to the demands Negroes made after the riot for justice was a reflection of the growing lack of concern of white New Yorkers for the increasingly serious impediments to Negro equality.

VI

In August 1900 New York City was in the midst of a heat wave. The weather bureau recorded stifling temperatures throughout the month: "The warmest August since the Local Bureau kept track of it." At noon on August 12, the temperature reached 91 degrees. New Yorkers spilled out of their tenements seeking relief. Stoops in the Tenderloin were crowded throughout the night. Local saloons were packed to capacity.[71]

Arthur J. Harris left his house at 241 West Forty-first Street on the evening of August 12 to buy some cigars and pass some time at McBride's Saloon. Harris, twenty-two, was typical of many young Negroes who came to New York City at that time. Born in Richmond, Virginia, of an unstable family (his mother lived in Washington, D.C., in 1900, his father in Cranford, New Jersey), he had left home at fourteen and lived in Washington for seven years. In 1899 he came north to visit his father and find work. The Washington police never had any trouble with him, his record showed "No Prior Convictions." When asked about his previous education, he responded "Yes"; he could read and write.[72] He called himself a Protestant.[73]

[70] Florence E. Gibson, *The Attitudes of the New York Irish toward State and National Affairs, 1848–1892* (New York, 1951), p. 66; *The New York Age,* January 26, 1905; W. L. Bulkley, "Race Prejudice As Viewed from An Economic Standpoint," *Proceedings of the National Negro Conference, 1909* (New York, 1909?), 94.

[71] This information and much that follows is derived from contemporary press reports.

[72] Of the fifty Negro migrants studied by William Fielding Ogburn, all read the daily newspapers. "The Richmond Negro in New York City: His Social Mind as Seen in His Pleasures" (M.A. thesis, Columbia University, 1909), p. 71.

[73] The People vs. Arthur J. Harris, October 29, 1900. Transcript and summary of trial in New York City Magistrates Court.

In Jersey City in 1899, he had picked up money working at odd jobs—as a cook, baker, carpenter and poolroom attendant—and lived with 20-year-old May Enoch, who had left the husband she had married at sixteen. Harris and "his woman," or, as he often referred to her, "my wife," came to Forty-first Street at the beginning of August 1900, rented a room at Annie Johnson's, and said they were looking for work. At 2 A.M. on August 13, May came down to McBride's: "I says to Harris, 'Kid come on up home.' " [74] While she waited for him at the corner of Forty-first Street and Eighth Avenue, Robert J. Thorpe, a plain-clothes policeman, approached her and charged her with "soliciting." To Harris he looked like a white man who was mishandling his woman: "The policeman grabbed my girl. I didn't know who he was and thought he was a citizen like myself," he maintained later at his trial. Harris was clubbed in a struggle with the policeman. He said the policeman pummeled him with his club and shouted, "Get up you black son-of-a-bitch." "I thought the man was trying to kill me, and I believed that he would kill me if I didn't protect myself." Harris pulled out a knife and "cut him twice." May ran home where she was later picked up and arrested; Harris took a train to his mother's home in Washington; Thorpe died in Roosevelt Hospital the next day.[75]

Little more was needed to set off the racial tensions that now lay so near the surface of everyday life in the Tenderloin. A Negro, a recent southern migrant, had killed a "cop"—the son-in-law to be of the acting captain of the local police station. Rumors of violence spread throughout the Negro sections. One woman went to the police and begged for protection: "the tenants of her house were terror-stricken," she said. "They had been warned of an attack in the late night." [76] "Feelings against the Negroes in the neighborhood of Thorpe's late home had been at white heat for a couple of days," it was reported. Large crowds, including sixty members of the Thirty-seventh Street station house, gathered at the home of the Thorpe family to pay their respects.[77]

The immediate cause for the outbreak was a fight between a Negro, Spencer Walters, and a white man, Thomas J. Healy. The Police Board, in its official findings on the riot, claimed that Walters attempted to shoot Healy on the night of August 15. The fight took place near Thorpe's home the evening before the burial. Negroes said that Walters had been set upon by some hysterical people who just visited the Thorpe family.[78] It makes little difference who was right. If it was not this, there would have been some other excuse for violence.

The entire neighborhood went wild with rage. Walters was immediately attacked by a mob. He "was a wreck when placed under arrest." "If there had been a carefully arranged plot and this had been the agreed signal, the outbreak could not have been more spontaneous," a journalist reported. "Men and women poured by the hundreds from the

[74] *Ibid.*

[75] *Ibid.; The World,* August 17, 1900.

[76] *New York Daily Tribune,* August 17, 1900.

[77] *Ibid.,* August 16, 1900.

[78] Bernard J. York, Chairman of the Committee on Rules and Discipline, to Police Board, December 8, 1900 (Mayor Van Wyck Papers, Municipal Archives).

neighboring tenements. Negroes were set upon wherever they could be found and brutally beaten." [79] The word spread that a "nigger chase" was on.[80] Up and down the
streets, through hotels and saloons, in cellars and streetcars, Negroes were attacked and
beaten. White street gangs mobbed the electric cars on Eighth Avenue ("Nigger,
nigger never die, black face and shiny eye"), pulled Negroes off at random and beat
them: "Every car passing up or down Eighth Avenue . . . was stopped by the crowd
and every negro on board dragged out. . . . The police made little or no attempt to arrest any of [the] assailants," The New York Times noted. One man brought a clothesline,
tied it to a lamppost, and looked for someone to lynch.[81]

A group of Negro waiters at a midtown hotel remained there all night rather
than tempt the mob. Stephen Small and Adolphus Cooks were beaten by the police and
decided to hide in a cellar all night. Zeb Robinson, a Negro barber, was attacked on the
streets and taken to Bellevue in a disheveled state. Charles Mitchell became hysterical
after repeated "blows on the head." [82] A friend of James Weldon Johnson never fully recovered from the beating he received with a lead pipe.[83] Affidavits were later collected
from eighty Negroes—waiters, porters, elevator operators, chimney sweeps, laborers,
longshoremen—attesting to police and mob brutality. Although there are no reliable estimates of the number of persons injured in the riot, any Negro who happened to be on
the streets of the Tenderloin that night was attacked and beaten. That serious injury
was done to many is attested in the individual complaints collected in Story of the Riot
(1900). Others never bothered to protest.

Acting Captain Cooney of the Twentieth Precinct called out the reserves to quell
the trouble. However, the predominantly Irish police force hardly acted as detached enforcers of the law. Some did protect Negroes, but most, at the height of the frenzy, encouraged the rioters: "It was said freely by witnesses of the disorderly scenes of
Wednesday night that the police had done as much as anybody to encourage and promote the abuse of inoffensive negroes," a reporter indicated. Policemen often led mobs
that attacked Negroes. Some dragged Negroes off streetcars and beat them. Others
looked the other way rather than witness trouble. A white woman, Mrs. Davenport,
sheltered a few Negroes in her home on the night of August 15. When she refused to
turn them over to the police, they replied: "What kind of woman are you to be harbor-
ing niggers?" It seemed their ambition to "club the life out of a nigger," a witness
said.[84]

William J. Elliott, a Negro waiter, was arrested for carrying a revolver. Reporters

[79] New York Daily Tribune, August 16, 1900.

[80] Ibid.

[81] The New York Times, August 16, 1900; Autobiography of Dr. William Henry Johnson (Albany, 1900), p.
148.

[82] [Frank Moss], Story of the Riot: Persecution of Negroes by Roughs and Policemen, in the City of New York,
August, 1900 (New York, 1900), p. 5; Richard O'Connor, Hell's Kitchen: The Roaring Days of New York's Wild
West Side (New York, 1958), p. 151.

[83] The New York Times, August 20, 1900; Johnson, Along This Way, pp. 157–158.

[84] New York Daily Tribune, August 16, 17, 1900.

saw him entering the Thirty-seventh Street station house uninjured. When he left the next morning he was beaten and bloody. Elliott told the Police Commissioners that as he passed through the muster room the lights were turned out and he was kicked, punched and clubbed into insensibility.[85] As he could not identify any specific assailant, however, the Commissioners found this evidence "contradictory," and ruled that "no conviction of a violation of the Rules of the Department could be sustained [on it]." [86]

At about 2 A.M. on August 16 a providential summer thunderstorm drenched the city. It ended the initial violence. Emergency staffs on all-night duty at Roosevelt, Belle-vue and New York hospitals handled the many cases of battered heads. The local police courts were jammed to capacity—with Negroes. One of the magistrates criticized the police and asked to see "some of the white persons who participated in this riot." By 1:30 A.M. his request was fulfilled. A teenager, Frank Minogue, was brought in and charged with trying to trip a policeman who was dispersing a crowd of rioters.

VII

Although the riot had ended, the neighborhood remained tense. Negroes began to arm. Revolvers and other weapons were easily purchased at local pawnshops and hardware stores. In a survey made of the Tenderloin, just one day after the riot, it was found that 145 revolvers and a substantial amount of ammunition had been sold—"all had gone to negroes." [87] Lloyd Williams, a Negro bartender, was seen leaving one store with an arsenal of weapons. When asked what he was going to do with them, he replied: "I understand they're knocking down negroes 'round here. The first man tries it on me gets this. . . ." Other Negroes warned that no white men were going to bother them. As policemen patrolled the Negro blocks they were showered with bricks, bottles and garbage from rooftops and tenement windows. They fired back with revolvers. It seems miraculous that no one was killed then.

Orders went out to keep the Negroes off the streets. Paul Laurence Dunbar went into the Tenderloin, visited Negro homes and attempted to restore peace. Innumerable arrests were made, practically all of Negroes, on the charge of carrying concealed weapons. For more than a month after the riot there were almost daily clashes between individual Negroes and whites. At least two people were killed in these fights. Slowly, the Tenderloin returned to its normal state of semipeace.

VIII

The white community was shocked.[88] Editorials appeared throughout the press criticizing the police for their brutality and the vicious for their violence. The tone of the re-

---

[85] Israel Ludlow to Bernard J. York, August 30, 1900 (Mayor Van Wyck Papers, Municipal Archives).

[86] Bernard J. York to Police Board, December 8, 1900. *Ibid.*

[87] *The World,* August 17, 1900.

[88] Less than a month before the riot, the New York press had bitterly criticized the South for a race riot in New Orleans. Southerners now responded gleefully; stressed the universality of race hatred; made some comments about casting the first stone; and warned against the "young country negro" who flocks to the city to "lead a life of idleness." *Ibid.,* August 17, 18, 19, 1900.

sponses, however, lacked sympathy for the injured Negroes. The riot was made a political issue as the Republican press and the Good Government Society attacked Tammany Hall. The *New York Daily Tribune* printed a cartoon of a massive Tammany tiger in police uniform swinging a club. Huddled on the floor in the background was a bloody Negro. The caption read: "He's On the Police Force Now." The "Respectable Citizenry" attacked the "white trash" and advised Negroes to vote Republican.[89]

Negro leaders demanded punishment of the guilty and compensation for the injured. The Reverend Dr. W. H. Brooks of St. Mark's Methodist Episcopal Church led the protest. Brooks, born on a Maryland plantation, had been at St. Mark's since 1897—well equipped with a voice that could drown out the clatter of elevated trains that ran near his church.[90] One of the most important leaders of the city's Negro community, he later became a founder of the NAACP and the National Urban League. From his pulpit, and from the pulpits of all the Negro churches in the city, the mobs and police were vilified. An honest public investigation was demanded,[91] and prominent members of the Negro community—lawyers, clergymen, politicians, businessmen— were urged to use their influence to seek justice.[92] An *ad hoc* defense committee, the Citizens' Protective League, was organized at a meeting in St. Mark's on September 3. Two lawyers, Frank Moss and Israel Ludlow, were hired. Moss vowed never to let the riot "fade into forgetfulness." Suits were filed for damages against the city in the names of persons injured by the police.[93] At a mass meeting at Carnegie Hall to raise money and gain public support, some speakers urged caution and peaceful agitation. D. Macon Webster, a Negro lawyer, wanted justice done for the "humblest citizen." "One might think we [were] all aliens" from the manner in which we were treated, he concluded.[94] Others, more belligerent, urged Negroes to arm and defend their homes.[95] All agreed that right must be done.

The protests were militant and idealistic, the results cold and bleak. There was no mass response to the appeal for public support: "I heard many native Americans . . . say after the riot," a contemporary noted in *Harper's Weekly*, "that they would have been glad if many of the negroes had been killed." "This is a mass in the midst of what is . . . an alien and hostile people," another believed.[96] The August Grand Jury refused to indict a single policeman, alleging that accusations were brought against groups

[89] *New York Daily Tribune*, August 19, 1900.

[90] Clement Richardson, ed., *The National Cyclopedia of the Colored Race* (Montgomery, Alabama, 1919), I, 223; Mary White Ovington, *The Walls Came Tumbling Down* (New York, 1947), pp. 25–26.

[91] *New York Daily Tribune*, August 27, 1900.

[92] Some of the original postcards sent out by the Reverend Dr. Brooks may be found at the Schomburg Collection.

[93] *New York Daily Tribune*, August 25, September 8, 1900; Israel Ludlow to Bernard J. York, President of Board of Police Commissioners, August 30, 1900 (Mayor Van Wyck Papers, Municipal Archives); Frank Moss to York, September 14, 1900, *ibid.*

[94] "Notes of D. Macon Webster for a speech at protest meeting" (Miscellaneous Manuscripts, Schomburg Collection).

[95] *The New York Times*, September 13, 1900.

[96] J. G. Speed, "The Negro in New York: A Study of the Social and Industrial Condition of the Colored People in the Metropolis," *Harper's Weekly*, XLIV (December 22, 1900), 1249.

rather than individuals. When cases were presented against individual policemen, they too were dismissed.[97] The Police Board set up a committee of investigation, which refused Moss and Ludlow permission to cross-examine witnesses, and concluded in its report that "there is nothing in the evidence taken by your committee which will justify preferment of charges against any officer. . . ."[98] The *Tribune* quipped: "The Police Board wants it understood that the riot inquiry is to be full and impartial, only no evidence against the police will be admitted."[99] Arthur J. Harris was arrested in Washington for killing policeman Thorpe, tried in New York, found guilty of murder in the second degree, and "sentenced to the State Prison at Sing Sing at hard labor for the term of his natural life."[100] The Reverend Dr. Brooks created "The Arthur J. Harris Liberation Fund" and continued to fight for his release, but Harris died in prison on December 20, 1908.[101] The Citizens' Protective League simply ceased to exist. It accomplished nothing. The little power it could wield ran into an almost solid wall of indifference and opposition. "It is like sheep proclaiming the law of righteousness to a congregation of wolves," Kelly Miller commented on another occasion. "A complaint is effective only in so far as there is power to enforce it."[102]

And the Police Department, in its *Annual Report,* provided its own conclusion to the sad affair: "In the month of August the west side of the city was threatened with a race war between the white and colored citizens. . . . Prompt and vigorous action on the part of the Police . . . kept the situation under control, and . . . quiet was restored in districts . . . which were affected."[103]

Was the riot and the reaction to it a sign of intensified racial alienation in New York City, as some people claimed? No, said a columnist for *The New York Times* in an emphatic rejoinder. There is no "settled race hatred . . . in New York. There are no signs that the citizen of African descent is distrusted or disliked. . . . His crude melodies and childlike antics are more than tolerated in the music halls of the best class."[104]

[97] *New York Daily Tribune,* September 9, 1900.

[98] John Hains vs. Herman A. Ohm, October 26, 1900; George L. Myers vs. John J. Cleary, October 26, 1900 (Mayor Van Wyck Papers, Municipal Archives).

[99] Bernard J. York to Police Board, December 8, 1900 (Mayor Van Wyck Papers, Municipal Archives).

[100] The People vs. Arthur J. Harris, October 29, 1900 (New York City Magistrates Court).

[101] Harold W. Folletta, Acting Warden, Clinton Prison, to author, August 14, 1961.

[102] Kelly Miller, "The American Negro as a Political Factor," *The Nineteenth Century,* LXVIII (August 1910), 297.

[103] *Report of the Police Department of the City of New York* (New York, 1901), p. 10.

[104] *The New York Times,* August 24, 1900.

Part 5

WORLD WAR I
AND AFTER

World War I is often considered a watershed in the history of the American people. There is ample support for this hypothesis as it concerns the entire American population. There is also support for the hypothesis as it applies to the special history of black Americans as a minority group in the United States. The tide of urban movement which began after the Civil War reached flood proportions during the First World War. This movement would eventually create a situation in which the typical experience of a black American was an urban experience and in which the major problems of race relations and racial justice became inextricably intertwined with problems related to the quality of urban life. In addition, World War I took large numbers of black Americans outside the country, from which perspective they were better able to view their experiences in their homeland. The meeting of great numbers of black people in the large cities and the realization, through experience, that there was a wider world of relations between people of different races than that suggested by American practice suggest strongly the importance of the war in the history of black Americans.

Students of political science tell us that people do not rise against a system when it is operating efficiently and when they are in the depths of despair. Consequently, the search for direction in the four decades following Reconstruction produced no violent upheaval or concerted attack on the entrenched system of prejudice, segregation and discrimination. Events related to World War I seemed to reduce the efficiency with which this system kept blacks "in their place." It also provided, because of increased income

and insight, the desire for more than mere survival. These were conditions from which
new approaches could emerge.

   Participation in the armed forces of the United States and work in war industries
produced no noticeable reduction of hostility toward blacks and no lowering of the barriers of prejudice. Instead, the war "to make the world safe for democracy" made it more
dangerous for blacks to seek democratic rights in this part of the world. The mass
movement to the cities and the confrontation of the races in new areas, under conditions
of tension and aggression, resulted in desperate efforts to strengthen some barriers and,
on occasion, in violence to suppress real or imagined efforts of blacks to push ahead.
These efforts and the accompanying attitudes carried over into the 1920s when, coupled
with the general reaction to the war, they produced another of those waves of nativism
which occur periodically in American life.

   In the selection from *Black Manhattan,* James Weldon Johnson briefly traces the
events of the war and the 1920s in Harlem. The patriotism of blacks and their hostility
to prejudice at home and its export abroad appear as twin themes. Mingled emotions of
bitterness, despair, and anger are presented as characteristic of the postwar period when
the high hopes of veterans and patriots were dashed by the realities of the twenties.
Black Manhattan is less important for its historical thoroughness than for its reflections
of the struggle for identity among black citizens of New York. The author was active in
this movement on two fronts between 1916 and 1930: he served as an official of the National Association for the Advancement of Colored People while continuing his literary
career.

   "The Participation of Negroes in World War I: An Introductory Statement,"
provides a view of the treatment of black servicemen by Special Assistant to the Secretary of War, Emmett J. Scott. In the selection from the 1943 article Mr. Scott recounts
the extent of black participation in the war and the nature of race relations. Descriptions
of these relations are reflected in "Documents of the War," a selection from the May
1919 *Crisis.* The documents show the attitudes of white Americans and their efforts to
export these attitudes to France where racism was not a general practice, as in the
United States.

   The postwar "Back to Africa" movement of Marcus Garvey and its appeal to
black Americans is discussed in *The New World of Negro Americans* by Harold R. Isaacs.
The selection bearing the same title as the movement reports Garvey's attractiveness to
many blacks and the intraracial conflict resulting from his demand for a pure black race.
This position was in opposition to the top social and economic strata of black society,
most of the members of which reflected in their ancestry the race mixing which had
long been a part of American society, albeit in violation of the legal and social codes in
those areas where it was most prominent.

   Foremost among the Garvey critics was William E. B. Du Bois, leader of the
Pan-African Movement, Director of Research for the NAACP, and editor of the *Crisis.*
Elliott Rudwick explores this conflict between the two men in "DuBois versus Garvey:
Race Propogandist at War," an article in *Journal of Negro Education.* Specifically the au-
thor examines the NAACP's *Crisis* and the Garvey-owned *Negro World* as a basis for his
study. Reflected in the conflict are problems which have plagued black leadership in the

past. Foremost among these is the difficulty of involving masses of blacks and the educated middle class in the same movement. That the intraracial conflict has been lessened attests to the quality of recent leadership.

Important in the postwar period were the artistic developments among blacks. Critics agree that the period variously known as the Harlem Renaissance, the Black Renaissance, or the Negro Renaissance was a time of enthusiasm and creativity. Alain Locke's "New Negro" was imbued with a new sense of his own worth. He wrote poetry and novels at fever pitch; he lauded his African past; he initiated the Jazz Age; he protected his future through investment in real estate. Beyond this, critics do not agree upon the permanence of the impact of the Renaissance or upon the validity of the talent it disclosed. It has been described as lasting the decade of the twenties or continuing into the sixties. The work of one author, Jean Toomer, is acclaimed as "that abstract and absolute thing called Art" [1] and condemned for drifting "off into a hazy poetic incoherence . . . too insubstantial to be remembered." [2]

Waiving the literary disagreements evident in critical comment of any age, however, the observer can assess this as a period when the black man replenished his spirit. After his migration from the South and the West Indies, he supported his urban condition with memories of earlier scenes. A literature shot with the color of the Caribbean emerged in the poetry of Claude McKaye and others. Professor Locke called for a black theatre. Beyond mere replenishment, however, the movement yielded a literary exuberance sparked by appearance of Negro characters in white works and developed and sustained by black writers' treatment of black themes.

The literary salon and the patron of Negro Art were prime movers of the Renaissance. Carl Van Vechten became the best known of the white patrons. Many early writers, Langston Hughes among them, saw his patronage as an aid, but in *The Crisis of the Negro Intellectual* (William Morrow and Co., N.Y., 1967), Harold Cruse condemns it as destructive paternalism. One of the most virulent Renaissance attacks upon the practice of whites swarming to Harlem to visit nightclubs and attend soirees and donation parties appears in Wallace Thurman's satirical novel, *Infants of the Spring*. It is included here as counterbalance to the copious favorable comment on literary patronage which is readily available. The selection is also interesting in its satire on black attitudes as well as white, for through this is revealed a call to self-assessment—germane to burgeoning race pride.

Of course, the mecca of literary and musical activity was Harlem. James Weldon Johnson's "Harlem: the Culture Capital" traces the historical and social development there. Here, however, exuberance outstrips objective prediction, and the writer concludes that "there is small probability that Harlem will ever be a point of race friction between the races in New York." (p. 310) Any study of black Americans' history would benefit from attention to the effect of Harlem and its sister communities in other states

---

[1] Toomer, Jean *Cane,* N.Y., Boni and Liveright, 1923, p. xi

[2] Littlejohn, David *Black on White: A Critical Study of Writing by American Negroes,* N.Y., Viking Press, 1966, p. 60.

upon their residents. In recent years, much material on "ghetto life" has appeared. Johnson recognized early that the Negro's ability to hold Harlem was imperative to his cultural and financial survival. His essay presages Le Roi Jones's "City of Harlem" (*Home: Social Essays,* William Morrow and Co., N.Y., 1966) with a challenging combination of naïveté and insight.

The selection from *Blues People: Negro Music in White America,* another collection by Jones, traces in a special way the migrations, city life, and methods of coping with that life adopted by the Black Renaissance man. The history Jones recounts emphasizes another of the business aspects of city life. Many blues lyrics grew out of plant and mill job experiences, stressing the perennial need for employment. Then, when phonograph "race records" were cut and sold on a large scale, the significance of the black worker as consumer increased. Bessie Smith embodied the soul of the blues; her mellow voice has been described as gripping and overwhelming. She and the Father of the Blues, W. C. Handy, limned the migrations in all their tortured and sweet variances. Finally, the "blues people" broadened their Renaissance fervor to include painting and sculpture. Quotations from Romare Bearden and others, included here in Cedric Dover's *American Negro Art,* are important for the moral direction they offer Negro artists. This didactic emphasis continues to the present. If, as some commentators hold, we are experiencing a continued period of creative expression, this emphasis is the constant. It reenforces the cultural activity of the Harlem Renaissance and of succeeding periods and gives them substance.

Black Manhattan*

James Weldon Johnson

At the beginning of the year 1917 Negro Harlem was well along the road of development and prosperity. There was plenty of work, with a choice of jobs, and there was plenty of money. The community was beginning to feel conscious of its growing size and strength. It had entirely rid itself of the sense of apology for its existence. It was beginning to take pride in itself as Harlem, a Negro community.

But it was far from being complacent. It was alive and quick with enthusiasm and energy. Plans were being drawn that took in many things which hitherto had been considered to lie in the field of the impossible. Even its members from the darkest South felt strange stirrings of aspiration and shed that lethargy born of hopelessness which so often marks Negroes from sections where they have for generation after generation borne physically and spiritually an unrelieved weight of white superiority. Harlem had begun to dream of greater and greater things.

There had also taken place a birth of new ideas—new, at least, to Negroes. There were Negroes in Harlem who envisaged the situation of the race in the light of economic and social revolution. Radicalism in the modern and international sense of the term was born. Nightly along Lenox and Seventh avenues dozens of speakers could be heard explaining to listening groups the principles of socialism and the more revolutionary doctrines; trying to show them how these principles applied to their condition; hammering away at their traditional attitude of caution. These were some of the important forces at work in Harlem when the United States declared war against the German Empire.

Like the average American community, Harlem did not exhibit any great enthusiasm about the war. However, the war for months had been a topic of discussion among high and low, educated and uneducated. As the probabilities that this country would be embroiled became greater, the discussions increased in frequency and intensity. Among those who had a knowledge of affairs outside of the United States, there

* From James Weldon Johnson, *Black Manhattan* (New York: Atheneum Publishers, 1968), pp. 231–45, 246–51. Copyright 1930 by James Weldon Johnson. Copyright renewed 1958 by Mrs. James Weldon Johnson. Reprinted by permission of Mrs. James Weldon Johnson.

had all along been deep sympathy for France, as the most liberal of all great white nations towards black peoples. Among others there had been little concern one way or the
other. The matter did not touch their lives; and when they were brought face to face
with it, they were apt to brush it aside with characteristic Negro humour. One coloured
man came into a Harlem barber-shop where a spirited discussion of the war was going
on. When asked if he wasn't going to join the Army and fight the Germans, he replied
amidst roars of laughter: "The Germans ain't done nothin' to me, and if they have, I
forgive 'em."

Nevertheless, after the declaration of war, patriotism was fanned to a flame as
quickly in Harlem as in the average American community. Indeed, six years before the
United States entered the World War, steps were taken, led by the Equity Congress, a
civic organization, to form a regiment of state militia. A provisional regiment was
formed with Charles W. Filmore as provisional colonel. But a great deal of unwillingness and opposition developed on the part of state authorities to the mustering of the
regiment. Several bills to that end were introduced in the Assembly, and those behind
the proposal worked without ceasing; but it was not until July 2, 1913 that legislation
authorizing the Fifteenth Regiment as a unit of the New York National Guard was
passed. Immediately after the declaration of war the Federal Government recognized the
regiment as a National Guard unit; and four months later, it was called to arms. It was
the first regiment of the New York Guard to reach the required war strength.

The Fifteenth Regiment, under the command of Colonel William Hayward, after
being awhile at Peekskill and at Camp Whitman, was sent to Spartanburg, South Carolina, where other units of the New York Guard were encamped. One day Sergeant
Noble Sissle (the same Sissle of later *Shuffle Along* fame) went into the lobby of the
local hotel, where there was a news-stand, to buy New York papers for himself and
some of his men. The proprietor demanded of him why he did not take off his hat. Sergeant Sissle, in ignorance or defiance of the local *mores,* replied that he was a United
States soldier and did not have to take off his hat. His hat was knocked off and he was
kicked into the street. When the news of this incident reached camp, the men of the
Fifteenth were for going into town and retaliating; but they were restrained by discipline. Men of other regiments of the New York Guard were indignant over the matter.
The upshot of it all was that the Fifteenth Regiment was quickly ordered away and
brought up to Camp Mills, on Long Island, where they were quartered with state troops
from Alabama and Mississippi. The first night in camp trouble broke out over the discrimination against Negro soldiers in the canteen. The next day the regiment was hur-
riedly embarked. It sailed for France on November 12, 1917, being one of the first units
from the National Guard of the whole country to go overseas; and this was, of course,
long before any drafted troops were sent.

When the Fifteenth reached France there was further embarrassment. What to
do with this Negro regiment became a serious question. Naturally, it should have remained a contingent of the New York National Guard; but for reasons held sufficient
by those in high command, this could not be permitted. A way out was found by bri-
gading the regiment with French troops. It was attached as a combat regiment to the
Eighth Corps of the Fourth French Army. So, wholly under French command and carry-

ing its state colours, it fought through the war. It was the only American unit to do either of these things. But "the stone that the builders rejected . . ." The first soldier of
the entire American Expeditionary Forces to receive the Croix de Guerre with star and
palm was Sergeant Henry Johnson of the Fifteenth Regiment, New York National
Guard. The entire regiment was cited for exceptional valour in action during the
Meuse-Argonne offensive, and its colours were decorated with the Croix de Guerre. The
Fifteenth was under shell-fire 191 days, and held one trench ninety-one days without relief. At the declaration of the armistice, the French command gave it the honour of
being the first of all the Allied forces to set foot on enemy territory; it went down as the
advance guard of the French army of occupation. On this side, no single regiment in the
A.E.F. was more often heard of or better known than the Fifteenth.

The regiment, now the 369th Infantry, arrived back in New York on February
12, 1919. On February 17 they paraded up Fifth Avenue. New York had seen lots of soldiers marching off to the war, but this was its first sight of marching veterans. The
beautiful Victory Arch erected by the city at Madison Square as a part of the welcome to
the returning troops was just nearing completion, and the old Fifteenth was the first
body of troops to pass under it. The parade had been given great publicity, and the city
was anxious and curious to see soldiers back from the trenches. The newspapers had in-
timated that a good part of the celebration would be hearing the now famous Fifteenth
band play jazz and seeing the Negro soldiers step to it. Those who looked for that sort
of entertainment were disappointed. Lieutenant Jim Europe walked sedately ahead, and
Bandmaster Eugene Mikell had the great band alternate between two noble French military marches. And on the part of the men, there was no prancing, no showing of teeth,
no swank; they marched with a steady stride, and from under their battered tin hats eyes
that had looked straight at death were kept to the front.

But before the Fifteenth left for France, while they were in camp, training to go,
there was another parade. On July 28, 1917 ten thousand New York Negroes silently
marched down Fifth Avenue to the sound of muffled drums. The procession was headed
by little children dressed in white, followed by the women in white, the men bringing
up the rear. They carried banners. Some of them read: "Unto the Least of My Brethren," "Mother, Do Lynchers Go to Heaven?" "Give Me a Chance to Live," "Mr. President, Why Not Make America Safe for Democracy?" "Treat Us so that We May Love
Our Country," "Patriotism and Loyalty Presuppose Protection and Liberty," "Pray for
the Lady Macbeths of East St. Louis." In front of the man bearing the flag of the United
States went a banner with the inscription: "Your Hands Are Full of Blood." This was
the "Silent Protest Parade," organized by Negro leaders in Harlem, and one of the
strangest and most impressive sights New York has witnessed. They marched in silence
and they were watched in silence; but some of those who watched turned away with
their eyes filled. Negro boy scouts distributed to the watchers circulars which, under the
caption: "Why We March," stated these reasons for the demonstration:

> We march because by the Grace of God and the force of truth, the dangerous,
> hampering walls of prejudice and inhuman injustices must fall.
> We march because we want to make impossible a repetition of Waco, Mem-

phis, and East St. Louis, by rousing the conscience of the country and bringing the murderers of our brothers, sisters and innocent children to justice.

We march because we deem it a crime to be silent in the face of such barbaric acts.

We march because we are thoroughly opposed to Jim-Crow Cars, Segregation, Discrimination, Disfranchisement, LYNCHING and the host of evils that are forced on us. It is time that the Spirit of Christ should be manifested in the making and execution of laws.

We march because we want our children to live in a better land and enjoy fairer conditions than have fallen to our lot.

We march in memory of our butchered dead, the massacre of the honest toilers who were removing the reproach of laziness and thriftlessness hurled at the entire race. They died to prove our worthiness to live. We live in spite of death shadowing us and ours. We prosper in the face of the most unwarranted and illegal oppression.

In view of the temper of the times, the Protest Parade was a courageous form of action to take. Behind all lay a culminating series of causes: lynchings, disfranchisement in the South, discriminations of many kinds, all of which assumed a magnified and more ironic cruelty in the face of the fact that Negroes were being called upon like all others to do their full part in the war as American citizens. But more immediate were the humiliations and injustices to which Negroes who had answered the call to arms were being subjected. And the cup overflowed with the East St. Louis massacre of July 2, 1917, in which four hundred thousand dollars' worth of property was destroyed, nearly six thousand Negroes driven from their homes, and hundreds murdered, a number of them burned alive in houses set afire over their heads. A resolution was introduced in Congress calling for an investigation of the East St. Louis riots. Some idea of the unbelievable savagery and its reaction upon the coloured people of the country may be gained from statements made at a hearing before the Committee on Rules of the House of Representatives by members of Congress.

Mr. Dyer of Missouri said in part:

I have visited out there and have interviewed a number of people and talked with a number who saw the murders that were committed. One man in particular who spoke to me is now an officer in the United States Army Reserve Corps, Lieut. Arbuckle, who is here in Washington somewhere, he having come here to report to the Adjutant General.

At the time of these happenings he was in the employ of the Government, but he was there on some business in East St. Louis. He said that he saw a part of this killing, and he saw them burning railway cars in yards, which were waiting for transport, filled with interstate commerce. He saw members of the militia of Illinois shoot Negroes. He saw policemen of the city of East St. Louis shoot negroes. He saw this mob go to the homes of these Negroes and nail boards up over the doors and windows and then set fire and burn them up. He saw them take little children out of the arms of their mothers and throw them into the fires and burn them up. He saw the most dastardly and most criminal outrages ever perpetrated in this country, and this is undisputed. And I have talked with others; and my opinion is that over five hundred people were killed on this occasion.

Mr. Rodenberg of Illinois (East St. Louis is in Illinois), among other things, said:

Now, the plain, unvarnished truth of the matter, as Mr. Joyce told Secretary Baker, is that civil government in East St. Louis completely collapsed at the time of the riot. The conditions there at the time beggar description. It is impossible for any human being to describe the ferocity and brutality of that mob. In one case, for instance, a little ten-year-old boy, whose mother had been shot down, was running around sobbing and looking for his mother, and some members of the mob shot the boy, and before life had passed from his body they picked the little fellow up and threw him in the flames.

Another colored woman with a little two-year-old baby in her arms was trying to protect the child, and they shot her and also shot the child, and threw them in the flames. The horror of that tragedy in East St. Louis can never be described. It weighted me down with a feeling of depression that I did not recover from for weeks. The most sickening things I ever heard of were described in the letters that I received from home giving details of that attack.

The Silent Protest Parade had hardly disbanded when there flashed up from Texas the news of the "Houston affair." A battalion of the Twenty-fourth Infantry, one of the Negro regiments of the regular Army, was stationed at the time at Houston, and during their service there a number of the men had been assaulted by the Houston police. The friction grew out of the fact that, instead of having the soldiers of the camp policed by the usual method of establishing a provost guard, that duty was placed in the hands of the local police. The most popular non-commissioned officer, and one of the most experienced soldiers in the regiment, Corporal Baltimore, had been seriously beaten; news reached the camp that he had been killed. On the night of August 23 the city of Houston was shot up; two Negroes and seventeen white people were killed, five of the latter being Houston policemen. As a result, sixty-three members of the battalion were court-martialled at Fort Sam Houston, and, on December 11, 1917, thirteen of them were hanged. A wave of bitterness and anguish, made more acute by a sense of impotence, swept over the coloured people. They did not question the findings of the court martial, but they did feel that the men should have been accorded their right of appeal to their Commander-in-Chief, the President. And they knew so well the devilish and fiendish baiting by which the men had been goaded.

A second court martial sentenced five more to be hanged and in addition sentenced fifty-one to life imprisonment and five to long terms. At this point a committee of four representatives from the National Association for the Advancement of Colored People—the Rev. George Frazier Miller, the Rev. Frank M. Hyder, the Rev. F. A. Cullen, and James Weldon Johnson, secretary of the association—proceeded from New York to Washington to see President Wilson, taking with them a petition signed by twelve thousand New York citizens asking executive clemency for the condemned men. Mr. Johnson acted as spokesman and in presenting the petition said:

> "We come as a delegation from the New York Branch of the National Association for the Advancement of Colored People, representing the twelve thousand signers to this petition which we have the honour to lay before you. And we come not only as the representatives of those who signed this petition, but we come representing the sentiments and aspirations and sorrows, too, of the great mass of the Negro population of the United States.
>
> "We respectfully and earnestly request and urge that you extend executive clemency to the five Negro soldiers of the Twenty-fourth Infantry now under sentence of death by court martial. And understanding that the cases of the men of the same regiment who were sentenced to life imprisonment by the first court martial are to be reviewed, we also request and urge that you cause this review to be laid before you and that executive clemency be shown also to them.
>
> "We feel that the history of this particular regiment and the splendid record for bravery and loyalty of our Negro soldiery in every crisis of the nation give us the right to make this request. And we make it not only in the name of their loyalty, but also in the name of the unquestioned loyalty to the nation of twelve million Negroes—a loyalty which today places them side by side with the original American stocks that landed at Plymouth and Jamestown.
>
> "The hanging of thirteen men without the opportunity of appeal to the Secretary of War or to their Commander-in-Chief, the President of the United States, was a punishment so drastic and so unusual in the history of the nation that the execution of additional members of the Twenty-fourth Infantry would to the coloured people of the country savour of vengeance rather than justice.
>
> "It is neither our purpose nor is this the occasion to argue whether this attitude of mind on the part of coloured people is justified or not. As representatives of the race we desire only to testify that it does exist. This state of mind has been intensified by the significant fact that although white persons were involved in the Houston affair, and the regiment to which the coloured men belonged was officered entirely by white men, none but coloured men, so far as we have been able to learn, have been prosecuted or condemned.
>
> "We desire also respectfully to call to your attention the fact that there were mitigating circumstances for the action of these men of the Twenty-fourth Infantry. Not by any premeditated design and without cause did these men do what they did at Houston; but by a long series of humiliating and harassing incidents, culminating in the brutal assault on Corporal Baltimore, they were goaded to sudden and frenzied action. This is borne out by the long record for orderly and soldierly conduct on the part of the regiment throughout its whole history up to that time.

"And to the end that you extend the clemency which we ask, we lay before you this petition signed by white as well as coloured citizens of New York; one of the signers being a white man, president of a New York bank, seventy-two years of age, and a native of Lexington, Kentucky.

"And now, Mr. President, we would not let this opportunity pass without mentioning the terrible outrages against our people that have taken place in the last three-quarters of a year; outrages that are not only unspeakable wrongs against them, but blots upon the fair name of our common country. We mention the riots at East St. Louis, in which the coloured people bore the brunt of both the cruelty of the mob and the processes of law. And we especially mention the savage burnings that have taken place in the single state of Tennessee within nine months: the burnings at Memphis, Tennessee; at Dyersburg, Tennessee; and only last week at Estill Springs, Tennessee, where a Negro charged with the killing of two men was tortured with red-hot irons, then saturated with oil and burned to death before a crowd of American men, women, and children. And we ask that you, who have spoken so nobly to the whole world for the cause of humanity, speak against these specific wrongs. We realize that your high position and the tremendous moral influence which you wield in the world will give a word from you greater force than could come from any other source. Our people are intently listening and praying that you may find it in your heart to speak that word."

The President received the delegation very cordially and granted them an audience lasting half an hour. He assured them, in effect, that he would carefully examine the record in the case of the condemned men and would give the whole matter his sympathetic attention. A surprising incident of the interview was that the President declared that he had not heard anything about the Estill Springs burning. He asked the committee to state the facts for him. His comment was that he could hardly believe that such a thing had happened in the United States. He promised to seek an opportunity and later he did make a strong statement against lynching.

President Wilson prohibited the execution of any more American soldiers—except in General Pershing's forces abroad—before the sentences of the courts martial had been reviewed by the War Department. Eleven more men of the Twenty-fourth, making sixteen, were condemned to die. The President, after review of their cases, commuted ten death-sentences and affirmed six. The men who were sent to prison finally had their sentences commuted and were released on parole through the efforts of the Advancement Association.

Exactly what happened at Houston on that night in August will probably never be known. The executed men went to death and the fifty-odd to prison without "talking." According to the military investigation that was made, Bartlett James, one of the white officers, a West Pointer and a splendid soldier, Captain of Company L, was in the company street that night with his men gathered round him; a detail from the men who had left camp came back to induce the rest of the battalion to join them; the corporal in charge of the detail is said to have appealed to the men of Company L to follow, but none made a move; in reply to an appeal to him, Captain James was reported as saying: "The men of Company L are going to stay with their captain"; and he did hold his company practically intact. Captain James was down as one of the most important witnesses in this remarkable military trial. But on Wednesday night, October 24, seven days before the date set for the trial to begin, he went to his tent and blew out his brains. So the one officer of the line who could have told a great deal about the matter did not testify.

These were some of the depressing happenings at home after our entry into the war. From the other side came tidings far from being glad. There came back reports of the practices of discrimination and "Jim Crowism" against Negro soldiers; of the efforts to belittle and discredit their fighting qualities; of the ceaseless endeavours at every turn on the part of many of the white American troops to create a prejudice against them where none had existed. By one means or another, copies of the order entitled "Secret Information Concerning Black American Troops" found their way from France into the United States. This order, issued at the instance of American authorities and through the French military mission, was for the instruction of French officers in dealing with American Negro troops. . . .

● ● ●

With the close of the war went most of the illusions and high hopes American Negroes had felt would be realized when it was seen that they were doing to the utmost their bit at home and in the field. Eight months after the armistice, with black men back fresh from the front, there broke the Red Summer of 1919, and the mingled emotions of the race were bitterness, despair, and anger. There developed an attitude of cynicism that was a characteristic foreign to the Negro. There developed also a spirit of defiance born of desperation. These sentiments and reactions found varying degrees of expression in the Negro publications throughout the country; but Harlem became the centre where they were formulated and voiced to the Negroes of America and the world. Radicalism in Harlem, which had declined as the war approached, burst out anew. But it was something different from the formal radicalism of pre-war days; it was a radicalism motivated by a fierce race consciousness.

A new radical press sprang up in Harlem, and those periodicals that were older took on fresh vigour. Among the magazines and newspapers published were: *The Messenger, Challenge, The Voice, The Crusader, The Emancipator,* and *The Negro World.* These periodicals were edited and written by men who had a remarkable command of forcible and trenchant English, the precise style for their purpose. And the group was not at all a small one; in it were: A. Philip Randolph, Chandler Owen, George Frazier Miller, W. A. Domingo, Edgar M. Grey, Hubert Harrison, William H. Ferris, William Bridges, Richard B. Moore, Cyril V. Briggs, William N. Colson, and Anselmo Jackson. Two of these men, A. Philip Randolph and W. A. Domingo, wrote in a very close-knit, cogent manner. The utterances of these publications drew the notice of the Federal Government, and under the caption "Radicalism and Sedition among the Negroes as Reflected in their Publications" they were cited in a Department of Justice report made by Attor-

ney General Palmer in 1919. The report of the Lusk Committee in New York State devoted forty-four pages to them. The radicalism of these publications ranged from left
centre to extreme left; at the extreme it was submerged in what might be called racial-
ism. It was to be expected that at such a time an organization like the National Association for the Advancement of Colored People would not escape scrutiny. The utterances
of Dr. Du Bois in the *Crisis,* the organ of the association, brought a visit to the office
from agents of the Department of Justice. In reply to the query: "Just what is this organization fighting for?" Dr. Du Bois said: "We are fighting for the enforcement of the
Constitution of the United States." This was an ultimate condensation of the program
of the association.

The *Messenger* preached socialism and the social revolution. It was the most
widely circulated of all the radical periodicals and probably the most influential. In an
editorial, "The Cause of and Remedy for Race Riots," it said in part:

> The solution will not follow the meeting of white and Negro leaders in love
> feasts, who pretend, like the African ostrich, that nothing is wrong, because their
> heads are buried in the sand.
>
> On the economic field, industry must be socialized, and land must be national-
> ized, which will thereby remove the motive for creating strife between the
> races. . . .
>
> The people must organize, own and control their press.
>
> The church must be converted into an educational forum.
>
> The stage and screen must be controlled by the people.

This editorial offered an "immediate program," which was summed up in the following paragraph:

> *Lastly, revolution must come.* By that we mean a complete change in the organi-
> zation of society. Just as absence of industrial democracy is productive of riots
> and race clashes, so the introduction of industrial democracy will be the longest
> step toward removing that cause. When no profits are to be made from race fric-
> tion, no one will longer be interested in stirring up race prejudice. The quickest
> way to stop a thing or to destroy an institution is to destroy the profitableness of
> that institution. The capitalist system must go and its going must be hastened by
> the workers themselves.

Challenge was, perhaps, the least restrained of the radical publications. It had no
theory of reform like the *Messenger.* It made a direct appeal to the emotions. It assaulted,
not the class-line, but the colour-line; and so spoke a language that the great majority
understood. Its editor, William Bridges, was master of a rhythmic, impassioned prose
that possessed the power of stirring masses of people. In the use of this sort of instrument he has been surpassed by few, if any, pamphleteering champions of a cause in this
country. In one of his editorials, in which he sought to bring about a union of forces
and a united front on the part of American Negroes and West Indians, he said:

There is no West Indian slave, no American slave; you are all slaves, base, ignoble slaves.

There is no more love in the hearts of the British statesmen when passing laws to curtail the liberties of their black subject than there is in the hearts of Americans when passing similar laws to abridge the liberties of theirs.

West Indian Negroes, you are oppressed. American Negroes, you are equally oppressed. West Indians, you are black. Americans, you are equally black. It is your color upon which white men pass judgment, not your merits, nor the geographical line between you. Stretch hands across the seas, with the immortal cry of Patrick Henry: "Give me Liberty or Give me Death."

Prayer will not do all. White men expect to keep you in eternal slavery through superstitions that they have long cast off. They delight in seeing you on your knees. They mean to remain on their feet. They want your eyes kept on the gold in heaven. They mean to keep their eyes on the gold of the world. They want you to seek rest beyond the grave. They mean to have all the rest this side of it.

Can't you see that with every tick of the clock and every revolution of the eternal sun your chains are fastened tighter? You are cursed with superstition and ignorance. You are not taught to love Frederick Douglass, L'Ouverture, Dessalines, and Tubman. You are always taught to love George Washington, Wm. Pitt, Abraham Lincoln, and Wm. Gladstone. . . .

West Indians, the only things you are wanted and permitted to do that white men do is worship the king and sing "Britannia Rules the Waves," no matter if Britannia rules you more sternly than she ever does the waves.

Americans, the only thing that you are wanted and are permitted to do that white men do is to be loyal and sing, "The Star Spangled Banner," no matter how many Southern hillsides are spangled with the blood of many another innocent Negro. . . .

Negroes of the West Indies and America, Unite! Slavery is just as bad under a king as under a president. We don't want white wives; we don't want to dine in the homes of white men; we don't want the things they have acquired; but by the eternal God that reigns on high listen to the rhythmic voice of the New Negro ringing at the court gates of kings and presidents like a raging tempest wind, furious as a curse of Hell, valorous, determined, unafraid, crying: "Give Us Liberty or Give Us Death."

In each issue of the magazine there was printed "An Oath," which the report of the Lusk Committee listed as "another typical example of inflammatory propaganda." The oath read:

BY ETERNAL HEAVEN—

I swear never to love any flag simply for its color, nor any country for its name.

The flag of my affections must rest over me as a banner of protection, not as a sable shroud.

The country of my patriotism must be above color distinctions, must be one of laws, not of men; of law and not lawlessness, of LIBERTY and not BONDAGE, of privilege to all, not special privilege to some.

Kaiser is not the only word synonymous with IMPERIALISM, TYRANNY, MURDER, and RAPINE.

PRESIDENT AND KING are not the only words synonymous with DE-MOCRACY, FREEDOM, PROGRESS.

I shall love not names but deeds. I shall pay homage to any and all men who strive to rid the world of the pestilential diseases of WAR, PREJUDICE, OP-PRESSION, LYNCHING.

I am a Patriot.

I am not merely of a Race and a Country, but of the World.

I am BROTHERHOOD.

These journals shook up the Negroes of New York and the country and effected some changes that have not been lost; but able as were most of the men behind them, as radicals, they failed almost wholly in bringing about any co-ordination of the forces they were dealing with; perhaps that was to be expected. This post-war radical move-ment gradually waned—as it waned among whites—and the organs of the movement, one by one, withered and died. The *Messenger,* which continued to be published up to last year, was the longest-lived of them all. The *Negro World* is still being published; but it falls in a classification distinctly its own.

The Harlem radicals failed to bring about a correlation of the forces they had called into action, to have those forces work through a practical medium to a definite objective; but they did much to prepare the ground for a man who could and did do that, a man who was one of the most remarkable and picturesque figures that have ap-peared on the American scene—Marcus Garvey.

The Participation of Negroes in World War I*

Emmett J. Scott

INTRODUCTION

The American Congress declared war upon Germany April 6, 1917, World War I. It declared war on Japan December 8, 1941 by vote of 82–0 in the United States Senate and by vote of 388–1 in the United States House of Representatives. On December 11, 1941 the Senate and House passed resolutions declaring a state of war existed between Germany and the United States and the United States and Italy. The Senate vote on the German resolution was 88–0; and 90–0 on the Italian resolution. In the House of Representatives the vote on the German resolution was 393–0; and on the Italian resolution, 399–0, World War II. Thus, twice in twenty-four years, the American people have found themselves facing the ruthless hostility of Germany and those associated with her in two wars which have come to be referred to as World War I and World War II.

The historical background of the causes of both of these conflicts is to be found in rooted racial hatreds, the international jealousies of peoples, rulers and dictators; and, primarily, the barbaric tyrannies of a self-called Master Race seeking the subjection and destruction of those governments and peoples that set themselves in opposition to such programs of subjection and destruction under the might of the arch enemy of civilized mankind.

Curiously enough, the United States was not directly a party to the contentions and resentments which finally brought on either of these wars. Yet, drawn by inescapable forces, it was compelled to enter both by broadminded sympathies which, long beforehand, had been resolutely expressed by outraged public opinion. The forces of aggression, seeking the domination of the world, have never been highly regarded by

* From Emmett J. Scott, "The Participation of Negroes in World War I: An Introductory Statement," *Journal of Negro Education,* XII (Summer, 1943), pp. 288–94, 295–97. Reprinted by permission.

our nation. Founded upon idealistic principles as declared in our Declaration of Independence, our Federal Constitution, and our Bill of Rights, a nation of freedom-loving people could not complacently sit by the wayside as treaties were regarded as scraps of paper, when innocent, independent nations were being atrociously outraged and subjected to every possible barbarity in the catalog of infamy by the Central Powers in World War I, and the enemy countries following the same pattern in World War II.

All of the catchwords of democracy, liberty, and freedom have been invoked in both wars to stir the emotions of the American people—"a fight for humanity," "equality," "republicanism against absolutism," "the rights and self-determination of small nations," "to make the world safe for democracy." Oppressed peoples were to be freed by us and our Allies in World War I. How the war came to America in 1917, a survey of the events leading up to World War I, has been set forth by the writer in his *The American Negro in the World War.*[1]

The causes which have brought us into conflict with the barbarous German Reich, bullying Italy, and treacherous Japan, World War II, are a part of contemporary history.

The slogans, catchwords, and shibboleths of 1917 have again been invoked in connection with World War II. The patriotism of the American Negro, always deeply stirred, has responded to these catchwords, to every call of the Government for man- and woman-power, and for investment in Government securities; to the appeals of the Red Cross (despite its flagrant discriminations and insults to the manhood and womanhood of the race), and of the Salvation Army, the Knights of Columbus, and nearly every other patriotic organization; and to every other effort that will give force and effect to our will to win an all-out victory over our enemies.

In truth, the American Negro, suffering under the burdens of second-degree citizenship, was aflame in 1917 as he is in World War II to play a significantly important part in any war for the destruction of oligarchies which deny him the full-rounded citizenship he has won on every battlefield as a member of the armed forces when the country has been in peril, in the world of industry, on plantation and farm, and in the performance of the varied activities of his normal life. It was for these reasons that American Negroes in World War I eagerly went to Europe to fight for the liberation of oppressed peoples.

NUMBER AND CLASSIFICATION OF NEGROES IN WORLD WAR I

The Tables of Organization drafted under the Selective Service Law passed May 18, 1917 called for the registration of 367,710 colored men. An amazing performance was the classification in Group I of 51.65 per cent of colored men registered; while only 32.53 per cent of whites were put in Class I. The Provost Marshal General offered more or less elaborate explanations of the reasons for the high figures for colored registrants

[1] Emmett J. Scott, *The American Negro in the World War.*

in Class I, but they did not seem at the time, and they do not seem now, to be tenable reasons. However, in his final report, discussing "The Negro in Relation to the Draft," he referred in terms of almost fulsome praise to the part played by Negroes in the world drama which came to an end with the signing of the Armistice on November 11, 1918:

> His race furnished its quota, and uncomplainingly, yes, cheerfully. History, indeed, will be unable to record the fullness of his spirit in the war, for the reason that opportunities for enlistment were not opened to him to the same extent as to the whites. But enough can be gathered from the records to show that he was filled with the same feeling of patriotism, the same martial spirit, that fired his white fellow citizen in the cause for world freedom.

Of the nearly 400,000 colored men who were called to the Colors, World War I, 200,000 were sent across the seas to fight on foreign soil.

After considerable controversy and persuasion, the War Department agreed to establish an Officers' Training Camp at Des Moines, Iowa, authorized on May 19, 1917. On October 14, 1917 commissions were awarded at Des Moines to 639 officers—106 Captains, 328 First Lieutenants, 204 Second Lieutenants. Two others served as Majors in the 92nd Division, Major Milton T. Dean, and Major Adam E. Patterson. These officers were ordered to report, after fifteen days' leave, to the following camps where they were sent in equally divided groups: Camp Funston, Kansas; Camp Dodge, Iowa; Camp Grant, Illinois; Camp Sherman, Ohio; Camp Meade, Maryland; Camp Dix, New Jersey; Camp Upton, New York. (Colored draftees and colored officers were so distributed that they were always a minority military group at the various camps, in order to obviate racial clashes which the War Department had been led to feel would follow, if there were extra large concentrations at the camps mentioned.) The men trained at the camps here mentioned were afterward organized into the 92nd Division under command of General C. C. Ballou.

Newton D. Baker, Secretary of War, established as a part of his office a Special Assistant to assist and advise with him in connection with problems attendant upon Negro participation in the war. This Special Assistant had ready and personal access to the Secretary at certain stated periods agreed upon in advance. In addition, General Robert I. Rees of the General Staff was assigned as a Liaison Officer between the Office of the General Staff and the Office of the Special Assistant to the Secretary of War. Secretary Baker personally devoted much time and attention to the consideration of many of the problems which arose. He heartily approved, almost invariably, the certain recommendations submitted to him for his general approval which were planned to improve the morale and efficiency of the colored troops, and the civilian population.

This organizational set-up, with six or eight assistants, was thus able to have clear understanding at all times with the offices of the Secretary of War, and of the General Staff, so that there could be decisive interpretations to the Government of the Negro point of view, and from the War Department to the Negro people.

Dean Kelly Miller of Howard University, under date of October 22, '17, in attempting to evaluate the importance of the appointment, stated that:

Secretary Baker in meeting the impending military emergency has laid the basis of a broad and far-reaching statesmanship. I have always contended, and shall always contend, that the fundamental grievance of the Negro against the American people consists in the fact that he is shut out from participation in the making and administering of the laws by which he is governed and controlled. The nation cannot expect that the Negro will always remain an ardent, enthusiastic citizen, eager to play his part, if he is to be forever shut out from equal participation in and protection under the law. It is imposing too great a tax upon the docility even of the Negro, to make him the victim of harshly enforced discriminatory laws and expect that he will forever exhibit this patriotism and loyalty with ecstatic enthusiasm and paeans of joy. The race may rest assured that its interest will be looked after and safeguarded so far as the military situation is concerned as long as Emmett J. Scott sits at the council table.

I regard the appointment of Mr. Scott, as Special Assistant to the Secretary of War, as the most significant appointment that has yet come to the colored race. Other colored men have been appointed to high office under different administrations, but the appointments have been mainly a reward for political service, or representation of a contributing element to party success. Such appointments are altogether worthy and desirable, but they are not supposed to carry with them any particular function affecting the welfare of the colored people. The appointment of Mr. Scott, on the other hand, is for the express purpose of securing the cheerful cooperation of the Negro race in the accomplishment of the greatest task to which our Government has committed itself. This is not merely representation for the sake of political reward, but representation carrying with it the vital governmental function.

The important thing to say is that the Secretary of War, with great understanding and sympathetic appreciation of the difficulties involved, sought to live up to the high expectations expressed in Dean Miller's comment.

NEGRO COMBAT UNITS

The War Department at once set about the organization of Negro Combat Units and, pursuant to War Department orders, the 92nd Division was organized November 29, 1917 from the first contingent of Negro draftees arriving at the various camps and cantonments throughout the United States during the latter part of the month of October 1917. The Staff and Field Officers, officers of the Supply Units, Quartermaster Corps, Engineers' Corps, and of the Artillery Units, with few exceptions, were white. The remainder of the commissioned personnel, comprising about four-fifths of the whole, were colored.

The 92nd Division Units were Division Headquarters, Headquarters Troop, 349th Machine-gun Battalion, Divisional Trains at Camp Funston, Ft. Riley, Kansas; 366th Regiment of Infantry, Camp Dodge, Des Moines, Iowa; 365th Regiment of Infantry and 350th Machine-gun Battalion at Camp Grant, Rockford, Illinois; the 317th

Engineers Regiment, 317th Engineers Train and the 325th Field Signal Battalion at Camp Sherman, Chillicothe, Ohio; 368th Regiment of Infantry and 351st Field Artillery at Camp Meade, Annapolis Junction, Maryland; the 349th Field Artillery, 350th Field Artillery and 317th Trench Mortar Battery at Camp Dix, Wrightstown, New Jersey; and the 367th Regiment of Infantry, 351st Machine-gun Battalion at Camp Upton, Yaphank, New York. Aside from these, the other combat units were the 369th Infantry —the "Old 15th" of New York; the 370th Infantry—the "Old 8th," Illinois; and the 371st and 372nd Infantry, composing the main body of fighting groups which made up the 93rd Division.

The story of their exploits, of honors won, and of the especially fine manner in which they carried themselves, could not successfully be discounted, in the light of their performances, although, viciously and violently, efforts were made by certain high-ranking military "experts" to do so.

Happily, from one point of view, it is well that the 369th Infantry Regiment— the "Old 15th" of New York—, the 370th Infantry Regiment—the "Old 8th" of Illinois—, and the 371st and 372nd Regiments were brigaded during their active service overseas with French troops. In this way they escaped the traditional prejudices, sneers, and insults of those officials of American military units who looked with disfavor upon the employment of Negroes as combat troops and who sought to carry their jaundiced opinions to France and impress them on the French people. The narration of the praises and the honors paid these Regiments which were brigaded with the French is set forth in detail in the individual histories of the several Regiments and by the author of this article in his *American Negro in the World War.*

The organization of combat units for World War II has not as yet been made altogether clear. An attempt to secure precise information has not been too successful. A study of "The Negro in the Army," especially prepared for a conference of Negro editors and publishers, does not throw much light upon this particular relationship. At Fort Huachuca, Arizona, a full Division of combat troops, the 93rd, was the first colored division activated in World War II. This Division has been sent to Louisiana on maneuvers. It has been succeeded at Huachuca by the 92nd Division, activated at Fort McClellan, Alabama.

I think it fair to say that more places for service in units of Army organizations have been opened to Negroes than was formerly true. This is natural, however, in that the same thing is true of white men as well because of new developments in offensive and defensive warfare. A unit of Negro Marines, it is reported, is already doing overseas duty and others are being trained in artillery, anti-aircraft, communications and other fields. Plans, it is said, call for recruitment up to 10,000 new men. It is also reported that 2,000 Negro Marines are now being trained at New River, North Carolina. The Marine Corps broke a tradition of 167 years when, in June, 1942, it began enlisting colored men as volunteers. Similarly, a minor branch of service has been opened in the Navy Department. Under compulsion, the Navy Department has been forced to admit approximately 6,000 colored men. Flight pursuit units of colored men during World War II have been established, which was not true in World War I. During World War II three ships have been named after notable Negroes—the S. S. *Booker T. Washington,* the S. S. *George W. Carver,* and the S. S. *Frederick Douglass.* These are all triumphs not to be unduly discounted despite the grudging attitude of officials who have had to yield to enlightened public opinion.

RACE RELATIONS

The story of race relations is a long, long one rather well known to those who have made any study of the problem. It appears that the difficulties which arose during World War I are being repeated almost identically during World War II. Many Negro soldiers returned from World War I bitter because of ignominies heaped upon them by American white soldiers who sought to transplant American prejudices and traditions. The colored press, week by week, in World War II, is filled with protests against homefront and battle-front conditions. Efforts are being made to revive the techniques of World War I in turning foreign populations against colored soldiers. The Negro is fighting a war for democracy, and for his dignity as a citizen; and, as a member of the armed forces, he is going to foreign fields to fight the same war all over again. This is carrying a 100 per cent additional burden to what the whites are carrying.

During World War I Secretary Baker held a number of preliminary conferences not only with reference to the establishment of an Officers' Training School, but also with reference to general policies to be followed so as to preserve a close relationship with the Negro population generally and to contribute to unified morale.

In addition, with the approval of the Secretary of War and the Chairman of the Committee on Public Information, George Creel, World War I, a conference of Negro Editors and responsible leaders of the race was called and assembled at Washington. At this time there were formulated certain recommendations which were laid before the President of the United States, the Secretary of War, and the Committee on Public Information.

They were (this group assembled) probably as full and complete a gathering of race leaders[2] devoted to securing positive results as had at almost any time assembled to present the case of the Negro along with his problems, particularly in war time. A three-day session was held, at which the Secretary of War, Mr. Creel, and the then Assistant Secretary of the Navy, Franklin D. Roosevelt, now President of the United States, were present, along with many other Government officials. There was no reser-

---

[2] Included in this representation were such outstanding and uncompromising persons as:

Charles W. Anderson, *U. S. Internal Revenue Collector of New York City;* Archibald H. Grimke of the District of Columbia; *Former Governor* P. B. S. Pinchback of Louisiana; William H. Steward of Kentucky; John C. Dancy; Harry C. Smith of Ohio; R. R. Moton of Alabama; *Judge* Robert H. Terrell, James A. Cobb, and W. L. Houston of Washington, D.C.; W. E. DuBois; Dr. A. M. Curtis of the District of Columbia; Dr. Sumner A. Furniss of Indiana; Henry Allen Boyd of Tennessee; George W. Harris and Fred R. Moore of New York; Robert E. Jones, now Bishop of the Methodist Episcopal Church; John H. Murphy of Maryland; Christopher J. Perry of Pennsylvania; Ernest Lyon of Maryland, Benjamin J. Davis of Georgia; Charles N. Love and W. E. King of Texas; Dr. Walter H. Brooks of the District of Columbia; Robert S. Abbott of Illinois; Ralph W. Tyler of Ohio; Nelson Crews of Missouri; John R. Hawkins of North Carolina and the District of Columbia; and many other notables of like prominence and influence.

vation of thought and opinion on the part of the participants. Government officials and participants spoke with equal candor. In addition, there was organized a group of speakers who were utilized by the Red Cross, Y.M.C.A., the Treasury Department, and by other agencies of that character. This group was organized as a Committee of One Hundred. It was made up of well prepared and thoroughly trained men representing practically every organization of Negroes in the United States, persons having undisputed influence among Negroes of all classes. Zones of activity were worked out and men of varying qualifications were given assignments. Reports were made by members of this Committee of One Hundred from time to time on the state of public feeling in their sections. These reports were digested and extracts placed before the Secretary of War, the General Staff, and officials of the Government filling positions relating in any way to colored civilians.

This Committee also cooperated with Herbert Hoover who was then Food Administrator and who had as a Field Worker and Assistant, Ernest T. Attwell. Mr. Attwell instituted a similar program with headquarters at the Food Administration Organization.

PUBLIC RELATIONS

During World War I recommendation was made to the Secretary of War that a trained newspaper writer of Negro extraction should be sent to France with instructions to report on the life and activities of Negro soldiers, in order that the Negro press of America might be furnished with first hand, accurate information for their readers of the precise conditions under which colored soldiers were working and fighting in France. After conference with George Creel, Chairman of the Committee on Public Information, the recommendation was approved and Ralph W. Tyler of Columbus, Ohio, a former newspaper man,[3] as well as a former auditor of the Navy Department, was accredited as a War Correspondent to supply information on conditions surrounding colored troops in France and to make reports of the activities and engagements in which colored soldiers were playing a part. Mr. Tyler was attached to the staff of General John J. Pershing, Commander in Chief of the American Expeditionary Force.

Mr. Tyler's reports came to the Office of the Special Assistant and were mimeographed and mailed to all of the colored newspapers, as well as to members of the Committee of One Hundred, already referred to, as material for addresses. At the same time a considerable mailing list was built up, so that officers of the Government might have these reports too.

By the time of World War II many of our colored newspapers had grown enterprising enough and were economically able to send their own correspondents at their own expense, with the approval of the War Department. For instance, the *Pittsburgh Courier* and its group of papers are served by Edgar T. Rouzeau and Randy O. Dixon; the *Afro-American* chain of newspapers is served by Ollie Stewart; the *Chicago Defender*

---

[3] Mr. Tyler had for 17 years served in various departments of the Columbus *Evening Dispatch* and the *Ohio State Journal.*

is served by David Orro; the *Norfolk Journal and Guide,* by Thomas P. Young. Aside from these correspondents who are serving overseas, these newspapers also have their special correspondents who travel from camp to camp and report on conditions in this country while men are undergoing preparation for overseas operation.

COLORED WOMEN FOR WAR SERVICE

One of the outstanding high lights of World Wars I and II is the patriotic service of colored women who have not hesitated to shoulder every burden possible in order to promote Negro morale. They have been vocal in denouncing the tragedy inherent in our own race prejudices and traditions in America with respect to the Negro, which prejudices and traditions run so counter to the professed ideals proclaimed by the Congress of the United States, the President of the United States in his "Four Freedoms," and all of the other high sounding pronouncements of that character. To catalog a list of these services would simply be to describe definite, constructive, far-reaching work being done in almost every community in the land.

•   •   •

NEGROES IN WAR INDUSTRY

The same long and protracted struggle of World War I is being repeated during World War II. Public opinion has forced the employment of large groups of colored men into many of the major industrial plants of the country.

Negro migration, on a scale almost unheard of and at first almost unheralded, was under way before the South awakened in 1917 and 1918 to the fact that the hitherto dependable Negro labor group was migrating to the North. Every conceivable type of opposition was instituted from municipal and state legislation to petty persecutions, but the onward march of these Negro laborers was not in the slightest degree halted. During World War I the American Federation of Labor was unwilling to break down its "regulations," preventing Negroes from becoming members. The restricted membership of the American Federation continues now as it existed during World War I.

Dr. George E. Haynes, Professor of Social Sciences at Fisk University, Nashville, Tennessee, was called to Washington by the Secretary of Labor, World War I, to make a scientific study of Negro labor and to establish an organization for its direction. State Councils of National Defense, Chambers of Commerce, the United States Employment Service, social welfare organizations, and personnel officers of industrial plants were approached, looking to wider employment of the valuable Negro group.

World War II has been repetition of the first World War, except that the techniques of pressure in opposition have been applied more drastically and larger and more important results have been secured. The President's Executive Order No. 8802 has been widely published and a Fair Employment Practices Committee (FEPC) was appointed, though with no arbitrary or legal power to enforce its demands. The Negro press, the various national organizations of the race, supported by enlightened editors of white magazines and white organizations, joined in the effort to force this larger employment and to absorb the great Negro unemployment situation which had existed throughout the depression.

At first only token employments were granted. At this time, however, under the force of public opinion and the needs of industry, thousands upon thousands of Negroes are now being employed at wages far beyond any previously earned. Probably, the most significant event was the announcement on May 27, 1942 by the Sun Shipbuilding Company at Chester, Pennsylvania, of its intention to open the way for 9,000 colored men to be employed in shipbuilding crafts. At that time, of 20,000 employees, only 2,000 were Negroes. As of June 1, 1943, more than 15,000 were employed in the four yards of the Company, with the larger proportion of these men and women distributed throughout the three "older" yards. Many aircraft factories and others holding Government contracts are using Negro labor to a larger extent than ever before.

GETTING A SQUARE DEAL

Neither the Negro soldier nor the Negro civilian population received a square deal during World War I, nor for many months succeeding. At one time the Negro population was very greatly depressed by reason of the many injustices being visited upon Negro soldiers overseas and in Army camps in the United States.

The Negro population was apprised of these injustices by articles and editorials, by reports of war correspondents which appeared in the Negro press, and by other publications based upon information received from letters of criticism written by colored soldiers and officers, by chaplains, Y.M.C.A. secretaries, special investigators and others concerned with conditions among Negro soldiers in camps at home and overseas. In many cases, criticisms were based upon official orders, both at home and abroad, issued in the form of official directives seeking to minimize the dignity and importance of Negro soldiers. In World War I, injustices began with many draft boards and extended to the battlefields of France. Grave questions arose in France with reference to the effort to discredit Negro officers and to exalt the efficiency of Negro soldiers when led by white officers. These discriminations took many forms and ran the gamut from gross brutality to sneering tolerance and lukewarm acceptance of Negro soldiers as fighting men.

The civilian population suffered no less than the soldiery. Colored medical officers, colored nurses and workers in Government departments at Washington suffered under discrimination on a par with present-day treatment and disdain.

Elsewhere in a somewhat extended statement I have attempted to answer the question, "Did the Negro Soldier Get a Square Deal," during World War I? An attempt was also made to set forth the advantages gained by the Negro as a result of the war.[4]

Despite the harsh treatment meted out on many sides, there nowhere appeared in the Negro press or in any publication of the country suggestions of anything less than the most complete loyalty to the United States. Necessarily, the morale of colored

[4] Emmett J. Scott, *op. cit.,* pp. 426–470.

Americans was affected from time to time by reason of unworthy and undeserved mistreatment and barbaric outrages during the war and immediately succeeding it, in riots at Washington, Chicago, New Orleans, East St. Louis, and New York.

The Negro, as has been proved, is willing to do his full share of fighting. Official records indicate that he, when called upon, will do more than his proportionate share. Under the administration of the Draft Act, 1917–18, he contributed 13.8 per cent to the total colored and white inductions from June 5, 1917 to November 11, 1918, while he represented only 10.7 per cent of the total population of the country at that time.

It is worthy of note that the most important publications in the country, North and South, contained editorials and articles reporting the outrageous treatment of colored groups both in the Army and as a part of the civilian population. Negro morale remained unshaken to the end, however, and disloyalty was never a charge leveled against the Negro population. Colonel Campbell C. Johnson's article, this volume, will adequately describe, I am sure, conditions under the Selective Service Act, World War II.

To paraphrase Lincoln at Gettysburg when, in referring to the establishment of the American Republic, he called attention to the fact that our forefathers had established upon this continent a new nation, conceived in liberty and dedicated to the proposition that all men are created equal: We are engaged in a great global war (as we were engaged in a great civil war when Lincoln spoke). We are now testing (as we were in 1861–65) whether this nation or any nation so dedicated and so consecrated can long endure without a healthy respect for the ideals of the democracy we profess and too seldom practice.

There are many struggles still ahead of the Negro people. As I have said elsewhere: This constant struggle of the Negro to establish himself as a serious factor in American life must become a reality. His plight is so serious that the Negro calls for a willing and ungrudging abandonment of every hindrance likely to interfere with the victory of American arms, and that oneness of spirit which triumphs over racial barriers, intolerances and bigotries of every kind and character.

In 1917–1918, we were waging a war then as now against ideals of racial superiority. The inalienable right to equality of opportunity was not only fought for in 1917–1918 but is being fought for now. The immorality of present-day discriminations, prejudices and hates is recognized by thoughtful men and women throughout the world. The Kaiserism of 25 years ago is reincarnated in the Hitlerism of 1941–1943. It must be crushed.

Documents of the War[*]

William E. B. Du Bois

FRENCH MILITARY MISSION
Stationed with the American Army
August 7, 1918.

SECRET INFORMATION CONCERNING BLACK AMERICAN TROOPS

1. It is important for French officers who have been called upon to exercise command over black American troops, or to live in close contact with them, to have an exact idea of the position occupied by Negroes in the United States. The information set forth in the following communication ought to be given to these officers and it is to their interest to have these matters known and widely disseminated. It will devolve likewise on the French Military Authorities, through the medium of the Civil Authorities, to give information on this subject to the French population residing in the cantonments occupied by American colored troops.

2. The American attitude upon the Negro question may seem a matter for discussion to many French minds. But we French are not in our province if we undertake to discuss what some call "prejudice." American opinion is unanimous on the "color-question" and does not admit of any discussion.

The increasing number of Negroes in the United States (about 15,000,000) would create for the white race in the Republic a menace of degeneracy were it not that an impassable gulf has been made between them.

As this danger does not exist for the French race, the French public has become accustomed to treating the Negro with familiarity and indulgence.

This indulgence and this familiarity are matters of grievous concern to the Americans. They consider them an affront to their national policy. They are afraid that contact with the French will inspire in black Americans aspirations which to them [the whites] appear intolerable. It is of the utmost importance that every effort be made to avoid profoundly estranging American opinion.

Although a citizen of the United States, the black man is regarded by the white

---

* From William Edward Burghardt Du Bois, collector, "Documents of the War," *Crisis*, XVIII (May 1919), 16–21. Reprinted by permission.

American as an inferior being with whom relations of business or service only are possible. The black is constantly being censured for his want of intelligence and discretion, his lack of civic and professional conscience and for his tendency toward undue familiarity.

The vices of the Negro are a constant menace to the American who has to repress them sternly. For instance, the black American troops in France have, by themselves, given rise to as many complaints for attempted rape as all the rest of the army. And yet the [black American] soldiers sent us have been the choicest with respect to physique and morals, for the number disqualified at the time of mobilization was enormous.

CONCLUSION

1. We must prevent the rise of any pronounced degree of intimacy between French officers and black officers. We may be courteous and amiable with these last, but we cannot deal with them on the same plane as with the white American officers without deeply wounding the latter. We must not eat with them, must not shake hands or seek to talk or meet with them outside of the requirements of military service.

2. We must not commend too highly the black American troops, particularly in the presence of [white] Americans. It is all right to recognize their good qualities and their services, but only in moderate terms, strictly in keeping with the truth.

3. Make a point of keeping the native cantonment population from "spoiling" the Negroes. [White] Americans become greatly incensed at any public expression of intimacy between white women with black men. They have recently uttered violent protests against a picture in the "Vie Parisienne" entitled "The Child of the Desert" which shows a [white] woman in a "cabinet particulier" with a Negro. Familiarity on the part of white women with black men is furthermore a source of profound regret to our experienced colonials who see in it an over-weening menace to the prestige of the white race.

Military authority cannot intervene directly in this question, but it can through the civil authorities exercise some influence on the population.

(Signed) LINARD

The following document is a specimen of the numerous and continuous requests made by white commanders of colored regiments to get rid of colored officers. It will be noted that at the date of this document was sent Colored officers had had very little chance to prove their efficiency.

G. H. G., A. E. F.

8/25/1918

11440–A124
Headquarters 372nd Infantry
S. P. 179, France
August 24, 1918.

From: The Commanding Officer, 372nd Infantry.

To: The Commanding General, American E. F.

Subject: Replacement of Colored Officers by White Officers.

    1. Request that colored officers of this regiment be replaced by white officers for the following reasons:

    First: The racial distinctions which are recognized in civilian life naturally continue to be recognized in the military life and present a formidable barrier to the existence of that feeling of comradeship which is essential to mutual confidence and *esprit de corp.*

    Second: With a few exceptions there is a characteristic tendency among the colored officers to neglect the welfare of their men and to perform their duties in a perfunctory manner. They are lacking in initiative. These defects entail a constant supervision and attention to petty details by battalion commanders and other senior officers which distract their attention from their wider duties; with harmful results.

    2. To facilitate the desired readjustment of officer personnel it is recommended,

    A. That no colored officers be forwarded to this regiment as replacements, or otherwise.

    B. That officers removed upon recommendation of efficiency boards be promptly replaced by white officers of like grade. But, if white officers are not available as replacements; white officers of lower grades be forwarded instead.

    C. That the opportunity be afforded to transfer the remaining colored combat officer personnel to labor organizations or to replacement units for other colored combat organizations according to their suitability.

    3. Reference letter No. 616–3s written by Commanding General, 157th D. I. on the subject August 21, 1918, and forwarded to your office through military channels.

        (Signed) Herschel Tupes,

        Colonel, 372nd Infantry.

Received A. G. O.

26th Aug., 1918,

G. H. Q., A. E. F.

1st Ind. [Endorsement]

G. H. Q., A. E. F., France, August 28, 1918

—To Commanding Officer, 372nd Infantry, A. E. F.

    1. Returned.

    2. Paragraph two is approved.

    3. You will submit by special courier requisition for white officers to replace officers relieved upon the recommendation of efficiency board.

    4. You will submit list of names of officers that you recommend to be transferred to labor organization or to replacement units for other colored combat organizations; stating in each case the qualifications of the officers recommended.

    By command of General Pershing:

        (Signed) W. P. Bennett,

        Adjutant General.

2nd Ind. [Endorsement.]
Hg. 372nd Infantry, S. P., 179, France,
September 4, 1918—To Commanding General, A. E. F., France.
    1. Requisition in compliance with par. 3, 1st. Ind. is enclosed herewith. Special attention is invited to the filling of two original vacancies by app.

The following letter was sent contrary to military regulations to a U. S. Senator by the man who was Chief of Staff of the colored Ninety-second Division; in other words, by the man who more than any other single person was responsible for the morale and efficiency of this Division. We shall prove later that every essential statement made in this letter against Negro troops is either false or misleading.

Headquarters VI Army Corps
American Expeditionary Forces
Dec. 6, 1918.

My Dear Senator:
    Now that a reorganization of the army is in prospect, and as all officers of the temporary forces have been asked if they desire to remain in the regular army, I think I ought to bring a matter to your attention that is of vital importance not only from a military point of view but from that which all Southerners have. I refer to the question of Negro officers and Negro troops.
    I have been Chief of Staff of the 92nd (Colored) Division since its organization, and shall remain on such duty until it starts its movement in a few days back to the United States, when I go to the 6th Corps as the Chief of the Operation Section of that unit. My position has been such that I can speak from intimate knowledge and what I have to say is based on facts which I know fully and not from secondhand information.
    To start with: all company officers of infantry, machine guns and engineers were Negroes; as were also most of the artillery lieutenants and many of the doctors. Gradually as their incompetence became perfectly evident to all, the engineers and artillery-men, were replaced by white officers. They remained with the infantry until the end, and also with a few exceptions with the machine guns.
    The record of the division is one which will probably never be given full publicity, but the bare facts are about as follows. We came to France in June, were given seven weeks in training area instead of the four weeks in training area usually allotted, then went to a quiet sector of the front. From there we went to the Argonne and in the offensive starting there on September 26, had one regiment in the line, attached to the 38th French Corps. They failed there in all their missions, laid down and sneaked to the rear, until they were withdrawn. Thirty of the officers of this regiment alone were re-ported either for cowardice or failure to prevent their men from retreating—and this against very little opposition. The French and our white field officers did all that could possibly have been done; but the troops were impossible. One of our majors com-manding a battalion said "The men are rank cowards there is no other word for it."
    Next we were withdrawn to another defensive sector where we remained until

the armistice; having some minor engagements against any enemy who had no offensive intentions.

During our career, counting the time in America, we have had about thirty cases of rape, among which was one where twenty-two men at Camp Grant raped one woman, and we have had eight (I believe) reported in France with about fifteen attempts besides. There have been any number of self-inflicted wounds, among others one captain.

There have been numerous accidental shootings, several murders, and also several cases of patrols or sentinels shooting at each other. And at the same time, so strict had been the supervision and training that many officers passing through our areas would remark that our men actually had the outer marks of better discipline than the other divisions. They were punctillious about saluting, their appearance was excellent. They kept their animals and equipment in good condition. General Bullard, commanding our Second Army, asked me my estimate and I said they could do anything but fight. They have in fact been dangerous to no one except themselves and women.

In these organizations where we have white company officers, namely the artillery and engineers, we have had only one case of rape. The undoubted truth is that the Colored officers neither control nor care to control the men. They themselves have been engaged very largely in the pursuit of French women, it being their first opportunity to meet white women who did not treat them as servants.

During the entire time we have been operating there has never been a single operation conducted by a colored officer, where his report did not have to be investigated by some field officer to find out what the real facts were. Accuracy and ability to describe facts is lacking in all, and most of them are just plain liars in addition.

The foregoing is just to give you an insight into the facts. Should any effort be made to have Negro officers, or for that matter Negro troops, the career of this division should be asked for; and every officer who has been a field officer of the 92nd Division should be summoned before the Committee to give his experience and opinions. Their statements, based on a year's experience should certainly carry a great deal of weight, and all of them state the same thing, only varying in extremes.

With best wishes, I am

Sincerely yours,
(Signed) Allen J. Greer,
Colonel, General Staff, U. S. A.

Hon. Kenneth D. McKellar,
United States Senate,
Washington, D. C.

The following letter written by a Negro officer to an American friend illustrates the temper and difficulties of the situation in France.

19 Feb., 1919.

I have been hoping that you would be able to drop in on us here before our departure. We are slated to leave here at 4 A. M. on the 21st supposedly aboard the *Aquitania*. It was my desire to talk with you about the offer to officers and men in the A. E. F. to attend a school in France or England. I made application and was shown the endorsement by the Regt. Commander, that the offer did not apply to transient officers. The knowledge was obtained from a telegram received from Hdq. One of our officers went to the Commanding General of this Camp to obtain a copy of the telegram which could not be or was not produced. Capt. —— ———— went in person to the General and requested permission to attend stating that he volunteered for service, left his practise and family at a sacrifice and that he thought the Govt. owed it to him to give him a chance and attend school here. The General took his name and the Organization to which he belongs promising to let him hear from him, but as yet nothing has been done. This Camp is practically a penal institution and prejudice against us is very strong. Some day there is likely to be some grave disturbance here. The conditions are simply awful: mud everywhere, leaky tents and barracks and lack of sufficient and proper toilets. The men are worked quite hard, some at night and others in the day, rain or shine. As a consequence there are quite a number of sick men in our organization. Since our arrival here, the roads have been improved quite a bit (due to the work of the 92nd div.) and you do not have to wade in ankle deep mud. Board walks here to nearly all the tents and barracks. There is so much talk about the rotten conditions that the Camp Officials are making feverish efforts to be ready for the proposed inquiry.

The work of each organization is graded by the Camp Officer in Charge of details and if not satisfactory, the organization may be placed at the bottom of the sailing list or removed temporarily. Commanding Officers of separate units or regiments are practically helpless and if they complain too much against the treatment accorded them, are kept here until the Commanding General sees fit to let them go.

I am beginning to wonder whether it will ever be possible for me to see an American (white) without wishing that he were in his Satanic Majesty's private domain. I must pray long and earnestly that hatred of my fellow man be removed from my heart and that I can truthfully lay claim to being a Christian.

NOTES
The following instances of color discrimination are taken at random from among numbers of similar cases.

This memorandum was sent to the Commanding Officer, 367th Infantry:

1. Company "D" of your organization has been designated by the Central Embarkation Office as a coaling detail for U. S. S. *Virginia*.

2. This detail with all officers and men will report at Naval Surgeon's Office, foot of Rue de Siam, Brest, at 8:30 a. m., February 9, 1919. Detail will march from camp not later than 7 a. m.

3. All equipment and officers' hand baggage will be taken. You will arrange for truck with Camp Transportation Officer Building No. 2, Camp Headquarters. Truck will be furnished at 5 a. m.

4. All embarkation regulation will be followed. The detail will be checked aboard the vessel by an officer from the Central Embarkation Office. *The detail will not return to camp.*

By Command of Brig. General Butler,

L. S. SCHMIDT,
Major A. G., Adjutant.

There was an order issued from the Central Embarkation Office to the effect that when troops were designated as a coaling detail, they would go on board with all regulations for embarkation completed and would not return to camp, but would proceed to the United States on board the ship that they had coaled. When the Executive Officer of the *Virginia* discovered that these troops were Colored, he requested Admiral Halstead to have these Colored troops taken off board, after having coaled the vessel, as it was a precedent in the navy that no Colored troops had ever traveled on board of a United States battleship. This request was then sent by Admiral Halstead to the Central Embarkation Office, and the Colored Troops were placed on board a tug and sent back to Brest. When they arrived in Brest, it was late at night, they had no orders as to where to proceed, were without a place to stay and anything to eat.

Before leaving the ship the Colored commanding officer of the troops received the following letter from the officer under whom the men worked:

U. S. S. *Virginia,*
Brest, France,
11 February, 1919

1. I take pleasure in commending you and the officers and men under your command in connection with the coaling of this ship, and at the same time wish to express my appreciation of the good conduct and the high state of discipline of your command.

H. J. ZIEGMINE,
Captain U. S. Navy,
Commanding.

During November, 1918, Colored Artillery officers were in school at Vannes; a number of dances was given by the French ladies which were called the Franco-American dances. These dances were given for charity and a fee was charged for admission. The Colored Officers, who composed what was known as the 167th Brigade Detachment, attended several of these dances, and were entertained by and danced with the French ladies of the town. The matter was then brought to the attention of General Horn, who was in command of the school, whereupon he issued an order that no officer of the 167th Brigade Detachment would be permitted to attend a dance where a fee was charged. The 167th Brigade Detachment was composed entirely of Colored officers, so that the order referred only to them, but had no effect upon the white officers who were in attendance at the school.

Headquarters, Area "D,"
January 25, 1919.

MEMORANDUM

To C. O. 367th Infantry:

White officers desiring meals in their quarters will have their orderlies report to Lieutenant Williams at the Tent adjoining Area Headquarters for cards to present at Officers' Mess.

All colored officers will mess at Officers' Mess in D-17.

F. M. CRAWFORD,
First Lieutenant Infantry,
Area "D."

HEADQUARTERS FORWARDING CAMP
AMERICAN EMBARKATION CENTER
A. P. O. 766, A. E. F.
January 21, 1919.

MEMORANDUM: No. 229, E. O.

To All Organizations:

1. For your information and guidance.

Program Reference Visit of General Pershing, 9:30 A. M. Arrive Forwarding Camp. All troops possible, except *Colored,* to be under arms.

Formation to be as designated by General Longan. Only necessary supply work and police work to be performed up to time troops are dismissed in order that they may prepare for reception of General Pershing. As soon as dismissed men to get into working clothes and to go to their respective tasks in order that Commander-in-Chief may see construction going on. (Work of altering dry delousing plant not to be interrupted). Colored troops who are not at work to be in their quarters or at their tents. . . . .

By command of

BRIGADIER-GENERAL LONGAN.
RICHARD I. LEVY,
Major, C.A.C., U.S.A. Camp,
Adjutant.

Will every Negro officer and soldier who reads these documents make himself a committee of one to see that the Editor of THE CRISIS *receives documents, diaries and information such as will enable* THE CRISIS *history of the war to be complete, true and unanswerable?*

Back to Africa[*]
Harold R. Isaacs

. . . In 1910 the Niagara group was succeeded by the National Association for the Advancement of Colored People, launched by a group of prominent white and Negro leaders, with Du Bois as its director of research and editor of its organ, *Crisis*. These events marked where the tide changed and a great pressing forward began. The NAACP launched the long struggle for rights through the courts, in the public prints and forums of the nation. Then came the First World War, bringing on its great upheavals and uprootings, its migrations, its mobilizations, and for Negroes its great new hopes of emancipation. Briefly roused, these hopes shriveled at the war's end as the walls of the white American world once more closed in around them. The historic dialogue resumed. The new taker of the ultimate option appeared directly on cue, a caller to the wishful dream, a black West Indian prophet named Marcus Garvey who summoned the weary Negroes of America to stop following after their false white gods and false white hopes and to follow after him, back to black Africa.

MARCUS GARVEY

Marcus Garvey, the "provisional President of Africa," never set foot on African soil and never sent a single Negro migrant back to settle there, but his name stands for the greatest "Back-to-Africa" movement in Negro history. His figure hovers somewhere in the memory of every member of our panel, and echoes of many things he said can be clearly heard now in the words of many who were embarrassed by him while he lived.

Garvey was a Jamaican who came to the United States in 1916. Over his Universal Negro Improvement Association he raised the banner of black-race purity, and he summoned the Negro masses to join him in returning to the African homeland, which he promised to win back for them from its white masters. By 1920 he claimed four million dues-paying members; by 1923, six million. Even his most ardent belittlers admit-

* From Harold R. Isaacs, *The New World of Negro Americans* (New York: The John Day Company, Inc., 1963), pp. 132–46. Copyright © 1963 by Massachusetts Institute of Technology. Reprinted by permission of The John Day Company, Inc.

ted he had hundreds of thousands of followers. He sank most of the money they gave him in his Black Star Steamship Line, which was going to provide the means for returning to the promised land but managed only to founder after a series of costly misadventures. He was convicted of using the mails to defraud in 1923, went to Atlanta Penitentiary in 1925, was pardoned and deported by President Coolidge in 1927, and died obscurely in London in 1940 at the age of fifty-three.

In the brief high years of his career Garvey became an international figure, center of turmoil and controversy, constantly attacked and attacking. European colonial authorities in Africa kept an eye cocked on him from afar and kept his paper, *Negro World*, from entering their precincts. In the United States all the best-known leaders among Negroes and most of the educated, aspiring American Negro middle class reacted strongly against him as a West Indian interloper, a bizarre mountebank, an irresponsible demagogue, a cheat and fraud, a wild dreamer, and, most of all, as a black racist who with brutal tongue and phrase rejected men of mixed descent far more violently than he rejected the whites themselves. But he was also the man who created the most spectacular mass movement seen among Negroes before or since. With his appeal to race pride, he reached into the lowest levels of the Negro masses and won a following that no Negro leader or group, not even the churches, had ever touched before. Instead of pie in the sky, Garvey promised Africa. For a brief flash of time Garvey made it seem that Africa did lie, reachable, at the end of the streets through which his followers marched; the homeland where a new life for the race could begin, where he saw "a new world of black men, not peons, serfs, dogs, and slaves, but a nation of sturdy men making their impress upon civilization and causing a new light to dawn upon the human race."

In his heyday Garvey wrote much and spoke much and was much written about. After his eclipse, his name and history were kept alive by small surviving bands of the faithful. His swift passage across the scene was only briefly noted in the appropriate places in occasional books. Garvey went largely unstudied and unchronicled for nearly a generation after his movement collapsed. Some re-examination of his movement has begun to appear in journal articles and theses in the last ten years or so. The first and so far still the only serious book-length study of him appeared in 1955. It is with material drawn from these sources[25] that we will attempt here to locate Garvey's place in this short history of Negro links to Africa.

In his appeal to Negroes to follow him back to Africa, Marcus Garvey gave his own shape and his own accent to every major theme that had already appeared on this subject in the past, and he added some themes that had never so explicitly been there

---

[25] Edmund David Cronon, *Black Moses, The Story of Marcus Garvey and the Universal Negro Improvement Association* (Madison, Wis., 1955); Robert Hughes Brisbane, Jr., "The Rise of Protest Movements Among Negroes since 1900," unpub. thesis, Harvard University, 1940, and "His Excellency the Provisional President of Africa," *Phylon*, 3rd quarter 1949; Record, "The Negro Intellectual and Negro Nationalism," *op. cit.* These studies provide ample bibliographical notes and footnotes which will lead any interested student back to the living details of the Garvey story. The quotations from Garvey that follow in these pages are, unless otherwise indicated, drawn from these sources.

before. Like all his predecessors in the Moses role, Garvey came offering an escape from despair, and the despair among Negroes in the aftermath of the First World War was as deep as, and perhaps less bearable than, any they had known before. The great sweeping events of the war had enormously dramatized both the rise of new hopes and their collapse. All the magnitudes were large—the movement of people from South to North, from lonely fields and furrows to crowded streets and factories, from smaller communities of known victimizers to the encounter in the great cities with large faceless masses of hostile whites. There was the experience in the armed forces, and for some the journey across the sea, the exposure to a great mass of new impulses and new ideas. The ideas were large too: the war was for freedom, to make the world safe for democracy. Like subject peoples all around the globe, Negroes in America thought this included them. All these hopes and expectations were struck down; the Ku Klux Klan, lynch mobs and rioters rode right over them while the rest of the society simply looked on. Most of the millions of Negroes in the country hugged what cover they could from this storm, as they always had in the past; most of them never even heard of Garvey. But there were other millions in large cities now who did hear of him; great numbers who heard him, and large numbers who stepped out after him when he called.

Like others before him who had seized this ultimate option, Garvey urged his people to leave the white man's land to the white man and to seek a place of their own where the black man could be his own man:

> If you cannot live alongside the white man in peace, if you cannot get the same chance and opportunity alongside the white man, even though you are his fellow citizen . . . then find a country of your own and rise to the highest position within that country . . . [We need] a government, a nation of our own, strong enough to lend protection to the members of our race scattered all over the world, and to compel the respect of the nations and races of the earth.

And the black man's nation, of course, was to be found in Africa, a homeland waiting to be reclaimed from the white men who held it. Garvey summoned up his Negro hosts—he counted them up to an imaginary 400,000,000—to fight for their own home soil:

> If Europe is for the Europeans, then Africa shall be for the black peoples of the world. We say it, we mean it . . . The other races have countries of their own and it is time for the 400,000,000 Negroes to claim Africa for themselves . . . The Negroes of the world say, "We are striking homewards toward Africa to make her the big black republic." And in making Africa a big black republic, what is the barrier? The barrier is the white man, and we say to the white man who now dominates Africa that . . . we mean to retake every square inch of the 12,000,000 square miles of African territory belonging to us by right Divine . . .

Garvey dressed himself and his followers in titles and fancy uniforms, organized them into Royal African Legions and Black Cross Nurses, and marched them through

Harlem. The bizarre show made the white world laugh and sensible Negroes wince, but some of his words stabbed deep into those who could hear him:

> The white man need expect no more Negro blood shed on his behalf. The first dying that is to be done by the black man in the future will be to make himself free [and when this is accomplished] if we have any charity to bestow, we may die for the white man. But as for me, I think I have stopped dying for him.

Garvey called not only for blood, but for *pure* blood. Garvey spoke the language of an all-out black racism. When he called upon his people to reforge their kinship and connection to Africa, Garvey called on *black* men for this, men without white taint. The racist note had been heard in this dialogue from the very beginning, but Garvey made it his central crashing theme. On this score he was bolder and more violent than the strongest-tongued "raceman" who had ever at any time pressed Negroes to meet the racist white man on his own terms. He called for a pure black race to stand by itself apart from a pure white race, and he reserved his most poisonous scorn for Negroes of mixed ancestry, who in his time made up virtually the whole top social and economic layer of the Negro population. Against them, Garvey unhesitatingly aligned himself with the white racists:

> The black and white races are now facing the crucial time of their existence. The whites are rightfully and properly crying out for a pure white race and the proud and self-respecting blacks are crying out for a morally pure and healthy Negro race. Between both we have a new school of thought, advanced by the "near white" or "colored man," W. E. B. Du Bois and his National Association for the Advancement of Colored People, who advocate racial amalgamation or general miscegenation with the hope of creating a new type of colored race by wiping out both black and white.

Garvey's black racism was a deep and vital part of his appeal, perhaps the deepest and most vital of all. It was addressed in the first place to the larger numbers of his fellow West Indians in New York, immigrants who had come out of the profoundly color caste-ridden system in the Caribbean and who formed a considerable part of his core following. But after them, Garvey's ultraracism also directly touched deep chords of response among the lower-class Negroes crowding the war-swollen ghettos of New York and a few other big cities. These people tended to be more commonly black, or at least blacker, than members of the predominantly "mulatto" or lighter-colored middle class. Garvey summoned up in them all the deeply stored resentment, even hatred, created by the American Negro's own deeply imbedded color caste system.

In lighter Negroes Garvey aroused fear and repugnance. They were stung to outrage—often complex and ambiguous—by his attempt to read them out of the race as impure "near whites." All the best-known and most articulate Negroes of the time fell into this category; they stood up against Garvey, fighting the Negro cause as they saw it but fighting also, desperately, for themselves. Under all the blows of the time, these men were suffering their own doubts, ambivalence, and alienation. But Garvey forced them to cling all the harder, despite all the adversity, to the hope for a future based on equal rights in American society. Even where they carried within them their own racial feeling (and who can say that men like Du Bois, A. Philip Randolph, and James Weldon Johnson did not?) Garvey denied it to them because they were not black or not black enough. Even if any one of them had felt the impulse to see if there was indeed any reality in the prospect of an escape to Africa, Garvey cut them off from it; they were not *black* enough. Garvey tied the race and Africa to *blackness,* and in ways deeper than most Negro leaders either knew or would acknowledge, this made him their mortal foe.

These leaders saw Garvey's movement primarily as a mad, capering chimera in which people could only be cruelly deceived and defrauded and the larger Negro cause damaged. Where Garvey also made the matter an issue of race and color in its bluntest and most personal form, he only sharpened and embittered the controversy, and in the fray he forced some notable men to dispute with him on his own terms. Randolph called Garvey a "supreme Negro Jamaican jackass" who had come out of "the mudsill of Jamaican society." In a phrase that Garvey gleefully hugged to himself and repeated to cheering admirers again and again, Du Bois called Garvey that "little fat black man, ugly, but with intelligent eyes and a big head." Garvey retorted that Du Bois was "a mulatto whose white blood despised the black within him." Du Bois, who had his own racial ideas and his own vision of a new Pan-Africa (his first Pan-African Congress had taken place in Europe in 1919), saw the Garvey threat in these terms:

> Here is Garvey yelling to life from the black side a race consciousness which leaps to meet Madison Grant, Lothrop Stoddard and other worshippers of the great white race. . . . If with a greater and more gifted and efficient Garvey, it sometimes blazes into real flame, it means world war and eternal hate and blood.

Partly under the pressure of his opponents—who successfully put the law on him—but mostly by his own actions, Garvey brought his own movement crashing down. He punctured much of his appeal and showed his essential lack of contact with American Negroes by carrying his racism to the point of making public common cause with the Ku Klux Klan. He approved its white racism; it supported his plan to take the blacks back to Africa. But even among his West Indian followers, to whom the Klan was perhaps a less meaningful symbol, the high emotion generated by his demagogy and showmanship began to need more substantial nourishment. There was some excitement in the sailings of two vessels which got to the Caribbean but never to Africa. But the Black Star Line soon went down in a storm of wild mismanagement. Garvey's high-handedness and lack of touch with reality finally overtook him. He went to prison, and his organization fell apart into fragments. The larger masses which had sought relief or escape through Garvey were forced to seek it elsewhere.

Marcus Garvey was well remembered by all but a few of the youngest members of our panel, and even they had heard or read of him. Some of the older and best-known members of the group, like Du Bois and Randolph, were among the most prominent of

Garvey's opponents. Others, like Frazier, had observed him closely at firsthand or had heard him speak, watched his parades, or followed from a distance the controversy about him in the press. Then there were those who had been children in Garvey's time and remembered how their families had reacted. All but a few of these individuals came out of backgrounds that were either already middle class or aspiring to that status or were of clearly mixed descent, and their responses to Garvey were patterned accordingly.

For some the recollection is dominated by the strong feeling about West Indians that ran among American Negroes in those days:

> As a kid I heard about Marcus Garvey. We used to sing a song ridiculing him. It went like this:

> Marcus Garvey is a big black monkey man,
> Marcus Garvey will catch you if he can.
> All you black folks get in line,
> Buy your tickets on the Black Star Line.

Other examples reflect the difference of class and education between those who followed Garvey and those who did not:

> I heard Garvey speak on a few occasions in Cleveland, once at Howard. I was never attracted. There was a certain intellectual snobbery about this. Garvey did not have a literate following and he was given to gaudiness, parades, and fantasy and grand eloquence. I looked down my nose at this sort of thing.

> I remember hearing my father talk about Garvey. He never liked him; thought he was a crook. He laughed about the Back-to-Africa movement . . .

> Among people of education, the idea of going back to Africa has always been absurd . . .

> Garvey was able to attract all Negroes who wore red underwear, I mean the lower class. I was too young or too ignorant to know too much about it . . .

> Garvey attracted frantic, insane people. My brother and I once had to run for our lives when we scoffed at some of them . . .

> The Garvey movement occurred while I was in college. . . . It was the uneducated who fell in line . . . a herd led by a skillful manipulator. . . . This was not for our kind of people, physicians, school-teachers, civil servants . . .

> His appeal was mostly to the lower masses. . . . He was the man who led big parades of ignorant people down the street selling pie in the sky.

Garvey came during my school days. He was much discussed and ridiculed in my family. He was playing into the hands of the Bilbos; he was unrealistic. He assumed we were not first and last of all Americans. My folks went too far back in Washington and Virginia to be interested in the Garvey movement . . .

For many the stronger focus was on the notion of going back to Africa:

I shared my father's views. This was *my* country, and I would rather fight for what I had here than go back to Africa . . .

I know of no well-educated Negro who believed Marcus Garvey was on the right track. Thirty years ago the average Negro with education or any advantages had very little interest in Africa; resented the implication that he should be. The popular phrase was: "I haven't lost anything in Africa and I'm not going there to find it." . . . Most trained Negroes rejected Garveyism as a burlesque act . . .

I rejected the idea of any Negro identification with Africa on a large scale. Any man who talked of Africa as a home for Negroes was simply foolish. It was pure hokum. Most Negro intellectuals looked at it this way. I saw a Garvey parade in Chicago. He wore a yellow cap and rode a horse. I thought he was a mountebank.

Mentioned somewhat less often but running through all these reactions, clearly visible even when it was being unnoticed or unstressed, ran the black thread of color:

It was a black chauvinistic movement . . .

The theory was to unite the Negroes to go black and do black . . .

Garvey was a transplanted black man who wanted to do everything black and establish a black country in Africa. . . . But *this* was *my* country, where *my* people were born . . .

Garvey was able to tear the Negroes apart in this country. He set Negro against Negro, the light against the dark. If he had been efficient and honest, there is no telling where the thing would have gone . . .

There was very little crossing of line then on the color question: black against light, West Indian against American, Garvey against Du Bois . . .

The Garvey story was clearly more than just a bizarre episode, and Garvey himself something more than a race-mad clown. He linked himself to ideas and emotions that have had a continuing relevance: Africa, the Negro's relationship to it, and the Negro's view of himself.

For one thing, Garvey made himself the first prophet of a free Africa. "I know no national boundary where the Negro is concerned," he proclaimed. "The whole world is my province until Africa is free." Whether addressing his West Indian followers or Americans, or in the last years in London, where young African expatriates were within hearing, Garvey never abandoned the messianic note: "No one knows when the hour of Africa's redemption cometh," he proclaimed. "It is in the wind. It is coming. One day, like a storm, it will be here." To some Africans his words came as a summons. One of his readers, for example, was a young African named Kwame Nkrumah studying in the United States in the late 1930's who later wrote: "Of all the literature I studied, the book that did more than any other to fire my enthusiasm was *The Philosophy and Opinions of Marcus Garvey.*" [26]

Barely twenty years later Nkrumah became head of the first of the new African republics. In December 1958 he opened the first All-African People's Congress at Accra with a tribute to Garvey, and when his new black state established its own fleet of merchant ships, he called it the Black Star Line.

What Garvey made Africa mean to the Negroes in America who briefly listened to him is still another matter. He summoned black men to rise with him and go back to Africa. He cast his words upon the winds, and the response came pouring in upon him in great human tides and floods of money. Yet no migration ever took place, nor did Garvey ever apparently make any serious moves toward launching one. He did send a probing mission to Liberia. (One individual I interviewed remembered that his brother had been a member of that mission. "He nearly stole Liberia for $50,000," he said.) But the would-be vanguard of the Garveyite mass was repulsed. The Liberians wanted no part of an invasion of freedom-seeking kinsmen from America led by a half-mad Jamaican prophet. No plans for anyone's actual return to Africa ever moved beyond this point; in Garvey's program the central theme, Back-to-Africa, remained pure fantasy. It was "not that he was a conscious liar," observed Du Bois in 1923, "but dream, fact, fancy, wish were all so blurred in his thinking that neither he himself nor his hearers could clearly extricate them." It was this fantastic quality, among other things, that led Ralph Bunche, in a study he made in 1940 for Gunnar Myrdal, to the view that Garveyism had been pure escapism, a large movement because there was a large desire for escape, but not to be taken seriously as a sign of the readiness of Negroes to go back to Africa.[27]

Garvey presumably meant himself to be taken quite literally when he spoke of the return to Africa, but apparently few of his followers did so. Even of Garvey's West Indian immigrant following, Claude McKay wrote:

---

[26] Kwame Nkrumah, *Ghana* (New York, 1957), p. 45.

[27] Garvey's widow, Amy Jacques Garvey, offered this interpretation in 1960: "As a matter of fact, the term Back-to-Africa was used and promoted by newspapers, Negro newspapers mostly, to ridicule Garvey. There was no Back-to-Africa movement except in a spiritual sense." "The Ghost of Marcus Garvey," *Ebony,* Mar. 1960.

They gave Garvey all the money he needed to institute his programme. But only an infinitesimal few of these people really desired to go—*back to Africa*. And obviously Marcus Garvey himself had no intention of going back to live in some corner of the vast land of his ancestors. But Back-to-Africa on a Black Star Line was magical propaganda.[28]

Perhaps what most of his listeners heard was a man calling them back to themselves, to stop forever seeing themselves in the white man's eye. As E. Franklin Frazier, then a young but already sharp-eyed observer of Negro life, remarked at the time: Garvey made people "feel like somebody among white people who have said they were nobody."

One of Garvey's attorneys at his trial tried to express a similar idea to the jury:

If every Negro could have put every dime, every penny into the sea, and if he might get in exchange the knowledge that he was somebody, that he meant something in the world, he would gladly do it. . . . The Black Star Line was a loss in money, but it was a gain in soul.[29]

Among all those I interviewed there were barely half a dozen who had either positive recollections about the Garvey movement or positive afterthoughts about it. These were in every case attached not to the Back-to-Africa theme or the color issue (these were minimized, indistinctly remembered or just "forgotten") but rather this element of pride in self. Here are three examples all from individuals of West Indian background who were children in Garvey's time:

My mother was a member of the UNIA. As a child I went to meetings with her. . . . I have no recollection of the color issue in connection with the Garvey time. . . . I don't think my mother ever seriously thought of going to Africa. She had no deep or burning desire to do anything like that. I think she joined the Garvey movement to get identity. She was an alien accepted by nobody, neither the Negroes nor the whites . . .

I was just a youngster and I was excited by the parades and the ritual. I only got a little of the content. It was glorious and uplifting for the Negro. I never even thought about the idea of going back to Africa. My people were already immigrants and certainly weren't thinking of making another move . . .

My mother was an intense Garveyite. She bought stock in it. I was very young and to me it meant excitement, fervor. I went to meetings with my mother to Liberty Hall. . . . She lost money in its ventures and was disillusioned, but not

[28] Claude McKay, *Harlem: Negro Metropolis* (New York, 1940), p. 150.
[29] Quoted in Ottley, *New World A-Coming*, p. 79.

in the principles involved. She kept a certain pride in it, and still does. The Back-
to-Africa part was not important. Pride was. Negroes should have something of
their own. And the blackness, this was not taken literally, as far as I can recall.
My mother isn't black. I don't recollect this part of it. All my memory of the
Garvey movement is positive. My mother's explanations, seeing the parades, my
mother's reproduction of the black Christ and the brown dolls.

But there is no way, even by the most selective kind of remembering, to get away
from the central theme in Garvey's appeal: in calling them back to Africa, back to
themselves, he was calling them back to their *blackness.* " 'Negro, Black, and Africa,' the
magic words repeated again and again," wrote McKay, "made Negroes delirious with
ecstasy." [30] Garvey did not mean this only symbolically, although many no doubt took
it that way and some of his lieutenants were far from black themselves. Garvey was not
merely summoning Negroes from the false lure of white values, white ways, white
cruelties. He meant it literally; he dreamed of a pure black race regaining a proud posture in the world, and he had as much contempt for "race mixers" as the most fanatic
white racist, and even more contempt for those whose race had already been mixed
beyond repair.

Garvey's brutal assault on the issue of color among Negroes forced it out onto
the surface of things where it had rarely been seen before. He dramatized it, deliberately
setting dark Negro against light Negro. By bringing them out into the open in their
most blatant and dangerous form, Garvey forced a certain change in the currency of
these prejudices though not in ways that he intended. The inner shame over blackness
was by no means exorcised but after Garvey it was never again quite the same as it had
been. It can be said that the beginning of the crumbling of the old color caste really
began from this time in the 1920's, because Garvey made so many more people so much
more sharply aware of the cleavage and of its cost. Color caste attitudes after that were
much less flagrantly held or expressed. Leaders of Negro protest movements in the
years after Garvey were made especially conscious of this problem and tried more strenuously than ever before to close the gap between themselves and the masses of darker
people below, and thereby to broaden the base of struggle for civil rights.

On the other hand, Garvey drove Africa still further away beyond the American
Negro's horizon. He did this partly by making Africa seem such an ephemeral dream
that the same emotions that had led many people to him guided them afterward to Father Divine, a newly risen religious cultist who said he was God and whose Kingdom
was made to look much closer than Garvey's Africa. Garvey also accomplished this by
linking the African dream so explicitly to blackness. If the call back to Africa did mean
a call back to blackness, there were simply too many Negroes of irretrievably mixed descent who not only could not respond to the call but desperately did not want to do so.
If any link was ever to be re-established between them and Africa, it would have to be
on some other plane not yet in sight. Meanwhile those Negroes who dreamed the

[30] McKay, *op. cit.,* p. 151.

black-African dream continued to do so only at the fringes of real life, whether it was shaped by Garvey's wild fantasies, by the cult of glorified black primitivism that also flourished in the Harlem Bohemia of the time, or by Du Bois' wider vision of Pan-Africanism.

Du Bois[a] Versus Garvey[*]
Elliott Rudwick

After World War I, large numbers of Negroes were stirred by race pride and demanded a "spiritual emancipation." They were encouraged to seek improvement of their own living conditions and work for the betterment of the natives on the African continent. During this post-war decade two prominent leaders, W. E. B. DuBois and Marcus Garvey, clashed in their separate plans to establish an African state and an international organization of Negroes. Both men were propagandists. DuBois was editor of the *Crisis*, the official magazine of the N.A.A.C.P. and Garvey owned the *Negro World*. (The Jamaican regularly wrote articles for his newspaper and the editorial writers he hired adopted his tone.) The present article is based primarily on a study of these two publications and seeks to examine the DuBois-Garvey debate which—especially from Garveyite quarters—was abusive and acrimonious.

In 1917, DuBois favored the formation of a "great free central African state" (the amalgamation of German East Africa and the Belgian Congo); later, he declared that the state should be enlarged to include Uganda, French Equatorial Africa, German Southwest Africa, and the Portuguese territories of Angola and Mozambique.[1] In his conception, a "Brain Trust" of Negro administrators were to be responsible for the establishment of an "industrial democracy," *i.e.*, a socialized system of production and distribution.[2] In 1919, through the help of Blaise Diagne, a Negro Senegalese representative in the French Chamber of Deputies, DuBois received permission from Prime Minister Clemenceau to organize the First Pan-African Congress in Paris. The delegates (from the United States, West Indies, Europe, and Africa) asked the League of Nations to guarantee political, social, and economic rights to the African natives and set up a legal code for the "international protection" of these people. The League was requested

[a] This study was made possible through a grant from the Albert M. Greenfield Center for Human Relations, Philadelphia.

[*] From Elliott M. Rudwick, "Du Bois versus Garvey: Race Propagandists at War," *Journal of Negro Education*, XXVIII (Fall, 1959), pp. 421–29. Reprinted by permission of author and journal.

[1] *Crisis* XV (1917–1918), p. 114.
[2] *Crisis* XVII (1918–1919), pp. 119–120.

to consider the Africans in "international labor legislation" and to provide for native representation within the organization.

According to the Pan-African Congress, "Negroes of the world demand" that the natives should hold title to all African land which they could "profitably" cultivate. The conclave petitioned for effective controls upon the white capitalists in order to prevent further economic exploitation. The conferees also maintained that the Africans should receive assurances that elementary, vocational, and college education would be available to them.[3] To create international racial unity, DuBois proposed to found the *Black Review* (with English, French, and perhaps Spanish and Portuguese editions). He hoped that American Negroes would learn to speak French and Spanish and he was certain that Negro literature and art would thereby gain momentum in all nations. He suggested that U. S. Negroes should travel to Europe on "*personal rencontres* for information and propaganda."[4] The League paid little attention to DuBois's Pan-African Congress, nor did any other group consider the conclave as "representative of the Negro race." The convention had no real grass roots organizational support; only on paper was the N.A.A.C.P. headquarters concerned and the N.A.A.C.P. branches simply ignored the Pan-African Congress. However, DuBois seemed undaunted and continued to grind out propaganda which was moderate in tone and intellectual in approach.

Unlike DuBois, Marcus Garvey was able to gain mass support and his propaganda had a tremendous emotional appeal. He established the Universal Negro Improvement Association in New York (with branches in many U. S. cities and several foreign countries). The aim of the organization was the liberation of Africa. By 1919, he set up the Black Star Line and the Negro Factories Corporation. In August, 1920, Garvey called a month-long convention of the U.N.I.A. in New York City. In the name of "400,000,000 Negroes of the World," he declared that Africa must be free. He did not bother to display the restraint which characterized Pan-African leaders and many of his remarks were inflammatory. He warned that his race was prepared to shed its blood to remove the whites from the natives' rightful land in Africa.[5] His convention delegates and members paraded through Harlem. Tens of thousands of Negroes were excited by the massed units of the African Legion in blue and red uniforms and the white-attired contingents of the Black Cross Nurses. Garvey's followers sang the new U.N.I.A. anthem, "Ethiopa, Thou Land of Our Fathers" and they proudly waved the Association's flag (black for Negro skin, green for Negro hopes, and red for Negro blood). Never again was the race to have a leader who could produce such a wonderful show.

DuBois publicly ignored Garvey until December of 1920 and this tardiness of editorial recognition was probably due to the *Crisis* editor's ambivalence toward him. DuBois was profoundly impressed by "this extraordinary leader of men," and he acknowledged that Garvey was "essentially an honest and sincere man with a tremendous vision, great dynamic force, stubborn determination and unselfish desire to serve." However, the *Crisis* editor also considered him to be[6]

[3] *Crisis* XVII (1918–1919), pp. 271–274.
[4] *Crisis* XVII (1918–1919), pp. 269–270.
[5] New York *Times,* August 3, 1920. See also, *Negro World,* September 11, 1920.
[6] *Crisis* XXI (1920–1921), pp. 58–60.

dictatorial, domineering, inordinately vain and very suspicious. . . . The great difficulty with him is that he has absolutely no business sense, no *flair* for real organization and his general objects are so shot through with bombast and exaggeration that it is difficult to pin them down for careful examination.

The following month, after DuBois had requested (and failed to receive) a financial statement from the Jamaican on the Negro Improvement Association and the Black Star Line, the *Crisis* editor wrote:[7]

When it comes to Mr. Garvey's industrial and commercial enterprises there is more ground for doubt and misgiving than in the matter of his character.

Originally, DuBois believed that his own hopes for Africa's reclamation and an international black economy could be achieved through Garvey's mass appeal. He concluded that the failure of the Garvey Movement, which had generated so much "spiritual" potential, might seriously damage racial self-confidence. He was impressed by the "bold effort and some success" of the Jamaican, who, after all, had sent ships ("owned by black men") to sea. However, the editor of the *Crisis* announced that Garvey was expending funds for current expenses instead of using the money for capital improvements. (The flamboyant Garvey seemed more interested in public relations than in buying ships.)

Nevertheless, the *Crisis* editor saw a bright future if Garvey was willing to eschew certain tactics which had been employed in the past:

1. Garvey "introduced" the Jamaican black-mulatto schism to the U. S., where DuBois claimed it had no relevance and only bred disunity. (One of DuBois's own errors was that he minimized this conflict.)

2. Garvey alienated the British by his tactlessness, and the help of Great Britain was required in his international trade plans.

3. He did not seem interested in establishing a friendly relationship with the N.A.A.C.P. and went out of his way to antagonize its officials.

4. His relations with the Liberian Government were less than satisfactory, even though he hoped to establish headquarters there.

5. With inadequate material resources, he still made bellicose statements about conquering Africa.

DuBois's comments showed remarkable temperateness in view of the fact that the Garvey Movement had been attacking him for more than a year. Just before the Pan-African Congress in 1919, Garvey alleged that DuBois talked so mildly and equivocally to French reporters about American race relations, that the Jamaican's "High Commissioner" abroad found his own work sabotaged.[8] DuBois denied the accusation. The *Negro World* instructed its readers that the *Crisis* was basically reactionary and was

[7] *Crisis* XXI (1920–1921), pp. 112–115.
[8] *Crisis* XXI (1920–1921), pp. 112–115.

published from an "aristocratic Fifth Avenue" office.[9] After a *Crisis* editorial on Wood-row Wilson's faithlessness, and following a DuBois comment on the post-war imperial-ist resurgence in England, the *Negro World* reminded the N.A.A.C.P. propagandist that Garvey had forseen these developments as early as 1918, when the editor was coun-seling cooperation with the United States Government. DuBois was pictured as a fallen old warrior whose contributions to the race were at an end. With relish the *Negro World* also took up the cry of A. Philip Randolph's *Messenger* that DuBois was "controlled" by white capitalist on the N.A.A.C.P. board.[10] When the *Crisis* editor was awarded the Spingarn Medal in 1920 for "founding" the First Pan-African Congress, Garvey's paper charged that the entire affair was "a discreditable fraud." [11] (The N.A.A.C.P. citation ignored a 1900 Pan-African conclave. By juggling words, DuBois had "founded" the first Congress because he argued that the 1900 organization was called the Pan-African *"Conference."*)[12] As far as Garvey was concerned, the 1919 Pan-African Congress had ac-complished little and he asserted that William Monroe Trotter's National Equal Rights League had contributed more to the race when it presented its petition to the Peace Conference in Paris:[13]

> But perhaps Mr. Villard [one-time N.A.A.C.P. board chairman] and the other gentlemen of the Committee on award regard Mr. Trotter as too radical, perhaps they do not regard him from a white man's point of view as safe and sane a leader as Dr. DuBois.

At the 1920 U.N.I.A. convention, Garvey called the *Crisis* editor "the associate of an alien race," and his remark received "the most enthusiastic applause" of the session. The *Negro World's* editorial reaction to DuBois' lengthy critique was typical: "subtle, shrewd, untruthful in its professed sincerity, cunning and adroit in its attempt to blow hot and cold at the same time." The N.A.A.C.P. propagandist was accused of petty jeal-ousy and of being quite possibly "more of a white man than a Negro and [he] seems to be only a professional Negro at that." Garvey mounted the platform to chide DuBois for ignoring the masses and believing in a "bastard aristocracy." In contrast, the Jamai-can recalled how he "always walked among [his own] ordinary humble people . . . (cheers)." Garvey proved his ability to write demagogic propaganda:[14]

> Where did he [DuBois] get this aristocracy from? He picked it up on the streets of Great Barrington, Mass. He just got it into his head that he should be an aris-tocrat and ever since that time he has been keeping his very beard as an aristo-

[9] *Negro World*, May 24, 1919.
[10] *Negro World*, March 13, April 3, 1920.
[11] *Negro World*, June 19, 1920.
[12] *Crisis* XXI (1920–1921), p. 198.
[13] *Negro World*, June 12, 1920.
[14] *Negro World*, January 8, 1921.

crat; he has been trying to be everything else but a Negro. Sometimes we hear he is a Frenchman and another time he is Dutch and when it is convenient he is a Negro (Derisive cheers and laughter). Now I have no Dutch. I have no French, I have no Anglo-Saxon in me, but I am but a Negro now and always (thunderous applause). I have no Frenchmen to imitate, I have no Anglo-Saxon to imitate; I have but the ancient glories of Ethiopia to imitate. (Great applause.) The men who built the Pyramids looked like me, and I think the best thing I can do is to keep looking like them. Anyone you hear always talking about the kind of blood he has in him other than the blood you can see, he is dissatisfied with something, and I feel sure that many of the Negroes of the United States of America know that if there is a man who is most dissatisfied with himself, it is Dr. DuBois.

In order to demonstrate that displeasure with DuBois was mounting in various quarters of the race, the *Negro World* reprinted several comments and editorials from other Negro papers. The Richmond *Planet* believed that DuBois was much out of his element for having the audacity to reproach Garvey, the "man of action." The Oakland *Sunshine* expressed similar sentiments: "DuBois is talking big things and Garvey is doing big things. We rather admire the man that does rather than talks." According to this newspaper, the N.A.A.C.P. propagandist was hurting the Association by his anti-Garvey campaign. The *Sunshine*'s editor contended that the Garvey organization was larger and more powerful than the N.A.A.C.P. and was dedicated to DuBois's principles of improving the status of Negroes in the United States. The *National Review* took Du-Bois to task for editorializing on Pan-African movements and omitting the U.N.I.A. For this incompleteness, DuBois was dubbed, "king of journalistic jugglers." [15]

The *Negro World* was resentful because of the *Crisis*'s tone of superiority and public omniscience. DuBois was castigated for thinking that Negroes who wanted to start race enterprises were obliged to appear before his inquisition.[16] A Garveyite published a pamphlet in 1921 entitled, "The Mistakes of Dr. W. E. B. DuBois," which was designed to show its victim's feet of clay:[17]

> Garvey's old, unseaworthy wooden ships are still plowing through the turbulent waters of old Father Neptune's salty domains. Unlike the wreck of the Niagara Movement, they are not lying high and dry upon the weather-beaten shores of Disaster.

Such remarks brought forth DuBoisian retaliation, and he blasted the Garveyites as "scoundrels and bubble-blowers" who were causing havoc within the race. He denounced them for damning all whites and exploiting the Negro masses. (He claimed that the white supremacists were retreating and that the N.A.A.C.P. would liberate the

---

[15] Reprinted in *Negro World,* January 29, March 5, and May 21, 1921.
[16] *Negro World,* May 14, 1921.
[17] Wheeler Sheppard, *Mistakes of Dr. W. E. B. DuBois,* pamphlet, New York, 1921.

Negroes in another quarter of a century.[18] In the past, DuBois had also condemned whites in wholesale fashion, but in fighting Garvey, he undoubtedly tried to appear more optimistic about interracial relations than he actually was.)

During the early months of 1921, DuBois was preparing for the Second Pan-African Congress which he announced for the fall. He promised to invite not only the Negro Governments, but "all Negro organizations interested in the peoples of African descent." He also mentioned that colonial powers would be encouraged to send delegates to the conclave which was to be held in Europe again.[19] Realizing that his organization would be confused with and compared with the Garveyites, he stressed that the Second Pan-African Congress was not convening to prepare a "scheme of migration." Shortly before the Congress, the Negro World reminded DuBois that only about one-fourth of the delegates to his first Congress were from Africa, and since the ratio had been so small, the term "Pan-African" was unrealistic. The N.A.A.C.P. propagandist had only recently printed a letter from the Liberian President, and the note was intended to rebuke the Garveyites. (The Liberian chief of state warned that his country would not allow itself to serve as a base of operations from which the Garvey Movement could harass other governments in Africa.)[20]

DuBois found it necessary to make a public statement after it became known that Garvey had not been invited to the coming conclave, and the Crisis editor announced that the U.N.I.A. leader was ignored because his movement was "dangerous" and "impracticable." [21] The Negro World told its readers that such studied neglect was all that could be expected of DuBois, who directed his Pan-African Congress like "an exclusive college function." [22] The newspaper followed up this criticism with another entitled, "Is Dr. DuBois Misled or Is He Misleading?" In this piece, DuBois was advised to join forces against the "white beasts." [23] (Garvey predicted a race war, and he asserted that DuBois and the old-time leaders were not really preparing for it.) The Crisis editor was invited to attend the second convention of the U.N.I.A.[24]

Strategically, Garvey decided to call his own international conclave in New York a few weeks before the Pan-African Congress. Unanimously, the U.N.I.A. delegates condemned DuBois's movement (and they dispatched their caustic comments to European newspapers.) Garvey considered it an absurdity for the Pan-African Congress leaders to ask white representatives of the imperialists to attend their meetings:[25]

> Just imagine that! It reminds me of the conference of rats endeavoring to legislate against the cats and the secretary of the rats convention invites the cat to preside over the convention.

[18] Crisis XXII (1921), p. 8.
[19] Crisis XXI (1920–1921), p. 101. Crisis XXII (1921), p. 5.
[20] Crisis XXII (1921), p. 53.
[21] New York Age note reprinted in Negro World, July 2, 1921.
[22] Negro World, July 2, 1921.
[23] Negro World, July 23, 1921.
[24] Negro World, July 23, July 30, 1921.
[25] Negro World, August 6, 1921.

The Jamaican tried to create the impression that DuBois represented "the antithesis" of the U.N.I.A.—on the alleged grounds that the *Crisis* editor's policy was racial amalgamation. Contending that the whites would always hold firmly to their racism, Garvey suggested that the Negro develop[26]

> a distinct racial type of civilization of his own and . . . work out his salvation in his motherland, all to be accomplished under the stimulus and influence of the slogan, 'Africa for the Africans, at home and abroad!'

His speech was delivered at a special meeting "called unexpectedly" after press dispatches of the Second Pan-African Congress (condemning the U.N.I.A.) arrived from Europe.

The Second Pan-African Congress met in London, Brussels, and Paris, in late August and early September of 1921. As in 1919, the conclave promulgated its belief in the physical, social, and political equality of all races. The Negroes were to be guaranteed "the ancient common ownership of the land and its natural fruits and defence against the unrestrained greed of invested capital." The League of Nations was asked again to set up one agency to study Negro problems and another to insure that native labor was not exploited. England, Belgium, and France were accused of taking advantage of the natives. However, within the Pan-African movement itself there was a rupture between the American-British delegation who favored a critical approach to colonialism and the French-Belgian delegates, who desired an accommodation to the status quo.[27]

In Belgium, the Pan-African leaders were regarded as Garvey's henchmen, and white European newspapers continually asked if DuBois expected to eject the whites from Africa.[28] Repeatedly, the Pan-African Congress spokesmen asserted that they eschewed "any policy of war, conquest, or race hatred." [29] However, the moderate propaganda approach received the sympathy of some newspapers. The Paris *Humanite* stated:[30]

> The black and mulatto intelligentsia which the Congress revealed or permitted us to know better, showed by its very existence that the black race is not naturally or essentially an inferior race, and that it is not destined to remain so forever.

After the Second Pan-African Congress, Marcus Garvey challenged DuBois's group "to fight to a finish (applause.")[31] He laughed at those who argued that they owed their primary allegiance to the nations in which they lived. When one Pan-Afri-

---

[26] *Negro World,* September 17, 1921.

[27] *Crisis* XXIII (1921–1922), pp. 5–8. See also, Jesse Fauset, "Impressions of the Second Pan-African Congress," *Crisis* XXIII (1921–1922), p. 13.

[28] *Negro World,* October 8, 1921.

[29] W. E. B. DuBois, "A Second Journey to Pan-Africa," *New Republic* XXIX (1921–1922), p. 41.

[30] Jesse Fauset, *op. cit.* pp. 12–18.

[31] *Negro World,* September 17, 1921.

can leader said that he would "lose everything" if he returned permanently to Africa, Garvey jibed that "everything" meant Parisian white women. Garvey charged that the American whites were encouraging European immigration in order to replace the Negro "and cause him to die by starvation." [32] The Jamaican argued that it was only a matter of time before the whites would exile Negroes from all countries. However, he declared that some members of the race would remain in the United States for another hundred years; he announced that they would occupy a higher status because their welfare would be guaranteed by the prestige of the African Republic.

Although he excoriated N.A.A.C.P. leaders, Garvey denied that he hoped for the demise of the organization. He announced that he would not "originate an attack" on the Association, but that he was prepared to defend the race against "our bitterest enemies [who] are not so much those from without as within; men who will continue to find faults where there are no faults." He asked the N.A.A.C.P. to send its representatives to the third convention of the U.N.I.A. and to permit "the real leadership" to assume command of the race.[33] The Jamaican wanted his followers to believe that DuBois lived in fear of being dropped by the Association—"the National Association for the Advancement of (Certain) Colored People." [34]

During all of this time, DuBois was still requesting the U.N.I.A. to issue a financial statement of its activities, and the Negro World's reply was that this interloper had no right "to say what people should do with their money and what other organizations should do." The Garveyites declared that their leader supplied jobs to twelve hundred Negroes, when one included such enterprises as the U.N.I.A., the Negro World, the Negro Times, a printing plant, the Negro Factories Corporation, a hotel, restaurant, steam laundry, and a doll factory.[35]

In sharp contrast to the Garveyite hysterics, DuBois's comments about Ntime maican's program were usually calmly delivered and based on objective data. Since he viewed the Black Star Line as crucial in a consideration of the leader's fame and influence, DuBois examined the development of this business venture. He proceeded to recount the history of Garvey's mismanagement of the enterprise. DuBois described the unseaworthy Yarmouth's voyage to the West Indies. The ship carried a cargo of whiskey, much of which was stolen; the American Government fined the vessel's owners. Since the ship was old, much money was spent on repair bills, and the Yarmouth was finally sold in order to pay off the creditors. Another vessel, the Antonio Maceo, was also lost to the Black Star Line after it was beached in Cuba because it required extensive repairs. A third ship, the Shadyside, suffered the same ignominious fate, after it served a short propaganda stint as an excursion boat up the Hudson. In early 1921, the Jamaican said he purchased the Phyllis Wheatley in order to handle the African trade, and later he stated that some of his associates had absconded with funds which had been designated as a deposit for the ship. Since Garvey had announced sailings and sold pas-

[32] Ibid.
[33] Negro World, October 29, 1921. Negro World, February 4, 1922.
[34] Negro World, September 9, 1922. Negro World, November 4, 1922.
[35] Negro World, July 8, 1922. Negro World, January 6, 1923.

sage on the Phyllis Wheatley, he was indicted for fraud. In 1922, after the Black Star Line collapsed, DuBois wrote feelingly, "Here then is the collapse of the only thing in the Garvey Movement which was original or promising." [36]

The *Crisis* editor also attempted to learn how many members of the U.N.I.A. there actually were. Garvey claimed four million by August of 1920[37] and for 1921 he listed two figures. (During the early part of the year he stated that there were still four million members, but two years later, he recalled that there were six million members in 1921.)[38] The year after Garvey's indictment, DuBois estimated the membership in the U.N.I.A. for the period of September, 1920 to July, 1921. (He divided the annual dues into the total sum which was collected.) The *Crisis* editor calculated that there were fewer than ten thousand "paid up members," between ten and twenty thousand "active members," and very much less than a hundred thousand "nominal members." [39]

DuBois reached a white public when he analyzed the Garvey Movement in *Century* magazine, and while he made no attempt to mask his disapproval of the organization, he did try to account for it. He viewed Garvey as a disoriented victim of the color line:[40]

All his life whites have laughed and sneered at him, and torn his soul. All his life he has hated the half-whites, who rejecting their darker blood, have gloried in their pale shame.

DuBois referred to the Jamaican as a "little, fat, black man; ugly, but with intelligent eyes and a big head." Garvey made the most of this description, replying that his physiognomy was "typical of the African:" [41]

Anything that is black, to him [DuBois] is ugly, is hideous, is monstrous, and this is why in 1917 he had but the lightest of colored people in his office, when one could hardly tell whether it was a white show or a colored vaudeville he was running at Fifth Avenue [the offices of the N.A.A.C.P.].

The *Crisis* editor was labeled as an apostle of "social equality," which in Garvey's thinking represented the kind of person who demanded to squire a white woman to a dance at the Waldorf-Astoria Hotel.[42] The Jamaican said that the U.N.I.A. was the only agency which was able to protect the darker-skinned Negro masses against the DuBois-

[36] *Crisis* XXIV (1922), pp. 210–214.
[37] Marcus Garvey, "The Negro's Greatest Enemy," *Current History* XVIII (1923), p. 955.
[38] Speech of Marcus Garvey to the Beulah Baptist Church of Cincinnati, Ohio. Typescript, February 19, 1921. (Located at Hampton Institute Library) See also Garvey, "The Negro's Greatest Enemy," *Current History* XVIII (1923), p. 956.
[39] *Crisis* XXV (1922–1923), p. 120.
[40] W. E. B. DuBois, "Back to Africa," *Century* CV (1922–1923), p. 544.
[41] *Negro World,* February 10, 1923. *Negro World,* February 17, 1923.
[42] *Negro World,* March 3, 1923.

led "caste aristocracy" of light mulattoes, many of whom were "intellectuals." [43] Paradoxically, Garvey denied that he was prejudiced against mulattoes, and he argued that all men had equal opportunity in the U.N.I.A.

In 1923, Garvey was convicted of mail fraud. After the trial, DuBois reprinted an editorial from a West Indies newspaper, wherein the U.N.I.A. leader was termed a "transparent charlatan." [44] Frustratedly, DuBois declared once again that his own attempt to settle the race problem on an international scale (through "cooperation" with the whites) was "harmed by the tragedy and comedy of Marcus Garvey." [45] The Jamaican refused to accept his defeat. In his prison cell, he continued to write diatribes, and DuBois angrily denounced him as "the most dangerous enemy of the Negro race in America and in the world. He is either a lunatic or a traitor." [46]

Since DuBois had been his chief critic, Garvey charged that the *Crisis* editor was responsible for his indictment and conviction. He blamed the N.A.A.C.P. propagandist for all of his difficulties and he asserted that the editor's malevolence had prevented the Black Star Line from sending "dozens" of ships to sea. During the summer of 1924, the U.N.I.A. exiled DuBois from the Negro race.[47] However, such sentiments were only the last breaths of the movement. The Liberian Government announced that no members of the Garvey organization were welcome in the country. In January, 1925, President King remarked that his administration would not support any organization which dedicated itself to stirring up racial animosity. DuBois, who had recently been in Liberia as American Envoy Extraordinary and Minister Plenipotentiary, was identified by Garvey as the leader in the Liberian plot to destroy him.[48]

During the same years in which the Garvey Movement attracted thousands of average Negroes, DuBois's Pan-African Congress barely managed to survive. However, in 1923 and 1927, he was finally able to persuade the National Association of Colored Women to sponsor his conclaves.[49] These Congresses attracted few people and DuBois's large hopes to arouse the Negro were unrealized. In his leadership of the movement DuBois did not seem to understand that a truly effective propagandist related his work to a functioning organization. Since he did not build a real machine and did not have N.A.A.C.P. aid, his movement faded away.

This article has examined the intraracial battles between DuBois and Garvey. During the 1920's, in the pages of the *Crisis* and the *Negro World,* they employed the same propaganda style and approach in their attacks on each other as they used in their organizational pronouncements on Africa. Garvey's expressions were explosive, irrational, and flamboyant. Their emotional appeal attracted large numbers of frustrated, uneducated blacks. DuBois's remarks were usually moderate, thoughtful, and analytical and were directed to a minority within the minority.

[43] *Negro World,* March 1, 1924.
[44] *Crisis* XXVI (1923), p. 230. See also, *Crisis* XXVIII (1924), pp. 8–9.
[45] *Crisis* XXVII (1923–1924), p. 9.
[46] *Crisis* XXVIII (1924), pp. 8–9.
[47] *Negro World,* April 10, 1924. New York *Times,* August 29, 1924.
[48] Edmund D. Cronon, *Black Moses* (Madison, 1955), pp. 129–131.
[49] *Crisis* XXVII (1923–1924), p. 122, 170. *Crisis* XXXIV (1927), p. 264.

Infants of the Spring*

Wallace Thurman

It was the night of the Donation Party. For ten days preparations had been made. For ten days Raymond's typewriter and the telephone had been overworked, bidding people to report to Niggeratti Manor on the designated night. The wolf must be driven from the door. Paul had scuttled through Greenwich Village, a jubilant Revere, sounding the tocsin. Euphoria and Eustace had canvassed their Harlem friends. Barbara had been called in for a consultation and departed ebullient, a zealous crusader. A large crowd had been assured. The audacious novelty of the occasion had piqued many a curiosity. And of course there was promise of uninhibited hijinks.

Ten o'clock. Only a few guests had arrived, laden with various bundles of staple foods. Eustace's studio and the nearby kitchen were to be the focal points for the party because in the basement there would be fewer stairs for the drunks to encounter, and more room for dancing.

Ten-thirty. The Niggeratti clique, supplemented by a few guests, had gathered around the punch bowl on the kitchen table. The concoction, fathered by Eustace, was tasty and strong.

"Ol' Mother Savoy has surpassed herself tonight," Paul murmured between drinks.

Also on the table were a half dozen bottles of gin, and Raymond noted that it was to one of these that Stephen was clinging tenaciously.

"Have some punch?"

"No," Stephen answered Raymond shortly and continued to gulp down glass after glass of straight gin.

"Go easy, Steve. The night's young."

"What of it?" He walked away from the table and leaned against the wall in a far corner of the room.

Before Raymond had time to consider his friend's unusual behavior, a host of people boisterously invaded the room, dropping packages, clamoring for drinks.

* From Wallace Thurman, *Infants of the Spring* (New York: The Macaulay Company, 1932), pp. 173–84, 229–43.

"Two cans of corn," someone shouted.

"Pound of sugar here."

"Some yaller corn meal. Hot ziggitty."

" 'Taters. 'Taters. Nice ripe 'taters."

"Wet my whistle, Eustace. I lithp."

Samuel emerged from the crowd and taking hold of Raymond's arm pulled him aside. It was the first time they had met since their quarrel some weeks before. Samuel was contrite, anxious for a reconciliation. He had reasoned to himself that he had been too quick to lose his temper. People like him—people with a mission in life—must expect to be the recipients of insults and rebuffs. How could he help others when he could not control himself? Samuel felt that he had betrayed his purpose in life by reacting positively to Raymond's drunken statements.

"Ray, I owe you an apology."

"For what?"

"For what happened."

"Oh, that. Forget it." Raymond turned away and rejoined the exuberant crowd centered around the kitchen table.

"Ray." It was Paul. "Meet a friend of mine."

By his side was a grinning black boy.

"Ray, this is Bud. He's a bootblack, but he has the most beautiful body I've ever seen. I'll get him to strip for the gang soon."

The boy grinned sheepishly. But he did not seem the least bit abashed. Before Raymond could make any comment, Paul had propelled his charge toward Eustace's studio. Raymond followed. The room was crowded with people. Black people, white people, and all the in-between shades. Ladies in evening gowns. Ladies in smocks. Ladies in tailored suits. Ladies in ordinary dresses of every description, interspersed and surrounded by all types of men in all types of conventional clothes. And weaving his way among them, green dressing gown swishing, glass tray held tightly in both hands, was Eustace, serving drinks to those who had not yet found the kitchen oasis.

"Folks," Paul shouted above the din, "this is Bud. He has the most perfect body in New York. I'm gonna let you see it soon."

"Bravo."

"Go to it."

"Now?"

Paul and his protegé were surrounded by an avid mob.

Raymond sauntered back into the kitchen. Stephen was still standing in his isolated corner, a full glass progressing toward his lips. His face was flushed. His eyes half closed. Raymond started toward him.

"Hi, Ray." Someone jerked the tail of his coat. It was Bull. Beside him was Lucille.

"Hen's fruit." Bull deposited a sack full of eggs on top of the refrigerator.

"Eve's delight." A bag of apples was thrust into Raymond's hand by some unknown person.

"An' my sweet patootie has the bacon," Bull continued, jerking an oblong package from beneath Lucille's arm. Raymond put the apples beside Bull's eggs.

"Hello, 'Cile. Thanks, Bull."

"Oh, Ray." It was Barbara. She was followed and surrounded by a group of detached, anemic white men and women, all in evening dress, all carrying packages of various sizes and shapes.

"This is Ray, folks," Barbara announced to her companions. They all smiled dutifully and began relieving themselves of their bundles.

Barbara appropriated Raymond's hand and placed something in his palm.

"For Negro art," she whispered, then, slipping quickly away, corralled her friends and ushered them toward the punch bowl. Raymond opened his palm and gasped at the sight of a twenty-dollar bill.

"Good God, what a mob." Lucille was beside him. He pocketed the money Barbara had given him and regarded Lucille coolly.

"Still hep on your man?"

"Why, Ray," she began, then quickly regaining control of herself, riposted merrily, "and *how.*" She then started to move away.

Raymond forestalled her by firmly clenching her wrist in his hand.

"How long you gonna play this game?" he asked sternly.

"What ol' black game?"

"You know damn well. . . ."

"Here's a drink, baby." Bull handed Lucille a glass of punch. Raymond released her wrist, glared at the two of them, walked to the table, pushed his way through the crowd, seized a glass, and handed it to Euphoria, now guardian of the punch bowl, to fill.

After having had several drinks, he threaded his way back into Eustace's studio. It was more crowded and noisy than before. Someone was playing the piano, and in a small clearing the ex-wife of a noted American playwright was doing the Black Bottom with a famed Negro singer of spirituals.

"Ain't I good?" she demanded of her audience. "An' you ain't seen nothin' yet."

With which she insinuated her scrawny white body close to that of her stalwart black partner and began performing the torrid abdominal movements of the "mess-around."

"How d'y'do, Ray."

Raymond turned to see who had spoken. On the davenette against the wall was a well known sophisticated author and explorer of the esoteric. He was surrounded by four bewildered-looking, corn-fed individuals. He introduced them to Raymond as relatives and friends from his native middle west. It was their first trip to Harlem, and their first experience of a white-black gathering.

Raymond sat down beside them, talking at random, and helping himself to the bottles of liquor which the cautious author had recruited from his own private stock.

Soon there was a commotion at the door. It cleared of all standees, and in it was framed the weird Amazonian figure of Amy Douglas, whose mother had made a fortune devising and marketing hair preparations for kinky-haired blackamoors. Amy, despite her bulk and size—she was almost six feet tall and weighed over two hundred pounds—affected flimsy frocks and burdened her person with weighty brilliants. A six months stay in Europe had provided her with a series of foreign phrases with which to interlard her southern dialect. Being very black, she went in for skin whiteners which had been more effective in certain spots than in others. As a result, her face was speckled, uncertain of its shade. Amy was also generous in the use of her mother's hair preparations, and because someone had once told her she resembled a Nubian queen, she wore a diamond tiara, precariously perched on the top of her slickened naps.

Majestically she strode into the room, attended as usual by an attractive escort of high yaller ladies in waiting, and a chattering group of effeminate courtiers.

Raymond excused himself from the people with whom he had been sitting and started once more for the kitchen. While trying to pierce through the crowd, he was halted by Dr. Parkes, a professor of literature in a northern Negro college, who, also, as Paul so aptly declared, played mother hen to a brood of chicks, he having appointed himself guardian angel to the current set of younger Negro artists.

"I've been trying to find you for the past hour."

"Sorry, Dr. Parkes . . . but in this mob . . ."

"I know. Perhaps I should await a more propitious moment, but I wanted to ask you about Pelham."

"Pelham?"

"Yes."

"Oh, he's still in jail. That's all I know. His trial isn't far off. I've forgotten the exact date."

"What effect do you think this will have on you?"

"On me? I don't know what you mean."

"Don't you think this scandal when publicized will hurt all of you who lived here with Pelham?"

Raymond laughed.

"I hadn't thought of that. This might be Paul's opportunity to get his name in the paper."

"Who's taking my name in vain?" Paul appeared, still leading his dark shadow by the hand. "Oh, Dr. Parkes," he continued excitedly, "meet Bud. He's got . . ."

Raymond escaped and worked his way over to the piano. He stopped to chat with Aline and Janet, who had staggered in some time before with a group of conspicuously and self-consciously drunk college boys.

"Hi, Ray."

"What say, keeds?"

"Where's Steve?" they asked in unison.

"Find the gin," he replied and moved away.

Meanwhile four Negro actors from a current Broadway dramatic hit harmonized a popular love song. Conversation was temporarily hushed, laughter subsided, and only the intermittent tinkle of ice in an upturned glass could be heard as the plangent voices of the singers filled the room.

There was a burst of applause as they finished, followed by boisterous calls for an encore. After a moment's conference, the singers obligingly crooned another mellifluous tune.

Raymond retraced his steps, greeting people, whispering answers to questions buzzed into his ear. Finally he was once more in the kitchen.

It was one-thirty. The twenty dollar bill had been given to Eustace, who had sent for another dozen bottles of gin. A deposed Russian countess was perched atop the gas range talking animatedly in broken English to Paul's Spartan bootblack. The famed American playwright's ex-wife had developed a crying jag. No one could soothe her but the stalwart singer of Negro spirituals. Near them hovered his wife, jealous, bored, suspicious, irritated rather than flattered by the honeyed, Oxonian witticisms being cooed into her ear by a drunken English actor.

The noise was deafening. Empty gin bottles on the floor tripped those with unsteady legs. Bull's bag of eggs had been knocked to the floor. Its contents were broken and oozed stickily over the linoleum. Someone else had dropped a bag of sugar. The linoleum was gritty. Shuffling feet made rasping sounds.

Two-thirty. Raymond began to feel the effects of the liquor he had consumed. He decided to stop drinking for a while. There was too much to see to risk missing it by getting drunk.

In the hallway between the kitchen and Eustace's studio, Euphoria sought to set a group of Negro school teachers at ease. The crowd confused them as it did most of the Harlem intellectuals who had strayed in and who all felt decidedly out of place. Raymond noticed how they all clung together, how timid they were, and how constrained they were in conversation and manner. He sought Stephen. He wanted to share his amusement at their discomfiture and self-consciousness. It gave him pleasure that he should have such a pertinent example of their lack of social savoir, their race conscious awareness. Unable to recover from being so intimately surrounded by whites, they, the school teachers, the college boys, the lawyers, the dentists, the social service workers, despite their strident appeals for social equality when among their own kind, either communed with one another, standing apart, or else made themselves obnoxious striving to make themselves agreeable. Only the bootblack, the actors, the musicians and Raymond's own group of friends comprised the compatible Negroid elements.

● ● ●

Thursday night came and so did the young hopefuls. The first to arrive was Sweetie May Carr. Sweetie May was a short story writer, more noted for her ribald wit and personal effervescence than for any actual literary work. She was a great favorite among those whites who went in for Negro prodigies. Mainly because she lived up to their conception of what a typical Negro should be. It seldom occurred to any of her patrons that she did this with tongue in cheek. Given a paleface audience, Sweetie May would launch forth into a saga of the little all-colored Mississippi town where she claimed to have been born. Her repertoire of tales was earthy, vulgar and funny. Her darkies always smiled through their tears, sang spirituals on the slightest provocation, and performed buck dances when they should have been working. Sweetie May was a master of southern dialect, and an able raconteur, but she was too indifferent to literary creation to transfer to paper that which she told so well. The intricacies of writing bored her, and her written work was for the most part turgid and unpolished. But Sweetie May knew her white folks.

"It's like this," she had told Raymond. "I have to eat. I also wish to finish my education. Being a Negro writer these days is a racket and I'm going to make the most of it while it lasts. Sure I cut the fool. But I enjoy it, too. I don't know a tinker's damn about art. I care less about it. My ultimate ambition, as you know, is to become a gynecologist. And the only way I can live easily until I have the requisite training is to pose as a writer of potential ability. *Voila!* I get my tuition paid at Columbia. I rent an apartment and have all the furniture contributed by kind hearted o'fays. I receive bundles of groceries from various sources several times a week . . . all accomplished by dropping a discreet hint during an evening's festivities. I find queer places for whites to go in Harlem . . . out of the way primitive churches, sidestreet speakeasies. They fall for it. About twice a year I manage to sell a story. It is acclaimed. I am a genius in the making. Thank God for this Negro literary renaissance! Long may it flourish!"

Sweetie May was accompanied by two young girls, recently emigrated from Boston. They were the latest to be hailed as incipient immortals. Their names were Doris Westmore and Hazel Jamison. Doris wrote short stories. Hazel wrote poetry. Both had become known through a literary contest fostered by one of the leading Negro magazines. Raymond liked them more than he did most of the younger recruits to the movement. For one thing, they were characterized by a freshness and naïveté which he and his cronics had lost. And, surprisingly enough for Negro prodigies, they actually gave promise of possessing literary talent. He was most pleased to see them. He was also amused by their interest and excitement. A salon! A literary gathering! It was one of the civilized institutions they had dreamed of finding in New York, one of the things they had longed and hoped for.

As time passed, others came in. Tony Crews, smiling and self-effacing, a mischievous boy, grateful for the chance to slip away from the backwoods college he attended. Raymond had never been able to analyze this young poet. His work was interesting and unusual. It was also spotty. Spasmodically he gave promise of developing into a first rate poet. Already he had published two volumes, prematurely, Raymond thought. Both had been excessively praised by whites and universally damned by Negroes. Considering the nature of his work this was to be expected. The only unknown quantity was the poet himself. Would he or would he not fulfill the promise exemplified in some of his work? Raymond had no way of knowing and even an intimate friendship with Tony himself had failed to enlighten him. For Tony was the most close-mouthed and cagey individual Raymond had ever known when it came to personal matters. He fended off every attempt to probe into his inner self and did this with such an unconscious and naïve air that the prober soon came to one of two conclusions: Either Tony had no depth whatsoever, or else he was too deep for plumbing by ordinary mortals.

DeWitt Clinton, the Negro poet laureate, was there, too, accompanied, as usual, by his *fideles achates,* David Holloway. David had been acclaimed the most handsome Negro in Harlem by a certain group of whites. He was in great demand by artists who wished to paint him. He had become a much touted romantic figure. In reality he was a fairly intelligent school teacher, quite circumspect in his habits, a rather timid beau, who imagined himself to be bored with life.

Dr. Parkes finally arrived, accompanied by Carl Denny, the artist, and Carl's wife, Annette. Next to arrive was Cedric Williams, a West Indian, whose first book, a collection of short stories with a Caribbean background, in Raymond's opinion, marked him as one of the three Negroes writing who actually had something to say, and also some concrete idea of style. Cedric was followed by Austin Brown, a portrait painter whom Raymond personally despised, a Dr. Manfred Trout, who practiced medicine and also wrote exceptionally good short stories, Glenn Madison, who was a Communist, and a long, lean professorial person, Allen Fenderson, who taught school and had ambitions to become a crusader modeled after W. E. B. Du Bois.

The roster was now complete. There was an hour of small talk and drinking of mild cocktails in order to induce ease and allow the various guests to become acquainted and voluble. Finally, Dr. Parkes ensconced himself in Raymond's favorite chair, where he could get a good view of all in the room, and clucked for order.

Raymond observed the professor closely. Paul's description never seemed more apt. He was a mother hen clucking at her chicks. Small, dapper, with sensitive features, graying hair, a dominating head, and restless hands and feet, he smiled benevolently at his brood. Then, in his best continental manner, which he had acquired during four years at European Universities, he began to speak.

"You are," he perorated, "the outstanding personalities in a new generation. On you depends the future of your race. You are not, as were your predecessors, concerned with donning armor, and clashing swords with the enemy in the public square. You are finding both an escape and a weapon in beauty, which beauty when created by you will cause the American white man to reëstimate the Negro's value to his civilization, cause him to realize that the American black man is too valuable, too potential of utilitarian accomplishment, to be kept downtrodden and segregated.

"Because of your concerted storming up Parnassus, new vistas will be spread open to the entire race. The Negro in the south will no more know peonage, Jim Crowism, or loss of the ballot, and the Negro everywhere in America will know complete freedom and equality.

"But," and here his voice took on a more serious tone, "to accomplish this, your pursuit of beauty must be vital and lasting. I am somewhat fearful of the decadent strain which seems to have filtered into most of your work. Oh, yes, I know you are children of the age and all that, but you must not, like your paleface contemporaries, wallow in the mire of post-Victorian license. You have too much at stake. You must have ideals. You should become . . . well, let me suggest your going back to your racial roots, and cultivating a healthy paganism based on African traditions.

"For the moment that is all I wish to say. I now want you all to give expression to your own ideas. Perhaps we can reach a happy mean for guidance."

He cleared his throat and leaned contentedly back in his chair. No one said a word. Raymond was full of contradictions, which threatened to ooze forth despite his efforts to remain silent. But he knew that once the ooze began there would be no stopping the flood, and he was anxious to hear what some of the others might have to say.

However, a glance at the rest of the people in the room assured him that most of them had not the slightest understanding of what had been said, nor any ideas on the subject, whatsoever. Once more Dr. Parkes clucked for discussion. No one ventured a word. Raymond could see that Cedric, like himself, was full of argument, and also like him, did not wish to appear contentious at such an early stage in the discussion. Tony winked at Raymond when he caught his eye, but the expression on his face was as inscrutable as ever. Sweetie May giggled behind her handkerchief. Paul amused himself by sketching the various people in the room. The rest were blank.

"Come, come, now," Dr. Parkes urged somewhat impatiently, "I'm not to do all the talking. What have you to say, DeWitt?"

All eyes sought out the so-called Negro poet laureate. For a moment he stirred uncomfortably in his chair, then in a high pitched, nasal voice proceeded to speak.

"I think, Dr. Parkes, that you have said all there is to say. I agree with you. The young Negro artist must go back to his pagan heritage for inspiration and to the old masters for form."

Raymond could not suppress a snort. For DeWitt's few words had given him a vivid mental picture of that poet's creative hours—eyes on a page of Keats, fingers on typewriter, mind frantically conjuring African scenes. And there would of course be a Bible nearby.

Paul had ceased being intent on his drawing long enough to hear "pagan heritage," and when DeWitt finished he inquired inelegantly:

"What old black pagan heritage?"

DeWitt gasped, surprised and incredulous.

"Why, from your ancestors."

"Which ones?" Paul pursued dumbly.

"Your African ones, of course." DeWitt's voice was full of disdain.

"What about the rest?"

"What rest?" He was irritated now.

"My German, English and Indian ancestors," Paul answered willingly. "How can I go back to African ancestors when their blood is so diluted and their country and times so far away? I have no conscious affinity for them at all."

Dr. Parkes intervened: "I think you've missed the point, Paul."

"And I," Raymond was surprised at the suddenness with which he joined in the argument, "think he has hit the nail right on the head. Is there really any reason why *all* Negro artists should consciously and deliberately dig into African soil for inspiration and material unless they actually wish to do so?"

"I don't mean that. I mean you should develop your inherited spirit."

DeWitt beamed. The doctor had expressed his own hazy theory. Raymond was about to speak again, when Paul once more took the bit between his own teeth.

"I ain't got no African spirit."

Sweetie May giggled openly at this, as did Carl Denny's wife, Annette. The rest looked appropriately sober, save for Tony, whose eyes continued to telegraph mischievously to Raymond. Dr. Parkes tried to squelch Paul with a frown. He should have known better.

"I'm not an African," the culprit continued. "I'm an American and a perfect product of the melting pot."

"That's nothing to brag about." Cedric spoke for the first time.

"And I think you're all on the wrong track." All eyes were turned toward this new speaker, Allen Fenderson. "Dr. Du Bois has shown us the way. We must be militant fighters. We must not hide away in ivory towers and prate of beauty. We must fashion cudgels and bludgeons rather than sensitive plants. We must excoriate the white man, and make him grant us justice. We must fight for complete social and political and economic equality."

"What we ought to do," Glenn Madison growled intensely, "is to join hands with the workers of the world and overthrow the present capitalistic régime. We are of the proletariat and must fight our battles allied with them, rather than singly and selfishly."

"All of us?" Raymond inquired quietly.

"All of us who have a trace of manhood and are more interested in the rights of human beings than in gin parties and neurotic capitalists."

"I hope you're squelched," Paul stage whispered to Raymond.

"And how!" Raymond laughed. Several joined in. Dr. Parkes spoke quickly to Fenderson, ignoring the remarks of the Communist.

"But, Fenderson . . . this is a new generation and must make use of new weapons. Some of us will continue to fight in the old way, but there are other things to be considered, too. Remember, a beautiful sonnet can be as effectual, nay even more effectual, than a rigorous hymn of hate."

"The man who would understand and be moved by a hymn of hate would not bother to read your sonnet and, even if he did, he would not know what it was all about."

"I don't agree. Your progress must be a boring in from the top, not a battle from the bottom. Convert the higher beings and the lower orders will automatically follow."

"Spoken like a true capitalistic minion," Glenn Madison muttered angrily.

Fenderson prepared to continue his argument, but he was forestalled by Cedric.

"What does it matter," he inquired diffidently, "what any of you do so long as you remain true to yourselves? There is no necessity for this movement becoming standardized. There is ample room for everyone to follow his own individual track. Dr. Parkes wants us all to go back to Africa and resurrect our pagan heritage, become atavistic. In this he is supported by Mr. Clinton. Fenderson here wants us all to be propagandists and yell at the top of our lungs at every conceivable injustice. Madison wants us all to take a cue from Leninism and fight the capitalistic bogey. Well . . . why not let each young hopeful choose his own path? Only in that way will anything at all be achieved."

"Which is just what I say," Raymond smiled gratefully at Cedric. "One cannot make movements nor can one plot their course. When the work of a given number of individuals during a given period is looked at in retrospect, then one can identify a movement and evaluate its distinguishing characteristics. Individuality is what we should strive for. Let each seek his own salvation. To me, a wholesale flight back to Africa or a wholesale allegiance to Communism or a wholesale adherence to an antiquated and for the most part ridiculous propagandistic program are all equally futile and unintelligent."

Dr. Parkes gasped and sought for an answer. Cedric forestalled him.

"To talk of an African heritage among American Negroes *is* unintelligent. It is only in the West Indies that you can find direct descendents from African ancestors. Your primitive instincts among all but the extreme proletariat have been ironed out. You're standardized Americans."

"Oh, no," Carl Denny interrupted suddenly. "You're wrong. It's in our blood. It's . . ." he fumbled for a word, "fixed. Why . . ." he stammered again, "remember Cullen's poem, *Heritage*:

" 'So I lie who find no peace
Night or day, no slight release
From the unremittant beat
Made by cruel padded feet
Walking through my body's street.
Up and down they go, and back,
Treading out a jungle track.'

"We're all like that. Negroes are the only people in America not standardized. The feel of the African jungle is in their blood. Its rhythms surge through their bodies. Look how Negroes laugh and dance and sing, all spontaneous and individual."

"Exactly," Dr. Parkes and DeWitt nodded assent.

"I have yet to see an intelligent or middle class American Negro laugh and sing and dance spontaneously. That's an illusion, a pretty sentimental fiction. Moreover your songs and dances are not individual. Your spirituals are mediocre folk songs, ignorantly culled from Methodist hymn books. There are white men who can sing them just as well as Negroes, if not better, should they happen to be untrained vocalists like Robeson, rather than highly trained technicians like Hayes. And as for dancing spontaneously and feeling the rhythms of the jungle . . . humph!"

Sweetie May jumped into the breach.

"I can do the Charleston better than any white person."

"I particularly stressed . . . intelligent people. The lower orders of any race have more vim and vitality than the illuminated tenth."

Sweetie May leaped to her feet.

"Why, you West Indian . . ."

"Sweetie, Sweetie," Dr. Parkes was shocked by her polysyllabic expletive.

Pandemonium reigned. The master of ceremonies could not cope with the situation. Cedric called Sweetie an illiterate southern hussy. She called him all types of profane West Indian monkey chasers. DeWitt and David were shocked and showed it. The

literary doctor, the Communist and Fenderson moved uneasily around the room. Annette and Paul giggled. The two children prodigies from Boston looked on wide-eyed,
utterly bewildered and dismayed. Raymond leaned back in his chair, puffing on a ciga-
rette, detached and amused. Austin, the portrait painter, audibly repeated over and over
to himself: "Just like niggers . . . just like niggers." Carl Denny interposed himself between Cedric and Sweetie May. Dr. Parkes clucked for civilized behavior, which came
only when Cedric stalked angrily out of the room.

Harlem:
The Culture Capital*
James Weldon Johnson

In the history of New York, the significance of the name Harlem has changed from
Dutch to Irish to Jewish to Negro. Of these changes, the last has come most swiftly.
Throughout colored America, from Massachusetts to Mississippi, and across the continent to Los Angeles and Seattle, its name, which as late as fifteen years ago had scarcely
been heard, now stands for the Negro metropolis. Harlem is indeed the great Mecca for
the sight-seer, the pleasure-seeker, the curious, the adventurous, the enterprising, the
ambitious and the talented of the whole Negro world; for the lure of it has reached
down to every island of the Carib Sea and has penetrated even into Africa.

In the make-up of New York, Harlem is not merely a Negro colony or community, it is a city within a city, the greatest Negro city in the world. It is not a slum or a
fringe, it is located in the heart of Manhattan and occupies one of the most beautiful
and healthful sections of the city. It is not a "quarter" of dilapidated tenements, but is
made up of new-law apartments and handsome dwellings, with well-paved and well-
lighted streets. It has its own churches, social and civic centers, shops, theaters and
other places of amusement. And it contains more Negroes to the square mile than any
other spot on earth. A stranger who rides up magnificent Seventh Avenue on a bus or in
an automobile must be struck with surprise at the transformation which takes place
after he crosses One Hundred and Twenty-fifth Street. Beginning there, the population
suddenly darkens and he rides through twenty-five solid blocks where the passers-by,
the shoppers, those sitting in restaurants, coming out of theaters, standing in doorways
and looking out of windows are practically all Negroes; and then he emerges where the
population as suddenly becomes white again. There is nothing just like it in any other
city in the country, for there is no preparation for it; no change in the character of the
houses and streets; no change, indeed, in the appearance of the people, except their
color.

* From James Weldon Johnson, "Harlem: The Culture Capital," in Alain Locke, ed., *The New Negro*
(New York: Atheneum Publishers, 1968), pp. 301–11.

Negro Harlem is practically a development of the past decade, but the story behind it goes back a long way. There have always been colored people in New York. In the middle of the last century they lived in the vicinity of Lispenard, Broome and Spring Streets. When Washington Square and lower Fifth Avenue was the center of aristocratic life, the colored people, whose chief occupation was domestic service in the homes of the rich, lived in a fringe and were scattered in nests to the south, east and west of the square. As late as the '80's the major part of the colored population lived in Sullivan, Thompson, Bleecker, Grove, Minetta Lane and adjacent streets. It is curious to note that some of these nests still persist. In a number of the blocks of Greenwich Village and Little Italy may be found small groups of Negroes who have never lived in any other section of the city. By about 1890 the center of colored population had shifted to the upper Twenties and lower Thirties west of Sixth Avenue. Ten years later another considerable shift northward had been made to West Fifty-third Street.

The West Fifty-third Street settlement deserves some special mention because it ushered in a new phase of life among colored New Yorkers. Three rather well-appointed hotels were opened in the street and they quickly became the centers of a sort of fashionable life that hitherto had not existed. On Sunday evenings these hotels served dinner to music and attracted crowds of well-dressed diners. One of these hotels, The Marshall, became famous as the headquarters of Negro talent. There gathered the actors, the musicians, the composers, the writers, the singers, dancers and vaudevillians. There one went to get a close-up of Williams and Walker, Cole and Johnson, Ernest Hogan, Will Marion Cook, Jim Europe, Aida Overton, and of others equally and less known. Paul Laurence Dunbar was frequently there whenever he was in New York. Numbers of those who love to shine by the light reflected from celebrities were always to be found. The first modern jazz band ever heard in New York, or, perhaps anywhere, was organized at The Marshall. It was a playing-singing-dancing orchestra, making the first dominant use of banjos, saxophones, clarinets and trap drums in combination, and was called The Memphis Students. Jim Europe was a member of that band, and out of it grew the famous Clef Club, of which he was the noted leader, and which for a long time monopolized the business of "entertaining" private parties and furnishing music for the new dance craze. Also in the Clef Club was "Buddy" Gilmore who originated trap drumming as it is now practised, and set hundreds of white men to juggling their sticks and doing acrobatic stunts while they manipulated a dozen other noise-making devices aside from their drums. A good many well-known white performers frequented The Marshall and for seven or eight years the place was one of the sights of New York.

The move to Fifty-third Street was the result of the opportunity to get into newer and better houses. About 1900 the move to Harlem began, and for the same reason. Harlem had been overbuilt with large, new-law apartment houses, but rapid transportation to that section was very inadequate—the Lenox Avenue Subway had not yet been built—and landlords were finding difficulty in keeping houses on the east side of the section filled. Residents along and near Seventh Avenue were fairly well served by the Eighth Avenue Elevated. A colored man, in the real estate business at this time, Philip A. Payton, approached several of these landlords with the proposition that he would fill their empty or partially empty houses with steady colored tenants. The suggestion was accepted, and one or two houses on One Hundred and Thirty-fourth Street east of Lenox Avenue were taken over. Gradually other houses were filled. The whites paid little attention to the movement until it began to spread west of Lenox Avenue; they then took steps to check it. They proposed through a financial organization, the Hudson Realty Company, to buy in all properties occupied by colored people and evict the tenants. The Negroes countered by similar methods. Payton formed the Afro-American Realty Company, a Negro corporation organized for the purpose of buying and leasing houses for occupancy by colored people. Under this counter stroke the opposition subsided for several years.

But the continually increasing pressure of colored people to the west over the Lenox Avenue dead line caused the opposition to break out again, but in a new and more menacing form. Several white men undertook to organize all the white people of the community for the purpose of inducing financial institutions not to lend money or renew mortgages on properties occupied by colored people. In this effort they had considerable success, and created a situation which has not yet been completely overcome, a situation which is one of the hardest and most unjustifiable the Negro property owner in Harlem has to contend with. The Afro-American Realty Company was now defunct, but two or three colored men of means stepped into the breach. Philip A. Payton and J. C. Thomas bought two five-story apartments, dispossessed the white tenants and put in colored. J. B. Nail bought a row of five apartments and did the same thing. St. Philip's Church bought a row of thirteen apartment houses on One Hundred and Thirty-fifth Street, running from Seventh Avenue almost to Lenox.

The situation now resolved itself into an actual contest. Negroes not only continued to occupy available apartment houses, but began to purchase private dwellings between Lenox and Seventh Avenues. Then the whole movement, in the eyes of the whites, took on the aspect of an "invasion"; they became panic-stricken and began fleeing as from a plague. The presence of one colored family in a block, no matter how well bred and orderly, was sufficient to precipitate a flight. House after house and block after block was actually deserted. It was a great demonstration of human beings running amuck. None of them stopped to reason why they were doing it or what would happen if they didn't. The banks and lending companies holding mortgages on these deserted houses were compelled to take them over. For some time they held these houses vacant, preferring to do that and carry the charges than to rent or sell them to colored people. But values dropped and continued to drop until at the outbreak of the war in Europe property in the northern part of Harlem had reached the *nadir*.

In the meantime the Negro colony was becoming more stable; the churches were being moved from the lower part of the city; social and civic centers were being formed; and gradually a community was being evolved. Following the outbreak of the war in Europe Negro Harlem received a new and tremendous impetus. Because of the war thousands of aliens in the United States rushed back to their native lands to join the colors and immigration practically ceased. The result was a critical shortage in labor. This shortage was rapidly increased as the United States went more and more largely into the business of furnishing munitions and supplies to the warring countries. To help meet this shortage of common labor Negroes were brought up from the South. The government itself took the first steps, following the practice in vogue in Germany of shifting labor according to the supply and demand in various parts of the country. The example of the government was promptly taken up by the big industrial concerns, which sent hundreds, perhaps thousands, of labor agents into the South who recruited Negroes by wholesale. I was in Jacksonville, Fla., for a while at that time, and I sat one day and watched the stream of migrants passing to take the train. For hours they passed steadily, carrying flimsy suit cases, new and shiny, rusty old ones, bursting at the seams, boxes and bundles and impedimenta of all sorts, including banjos, guitars, birds in cages and what not. Similar scenes were being enacted in cities and towns all over that region. The first wave of the great exodus of Negroes from the South was on. Great numbers of these migrants headed for New York or eventually got there, and naturally the majority went up into Harlem. But the Negro population of Harlem was not swollen by migrants from the South alone; the opportunity for Negro labor exerted its pull upon the Negroes of the West Indies, and those islanders in the course of time poured into Harlem to the number of twenty-five thousand or more.

These new-comers did not have to look for work; work looked for them, and at wages of which they had never even dreamed. And here is where the unlooked for, the unprecedented, the miraculous happened. According to all preconceived notions, these Negroes suddenly earning large sums of money for the first time in their lives should have had their heads turned; they should have squandered it in the most silly and absurd manners imaginable. Later, after the United States had entered the war and even Negroes in the South were making money fast, many stories in accord with the tradition came out of that section. There was the one about the colored man who went into a general store and on hearing a phonograph for the first time promptly ordered six of them, one for each child in the house. I shall not stop to discuss whether Negroes in the South did that sort of thing or not, but I do know that those who got to New York didn't. The Negroes of Harlem, for the greater part, worked and saved their money. Nobody knew how much they had saved until congestion made expansion necessary for tenants and ownership profitable for landlords, and they began to buy property. Persons who would never be suspected of having money bought property. The Rev. W. W. Brown, pastor of the Metropolitan Baptist Church, repeatedly made "Buy Property" the text of his sermons. A large part of his congregation carried out the injunction. The church itself set an example by purchasing a magnificent brownstone church building on Seventh Avenue from a white congregation. Buying property became a fever. At the height of this activity, that is, 1920–21, it was not an uncommon thing for a colored washerwoman or cook to go into a real estate office and lay down from one thousand to five thousand dollars on a house. "Pig Foot Mary" is a character in Harlem. Everybody who knows the corner of Lenox Avenue and One Hundred and Thirty-fifth Street knows "Mary" and her stand, and has been tempted by the smell of her pigsfeet, fried chicken and hot corn, even if he has not been a customer. "Mary," whose real name is Mrs. Mary Dean, bought the five-story apartment house at the corner of Seventh Avenue and One Hundred and Thirty-seventh Street at a price of $42,000. Later she sold it to the Y. W. C. A. for dormitory purposes. The Y. W. C. A. sold it recently to Adolph

Howell, a leading colored undertaker, the price given being $72,000. Often companies of a half dozen men combined to buy a house—these combinations were and still are generally made up of West Indians—and would produce five or ten thousand dollars to put through the deal.

When the buying activity began to make itself felt, the lending companies that had been holding vacant the handsome dwellings on and abutting Seventh Avenue decided to put them on the market. The values on these houses had dropped to the lowest mark possible and they were put up at astonishingly low prices. Houses that had been bought at from $15,000 to $20,000 were sold at one-third those figures. They were quickly gobbled up. The Equitable Life Assurance Company held 106 model private houses that were designed by Stanford White. They are built with courts running straight through the block and closed off by wrought-iron gates. Every one of these houses was sold within eleven months at an aggregate price of about two million dollars. To-day they are probably worth about 100 per cent more. And not only have private dwellings and similar apartments been bought but big elevator apartments have been taken over. Corporations have been organized for this purpose. Two of these, The Antillian Realty Company, composed of West Indian Negroes, and the Sphinx Securities Company, composed of American and West Indian Negroes, represent holdings amounting to approximately $750,000. Individual Negroes and companies in the South have invested in Harlem real estate. About two years ago a Negro institution of Savannah, Ga., bought a parcel for $115,000 which it sold a month or so ago at a profit of $110,000.

I am informed by John E. Nail, a successful colored real estate dealer of Harlem and a reliable authority, that the total value of property in Harlem owned and controlled by colored people would at a conservative estimate amount to more than sixty million dollars. These figures are amazing, especially when we take into account the short time in which they have been piled up. Twenty years ago Negroes were begging for the privilege of renting a flat in Harlem. Fifteen years ago barely a half dozen colored men owned real property in all Manhattan. And down to ten years ago the amount that had been acquired in Harlem was comparatively negligible. To-day Negro Harlem is practically owned by Negroes.

The question naturally arises, "Are the Negroes going to be able to hold Harlem?" If they have been steadily driven northward for the past hundred years and out of less desirable sections, can they hold this choice bit of Manhattan Island? It is hardly probable that Negroes will hold Harlem indefinitely, but when they are forced out it will not be for the same reasons that forced them out of former quarters in New York City. The situation is entirely different and without precedent. When colored people do leave Harlem, their homes, their churches, their investments and their businesses, it will be because the land has become so valuable they can no longer afford to live on it. But the date of another move northward is very far in the future. What will Harlem be and become in the meantime? Is there danger that the Negro may lose his economic status in New York and be unable to hold his property? Will Harlem become merely a famous ghetto, or will it be a center of intellectual, cultural and economic forces exert-

ing an influence throughout the world, especially upon Negro peoples? Will it become
a point of friction between the races in New York?

I think there is less danger to the Negroes of New York of losing out economically and industrially than to the Negroes of any large city in the North. In most of the
big industrial centers Negroes are engaged in gang labor. They are employed by thousands in the stockyards in Chicago, by thousands in the automobile plants in Detroit;
and in those cities they are likely to be the first to be let go, and in thousands, with
every business depression. In New York there is hardly such a thing as gang labor
among Negroes, except among the longshoremen, and it is in the longshoremen's unions, above all others, that Negroes stand on an equal footing. Employment among Negroes in New York is highly diversified; in the main they are employed more as individuals than as non-integral parts of a gang. Furthermore, Harlem is gradually
becoming more and more a self-supporting community. Negroes there are steadily
branching out into new businesses and enterprises in which Negroes are employed. So
the danger of great numbers of Negroes being thrown out of work at once, with a resulting economic crisis among them, is less in New York than in most of the large
cities of the North to which Southern migrants have come.

These facts have an effect which goes beyond the economic and industrial situation. They have a direct bearing on the future character of Harlem and on the question
as to whether Harlem will be a point of friction between the races in New York. It is
true that Harlem is a Negro community, well defined and stable; anchored to its fixed
homes, churches, institutions, business and amusement places; having its own working,
business and professional classes. It is experiencing a constant growth of group consciousness and community feeling. Harlem is, therefore, in many respects, typically
Negro. It has many unique characteristics. It has movement, color, gayety, singing,
dancing, boisterous laughter and loud talk. One of its outstanding features is brass band
parades. Hardly a Sunday passes but that there are several of these parades of which
many are gorgeous with regalia and insignia. Almost any excuse will do—the death of
an humble member of the Elks, the laying of a cornerstone, the "turning out" of the
order of this or that. In many of these characteristics it is similar to the Italian colony.
But withal, Harlem grows more metropolitan and more a part of New York all the
while. Why is it then that its tendency is not to become a mere "quarter"?

I shall give three reasons that seem to me to be important in their order. First,
the language of Harlem is not alien; it is not Italian or Yiddish; it is English. Harlem
talks American, reads American, thinks American. Second, Harlem is not physically a
"quarter." It is not a section cut off. It is merely a zone through which four main ar-
teries of the city run. Third, the fact that there is little or no gang labor gives Harlem
Negroes the opportunity for individual expansion and individual contacts with the life
and spirit of New York. A thousand Negroes from Mississippi put to work as a gang in
a Pittsburgh steel mill will for a long time remain a thousand Negroes from Mississippi. Under the conditions that prevail in New York they would all within six months
become New Yorkers. The rapidity with which Negroes become good New Yorkers is
one of the marvels to observers.

These three reasons form a single reason why there is small probability that Har-

lem will ever be a point of race friction between the races in New York. One of the
principal factors in the race riot in Chicago in 1919 was the fact that at that time there
were 12,000 Negroes employed in gangs in the stockyards. There was considerable race
feeling in Harlem at the time of the hegira of white residents due to the "invasion," but
that feeling, of course, is no more. Indeed, a number of the old white residents who
didn't go and could not get away before the housing shortage struck New York are now
living peacefully side by side with colored residents. In fact, in some cases white and
colored tenants occupy apartments in the same house. Many white merchants still do
business in thickest Harlem. On the whole, I know of no place in the country where
the feeling between the races is so cordial and at the same time so matter-of-fact and
taken for granted. One of the surest safeguards against an outbreak in New York such
as took place in so many Northern cities in the summer of 1919 is the large proportion
of Negro police on duty in Harlem.

To my mind, Harlem is more than a Negro community; it is a large scale laboratory experiment in the race problem. The statement has often been made that if Negroes were transported to the North in large numbers the race problem with all of its
acuteness and with new aspects would be transferred with them. Well, 175,000 Negroes
live closely together in Harlem, in the heart of New York—75,000 more than live in
any Southern city—and do so without any race friction. Nor is there any unusual record
of crime. I once heard a captain of the 38th Police Precinct (the Harlem precinct) say
that on the whole it was the most law-abiding precinct in the city. New York guarantees its Negro citizens the fundamental rights of American citizenship and protects
them in the exercise of those rights. In return the Negro loves New York and is proud
of it, and contributes in his way to its greatness. He still meets with discriminations, but
possessing the basic rights, he knows that these discriminations will be abolished.

I believe that the Negro's advantages and opportunities are greater in Harlem
than in any other place in the country, and that Harlem will become the intellectual,
the cultural and the financial center for Negroes of the United States, and will exert a
vital influence upon all Negro peoples.

....The City*

LeRoi Jones

At the turn of the century most Negroes still lived in rural areas of the South, but by 1914 the largest exodus began. Masses of Negroes began to move to the Northern industrial centers such as Chicago, Detroit, New York. Between the years 1910 and 1920, for example, 60,000 Negroes migrated from the South to the city of Chicago. There were many reasons for this mass flight from the South, not all of them as obvious as the phrase "greater opportunity" would seem to indicate. Economically, the South was lagging behind the rest of the country in its move toward industrialization. America had once been primarily an agricultural country, but now, a few years after the turn of the century, the country was fast on its way to becoming the largest industrialized country in the world. But the South was behind, and as always, it was the black man who suffered most because of it. The North became the Promised Land, another Jordan—not only because of the tales of high-paying jobs for everyone there but because the South would always remain in the minds of most Negroes, even without the fresh oppression of the post-bellum Jim Crow laws, the scene of the crime.

What seems to me most important about these mass migrations was the fact that they must have represented a still further change within the Negro as far as his relationship with America was concerned. It can be called a psychological realignment, an attempt to reassess the worth of the black man within the society as a whole, an attempt to make the American dream work, if it were going to. It was a *decision* Negroes made to leave the South, not an historical imperative. And this decision must have been preceded by some kind of psychological shift; a reinterpretation by the Negro of his role in this country. It was the same kind of human "movement" that made jazz and classic blues possible—the discovery of America or its culture as would-be Americans. And the idea of a Jordan persisted, albeit this Jordan, to be sure, was of a much less supernatural nature. It was a Jordan that could almost be identified within the general emotional tenor of the whole of the American people. "Jobs, Homes, Dignity" was the way one Negro paper put it in the early twenties in constant editorials proselytizing for Negro migration to the North. But even more, the North suddenly represented a *further* idea of what this country and what a black man's life might be. Not every Negro left the South to get a better job. Some left so they could find a greater degree of freedom, and some so they could walk the streets after 10 P.M. (many Southern towns having ordinances against "night rambling nigras"). Some, like my father, left very suddenly after unfortunate altercations with white ushers in movies; some, like my grandfather, to start small thriving businesses (having had two grocery stores and a funeral parlor burned out from under him in Alabama). But whatever the peculiar reason for any one individual's flight northward, the significant idea is that the North now represented for Negroes a place where they could begin again, this time, perhaps, on more human footing.

The *Negro,* now, becomes more definitely *Negroes.* For the first time, after and during these mass flights to the North, Negroes spread out throughout the country. The South was no longer the only place where there were Negroes in great numbers. Chicago, Detroit, New York, Los Angeles, Washington, Philadelphia, all received in very short periods of time relatively large Negro populations. But more important, one essential uniformity, the provinciality of place, the geographical and social constant within the group, was erased. There were now such concepts as a Northern and a Southern Negro, and they would soon be, to a certain extent, different people.

By 1920, the proportion of Negroes in the North had increased to 14.1 per cent; five-sixths of those in the North were in large cities. Of course the new Jordan proved to be almost as harsh and slighting to Negroes as the South. Negroes received the lowest wages and did the hardest and most socially debasing work. Paul Oliver reports that "In the steel factories many of the jobs were restricted, but the 'open hearth' sections offered ready employment for Negroes; few others would work under the almost insufferable heat from the furnaces. Field hands weighed their chances against the disadvantages of severing themselves from their homes; the mills of Bessemer and Gary called, and they were gone." [1] But even faced with such a situation, the very idea of working inside a steel mill seemed glamorous to most Negroes, who had never done any work but agricultural labor in their lives. Five dollars a day was what Mr. Ford said, and Negroes came hundreds of miles to line up outside his employment offices.

It is interesting to note that there are a great many blues written about the Ford company and Ford products. One reason for this is the fact that Ford was one of the first companies to hire many Negroes, and the name *Ford* became synonymous with Northern opportunity, and the Ford Model-T was one of the first automobiles Negroes could purchase—"the poor man's car."

---

[1] *Blues Fell This Morning* (London, Cassell, 1960), p. 30.

Oliver, however, writes about Ford's policies of hiring Negroes:

"In 1914 the continual flow of immigrants from Europe to the United States ceased and the Northern industrialists, whose work was expanding with the demands of impending war, required cheap labor in quantity. Restricted immigration still operates today but it now has no major influence on the national economy; during the years of World War I when the stream of European unskilled labourers was halted, there was an acute labour shortage in the industrial North. Recruitment officers were sent South to draw Negroes from the plantations, and special freight cars were chartered to bring them to the North. . . . The cessation of the influx of European immigrants coincided with Henry Ford's announcement, in 1914, that none of his workers would earn less than five dollars per day, and it was in that year also that he commenced to employ Negroes on his assembly lines. As his huge plants in Detroit continued to expand and more coloured workers were taken on, the news reached the remotest corners of the South and attracted men who had been living in penury." [2]

Say, I'm goin' to get me a job now, workin' in Mr. Ford's place
Say, I'm goin' to get me a job now, workin' in Mr. Ford's place,
Say, that woman tol' me last night, "Say, you cannot even stand Mr. Ford's ways."

Blues, until the time of the classic blues singers, was largely a *functional* music; and it emerged from a music, the work song, that did not exist except as a strictly empirical communication of some part of the black slave's life. But the idea of the blues as a form of music that could be used to entertain people on a professional basis, *i.e.,* that people would actually pay to see and hear blues performed, was a revelation. And it was a revelation that gave large impetus to the concept of the "race" record.

Race records were commercial recordings aimed strictly toward the Negro market (what large companies would call their "special products division" today, in this era of social euphemism). The appearance and rapid growth of this kind of record was perhaps a formal recognition by America of the Negro's movement back toward the definable society. This recognition was indicated dramatically by the Okeh Record Company's decision to let a Negro singer make a commercial recording. Strangely enough, the first Negro blues singer to make a commercial recording was not Ma Rainey or Bessie Smith, or any of the other great classic or country blues singers, but a young woman, Mamie Smith, whose style of singing was more in the tradition of the vaudeville stage than it was "bluesy." Mamie's style, ironically enough, though blues-oriented, was much closer in overall effect to the woman she replaced at that first recording session— Sophie Tucker (Miss Tucker was too ill to record). Nevertheless, Mamie Smith and her recording of Perry Bradford's *Crazy Blues* ushered in the era of race records.

I can't sleep at night
I can't eat a bite

[2] *Ibid.,* pp. 31–32.

Cause the man I love
He didn't treat me right.

Now, I got the crazy blues
Since my baby went away
I ain't got no time to lose
I must find him today.

Actually, *Crazy Blues* was Mamie Smith's second recording. Her first recording
for the Okeh Company in New York was a disc containing two songs, *You Can't Keep
a Good Man Down* and *That Thing Called Love,* and although the immediate sales of the
first record weren't that spectacular, the company did see fit to have Miss Smith record
again. The next recording made history. This was on February 14, 1920, the beginning
of the "Jazz Age." (But a really strange phenomenon was the fact that the first jazz records had been made three years before, in 1917, by a white group, the Original Dixie-
land Jazz Band. So actually the Jazz Age had begun three years before the first blues recording. By 1920 Paul Whiteman was making millions as "King of Jazz"—the word, at
least, had entered the popular vocabulary. With such displays as Whiteman's Aeolian
Hall concert, complete with "European Style" orchestra and Heifetz and Rachmaninoff
in the audience, jazz had rushed into the mainstream without so much as one black face.
Whiteman's only reference to the earlier, less lucrative days of this "new" music ("sym-
phonized syncopation") was the first selection of his concert, which was *Livery Stable
Blues* done à la minstrel show jazz to demonstrate, as Whiteman said, ". . . the crude
jazz of the past." The Jazz Age can also be called the age of *recorded* blues and jazz because it was in the twenties that the great masses of jazz and blues material began to be
recorded, and not only were the race records sold in great numbers but Americans began
to realize for the first time that there was a *native* American music as traditionally wild,
happy, disenchanted, and unfettered as it had become fashionable for them to think they
themselves had become.

Of course, looking at the phenomenon of race records from a more practical
point of view, as I am certain the owners of Okeh must have done, Mamie Smith's records proved dramatically the existence of a not yet exploited market. *Crazy Blues* sold
for months at a rate of 8,000 records a week. Victoria Spivey's first record, *Black Snake
Blues,* recorded six years later, sold 150,000 copies in one year. So it is easy to see that
there were no altruistic or artistic motives behind the record companies' decision to continue and enlarge the race category. Race records swiftly became big business. The companies also began to hire Negroes as talent scouts and agents so that they would be able
to get the best Negro talent available for their new race catalogues.

Early advertising for the race records might now seem almost ridiculously crass,
but apparently it was effective and very much of the times. This is an example taken
from a Columbia Records advertisement that appeared in 1926; the song being advertised was something called *Wasn't It Nice:* "There sure am mean harmonizing when
Howell, Horsley and Bradford start in on 'Wasn't it Nice.' You're a gonna think it's
nice when you once get the old disc a-spinning. The boys are still going strong when

they tackle the coupling 'Harry Wills, the Champion.' This trio sneaks right up on a chord, knocks it down, and jumps all over it." [3] Certainly this is a far cry from the light-skinned well-groomed Negroes who sip their sociable Pepsi Colas in the pages of to-day's Negro periodicals; but the intent, I think, is quite similar.

The Negro as *consumer* was a new and highly lucrative slant, an unexpected addition to the strange portrait of the Negro the white American carried around in his head. It was an unexpected addition for the Negro as well. The big urban centers, like the new "black cities" of Harlem, Chicago's South Side, Detroit's fast-growing Negro section, as well as the larger cities of the South were immediate witnesses to this phenomenon. Friday nights after work in those cold gray Jordans of the North, Negro working-men lined up outside record stores to get the new blues, and as the money rolled in, the population of America, as shown on sales prognostication charts in the offices of big American industry, went up by one-tenth.

Another important result of the race records was that with the increased circulation of blues, certain styles of singing became models for a great many aspiring blues artists. (The classic urban singers were recorded first, for obvious reasons; it was some years later before the country singers were recorded.) Before race records, blues form was usually dependent on strictly local tradition. Of course, the coming of the traveling shows changed this somewhat, as I have mentioned, but the race recordings really began to put forth extra-local models and styles of blues-singing which must have influenced younger Negroes. (Even in rural areas of the South, there was always at least one family that had a "victrola," which drew their neighbors from miles around. The coming of radio, which I will discuss later, also had a profound effect on blues in a similar fashion.) It has been said, for instance, that a great many of the blues singers from Missouri, St. Louis especially, sing through their noses. A woman like Ida Cox, who certainly does sing through her nose, would, in the pre-vaudeville, pre-phonograph era only have influenced people in her immediate vicinity. But when Ida began to work with the traveling shows, her style was heard and copied by a great many more people. And in one sense, as I have explained, this was why the so-called classic blues singers were classic. Not only because their styles were a kind of beautiful balance between the urban and country styles of blues, but because these classic singers were heard by more people and were widely imitated. The phonograph record increased one thousandfold the widespread popularity and imitation of certain blues singers; and because of this, phonograph records themselves actually *created* whole styles of blues-singing. And time though the local traditions remained, the phonograph record produced the first blues stars and nationally known blues personalities. For instance, a singer like Victoria Spivey, who was a typical example of the popular, post-classic, race-record blues singer (she became so popular she had a starring role while still under twenty, in King Vidor's "experiment" *Hallelujah*), was first drawn to blues-singing by the records of Bessie Smith and Sarah Martin, who, at the time, sold more blues records than anyone else. It is easy to see how this must have affected the existing folk tradition and created another kind

[3] From Samuel B. Charters, *The Country Blues* (New York, Rinehart, 1959), illus. opposite p. 160.

of tradition that was unlike any other in the past. And if the old calendar picture of Negroes sitting around a little shack, strumming guitars and singing happily and carelessly, had by the nature of certain sociological factors been caused to dim, certainly the new stereotype to replace that vanishing paternalistic image could have been a group of Negroes sitting around listening to records by their favorite blues artists.

Martin Williams mentions another effect the phonograph record had on blues form. Blues was traditionally an improvised music that could be sung or played as long as the performer could come up with fresh improvisations, but recorded performance meant that there was a certain definite and limited space of time in which the singer could perform. "At their own right tempo each of these singers could get in about four blues stanzas on a ten-inch recording. Many singers . . . responded to the limitations of time on records by simply stringing together four stanzas on (more or less) the same subject; others . . . attempted some kind of narrative continuity." [4]

Speaking of classic blues singers Sarah Martin and Ida Cox, Williams says: "Both of these singers do more; they give each blues a specifically poetic development which takes subtle advantage of the four-stanza limitation and creates a kind of classic form within it." [5]

FOGYISM

Why do people believe in some old sign?
Why do people believe in some old sign?
You hear a hoot owl holler, someone is surely dyin'.

Some will break a mirror and cry, "Bad luck for seven years,"
Some will break a mirror and cry, "Bad luck for seven years,"
And if a black cat crosses them, they'll break right down in tears.

To dream of muddy water—trouble is knocking at your door,
To dream of muddy water—trouble is knocking at your door,
Your man is sure to leave you and never return no more.

When your man comes home evil, tells you you are getting old,
When our man comes home evil, tells you you are getting old,
That's a *true* sign he's got someone else bakin' his jelly roll.

While the classic singers were making records, theater appearances, national tours, another more private kind of blues had grown up, given the catalyst of the Negro's move to the large urban centers. A new city, or urban, blues had appeared outside the main theatrical tradition being created by the classic singers. The city blues grew in

[4] "Recording Limits and Blues Form" in Martin T. Williams, ed., *The Art of Jazz* (New York, Oxford University Press, 1959), pp. 91–92.
[5] *Ibid.*, p. 92.

the various after-hours joints, house rent parties (parties where the low admission helped pay the rent—or at least that was used as the excuse for the party), and barbecue and gut parties (where either chitterlings or hog maws were served). This music, like the country blues, was something directly out of the lives of the people involved:

> My baby she found a brand new place to go
> My baby she found a brand new place to go
> She hangs across town at the Monte Carlo.
>
> She likes my money, tells me she goin' to the picture show
> She likes my money, tells me she goin' to the picture show
> But that girl's been throwin' my money away at the Monte Carlo.
>
> (From *Monte Carlo Blues* by Roosevelt Sykes)

Classic blues was entertainment and country blues, folklore. The blues and blues-oriented jazz of the new city dwellers was harder, crueler, and perhaps even more stoical and hopeless than the earlier forms. It took its life from the rawness and poverty of the grim adventure of "big city livin'." It was a slicker, more sophisticated music, but the people, too, could fit these descriptions. The tenements, organized slums, gin mills, and back-breaking labors in mills, factories, or on the docks had to get into the music somehow.

To most Negroes, urban living was a completely strange idea. They had come from all over the South, from backwoods farms as sharecroppers who had never even been to the moderately large cities of the South, into the fantastic metropolises of the North. It must have been almost as strange as that initial trip their ancestors made centuries before into the New World. Now the Negroes had not even the land to walk across. Everywhere were cement, buildings, and streets filled up with automobiles. Whole families jammed up in tiny, unbelievably dirty flats or rooming houses. But the sole idea was "to move," to split from the incredible fabric of guilt and servitude identified so graphically within the Negro consciousness as the white South. However, there was a paradox, even in the emotionalism of this reasoning. The South was *home.* It was the place that Negroes knew, and given the natural attachment of man to land, even loved. The North was to be beaten, there was room for attack. No such room had been possible in the South, but it was still what could be called home. The emigrants sang, "I'm a poor ol' boy, a long ways from home," or "I rather drink muddy water and sleep in a hollow log/Than go up to New York City and be treated like a dirty dog."

Still after a time, the newly arrived Negroes from the South were the brunt of the Northern Negro's jibes. Nothing was quite as disparaging as to be called "a country boy." It was an epithet delivered with almost as much scorn as when the religious people might call some backslider a "heathen." To the new city dwellers, the "country boy" was someone who still bore the mark, continued the customs, of a presumably discarded Southern past. But the displaced persons made quick movements toward the accomplishment of the local sophistication and in a few months could even join in to taunt a new arrival with greetings like, "Hey, Cornbread!"

My home's in Texas, what am I doin' up here?
My home's in Texas, what am I doin' up here?
Yes, my good corn whisky, baby, and women brought me here.

The local sophistication for the newly arrived Negroes was swift acclimatization to the conflicts and strangeness of the city. And acclimatization could mean so many things. The "rent party" was a form of acclimatization, the relief check, another. The early twentieth century was a very significant time for the Negro in the United States. In the city there was a wider psychological space for everybody. Things spread out in the cities, dispersed as was never possible in the South. The hand of the paternalistic society was subtler, and that subtlety enabled the Negroes to *improvise* a little more in their approach to it. There was even the simple fact that people could make their living now, when they did, in a greater variety of ways. You could work for Ford or run an elevator, be a pimp or (soon) a postman, etc.—but the idea was to "get in," to "make it" as best one could. This acclimatization had to occur in all facets of the urban Negro's life. But the "new people" brought with them the older customs and the older attitudes, and even though they rushed with all speed (in relation to their economic, hence *social,* status) into the cool waters of American culture, they brought with them at least, their songs.

I used to have a woman that lived up on a hill,
I used to have a woman that lived up on a hill,
She was crazy 'bout me, ooh well, well, 'cause I worked at the Chicago mill.

You can hear the women hollerin' when the Chicago Mill whistle blows,
You can hear the women hollerin' when the Chicago Mill whistle blows,
Cryin', "Turn loose my man, ooh well, well, please and let him go."

If you want to have plenty women why not work at the Chicago Mill?
If you want to have plenty women why not work at the Chicago Mill?
You don't have to give them nothin', oooh well, jest tell them that you will.

(From *Chicago Mill Blues* by Peatie Wheatstraw)

The "balance" that the constant, northward flow of Southern Negro culture provided for Negroes in the North manifested itself in innumerable ways. Tom Davin's interviews with James P. Johnson, one of the masters of what came to be known as "New York stride piano" mentions the phenomena of "acclimatization" and "balance":

"One night a week, I played for Drake's Dancing Class on 62nd Street, which we called 'The Jungles Casino.' It was officially a dancing school, since it was very hard for Negroes to get a dance-hall license. But you could get a license to open a dancing school very cheap.

"The Jungles Casino was just a cellar, too, without fixings. The furnace, coal, and ashes were still there behind a partition. The coal bin was handy for guests to stash their liquor in case the cops dropped in.

"There were dancing classes all right, but there were no teachers. The 'pupils' danced sets, two-steps, waltzes, schottisches, and 'The Metropolitan Glide,' a new step.

"I played for these regulation dances, but instead of playing straight, I'd break into a rag in certain places. The older ones didn't care too much for this, but the younger ones would scream when I got good to them with a bit of rag in the dance music now and then.

". . . The dances they did at The Jungles were wild and comical—the more pose and the more breaks, the better. These Charleston people and the other southerners had just come to New York. They were country people and they felt homesick. When they got tired of two-steps and schottisches (which they danced with a lot of spieling) they'd yell: 'Let's go back home!' . . . 'Let's do a set!' . . . or 'Now, put us in the alley!' I did my *Mule Walk* or *Gut Stomp* for these country dances.

"Breakdown music was the best for such sets, the more solid and groovy the better. They'd dance, hollering and screaming until they were cooked. The dances ran from fifteen to thirty minutes, but they kept up all night long or until their shoes wore out—most of them after a heavy day's work on the docks." [6]

The Southerners brought the blues north with them, and it was the fusion of the older traditions with "the new learning" that produced the urban blues, though the earlier blues forms still persisted. But for most Negroes who were raised in the North, blues was something quite *new*. The Northern Negro, *i.e.,* the one raised in the North, had from the outset of his life been exposed to the kind of *centerless* culture to which the new Northerners were just now adjusting. The young Negro who had always lived in the North was never aware of a "purer" Negro culture than the consciously diluted model that existed there. Before the great movements north, many Northern Negroes were quite purposely resisting what could be called their cultural heritage in an attempt to set up a completely "acceptable" route into what they had come to think of as the broadness of American society. Blatant references to "the South," and all the frightening associations that word produced, were not tolerated. But with the coming of the black hordes, it was no longer possible to completely suppress these references and their associations. Whereas the older Northern Negroes might have forbidden their children the blues or simply refused to expose them to it, with the coming of the new citizens whole areas of "Southern Negro" culture were thrust upon these innocent youths.

The Negro musician in the North, before what are called the "jazz years," was usually well within the tradition of white "show" music (and brass-band style), if he played "popular" music, or else he was a "serious" musician. Just as the New Orleans Creoles had learned European music on European instruments from European teachers, so had the Northern Negro been trained. In an interview by Nat Hentoff, Garvin Bushell, a clarinetist with some of the pre-blues "Northern" Negro groups, placed the situation in its proper perspective.

"[The playing of] New York musicians of the time was different than the

---

[6] "Conversations with James P. Johnson," *Jazz Review* (July, 1959), pp. 11–12.

playing of men in Chicago, St. Louis, Texas and New Orleans. New York 'jazz' then was nearer the ragtime style and had less blues. There wasn't an Eastern performer who could really play the blues. We later absorbed how from the Southern musicians we heard, but it wasn't original with us. We didn't put that quarter-tone pitch in the music the way the Southerners did. Up North we learned the ragtime conception—a lot of notes.

"On Sundays I rehearsed with a band from Florida. The way they played reminded me of my uncle's work in the circus band. They played real blues.

"Gradually, the New York cabarets began to hear more of the real pure jazz and blues by musicians from Florida, South Carolina, Georgia, Louisiana, etc. What they played was more expressive than had been heard in New York to that time.

"You could only hear the blues and real jazz in the gutbucket cabarets where the lower class went. The term 'gutbucket' came from the chitterlings bucket. Chitterlings are the guts of a hog and the practice used to be to take a bucket to the slaughterhouse and get a bucket of guts. Therefore, anything real low down was called gutbucket." [7]

Again, the marvelous paradox created by ghetto reasoning and the social predicates out of which it issued. The Northern musicians who wouldn't play blues or "jass" were quite happy playing American and European popular music, including light opera —anything within the shadowy world of semiclassical music—but all was played in the raggy style of the day, which, of course, had been the result of white dilutions of Negro ragtime styles. And even though the Negro musicians who imitated "popular" ragtime styles were merely trying to reflect the dominant tastes of the day, they still managed to bring a separate cultural knowledge (maintained by the "blue" tones of the Negro church) to their "syncopated music," as it was called then.

Northern Negro pre-jazz music was almost like the picture within a picture within a picture, and so on, on the cereal package. Ragtime was a Negro music, resulting from the Negro's appropriation of white piano techniques used in show music. Popularized ragtime, which flooded the country with songsheets in the first decade of this century, was a dilution of the Negro style. And finally, the show and "society" music the Negroes in the pre-blues North made was a kind of bouncy, essentially vapid appropriation of the popularized imitations of Negro imitations of white minstrel music, which, as I mentioned earlier, came from white parodies of Negro life and music. And then we can go back even further to the initial "steal" American Negro music is based on, that is, those initial uses Euro-American music was put to by the Afro-American. The hopelessly interwoven fabric of American life where blacks and whites pass so quickly as to become only grays!

Typical of the kind of black orchestras that thrived in the North at the beginning of the century were James Reese Europe's various Clef Club and Tempo Club orchestras. As accompanist for Vernon and Irene Castle, it was Europe who with his Europe's Society Orchestra was largely responsible for introducing the Castle Walk and

[7] "Garvin Bushell and New York Jazz in the 1920's," *Jazz Review* (January, 1959), p. 12.

Fox Trot to America. Europe had concerts at Carnegie Hall where he played such music as *Indian Summer, Concert Waltz,* and other semi-classical, mildly ragged items, and at one concert the orchestration of his 100-piece orchestra included ten pianos and forty-seven mandolins! Needless to say, Europe's orchestra was the first Negro "dance band" to be recorded.

The invasion of the North by Southern musicians was augmented by the closing of New Orleans' red light district, Storyville, in 1917. This threw a great many Negro and Creole musicians out of work, and they joined the trek northward. The larger Northern dance bands began to hire some of the Southern musicians because at the time the "dada strain" of the blues-oriented instrumentalists was thought to be an added "novelty" feature that could increase an orchestra's commercial value. But usually the Northern Negro musician came under the influence of these Southern musicians with their "hot" or bluesy intonations. And by the time the phonograph record became popular, this "hot" style was spread to an even broader Northern audience, black and white alike.

World War I was an extremely significant phenomenon insofar as it related to the movement of the Negroes into the mainstream of American life. The rudeness with which "the great war" dragged America and most of the Western world into the twentieth century served also to produce the "modern" American Negro. The war proposed to the great masses of Negroes that the world was indeed much more than America. The idea of Europe as a place where other people lived who had a consistent social definition as "white people" just like American white people was to most Negroes a major revelation. And when Negroes went into the services in their special black units, even though they were designed to utilize black bodies while continuously avoiding any recognition of these bodies as belonging to other human beings, there was still a sense of actual *participation* in the affairs and fortunes of the country that was heightened by the recognition these black troops received in various parts of Europe, France notably. After the war, the returning soldiers with their tales of Europe and its white people so like but so very unlike the American whites caused a great deal of open resentment among Negroes about the racially restrictive social mores of American life.

In Richard Wright's novel *Black Boy,* there is a passage that in part describes the white man's reaction to this newly acquired "international" sense World War I produced in many Negroes, North or South: "Among the topics that southern white men did not like to discuss with Negroes were the following: American white women; The Ku Klux Klan; France, and how Negro soldiers fared while there; French women; Jack Johnson; the entire northern part of the United States; the civil war, Abraham Lincoln; U. S. Grant; General Sherman; Catholics; the Pope; Jews; the Republican Party; Slavery; Social Equality; Communism; Socialism; the 13th, 14th, and 15th Amendments to the Constitution; or any topic calling for positive knowledge or manly self-assertion on the part of the Negro." [8] (Nor, I suppose, could many Negroes before the northward movement or World War I discuss these things. They simply did not exist.)

---

[8] *Black Boy* (New York, Harper Bros., 1937), p. 202.

For the first time, Negroes began to feel the singularity of their plight as American black men. And there have never been so many race riots in this country as during and immediately after World War I. Race relations, as our peculiar mode of mutual mistrust between blacks and whites is termed, reached a terrifying nadir, manifested by such bloody episodes of violence as the East St. Louis race riots of 1917. It was the war also that was responsible in many ways for swelling the numbers of Negroes leaving the South. As I mentioned before, the wartime economy of this country created a great many factory jobs in the North that were open to Negroes. Also, after the war was over, a great many younger Negroes who had been in the army could no longer be satisfied with "the mind of the South." The tradition of silent acceptance had become much too stifling. It is significant that World War II produced a similar social crisis in this country.

World War I not only pointed up the social inequities of American life as being peculiar to America, but also, because of this delineation, these social inequities suffered by the black man could for the first time be looked at somewhat objectively by Negroes as an *evil,* and not merely as their eternal *lot.* It was during these times that the first widespread organized resistance by Negroes against these evils began to form. The race riots were one manifestation of this tendency, also the appearance of groups like Marcus Garvey's black nationalist organization, which advocated that Negroes return to Africa. (The NAACP, which had been formed some years earlier in 1909, enjoyed during the first years after the war its greatest support from poorer Negroes, a support it has since lost in favor of the support of white liberal philanthropists and the Negro bourgeoisie.) The Garvey movement, even though ill-fated, enjoyed a great deal of popularity among poorer Negroes, and it is important to realize that even at the time of World War I and the years directly following, the Negro masses had not moved so far into the mainstream of American life that they could forget there was an Africa out of which their forebears had been taken and to which they themselves might yet have to return.

Another blues music to appear in the cities around this same time was what was called boogie woogie. Basically a piano music, boogie woogie rose to its greatest popularity in the rent parties and juke joints of the North, even though, characteristically enough, it had its origins in the primitive blues of the Southern country Negro. It seemed to be a fusion of vocal blues and the earlier guitar techniques of the country singers, adapted for the piano. The old blues singers called it "Western" piano, meaning that the music had originated in the mining and lumber camps of the West and Midwest. In some ways boogie bears strong resemblance to ragtime piano style, although the repeated "rolling" (*ostinato*) figure used in boogie piano identifies it immediately. Ragtime was the first appropriation of white pianistic techniques by Negro musicians, boogie woogie was the second appropriation of a "pianistic" approach to the instrument, but in such a blatantly percussive and blueslike manner as to separate it immediately from any more Europeanized music. In keeping with the traditional styles of Negro music, boogie woogie also was predominantly a music of rhythmic contrasts rather than melodic or harmonic variations.

Most of the great boogie pianists came north in the general exodus during the first three decades of the century (although a few of them, like Jimmy Yancey and Albert Ammons, were born in Chicago, the city where boogie received its first popularity). The boogie pianist achieved a special social status, playing at the various Chittlin' Struts, Gumbo Suppers, Fish Fries, Egg Nog Parties. His services were much sought after, and he could gain entrance to all these "pay-parties" without being expected to pay. "If you could play piano good, you went from one party to another and everybody made a fuss about you and fed you ice cream, cake, food and drinks. In fact, some of the biggest men in the profession were known as the biggest eaters we had. At an all-night party, you started at 1 A.M., had another meal at 4 A.M. Many of us suffered later because of eating and drinking habits started in our younger socializing days." [9]

I don't mind playin' anytime y'all can get me drunk,
But Mr. Pinetop is sober now.
I been playing the piano round here all night long
And y'all ain't bought the first drink somehow.
(From *I'm Sober Now* by Clarence "Pine Top" Smith)

One reason perhaps why boogie woogie remained predominantly a piano music (until its eventual dilution and commercialization) was because of the general environment that served as catalyst for its development. Although ragtime was also a piano music, the very fact that it was a "composed" music (and sheet music could be issued so quickly on a large scale) meant that it could be performed by any number of pieces and in almost any environment. It took much longer for boogie sheet music to arrive, because boogie woogie was still a largely improvised music.

Small, very amateurishly lettered signs would appear in the local stores and restaurants, advertising the larger parties. (The number of grocery stores and restaurants offering "Southern Specialties" had increased tenfold throughout the North, and in any Negro neighborhood it was possible to find the hogmaws, chitterlin's, collards, pig knuckles, tails, feet, snouts, that were so integral to Southern Negro cuisine. This was one of the first organized industries Negroes in the North got into, packaging and selling their traditional foods. Today, some of these same foods are packaged and sold by large white companies for Negro consumption, but foods like yams and collard greens have also found their way into a great many non-Negro kitchens.) On the weekends, after a hard week of work, hundreds of dancers would crowd into the "blue light" parties to "grind" or "slow-drag" or belly-rub." There would usually be four or five pianists at any really popular affair, and each would take his turn at the "box." The parties could last all weekend, and for some intrepid souls, well into the week. The Third Ward of Newark once boasted for several months, until the law moved in, a rent party promoted by two blues singers which was called "The Function" and which advertised

[9] "Conversations with James P. Johnson," p. 10.

that one could "Grind Till You Lose Your Mind." It was at these kinds of parties that boogie woogie developed.

> I want you to pull up on your blouse, let down on your skirt,
> Get down so low you think you're in the dirt . . .
> Now when I say "Boogie!" I want you to boogie;
> When I say "Stop!" I want you to stop right still . . .
>
> (From *Pinetop's Boogie Woogie*
> by Clarence "Pine Top" Smith)

The success of race recordings soon led the companies to record not only the classic blues singers but also a few boogie-woogie pianists and country singers as well. The larger record companies began setting up permanent Southern offices for the discovery of new talent, and some really ambitious companies like Columbia even had a mobile unit that roamed the South, recording people like Barbecue Bob, Peg Leg Howell, Blind Willie Johnson, Lillian Glinn, Pink Anderson, Blind Willie McTell (recording then under the name "Blind Sammie"), Bobby Cadillac, Aaron T-Bone Walker, and many other singers who sang what was essentially folk material. But, for the most part, the rent-party pianists, with exceptions like Clarence "Pine Top" Smith, Eurreal Montgomery, Hersal Thomas, remained unrecorded. The music, boogie woogie, still remained so extremely functional that it could be considered by its exponents as strictly an avocation, rather than a way to make a living. Most of the better boogie-woogie pianists had other jobs, just like the earlier blues singers, and their boogie was something they created for themselves within the environment of those "new" black cities of the North.

American Negro Art*
Cedric Dover

The only Negro artist presented by *The New Negro* was Aaron Douglas. The geometric symbolism of his illustrations for it moved forward quickly into the illuminated shades and contrasts, integrated with a classical sense of proportion and interval, of his suggestive illustrations for James Weldon Johnson's *God's Trombones: Seven Negro Sermons in Verse* (1927). These transformed folk sermons conveyed the imagery and manner of the fundamentalist Negro minister in highly sophisticated verse; and Douglas pictorialized that imagery in a way that remains unique in book illustration.

Deprived of the opportunity to collaborate again with a creative writer of equal stature, Douglas developed his particular symbolic style in his murals. Criticisms of them in terms of elongation and angularities, patterns of mystical light, implausible exoticism and so on are merely trite. The importance of his murals is that they communicate their intentions in an original and satisfying way, without benefit from any school. His expression of light, in Sir Kenneth Clark's phrase, is an 'expression of love'.

Other artists soon followed Aaron Douglas into the Renaissance and some were dragged, temporarily, into it. His own description of what happened is just enough exaggerated to emphasize the truth:

> Harlem was sifted. Neither streets, homes nor public institutions escaped. When unsuspecting Negroes were found with a brush in their hands they were immediately hauled away and held for interpretation. They were given places of honour and bowed to with much ceremony. Every effort to protest their innocence was drowned out with big-mouthed praise. A number escaped and returned to a more reasonable existence. Many fell in with the game and went along making hollow and meaningless gestures with brush and palette.
> But . . . the Negro artists have emerged . . .

Their emergence was celebrated in January 1928 by the Harmon Foundation at

* From Cedric Dover, *American Negro Art* (New York: New York Graphic Society, 1960), pp. 31–33, 34–35. Reprinted by permission of Studio Vista Limited.

International House, New York, in the first all-Negro exhibition in America. Some of the eighty-seven items were oddments of schoolgirl standard, but the majority were more than creditable. Apart from Aaron Douglas, many of the exhibitors became, and remained, eminent in American Negro art: Augusta Savage and Sargent Johnson among the sculptors, Allan Freelon, John Hardrick, Palmer Hayden, Malvin Gray Johnson, James Porter, William Scott, Laura Wheeler Waring and Hale Woodruff among the painters. The photographic work involved was done by James Latimer Allen, the pioneer Negro creative photographer.

Archibald Motley, winner of the Harmon Gold Award for 1928, was not included as his pictures were being shown at the New Galleries. May Howard Jackson received the Bronze Award, though her work was also not available. William Johnson won the Gold Award in 1929, though he did not exhibit until 1930; and Nancy Elizabeth Prophet took a prize, though she too did not exhibit until 1930. Motley and Richmond Barthé joined the Harmon exhibit in 1929; Allan Crite, Lois Jones and Ellis Wilson in 1930; William Cooper, Meta Fuller, James Wells (winner of the Gold Award in 1930), Edwin Harleston and May Howard Jackson in 1931.

By 1933, William Artis, Henry Bannarn, Leslie Bolling, Joseph Carter, Samuel Brown, Beauford DeLaney, Elton Fax and Romeyn Van Vleck Lippman were among the hundred and twenty-five artists who had taken advantage of the facilities offered by the Foundation. These included five exhibitions, travelling exhibits seen by nearly half a million people in fifty cities, co-operation in several exhibitions, the promotion of art education in Negro schools and colleges, and much other assistance. A new situation, marked by the Whitney Museum's purchase of Nancy Prophet's *Congolaise* and three works by Barthé, had been created.

Critics of the Harmon Foundation's activities failed to realize that, while patronizing mediocrity, it was also sponsoring the makers of modern Negro art; and that one of its most important services was the provision of opportunities for critics to criticize. Romare Bearden, then a student, was severe:

> Many of the Negro artists argue that . . . since the Negro is becoming so amalgamated with the white race, and has accepted the white man's civilization he must progress along those lines. Even if this is true, they are certainly not taking advantage of the Negro scene. The Negro in his various environments in America, holds a great variety of rich experiences for the genuine artists. . . . Instead, the Negro artist will proudly exhibit his 'Scandinavian Landscape', a locale that is entirely alien to him. This will of course impress the uninitiated who, through some feeling of inferiority toward their own subject matter, only require that a work of art have some sort of foreign stamp to make it acceptable. . . .
>
> No one can doubt that the Negro is possessed of remarkable gifts of imagination and intuition. When he has learned to harness his great gifts of rhythm and pours it into his art—his chance of creating something individual will be heightened. At present it seems that by a slow study of rules and formulas the Negro artist is attempting to do something with his intellect, which he has not felt emotionally. In consequence he has given us poor echoes of the work of white artists—and nothing of himself. . . .

There are quite a few foundations that sponsor exhibitions of the work of Negro artists. . . . Take for instance the Harmon Foundation. . . . It has encouraged the artist to exhibit long before he has mastered the technical equipment of his medium. By its choice of the type of work it favors, it has allowed the Negro artist to accept standards that are both artificial and corrupt. . . .

The artist must be the medium through which humanity expresses itself. In this sense the greatest artists have faced the realities of life, and have been profoundly social. . . . An intense, eager devotion to present day life, to study it, to help relieve it, this is the calling of the Negro artist.

The fundamental truths in Mr. Bearden's assessment remain true. What it overlooked was that the making of good art amongst underprivileged peoples is necessarily accompanied by the making of much more bad art; that it would be unwise for an encouraging organization to pontificate on what is good and bad, especially as time changes viewpoints and matures some artists at least; and that most of the artists for whom the Harmon Foundation opened doors were doing just what Mr. Bearden required. They were facing realities; they were relieving the burdens of living; they were chronicling, interpreting and sometimes transforming. In doing so, they were meeting the needs of their own people—and the ultimate test of any work of art is its value to the society in which it is produced, not its reception by the coteries as amusing, exotic, exciting, interesting, original or universal.

Universal art does not arise from the intention to be universal: it is sifted out of deeply rooted community art. 'The artist must work in contact with society,' Henry Moore told a Unesco conference a few years ago, 'but that contact must be an intimate one. I believe that the best artists have always had their roots in a definite social group or community, or in a particular region. We know what small and intimate communities produced the great sculpture of Athens, or Chartres, or Florence.'

The Negro artist is fortunate in belonging to a definite group organized as regional communities; and within the group is a pulsing folkart, and pervading urgencies of mythology, conditions, circumstances and viewpoints, for absorption, transformation and return to the group as works of art. The Negro Renaissance began the work of drawing upon the inspirations of this living classicism, but was inevitably motivated much more by 'race' pride. The fact that there are no races, that all human groups are mongrelized, has seldom disturbed such satisfactions.

The rediscovery of African culture, and 'the legacy of the ancestral arts', therefore offered hopes of racial inheritance, but actually produced little more in poetry than desires to see 'slim palm trees pulling at the clouds' or other arboreal phenomena. The visual arts accordingly gained colour, but Alain Locke was compelled to admit in 1940 that 'when the younger Negro artists first became aware of this heritage, a sudden and hectic interest flared up which led, unfortunately, to relatively superficial understanding and shallow artistic results. African art could yield little through direct imitation or sophisticated racial pride.'

Nevertheless, he thought that African art could 'still have rich inspiration to offer to any artist, but especially to a group of artists who may sense or cultivate a close spiritual kinship with it'. It may be that he was more prophetic than his critics knew, for there are indications that the upsurge of African nationalisms will give American Negroes greatly increased opportunities for extending their cultural understanding and contributing to African needs. The activities of the American Society of African Culture, New York, and the superb special number of *Présence Africaine* edited by the Executive Director of the Society, John A. Davis, promise a happy future for co-operation between Africans, West Indians and American Negroes. One hopes it will not be afflicted, as Indian friendships were by J. Saunders Redding *(An American in India),* by ex-radicals turned near-pukka sahibs.

It should be recognized, too, that sentimental Africanism prompted new values basic to group pride. Concepts of feminine beauty in Negro literature, so important in this respect, moved conspicuously in the direction of the variously expressed preferences of the common people: 'a sealskin brown make the preacher lay his Bible down'; 'the blacker the berry, the sweeter the juice'. A study, for example, by Cynthia Mathis (in the thesis Library of Fisk University) of seventy-one novels by Negroes from 1886 to 1936 showed an increasing preference for dark skins, especially after 1920: of 147 beautiful women among their characters, twenty-five were white, fifty-six yellow, fifty-six brown and ten black, the whites being in the earlier, and the blacks in the later, works.

• • •

And, as artists are poets too, they soon joined this ferment of awareness. Some came out of the studios of yesterday to add inspired documentation of people and places; others interpreted the spirit of their time. A glimpse of their achievements is afforded by several pictures in the text and plates of this book.

Aaron Douglas found no rival in the symbolic treatment of themes, but in realistic portraiture he acknowledged an equal in Archibald Motley epochs lived in Mr. Motley's portraits, James Porter, then barely past the young student stage, was moving into the company of these older men as an interpreter of the Negro face. His drawings had the swift gripping precision of a Delacroix; his oils were revelations of the soul. Unfortunately destroyed by fire, his very early *Sarah* (1928) remains in reproduction one of the most haunting portraits in Negro art. The same quality of brooding beyond personal distress lives in his *Woman Holding a Jug,* but it gives more than a hint of previously resisted indulgence in the decorative temptations to which his mature style succumbed. His attractive tribute to Dorothy Porter, a leading figure in the world of Negro scholarship, is an example.

Neither Douglas nor Porter painted a period. Motley did. In fact, no other Negro artist reflected the preoccupations of the 'twenties and their aftermath more typically and interestingly: a Roman Catholic born in New Orleans, with a proud claim to part-Pygmy ancestry, he was emotionally fitted to do so. He gave a decade tortured by racial mystiques the exquisite torture of superb pictures of the *fille de couleur* which brought Lafcadio Hearn's ecstasies to the eye, for each one was a 'thoroughbred representing the true secret of grace—economy of force'.

He also left us a series of evocative impressions of Negro and Parisian night life which belong to the history of an age. They are social comments but not satires. The compassion of true artistry, the communicated flow of rhythm and misdirected vitality, raise them above caricature.

Mr. Motley was alone, too, in taking Africanism seriously. He did not look to it for motifs or lessons in design; he did the artist's job of trying to transform various tribal myths in his own manner. His 'symbolic realism' visualized the control of nature by magic, but the dark continent was still so dark and full of Voodoo that critics saw in his African pictures no more than the exuberant treatment of rank vegetation, lurking terror, the mystery of tropical moons, and savage submission to sorcery. Edward Alden Jewell stood before them bewitched:

> Vivid pictures they are and weirdly unique their subjects. Here are steaming jungles that drip and sigh and ooze, dank in the impenetrable gloom of palm and woven tropical verdure, or ablaze with light where the sun breaks fiercely in. Here are moons that rise, yellow and round, quizzical and portentous, aureoled with a pallor of sorcery; crescent moons with secrets cryptically packed in the shining scimitar, and moons that wane and die with a shudder of spent prophecy. . . . There are devil-devils watching in the solemn night or poised to swoop on hapless human prey. There are thunders and lightnings with revelation imprisoned in their heart of death. There are charms, simple or unsearchable, to lure a smile or to ravage with the hate of vampires.
>
> Glistening dusky bodies, stamping or gliding, shouting or silent, are silhouetted against hot ritual fires. Myriad age-old racial memories drift up from Africa and glowing islands of the sea. . . .

Part 6

PRELUDE TO PROTEST

In the study of Afro-American History, the period of the 1930s and 1940s can, with much justice, be called the prelude to protest. To be sure, protest had existed from the first arrival of Africans in the Americas, but the systems which developed under slavery and in the post-Civil War days were characterized more by accommodation than by protest. Many factors at home and abroad influenced the changes which took place in the twentieth century. The attacks of non-white Asians on Europeans and Americans and the postwar influences of independence movements in Africa are important. However, the main reasons are to be found within the United States.

The *modus vivendi* of relations between the races was seriously shaken by the late 1920s so that efforts of some whites to restore prewar race relations were without success. Large-scale migration to northern cities, wartime experience of those blacks who entered military service, and the results of war propaganda regarding democracy all had their influences. The black man's view of himself and the American system was reflected in the works of the Harlem Renaissance, the rise of black nationalism, and the increased activities of the National Association for the Advancement of Colored People. More was to come which would raise the hopes and aims of blacks and demonstrate weaknesses in the system of white supremacy. By the 1930s concentration of large black populations in urban areas and the growing expressions of self-esteem resulted in increased hostility on the part of some whites but great respect and concern on the part of others. On the one hand anti-black nativism produced the Scottsboro case; on the other, concern for the conditions of life of black citizens was important to some New Deal reformers. The most important aspects of the changes occurring, however, were in the actions of blacks.

The extent to which some New Dealers had genuine concern for the welfare of blacks, as opposed to recognition of the political potential, is difficult to say and probably unknown even to those people directly involved. What is significant is the shift of blacks from their historical political loyalty to the Republican party to support of the Democrats. Consideration of this shift is the subject of *The Changing Political Thought of the Negro, 1915–1940* by Elbert Lee Tatum. As educational director for the Civilian Conservation Corps camps in Illinois, the author's pro-Democratic position is probably more than scholarly. Nevertheless, his tracing of the factors involved in the shift of political allegiance points up the major change in the political activity of blacks. The section from his chapter on "The Negro and the Republican Party, 1932–1940" appears here.

Republican lack of concern for the welfare of blacks and insensitivity to the forces at work in the black community occurred as the Democrats were taking special care to cultivate ethnic groups, according to *The Politics of Upheaval,* by Arthur M. Schlesinger, Jr. In "The Roosevelt Coalition," the author deals with the failure of Republicans, especially Hoover, to maintain the support of blacks and with the approach to this group taken by Franklin D. Roosevelt and the New Deal. New Deal aid to blacks appeared not in the area of civil rights, where very little was done, but in the area of relief for the poor and unemployed, among whom blacks were to be found in large numbers. In return they used their growing political strength to support Roosevelt and those northern Democrats who were willing to consider their welfare.

The *Negro's Share,* Richard Sterner, is a study of income, consumption, housing, and public assistance during the 1930s. It grew out of the study of black Americans made by Gunnar Myrdal and sponsored by the Carnegie Corporation. "The Negro on Relief," taken from this source, is concerned with the significance of relief for blacks, the extent and nature of the relief, and the conclusions to be drawn from an examination of this information. The author cites, as a major problem, the efforts to reconcile the demand that people not earn more on relief than people working, the low level of income for blacks, and the desire for adequate and uniform relief standards. One concludes from the selection that discrimination existed in relief under the New Deal as in other aspects of American life and that it was probably more severe than the writing would suggest. The author supports this in his preface, describing certain of his comments on this matter as "conservative statements" and "understatements." Thus, in spite of a more favorable attitude toward blacks than any other twentieth-century administration, the New Deal reflected the typical American position on race.

One aspect of the general issue of black reactions to the situation in the 1930s is the subject of Wilson Record's *Race and Radicalism: The NAACP and the Communist Party in Conflict.* The book is part of a series on communism in American life by an author who has done pioneer work in the study of black Americans and communism. The chapter, "The Depression Era: 1929–1935," examines the efforts of the Communist Party of the United States to gain support from blacks and the conflicts of the party with established black organizations, principally the NAACP. The Scottsboro case is the focus of conflict between the two organizations. In these efforts the Party was singularly unsuccessful.

After 1941 the country found itself engaged in a military conflict in which the most powerful enemy embodied a form of racism even more brutal and destructive than that produced in America. Efforts to mobilize opinion in support of the war demanded reenforcement of the national ideals of democracy and justice in opposition to racism. This action made more obvious the conflict between ideals and reality in the treatment of blacks and led idealists to envision improved conditions after the war. More important, it, along with wartime experiences of large numbers of blacks, decreased the degree to which the old racial controls were operative. For those who expected significant change the realities, as reflected in the following selections, were unsettling.

Negro Labor: A National Problem, Robert C. Weaver, concerns black civilian workers before and during the war. The author, a Harvard-trained economist and a member of the so-called Black Cabinet of New Deal days, worked during the war for the Office of Price Management and for the War Production Board. The selection from his work which is included here pictures the limited effort of the government during World War II to make effective use of the pool of black labor and the continuation of discrimination in employment, unaffected by an unenforced executive order to the contrary. In spite of this and because of pressure from blacks, some gains in the area of employment are reported to have been made.

Two excerpts from *A Man Called White* by Walter White expand this examination of prejudice and discrimination toward the black soldier and the returning veteran. During World War II and at the time the book was written, the author was Executive Secretary of the National Association for the Advancement of Colored People. In appearance he was blond and white-skinned. This combination placed him in various situations of racial sensitivity and enabled him, through "passing," to encounter those remarks about blacks which whites often passed along to other whites. Significant in the record of his experiences is the near universal acceptance by racist whites that other whites shared their views, a matter so widely accepted as to lead one to deduce that it was well founded.

"Summary Justice—The Negro G I in Korea," Thurgood Marshall, explores the influences of racism on justice for soldiers in the Korean conflict. In this article from *Crisis* the special counsel for the NAACP, later to become Associate Justice of the Supreme Court, examines specific cases of army justice in Korea and concludes that serious problems exist when justice for blacks depends on whites.

More than any other one event, the Supreme Court decision in *Brown* vs. *Board of Education* in 1954 is a symbol of the end of the prelude to protest. The selection from the 1968 Bancroft Prize-winning book, *A History of Negro Education in the South,* Henry Allen Bullock, explores the reaction of whites to the 1954 decision. The hostility to school integration on the part of many was viewed by blacks as opposition to quality education, the absence of which was often used as rationalization for limits placed on opportunities for minority citizens.

The stage was set for protest!

The Negro and the Republican Party, 1932–1940*

Elbert Lee Tatum

There is little reason, if any, to doubt that prior to 1932 the American Negroes as a group were generally loyal to the Republican party. The loyalty had its foundation, at least in part, in traditions and sentiments which extended back to the time when that party was organized in 1854. In the early days of the party's history one of the ablest Negro statesmen played at least a minor role and for that cause, if no other one existed, the Negroes thought the Republican party was the one with which they should align themselves.[1] Beginning about the middle of the nineteenth century and continuing without serious interruption until 1932 the political affiliation and political thought of the American Negroes was that of a single party—Republican—which had since that date (1854) consistently held sway over them. Indeed, prior to 1933 there had been little difference of opinion among Negroes over what party to support although there are examples of differences among some of their leaders over what Republican candidate to support. With rare exceptions, they could be counted upon to follow loyally the party label in the state and national politics. The distinction between men and measures, issues and "isms," was not clear to them, and in many cases that distinction was ignored. Out of such a situation the Hoover Administration began in 1929.

The four years during which Mr. Hoover was President, 1929–1933, were in several ways heart-rending to the Negro as well as to the nation at large. The economic cri-

---

* From Elbert Lee Tatum, *The Changing Political Thought of the Negro 1915–1940* (New York: Exposition Press, 1951), pp. 113–16, 132–33, 137–41. Reprinted by permission.

[1] Frederick Douglass, *Life and Times of Frederick Douglass,* 358–66. See also Carter Woodson, editor, *Journal of Negro History,* Association for the Study of Negro Life and History, Washington, D.C., Volume XXIV, 1941, 413–84.

sis which occurred shortly after the beginning of his term not only caused much suffering but it served to render Mr. Hoover increasingly unpopular. There were other occurrences, which will be discussed shortly, some of which can justly be attributed to Mr. Hoover while others were beyond his control. The occurrence which taxed the Negro's continued Republican loyalty was one that Mr. Hoover could not control and prevent. This was the depression which struck the country in 1929 and continued throughout his administration. Those who suffered as a consequence of the depression held Mr. Hoover responsible for it. That fact is shown by the frequent references to "Hoover's Depression." If the views of certain economists were taken for it, there would be little or no ground for making Mr. Hoover wholly responsible, for they had many years before propounded a theory which claimed that business disturbances, sometimes called crises or depressions, were predictable and occurred naturally at about seven-year intervals.[2] Under that theory the year 1929 was overdue for a depression, since the previous one had occurred in the fall of 1921.

A discussion in an effort to demonstrate the value of that law has value in the immediate undertaking only insofar as it helps to fix or not fix responsibility on Mr. Hoover. If it can be shown, as some people claimed, that Mr. Hoover's grant of a moratorium to the debtor nations caused American businessmen to distrust generally the soundness of his policies and that as a consequence they would not expand domestically or make foreign investments, then Mr. Hoover was at least partly responsible for the depression. But if, on the contrary, depressions are the results of natural forces, even when they are predictable, and may not be controlled by finite man, then, Mr. Hoover was not responsible. There exists abundance of literature which supports both views, but for the purpose here it is significant that a depression occurred and as a result of it Negroes, like many other people, left the Republican party in large numbers.[3]

The intensity of the depression was increased in regard to the Negro because he had recently witnessed the greatest era of prosperity he had ever known in this country. In both the North and the South, many Negroes had purchased homes, made investments in life insurance, started small businesses, and in numerous other ways invested their savings and pledged their income from whatever source derived to meet their obligations.[4] When that depression struck the country it not only destroyed their savings in the banks and their investments, but it robbed them of an opportunity to continue to earn a livelihood by gainful employment; for, it is well known, the Negro is last to be hired and the first to be discharged when depressions or crises occur in the industrial world. It was in part for those reasons they accepted the current slogan that this depression was caused by Mr. Hoover. They were led to believe that if Mr. Hoover were out

[2] S. J. Chapman, *Elementary Economics,* Longmans, Green and Company, New York, 1913, 45–97; Hugo Bilgram, *The Cause of Business Depression,* J. P. Lippincott Company, Philadelphia, 1913, 1–16; T. N. Carver, *Principles of Political Economy,* Ginn and Company, New York, 1919, 329–38.

[3] R. G. Tugwell, "Flaws in the Hoover Economic Plan," *Current History,* New York Times Company, New York, Volume XXXV, 1932, 525–31; also, in the same issue, Robert W. Morse, "President Hoover's Plan to Check the Depression," 263–64.

[4] Monroe N. Work, *The Negro Yearbook, 1931–1932,* 118–38.

of the White House, their opportunities to find security would be increased in business and industry. They cast their lot with that group in the campaign of 1932 which had adopted the slogan "Who but Hoover," not meaning that he was indispensable, but that anyone was more to be desired than he.[5]

• • •

Mr. Hoover was nominated and elected, largely because he had been successful in building up a "Lily White" organization in the South and because he was able to play upon the emotions of the people there in such a way as to turn them against his "wet, Catholic, Tammany" dominated rival, as Lamont Rowland of Mississippi puts it.[52] After Mr. Hoover had taken office as President of the United States he made other utterances that had not clarified his position and policies relative to Negro consideration and deference but re-emphasized his determination to "play ball" with the "Lily White" factions of the Republican party.

"Successive presidents have long wished to build up a Republican party in the South such as would commend itself to the citizens of those states," he declared. (The implication here is that he did not regard the Negro as a citizen.) Then he commended the "Lily White" state committees in Virginia, North Carolina, Alabama, Arkansas, Louisiana, Texas, and Florida; but said he,

> In South Carolina, Georgia, and Mississippi, recent exposure of abuses in the sale of patronage obviously render it impossible for the old organization . . . to command the confidence of the administration. . . . The duty of reorganization rests with the people of those states, and all efforts to that end will receive the hearty cooperation of the administration. . . . If these three states are unable to initiate such an organization . . . the different federal departments will be compelled to adopt other measures to secure advice as to the selection of federal employees.[53]

This is by far the boldest and most expansive public gesture toward the "Lily Whites" made by a responsible Republican spokesman to be found. It let the Negroes know anew that the Hoover administration did not want them and furthermore was not going to do anything politically new for them. The situation then confronting the Negro in the South was this: The Republican party, was indifferent toward him; the administration in Washington had repudiated him; and the Democrats as a whole would not have him.

• • •

It would be missing the point to see the Negro bolting the Republican party fully in the 1932 election or to think that he became aware, for the first time, of Repub-

[5] "Who But Hoover," editorial in *Collier's,* Crowell-Collier Publishing Company, New York, Volume LXXXVI, 1932, 12.

[52] *Corinthian,* Klyce and Bishop, editors and publishers, Corinth, Mississippi, November 14, 1928. A clipping from the above paper was sent to the writer in March, 1933, by Lamont Rowland.

[53] *New York Times,* March 27, 1929.

lican insincerity and indifference during the Hoover administration. The truth of the matter is that certain Negroes had been cognizant of such a tendency since 1876 when it was thought that the Republicans made a deal with the South during the Hayes-Tilden deadlock whereby Hayes, the Republican candidate, was to be made President, in return for which Mr. Hayes was to take the United States Army out of the South and leave the Negroes in the hands of their former slave masters.[66] Nearly every anti-Negro policy found in any of the former Republican administrations was used by Mr. Hoover while he was in the White House. He neither showed deference to the Negro nor gave any unique positions to him.

Such indifference seemed to increase the political friction between the Negro and the white of the South as was evidenced by the formation of the "Loyal League" in Georgia. That League was a sort of bureau of the radical Republican party whose chief object was to control the Negro vote.[67] The League did not oppose use of the franchise if it would aid in electing the kind of officers the whites had had since the overthrow of the Reconstruction government. All students of political science know that Mr. Hoover was badly beaten in the election of 1932 by Franklin Delano Roosevelt. Since 1933 the Republicans have tried to recapture the Negro vote in a variety of ways, but their vitriolic expressions, their skill in the manipulation of propaganda symbols, their emotional pleas, and their expenditures of large sums left Mr. Landon in 1936 and Mr. Willkie in 1940 in no better circumstance with the Negro than Mr. Hoover was in November, 1932.

The Republicans blamed the New Deal relief, which was partly correct, for their losing the Negro vote, but they are equally at fault, for they did nothing to prevent it. Earl Brown, writing for *Opportunity* in December, 1936, estimates that over 2,000,000 Negroes voted in the election of that year. He asserts:

> That was the first time since the Reconstruction Amendments that the majority of Negroes voted for a Democratic president. That situation made the race an integral part of both major parties and increased them in political stature and importance.[68]

He continued by pointing out four additional things this election implied or achieved. First, the increased political activity among Negroes in the South was the most important political movement for them and for the poor whites. The latter saw that because the Negroes were disfranchised, they were too. Secondly, more Negroes voted in the South than at any time since Reconstruction. In Durham, North Carolina, over 4,000 voted as contrasted with about 500 in previous national elections. Thirdly, there was little opposition to the Negroes voting in many places; the press carried no releases about

---

[66] Editorial, *Chicago Bee*, October 1, 1944. See also John R. Lynch, *The Facts of Reconstruction*, 156–61.

[67] Robert F. Carson, "The Loyal League in Georgia," *Georgia Historical Quarterly*, Savannah, Volume XX, Number I, March, 1936, 125–53.

[68] *Opportunity*, Volume XIV, Number 12, 359–61.

the whites intimidating the Negroes because some of them (Negroes) went to the polls. Fourthly, he claimed that the New Deal had abolished sectionalism to a greater extent than any other force in history.[69]

Between 1932 and 1940 the nation had seen the Negroes swing far to the left, not only by electing liberal-minded white men as Democrats to offices in the nation's capital, but it had also seen them elect a politically unknown Negro, Arthur Mitchell, who at the time had been in the district from which he was elected for less than six years. This election is all the more significant because he was elected over the militant Republican Negro Congressman, Oscar DePriest. Mitchell used as a slogan "Forward with Roosevelt" while Oscar DePriest, the Republican, constantly appealed to the people to give him support because, first, he was a Republican, and, secondly, because of his record. In 1936 we find that in the United States as a whole, sixteen Negroes were elected to the state legislatures—eleven Democrats and five Republicans. The state of Pennsylvania led with electing five from the city of Philadelphia—one being Reverend Marshall Shepard who later offered prayer in the Democratic Convention meeting at Philadelphia in July, 1940. His recognition caused some of the southern whites to bolt their party, for example, Senator Edward (Cotton Ed) Smith of South Carolina.[70] The significant thing about that election is that the Negro showed a change in political thought that was far-reaching in that he not only left the Republican party in national politics but was seeking positions in state and local government on the Democratic ticket.

The Landon campaign was supported very mildly even by the Negro Republicans. In fact, some of the best Negro political minds which had formerly been Republican fought him ferociously. For example, the learned Kelly Miller wrote a series of articles for the ANP in which he urged the Negroes to support President Roosevelt.[71] Bishop R. R. Wright of the African Methodist Episcopal Church not only wrote articles for the ANP but organized a committee, the purpose of which was to fight Landon and the Republicans.[72] How well they succeeded is seen in the election returns—Landon carried only two states and neither of those has a Negro population large enough to have swung the election for him even had all Negro residents supported the Republican candidate.

Mr. Wendell Willkie, the Republican standard-bearer in the 1940 campaign, was given far more support by Negroes than Mr. Landon had received four years earlier. The Negro press seemed less critical of him than of Mr. Landon, even though there was no outstanding Negro paper which unconditionally supported his candidacy.[73] Some of the minor Negro papers were found supporting both of the candidates.[74]

[69] *Ibid.,* 360.

[70] For the states from which Negroes were elected, other data relative to the votes received, the opposing candidates, etc., see the *Chicago Bee,* November 15, 1936.

[71] *Ibid.,* October 11, 1936, and all of the November, 1936, issues.

[72] *Ibid.,* November 3, 1936.

[73] The most popular Negro papers are: *Pittsburgh Courier, Chicago Defender, The Afro-American, Kansas City Call,* and *Amsterdam News.* Issues for October and November of those papers were consulted; although they did not fight Mr. Willkie, they did not give open support to him.

[74] *Chicago Bee, St. Louis Argus,* and *Black Dispatch* were for Roosevelt; *New York Age* and *Cleveland Plain Dealer* supported Willkie. See October and November, 1940, issues.

The Republican situation as far as the Negro was concerned had made the Negro conscious of the party's lack of divinity. By 1940, he had come to look upon political parties somewhat as though they were two bottles which still retained on them their labels after the contents had been emptied. It was then (1940) a man-measure matter with the Negro, not an emotional attachment to a party label.

The Roosevelt Coalition*
Arthur M. Schlesinger, Jr.

. . . The New Deal took special care to cultivate ethnic groups. Thus Roosevelt named the first Italo-American and the first Negroes ever appointed to the federal bench. Catholics and Jews were recognized as never before. Of the 214 federal judges appointed by Harding, Coolidge and Hoover, according to the computations of Samuel Lubell, only 8 were Catholics and 8 Jews. Of the 196 judicial appointments made by Roosevelt, 51 were Catholics and 8 Jews. Roosevelt cared deeply about speeding the assimilation of minorities into all parts of national life. "If I could do anything I wanted for twenty-four hours," he once said, "the thing I would want most to do would be to complete the melting of the melting-pot." "Remember, remember always," he told the Daughters of the American Revolution, "that all of us, and you and I especially, are descended from immigrants and revolutionists."

The appeal to the Negroes represented the most dramatic and risky innovation in the New Deal design. After all, the Democratic party had shown a capacity to absorb whites of foreign stock since the days of Jefferson. But the inclusion of Negroes struck vitally at the conception of a party which had also, since the days of Jefferson, respected the peculiar claims of the white South. Moreover, it challenged a tradition in America politics almost as sacred as the one which kept the South voting Democratic—the tradition that the Negroes should vote Republican. Nothing in the politics of the New Deal was more daring than the project of combining in the same party the descendants of the slaveholders and the descendants of the slaves.[2]

By the turn of the century, when the last Negro congressman from the South retired from the House of Representatives, the Negro seemed extinct in national politics. In the South he was effectively excluded from political life. In the North, he was a negligi-

---

* From Arthur M. Schlesinger, Jr., *The Politics of Upheaval* (Boston: Houghton Mifflin Company, 1960), pp. 425–38. Copyright © 1960 by Arthur M. Schlesinger, Jr. Reprinted by permission of the publisher, Houghton Mifflin Company.

[2] Samuel Lubell, *The Future of American Politics* (New York, 1952), 78; interview with George Fischer, Dec. 13, 1956; F.D.R., *Public Papers* (1938), 259.

ble minority, tamely voted by the local Republican machine. Then the First World War provoked a massive change in the life of the Negro. He began to go north, partly because of increasing troubles in southern agriculture, but mostly because of expanding job opportunities in northern cities. The industrial boom of the twenties furthered the great migration. By 1930, almost two million Negroes had moved out of the realm of political impotence into that of political potentiality. Between 1910 and 1930 the Negro population of Detroit, for example, increased nearly twentyfold; that of Chicago, nearly sixfold; of New York, well over threefold; of Philadelphia, nearly threefold.

The result was a dazzling new opportunity for urban politicians. Some Republicans, like William Hale Thompson of Chicago, worked hard to keep the Negroes faithful to the Grand Old Party. But Republicans too often assumed Negro devotion as unalterable, just at the time that the Democrats, the urban politicians par excellence, began to awaken to the existence of this new voting group. The first Democratic boss to woo and win the Negro electorate was Tom Pendergast of Kansas City. Though Al Smith in his personal brushes with James Weldon Johnson and Walter White of the National Association for the Advancement of Colored People displayed reserve about Negroes and cynicism about their political motives, he was ready, as the specialist in urban coalitions, to consider a national Democratic appeal to colored people.

In 1928 he told White, "I know Negroes distrust the Democratic Party, and I can't blame them. But I want to show that the old Democratic Party, ruled entirely by the South, is on its way out, and that we Northern Democrats have a totally different approach to the Negro." At his request, White drafted a statement making it clear that Smith, if elected, would be president of all the people, white and colored. As the campaign developed, however, Joe Robinson, the vice-presidential candidate, and other southern Democrats, already sufficiently fearful about the South and Smith, succeeded in killing the statement. Indeed, during the campaign anti-Smith forces inundated the South with photographs of the Negro Civil Service Commissioner of New York City dictating to his white secretary—a tableau presented as ominous indication of what northern Democrats planned for the country.

Nonetheless, the political urgencies behind Smith's interest in the Negro vote remained ceaselessly at work. Thus the 1928 election gave Northern Negroes their first representative in the House in Oscar De Priest of Chicago, a Republican. Tammany Hall began to make inroads in Harlem. Hoover himself, however, failed to read these lessons. Not only had he backed lily-white against black-and-tan (*i.e.* mixed) delegations from southern states in the 1928 Republican convention; not only had he failed to rebuke racist attacks on Smith; but his success in splitting the solid South evidently persuaded him and other Republican strategists that if he continued to behave with circumspection, he might permanently attach a large number of southern whites to the Republican party. So he disregarded the portent of Oscar De Priest and proceeded to act in a way which soon led Walter White to dub him "the man in the lily-White House."

For all his Quaker background, Hoover showed little personal sympathy for Negroes. The White House shortly faced what the Hoovers apparently regarded as an insoluble social problem. Mrs. Hoover wanted to invite the wives of members of Congress to a series of teas; but what was to be done about Mrs. De Priest? The White House social secretary insisted that she must be invited; others were doubtful; and four parties, covering nearly all the congressional ladies, went by while Mrs. De Priest remained under prayerful consideration. "The official angle was referred to the Executive Offices," reported the White House usher, "one of the President's secretaries pondering over it for days and days." Finally Mrs. Hoover decided to ask Mrs. De Priest to a special tea at which guests could be individually warned in advance about the ordeal to which they were about to be subjected. When the day arrived, Mrs. De Priest seemed to the White House usher the most composed person there. "In a short while Mrs. Hoover retired from the room, and Mrs. De Priest in perfect form made her exit, no doubt to the relief of all and yet leaving behind a feeling of admiration at the way she conducted herself."

For the rest, Hoover ignored the Negroes. He made, said W. E. B. Du Bois, "fewer first-class appointments of Negroes to office than any President since Andrew Johnson." Negroes were not admitted to government cafeterias in the federal buildings. When the administration sent the Gold Star mothers to visit their sons' graves in France, Negro mothers went on separate ships with inferior accommodations. When a mixed delegation called on Vice-President Charles Curtis, the Vice-President refused to shake the hands of the Negro. The lynching of fifty-seven Negroes during his term provoked no expression of presidential disapproval. And Hoover's nomination to the Supreme Court in 1930 of Judge John J. Parker of North Carolina, who had been quoted ten years earlier as saying that the participation of the Negro in politics was "a source of evil and danger," drove Negro leaders into open opposition. The NAACP played an important role in preventing Parker's confirmation.[3]

In March 1931 a new event occurred to heighten the determination of Negroes to fight for their rights. In the swirl of the depression, wandering boys, some white, some Negro, were caught together on a slow freight train out of Chattanooga into Alabama. As the train jolted along, the two groups began to pick at each other. "Nigger bastard, this is a white man's train. You better get off. All you black bastards get off!" Soon, with quiet, repressed bitterness, they began to fight. Some of the white boys, thrown off the train at Stevenson, Alabama, complained to the station master, who obligingly called ahead to the next stop. When the train chugged into Paint Rock, a posse cleared the freight cars and took the Negroes to the county seat at Scottsboro. They also found somewhere in one of the cars two girl hobos, who promptly claimed to have been raped by the Negroes. The colored boys denied ever having touched them. But Scottsboro justice knew better. In two weeks the Negro boys, whose average age was about sixteen, were tried, convicted, and sentenced to death.

[3] E. Franklin Frazier, *The Negro in the United States* (New York, 1957), 230; Walter White, *A Man Called White* (New York, 1948), Chs. 13–14; White, *How Far the Promised Land* (New York, 1955), 77; I. H. Hoover, *42 Years in the White House* (Boston, 1934), 301–03; Henry Lee Moon, *Balance of Power: The Negro Vote* (New York, 1948), Ch. 6; W. E. B. Du Bois, "Herbert Hoover," *Crisis,* Nov. 1932; James Weldon Johnson, *Along This Way* (New York, 1933), 239, 407; Ella Reeve Bloor, *We Are Many* (New York, 1940), 239.

Somehow the incident did not stop there. Negro organizations rallied behind the Scottsboro boys. Then the Communists moved in and, with cold disregard for the boys themselves, exploited the case as a means of raising money for the party and of dramatizing their portrait of capitalist society. ("Had it not been for their senseless interference," W. E. B. Du Bois, who was no enemy of Communists, wrote in 1940, "these poor victims of Southern injustice would today be free.") The Alabama Supreme Court affirmed the conviction; but late in 1932 the United States Supreme Court threw the case out because the boys had not had proper legal representation. At a new trial in 1933, one of the girls recanted her testimony. By now Samuel Liebowitz had come down from New York to take over the defense. The prosecutor said ominously that "no Alabama jury would listen to witnesses bought with Jew money in New York." After a notably fair charge from the judge, the jurors found the boys guilty again. "If you ever saw those creatures," Leibowitz later said, "those bigots, whose mouths are slits in their faces, whose eyes pop out at you like frogs, whose chins drip tobacco juice, bewhiskered and filthy, you would not ask how they could do it." The judge, outraged at the result, ordered a new trial and thereby insured his own political death at the next election. And the next trial produced the same result.

The Scottsboro case had profound emotional impact on the Negro community. It made white indifference to wrongs perpetrated against Negroes more intolerable than ever. It strengthened Negro determination to strike out on their own. It increased Negro militancy and Negro despair.[4]

By 1932 Negro leadership had fairly well soured on Republican indifference. In addition, since the Negroes were at the bottom of America's economic structure, Hoover's resistance to federal relief hurt them more than any other group. The result was a new impulse toward political action.

For many years, for example, James Weldon Johnson, secretary of the NAACP and the most eminent Negro literary figure, had been a devoted Republican. But as early as 1928 Johnson, increasingly disturbed over Republican passivity, declined a Republican nomination for Congress in New York City. Now he openly counseled political independence. "An uprising of Negro voters against Mr. Hoover and his party," said Bishop R. C. Ransom of the African Methodist Episcopal Church in the autumn of 1932, "would free our spirits equally as much as Mr. Lincoln's Proclamation freed our bodies." "For the Negro people of this country," said the *St. Louis Argus*, "Mr. Hoover is a dangerous man. In his palmiest days Tillman was a better friend to the colored brother than is President Hoover."

One day in Pittsburgh her Negro manicurist told Emma Guffey Miller, the

---

[4] Haywood Patterson and Earl Conrad, *Scottsboro Boy* (New York, 1950), Part I; Walter White, "The Negro and the Communists," *Harper's*, Dec. 1931; W. E. B. Du Bois, *Dusk of Dawn* (New York, 1940), 298; Mary Heaton Vorse, "The Scottsboro Trial," *New Republic*, April 19, 1933; editorial note, *New Republic*, April 26, 1933; F. Raymond Daniell, "Land of the Free," in Hanson Baldwin and Shepard Stone, eds., *We Saw It Happen* (New York, 1938).

Democratic National Committeewoman, that "Mr. Vann" would like to see her brother Joseph F. Guffey. This was Robert L. Vann, publisher of the influential *Pittsburgh Courier*, the largest Negro paper in the state. When Vann and Guffey met, Vann said that the Democrats had a chance of winning a large share of the 280,000 Negro votes in Pennsylvania. Guffey was quick to press the opportunity. "It was hard work," he later said, "but I finally persuaded Jim Farley and Louis McHenry Howe to establish the first really effective Negro division a Democratic campaign committee ever had." Vann was put in charge. "My friends, go home and turn Lincoln's picture to the wall," Vann told Negro voters. "That debt has been paid in full."

The swing away from Hoover was still essentially a defection from the top. Negro voters on the whole stuck with the Republicans in 1932. But the opinion-makers had abandoned the Republicans, and it might only be a matter of time before opinion followed their example.[5]

The new President's history up to 1933 was of a man fairly conventional in his racial attitudes. Back in 1911 he could pencil on the margin of a speech text a crisp reminder: "story of nigger." As Assistant Secretary of the Navy, he served with no visible discomfort under Woodrow Wilson and Josephus Daniels—two liberal southerners who rapidly dropped their liberalism when it came to the race question. In the middle twenties he made Georgia his "second home" with no thought to its peculiar folkways.[6] As late

---

[5] White, *Man Called White,* Ch. 16; Johnson, *Along This Way,* 393; Bishop R. C. Ransom in *Crisis,* Nov. 1932; *St. Louis Argus,* Sept. 16, 1932; Joseph R. Guffey, *Seventy Years on the Red-Fire Wagon* (privately printed, 1952), 170; Joseph Alsop and Robert Kintner, "The Guffey," *Saturday Evening Post,* March 26, 1938.

[6] On the other hand, he did not, as has been charged, insert a racial restriction clause into deeds conveying farmlands in Georgia. On May 27, 1957, Senator Herman Talmadge put into the appendix of the *Congressional Record* a letter from R. Carter Pittman of Dalton, Georgia, making this charge and adding that the clause was known locally as "the Roosevelt restriction." (The rest of the Pittman letter was a denunciation of the Supreme Court, suggesting that Alger Hiss "led the Court away from the Constitution" in the restrictive-covenant case of *Shelley v. Kraemer* in 1948.)

I am indebted to William F. Snyder, general counsel of the Georgia Warm Springs Foundation, for the following comment: "The statement . . . that the restriction is referred to by some Georgia lawyers as the Roosevelt restriction 'because Mr. Roosevelt was one of the few persons ever to insert such a clause in a deed conveying farmlands in Georgia' is not true. (1) Thousands of deeds contained such restriction before Mr. Roosevelt ever went to Georgia. (2) The restriction was not inserted by Mr. Roosevelt in any deed of his own property. (3) The restriction was included in the printed form used by Meriwether Reserve, Inc. for the conveyance of subdivision lots [for private dwelling purposes]—not farm lands. (4) Neither of the deeds referred to by Mr. Pittman was a conveyance by Mr. Roosevelt personally and both deeds conveyed subdivision lots. As a matter of fact the deed recorded in Book 24, page 388, was a conveyance *to* Mr. Roosevelt. When he later conveyed this property to Meriwether Reserve, Inc. (Book 29, page 183) the deed merely stated that the property was conveyed subject to restrictions of record, which is the uniform practice in all states.

"It is true that Mr. Roosevelt, as President of Meriwether Reserve, Inc. signed some of the deeds containing the said restriction (the last such deed appears to have been on May 23, 1932), but it is doubtful that he knew the deed contained such restriction. In every case the deed was completed by a Georgia attorney and was sent to Mr. Roosevelt. . . . The form consisted of three full legal-size pages. The restriction was printed in small type on the second page and Mr. Roosevelt signed on the third page. It should also be remembered that lawyers of one state are not familiar with the real estate laws of another state and when a deed is prepared

as 1929, he wired the chairman of the Democratic State Committee in Virginia indignantly denying a Republican charge that he had entertained a large number of Negroes at a public luncheon. As Governor of New York, he showed no special concern for Negroes either in appointments or in legislation. In seeking the nomination in 1932, he courted southern support; and he took as running mate a man whom Negroes regarded as hopeless (unjustly: Garner, who came from west Texas, was relatively fair-minded on the race issue).

Still, Roosevelt had no more a closed mind on this than on other subjects. Both his natural openness of heart and his early training in Christian responsibility inclined him, when he thought of it, to sympathy for Negro aspirations. As far back as his student days, he had written an essay urging southern colleges to follow the Harvard example and admit Negroes. During the Wilson administration he had harassed the Surgeon General to get a commission for a Negro doctor. As the Negro vote increased, his astute political sense doubtless made him think of these things more often. If a decent policy toward the Negro was not in his own first order of priorities, he was responsive enough to the idea when anyone else proposed it. Negro leaders felt in his general stance a greater accessibility to Negro issues. "A liberal in politics and in economics," as *Opportunity,* the organ of the Urban League, said shortly after the election, "might well be expected to be a liberal in race relations and to adopt the viewpoint of the more advanced thinkers on the problems of race adjustment. As he assumes his duties, he will carry the hopes of millions of Negroes who see in him an exponent of the finest ideals of this great Democracy."

For a time, however, the Negro had little more than these hopes to live on.

---

by a lawyer of another state they assume that the printed terms, conditions and restrictions therein are in accordance with the laws of that state.

"Mr. Roosevelt was also President of the Georgia Warm Springs Foundation. . . . The [Warm Springs] property was acquired by Georgia Warm Springs Foundation from Meriweather Reserve, Inc. in 1940. No deed containing a restriction such as appeared in the Meriweather Reserve, Inc. deeds was ever executed by Mr. Roosevelt as President of Georgia Warm Springs Foundation. . . . It is noteworthy that the deed from Meriweather Reserve, Inc. to Georgia Warm Springs Foundation did not contain the restriction as to racial usage because in this case a Georgia printed form was not used and also the property conveyed by this deed included farm land."

Cf. *Congressional Record,* 85 Cong., 2 Sess., A4048 (May 27, 1957); and W. F. Snyder to author, Nov. 20, 1957.

One other incident reflecting Roosevelt's attitude toward the Negro should perhaps be noted. In 1923, a Harvard graduate wrote Roosevelt, as a Harvard overseer, and asked him to do something for "the maintenance of the Harvard tradition of liberal and democratic treatment" by speaking up for a Negro boy excluded from the freshman dormitories. Roosevelt replied, "It seems to be a pity that the matter ever came up in this way. There were certainly many colored students in Cambridge when we were there and no question ever arose." Mrs. Merle Fainsod informs me that two Negro students in particular, both prominent in Harvard College, lived in dormitories in 1904, Roosevelt's last year at Harvard. Southerners who didn't like it could live elsewhere. The issue of 1923 apparently arose over a recent ruling that, up to capacity, all members of the freshman class should reside in freshman halls. There is no indication of further action by Roosevelt in this matter. Cf. R. S. Wallace to Roosevelt, February 1, F.D.R. to Wallace, February 7, 1923, Roosevelt Papers.

Under AAA, Negro tenant farmers and sharecroppers were the first to be thrown off farms as a consequence of the crop-reduction policy. Under NRA, Negroes either had to accept racial differentials in wages or run the risk of displacement by unemployed white men; in the case of jobs still reserved for Negroes, a complicated system of exemptions minimized the application of the codes; and local control of compliance machinery made it almost impossible for the Negro to seek effective redress. TVA, for all its high ideals, adopted surrounding southern folkways in order not to risk its central program by fighting marginal battles. It hired Negroes as unskilled labor but would not admit them to the training programs; in the model government town of Norris, Tennessee, as one Negro writer bitterly commented, the Negro could not "even live on the outskirts of town in his customary hovel." Subsistence homesteads were no better: more than two hundred Negroes applied for admission to Arthurdale, West Virginia, to be told by the manager the project was open only to "native white stock." The Federal Housing Administration sponsored restrictive covenants in its building and rental programs. "The Attorney General," said Walter White with scorn of the Department of Justice, "continues his offensive against crime—except crimes involving the deprivation of life and liberty to Negroes." Even the administration's support of independent labor organization meant little to Negroes who, up to this time, had been largely rejected by organized labor and found their main haven in company unions (not out of managerial idealism, but because Negroes offered a convenient supply of strikebreakers).[7]

There was nothing new about such a record of discrimination. What was new was that anyone cared about it. In the summer of 1933 Edwin R. Embree of the Julius Rosenwald Fund suggested to Roosevelt that someone in government be responsible for seeing that Negroes got fair treatment. Roosevelt approved the idea, adding that this person should be attached to a department; he suggested Harold Ickes as the cabinet member most likely to be sympathetic. When Embree approached Ickes, Ickes said he would be glad to have such a person on his staff but had no money for it. The Rosenwald Fund then offered to pay the salary. Dr. Clark Foreman, a forceful young Georgian who had been director of studies for the Fund, was now appointed to the Department of the Interior.

    Ickes made clear to Foreman that, though located in Interior, he was expected to

---

[7] F.D.R., speech before Saturn Club of Buffalo, Dec. 23, 1911, F.D.R. to W. C. Gorgas, Aug. 7, 1917, F.D.R. to J. Murphy Hooker, Oct. 31, 1929, Roosevelt Papers; Ickes, *First Thousand Days,* 16; editorial, *Opportunity,* Dec. 1932; Report of the Agricultural Committee of the Inter-Departmental Group concerned with the Special Problems of Negroes, May 1934, National Archives; E. E. Lewis, "Black Cotton Farmers and the AAA," *Crisis,* March 1935; NRA Division of Research and Planning, Report on Effect of NRA Codes Upon Negroes, March 21, 1934, NRA Papers; John P. Davis, "Blue Eagles and Black Workers," *New Republic,* Nov. 14, 1934; Davis before Senate Finance Committee, *Investigation of the National Recovery Administration: Hearings,* 74 Cong., 1 Sess. (1935), 2140 ff.; Davis, "The Plight of the Negro in the Tennessee Valley," *Crisis,* Oct. 1935; Davis, "A Black Inventory of the New Deal," *Crisis,* May 1935; Cranston Clayton, "The TVA and the Race Problem," *Opportunity,* April 1934; Walter White, "United States Department of (White) Justice," *Crisis,* Oct. 1935; Charles Abrams, *Forbidden Neighbors* (New York, 1955), 8, 162.

function in the government generally. Foreman brought in Dr. Robert C. Weaver, a Harvard Ph.D. in economics, as his assistant, as well as a Negro secretary. Shortly after, Dan Roper, though a South Carolinian, appointed E. K. Jones of the Urban League as an adviser on Negro affairs in Commerce. Foreman and Jones began to work together to stimulate Negro appointments in other departments. In addition, they tried to protect the interest of the Negro in the operations of the emergency agencies.

By February 1934 Foreman succeeded in setting up an interdepartmental committee to consider the problems created for Negroes by NRA minimum wages and by AAA crop-reduction policies. The NRA representative frankly admitted to the committee that NRA's effect in "decreasing the spread between the wages of white and colored labor has been nullified to an undetermined extent by discriminations against Negroes." AAA added, "It may be said that the smaller the administrative unit and the greater the degree of local control, the worse the conditions to which Negroes are subjected." But neither NRA nor AAA could figure out any solution which would safeguard the Negro within the program without threatening the program's essential objectives. The interdepartmental committee reached the reluctant conclusion that it had no choice but to expect displacement of Negroes and to try and salvage them by relief programs.

This situation, as well as the exhaustion of savings, accounted for the steady increase of the number of Negroes on relief—from about 18 per cent of the Negro population in October 1933 to almost 30 per cent in January 1935. The various Hopkins organizations rose nobly to the challenge, though their efforts provoked angry southern resentment. As Lorena Hickok reported from Georgia early in 1934, "For these people to be getting $12 a week—at least twice as much as common labor has ever been paid down there before—is an awfully bitter pill for Savannah people to swallow. . . . The Federal Reemployment director observed yesterday: 'Any Nigger who gets over $8 a week is a spoiled Nigger, that's all.' "

Still, Hopkins and his people persisted in their efforts to end racial discrimination in relief. As *Crisis,* the NAACP journal, conceded in 1936, "Even with their failures, they have made great gains for the race in areas which heretofore have set their faces steadfastly against decent relief for Negroes." Other New Deal agencies followed this example. CCC took in 200,000 Negroes—30,000 of these, mostly in New England and the West, in integrated camps. One Negro described his CCC life in *Crisis*: "As a job and an experience, for a man who has no work, I can heartily recommend it." PWA built houses, schools, and hospitals for Negroes. It granted $3 million to Howard University and another $7.5 million to Negro schools and colleges in the South. The National Youth Administration set up an Office of Minority Affairs with a leading Negro educator, Mary McLeod Bethune, as director, and helped thousands of Negro students. Southern Negroes, denied the right to vote for political office, could vote in NLRB elections and AAA referenda. Over a million Negroes took part in the government's emergency education program, where 300,000 learned to read and write.[8]

[8] Report on Special Problems of Negroes; Agric. Com. NRA Div. of Res. and Planning, Effect of NRA Codes Upon Negroes; Minutes of the Third Meeting of the Inter-Departmental Group, March 20, 1934, NRA Papers; C. F. Roos, *NRA Economic Planning* (Bloomington, 1937), 173; Davis, "Black Inventory";

Quite as important as what the administration did was how it felt. The fact that it felt about the Negro at all was a startling novelty. And, Roosevelt, in particular, was a figure to stir the imagination. His physical handicap, John Hope Franklin has suggested, was a special inspiration for Negroes: "He had overcome his; perhaps some day, they could overcome theirs." Privately Roosevelt for a time still kept the problem at arm's length. "I am told," he wrote a southern correspondent in 1933, "that many of the colored brethren of South Carolina are very certain that NRA means Negro Relief Association. They are at least partly right!" The tone suggested a certain detachment. But later, when Mrs. Bethune, as a member of the NYA advisory committee, told Roosevelt how much the agency meant to Negro young people—"We are bringing life and spirit to these many thousands who for so long have been in darkness"—she thought she saw, at the end of her discourse, tears streaming down the President's cheeks. If tears seem unlikely, Roosevelt may well have been moved enough by her recital to justify this impression in recollection.

Roosevelt always remained on the cautious side. Mrs. Bethune reports that, when she proposed drastic steps to him, he usually demurred, saying that a New Reconstruction in the South would have to keep pace with democratic progress on a national scale. "Mrs. Bethune, if we do that now, we'll hurt our program over there. We must do this thing stride by stride, but leaving no stone unturned." Yet he communicated a genuine sense of commitment in the midst of his recognition of complexity. "People like you and me are fighting and must continue to fight for the day when a man will be regarded as a man regardless of his race or faith or country," he once said with great earnestness to Mrs. Bethune. "That day will come, but we must pass through perilous times before we realize it."

Eleanor Roosevelt, operating as the extension of the generous side of the President's personality, was openly and vigorously identified with the cause of the Negro. Although some of the White House staff, notably Steve Early, regarded this enthusiasm with dismay, Louis Howe, always alert to new sources of political backing, wrote letters in support of Clark Foreman's eventually successful campaign to use Negroes as advisers and specialists in CCC camps (getting a reply, for example, from Douglas MacArthur that, so far as the CCC educational program was concerned, "The position taken by the Army representatives on this committee on every occasion is that there should be no discrimination on account of race, religion, or color").

In the cabinet Harold Ickes, who had once served as president of the Chicago chapter of the NAACP, now functioned as an informal Secretary of Negro Relations. He quickly ended segregation in Interior, employed Negro architects and engineers in

Lorena Hickok to Harry Hopkins, Jan. 16, 1934, Hopkins Papers; "The Campaign," *Crisis,* Nov. 1936; Luther C. Wandall, "A Negro in the CCC," *Crisis,* Aug. 1935; C. P. Harper, *The Administration of the Civilian Conservation Corps* (Baltimore, 1937), 89–90; Kenneth Holland and F. E. Hill, *Youth in the CCC* (Washington, 1942), 111–12; Stanley High, *Roosevelt—And Then?* (New York, 1937), 201–02; Robert C. Weaver, "The New Deal and the Negro," *Opportunity,* July 1935.

PWA, brought in a brilliant young Negro lawyer, William H. Hastie, as assistant solicitor of the Department, and backed him for appointment as federal judge in the Virgin Islands. When Foreman left his post as adviser on Negro problems, Ickes replaced him by his Negro aide, Robert C. Weaver. In the next years Weaver became the center of a group of Negroes scattered through the administration, known—reviving a term in disuse since the administration of Theodore Roosevelt—as the "Black Cabinet." In 1936 Ickes, addressing the annual convention of the NAACP, could begin by saying, "I feel at home here"—an unprecedented declaration from a member of a Democratic administration. Roosevelt, Ickes continued, had changed the old attitude of laissez faire in race relations. "Under our new conception of democracy, the Negro will be given the chance to which he is entitled. . . . The greatest advance since the Civil War toward assuring the Negro that degree of justice to which he is entitled and that equality of opportunity under the law which is implicit in his American citizenship, has been made since Franklin D. Roosevelt was sworn in as President." Perhaps the testimony delivered later that year by Mary McLeod Bethune was even more impressive, coming as it did from a Negro. "Never before in the history of America," Mrs. Bethune said, "has Negro youth been offered such opportunities." [9]

Word got round among Negroes, and intelligent Democratic politicians were quick to exploit the new possibilities. After the 1932 election, Joe Guffey got the administration to appoint Robert L. Vann assistant to the Attorney-General. This was only the beginning of the federal recognition which descended on Pennsylvania Negroes in the next two years. Democratic professionals watched the Guffey experiment with some skepticism, but not without interest. Then, in 1934, in an upset, Republican Pennsylvania sent Guffey to the Senate and George Earle, another Democrat to Harrisburg. It was guessed that about 170,000 Negroes had voted for the Democratic ticket. There were other omens in 1934. In Louisville, the traditionally Republican Negro vote shifted and elected a Democratic mayor and congressman. In Chicago, Oscar De Priest fell before a Democratic Negro, Arthur W. Mitchell, who himself had been a Republican a few years back. Impressed, the Democratic National Committee quietly began to cultivate Negro leaders.

In national politics, one issue mattered more to Negroes than any other. This was federal legislation against lynching—an objective long sought by the NAACP. As far back as 1922 an antilynching bill had come to vote in the Senate only to be defeated by a southern filibuster. The issue then lay dormant through the years of Republican supremacy; lynching itself declined after the big year of 1926. With depression, the art re-

[9] F.D.R. to Mrs. William C. Eustis, Dec. 12, 1933, Roosevelt Papers; Mary McLeod Bethune, "My Secret Talks with President Roosevelt," *Ebony*, April 1949; Allan Morrison, "The Secret Papers of F.D.R.," *Negro Digest*, Jan. 1951; J. H. Franklin, *From Slavery to Freedom* (New York, 1947), 516; Eleanor Roosevelt to Hopkins, July 16, 1935, Hopkins Papers; Douglas MacArthur to Louis Howe, March 30, 1934, Howe Papers; Harold Ickes, "My Twelve Years with F.D.R.," *Saturday Evening Post*, June 26, 1948; Ickes, *First Thousand Days*, 416; Ickes, "The Negro as a Citizen," *Crisis*, Aug. 1936; Mary McLeod Bethune, radio address, Oct. 26, 1936, Roosevelt Papers.

vived—over 60 Negroes were hanged or shot or burned by mobs between 1930 and 1934. In 1933, after the Republican Governor of California defended a lynching (in this case, of two white men) as "the best lesson California has ever given the country," Roosevelt spoke sharply against "that vile form of collective murder. . . . We do not excuse those in high places or in low who condone lynch law." In his annual message in January 1934, he denounced lynching, kidnaping, and other crimes, adding that "these violations of law call on the strong arm of Government for their immediate suppression." Two Democrats, Wagner of New York and Costigan of Colorado, promptly introduced a federal antilynching bill. It had been drafted by the NAACP and bore the endorsement of nearly a dozen northern governors.

The bill got nowhere in 1934, a year in which Negroes were lynched at a rate of better than one a month. Louis Howe put it in his files with a typewritten note: "Not favored at this time—may create hostility to other crime bills." In 1935 Wagner and Costigan reintroduced their bill. (Among those who now testified for it was H. L. Mencken: "No government pretending to be civilized can go on condoning such atrocities. Either it must make every possible effort to put them down or it must suffer the scorn and contempt of Christendom.") Late in April 1935 the Wagner-Costigan bill, with a favorable report from the Judiciary Committee reached the floor. Southern senators quickly deployed for their traditional response.

Except for a few demagogic interpolations about southern womanhood by Cotton Ed Smith of South Carolina, the filibuster was on a relatively high level. Josiah Bailey of North Carolina condemned the Wagner-Costigan proposal as a force bill and praised states' rights ("that's a cause worth dying for"). Hugo Black of Alabama said it was an antilabor bill ("in the name of antilynching, to crucify the hopes and the aspirations of the millions of workers of the country is beyond my conception") and would drive a wedge between the races ("is it fair to us at this time, when we are working in peace and harmony the one with the other, to do something which will bring about again the spread of the flame of race antagonism, and instill prejudices which, thank God! have been stifled in the hearts of most of the people of Alabama and the other States of the South?"). James F. Byrnes denounced the bill as unconstitutional.

As the filibuster droned on into May, the administration grew increasingly concerned about the rest of its legislative program. On a lovely spring Sunday, Eleanor Roosevelt brought Walter White to the White House. "I did not choose the tools with which I must work," Roosevelt told White. "But I've got to get legislation passed by Congress to save America. The Southerners by reason of the seniority rule in Congress are chairmen or occupy strategic places on most of the Senate and House committees. If I come out for the antilynching bill now, they will block every bill I ask Congress to pass to keep America from collapsing. I just can't take that risk."

Nonetheless Roosevelt, while not sure himself about the constitutionality of the measure, induced Joe Robinson to permit consideration of the motion to bring up the bill. "I am absolutely for the objective," the President told his press conference, "but am not clear in my own mind as to whether that is absolutely the right way to attain the objective. However, I told them to go ahead and try to get a vote on it." Other liberals shared Roosevelt's constitutional doubts. George Norris, for example, opposed the bill;

and toward the end of the filibuster William E. Borah delivered a powerful attack on it. It was Borah's speech which tipped the balance; the Senate now voted to adjourn, after having refused to do so on earlier occasions, and Costigan's original motion to bring up the bill was thereby vacated. . . . In that year, Negroes were lynched in America at a rate of a little better than one every three weeks.

Crisis, while deploring "the Great Silence of the Man in the White House," called the 1935 fight "the best of the many crusades against lynching." No one could miss the fact that the fight was initiated and largely conducted by northern Democrats. And Roosevelt's painful dilemma was understood, if not excused, in Negro circles. The antilynching fight further dramatized the northern Democrats as the only men to appear in national politics for years prepared to work and struggle for Negro rights. It provided new incentives for the Negro to sign up with the New Deal coalition.[10]

[10] Guffey, *Seventy Years on the Red-Fire Wagon,* Ch. 21; Alsop and Kintner, "The Guffey"; Harold Gosnell, *Negro Politicians: The Rise of Negro Politics in Chicago* (Chicago, 1935), 90–92; Mary White Ovington, *The Walls Came Tumbling Down* (New York, 1947), 258; F.D.R., *Public Papers* (1933), 519, (1934), 12–13; antilynching file in Howe Papers; Senate Judiciary Committee, *Punishment for the Crime of Lynching: Hearings,* 73 Cong., 2 Sess. (1934), 17–20; Senate Judiciary Committee, *Punishment for the Crime of Lynching: Hearing,* 74 Cong., 1 Sess. (1935), 23; *New York Times,* Nov. 21, 1933, April 25–May 2, 1935; *Congressional Record,* 74 Cong., 1 Sess., 6529, 6533 (April 29, 1935); White, *Man Called White,* 169–70; O. G. Villard, "The President's Worst Failure," *Nation,* June 5, 1935.

The Negro on Relief*

Richard Sterner

SIZE OF RELIEF GRANTS, BY TYPE OF RELIEF

Not only did Negro families in most rural and many urban areas of the South have greater difficulties than whites in similar economic circumstances in obtaining public assistance; also those who did get relief received smaller benefits, on the average, than white families. In many cases, however, the general level of the relief benefits for all families regardless of race appears to have been a more significant problem than the occurrence of any racial difference in size of grants. Yet those differences cannot be overlooked, for the greater difficulties of Negroes than whites in similar economic circumstances in obtaining any public assistance at all means that the Negro relief group tended to consist of families in greater average distress than white families. Under such conditions uniform treatment in the true sense of the word would actually have resulted in higher relief grants for Negroes than whites.

Average monthly relief benefits in southern states usually were much below the general national average. Virginia, for example, had an average of $6.94 in July, 1933, for all cases as against $15.51 for the country as a whole and $30.59 for New York state. . . . There was a general increase in benefits during the following two years which brought Virginia up to $17.65 as against $29.64 for the entire country and $49.06 for New York state.[38]

The low general averages for the South are due in part to the small benefits given to rural and Negro relief cases. In 1935 the monthly averages for rural relief cases in the Cotton areas ranged around $10, whereas the corresponding averages for all rural areas were in the neighborhood of $15. . . . The Negro relief cases in the Cotton areas with only one exception (Western Cotton area in October, 1935) received from $2 to $6 less than the white families on relief in those areas. Negroes on both direct relief and work relief usually received somewhat smaller amounts than whites. Since there was a tend-

* From Richard Sterner, *The Negro's Share* (New York: Harper & Bros., 1943), pp. 233–38, excluding tables. Copyright 1943 by Harper & Row, Publishers, Inc. Reprinted by permission of the publishers.

[38] Unless otherwise specified, available data on monthly relief benefits are general averages for all relief cases, regardless of whether they received full or supplementary relief or whether they were on relief for the whole month or for only part of the month.

ency to give work relief with its higher benefits to a smaller proportion of Negro than white relief recipients, this reduced the average size of all Negro benefits in comparison with those received by whites. . . .

Part of the discrepancy can be explained on the ground that Negro relief cases usually were somewhat smaller than white cases. That was not always true, however, as in February, 1935, Negro rural relief cases (5.1 persons) were larger than white cases (4.2 persons) in the Western Cotton area,[39] and yet Negroes received $2 less per month on the average. Even when Negro relief cases were smaller, it was largely due to the fact that they were selected in such a way as to reduce the average size. After all the total Negro population included a larger proportion of both small and large families than the white population, and the average Negro rural household was no smaller than the white one.

In urban areas also Negro relief grants were smaller than white grants. The previously cited urban study of 13 cities for 1935 indicates that Negro general relief grants averaged $24.18 in May, 1935, in comparison with $29.05 for whites. The average general relief benefit in Atlanta, Georgia, was $32.66 for whites but only $19.29 for Negroes. In Houston, Texas, the difference, while smaller ($16.86 for whites and $12.67 for Negroes), tended to be larger proportionately than the racial differences in the northern and western cities surveyed.[40]

In comparing relief grants with earnings from private employment, it is found that the change from direct relief to private employment raised the income substantially for the average urban relief case in both the Negro and white groups. . . . There were individual differences, however; of the Negro cases securing private employment 8.8 per cent received less than before, while the corresponding figure for whites was 2.7 per cent. The loss sometimes amounted to as much as $20 or more. For 6.5 and 2.9 per cent of the cases, respectively, the wage rates in private employment were within the same $10 interval as the previous relief grants, while for 94.4 per cent of the whites and 84.7 per cent of the Negroes wage rates exceeded relief grants.[41] Works-program earnings, while less than earnings from private employment, were approximately twice as high as relief grants for both whites and Negroes.[42]

Such data emphasize one of the basic dilemmas in relief policies. To reconcile the demand, on the one hand, that nobody should receive more money on relief than he would earn at his usual work with the demand, on the other hand, that relief standards should be adequate and uniform is hard enough under ordinary circumstances. This con-

[39] See p. 230.
[40] Enid Baird and Hugh P. Brinton, *Average General Relief Benefits, 1933–1938*, Works Progress Administration, Washington, 1940, p. 32.
[41] F. L. Carmichael and R. Nassimbene, *op. cit.*, p. 86.
[42] Among rural relief cases in North Carolina closed from July through November, 1935, Negro heads of households employed for the full month of December, 1935, in private industry earned an average of $15 as compared with $35 for whites. Works-program earnings during that month averaged $24 for whites and $19 for Negroes. In both types of employment average earnings were considerably higher than former relief grants (Rebecca Farnham and Irene Link, *op. cit.*, pp. 44 and 55).

flict becomes particularly pronounced when the Negro is involved, for a large proportion of the Negro population has such a low earning power in the labor market that some Negroes must inevitably receive larger incomes when on relief than when engaged in ordinary work. The less the Negro is discriminated against as a relief client, the higher the general relief standards become; and the greater the Negro-white wage differentials on the labor market are, the more numerous such cases become. At any rate the cases in which relief grants exceed usual earnings must be frequent among large Negro families. Otherwise the principle that public assistance should be apportioned among families of various sizes in accordance with their relative needs could not be maintained.

The NAACP and the Communist Party*

Wilson Record

A new era in relations between the NAACP and the CPUSA was introduced in the late 1920's and early 1930's. It was precipitated by two developments: (1) a drastic shift in the Communist Party's program in general and on the Negro question in particular, growing out of directives from the Sixth World Congress of the Communist International in 1928, and (2) onset of the great American depression, whose impact was felt particularly by Negroes, most of whom were in marginal economic positions. The changes in the Communist Party program had wide implications for its approach to and work among Negroes, fostering a militancy which the NAACP could not take lightly. On the other hand, the depression, initially at any rate, confused and weakened the NAACP and precipitated problems, organizational and programmatic, with which it was poorly equipped to deal. Since an understanding of these two novel elements in the American racial scene is essential to a grasp of the detailed relations of the CP and the Association during the interval from 1929 to 1935, it might be well to examine the elements in some detail.

The new Communist Party line abandoned the "boring from within" tactics of the preceding period. Why? First, the evidence was impressive that the previous approach was a failure, the attempts to penetrate trade-unions, left-of-center parties, and racial and ethnic groups having produced few concrete results. Although the efforts had not been uniformly unrewarding, they had fallen so far short of the mark that leaders of the Communist International were convinced that only a complete reorientation of the CP strategy in the United States would do. Second, the serious internal crises in the Soviet Union had abated somewhat by the late 1920's, and the Communist International

* From Wilson Record, *Race and Radicalism: The NAACP and the Communist Party in Conflict* (Ithaca: Cornell University Press, 1964), pp. 52–56, 58–83. Copyright © by Cornell University. Used by permission of Cornell University Press.

leaders, now subservient to Stalin, believed that a more vigorous assault on capitalist systems, including that in the United States, should be launched.

At its core the new strategy entailed development of separatist organizations dedicated to an independent, uncompromising assault on capitalism, not only by fomenting proletarian revolutions in the more highly developed countries but also by fostering "national liberation" movements in colonial areas. Anticolonial activity would be an indirect way of attacking the major industrial powers. The new strategy, originating in the Kremlin and imposed on the affiliated sections of the Communist International over the doubts of some and the opposition of others, was to become the operating code of the CP in the United States.[1] What were its specific implications for American Negroes?

Generally, the new program required development of revolutionary, dual organizations in all areas of CP activity. The targets included industrial workers, intellectuals, sharecroppers, tenants, nationality groups, Negroes, and such other potentially dissident elements as might be brought, for whatever reasons, under Communist influence. The old in-boring apparatus was dismantled; instead of trying to capture indigenous protest groups from within, the party began a program to try to drain off members from those groups to swell the ranks of the new party organizations. To that end, unsympathetic leaders of indigenous groups were to be subjected to continuous, merciless attack which would brand them as "social fascists," "misleaders of labor," and "betrayers of the Negro people." [2]

Revolutionary trade-unions were to be organized through the Trade Union Unity League (TUUL), which quickly supplanted the Trade Union Educational League. Radically inclined members of the Socialist Party and unhappy members of other left-wing political movements were to be enticed directly into the Communist Party. In the Midwest and South separate revolutionary organizations of farmers, tenants, and sharecroppers were to be built on a program of land confiscation and redistribution and posed against older agrarian organizations such as the Grange. For Negroes there would be new agencies arrayed against the NAACP and the Urban League. If possible, revolutionary organizations of artists and writers were to be established with a view to using their talents for propaganda work.[3]

Specific organizations which eventually emerged were, in addition to the TUEL for industrial workers, the Sharecroppers Union for southern farm laborers and tenants, the American Student Federation for the left-wing college crowd, the League of Struggle for Negro Rights (LSNR) for colored people, and the League Against War and Fascism to accommodate a wide range of people sympathetic to Soviet foreign policy. Some of the new organizations got under way only slowly and might have died a-borning except for the worsening depression, which fostered radical upsurges that Communists were to some extent able to capitalize.

---

[1] Jay Lovestone, "The Sixth World Congress of the Communist International," *Communist,* VII (Nov., 1928), 659–675.

[2] William Z. Foster, "The Decline of the American Federation of Labor," *Communist,* VIII (Jan., 1929), *passim.*

[3] Eugene Gordon, "Negro Novelists and the Negro Masses," *New Masses,* VIII (July, 1933), 16.

The party developed a systematic analysis of the American Negro question for the first time. A new program, "Self-Determination for Negroes in the Black Belt," was adopted by the Communist International over the skepticism of American Communists, who, having made little headway among Negroes in the previous period, were in no position to say "no" effectively. The Communist International had long been aware of the American Negro's indifference to the CPUSA. It was also aware that the only mass movement ever organized among American black folk was Marcus Garvey's UNIA. And what did Garvey stress? Racial separation.

Prior to the 1928 meeting of the CI, its Executive Committee circulated a series of "theses" on the Negro question in the United States. They declared that Negroes in this country constituted a nation and that their exploitation was part and parcel of the same capitalist imperialism which crushed other colored peoples under foot in Asia and Africa. Therefore, it was argued, a solution of the Negro problem in the United States could be found in the doctrines on minorities, imperialism, and nationalism developed by Lenin and presumably applied by the USSR in dealing with Russian racial and cultural minorities.

Negroes in the United States were deemed by the party to meet every criterion of nationhood. They were a distinctive racial and cultural group—an "historically evolved, stable entity, defined by language, territory, economic life and psychological make-up manifested in a community of culture," a definition suggested by Stalin, presumably drawn from Lenin's works on nationalism. If American Negroes were a nation, they should be approached on the same basis that Communists had approached oppressed, racially homogeneous, colonial peoples elsewhere. Moreover, it logically followed that American Negroes had the same right to self-determination, which would presumably lead to the establishment of an independent Negro republic in the area of "black majority" in the South. The significance of the new line of thought can scarcely be overstated, for it was to become the guiding theory of CP work among American Negroes.[4]

• • •

With unemployment mounting, with Negroes unable to find jobs, and with those on relief proportionately twice as numerous as in the general population, the NAACP leaders knew the old methods had to be reviewed. They publicized the growing poverty and degradation of Negro communities. They encouraged organization of the black workers and the unemployed. Although they had reservations about the auspices under which such collective action took place, they were loath to counsel against the action, especially since they themselves could not come up with a workable alternative. The National Urban League took a similar position, even sponsoring workers' study groups in an effort to train Negroes for union participation. Even so, during the early depression years the NAACP and the NUL were more spectators than participants in the struggle to organize Negro workers into trade-unions.

[4] James S. Allen, *The Negro Question in the United States* (New York: International Publishers, 1936), *passim.*

Therefore the most forthright clashes between the NAACP and the Communists came in other spheres, specifically when the Association confronted the League of Struggle for Negro Rights and the International Labor Defense. The LSNR was organized in November, 1930, for the purpose of aligning a broad cross section of Negro groups behind a comprehensive race program under the firm control of the Communist Party.[10] Although a number of non-Communists held office in the League, there was never any doubt about where the power, such as it was, lay. The broad and ambitious League program was directed, as was that of the later National Negro Congress, toward Negro women, sharecroppers, workers, businessmen, soldiers, and students. In other words, in line with the self-determination theory, it proposed to cut across class lines.

The League did not have something for everybody; to the NAACP, for example, it offered no comfort. In an official declaration the League said it would have no truck with the leaders of the Association who "aped" their ideal, Booker T. Washington, in bowing and scraping in "the ante-rooms of the mighty." [11] Specifically it attacked W. E. B. Du Bois, William Pickens, and Walter White. Such charges had to be answered. The method the Association leaders employed was to stress the basic differences between the NAACP and the Communists and to expose the Communist affiliations of most of the League officers, sharpening its indictment by pointing out that the League had accepted without question the whole self-determination-for-Negroes program that originated in the party.

Although the League was committed to obtaining a broad Negro following, it quickly alienated itself from the institution in which most Negroes were to be found— the church. Proclaiming its acceptance of Marxist materialism, identifying religion with ignorance and superstition, and branding colored ministers and their followers as, at best, victims of unfortunate historical circumstance and, at worst, "lickspittles" of their white masters, the League cut itself off from black men and women who had found their main solace in the pews of rural churches. Even the more sophisticated city dwellers were offended by the party's rude rejection of the Negro's faith. For most Negroes the gospel according to Matthew continued to have more appeal than the gospel according to Marx.

In contrast, the NAACP had long recognized that religion was too deeply engrained in American Negro life to be discarded as an instrument for rallying Negroes against oppressive racial practices. Indeed, both leaders and members of the NAACP were usually men of rather firm religious commitments; for them an acceptance of the League's position would have meant not only organizational disaster but personal apostasy as well. The local minister was often the local Association president and attempted to persuade his flock that, far from being at cross-purposes, the NAACP and the Christian church were striving for the same goals.

Both the NAACP and the League were compelled to involve themselves in the immediate economic and social problems of Negroes. Both were handicapped by the fact

[10] LSNR, *Equality, Land and Freedom: A Program for Negro Liberation* (New York: LSNR 1933)
[11] *Ibid.,* pp. 12–13.

that the problems were of such magnitude that no private efforts could deal with them adequately; the situation called for a concerted national attack, which was eventually undertaken by the New Deal. At the end of its short career the League could point to no significant contribution on any of the specific, immediate issues with which Negroes were concerned: employment, voting, education, housing, and civil rights. As the party itself was later to admit, the League, in addition to the major handicap indicated above, was hobbled by a narrow, sectarian ideological image. Even Negro intellectuals, who might have been expected to be impressed by its radical ideology and ambitious program, were, with very few exceptions, unresponsive. Although the NAACP took cognizance of the League's existence and issued periodic blasts against it, the portion of its energies expended on the League was small; they were needed elsewhere, and the threat posed by the League seemed mild compared to the threat posed by the depression. During the 1929–1935 period the NAACP gained few recruits; the League fared even more poorly, despite energetic moves to enlist Negro nationalists who had earlier responded to Garvey.

The International Labor Defense, however, was another story. From it came the most effective Communist challenge to the NAACP during the 1929 to 1935 period. The central purpose of the ILD was to use the courts not for the usual juridical purposes but as a means of criticizing capitalist justice and spreading Communist propaganda.[12] Its technique was to intervene in trials in which members of Communist organizations or of some group to which it wanted to make a special appeal were defendants. It would then proceed to make financial, organizational, and propaganda hay out of such trials by appealing for defense funds, organizing special committees, and widely publicizing the issues to ILD and Communist Party advantage. There was no way to lose—if a case was decided against it, the ILD could charge injustice by class courts; if the decision was favorable, it could emphasize the power of mass pressure exerted through Communist leadership.

From the time of its formation until the early 1930's the ILD, although handling some Negro cases, had not found one which deeply stirred the colored community. Furthermore, not one of the cases that did attract attention had been in the South. The Scottsboro case, which emerged from rural Alabama in 1931, was a godsend.[13] Nine Negro youths, some of them mere boys, were accused of raping two white girls while traveling in an open freight car through northern Alabama. Although the girls were of bad repute and gave testimony which did not hang together, a local court overrode the boys' protestations of innocence, found them guilty, and sentenced eight of them to death. The long legal struggle that followed dramatized more than any other experience of that period the inherent differences between the NAACP and the ILD; moreover, it brought into major battle two organizations and ideologies which theretofore had merely skirmished.

---

[12] Bunche, *op. cit.*, p. 695.
[13] Harry Haywood, "The Scottsboro Decision," *Communist*, XI (Dec., 1932), 1075.

When it entered the Scottsboro case, the NAACP knew it would be bucking the white reactionaries of the South; it did not anticipate that on that particular issue it would be fighting the Communists as well or that so long a struggle would ensue.[14] The NAACP was disconcerted not only by the violence of southern reaction to the alleged rape of two loose white girls by nine Negro boys but also by the swiftness and the resourcefulness with which the party moved into the case.

The Association's remaining faith in "responsible" southern judges and other "decent" white elements in the South was shaken to its very roots when the most crucial of all tests was applied. The confidence of its leaders in themselves, the organization, and its techniques was, if not shattered, weakened at many points. At the same time there appeared on the scene a rival organization which, for the moment at least, appeared more able to challenge the prejudiced white newspapers, bigoted judges, demagogic prosecutors, and tobacco-chewing, near-hysterical jurors. All had to be overcome if the Negro youngsters were to obtain fair trials. Deserted by most of its white Southern friends and sympathizers, criticized even by some of its own moderate Negro supporters for its ineffectual action, under attack from the left, and in the throes of an internal crisis, with resources at a low ebb, the NAACP occupied a precarious position.

For the party, on the other hand, Scottsboro was an opportunity of the first magnitude. For the first time the ILD had an issue on which it could make an effective bid for Negro attention; the case was loaded with propaganda possibilities, the like of which not even the most imaginative party devotee could have foreseen. Here was a chance not only to carry its message to the Negro masses but also to link racial injustice to the very foundations of the bourgeois order. Finally, the Scottsboro case provided grist for the world-wide propanganda mill of the Comintern, which was committed to undermining the capitalist hold on colored peoples.

Few Negroes could understand the finer points of Marx's materialism, grasp the meaning of Lenin's theory of imperialism, or fathom the intent of the self-determination doctrine. They did know, either directly or indirectly, the face of southern white justice. No one needed to draw them a picture of the consequences for an accused Negro when an Alabama white woman, however unsavory of background or for whatever motives, yelled "rape." What black man did not identify to some degree with the accused Scottsboro boys?

When the nine Negroes were indicted, convicted, and with one exception given the death penalty—all within a period of less than three weeks—the NAACP intervened and attempted to handle the defense against obviously overwhelming odds. The ILD prejudiced the case still further by sending the presiding judge a telegram in which it threatened that he would be held "personally responsible" unless the defendants were released immediately.[15] It is now apparent, although it might not have been to some people at the time, that the ILD was more concerned with the propaganda aspects of the trials than with the guilt or innocence, the conviction or acquittal of the nine defend-

---

[14] White, *Promised Land,* p. 214.
[15] Walter White, *A Man Called White* (New York: Viking Press, 1949), 128.

ants. A quick acquittal would have disarmed the Communists; a quick conviction and execution would have demonstrated the ILD's ineffectiveness. But a case that would drag on and on through the courts was made to order for the comrades.

Having lost the first round, the NAACP moved to appeal the convictions to higher courts, sticking to strict legal procedures. In the interim, however, the ILD, spotting the propaganda gold glistening there for the taking, approached the parents of the condemned youths and persuaded some of them to entrust further handling of the cases to the ILD itself. ILD representatives told the parents that the NAACP was planning to desert the boys and possibly would have them plead guilty in exchange for promises of life imprisonment. Knowing little about the NAACP or the CP and convinced of the innocence of their offspring, some parents were relieved to accept ILD help.[16] Simultaneously the CP, the ILD, the LSNR, and the TUUL loosed an all-out propaganda campaign against the Association and its leaders. Having discredited the NAACP in the eyes of some Negroes because it refused to denounce the whole judicial system, the ILD set about to make Scottsboro not only an American but a world *cause célèbre*. With the aid of Communist-affiliated organizations over the globe it was able to accomplish its objectives.

In those circumstances the NAACP whose orderly, juridical approach had been frustrated by the ILD, withdrew from the Scottsboro defense. Realizing that it would then have to demonstrate concrete results acceptable to Negroes by doing something more than stirring up a propaganda fuss, the ILD retained the famed criminal lawyer, Samuel Liebowitz, to handle the case (the singular form is used though technically the charges were handled individually), which in time reached the United States Supreme Court. Although Liebowitz had been told about the ILD's ideology and methods, he could not at first believe that the organization would put political and propaganda concerns so far above the immediate legal interests of the defendants. Gradually, however, it dawned upon him what the ILD was up to, whereupon he withdrew, denouncing the ILD for its machinations and calling attention to the fact that in the name of Scottsboro it had raised large sums of money, presumably for defense purposes, and then diverted it to wholly unrelated party activities. Liebowitz had handled the case without compensation. While he was still the counsel of record, the ILD began to subject him to biting criticism.[17]

During the period from 1931 to 1935 the Scottsboro case received almost continuous attention in the Communist press; the party never let pass any opportunity to belabor the NAACP and its leaders for their insistence that nonrevolutionary approaches to the courts were the essential—in fact, the only—paths to racial justice. The invective heaped on the Association and its leaders reached a new high in volume and intensity. By 1935, however, the ILD was prepared to make overtures to the NAACP and other Negro organizations concerning the Scottsboro case, which was still plodding through the courts while the accused remained in prison.[18] The move was dictated not by a belief that some cooperative endeavor of the two organizations would possibly free the boys; it was a result of two factors that have not been accorded the attention they de-

[16] Quentin Reynolds, *Courtroom* (New York: Popular Library, 1957), p. 244.
[17] *Ibid.*, pp. 277–278.
[18] Editorial, "Betrayal by the NAACP," *New Masses*, XIV (Jan. 8, 1935), 6.

serve in the voluminous literature on Scottsboro. These were the beginning of a shift in the Communist Party line from dual, separatist, revolutionary action to nondirect, nonviolent, "united front" endeavors in concert with moderate and leftist movements, and the fact that the law of diminishing political and propaganda returns had set in for that particular issue. At one time many Negroes were inclined to believe that the ILD's concern for the defendants was genuine and that its methods were appropriate, perhaps even necessary; accordingly, they contributed money and other kinds of support. Eventually they began to raise questions about the noisy talk, the aggressive gestures, the appeals for more money—and the few concrete results. The Communists could not go on indefinitely appealing for sacrifices when consequences that Negroes expected—and could understand—were so few. Scottsboro had thus become something of a liability for the CP and the ILD.

Meanwhile the NAACP had fought the ILD, pointing out time and again the nature of the latter's interest in the case, calling attention to the misuse of defense funds, and insisting that the cause of racial justice could but fail when judicial processes were linked to revolutionary aims and became secondary to political purpose. One obviously cannot simultaneously pursue and denounce established legal procedures; how can serious appeals be made when the appellants are at the same time denying that the courts can act independently of political considerations? Although the Association's desire to free the defendants was never dampened, its hands were tied during the very time when legal appeals should have been pushed most vigorously through the courts. When a new coalition of organizations was formed in 1935 to try again to win acquittal, the NAACP went along even though the coalition included the ILD. The new Scottsboro Defense Committee included representatives of the American Civil Liberties Union, the Methodist Federation for Social Action, the Socialist League for Industrial Democracy, the Church League for Industrial Democracy, and the National Urban League (representatives of the latter served in an unofficial capacity), as well as the NAACP and the ILD. Significantly, it was the moderate organizations, especially the NAACP, that were responsible for the new round of long and involved court appeals and negotiations with Alabama officials which eventually led to freedom for most of the defendants. The CP and the ILD welcomed the outcome, which could be interpreted as verification of the "united front" approach, and which diverted attention from the failure of the Communists to accomplish anything by themselves. Later the Stalinists were to revive memories of the Scottsboro case, using them as a means of attacking the NAACP and the NUL in the post-World War II period.

The NAACP's cooperation with the ILD on the last push to free the Scottsboro defendants was not the forerunner of a new era of peace and harmony. Like the child once burned who is afraid of fire, the NAACP viewed the sudden change of party heart with skepticism. Association leaders feared the party's embrace more than its enmity, for they foresaw new party efforts in (1) to infiltrate local branches by pointing to cooperation at the top, (2) to form local front groups for which NAACP members would be courted, and (3) to gain respectability for party causes by pointing to the party's new allies in the Scottsboro case. Torn between such risks and a genuine interest in the nine defendants, the NAACP reluctantly joined the coalition.

The period of the United Front will be dealt with in detail in the next chapter. Before that time arrived the party continued to lambaste the NAACP, its foremost rival for Negro allegiance, and other reformist Negro organizations as well. The Communists attempted to discredit such agencies among their own followers and to undermine their frequently tenuous structures. Establishing rival organizations in whatever areas of Negro life the party thought might be penetrated, it tried to widen schisms within the Negro community and to capitalize the class, color, and social differences it found there.

The indigenous reformist groups were struggling with internal and external crises of the first magnitude. Lacking both the funds and the organizational apparatus for dealing with the major economic problems confronting most Negroes, the NAACP nearly went under. It was prepared to work slowly and carefully on such matters as education, voting, housing, and civil rights for Negroes, but it was poorly equipped to tackle mass unemployment and its myriad consequences. For many Negroes, including even some in the relatively small middle-class group, the basic problems were now those of physical survival and maintenance of a modicum of social and psychological well-being in the face of immense, impersonal, dislocating economic forces.

Lower-strata Negroes encountered in more intensified form the old problems of getting a job, enough to eat, and a place to live, so as to keep the family together. Highly disproportionate numbers of Negroes were unemployed, underemployed, without housing, on relief. They had never been particularly attracted to the Association; now the kind of issues the NAACP had been struggling with—breaking the white primary, gaining admittance to graduate schools, defending individual rights in the courts —seemed even further removed from the common colored man's world of reality. Even so, the lower classes probably weathered the depression better socially and psychologically than did the middle class, which found its hard-won respectability ebbing away as the prosperity of the twenties receded. As rural Negroes sometimes put it, "Them that ain't flew so high ain't got so far to fall." The NAACP could offer neither group a real solution.

In reacting to the depression the NAACP was characteristically slow. Its leaders were hesitant. But if they knew not what to do or how to do it, they had for company the American Federation of Labor, the Chamber of Commerce, and the President of the United States. Some kinds of crises in American life have provided opportunities as well as problems. The crisis of war, for example, had in the past offered colored workers a chance to improve their bargaining position in the tightening labor market. Crises also had precipitated Negro migrations to areas where there was greater personal freedom, social opportunity, and political participation and fewer restraints by law, tradition, and racial prejudice. The result had been a changed outlook, with Negroes seeing more clearly the nature of the gap between professed democratic ideals and existing racial practices. Although Negroes had received less than any other group from the society they had been called upon to defend in war, they had viewed war, as had other disadvantaged minorities, in terms of both sacrifice and new horizons. World War I, for example, had demonstrated that they could do as well as the next man when the avenues of opportunity were opened. Perhaps that fact helps to account for the virtual absence of pacifist sentiment among colored Americans in World Wars I and II, though there was also the feeling that Negroes, until recently politically powerless, could do little to shape the main drift of national policy and should make the best of the white man's war, if he insisted on having it.

A depression, or even a limited recession, is a different kind of crisis. The NAACP rolls withered rather than fattened during the early years of the depression decade. Marxist theory might have it that the ranks of the poor should close and tighten in unity when capitalism falters and economic catastrophe strikes; correlatively, prosperity might be supposed to dispel unity as proletarians find they can make it alone. In the actual case just the opposite is true. Unions and other ameliorative organizations have waxed in boom and waned in slump, at least in the United States. When the economy is healthy and opportunity levels are high, prodding and pressuring by reformist groups get results; dissenters' hopes are high; and there is money to pay dues. When a great depression strikes, the problem of survival is so pressing as to blot out other issues, and the gradualist, piecemeal programs of groups such as the NAACP fall into ineffectuality. An unemployed Negro need not be a Marxist in order to act like an economic determinist.

Until the depression struck, the Association's concern for the franchise, residential segregation, equal education, and civil rights, reflecting the values of the Negro middle class and the elitist outlook of its leaders, took the capitalist order for granted. Specifically rejected was the Communist contention that racial prejudice was peculiar to a given stage of economic development and could be overcome only when capitalism was abolished.

Even prior to the general depression, the Negro's economic position was largely marginal because of a concentration of the black population in the rural South, where agricultural crisis was chronic. There, in the 1920's, Negroes were being edged out of what skilled and semiskilled jobs they had managed to secure, while the hoped-for break in the dreary cycle of sharecropping and farm tenancy, leading to eventual independent land ownership, never materialized. Depression developments drove even deeper wedges between Negro and white workers. The 1930 convention of the Association indicated some awareness of the rapid impact of the burgeoning depression on Negro welfare. However, its leaders, along with Mr. Hoover, seemed to feel—or hope—that prosperity was no further away than the next corner. The resolutions adopted mirrored certain misgivings about the ability to achieve full citizenship in the absence of minimum economic security. But the means for attaining the latter objective were not explored with rigor.

With the depression deepening, the 1931 convention of the Association took a more questioning and inclusive view of the problems affecting Negroes. For the first time a forthright call for the alliance of Negroes with organized labor, qualified only by the demand that the latter's racial barriers be dropped, was issued, indicating quite a shift in outlook. However, the leaders remained uncertain about the specific things to be done. Even in 1932 the Association was prepared to go no further than the general dictum that Negroes and white workers faced common problems calling for a common, cooperative solution. One thing was clear: the inability of the Association to go it alone, even in the action areas where it had presumably perfected its approach and techniques. It needed allies. But where to turn? The trade-unions were something less than eager for racial cooperation, and the CP, before the United Front period, would have responded favorably only on the condition of complete capitulation by the NAACP. As a means of wringing concessions from the white community, NAACP leaders issued caveats about the possibility of Negroes turning "radical" if their plight was not alleviated; but this was an ancient stratagem, and those who voiced the warning scarcely believed it themselves.

The Association's leaders were committed to maintaining the NAACP as a continuing force in Negro life while keeping its structure intact and their own positions secure. That was understandable in men who equated race welfare with the welfare of the NAACP. To have embraced economic radicalism would have meant indictment of the very class on whose support the Association depended. Even so mild a thing as hinting that the NAACP might well make overtures to the labor movement caused some rumblings among conservative members, especially the Negro professionals and businessmen.

During that time Du Bois gave expression through the columns of *Crisis* to a ferment within the NAACP hierarchy. He demanded that the Association identify itself more closely with the mass of Negroes, a rather striking proposal from the originator and personal embodiment of the Talented Tenth concept. Going further, he called for decentralization of the NAACP's internal structure, with more autonomy for local branches. He wanted the annual convention rather than the self-perpetuating Executive Board to be the final arbiter of policy. Moreover, he was disturbed by the Association's lack of concern about foreign affairs, particularly relations with the colonial peoples of Africa and Asia; he wanted the NAACP to commit itself unequivocally to their liberation. Finally, he demanded that the NAACP appeal more effectively to younger Negroes and intellectuals.[19]

While the Du Bois proposals bore rather close outward resemblance to those advocated at the time by the Communists, they were original with Du Bois. He did not link them to an over-all theory of history or social change. If implemented, they might have caused a radical transformation of the NAACP, but he regarded them as nothing more than pragmatic solutions for immediate organizational and racial issues. Such similarity as they had to the party's offerings were a matter of coincidence. The *Crisis* editor was voicing misgivings and demands which were less forcefully put but perhaps just as keenly felt by other members of the Association. Significantly, at the very time he was advocating those measures, Du Bois was under almost continuous attack from the CP.

On economic matters Du Bois' proposals were something of a throwback to Garvey and Washington. He suggested that Negroes make a group effort to hold their present employment and pool their resources to start new all-Negro businesses. Economic separatism was combined with racial radicalism in his plan to form Negro group-purchasing institutions and a Negro economic "general staff" to develop an independent racial economic life in the United States. At the same time Negroes were to con-

---

[19] Lawrence, *op. cit.*, p. 138.

tinue to press for full civil and social rights. Some of his organizational proposals were later adopted in watered-down form, but the Association's leaders, who have always been primarily integrationists, rejected his separatist economic measures. By continuing to advocate the latter he incurred increasing disfavor, which partly led to his resignation in 1934.

A lateral development to Du Bois' economic separatism was found in the "Don't Buy Where You Can't Work" movement, which caught on in a number of cities during that period. The NAACP preferred to remain aloof from such campaigns. However, they were popular among northern urban Negroes and at times received the backing of local NAACP branches. The national officers considered it expedient to "go along," realizing that otherwise they might alienate members who saw concrete changes resulting from this form of direct action, from which they derived a sense of effectiveness. They sensed also that Negro extremists, left and right, would attempt to capitalize the issue. Even in the 1960's, sporadic campaigns, such as the San Francisco branch's effort to obtain jobs for Negro drivers in the Yellow Cab Company, receive official support from the national office.

During the depression it became increasingly clear that the race's economic problems would have to be dealt with primarily by political means. Whereas the Association's political participation had been spotty in the past, by 1932 the plight of Negroes was so desperate that a reluctance to use politics on a systematic and sustained basis was largely overcome. The Association was concerned not only that Negroes have the right to vote but also that they use their franchise to support reform measures of benefit to lower-strata groups generally and to Negroes in particular. While maintaining its nonpartisan pose, the NAACP strongly supported Roosevelt and most of the ensuing New Deal relief and employment measures from which Negroes benefited disproportionately because they had been hardest hit. Here was an indication of firm commitment to pragmatic, and often liberal, political action. Again, however, the development was sparked not by the Communists or other Marxian-oriented groups, or by radical ideologies, but by day-to-day experiences of Negroes and the Association's need to come up with a program adequate for the challenge.

Indeed, until about 1936 the CP was a vociferous critic of Roosevelt and his reform measures. The Communists believed rightly that the man in the White House and his wife had cut much of the ground from under the party's propaganda appeals to Negroes. The Communists' opposition to the early New Deal, which brought Negroes their first real measure of relief, was based partly on a recognition that colored citizens would turn to radicalism only as a last, desperate measure. The Communist shift in 1935 moved the Stalinists' immediate political outlook closer to that of the average Negro— not the other way around. Although Negroes at last had broken with the Republican Party, which could exploit the Lincoln legend only so far, they did not move to the opposite extreme and identify with radical political movements.

Even where Negroes did respond tentatively to Communist organizations— among the unemployed, sharecroppers, workers, and intellectuals—there was a pronounced tendency to conceive objectives in immediate, pragmatic terms, definitions which the party momentarily accepted and acted on. In contrast to the moderate organizations, the Communists were willing and to some extent able to work among the lower-strata Negroes on a grass-roots basis, organizing unemployed councils, relief demonstrations, hunger marches, and protests. This was plodding, unscintillating work, calling for dedicated acolytes who truly believed the future lay with the working classes. The party could staff such campaigns better than could the NAACP, for obvious reasons. The ideological commitments of most Negroes participating in the actions were limited, tenuous, and lacking in a broader sophistication the party would have welcomed. But though the Negro in distress could not grasp the finer points of Communist doctrine, he could understand the slogans for more relief, the halting of evictions, and the availability of more jobs with higher pay in public-works programs. And if he found himself associating with the Communists on those terms, he was nonetheless disinclined to make an over-all commitment to the party's larger objectives.

Understandably, NAACP leaders were disturbed by efforts of the party to capitalize the Negro's plight. They were convinced that once the stirring-up was done with, little would remain in the way of concrete gains, and that the noise itself was the main objective. Equally important, however, was a fear that Communist-led movements would challenge the Association itself, threatening both its ideological base and its organizational structure. Realistically, perhaps, NAACP spokesmen feared not the radicalism but the susceptibility of the Negro masses, who might fall in behind the red banner of James Ford as they had earlier followed the black flag of Garvey. In that respect Association officials voiced a sentiment that is one of the historic traits of both the conservative and the ultraradical: the masses must be held in check and led by elites.

The halting and inconsistent steps the NAACP took on various issues underscored the difficulties in modifying its traditional program and developing a suitable apparatus. Yet the pressures to do so remained strong. That the organization was able to shift, however slowly, is testimony to the flexibility of its leaders and to the value of intraorganizational conflict as an antidote to stagnation. The interaction between what John Roche has termed the "enthusiasts" and the "bureaucrats," although a source of personal animosities, was also the locus of organizational adaptability.

Without doubt, the CP influenced the NAACP in a number of indirect ways, as, indeed, it was to influence other organizations, for example, the trade-unions. The shifts within the Association were in part a response to the party's challenge; had they occurred sooner, the party's influence, such as it was among Negroes, would have been even more limited. Here and there the party demonstrated that lower-strata Negroes could be aroused and organized around immediate issues. It showed that racial discontent could be turned to political account, particularly when underscored by economic catastrophe. Although the party was unable to build a mass Negro following, it approached a stratum of the race frequently regarded by the NAACP as the middle-class Negro's burden. More sophisticated than their rank and file and having a personal identity with the Association, NAACP leaders showed little inclination to sever old ties to join a movement that was as unpredictable as it was radical. Significantly, no top or intermediate leader of the Association, as far as has been determined, defected to the party during that period, and no Communist held any position of consequence in the national office.

Authority in the NAACP was centralized in the Executive Board, which controlled the selection of the executive secretary and the rest of the national staff; indeed, the Board could hire and fire at will without accounting to the membership. Given the composition of the membership at that time, however, it is highly unlikely that it would have approved Communists for any important posts. The Association could not afford to be too restrictive about the political coloration of mere members, however, since they were hard to come by.

Criticism by Negro newspapers and young intellectuals was yet another force pushing the NAACP toward a broadened program. In the spring of 1932 Du Bois polled seventeen editors of leading papers about communism and the activities of the party among Negroes. Carl Murphy of the *Baltimore Afro-American* praised the party for its insistence on internal racial equality and its concern for the plight of lower-strata Negroes. William M. Kelly of the *Amsterdam News* voiced agreement in principle with what he described as Communist objectives in the race field but expressed serious doubts concerning their practicability in the United States. Young of the *Norfolk Journal and Guide* and Dungee of the *Black Dispatch* (Oklahoma) conceded that the Communists had made some contribution to Negro betterment but emphasized the party's limitations and questioned its final objectives. Five of the editors voiced the opinion that communism was making some headway among Negroes but saw no cause for alarm, since the party's influence was predicated on immediate issues and Negroes showed little concern for its ultimate objectives. Frank M. Davis, editor of the *Atlanta Daily World,* held that the party was making few gains among Negroes. Although glad that that was the case, he did not condemn the Communists outright. In contrast, Willis Cole of the *Louisville Leader* felt that the party was making serious inroads and deplored what he thought was a widespread favorable response to Communist appeals. Two editors, Robert L. Vann (*Pittsburgh Courier*) and Fred R. Moore (*New York Age*), condemned the party roundly, expressing the hope that Negroes would steer entirely clear of it.[20]

That few of the Negro newsmen were wholly critical of the party was an eye opener for the NAACP. In a sense their responses were back-handed slaps at the Association, whose frailties became more apparent as the depression deepened. NAACP officials could hardly afford to ignore the opinions and implied recommendations of such influential race spokesmen. It must be kept in mind, however, that the editors' responses were intended for white eyes and ears as well, by indirection suggesting that Negroes would seek radical alternatives if their most pressing needs were not met.

In 1933 the discontent of young colored intellectuals with the NAACP was brought to the fore at the second Amenia Conference, the first having been held in 1916. Some forty prominent young Negroes participated in the sessions held on the Spingarn estate in New York. Present also were a number of the "elders," including NAACP officials. The latter were shocked at the critical mood and the radical reactions of

[20] *Ibid.,* pp. 174–178.

their would-be protégés. Although there were diverse views among the younger set, there was general agreement that large-scale, militant political and economic action was the best means for improving the position of the Negro. Implicit was the assumption that the old guard didn't have the answers.[21]

Time and again the NAACP was criticized by the conference for its exclusiveness, hesitancy, conservatism, and shortsightedness. There were charges of reluctance to undertake mass organization among Negroes and of too slavish adherence to time-honored and timeworn tactics which were no longer sufficient. But though young Amenia participants were racially militant and showed a surprising acquaintance with Marxian theories and movements, few of them were Communists. Growing up in a political and social environment different from that of their elders, victimized by the depression, operating in a context of institutional as well as personal crisis, and seeking positions of racial leadership, they were understandably unhappy with the ineffectual role being played by the NAACP in the great drama taking place before them. But to whom could they turn and what could they do?

Marxism, emerging from the immigrant ghettos in the 1930's, began to reach the colleges and universities, even the Negro campuses in the South. Not many colored students turned True Believer, but some were influenced by the Communists' explanation of the old order in crisis and were responsive to its emphasis on economic forces as the root of most, if not all, evil. Some students wished to rally the black masses to a new faith and lead them along a leftward-curving road to salvation. Yet few of them paused, at Amenia or elsewhere, to consider that they themselves were neither from nor of the masses. Indeed, in acquiring intellectual status, they had increased the barrier between themselves and those they would lead. Since few had yet wet their feet in organizing the lower echelons, their innocence was virtually intact; the thought that sharecroppers and coal miners might not come rushing into the fold if invited to do so was submerged in the general enthusiasm.

There is a temptation, from the perspective of the 1960's, to treat the concern of those young militants for the masses with condescension or contempt. The fact that their enthusiasm came to little should not enhance the temptation. Unsuccessful radicals do not write the accepted histories. But before the Amenia insurgents are cavalierly dismissed, one might pause to honor them for having embodied in their own time and in their own way the "dissident impulse" in American life, an impulse whose lack of vitality in the present era undergirds a stultifying conformity.

In any event, the stir which the "young Turks" caused at Amenia was duplicated in other places where the elders gathered with youths to discuss problems of the race in the early 1930's. The discontent of the angry young men almost always included criticism of the NAACP, whose leaders accepted with few qualifications the existing capitalist order as a framework within which racial rights could be won. By late 1933 the NAACP leaders, while retaining their ideological focus, were changing their emphasis and broadening their sights. They insisted that their response was autonomous and predicated on

---

[21] Bunche, *op. cit.*, pp. 209–210.

a calm analysis of the scene, but there can be little doubt that the Amenia needle prick had struck blood.

Structurally the NAACP remained much the same, with real authority still vested in the Executive Board, though a few concessions were made to internal criticism and outside pressure. The concessions—for example, some of the critics were put on the Board—only whetted the appetite of the dissenters for a more thorough overhaul. The annual conference held in St. Louis in June, 1935, was publicized in advance as a turning point in the Association's history. It was thought that the conference would broaden and make official the adaptations of the past several years. In particular it was believed that prolonged criticism of the oligarchic apparatus would culminate in steps to provide real internal democracy with greater autonomy for local branches. The advocates of reform represented varying shades of political opinion, including radical intellectuals. Although their discontent reflected some Communist infiltration and pressure, the unrest was largely indigenous.

Much of the discontent cut across regional and political lines. However, it was never effectively centered in a disciplined group or articulated by a recognized spokesman. Some dissenters criticized the Association on its own ground; specifically they claimed that even in its chosen field, the prosecution of civil rights cases, the NAACP had fallen short of any acceptable mark.

The NAACP leaders, it had been conjectured beforehand, would accept some rather thoroughgoing changes at St. Louis. Membership was still only 85,000; dues were insufficient for the tasks at hand. Negro intellectuals were beginning to be disenchanted and could no longer be counted on to perform their ideological and agitational roles for the NAACP. Rival organizations, especially the left-wing groups, were making a lot of noise among the white-collar and industrial workers as well as among the tenants and sharecroppers in the South. While the Association's leaders went along with many of the reformers' economic and political proposals and even spoke in behalf of them, they in characteristic bureaucratic fashion did not relinquish their grip on the national office or extend branch autonomy or divest the self-perpetuating Executive Board of final authority on policy matters. The critics appeared to have won a victory if judged from the resolutions adopted, but the reins were still held firmly in the same old hands.

J. E. Spingarn, white philanthropist who had been one of the Association's founders and who acted as spokesman for the officialdom, insisted on a gradualist approach, stressing the difficulties inherent in carrying out the new economic and political program called for by the convention. He launched a vigorous attack on the Communists, warning delegates not to associate with them and calling attention to the party's designs on the NAACP. Fear of Communist infiltration of local branches or of the defection of Association members to the party was an important factor in retaining the centralized organizational structure and continuing the restraints on local branches. If the party could capture enough branches and if the locus of policy were shifted from the Board to the convention, the Communists could conceivably control the organization. The fear, though not wholly imaginary, was overdrawn. Of at least equal importance in the leaders' eagerness to retain the existing power structure was their belief that by experience, knowledge, personal dedication, and long commitment to the NAACP they were the natural guardians of the Association's welfare. In typical bureaucratic fashion, the incumbent officialdom identified its own interests with those of the organization. The Board had no intention of diluting its power, and dissenters at St. Louis could either go along or withdraw from the NAACP.

The party's attitude toward the Association was not immediately modified. The Communists kept up their attack through the party, the ILD, the LSNR, and other organizations. Even as the United Front was being launched during that year, the Stalinists could find little to justify inclusion of the NAACP, assuming that the Association, like Barkis, was willing. However, by the end of 1935 the United Front was in full swing, and the CP was finally willing to extend the left hand of fellowship to an organization which only a few months before it had denounced as a hopeless supporter of "imperialist reaction" and a saboteur of the "mass aspirations of the Negro people."

The gains the CP made from 1929 to 1935 were realized primarily on issues of everyday importance; the response of Negroes could rarely be projected into visions of a new society. In fact, to keep the picture in focus, one must remember that the party's following among Negroes was disproportionately low. The party's strength, such as it was, rested chiefly on its ability to appeal ideologically to a few Negro intellectuals and to stir some lower-strata Negroes on immediate issues.

From the standpoint of membership the NAACP was somewhat better off at the close of the six-year period than at the beginning, though its coffers were far from full. So far as concerns influence, particularly outside the Negro community, it had made gains. The improvement was a result in part of the general upsurge of reform that came with the New Deal. Ameliorative groups had become respectable in the general ferment of the Roosevelt era, and the NAACP's public image brightened accordingly. There was official recognition of its voice as a spokesman for the Negro's aspirations, and its leaders found men of power in Washington more accessible.

By turning, however slowly, to economic and political action, the NAACP was beginning to develop promising organizational skills whose value was to be demonstrated time and again during the following three decades. Having undergone an organizational crisis, a part of which flowed from efforts by the Communists to destroy it, the Association emerged with a somewhat broader vision, increased political sophistication, and restored confidence in its ability to function as an agency of racial protest. What impresses one as paradoxical is the fact that the NAACP weathered both organizational and racial crises with few ideological and structural changes. It might be argued that if NAACP leaders had been more imaginative in going to the masses, had taken the wraps off local units, had fired the hopes of the intellectuals, and had mapped out a comprehensive blueprint of the good society, they might have accomplished more. Unfortunately, there is no way of testing such conditionals conclusively, and the student is left with the possibility that just the opposite might have been the result.

The period 1929 to 1935 may be viewed as one in which differences between the NAACP and the CP became increasingly clear, erupting in open conflict in Scottsboro and a few other places. The differences were fought out also in the columns of the *New Masses* and the *Daily Worker* and on the pages of *Crisis* and *Opportunity*. Eventually they would have to be fought out in the minds of thoughtful Negroes; but that would come in a later era. What is perhaps most significant about those years, given the crisis in Negro life and the energetic efforts of the CP to win black men to its cause, is that so many Negroes chose, either positively or by default, the course charted by the NAACP.

Negro Labor and the Government*

Robert C. Weaver

The Negro was considered, if not included, from the outset of the defense effort. When the National Defense Advisory Commission was set up as the first over-all defense agency in World War II early in 1940, an administrative assistant was appointed in the Labor Division of the commission to facilitate the employment and training of Negroes. Shortly thereafter, the United States Office of Education announced that there *should be no* discrimination on account of race, creed, or color, in the expenditure of federal funds for vocational training. This was followed by a statement that workers in defense industries *should not* be discriminated against because of age, sex, race, or color. And Congress inserted an ambiguous non-discrimination clause in the appropriation for defense training passed in October, 1940.

These statements of policy were significant as pronouncements of official intent. Earlier chapters have indicated how little influence they had upon employers and how they were ignored by school officials. As a matter of fact, management paid only slight attention to any of the federal policies for labor supply; it paid even less attention to statements that minorities *should not* be discriminated against on defense work. Earlier experience with federally financed public construction programs illustrated graphically that non-discrimination statements mean little unless they are implemented. And, with the exception of some construction projects, there were few instances where the commission's policies were translated into action.

Out of the experience with craft organizations in the building trades, it became clear that certain unions were often serious impediments to the utilization of Negro artisans. Accordingly, the National Defense Advisory Commission began to discuss the matter with leaders of labor. Out of these discussions came an agreement that the

* From Robert C. Weaver, *Negro Labor: A National Problem* (New York: Harcourt, Brace & World, Inc., 1946), pp. 131–37, 141–42, 145–52. Copyright 1946 by Robert C. Weaver. Reprinted by permission of Harcourt Brace Jovanovich, Inc.

American Federation of Labor and the Congress of Industrial Organizations would assume responsibility for removing barriers against Negro workers in defense industries. This helped some, but it did not come to grips with the problem of union discrimination. It was ineffective chiefly because the agency which negotiated it had no powers of enforcement.

In recognition of the general inadequacies of the commission, a new agency, the Office of Production Management, was created in 1941, and its Labor Division assumed responsibility for labor supply. In response to great pressure from Negroes and the liberal press, Sidney Hillman, as co-director and head of the Labor Division of OPM, issued a letter to all holders of defense contracts urging them to "examine their employment and training policies at once to determine whether or not these policies make ample provision for full utilization of available and competent Negro workers." At the same time that this letter was issued, the Negro Employment and Training and Minority Groups Branches were created in the Labor Division of OPM. These new offices had small field staffs operating out of Washington, and they were assigned responsibility for encouraging and facilitating greater participation of minorities in war production.

As a result of these steps, a few defense contractors indicated their willingness to co-operate with government policy; some of them began to expand their Negro employment. It is interesting to observe, however, that up to this point the labor member of the directorate of OPM had taken all steps for the agency in dealing with minority groups' employment on defense contracts; the management representative had never given an official endorsement to the program. And the growing corps of business representatives, temporarily in government service with OPM, had almost universally taken a hands-off attitude. Small wonder that industrialists outside the government paid little attention to the appeals of OPM for full utilization of minorities.

Continuing discrimination in a federally financed program of defense training was most embarrassing to defense agencies. Negroes and others constantly pointed out the inefficacy of the federal government in translating its policies of non-discrimination into reality even in a program which it directed. As a result of these and other pressures, OPM urged more direct action. In June, 1941, the director of defense training in the Federal Security Agency set forth an official policy calling for the training of Negroes even where there were no immediate employment opportunities, but where there was a probability that their services would be used at a later date. This was the first official statement which clearly indicated that the traditional approach of vocational education to train workers for immediate job opportunities only was not to be followed in defense training. It accelerated the opening of such training to Negroes in some cities with mixed schools, but it had little immediate effect in the South.

As slight improvements in Negro training and employment were taking place, the total volume of defense employment grew appreciably. In many areas, all local white male labor had been absorbed and white women were entering defense plants. White workers from elsewhere were moving into tight labor markets, while local Negroes were still finding few jobs and most of those which they secured were in non-defense work. The proportion of Negroes among the unemployed steadily increased, and the degree of minorities' participation in defense industries showed no signs of expanding appreciably; in face of these developments the Negro community became aroused. OPM responded feebly to the new demands of Negroes. The staff of the Negro Employment and Training Branch was slightly expanded, and other branches of the Labor Division of OPM expressed concern about the situation. For the most part, however, the majority of those in the Labor Division was content to rely upon persuasion (to be applied by the numerically small staffs of the Minority Groups and the Negro Employment and Training Branches) and looked to economic necessity as the source of needed pressure to enforce official pronouncements of non-discriminatory hiring policies. The Management Division of OPM remained apathetic and continued to evade the issue. Meanwhile, the Labor Division had sponsored stabilization agreements which assured closed shops in certain shipyards, in aircraft plants, and on construction projects. As has been indicated in Chapter III, many of these agreements involved craft unions which either barred or discriminated against Negroes. Where, in such instances, there was a conflict between the operation of these agreements and the announced policy of non-discrimination in defense employment, OPM supported the stabilization pacts.

With this minimum support, the Negro Employment and Training Branch was able to get a few things done. By negotiation and persuasion, it facilitated the employment of Negro craftsmen on war construction projects, opened some new plants, secured greater participation in training, and laid the groundwork for the use of Negroes in new types of jobs in aircraft, electrical machinery, ordnance, shipbuilding, and machine-tools. In a score of cities, particularly in New England and New York, it secured the acceptance of Negroes in new industries and establishments. But the problem was not one of a score of cities or a few hundred plants in selected industries. It was a national issue, and it involved thousands of defense contractors. It could not be met by the Labor Division of OPM alone; certainly, it could not be handled effectively by a staff of about ten field representatives.

Negroes and their friends protested in all parts of the country. Conferences seemed to produce but small results, and a plan was developed for more drastic action. Representative Negro leaders met and devised strategy. Under the inspiration of A. Philip Randolph, president of the Brotherhood of Sleeping Car Porters, they finally decided upon a March on Washington as a means of dramatizing the plight of Negroes in war industries. A date was set for 50,000 colored men and women from all sections of the nation to march down Pennsylvania Avenue in protest. To many government officials, the prospect of 50,000 Negroes in a mass demonstration was most frightening. Representatives of the administration tried to get the march called off, but the leaders would not budge.

In the midst of these developments, President Roosevelt spoke. On June 12, 1941, in a memorandum addressed to Messrs. Knudsen and Hillman, he placed the full support of his office behind the Hillman letter to defense contractors. The President declared, in part, "Our government cannot countenance continued discrimination against American citizens in defense production. Industry must take the initiative in opening the doors of employment to all loyal and qualified workers regardless of race, creed, color, or national origin. American workers, both organized and unorganized, must be prepared to welcome the general and much-needed employment of fellow workers of all racial and nationality groups in defense industries."

This statement, the most forthright in the defense effort to that date, was too late. Negroes were suspicious of words, and their leaders insisted upon machinery for direct action. On June 25, 1941, President Roosevelt issued Executive Order 8802 reaffirming a policy of full participation in the defense program by all persons, regardless of race, creed, color, or national origin. By July, the Labor Division of OPM had established regional offices to deal with matters of labor supply. On the national level and in the regions, there were labor supply committees to coordinate the work of federal agencies in this field. The chiefs of the Negro Employment and Training and the Minority Groups Branches were among the twelve officials on the federal Labor Supply Committee, and field representatives of the branches served in a similar capacity on the regional Labor Supply Committees.

During the period from July, 1941, until January, 1942, FEPC functioned within the Labor Division of OPM. When, on January 26, 1942, OPM was abolished, the committee was transferred to WPB where it remained until the War Manpower Commission was set up in the summer of 1942. During this one-year period, the Negro Employment and Training Branch of the Labor Division of OPM and later of WPB continued to operate in close co-operation with the committee. The branch conducted systematic visits to industrial employers in order to promote the utilization of Negro workers, conducted preliminary investigations of individual complaints for the committee, reviewed the training programs in various communities, encouraged compliance with federal policy on defense training, and worked with the United States Employment Service in order to secure placement of Negroes. During the period it was within OPM, the Committee on Fair Employment Practice served as a board of appeal for the Negro Employment and Training Branch and the Minority Groups Branch, dealt with discrimination in federal agencies, urged the contracting agencies of the federal government to enforce the non-discrimination clauses in defense contracts, and maintained contacts with state and local agencies in order to combat discrimination. The committee received individual complaints and held formal hearings.

With the advent of Executive Order 8802, federal offices concerned with combatting discrimination were strengthened. In the first place, the executive order directed vocational training officials to take special measures to assure the administration of their programs without discrimination. Secondly, and more important, it stipulated that all future defense contracts should include nondiscrimination clauses. Finally, it established a Committee on Fair Employment Practice (subsequently known as the President's Committee on Fair Employment Practice, or FEPC) to receive and investigate complaints, take appropriate steps to redress grievances, and recommend to the various federal agencies and the President such measures as the committee deemed necessary to carry out the provisions of the order. A supplementary communication to the committee and a letter to the heads of all federal departments and independent establishments indicated that the order covered government employment and that federal agencies were expected to put into effect the policy of nondiscrimination.

With Executive Order 8802 and with the needs for labor in war industries mounting steadily, there were gains in Negro training and employment. It is impossible to discover how much influence each of these developments had on the final results, but both were extremely important. The experience and contacts of the field representatives of the Negro Employment and Training Branch permitted them to use the new executive order as a pressure to accelerate their work with management and training officials as well as with labor unions. Plants which had given them the run-around in the past were less unconcerned after Executive Order 8802 had been issued. Some began to employ and up-grade Negroes; others resorted to tactics of delay and evasion. FEPC, however, selected certain cities, Los Angeles, Chicago, and New York, where there were outstanding instances of racial discrimination and conducted public hearings. These hearings were fully reported in local newspapers, and they made the news wire services. As a result there was widespread publicity about firms and unions which discriminated against minorities in war employment.

Since large and powerful corporations, such as Vultee Aircraft in California, Buick Aircraft in Chicago, and Wright Aeronautical in Paterson, New Jersey, were cited, it was firmly established that the committee was prepared to focus the searchlight of public censure upon malpractices regardless of the economic power of the corporation involved. The exposure and pressure upon the International Association of Machinists at the Los Angeles hearings and the mechanical building craft unions at the Chicago hearings served a similar purpose in regard to labor unions. Plants and unions which persisted in barring Negroes from employment were constantly needled and faced the threat that they might be brought before the whole committee in a public hearing. All of these efforts led to greater employment of minorities.

There was one phase of the committee's work which could soon be measured; it was employment in the federal agencies. By the fall of 1942, there were dramatic evidences that Executive Order 8802 was effective in increasing the participation of Negroes in government service. In agency after agency, the old barriers to Negro clerical workers were giving way, and colored women, in particular, were entering the government in increasing numbers. This was especially true in Washington where, in 1938, less than 8.5 per cent of the federal employees were colored and 90 per cent of the Negroes were in subclerical capacities. By November, 1942, about 17 per cent of the federal workers in Washington were Negroes, and almost half of the colored employees were in clerical and professional capacities. (These figures must be considered in light of the fact that over 20 per cent of Washington's population is Negro.) In the field and regional offices of government agencies, however, progress was much slower and, in most areas, imperceptible.

•   •   •

No better key to the weaknesses of the approach of the War Manpower Commission to full utilization of Negro labor can be found than in the commission's operating instructions relating to its responsibility for facilitating the enforcement of the President's executive order. This document was issued in September, 1943, as a result of the previously negotiated operating agreement between FEPC and the commission. Even at that late date, it was necessary for the commission to urge regional, state, area, and local offices to take specific action to insure the inclusion of Negroes and other minority groups in all recruitment programs.

Since WMC had often certified housing needs for an area where resident Negroes were unemployed or under-employed, the instructions stated that in any future certification of such needs the availability of resident minority groups' labor and the needs of such groups for housing should be considered. In addition, the instructions specified that each voluntary agreement between WMC, management, and labor for the stabilization of the labor market should contain a specific provision for full utilization of all sources of labor. This provision was in recognition of the fact that some of the stabilization agreements had either evaded or watered down references to Negro workers' utilization. The ultimate responsibility for determining the adequacy of adjustments made in cases of alleged discrimination was vested in FEPC, although WMC assumed an initial responsibility for eliminating discrimination. The instructions provided for adequate liaison to co-ordinate the activities of the committee and the commission and stipulated that there should be personnel designated to perform this function in each regional office of WMC.

The operation of federal agencies was important in opening new job opportunities for Negroes. Their efficacy was due largely to Executive Orders 8802 and 9346. Prior to 1942, the over-all labor supply agencies through their Minorities Groups and Negro Training and Employment Branches established the framework in which future gains were achieved. Subsequently, FEPC established its own field staff and assumed many of the functions which the service branches of OPM and WPB had originally performed. Fortunately, however, by the time that the committee had largely displaced the branches, it had begun to call upon the operating agencies of the government to assume responsibility for enforcing non-discrimination clauses in their contracts.

•   •   •

No account of government activity in minority or any other groups' employment would be complete without some consideration of the United States Employment Service. It is difficult to present a short and, at the same time, accurate account of this agency. Like the United States Office of Education, it had been operating before the war, and its personnel was conditioned to certain procedures and attitudes. The most important of these was the desire to comply fully with employers' specifications.

There were other serious carry-overs too. The defense program was initiated after a long period of depression. During that depression, the Employment Service had become extremely conscious of soliciting employers' business, and it never dared alienate its customers. It had, in addition, developed a fetish for reporting a large volume of placements, and its budget requests were often evaluated on the basis of its placement figures. Most of its Negro placements were in common laboring work and in domestic service. Seldom did it place a skilled Negro, save in a few building trades; as a result, few skilled Negroes registered with it. It was natural, though unfortunate, that USES would continue in wartime to seek the favor of employers. This attitude was re-enforced by the fact that during the earlier phases of the war effort, management was free to seek its workers on the labor market, and most of the larger plants called on the Employment Service only for workers in occupation in which there was a scarcity of labor.

At the outbreak of World War II, and during the first years of the war, the United States Employment Service was, in fact, a series of state employment offices. The people who actually made placements were not federal employees but were responsible to a state organization. The United States Employment Service Division of the Bureau of Employment Security of the Social Security Board had an over-all supervisory position. Its most effective service, prior to the war, had been the development of good practices and the collection of accurate statistics. Policies issued from Washington were in the form of regulations which were issued to state offices.

The Washington officials of the United States Employment Service were conscious of the deficiencies of local employment offices from the start. As contrasted to the United States Office of Education, they collected and released current data indicating the condition of the labor market and the need to utilize minorities in war industries. After much urging, they issued specific regulations which set forth official policy, but they did not pursue them forcefully. In some states, local officials completely ignored the Washington bulletins dealing with minority groups. In other states, they were read and forgotten.

At the outset of the defense effort, there were four general practices of the United States Employment Service which delayed the acceptance of Negro workers in war plants. In many areas of the country, skilled Negro workers were encouraged to register in unskilled capacities on the theory that they could more easily be placed in such work. Statements of policy from Washington urging proper classification for all workers were ignored; and as a matter of fact regulations, even if followed, would have been inadequate since, from bitter past experience, many skilled Negroes had ceased seeking work through the USES.

When an employer requested a worker, many local employment offices in the North and South alike would ask him what racial type he preferred. Faced with such an abstract question, the average employer made an abstract answer to the effect that he desired white workers. The Employment Service justified this practice by saying that it did not want to embarrass colored workers or send them on a wild goose chase. As a matter of fact, such a procedure protected the employer from charges of discrimination and denied the individual Negro worker a chance to sell himself and his qualifications to the employer.

In southern and border cities there were separate Negro USES offices. Most of them received calls for unskilled and domestic workers only. In few instances were these offices exposed to the over-all demands for workers which came to the local Employment Service. Nor did the personnel of the Negro office have a chance to participate in discussions about job specifications, and most of the specifications for desirable openings were drawn up in terms of the white labor supply. The directors of the Negro offices usually were not afforded an opportunity to have direct contacts with employers. Consequently, most employers knew nothing about the qualifications of the available Negro registrants and did not consider employing them.

Few Employment Services exerted any effort to sell Negro labor to employers. Even in instances where tight labor markets developed early in the defense program, Employment Service offices accepted "white" specifications and imported white workers without calling employers' attention to the fact that qualified local Negroes were available.

Although the Washington office sent out statements suggesting reforms, no significant changes were made until after Executive Order 8802 was issued. And even then, improvements were slow and spotty. As late as October, 1941, four months after Executive Order 8802 had been issued, the Chief of the United States Employment Service Division of the Bureau of Employment Security was not prepared to take a forthright stand on non-discrimination in referrals. His thinking was in accord with the traditions and the then current position of the Employment Service.

When, for example, it was suggested that the United States Employment Service refuse to accept discriminatory orders (which were in effect evidences of violation of Executive Order 8802), the chief of the USES was quick to observe that it was not the Employment Service that was discriminating but rather the employer. And he added, despite the President's statement, that this discrimination on the part of the employer was not illegal. In his opinion, it was an undesirable social and economic practice and, as such, could not be eliminated by the Employment Service. If the USES refused to accept discriminatory orders, he observed, the Service would lose the employer's business, the employer would get workers elsewhere (applying the same discriminatory criteria), and the USES would become a less vital factor in the labor market.

There was much validity in this last argument. It is another illustration of the crucial influence of the general inefficacy of government's controls over the labor market upon its programs for full utilization of all sources of labor supply. As long as employers were free to secure their workers on the open labor market, it was futile to expect a labor exchange which was constantly selling itself to employers to attempt aggressively to modify its customers' specifications. In only two states did the Employment Service take effective steps in this direction. In New York, where a state law prohibited discrimination in referrals, the State Employment Service refused discriminatory orders. The Regional Director in Cleveland ordered the directors of the State Employment Services in Michigan and Ohio to take similar action, but was subsequently instructed by Washington to conform with federal policy and rescind the order.

When it was suggested, in a more realistic vein, that the USES accept discriminatory orders but ignore the discriminatory specifications, the chief of the service was not responsive. Again, he indicated the possibility of antagonizing the employer and losing his business and again he expressed fear of embarrassment to the applicant so referred. In order to prevent such embarrassment and to comply with employers' preferences, he felt that the race of the applicant should be on his referral card. All the Washington office felt it could do in the fall of 1941 was to take steps to see that its personnel did not inject their own prejudices in their official acts, not take the initiative in raising questions about racial or religious preferences, and encourage employers to remove racial and religious specifications when such specifications prevented full utilization of the local labor supply. In a word, the USES was an agency to serve the employer, and, as a labor exchange, it should avoid, as far as possible, questioning employers' discriminatory requests.

Within the limited area in which it could be induced to act on the matter of minorities' utilization, the USES slowly began to effect changes. The first reform was relative to the classification of workers. In most areas outside the South, Negroes were generally being registered in their proper skills by 1942. The practice of inquiring about employers' racial preferences was more deepseated. Some state Employment Services, notably New York, took direct and effective action to correct this practice; but in general, although more regulations on this matter were issued, the practice continued until well in 1943. Even after that date, it still occurred in certain areas. In Philadelphia, for example, some USES staff members were still asking employers if they would accept Negroes as late as the spring of 1945. But FEPC has constantly put pressure on the United States Employment Service, and the practice slowly declined.

The USES in New York State has been the most effective branch of the agency in securing employment equality for minorities during World War II. Yet, as late as the spring of 1945, there were flagrant violations of the non-discriminatory executive order in local USES offices. At Niagara Falls, many registration cards contained racial and religious identification, despite the fact that such labels were prohibited by regulations. The local officials were unfamiliar with the WMC policies of the region and did not seem anxious to correct violations of these policies. In Buffalo similar bad practices were followed in at least one USES office, and the local manager, when questioned about his failure to refer Negro registrants properly, expressed fear of losing employers' business if his office attempted to enforce the federal non-discrimination policy.

Although some feeble efforts were made to do away with the Negro offices, many still existed on V-E Day, and they occasioned protest. In January, 1945, for example, a vigorous complaint of Jim Crow practices in the Birmingham USES was reported. Manpower requirements and official pressures caused some southern cities to expose Negro registrants to skilled and semi-skilled jobs, but the system permitted of evasion, and such evasion often existed. Investigation of the Savannah, Georgia, USES in 1944 indicated that orders for skilled workers were centered in the white office and practically no skilled or semi-skilled workers were referred from the colored office. Both offices placed workers who had completed defense training; the Negroes were placed in helper jobs where they were frozen. White trainees were so placed as to assure future up-grading.

Starting at the Washington level, the USES made efforts to sell Negro labor to employers. The initial steps were directed primarily at the employees of local and state offices. An issue of the Employment Service's monthly magazine was devoted exclusively to the need and methods for minority groups' placement. Led by New York City, many local Employment Services developed elaborate and effective regulations for interviews, and there have been definite and unambiguous regulations setting forth the responsibilities of the Employment Services' personnel. As the War Manpower Commission assumed direction of the United States Employment Service, it extended these activities.

In order to prevent the Employment Service's being used as a tool for hiding em-

ployers' discriminations and violations of Executive Orders 8802 and 9346, FEPC induced the USES to require a report on each case of discrimination which came to its attention. The regulations provided instructions for attempting to overcome
discriminatory specifications and required individual reports for each instance where the
employer was guilty of discrimination. Few such reports had been filed before 1943.
Even at that late date, some states did not report a single case of this discrimination.
Field investigations indicated that many offices failed to discuss discriminatory specifications with employers; others simply did not refer Negroes to firms which indicated
orally their preference for white workers. There had been some improvement by 1945.
For the most part, this was a result of the WMC order of July 1, 1944, requiring that all
essential employers would thereafter be able to get new male (and sometimes female)
workers only by referrals from the USES or under arrangements made by USES. At the
same time, WMC stipulated that because of manpower shortages, no essential employer
would be permitted to refuse any qualified applicant because of race, color, creed, or national origin.

In the spring of 1945, the southern USES offices were still generally practicing
discriminatory acts. In many cities Negroes continued to encounter difficulties in securing proper classification in Employment Service offices which were often manned by
white clerks who had definite concepts of the Negro's place. This problem occasioned
much negotiation between WMC and FEPC in the southeastern region and adjustments
were being made in Georgia, Florida, and Alabama. In these three states and in Texas,
the USES submitted reports on employer discriminations. Elsewhere in the South, such
reports were rare or nonexistent. Seldom in the South were colored registrants referred
freely to skilled work, and Negroes were usually sent only to those firms which had
used colored labor in the past. In New Orleans, for example, a war contractor was induced to modify his discriminatory hiring specifications. When, however, this employer
placed an order for workers, the local USES directed him to specify whether he wanted
white or colored workers. And this occurred in December, 1944.

In many cities of the South and often in the North and West local USES personnel had verbal agreements with employers engaged in war production not to refer colored workers to certain plants or for certain types of work. Since the few Negro USES
employees in the South have no contacts with employers, these agreements were seldom
challenged or brought to light in that region; elsewhere, they were constantly being
challenged in 1944 and 1945. There was little real effort in most southern USES offices
to encourage employment of Negroes except in traditional types of work; despite the
labor shortages in textiles, for example, USES in the South accepted the industry's traditional discrimination and made no real effort to introduce Negro workers.

This brief resumé of the United States Employment Service's approach to Negro
placement indicates that the agency hesitated to face the problem squarely. It instituted
some reforms, and the situation outside the South in 1945 was vastly improved over
that which existed prior to the war. But even when the United States Employment
Service became the exclusive referral agency for war plants, it often failed to take aggressive action to secure compliance with the federal policy of non-discrimination.

As the only consumer of war material, the federal government could have insisted upon full utilization of minority groups from the start of the defense program. Such an approach, however, would have been inconsistent with the over-all method of securing war production. At the outset, few things were required of war contractors, and the initial defense agency was advisory. As time went on, controls were introduced, but most problems of labor supply were dealt with through negotiation and voluntary agreements. Beneath these agreements were many controls and the threat of more. Yet few controls were exerted to get fair racial employment practices. Those responsible for the earlier over-all problems of labor supply were hesitant to insist upon Negro employment in war industries. They believed that economic forces would eventually require it, and they were waiting until the necessity became greater.

But the Negro people who suffered from this situation were not so patient. They insisted upon and got more positive action. The result was a non-discriminatory executive order and a Committee on Fair Employment Practice to enforce it. This machinery and the economic necessity led to the employment gains which Negroes made during the war. They also occasioned some real improvements in the United States Employment Service. Since the latter agency is continuing a program of education for its personnel, some of these changes may persist after the war emergency has passed. It is regrettable, however, that little of the good training material and few of the training courses developed by USES were being given in the South where the need for them was greatest.

A Man Called White*

Walter White

JIM CROW IN THE SOUTH PACIFIC

The red-headed Army orderly with a luxuriant Southern accent leaned over the bucket seat of the C-54 to point out the tiny green and brown speck in the Pacific blue which was Guam. We had left Kwajalein sixteen hundred miles behind us the night before. A brigadier general and pfc. were asleep on the floor at our feet. Considerate of their slumber, the orderly spoke softly about the number of times he had made the round trip shuttling back and forth between Guam and Kwajalein on an army transport.

"They almost had a race riot in Guam a few days ago," the orderly said as casually as he would have mentioned a slight thunder shower as being in the natural order of things.

"Race riot?" I echoed. "What happened?"

"Oh, some Navy niggers got uppity, but the MP's cooled them off in a hurry," was the nonchalant reply.

We landed a short while afterward, dragging our gear out of the plane and into a truck under a sun so hot, despite the fact that it was two days after Christmas, that it made the earth seem like a hamburger grill. We bumped over roads still in the making by Seabees and Army engineers until we arrived and reported to Island Command. An Army public relations officer escorted me to a tent filled with "jungle bunks"—Army cots with mosquito nets—so close together that one had to step carefully from his own cot in the morning lest his feet collide with the man in the next bunk. I put down my barracks bag and mopped the sweat from my face. Without preliminaries of any sort the Army officer, who was, incidentally, not from the South but from Pennsylvania, began telling me of the way "niggers" had been "raising hell" on Guam.

"The black sons-of-bitches are getting out of hand and we are going to teach 'em a lesson," he angrily declared. According to the story he told me, all of the white people on Guam of the Army, Navy, and Marine Corps had been perfect gentlemen, but the

* From Walter White, *A Man Called White* (New York: The Viking Press, Inc., 1948), pp. 277–93, 322–28. Copyright 1948 by Walter White. Reprinted by permission of The Viking Press, Inc.

Negroes had stolen weapons and had gone on a rampage against the nice, kind white folks. It was manifest that the officer knew of me only as a war correspondent and had not the faintest idea either of my race or of my connection with the NAACP, if he knew there was such an organization. I decided, therefore, to let him talk as freely as he wished so that I might learn the worst.

Because what I heard and saw during the next few weeks in Guam is so tragically typical of the racial practices our country transported overseas during World War Two, the story of the trouble at Guam in December 1944 deserves recital here.

At that time the war in the Pacific had moved northward and westward to the Philippine Islands. Leyte had finally been taken and the mopping-up process of killing or driving into the jungle the Japanese yet on Leyte was being completed. Guam was, therefore, the chief base of supply, and frantic efforts were being made to speed the building of roads, supply stations, and fortifications. The Third Marines were undergoing there at that time final training for the assault on Iwo Jima. With the almost superhuman efficiency of American engineering genius, jungle land had been cleared and three magnificent B-29 airfields were being rushed to completion. Long, orderly rows of Quonset huts were packed tight with ammunition, food, clothing, and medical supplies. Apparently endless rows of refrigerators held enormous supplies of meats and other perishables.

But as was the almost invariable rule of the Army and Navy, the bulk of the hard, dirty work of construction and handling supplies had been given to Negroes. There were white construction units of the Army and white Seabees in Guam. But there were no Negro combat troops of the Navy or Army but only engineering, base company, sanitation, and other service units. Combat troops, as is their custom, looked with either indifference or contempt on noncombat troops, particularly if they were Negroes. But even more provocative than this was the fact that the traditional American attitudes of race had been brought from the United States to Guam, especially among the Marines, many of whom came from the South.

The very efficiency and progress of the transformation of Guam into a highly organized military and naval base increased the opportunity of some of the Negrophobes to translate their prejudices into action. Thanks to American mechanical equipment, a superb six-lane highway was built almost literally overnight from Island Command at one end of Guam to the Navy Supply Depot twenty-two miles away at the other end of the Island. Near the latter on one side of the new road were stationed the camps of four Negro Navy base companies. Everybody in Guam worked for long hours at top speed during that period, but the Negro base companies worked twelve hours a day, seven days a week at hard, sweaty work, handling supplies, cleaning up the area, and doing other necessary but menial chores. None of the excitement or glamour of war was theirs. One of the four Negro base companies had been made up of so-called "trouble makers" from Esperita Santos, their last base before moving to Guam. It was a case in human society of "giving a dog a bad name." The literacy rate was low, although there were a number of men with fair education and some with better than fair training and family background. But many a Negro was officially and privately classified as a "bad actor" by prejudiced superiors when he objected to discrimination or injustice. Thus this particular base company was made up of men who felt they had been given a raw deal, and who were understandably resentful.

But their resentment would probably never have been translated into action had not a long series of unchecked and unpunished insults and attacks been made upon these Negro sailors. Trucks rolled night and day along the Agat-Sumay Road from the part of the Island where the Third Marines were in training to the supply depots at the other end of the Island. Stones, empty beer bottles, and other missiles were thrown from the trucks into the Negro camp accompanied by such epithets as "niggers," "night-fighters," and "black sons-of-bitches." Twice hand grenades were hurled into the Negro camp. On one occasion, one of the Negroes had enough presence of mind and courage to pick up the hand grenade and throw it into a ravine back of the camp where it exploded a few seconds later. On the other occasion, injury or loss of life was prevented only by the fact that the grenade was a dud.

Near the Third Marines encampment was located a fuel dump where vast quantities of hundred-octane high-explosive gas was stored. One day a live grenade was thrown into the camp from a truck by four Marines. A tragedy was averted by one of the Negro soldiers who picked it up and threw it into a ravine outside the camp before it exploded. On another day a smoke bomb was thrown into the fuel dump. One of the Negroes working there smothered the bomb before it could explode.

And as in the United States, sexual jealousy and rivalry played a major role in fostering racial conflict.

Many of the Americans, particularly Southern-born Marines, bitterly resented the sight of a Negro talking to a female Guamanian. Small gangs of Marines began to run Negroes out of Agana—or what remained of that town, which was the largest on Guam before it was leveled by the sixteen inch guns of the American Navy. Negroes at first reported the attacks on them by whites to their commanding officers. Instead of acting to protect their men, these officers sought to cover up the attacks or to justify them. Negroes learned that it was a waste of time even to report the insults and assaults.

Events rapidly approached a climax on the afternoon of Christmas Eve, 1944. A group of Negroes had obtained liberty passes and had gone into Agana, where they were fired upon and driven out of town. Eight of them got safely back to camp. A ninth had disappeared. It was assumed that he had been injured or killed. Some forty men piled into two Navy trucks and set out for Agana to find their comrade. But a Negro assistant master-of-arms telephoned Military Police in Agana to inform the authorities that Negroes were headed into town. A road block was thrown up and the trucks stopped. When the men learned that their missing companion had not been killed or injured but instead had hidden in a ditch until nightfall and then had made his way back to camp, the Negroes climbed aboard the trucks and returned to their area.

Shortly after midnight a truck filled with white Marines drove into the Negro camp. The Marines angrily alleged that one of their number had been hit by a piece of coral thrown from a truck by a Negro. The spineless and scared white commanding officer of the Negro company, instead of arresting the men who were shouting threats that "if you don't do something about this, we are going to take the matter into our own hands," pleaded with the Marines to go away, which they finally did.

The invasion of the Negro camp shortly after midnight occurred just as the night crew came off duty and was going into the mess hall from which emerged the crew going on duty. Thus it was only a matter of a few minutes before all the Negroes in the four base companies knew about the invasion of the camp and the weakness on the part of their commanding officers. Apprehension mounted steadily throughout Christmas Day. Shortly before noon two intoxicated Marines shot and killed a Negro sailor. He and two companions were walking down the road past a native house. The Marine emerged, saw the three Negroes, whom he had never seen before, and went back into the native house to emerge with a carbine, which he raised to his shoulder and fired. On the afternoon of Christmas Day a white sailor shot and seriously wounded another Negro sailor. Neither of them had even been arrested when I reached Guam two days later.

Around nightfall, a jeep with a machine gun mounted on it drove past firing into the Negro camp and returned again firing. Guards who had been posted somewhat belatedly around the Negro camp returned the fire as did some of the Negro sailors. By this time the camp was in a state of almost hysterical apprehension. Negroes fired on a jeep containing two military police, which many of the Negroes believed was the same jeep which had fired into the camp shortly before. One of the MP's was injured. Again Negroes climbed aboard two trucks and set out for Agana. Again a road block was thrown up and this time all of them—forty-four in number—were arrested. The next morning a shakedown was given to the Negro camp. A considerable number of weapons, some of them handmade in the form of knives, and others stolen from the Navy Supply Depot, were found. A number of the Negroes later testified that, despairing of any protection from the responsible authorities, they had been driven to the conclusion that they could hope for no protection save that which they gave themselves.

The book was thrown at the forty-four men arrested at Agana. Among the crimes charged against them were unlawful assemblage, rioting, theft of government property, and attempted murder.

Either because they were too busy or had not taken the trouble to find out what had been going on even on so small an island as Guam, the Island authorities had done virtually nothing up to that time. Then suddenly they awoke to the explosive character of the situation and a Navy Board of Inquiry was ordered before which I was invited to appear as an "expert witness" on race relations. The presiding officer of the three-man Board was a Marine colonel from South Carolina. His associates were a lieutenant colonel from New York and a Navy lieutenant from Philadelphia. The Judge Advocate or prosecutor for the Navy was a lieutenant commander who had practiced law for nineteen years in Dallas, Texas, whose attitude toward Negroes was traditionally Southern despite the fact that not infrequently he invited me to the Navy Officers' Club for a drink after adjournment of Court.

Toward the end of my testimony, the Judge Advocate, Lieutenant Commander James Swift, asked me if it were not true that I held the degree of Doctor of Laws. I admitted this to be true.

"Then you are competent, aren't you, to represent the defendants in this case, as defense counsel?"

I hastened to explain to him that the degree of Doctor of Laws (given to me by both Howard and Atlanta Universities) was an honorary one and did not mean that its possessor had any knowledge of the law. To this he replied that procedure in the Navy Board of Inquiry was more informal than legalistic and that I did not have to be a lawyer to serve as defense counsel. My first impulse was to decline, for I did not want to jeopardize the legal rights of any defendant because of my ignorance of the law and of Navy court-martial procedure. I suspected, as well, that the request for me to serve was at least in part based upon a determination to excuse whatever convictions or sentences might be imposed by saying that there could have been no injustice because the secretary of the NAACP had represented the accused. But as the words were forming on my lips, I looked at the forlorn and pleading faces of the defendants. They appeared to say, and later some of them did put their inner emotions into words, that they were without friends on Guam deep in the Pacific and if I failed them by refusing to do what I could, they were without hope, since there was no one else they trusted to do so.

I stated to the Court that I would serve as defense counsel if the Court and the Judge Advocate would agree officially for the record that no legal right of any of the defendants would be abridged or jeopardized by my ignorance of the law and that I be given complete latitude and not held strictly to legal procedure in the introduction of testimony or the examination and cross-examination of witnesses. The Court inquired as to the extent of the latitude desired. To this I replied that what had occurred on December 24th to 26th could not be isolated but was a direct outcome of the attacks which had been made on Negro service men over a period of many weeks and of the racial attitudes of Negroes and whites which had developed out of racial proscription in the United States. Somewhat reluctantly the Court agreed to the stipulations.

And then began one of the most trying and revealing experiences of my life. The Judge Advocate was an able lawyer and was assisted by a younger man who was also well versed and experienced in legal procedure. I had no assistants or investigators. The Judge Advocate also had at his disposal all of the confidential records of the Navy from which I was barred by Navy regulations and customs.

The Court sat during the day, so that the only time left for me to do my own work of locating witnesses and evidence was after nightfall, which required going through areas where American soldiers had quite recently been ambushed and either killed or wounded by Japanese lurking in the vicinity. (There were still 40,000 of them on the Island, hiding in the jungle, getting what food they could by foraging.)

But, despite the difficulties, the job had to be done as best it could be done. For three weeks, witness after witness told the story either from the white or the Negro angle with varying degrees of veracity. As I look back on it, the abysmal failure of both civilian and military America to face the race question honestly was epitomized by the testimony of a handsome, sensitive young Negro whose deep ivory skin and wavy dark brown hair reminded me of my own son. He had come to me and requested an opportunity to tell the Board of Inquiry what he had seen and experienced in Guam. The lad had been born and lived all of his nineteen years in an Eastern seaboard city. His parents were fairly prosperous and highly respected citizens. Earnestly and simply the young man told a straightforward story.

He said he had voluntarily enlisted in the Navy on his seventeenth birthday "to help my race and my country." Almost savagely, the Judge Advocate jumped on the young man's sequence of desire for service, challenging him, "So you place race above country, do you?"

And then the Judge Advocate demanded, "Isn't it true that you have been convicted before Captain's Mast [informal Navy hearing before the Captain] and served sentences for violation of Navy regulations?"

This was a bolt from a clear blue sky. I whispered to the Judge Advocate a request that I be permitted to examine the records of the Captain's Mast to learn the circumstances. This request was curtly refused by the prosecutor who suggested, "Ask him yourself to find out."

It was a tough decision to make. The young man's honest and open countenance might be deceptive. My querying him as defense counsel might put damaging evidence into the record of some crime or at least of moral turpitude. But I decided to take a chance anyway because the Judge Advocate's question and the young man's affirmative answer would look bad in the record and weaken the story he had told up to that point which had been most moving in its recital of the slurs and discriminations to which Negroes in the Navy, eager to serve their country, had been subjected. So I asked the questions which brought forth answers which explained in part the Judge Advocate's refusal to permit me to see the record.

Here are the "crimes" for which the young volunteer had been convicted and sentenced on each occasion to five days in solitary confinement on bread and water. One of them had been committed when he, after completion of boot training at the Great Lakes Naval Training Station in Illinois, had been ordered to service in the Navy Mine Depot at Yorktown, Virginia. One day he had boarded a bus within the Naval reservation in which, in accordance with Virginia law, a sign hung from the roof of the bus separating white from Negro passengers. As eleven of the seats to the rear of the sign were filled, the young man sat under the sign, part of his body being in the "Negro" section and part in the "white" section. The bus driver had driven the vehicle to the nearest shore patrol and caused the boy to be arrested, as a result of which he was convicted and sentenced. The other "crime" had been his entering a "white" restaurant in Virginia to purchase food.

Jubilant at the results of my fishing expedition, I asked the young man if in his native city he had been accustomed to patronizing restaurants and other places of public accommodation and if he had ever had to conform to jimcrow laws in public conveyances. The answer had been that until ordered to Virginia, he had never been in the South before in his life.

After I left Guam, the recommendations of the Board of Inquiry, despite the evidence, resulted in courts-martial and the sentencing of all forty-four men to prison terms, which, happily, were later reversed when we appealed the convictions. But we had to take the cases all the way to the Secretary of the Navy and the White House to achieve this.

A story I wrote in Guam on January 20, 1945, was passed by the censor before I left the Island and a promise was made to me that it would be cabled to the *New York Post* at once.

Fully aware that no dispatch telling the full story would ever be passed, I wrote my story as carefully as possible and leaned over backward in understatement. But it was never published. When I returned to the States some months later, I learned that the *New York Post* had never received it.

I found out what had happened to it only after I had told the story of the trouble on Guam on a nation-wide broadcast, my speech having been passed without alteration by both Army and Navy censors in the United States. Several days later I received a photostatic copy of the story which is for me one of the most amusing examples of the stupidity of military censorship I have ever encountered.

"For Release July 11, 1945" is written in large letters above my typed "Guam 20 January 1945" and the release date of July 11 is written in again four additional times in a three-page story. Throughout the story were interpolated phrases such as "I was told," "reportedly" and "allegedly."

I had written that the officer who had so spinelessly submitted to threats and abuse from enlisted men of the Marines had been relieved from duty following the Naval Board of Inquiry hearings. The censor had inserted "steps having been taken before the holiday incident," which I know was false. A general closely identified with the affair had told me that nothing had been done against the officer until the facts were uncovered in the hearings because the officer's unfitness was not known until that time.

There were other alterations and insertions of the censor's personal opinions— and prejudices—which would be ludicrous were not the episode and circumstances so filled with tragedy and oppression.

Later, in Leyte, I first ran into the oft-repeated and completely unjustified canard about the cowardice shown by Negroes of the 93rd Division. A public relations officer who believed that I was just another white newspaper correspondent went out of his way to tell me that Negroes were no good in combat. I asked him on what evidence he based his statement, and he told me that in the invasion of Bougainville the 93rd had been given an easy beachhead to take, but that the division had broken and run under fire, "causing death to many officers and men in the white divisions on either side of them."

I traced the story carefully, looked into the records, and talked with the commanding general of the 93rd (who was a Texan), to a brigadier general who had been with the division at Bougainville, and with officers of the white units who had been with the Negro division. The truth was that the 93rd had not been in the original invasion, which had taken place in October 1943, but had been sent in in March of the following year, after the island had been declared "secure." The 93rd had been given the task of pushing back the perimeter of the Japanese line, driving it deeper into the interior. The infantry had done a routine, but competent, job. The 93rd artillery, however, had been officially cited by General Dunckel of the 37th Division for the excellence and accuracy of its firing.

The story had apparently come from an actual instance in which the cowardice of a white officer had disorganized the men under him. A white captain had disobeyed orders to attack a Japanese position on either or both sides of what was roughly a horseshoe area. He had ordered his men to attack down the center. Doing so, they had found a much larger number of Japanese than scouts had reported. A Negro lieutenant and thirteen of his men had been killed. The captain had thereupon become hysterical, given conflicting orders, and eventually had fled in terror back to the safety of the command post far in the rear. He was quietly transferred to another division instead of being court-martialed.

My investigation also revealed that the 93rd, like other divisions in the Army, had been used as a promotion mill and a dumping ground for white officers who had failed in other divisions. Many of them were prejudiced against the men under their command, which the men were not long in sensing. After Bougainville, the 93rd had been broken up and relegated to unloading ships and other menial chores.

When I got to Luzon, and saw General MacArthur, I told him of the maligning of the 93rd Division and other Negro troops and the conditions which I had found. He told me of having served with the 24th Infantry in his youth and of his high regard for the fighting ability of Negroes. He questioned me closely about the morale and the possible effect on the fighting ability of the 93rd as a result of the Division's performing Quartermaster and port battalion duties for so long a time as to make them rusty in combat.

He assured me that the Division would be almost immediately reassembled as a unit and given refresher courses in combat so as to be used in action as soon as practicable. I think that at the time he meant it, but except for mopping up duties on the Island of Morotai, the 93rd Division was never used in any major engagement.

MacArthur promised to stop the practice of dumping on the 93rd officers who had been failures with other divisions. Some other officers had remained in the 93rd Division only long enough to achieve far more rapid promotions there than were possible in other divisions. Not all of these men were inefficient but unfortunately most of them were. Their rapid advancement had an effect on the morale of qualified Negro officers which needs no description here.

In Pacific Islands such as Dutch New Guinea I saw, as I had seen in North Africa, how swiftly the brave, beautiful promises born of fear of defeat in war were forgotten as soon as fighting ceased. But I also was stirred by the devoted and brilliant work of scientists in conquering the tropical diseases which have kept millions of human beings from achieving their fullest development.

I worked and lived for some weeks with the 93rd Division, but there was time, fortunately, to learn about other things which were happening in Dutch New Guinea. By this time I had grown weary of battle operations and of the equally difficult struggle with Army and Navy censors to get passed by them any but the most innocuous stories. I found myself becoming increasingly interested in the kind of life which would be established in these far-off places by the colonial powers. I had read the sweeping promises made by Queen Wilhelmina in London, promising on behalf of the Netherlands

Government in Exile citizenship and better educational, health, and economic opportunities to the Dutch colonials after the war.

One day John Dos Passos and I went to see a new tropical hospital for the natives which had recently been erected not far from Hollandia. Set in a clearing surrounded by towering trees, it was a pleasant place although quite different from any hospital we had ever seen in the States or Europe. There were four large buildings of bamboo with thatched roofs and open sides. The beds were of bamboo with wooden pillows and no mattresses or linen. There were about a hundred patients and a daily average of two hundred out-patients were treated by a staff consisting of one Javanese doctor, two white Dutch nurses, and about a dozen native nurses. Two blond rosy-cheeked young Dutch civil servants guided Dos Passos, several medical officers of the 93rd Division, and me proudly through the buildings.

I told the civil servants how delighted I was to see Queen Wilhelmina's promises being put into practice and congratulated them on the fact that the Dutch government was spending money on improvement of health conditions and facilities in New Guinea even before the Netherlands were rebuilt. To my surprise he smiled deprecatingly and told me, "It isn't our money we are spending—we got this from your government through Lend-Lease."

I asked him, somewhat taken aback, how many additional hospitals were contemplated and was told that no more were being planned.

"We've got a small hospital in Hollandia [which I learned later was used almost entirely by Dutch officials] and these are sufficient for the Island."

I could see no brave new world for the many thousands of disease-burdened natives with only a hundred or so beds available.

Dos Passos then asked him what would be done about education and received the airy reply, "we'll continue to let the missionaries supply schools." Our questions as to the number of schools and the type of education supplied in them received the vaguest of answers and subsequently I saw no schools outside of Hollandia.

Our questions about plans to raise the living standards and economic status of the natives were treated with equal casualness.

"America is too far away to be a profitable market for the fruits, grains, and vegetables we could raise here in abundance. There are great possibilities in the mineral and natural gas resources which we will exploit after the war because our government will need every guilder it can obtain to restore our homeland."

As to native self-government which Queen Wilhelmina had promised, we were told, "We don't intend to do anything about that because we can rule the natives much better than they could rule themselves."

The civil servants were neither evil nor unkindly men, but it was not reassuring so far as solution of the rapidly rising demands of colonials for freedom was concerned.

Later with the aid of interpreters I talked with some of the native leaders. Isolated from the world, they were far less educated and in touch with the trends of world politics than the natives of other Dutch colonies like Java, Sumatra, and other units of Indonesia. But the war for human freedom had penetrated even into the most remote areas where neither newspapers, radio, or the omnipresent movies had reached before the war. These native leaders revealed only a meager knowledge of the details of the war, but they knew as clearly as any European or American the significance of the war to their own welfare. I found it both futile and unnecessary to spend much time attempting to convince them that I too belonged to a "colored" race. But they seemed in some uncanny way to sense that my questions were motivated by sympathy and honesty and they talked freely of the kind of world they were determined to achieve. They dreamed of freedom not only because the Japanese had done an excellent job of propaganda about the racial arrogance and imperialism of the white man, but because they were tired of being exploited.

It is not difficult for me to imagine from these conversations what these native leaders thought when later American airplanes, tanks, and guns bearing the familiar insignia of the United States Army were used by the Dutch and British in a futile effort to crush the independence movement in Indonesia. The white world had used the creative genius of mankind to make a word called "freedom" a dream and a goal wherever men live. All the war weapons now in existence or which may be devised will never be able to stifle the demands of non-white as well as white men for a more decent and just way of life. We seem so pathetically and abysmally unable to comprehend this simple fact.

Shortly after I reached Hollandia I met Major Hildrus Poindexter, a gifted Negro scientist, who reminded me of the late Dr. Robert Russa Moton of Tuskegee Institute. He had recently been awarded the Bronze Star for reducing the malaria rate in the Solomon Islands by 86.4 per cent in three months. He had done important work in the diagnosis and treatment of schistosomiasis, a disease which had taken heavy toll of American soldiers, caused by a tiny worm entering the bloodstream; was a holder of three degrees from the medical schools of Harvard and Columbia universities; and, having done extensive research in tropical diseases at the Institute of Tropical Medicine in San Juan, Puerto Rico, had taught for fourteen years in the medical school of Howard University in Washington. But his major passion was doing all that he could and learning as much as possible about tropical disease, which he believed to be the principal cause of the backwardness of dark-skinned people living in tropical countries.

Major Poindexter and I talked often of his specialty and plans.

"Because of my conviction that tropical disease is the largest handicap of the darker races of the world who live in the tropics," he told me one day as we sat in my tent, "I plan to devote my life to fighting it. Men with too much brain damage from sleeping sickness cannot think. Men suffering from malaria are too anemic to work. The muscles of men with hookworm are too flabby. Men who cannot think or work cannot contribute to civilization or compete with other men.

I found that even Major Poindexter's ability and devotion did not exempt him from the evil effects of prejudice. He expressed an almost heartbreaking eagerness to work in the Army Medical Laboratory which had been set up there because he believed that in the laboratory he could obtain the most practical experience with tropical maladies to be gained anywhere in the world.

The commanding officer was a kindly man, but he was from Kentucky. Both his education in medicine and his scientific contributions were considerably less than those of Major Poindexter. He freely expressed his admiration for the Negro doctor's ability when I talked to him a few days later, adding "and Major Poindexter works three times as hard as any of us and all of us work hard!"

The commanding officer, however, feared that some of the white officers would object to Major Poindexter's eating in the general mess hall and occupying a tent in Officers' Row.

The device to save the sensibilities of the white officers turned out to be one of those contradictory and ludicrous color-line stratagems, particularly as it had bearing on the hysterical fears of some white people regarding sexual relations between white women and Negro men. A special tent was erected for Major Poindexter at some distance from those of the white officers, but the isolated tent was placed near the quarters where the white nurses lived and was so remote, I reminded the commanding officer, that "you won't be able to keep as close an eye on Major Poindexter as you would if he were billeted with the other officers." This seemed to disturb the commanding officer, and shortly afterward Major Poindexter was assigned a tent close to that of the CO himself.

The eating arrangements in the officers' mess were solved in an amusing way by the arrival of Surgeon General Normal Kirk on a tour of inspection of the Pacific Islands. In General Kirk's party was an officer who demanded immediately upon arrival that he be permitted to see Major Poindexter to get him to check certain statements in an article for a scientific journal which he had written. The conference in the office of the commanding officer lasted all morning until time for luncheon. Impatient at the interruption, the officer who had accompanied General Kirk told Major Poindexter that they would continue their discussion over the luncheon table. There was no alternative to inviting Major Poindexter to join the official party at the commanding officer's table.

Thereafter Major Poindexter ate at that table because, as the commanding officer explained to me, "I felt I did not have the right to force any of my subordinates to eat at the same table with Major Poindexter, but I do have the right to invite whom I please to eat at my table."

In Australia, from Prime Minister Curtin and other officials of the Australian government I met at Canberra to barmaids and taxi drivers in Sydney, I encountered the familiar stories of bewilderment at the incessant conflict between white and colored American soldiers. I was forced to spend almost an entire afternoon answering questions from members of the Australian Sociological Society about the race question in the United States when I was much more eager to ask them questions about Australia and especially the "white Australia" policy. The American Red Cross had pursued its policy of setting up segregated clubs even though by that time the war had moved so far from Australia that relatively few American troops were left there. Again I encountered traces of the stories by some American whites that all Negroes had tails and belonged to a lower order of human kind indistinguishable from the Australian bushmen. But many of the Australians had met and learned to know and to like the American Negro soldier. Learning that many of them were graduates of high schools, colleges, and universities had offset the falsehoods about Negro ability and behavior. Prime Minister Curtin told me he personally opposed any change in the "white Australia" policy so far as orientals were concerned, but that the impression which many of the American Negroes had made in Australia had caused him and others to favor a change in the regulations to permit American Negroes to settle there if they desired.

If these incidents—and many like them could be added—give a gloomy picture of the treatment accorded Negro troops in the Pacific, I have precisely accomplished my purpose.

The rigid pattern of segregation, the virtually unbroken custom of assignment of Negroes to service units, the heritage and pattern of prejudice brought from the United States was altered only in isolated instances where in athletics, music, or other diversions, Americans—white and black—were permitted to escape segregation and learn to associate as normal human beings joined in a common cause.

It was this pattern which was responsible for the cynical remark I heard so often from Negro troops—"We know that our battle for democracy will begin when we reach San Francisco on our way home!"

• • •

JOHNNY (BLACK) COMES MARCHING HOME

Early on the morning of July 26, 1946, I received a long-distance telephone message which told me that four Negroes, two men and their wives, one of the men recently honorably discharged from the United States Army, had been lynched the previous day in Walton County, Georgia.

I immediately telephoned Atlanta to find great surprise and doubt that such a lynching had taken place since no news of it had been published there. But because my informant was utterly reliable I asked that the most competent and trustworthy investigators, white and colored, who could be secured be sent to Walton County as quickly as possible.

Georgia was torn asunder at the time by one of the most bitterly contested gubernatorial elections in its dark and bloody history. The notorious "Gene" Talmadge was using every possible appeal to bigotry to get himself elected governor again. Walton County was one of the strongholds of the rural electorate which followed Talmadge and his kind with blind devotion.

Monroe, the county seat of Walton County, was an attractive little Georgia community. In proportion to population it had an unusually large number of churches. It numbered among its citizens several whites who were as appalled by the lynchings and condemnatory of the mob as were the Negroes. But few of them dared express their opinion. Most of their fellow townsmen and even a larger percentage of the farmers who traded in Monroe were rabid believers in the Ku Klux Klan, Gene Talmadge, lynching, and white superiority.

The facts discovered by our investigators revealed a sordid background of twisted,

sadistic sexuality. One of the lynched Negroes had become involved in a fight with a
white man over the attentions which the latter had been paying to the Negro's wife.
The white man went to the hospital and the Negro to jail. In a manner which unmis-
takably established official connivance with the mob, the Negro had been released from
jail and driven down a back road by the white man on whose plantation he worked. In
the car were also the Negro's wife and another Negro friend and his wife. The car was
driven directly to the spot where the mob was lying in wait. We turned over to the FBI
and the Georgia Bureau of Investigation the evidence gathered by our investigators,
naming seven ringleaders of the lynching party. We offered a reward of ten thousand
dollars for the arrest and conviction of these men, which, added to the rewards offered
by the State of Georgia through Governor Ellis Arnall and other groups, brought the
total sum to more than one hundred thousand dollars. But even this sum, which was
undreamed-of wealth to the impoverished backwoodsmen of Georgia, was insufficient to
cause them to risk physical violence from the lynchers and their supporters. A reign of
terror and fear swept over Walton County and effectively shut the mouths of both
whites and Negroes. One man was beaten almost to death for having testified before
the Federal Grand Jury. Even nation-wide condemnation of the lynchings had no more
appreciable effect than water on a turtle's back.

A fortnight later a less-publicized but even more brutal lynching of another
Negro veteran occurred at Minden, Louisiana. Honorably discharged Ex-Corporal John
Jones had been thrown into jail charged with "loitering" in the backyard of a white
woman resident of Minden. Jones had been kept in jail along with his seventeen-year-
old cousin Albert Harris, despite the fact that the woman had steadfastly and indignantly refused to prefer charges against them. It was later revealed that Jones had incurred the enmity of a local white citizen for refusing to give the latter a war souvenir
which he had brought back from overseas.

One night Jones and Harris had been told by the jailer that they were free to
leave because the charges against them had been proved groundless, but there was
something about the manner in which this news was imparted which aroused Jones'
suspicion. He refused to leave the jail and insisted on remaining there until daybreak,
whereupon he was seized by several of the jailers and carried forcibly from the building
and put into an automobile filled with armed white men. His young cousin was forced
into another car also filled with hostile whites. The two men were driven to a lonely
spot. Jones was beaten terribly and left for dead. A blowtorch so charred his flesh that
the undertaker described him to us later as having been jet black in color though his
skin had been light yellow. The handsome and terrified seventeen-year-old Albert Harris had been beaten also unmercifully in a futile attempt to force him to "confess" that
he and Jones had been in the white woman's yard. Albert had been struck on the forehead with the butt of a forty-five caliber pistol and also left for dead. But he did not die.
Reviving some time after the mob had gone, he heard his cousin moaning in agony and
crawled to his side to hear the dying man beg for water. Albert, using a shoe for a dip-
per, had brought him water from a stream and had held the war veteran's head in his
arms as he died.

Despite his weakened condition from the terrible beating, the boy made his way by back roads to his father's house. The family knew that if it was discovered that Albert was still alive, he would surely be killed, to prevent his testifying against the mob (which included a number of prominent men of Minden and vicinity and several deputy sheriffs). Albert and his father climbed into the family automobile and set out under cover of darkness for a town in Arkansas where the boy could be hidden with a relative.

I telephoned the president of the NAACP branch in that town and asked him to put the Harrises on a plane and send them to New York. I wanted first to get them out of the clutches of the mob which, we learned from Daniel Byrd of our New Orleans branch who had gone at my request to Minden, was already on its way to the Arkansas town to complete its job of killing.

But hour after hour and day after day passed with no arrival of the Harrises. I talked with the Department of Justice and the FBI and solicited their aid in locating and protecting them. But even the vast and efficient manhunting machinery of the FBI was unequal to the task. We learned of other relatives of the Harrises in Texas and sought information from them, thinking that the Harrises might have learned of the mob seeking them in Arkansas. Our search in various parts of Texas was equally unsuccessful. We spread our search and eventually found them in a small town in northern Michigan after one of the most taxing and exciting manhunts in which we had ever engaged.

But even in Michigan we feared for their safety. The very success of the efforts we had made over the years to arouse public opinion against lynching and to stir the machinery of the federal government to activity against lynchers might have increased their danger, wherever they were. We knew from our representatives in Louisiana that the lynchers were so terrified by the prospect of being arrested and convicted in federal courts that they would let nothing be left undone to close Albert's mouth forever. We notified the Department of Justice that we had found the Harrises and I was asked to send them to Washington to tell their story. I sent Madison Jones, administrative assistant in our national office, to Michigan to bring them to New York, and Robert Carter of our legal staff and I took them to Washington. Never before had we been able to locate an eyewitness who could and would give firsthand evidence of what had taken place during a lynching.

Indictments of several members of the mob were handed down by the federal grand jury after Albert Harris, heavily guarded by U.S. marshals and by NAACP representatives, had gone from Michigan to Louisiana to testify. But a jury acquitted the lynchers despite the fact that the Department of Justice had utilized every possible section of the ineffective federal statutes which were then in effect.

Still another veteran was the target of violence during that terrible summer of 1946. After three years in the Army, fifteen months of which was spent in the jungles of the South Pacific, Isaac Woodard was discharged from the Army at a camp in Georgia. He eagerly boarded a bus for his home in North Carolina to see his wife and family after the long absence. On the bus he asked to be allowed to go to a restroom and, when he returned, he was cursed and threatened by the driver because he had been gone longer than suited the driver's wishes. At a town in South Carolina, the name of which Woodard did not know, the driver asked the chief of police to arrest the veteran for being "drunk and disorderly," although Woodard did not drink. When Woodard protested that he had been neither drunk nor disorderly the chief beat him unmercifully with a blackjack and struck him in both eyes with the end of his nightstick, blinding him forever. The soldier was then thrust into a cell and kept there overnight without food or medical treatment.

The next morning his cell door was opened and a policeman ordered him to go with him to court to be tried. He told the officer that he was unable to see. The policeman led him to a sink where he could wash the blood from his face and then conducted him before the judge. The latter promptly found him guilty and fined him fifty dollars and costs. The veteran fumbled in his pockets and proffered the contents totaling forty dollars in payment of his fine. This was peremptorily refused and he was told that the full amount must be paid in cash or he would return to jail. Woodard also had a severance-pay check of six hundred and ninety-four dollars which he was told he could sign to obtain the balance of his fine. Woodard shrewdly refused to do this, suspecting from the treatment which had been given him and from his own knowledge of the South that, being blind he would receive very little of the check. The court officials were apparently afraid to endorse the check themselves lest they get into difficulties with the federal government. By this time, moreover, the condition of Woodard's eyes was apparently so terrifying that either the consciences or the fears of the court were disturbed. A telephone call was put in to the U. S. veterans hospital at Spartanburg to ask that doctors be sent to examine him and take the Negro veteran to the Army hospital. Examination by Army doctors revealed that Woodard had been beaten so brutally that the corneas of both of his eyes had been injured beyond repair.

Orson Welles read of the case and with magnificent fury devoted most of the time of several weekly broadcasts to denunciation of the barbarism and a demand for punitive action, bringing about unsuccessful efforts on the part of Southern groups to have him removed from the air. Veteran, church, labor, and other groups joined us in our work of tracking down the culprit and insisting upon action.

The investigation launched by the FBI and the NAACP was hampered by the fact that Woodard didn't know the name of the town in which he had been beaten, imprisoned, and tried. But eventually we located after long search civilian and military fellow passengers on the bus who were able to identify the place of the assault and the man who had administered the barbarous beating as the chief of police. The chief of police was eventually indicted, so great was the public indignation against him, but upon being brought to trial he was acquitted to the cheers of a crowded courtroom. The U. S. Army denied our appeal in Woodard's behalf for a pension on the ground that his disability had not been incurred in service despite the fact that an Army ruling makes a discharged veteran subject to army discipline until midnight of the day of his discharge. We sought damages from the bus company but a jury ruled against Woodard. We arranged a tour for Woodard, accompanied by Franklin Williams, to publicize the case and to raise money for Woodard's relief. With the money obtained in this fashion, and through voluntary contributions totaling ten thousand dollars, we purchased an annuity to aid him.

There are two poignant memories connected with Isaac Woodard which I shall never forget. The first of these was the occasion when Woodard was led by his cousin into my office for the first time. Faltering with the unsureness of the newly blinded, Woodard extended his hand into open space in greeting, pathetically attempting to find my hand through the sound of my voice. Not yet skilled enough, his hand wavered a full two feet away from where my hand was, in the manner of one feeling his way in the darkness of a strange place.

"I saw you, Mr. White, when you visited my outfit in the Pacific," he told me. "I could see *then*."

The other memory is of the day when we invited representatives of several organizations and other individuals to meet in the Willkie Building to hear Woodard tell the story of what had happened to him. Although he could not see the audience, he was terrified by the ordeal of making a speech. I had to tell him over and over again that he need do no more than relate the facts and to assure him that his auditors were friends. It was one of the most moving speeches I have ever heard. With not the slightest trace of either bitterness or self-pity, and in a voice almost totally devoid of emotion, he told of the long and trying months in the Pacific and how eagerly he had looked forward to the end of the war when he could rejoin his family and resume normal civilian life. His voice swelled with modest pride as he told of receiving and reading his honorable discharge from the Army. We shared with him his impatience and anticipation as he waited for the bus which would take him to the North Carolina town where his wife awaited him. He made us in simple fashion look forward to the trip he and his wife were planning to New York to visit his mother and father. And we suffered with him the agony he endured during the unmerciful beating, the long night of pain without medical attention or food in a filthy prison cell, and his uttermost despair when he was told that he would be blind the rest of his life. Such was the pathos and understatement of Woodard's story that many in the audience, including hardboiled New York newspapermen, hardened to tales of misery and brutality, had tears in their eyes as he finished.

We were certain that the next morning's papers would give prominent and lengthy treatment to the story. I wanted this very much, because it had become evident that only the pressure of public opinion could force any redress for Woodard and stop the terrifying epidemic of violence against Negro veterans which threatened to spread. I knew from conversations with many veterans and from the reports of other conversations which members of our staff had had with Negro soldiers that a dangerous rebellion was rapidly growing among them. Many of them were beginning to feel that their service in the Army and Navy had intensified prejudice instead of diminishing it, and that there was no defense for them except that which they gave themselves.

But during the very time when Woodard was telling the story of what had happened to him in South Carolina, a Negro named Caraway killed the wife of a Long Island banker and shot and criminally attacked her daughter. This terrible crime, for which Caraway was later executed, was emblazoned in enormous headlines on the front page of every New York newspaper and the Woodard meeting was totally unmentioned by most papers and only briefly reported by the others.

The Negro GI in Korea*

Thurgood Marshall

. . . Who were the individuals condemned to serve out their lives in army prisons, or endure terms of 10, 15, 20, 25 and 50 years at hard labor for being cowards?

One boy convicted of cowardice had enlisted when he was fifteen. He remained in that bloody, frozen Korean fighting without telling anybody he was under age, knowing full well that he could at any time be returned to the United States as a hero. This coward remained in the front lines of his own free choice until he was confronted with court-martial charges. We checked, and found he told the truth. His 18th birthday occurred 11 days after his court martial convicted him of being a coward.

One unit of the 159th Field Artillery consisting of Negro enlisted men and white officers was in a river bed, where it was very peaceful and quiet. It was so quiet that the officers went back to town that evening. At fifteen minutes after midnight, enemy mortar shells dropped down on that unit in rapid succession. There was considerable confusion.

The captain in charge of the unit gave the command to Close Station and March Order. Artillerymen do not expect to have enough time to spell out every word in such a situation. The specific order is given by the letters, CSMO. When an officer says CSMO, he means *Get Ready to Get Out.*

They coupled the guns to vehicles called prime movers, a kind of big truck. None of the court-martial testimony is disputed except the application of the CSMO order. The captain admitted he gave it, but says it was for only one gun crew to move out and not the other batteries. He further admitted that his commanding officer had instructed him over the field telephone, *"Don't issue any order. You stay there and fight."*

Even though the batteries were all coupled up to leave, the word was given to uncouple and get back to firing shells. One gun crew of fourteen Negroes, however, had heard the order CSMO and had moved out too fast to get the new order. Twelve men were back the very next morning, even though the battery had moved to a new position that night. The other two men reported to duty shortly afterward. Even with the emergency CSMO order they had all taken the trouble to learn the location of their new firing position.

* From Thurgood Marshall, "Summary Justice—The Negro GI in Korea," *Crisis,* LVIII (May 1951), 304, 350–55. Reprinted by permission.

CONFUSION CONFOUNDED

The commanding officer told them that there had been so much confusion and misunderstanding that nobody knew what was going on. They were to forget about the incident, to go back to work and fight the war. And so the fourteen men forgot about it and were back on duty as before. Nevertheless, even though every one of the fourteen men had returned, charges of misbehavior were made subsequently.

Two of the men were court martialed. Three others, who testified for the two soldiers on trial, were also court martialed. At the two trials the captain gave three distinctly different stories under oath as to what had happened.

It is safe to say that this captain did not know what happened. He was confused. I talked with him and he still does not know what happened. But he has been promoted to Major, while five Negroes are in prison. Three of them are serving twenty years at hard labor and two of them received life sentences for "misconduct in the presence of the enemy."

As General MacArthur indicated in his cable to Walter White, when he first vetoed my visit overseas, under any decent system a man is treated as an individual. The terrible thing about these trials was the hopeless feeling common to every individual defendant. They felt they had no chance. The files showed these trials were held without any respect for the rights of individuals. The courts-martial were carried out with efficient haste, almost as on an assembly line. As many as four cases in a single day were tried, running on through the night, with all concerned anxious to get them over with.

QUICK JUSTICE

In four cases the trials which sentenced men to life imprisonment ran 42 minutes, 44 minutes, and the other two for 50 minutes each. This included the entire process of hearing the charges read, swearing in witnesses, examining all the evidence presented, hearing arguments (if any), explaining to the men their rights under the manual of courts-martial, the recess periods, discussion by the court and pronouncing sentence. Other trials ran an hour or an hour and ten minutes. I have seen many miscarriages of justice in my capacity as head of the NAACP legal department. But even in Mississippi a Negro will get a trial longer than 42 minutes, if he is fortunate enough to be brought to trial.

The men in the stockade had a common feeling of hopelessness. Some men with air-tight defenses had not presented evidence clearly demonstrating their innocence of the charges. Time and again I would ask them, *"Why didn't you tell your lawyer what really happened? Why didn't you tell the court? Why didn't you tell somebody?"*

Even though each man is an individual in the eyes of God and under our Constitution, these individuals gave me the same answer. *"It wasn't worth trying. We knew when we went in there we were all going to come out the same way. Each one of us hoped and prayed we would only get life. They gave that officer, Lt. Gilbert, death, only because he is a Negro. What did you expect them to give a Negro enlisted man? We know what the score is."*

Such a spirit of hopelessness will strip away from any man the ability to defend himself adequately. One particular sergeant imprisoned in the stockade outside Tokyo was representative of the devotion we have come to associate with our armed forces. Under fire in Korea three of his commanding officers were killed in a period of two days. This man had kept his company together. He did not lose a single wounded man in ninety days. He brought every injured man out, sometimes on his own back. He saw to it that his men received hot food, regularly, which he took up to them at the remoter points along the firing line. One after another he saw his friends killed, but refused to be relieved. Day in and day out, he kept on fighting, several times in command of the entire company because there weren't officers around.

BATTLE FATIGUE

This sergeant is charged with wilful disobedience of an order. When he was charged, when he talked to his lawyer, when he went into the courtroom, during the trial, and even after the sentence he never told any of them that right in his pocket was a slip from a doctor, a medical corps captain, certifying that this man was suffering from battle fatigue and should be returned to the rear for treatment. He never told anyone about this slip until he talked to me. I called the captain of the guard immediately and asked to have the sergeant's belongings searched. In the condemned man's wallet, taken away from him with the rest of his personal effects upon his reception at the stockade, was the slip of paper.

"Why didn't you tell them?" I asked.

"It wasn't worth it," he said. *"It wouldn't help me. You saw what happened to Sergeant B   , didn't you, when you talked with him? Sergeant B   put in as evidence the official record book kept by the Army hospital showing he was there on the days they charged him with being away from duty. The court didn't pay any attention to it. They are not paying attention to anything we say."*

There were men who were punished more than once for same alleged offense. Four Negro soldiers were attached to a mess hall miles behind the front lines. When they finished work one day, their sergeant told them they could go off and do what they liked. They told me it was customary to drive a jeep to a place where showers had been set up. When they returned from their shower the sentry told them there was supposed to be no movement in that section, but they could drive around by the road to the back part of the mess-hall area.

These men were picked up on the road going to Pusan. They said they were lost. When these men were brought in by the M.P.'s, their commanding officer said, *"You fellows have had easy jobs behind the lines, but you haven't appreciated it. For your punishment, I am going to put you in the front lines."*

Perhaps this captain was right. He put two of these men in a heavy mortar outfit and two others with a machine-gun unit. They were in fierce front-line fighting for twenty-one days and twenty-one nights. Perhaps they deserved this, since other men had been on prolonged duty in battle without mess-hall duty behind the lines or shower baths after work.

Their record in battle was never questioned. But these four men were pulled out, brought back and court martialed for violation of the 75th Article of War because of the incident that had happened three weeks before, miles behind the lines. They were sentenced to twenty years each for misbehavior before the enemy. The only crime which they could conceivably have been charged with involved the use of a jeep, without permission, which has not yet been charged against them.

OFFICER BEHAVIOR

How could officers of our Army behave in such a way? The official records proved that they did, but the explanation for their behavior was still lacking. My last Sunday in Korea was spent at a very forward position of the 24th Infantry Regiment, where I talked to the key man in every company of the regiment and of the 159th Field Artillery battery. These men knew what was behind these courts-martial operations.

The Regiment's forward positions were then moved north of Seoul. They had just taken an airstrip six hours before we got there.

These soldiers were survivors of the action occurring prior to and during the three months of courts-martial. There was one man whose father had been in the regiment for twenty years, and he's been in it for nine. I talked to about seventy of these veterans, asking them to tell me what had been going on last summer and fall.

One after another, they all said the same thing. The regiment's morale had been at a disastrously low ebb. Their white officers were in many instances Southerners who had brought their prejudices with them when assigned to duty with the 24th Infantry.

Time and again these officers told the men whom they were going to order into battle, *"I despise nigger troops. I don't want to command you or any other niggers. This Division is no good, and you are lousy. You don't know how to fight."*

I cannot imagine a worse situation in combat, where a man does not care what happens to those serving under him. There is no way to make the soldiers care less what is going to happen to the outcome of the fighting, or to their officers.

CASUALTIES HIGH

The casualty rates among the enlisted men and officers was disproportionately high. And how could it help but be high, when you are following such leaders? This wasn't told about one officer, but about several, by fighting men who were not court martialed and certainly had no reason to tell anything but the truth.

This explained these courts-martial proceedings to me. I think the high rate of casualties among officers made it necessary to assign the blame. The answer was a wholesale conviction of Negro soldiers who had survived this prejudiced leadership.

When I talked to the men that Sunday, morale in the 24th Infantry was certainly high. They had a new commanding officer, Colonel John T. Corley. They were proud of his having earned more battlefield decorations than any officer in the active Army. He respects them, and every man with whom I talked admired him. They repeatedly told me how, instead of ordering them forward into action, Colonel Corley goes out himself and commands, "Come!"

There are still some other officers in the regiment whom the men do not respect, and have little reason to respect. So long as that sort of officer is in command of jim-crow troops, we may expect the same pattern of injustice in the future. These soldiers are fighting and dying for us, who should see to it that they are not subjected to the kind of leadership which despises them.

MADE REPORT

I now had the information for a complete report to General MacArthur, with recommendations. According to Army procedure, MacArthur did not have official responsibility for the disposition of the individual courts-martial cases. After the trials were approved by the major general in command of the 25th Division, the records were forwarded for review to the Judge Advocate General's office in the Pentagon in Washington. There the NAACP has been representing the condemned men, and has already arranged for a number of the sentences to be reversed or reduced.

But in my report it was necessary to place the ultimate responsibility for these courts-martial squarely upon General Douglas MacArthur. He had both the authority and the responsibility for maintaining or ending racial segregation in the Army's Far East Command.

In the large headquarters staff of MacArthur's Far East Command at the time, in the Dai Ichi building, there were no Negroes except for three civilian clerks. This is but one of several buildings with thousands of army personnel; nowhere were there more than one out of four men fighting with the 25th Division in Korea is a Negro American. There was a handsome, elite honor guard of crack riflemen which used to guard the headquarters and the person of MacArthur, but there was not a Negro among them. Headquarters had a football team, all white. There wasn't even a Negro in the headquarters band.

MacARTHUR RESPONSIBLE

This was General MacArthur's responsibility. He was at the time the Supreme Commander of American and United Nations troops then engaged in battle with a Communist enemy which seeks to divide us from the rest of the world. The Communists preach and propagandize how Americans abuse colored people, and MacArthur had allowed discrimination in his own headquarters. Negro troops in Korea are not succumbing to the Communist propaganda any more than they believed the Germans in the last war. They see how the Communists are killing Negroes as thoroughly as they are killing others.

Major General Doyle O. Hickey, who was MacArthur's chief of staff, told me that the General was aware of these things and that a study was being made to find ways and means for correcting them. I told him that the United States Air Force took just one day to end segregation. They gave a single order, and the Air Force is now an integrated, American body of men using the best efficiency and skill each man can provide in his country's service.

Three blocks down Avenue A from the Dai Ichi building is the Far East Air Force headquarters. Negroes work alongside white soldiers there in the guard, in the offices, wherever they are capable of doing good work. The first time I went by the Air Force building there were two guards of the Air Police standing at attention. One happened to be white; the other was colored. And after the Dai Ichi building, it was a very pleasant experience to see the guard being checked by the Sergeant of the Guard, who on that day happened to be a Negro. The same policy is now in force in the U. S. Navy.

I told General MacArthur that if the Air Force and the Navy, both drawing men from the same forces as the Army, frequently from the same families, have done this without any disadvantageous results, there was no reason why the Army couldn't do it. The Army is eliminating segregation in other places, and the Far East Command has no special problems which would place it at an extra disadvantage. It is disgraceful to have the Japanese clerks in the canteens told to discriminate against Negro service men during their five day recreation rotation from Korea.

In every war in which this country has participated, Negro Americans have had to fight for the right to fight. At the start of each war, military leaders have questioned the Negro's abilities and finally accepted Negro participation under the pressure of necessity.

Although 920,000 Negroes served in the Army during the Second World War, the Army didn't take most of them until manpower shortages impelled their acceptance, using them for menial jobs wherever possible. These men were treated as inferiors in southern training camps. The great majority were used for arduous, dirty work overseas, but they covered themselves with glory just the same.

To date, the Cold War has erupted into violent action in one area, the Far East. There we face the potential enmity of hundreds of millions of men whose skins are not white, who look with extreme care to see how white men feel about colored peoples.

The NAACP believes that the men and women in our Armed Services shall have first preference on our time and efforts. But we are not only a group of Americans seeking *correction* of vicious practices and for the survival of this country, we also work to prevent injustice. The best way to accomplish this in our Armed Services is to work to bring about complete abolition of segregation now.

To date the legal department of the NAACP has secured reduction of sentence for twenty of these soldiers, but we have just begun. The NAACP is working to secure the appropriate exoneration or abbreviation of sentence for every man treated unjustly because of his race or color.

The Bid
for Desegregation[*]

Henry A. Bullock

Resistance and compliance were twin born. While the people and officials of some states vigorously searched for a way to mix the races in their schools, others searched, with greater diligence, for a way to keep the races apart. The scale was never balanced for popular sentiment kept the force pointed in the direction of the old tradition. Whereas those who deliberated accepted desegregation as an inevitable policy but tried to postpone the changeover as long as they could, those who resisted bluntly rejected the policy and tried vainly to erect barriers that would protect them forever against it. Although patterns of resistance were varied and can be classified in many ways, one can say with certainty that they assumed two forms: those that operated outside the legal machinery and those that operated within it. One can say, too, that the degree of success experienced through the use of either method depended squarely upon the extent to which actions of resistance were able to break through such lines of legal and moral defense as were thrown up by the constituted authority and the general citizenry of the desegregating communities.

There were dramatic instances in which popular discontent exploded into violence and fostered open rebellion against constituted authority. One of these occurred at Baltimore, where the nation's first step toward compliance with the Supreme Court's decision had to be fought for vigorously partly because no adequate preparation had been made for it. Here, desegregation proceeded smoothly for a month but in nearby Milford, Delaware, a spark destined to become a conflagration was lighted. Bryant Bowles, head of the "expedient" National Association for the Advancement of White People, closed a desegregated school, forced the school board to resign, and drove Negro students from the school which was formerly all white.

Moved by this action of defiance, some discontented citizens of Baltimore began

* From Henry Allen Bullock, *A History of Negro Education in the South* (Cambridge, Mass.: Harvard University Press, 1967), pp. 250–62. Copyright 1967 by the President and Fellows of Harvard College. Reprinted by permission of the publishers.

a duplication of the Milford rebellion on the same day. In a neighborhood near the B & O Shops, inhabited largely by home-owning semiskilled workers, women picketed an elementary school containing about 12 Negroes and 700 whites. Parents who were apprehensive about what was happening took their children out of school. On the following day resistance spread to Southern High School, where 50 Negro children had been placed as a result of desegregation. Conditions reached riotous proportions, and the operation of the desegregated schools was disrupted.

Nevertheless, such determination as school officials had shown in developing the desegregation program withstood a most violent test. Civic leaders rallied courageously to its defense. Ministers preached brotherhood in their churches; the Mayor pleaded for calm; and the school board stood firm. Both the school officials and the police adopted tougher policies when things were at their worst. School officials telephoned parents and warned them that it was illegal for them to keep their children out of school. The police commissioner went on television to declare that anybody who disturbed the school or induced a student to be a truant would be arrested.

At Baltimore constituted authority kept faith with its responsibilities. This worked. One day after school officials and police authorities had spoken, school reopened, and the pickets were chased home. Three days later attendance was back to normal. By 1957, three years after the city's school board had announced its desegregation plan, 28.7 percent of the Negro pupils were attending mixed schools. Faculties had been desegregated also, and more than one hundred Negro teachers were working in formerly all-white schools. Indicating a collapse of the will to resist at Baltimore, one man said, "there aren't many people really cheering but there aren't many trying to halt or delay it either." [36] As Superintendent Fischer concluded, the plan had succeeded because the school board was unanimous and unwavering in its stand, and the move was backed by the local government and the community's leaders.

In Sturgis, Kentucky, less than 200 miles away from Louisville—where later developed one of the best desegregation programs in the nation—constituted authority did not show official courage so great as that shown at Baltimore, and violent rebellion did not suffer so decisive a defeat. There, discontented citizens sought to block with mob action what school officials had done with too little deliberation. The rebellion started when, on September 4, 1956, Negro children who had been admitted to all-white schools at Sturgis and nearby Clay appeared for assignment to class. They were turned back in each instance by jeering crowds of five hundred at Sturgis and one hundred at Clay.

In taking this step as Kentucky's first desegregated students, the Negro children were not facing a community that had been prepared for them in any way. The superintendent had merely given his approval for their enrollment. School officials had hinted that Dunbar High School for Negroes would be closed in 1957 because of its small enrollment, and all Negro students would be integrated at Sturgis or Morganfield High Schools. However no announcement of this was ever made. Back of the plan was no history of planning for desegregation and no involvement of the communities.

---

[36] John B. Martin, *The Deep South Says "Never"* (New York: Baltimore Books, 1957), pp. 79–83.

On hearing that the Negro children had been admitted to these two formerly all-white schools, members of the White Citizens Council began writing antidesegregation letters to local newspapers and spreading "hate literature" throughout the communities. Their actions fostered a boycott that kept Negroes out of Clay High School, and they began action to secure the same results at Sturgis, where a boycott had begun but was fading. Mass meetings held by the council in Mansfield on September 15 and in Sturgis two days later rekindled a boycott of Sturgis High School by white students. Attendance dropped to about fifty whites and eight Negroes. Believing local law enforcement agencies incapable of handling the situation, Governor A. B. Chandler called in the Kentucky National Guard. Order was restored but not before the county board, responding to the pressure of lawlessness, had ousted the Negro students.[37]

Violence also won a temporary victory over weak authority in Mansfield, Texas. There bitterness followed desegregation despite the fact that San Antonio schools made the transition with relative ease. Desegregation was ordered at Mansfield in November 1955, when the Fifth District Circuit Court mandated the school board to admit students without regard to race. No organized preparation was made for the changeover, however, although the city's climate of race relations warranted it.

Relations between the races had been quite strained. The Ku Klux Klan had been active in Mansfield fifteen or twenty years before, and at least one lynching had occurred in the history of the city. A long-standing enmity had existed between a white cafe owner and a Negro operator of a barbecue stand. The white owner had been waging a vicious campaign in an effort to get school officials to prohibit white students from patronizing the Negro's stand. In addition the conditions of the Negro school had been considered deplorable by the Negro citizens. The school had no indoor toilet; no running water, no teaching materials, no flagpole on the grounds, and no school bus. Since all the city's Negro students who wanted a high school education had to go to Fort Worth to secure accommodations, the local chapter of the NAACP had brought suit in an effort to gain relief for these children. Their effort had resulted in the district court's decision.

It was against this background that the Negro students marched when they presented themselves for proper registration at the all-white high school. There on the school grounds a crowd of about 250 disgruntled citizens had gathered to stop them if they tried to register. They carried threatening signs that read: "Nigger stay out, we don't want niggers, this is a white school"; "A dead nigger is the best nigger"; "Coons ears $1.00 a dozen." A dummy figure of a Negro was displayed hanging from the school building.

Quantities of hate material had been so well distributed that the organizers of the antidesegregation demonstration developed a "little dictatorship" where once law and order had ruled. Despite the large number of law enforcement agents on hand, the

---

[37] A full account of this case may be found in Roscoe Criffin, *A Tentative Description and Analysis of the School Desegregation Crisis in Sturgis, Kentucky, August 31–September 19, 1956* (New York: Anti-Defamation League of B'nai B'rith, 1956).

Negro children who sought to register got no protection. In fact, the superintendent who had stayed away from school during the first day of the protest, came the second day and told the crowd: "Now you guys know I'm with you, but I've got this mandate hanging over my head." The Fort Worth attorney who represented the Negro children vainly issued a plea for additional law enforcement officials. He sent a telegram to the governor, requesting his aid. He tried to get the governor by telephone without success. He telephoned the director of public safety at Austin, but the director merely said that it was his policy to respond only to requests from local law enforcement agents and that such a request had not been forthcoming. The Mansfield press did not prove to be a responsible community force. Instead of pouring water on the conflagration, it added oil. It said that the Supreme Court could not make laws, cited biblical quotations in defense of segregation, and claimed that the "separate but equal" policy works no injustice against the Negroes. The *Mansfield News,* sole newspaper of the town, wrote a scorching editorial claiming that "Our Precious American Heritage is at stake." Only ministers raised a dissenting voice against lawlessness, but they were criticized by the editor of the local paper and called "pin-headed preachers." Frightened by their exposure to lawlessness, the Negro children failed to appear at the school for a chance at registration which was due them by law. They retreated to fight another day.[38]

On January 4, 1956, District Judge Taylor ordered the desegregation of all three high schools of Anderson County, Tennessee, by the fall of that year. Consequently, twelve Negro children registered for admission to the all-white high school in compliance with this order. They did this against a background that was steadily becoming more favorable to them and with the cooperation of a constituted authority that was not to yield to the pressure of extra-legalized violence.

The situation in Clinton, Tennessee, where the trouble centered, was already in transition. "Creeping integration" had already begun as a result of the economic expansion of nearby Oak Ridge, where Negro professionals were being employed. A Negro had been elected to the city council there; the public swimming pools had been desegregated; and, in the light of the Court's decision, the junior and senior high schools had been open to all races. There had been no high school for Negroes in the county prior to this time, and Negro high school pupils had been compelled to travel to La Follette, 24 miles away, or to Knoxville, which was 15 miles distant.

Nevertheless, the Anderson County Federation for Constitutional Government responded to the desegregation move by circulating petitions in protest against the change. Its members filed an injunction suit, demanding that the state cut off funds to Clinton High and restrain the county officials from desegregating the school. They invited others of the county to join them in working toward "an orderly solution to the problem." But on August 25, several days before the opening of school, Frederick John Kasper, twenty-six-year-old executive secretary of the Seaboard White Citizens Council, arrived in Clinton and began gathering support for a picket line against desegregating the school. He made house-to-house visits, talked with members of the Anderson

[38] John Griffin and Theodore Freedman, *What Happened in Mansfield* (New York: Anti-Defamation League of B'nai B'rith, 1957).

County Federation, and made speeches before mass gatherings. Agencies of law enforcement, accepting desegregation as their duty, met with Kasper and tried to persuade him to leave town. This failing, the agitator was arrested for inciting to riot. Although he succeeded in stimulating even greater demonstrations after his release from jail, lawlessness was controlled by the Tennessee National Guard. School enrollment returned to normal, and the Negro children enrolled in school as the Court had intended.[39]

It was at Little Rock, Arkansas, however, that the national government exercised its greatest force against violent reactions to desegregation, by taking decisive steps in support of a local school board that had begun to weaken.

After more than two years of careful planning and the development of a Court-accepted scheme for desegregation, Little Rock's school board experienced serious trouble. On September 3, 1956, its school desegregation program was blocked temporarily by troops of the Arkansas National Guard whom Governor Orval Faubus had prematurely ordered into action for the purpose of restoring a peace that had not been broken. On the evening before the schools were to open, these troops appeared at Little Rock Central High School and surrounded it. Governor Faubus, speaking on radio and television an hour later, said the guardsmen were there to maintain or restore peace and good order; that they were not to act as segregationists or integrationists; that peace and good order would not be possible "if forcible integration" were carried out; that the schools "must be operated on the same basis as they have operated in the past."

The school board, completely surprised by this action, responded by an attempt to gain time. It issued a statement which in effect recognized the Court's order, announced the presence of troops, and asked the Negro students not to try to enter the school the following morning. The ten Negro students who had registered in the all-white Central High School complied with this request. None of them went to school on the opening day. In the afternoon, the school board sought directions from the Federal court as to what it should do. Federal Judge Ronald N. Davis, who was serving the Little Rock District temporarily, ordered the board to go ahead with the desegregation schedule. He said he was taking the governor at his word—that the troops were there "to preserve peace and not to act as segregationists or integrationists." Nine Negro students appeared on the second day of school, but the troops turned them away. After refusing the school board's second plea, which asked, this time, that the desegregation plan be delayed indefinitely, Judge Davis ordered injunction proceedings against Governor Faubus, Major General Sherman T. Clinger, and Lt. Col. Morrison E. Johnson—all connected with the presence of the National Guard at Central High School. While a Faubus conference with President Eisenhower was breaking down, Judge Davis was hearing and ruling on the injunction proceedings which he had ordered. A temporary injunction against interference with the court desegregation order by Governor Faubus or the National Guard was promptly granted, and the governor ordered removal of the guardsmen three hours later.

---

[39] Anna Holden and Bonita Valien, *A Tentative Analysis of the School Desegregation Crisis in Clinton, Tennessee* (New York: Anti-Defamation League of B'nai B'rith, 1956).

In this collision between a state's chief executive and Federal authority, the American people had won. Despite the presence of a crowd of approximately 1,000 people, who had assembled before the school on the following Monday morning, the Negro children did enter the school. Once again, however, the school board registered fear and removed the Negro students. But President Eisenhower, after an appeal to the interfering crowd, ordered the Arkansas National Guard into Federal service along with a part of the 101st Airborne Division. Their orders were simple. They were to surround the school and see that the Court's will was enforced. On Wednesday morning, nine Negro boys and one girl entered the school.[40] President Eisenhower had done what his successor was to do later and in the deeper South: He had preserved the constitutional authority of the United States.

Resistance to school desegregation was most persistent in the field of legislative action, where several states, particularly those of the Deep South, attempted to avoid compliance with court orders by means of complicated administrative procedures. As James M. Nabrit, Sr., occasional attorney for the NAACP, described these procedures, they were "worded so as to make it difficult to separate pseudo-administrative difficulties from valid ones." [41]

One of the major techniques of resistance along these lines was the pupil placement law. Two years after the 1954 decree, laws of this type were passed by Alabama, Georgia, Florida, Louisiana, Mississippi, North Carolina, South Carolina, Tennessee, and Virginia. Alabama created a pupil assignment act providing that boards of education may assign pupils to schools on the basis of such factors as psychological aptitude for types of teaching and association involved, effects of the pupil's admission upon the prevailing standards of the school, and the possibility of threat or friction or disorder among pupils and others. A Florida law permitted the assignment of students to the school "for which he is best fitted." Louisiana legislation authorized local school superintendents to designate each school a student may attend. North Carolina, pioneering in this type of legislation, transferred complete authority over enrollment and assignment of pupils from the state board of education to local boards. And a South Carolina legislation not only gave local boards exclusive authority to operate any public school and to transfer pupils "so as to promote the best interest of education," but it also gave them permission to transfer pupils from one county to another without the necessity for the parent to own property in the county to which the transfer was made.

These various kinds of "resistance laws" were designed to serve three purposes: to make it necessary for Negroes to sue each school board or superintendent and thereby diffuse the impact of litigation aimed at desegregating the schools; to make it possible for desegregated schools to disappear for want of white students; and to make

---

[40] This summary report of the Little Rock incident was taken from the very complete account reported in *Southern School News,* October 1957.

[41] James M. Nabrit, Sr., "Legal Inventions and the Desegregation Process," *The Annals of the American Academy of Political and Social Science* 304:36 (March 1956).

it possible for superintendents caught under the force of a court mandate to exclude Negro pupils from all-white schools on spurious grounds that were not susceptible to clear validation.

Another device of legal resistance was that of putting discretionary control over the purse string of public education. Georgia made it a felony for any school official—whether state, county or municipal—to spend tax money for public schools in which the races are mixed. It fixed the penalty for such a violation at two years in prison in addition to an imposed personal liability for the money expended. Provisions for cutting off state financial aid for any school which mixed the races were planted in the state's constitution before 1952. However, a constitutional amendment was ratified in 1954 to allow the general assembly to provide for grants of state, county, or municipal funds to citizens of the state for educational purposes. Louisiana gave its state board of education authority to withhold approval from any school violating the state's segregation provisions, and prohibited the granting of free textbooks and other supplies or state funds for the operation of a school lunch program to any school violating the segregation provision. The South Carolina legislature of 1955 wrote into Clarendon and Calhoun County supply bills and the general appropriation act provisions for cutting off funds to any school from which or to which a child may be transferred in compliance with a court order contrary to the assignment of the school authorities. This state also joined North Carolina in placing disciplinary pressure upon teachers. In both instances continuing contracts were eliminated. As additional means of intimidation, laws were created to allow school boards to cancel the contracts of any teachers advocating desegregation or to require teachers to sign an oath to uphold and defend the constitution and law of the state. Such laws were enacted by Georgia and North Carolina. The Texas legislature also passed a series of resistance laws, the most threatening of which was the requirement that desegregation occur where public approval by referendum was secured.

Some states, rather than comply with the desegregation order, prepared to abolish their public schools if it should become necessary. They created "readiness legislation" along these lines soon after the court decree was rendered. Mississippi amended its constitution to provide for the abolition of public schools by a two-thirds vote of both the houses of the legislature. The amendment provided that a county or school district may be empowered to abolish its schools by a majority vote of both houses. South Carolina made similar enactments. It repealed its compulsory school attendance laws and its code authorizing school boards to regulate the opening and closing of school terms. Alabama legislation permitted the state to discontinue the public schools whenever necessary to avoid friction or disorder, and allowed the state and its subdivisions to appropriate public money for the aid of private education when adequate public facilities were lacking or public operation involved the adoption of coercive policies.

While enacting laws of resistance, Mississippi was building another defense line —one, it was hoped, which would make school desegregation less desirable to Negroes. The state tabled its move toward interposition, slowed down its laws of "massive resistance," and started a program of public school equalization. It appropriated large sums of money in an attempt to bring Negro schools up to the standards enjoyed by the white.

Salaries of teachers in the Negro schools were increased, new buildings were con-structed, and more varied courses were offered.

Despite all the law making, these resistance patterns gradually lost their power under the force of litigation that proved them unconstitutional. During the period from 1954 to 1958, eleven states passed 145 laws in defense of the maintenance of their segre-gated schools. Pupil placement acts were held invalid, teacher firing laws were over-thrown, voluntary segregation was ruled insufficient, and control of public education through police power was outlawed in Virginia, Tennessee, and Louisiana. Further col-lapse of the massive resistance movement appeared with the opening of the 1960s. The attorney general of Texas ruled unconstitutional the state's 1957 law requiring referen-dum approval by public school districts before desegregation could begin. And the United States Fifth Circuit Court of Appeals declared that Houston's "brother and sister rule" on pupil placement assignment was discriminatory.

Although the validity of many of these laws is still untested, the degree of their effectiveness in halting the desegregation program is currently assessable.[42] By 1961 small but definite progress had been made toward school desegregation. Of the 2,804 school districts which had Negro and white children in separate schools in 1954, ap-proximately one third had been desegregated by this time, and 233,509 of the 927,146, or 7.3 percent of the Negro children as of early 1960, were in school with white chil-dren. Only Alabama, Mississippi, and South Carolina had managed to escape desegrega-tion at this time.

When viewed over-all, the pace of public school desegregation in the South has been embarrassingly slow, and the Supreme Court's order that desegregation be carried out "with all deliberate speed" has come to be the most disregarded edict the high tri-bunal has ever handed down. Ten years after the historic decision, only 1.18 percent of the 2.9 million Negro children enrolled in schools of the Deep South were attending with white children. No child was attending a desegregated class in Mississippi prior to September 1964, and less than 600 Negro pupils in all had been admitted to formerly white schools in Alabama, Arkansas, Georgia, and South Carolina. Mississippi had Negro students registering in some of its schools for the first time in September 1964. When the six border states and the District of Columbia are added to the Southern to-tals, the record still shows that Negro children had not been able to derive significant benefit from the May 17 decision. Less than one in ten had been desegregated.[43]

In the border states—Delaware, Kentucky, Maryland, Missouri, Oklahoma, and West Virginia—the Court's order had meant complete desegregation in some instances, slow and token compliance in others. Approximately 55 percent of the Negro children in these states and the District of Columbia were attending schools with white pupils

[42] Various patterns of legislative resistance in the various Southern states have been reported serially by the *Southern School News*. For the ineffectiveness of these laws in their efforts to block desegregation, see Southern Education Reporting Service, *Statistical Summary*, November 1961, p. 3.

[43] Erwin Knoll, "10 Years of Desegregation," a series of articles published in the *Houston Post*, May 13–18, 1964.

ten years after desegregation was ordered. Almost all or 97 percent of the total Negro enrollment in the border region were in desegregated districts. Nevertheless shifting neighborhood patterns and deteriorating downtown districts have contributed heavily to resegregation in the cities of the border states.

In complete defiance, Prince Edward County, Virginia, closed her schools in 1959 and spent $2 million to support a white students' private academy and to fight legal efforts to compel desegregation. The approximate 1,600 Negro pupils who were left without schooling finally won access to education through the "free schools" which Attorney General Robert F. Kennedy initiated three years later. Financed by $1 million in private contributions and staffed by a crack faculty of 93 teachers recruited from all parts of the United States, the "free schools" claimed, through standardized test evidence, significant success in building the national achievement rates of the Negro pupils. Nevertheless, this movement was merely a stop-gap, not at all causing the traditional public schools which Negroes had lost to be no longer necessary. In fact the Court took this position while showing its impatience with the delay so obvious in the entire school desegregation program. On May 25, 1964, Justice Hugo Black wrote this statement in his opinion directing the Prince Edward County to reopen its public schools: "The time for more 'deliberate speed' has run out, and the phrase can no longer justify denying these school children their constitutional rights to an education equal to that afforded by public schools in other parts of Virginia." [44]

It is fair to say that although there has been some small progress in desegregation in the South, the national desegregation record had hardly improved by the end of 1966. "The great majority of American children attend schools that are largely segregated," stated James S. Coleman in the summary of a comprehensive report that he and his associates submitted to the United States Office of Education. [45] More than 65 percent of all Negro pupils in the first grade in the United States were attending schools that were between 90 and 100 percent Negro. In the South most public school children were attending schools that were 100 percent white or Negro. Court orders for school desegregation now blanket the South. Only the strength of human patience remains to be broken.

    [44] *Southern School News,* June 1964.

    [45] James S. Coleman, *Equality of Educational Opportunity* (Washington, D. C.; Government Printing Office, 1966), p. 3.

Part 7

PROTEST

In *Crisis in Black and White,* Charles E. Silberman, the introduction is addressed to both blacks and whites. Referring to relations between the races, the author observes, "The truth is too terrible . . . [so that] neither white nor Negro Americans have been willing to face, or even to admit, the truth." For black Americans who have sought improved conditions as individuals and as groups through the "American way"—work, political action, and education—the central feature of the last two decades has been the increased recognition of the realities of racism and the protests as a result of that recognition. This chapter omits attention to other matters and is concerned with the central feature, that of protest.

The selection from "Lawlessness and Violence in America and Their Special Manifestations in Changing Negro-White Relationships," Allen D. Grimshaw, examines the heritage of violence in the U. S. in light of the growing militance evident in 1959. The material implies that, even in its most extreme form, black protest follows established American patterns. Beginning in 1963 many instances of such violence appeared in urban areas of the country. The excerpt from the *Report of the National Advisory Commission on Civil Disorders* provides a brief description of a riot in Cincinnati in 1967 and gives a concise overview of the increasing black protest of the post-World War II period. Characteristic of these is more aggressive action by blacks than had been the case in previous eras.

The violence of the riots represents only one of the many forms of protest by blacks. Well before the first of the major disorders occurred in 1963 Martin Luther King, Jr., a Baptist minister, typified the new black protest leader of the period. Middle class in family background, educated in an all-black college, committed, skilled in leadership, and able to articulate the feelings of many blacks, he differed from others in methods of securing the goal of full manhood. *Why We Can't Wait*, written by King in 1963, provides insight into the nonviolent direct protest method which he espoused until his assassination in Memphis, Tennessee, in 1968. "Letter From Birmingham Jail," the selection included here, is King's response to a statement by white Alabama clergymen who were critical of the action leading to King's arrest. The letter is an eloquent defense of nonviolent direct action, an approach considered by its white critics to be radicalism bordering on anarchy.

The Fire Next Time, James Baldwin, and "Mission Accomplished," Ben Caldwell, are examples of literature as instruments of protest. Baldwin's essay, which provides the title for the book, takes the United States to task for its failure to deal effectively with racism and indicates the growing danger to the nation if the rights of black citizens cannot receive the concern and support needed to make reality of the national ideals. Caldwell's work in *The Drama Review* is one of a number of plays which have developed as voices of literary protest. They are protest in the sense of the description of Revolutionary Theatre given by LeRoi Jones in his book *Home*. He describes it as ". . . a political theatre, a weapon to help in the slaughter of these dim-witted fatbellied white guys who somehow believe that the rest of the world is here for them to slobber on." This is didactic literature written by blacks for black audiences. Not only does it rail against the "evil," but it instructs the reader in what must be done to correct the wrong.

"A Black at the Gridiron Dinner" from the March 26, 1970 *Washington Post* represents another expression of discontent. The writer Roger Wilkins, former Assistant Attorney General of the U. S., points up the tokenism of the situation in which he finds himself and protests the insensitivity of whites and white society to the problems inherent in the situation.

The slogan "Black Power" expresses much that is inherent in the protest of this period. John H. Clarke describes it as ". . . no more or less than the right to determine your own destiny, starting with the control of your own communities." His article "Black Power and Black History," published in the February 1969 issue of *Negro Digest*, protests the unwillingness of white Americans to allow black Americans to make such determinations. He argues that the implementation of the Black Power concept depends on the development of self-respect and black identity which, in turn, depends heavily on knowledge of the history of black people in Africa and the United States.

The protest of Black Muslims and hundreds of thousands of non-Muslims found expression in the words of Malcolm X. The selection from his autobiography reflects the hopelessness felt by many that white Americans will or can make any significant change in their racial attitudes. As onetime leading spokesman for the Nation of Islam Malcolm X describes whites as devils and the enemies of black men. Self-educated, brilliant, and charismatic, he had developed a large personal following before his assassination in 1965 not long after his break with Elijah Muhammed, the head of the Muslim movement.

Among the most active and most radical of the protest groups is the Black Panther Party. As in the case of Malcolm X, it speaks for and has the support of many who are not numbered among its members. One of its spokesmen was Eldridge Cleaver, former party Minister of Information. In the selection "Domestic Law and International Order" from his book *Soul On Ice,* he attacks the inequality of law enforcement, the "accidental violence" against black people, and most important the "policies of those who make the decisions." In his final sentence he intimates that the full exercise of the black revolt is yet to occur.

As Cleaver implies, Afro-American history is a story with a climax yet to come. Thus, for the student of Afro-American history the unanswered questions exist. What sources and what observations of what events and current movements should students examine in an effort to be better prepared to understand the outcome? Or better yet, what should the student do to play an active and effective part in shaping that outcome?

Lawlessness and Violence in America[*]

Allen D. Grimshaw

Ours has been a lawless and violent nation.[1] Indeed, race riots and bombings, although they are particularly dramatic manifestations of conflict, have claimed fewer lives than many other varieties of violence, individual or social. There are more criminal homicides in some American metropolises every year than there have been deaths from all the urban race riots of the 20th Century combined. A few famous feuds, and some important labor disputes have rolled up casualty lists which compare in length with the most spectacular interracial disorders. Social violence,[2] and lawlessness generally, have not been phenomena expressed only in interracial relations in this country. This article reviews briefly two sets of historical data relevant to an understanding of those patterns of race relations in urban areas which have culminated in violence. An introductory section consists of a simple listing of some other varieties of social violence which have characterized inter-group relations in the United States and notes a wide-spread tradition of lawlessness, a tradition which has been manifested in every area of civic life. The remainder of the article reviews the changing character of interracial relations and their more specific manifestations in social, interracial violence.

* From Allen D. Grimshaw, "Lawlessness and Violence in America and Their Special Manifestations in Changing Negro-White Relationships," *Journal of Negro History*, XLIV (Jan. 1959), 52–56. Copyright © by The Association for the Study of Negro Life and History, Inc. Reprinted by permission.

[1] The research reported in this article is part of a larger study on urban race riots in the United States as a manifestation of social violence under supporting grants from the Samuel S. Fels Fund and the George Leib Harrison Foundation. Strict limitations on space have necessitated the elimination of completer documentation which will be available in the full study. This fuller documentation is available from the author.

[2] Social violence, as the term is here used, refers to assault upon individuals or their property solely or primarily because of their group (ethnic, religious, or racial) affiliations.

OUR LAWLESS HERITAGE [3]

It is possible to make a rough classification of types of lawlessness and violence by reference to the areas of social interaction in which such lawlessness and violence occur. The two categories which emerge from such simple classification overlap, but are nonetheless distinguishable. The first category, that of ethnic violence includes, in addition to Negro-white social violence, conflict and violence focussed on religion and nativity. While the motivation behind much of this violence falls more accurately into the secular area of economic and political violence, the manifest reasons for "punishing" religious and nationality and racial groups have usually referred to religious, cultural and "racial" differences distinguishing these groups from "real Americans."

An anti-Catholic tradition, which has been expressed even in the 20th Century, was responsible for frequent eruptions in the last century, particularly in the period before the Civil War. In the three decades immediately preceding that war, street fights were frequent; sometimes taking on the proportions of major riots, convents and other religious edifices were attacked and sometimes destroyed, and Catholics both within and without the Church hierarchy were subject to constant vilification and occasional physical assault. This anti-Catholicism, particularly as related to an expression of Native-Americanism and the "Know-Nothing" movement, was most frequently directed against Irish Catholics, perhaps because they were resistant to accepting a subservient accommodative status, and had significant economic and political overtones. Jews and Mormons, to mention only two other religious communities, have also been the focus of hostility and violence.

While the Irish Catholics may have received the brunt of the animus and overt violence in Native American riots, they were by no means the only ethnic group attacked. Almost all immigrant groups went through a period of unpopularity, an unpopularity inextricably tied up with their status as perceived economic and political threats to the "older" immigrant groups. Groups distinguishable from the larger population by virtue of physical characteristics were a particular focus of hostility. Assaults upon the indigenous Indian population, commonplace throughout the historical period, were certainly not always necessary for the protection of the white population. A growing resentment toward the Chinese, originally imported as laborers on the transcontinental railroads, culminated in anti-Chinese riots in the closing decades of the 19th Century. Treatment of Mexican-Americans in the American Southwest has been similar to treatment of Negro-Americans in the American South. And the decade of the 1940's saw attacks not only on the civil rights of, but also against the persons and property of Japanese-Americans and Mexican-Americans as well as against Negroes.

The second general category includes a variety of secular types of violence. Most important here are lawlessness and violence growing out of politics and the relations of the populace to the government and out of economic competition. The Republic itself

---

[3] The title of this section is taken from James Truslow Adams, "Our Lawless Heritage," *Atlantic Monthly*, 142, 6, Dec. 1928: 732–740.

originated in an armed rebellion against the then established government. Like all civil wars and internecine strife, the Revolutionary War was a particularly vicious one, and the treatment accorded Loyalists by "Patriots" was no more gentle than that accorded the central figure in any lynching. The new government hardly found its constituents more tractable. Revolt against the new Republic was manifested in Shay's Rebellion in Massachusetts in 1787, in Pennyslvania's Whiskey Rebellion in 1794, in smuggling and trading with the enemy in the War of 1812 and in the Draft Riots of the Civil War. In the Depression of the 1930's the agrarian population manifested its hostility to the government in the "Penny Bankrupt Sales" and in other rural disturbances. Political hostility has not been limited to direct action against the government. The last century saw spectacular election riots, and elections even today are often characterized by sharp violations of the law.[4]

Economic strife has erupted into violence countless times in the last one hundred years. No major industry accepted unionization without a struggle, but in some, such as the railroads and the mines, the struggle assumed the character of wars. "Bloody Harlan" and the "Herrin Massacre," the Haymarket riot and the Homestead strike, these names conjure up a pageant of lawlessness and violence continuing well into the present century. Assassination and terrorism have been used by both labor and management, and in the "Big Steel" strikes of the 'Thirties the steel companies spent thousands upon thousands of dollars on machine guns and tear gas. Indeed, organizing strikes of today, such as that at Koehler, and similar protracted work stoppages, are still occasionally productive of violence.

America has been, then, a land of lawlessness and violence, ranging from spontaneous brawls between servicemen of different branches and schoolboys from different schools, through the "blood feud" and gangster warfare, to the full-fledged military campaigns which have occurred in struggles between class and class and between adherents of different religious faiths. The tradition of lawlessness includes both a contempt of parking regulations and an admiration of gangster heroes and, on the other hand, an excess zeal in the administration of "vigilante justice," "lynch law," and "six-shooter law" on the frontier. Some areas, such as Harlan County in Kentucky and "Bloody" Williamson in Illinois,[5] have run practically the full gamut of types of social violence suggested above. But there is practically no section of the United States which has not, at one time or another, been a center of lawlessness and violence. If there is less actual participation in violence today, and if Americans must sublimate their propensities to violence by watching television, the potentiality still remains.

The violence and bloodshed which has accompanied adjustments in the accommodative pattern between whites and Negroes in the United States is not unique to interracial relations. It is a thesis of the research on which this article is based that the violence which occurs in interracial relations is an inevitable product of assaults upon the

---

[4] E.g., illegal disfranchisement of the Negro electorate in some Southern States.

[5] For a journalistic but suggestive account of violence in one such area see Paul M. Angle, *Bloody Williamson,* New York, 1952.

accommodative pattern. Further research on the forms of violence which have been listed in this brief outline will, the writer believes, demonstrate that all social violence results from the interaction of conceptually similar forces in defining patterns of accommodation.

Civil Disorders*

The National Advisory Commission

CINCINNATI

On Monday, June 12, before order had been restored in Tampa, trouble erupted 940 miles away in Cincinnati.

Beginning in October, 1965, assaults on middle-aged white women, several of whom were murdered, had generated an atmosphere of fear. When the "Cincinnati Strangler" was tentatively identified as a Negro, a new element of tension was injected into relations between the races.

In December, 1966, a Negro jazz musician named Posteal Laskey was arrested and charged with one of the murders. In May of 1967 he was convicted and sentenced to death. Two of the principal witnesses against Laskey were Negroes. Nevertheless, many Negroes felt that, because of the charged atmosphere, he had not received a fair trial.

They were further aroused when, at about the same time, a white man, convicted of manslaughter in the death of his girlfriend, received a suspended sentence. Although the cases were dissimilar, there was talk in the Negro community that the difference in the sentences demonstrated a double standard of justice for white and for black.

A drive began in the Negro community to raise funds for an appeal. Laskey's cousin, Peter Frakes, began walking the streets on behalf of this appeal carrying a sandwich board declaring: "Cincinnati Guilty—Laskey Innocent." After warning him several times, police arrested Frakes on a charge of blocking pedestrian traffic.

Many Negroes viewed his arrest as evidence of police harassment, similar to the apparently selective enforcement of the city's anti-loitering ordinance. Between January, 1966, and June, 1967, 170 of some 240 persons arrested under the ordinance were Negro.

Frakes was arrested at 12:35 A.M. on Sunday, June 11. That evening, concurrently with the commencement of a Negro Baptist Convention, it was announced in one of the churches that a meeting to protest the Frakes arrest and the anti-loitering or-

* From *Report of the National Advisory Commission on Civil Disorders* (New York: Bantam Books, Inc., 1968), pp. 47–52, 224–36.

dinance would be held the following night on the grounds of a junior high school in the Avondale District.

Part of the significance of such a protest meeting lay in the context of past events. Without the city's realizing what was occurring, over the years protest through political and nonviolent channels had become increasingly difficult for Negroes. To young, militant Negroes, especially, such protest appeared to have become almost futile.

Although the city's Negro population had been rising swiftly—in 1967, 135,000 out of the city's 500,000 residents were Negroes—there was only one Negro on the city council. In the 1950's, with a far smaller Negro population, there had been two. Negroes attributed this to dilution of the Negro vote through abolition of the proportional representation system of electing the nine councilmen. When a Negro received the largest total vote of any of the councilmen—traditionally the criterion for choosing the mayor—tradition had been cast aside, and a white man was picked for mayor.

Although by 1967, 40 percent of the school children were Negro, there was only one Negro on the Board of Education. Of 81 members of various city commissions, only one was a Negro.

Under the leadership of the NAACP, picketing, to protest lack of Negro membership in building trades unions, took place at the construction site of a new city convention hall. It produced no results. When the Reverend Fred Shuttlesworth, who had been one of the leaders of the Birmingham demonstrations of 1963, staged a protest against alleged discriminatory practices at the County Hospital, he and his followers were arrested and convicted of trespassing.

Traditional Negro leaders drawn from the middle class lost influence as promises made by the city produced petty results. In the spring of 1967, a group of 14 white and 14 Negro business and community leaders, called the Committee of 28, talked about 2,000 job openings for young Negroes. Only 65 materialized. Almost one out of every eight Cincinnati Negroes were unemployed. Two of every five Negro families were living on or below the border of poverty.

A study of the West End section of the city indicated that one out of every four Negro men living there was out of work. In one public housing area two-thirds of the fathers were missing. Of private housing occupied by Negroes, one-fourth was overcrowded, and half was deteriorated or dilapidated.

In the 90-degree temperature of Monday, June 12th, as throughout the summer, Negro youngsters roamed the streets. The two swimming pools available to them could accommodate only a handful. In the Avondale section—once a prosperous white middle class community, but now the home of more than half the city's Negro population— Negro youths watched white workers going to work at white-owned stores and businesses. One youth began to count the number of delivery trucks being driven by Negroes. During the course of the afternoon, of the 52 trucks he counted, only one had a Negro driver. His sampling was remarkably accurate. According to a study conducted by the Equal Employment Opportunities Commission, less than 2 percent of truck drivers in the Cincinnati area are Negro.

Late in the afternoon the youth began to interfere with deliveries being made by white drivers. Dr. Bruce Green, president of the local NAACP chapter, was notified. Dr. Green asked his colleague, Dr. Robert Reid, the director of the Opportunities Industrialization Center, to go and try to calm the youngsters. Dr. Reid found several whom he knew, and convinced them to go with him to the Avondale Special Services Office to talk things over.

They were drawing up plans for a meeting with merchants of the Avondale area when word came of an altercation at a nearby drugstore. Several of the youths left the meeting and rushed over to the store. Dr. Reid followed them. The owner of the store was complaining to the police that earlier the youths had been interfering with his business; he declared that he wasn't going to stand for it.

Dr. Reid was attempting to mediate when a police sergeant arrived and asked the officers what was going on. One allegedly replied that they had been called in because "young nigger punks were disrupting deliveries to the stores."

A dispute arose between Dr. Reid and the sergeant as to whether the officer had said "nigger." After further discussion the sergeant told the kids to "break it up!" Dr. Reid, together with some of the youngsters, returned to the Special Services Office. After talking to the youngsters again, Dr. Reid left to attend a meeting elsewhere.

Soon after, some of the youngsters headed for the junior high school, where the meeting protesting the Frakes arrest and the anti-loitering ordinance was scheduled to take place.

The police department, alerted to the possibility of a disturbance, mobilized. However, the police were wary of becoming, as some Negro militants had complained, an inciting factor. Some months earlier, when Ku Klux Klansmen had been attracted to the scene of a speech by Stokely Carmichael, a Negro crowd, reacting to the heavy police patrolling, had gathered about the car of a plainclothesman and attempted to overturn it. On Monday, June 12, the department decided to withhold its men from the immediate area of the meeting.

It appeared for a time as if this policy might be rewarded. Near the end of the rally, however, a Negro real estate broker arose to defend the police and the anti-loitering ordinance. The crowd, including the youngsters who had had the encounter with the police officers only a short time earlier, was incensed. When the meeting broke up, a missile was hurled through the window of a nearby church. A small fire was set in the street. A Molotov cocktail was thrown through the window of a drug store.

The police were able to react quickly. There was only one major confrontation between them and the mob. Little resistance was offered.

Although windows were broken in some two dozen stores, there was virtually no looting. There were 14 arrests, some unconnected with the disturbance. Among those arrested was a community worker, now studying for a doctorate at Brandeis University. When he went to the area to help get people off the streets, he was arrested and charged with loitering.

The next morning a judge of the Municipal Court, before whom most of the persons charged were to be brought, said he intended to mete out the maximum sentence to anyone found guilty of a riot-connected offense. Although the judge later told the Commission that he knew his statement was a "violation of judicial ethics," he said that he made it because the "city was in a state of siege," and he intended it to act as a deterrent against further violence.

Maximum sentences were, in fact, pronounced by the judge on all convicted in his court, regardless of the circumstances of the arrest, or the background of the persons arrested. Police were charging most white persons arrested with disorderly conduct—for which the maximum sentence is 30 days in jail and a $100 fine. Many Negroes, however, were charged with violation of the Riot Act—for which the maximum sentence is one year in jail plus a $500 fine. The consequent impression among a major portion of the Negro community was of discriminatory justice.

Tuesday morning Negro leaders presented a list of 11 demands and grievances stemming from the Monday night meeting to the municipal government. Included were demands for repeal of the anti-loitering law, release of all prisoners arrested during the disturbance, full employment for Negroes, and equal justice in the courts.

Municipal officials agreed that the city council would consider the demands. However, they rejected a suggestion that they attend an open-air meeting of residents in the Avondale section. City leaders did not want to give stature to the militants by recognizing them as the *de facto* representatives of the community. Yet, by all indications, the militants were the only persons with influence on the people on the streets.

Mayor Walton H. Bachrach declared that he was "quite surprised" by the disturbance because the council had "worked like hell" to help Negroes. Municipal officials, whose contacts were, as in other cities, generally with a few middle-class Negroes, appeared not to realize the volatile frustrations of Negroes in the ghetto.

Early in the evening a crowd, consisting mostly of teenagers and young adults, began to gather in the Avondale District. When, after a short time, no one appeared to give direction, they began to mill about. A few minutes before 7:00 P.M. cars were stoned and windows were broken. Police moved in to disperse the gathering.

Fires were set. When firemen reached the scene they were barraged with rocks and bottles. A full-scale confrontation took place between police riot squads and the Negro crowd. As police swept the streets, people scattered. According to the chief of police, at approximately 7:15, "All hell broke loose."

The disorder leaped to other sections of the city. The confusion and rapidity with which it spread made it almost impossible to determine its scope.

Many reports of fires set by Molotov cocktails, cars being stoned, and windows being broken were received by the police. A white motorist—who died three weeks later—and a Negro sitting on his porch suffered gunshot wounds. Rumors spread of Negro gangs raiding white neighborhoods, of shootings, and of organization of the riot. Nearly all of them were determined later to be unfounded.

At 9:40 P.M., following a request for aid to surrounding communities, Mayor Bachrach placed a call to the Governor asking for mobilization of the National Guard.

At 2:30 A.M., Wednesday the first Guard units appeared on the streets. They followed a policy of restraint in the use of weapons. Few shots were fired. Two hours later, the streets were quiet. Most of the damage was minor. Of 40-odd fires reported before dawn, only 11 resulted in a loss of more than $1,000. The fire department log listed four as having caused major damage.

That afternoon the city council held an open session. The chamber was jammed with Negro residents, many of whom gave vociferous support as their spokesmen criticized the city administration. When the audience became unruly, a detail of National Guardsmen was stationed outside the council chamber. Their presence resulted in a misunderstanding, causing many of the Negroes to walk out, and the meeting to end.

Wednesday night there were virtually no reports of riotous activity until 9:00 P.M., when scattered incidents of violence again began to take place. One person was injured by a gunshot.

Despite fears of a clash between Negroes and SAMS—white Southern Appalachian migrants whose economic conditions paralleled those of Negroes—such a clash was averted.

H. "Rap" Brown, arriving in the city on Thursday, attempted to capitalize on the discontent by presenting a list of 20 "demands." Their principal effect would have been total removal of all white persons, whatever their capacity, from the ghetto area. Demand No. 18 stated that "at any meeting to settle grievances . . . any white proposal or white representative objected to by black representatives must be rejected automatically." No. 20 demanded a veto power over police officers patrolling the community.

His appearance had no galvanizing effect. Although scattered incidents occurred for three days after the arrival of the National Guard, the disorder never returned to its early intensity.

Of 63 reported injuries, 12 were serious enough to require hospitalization; 56 of the persons injured were white. Most of the injuries resulted from thrown objects or glass shards. Of the 107 persons arrested Tuesday night, when the main disturbance took place, 75 were 21 years of age or younger. Of the total of 404 persons arrested, 128 were juveniles, and 338 were 26 years of age or younger. Of the adults arrested, 29 percent were unemployed.

•   •   •

THE POSTWAR PERIOD

White opinion in some quarters of America had begun to shift to a more sympathetic regard for Negroes during the New Deal, and the war had accelerated that movement. Thoughtful whites had been painfully aware of the contradiction in opposing Nazi racial philosophy with racially segregated military units. In the postwar years, American racial attitudes became more liberal as new nonwhite nations emerged in Asia and Africa and took increasing responsibilities in international councils.

Against this background, the growing size of the Northern Negro vote made civil rights a major issue in national elections and, ultimately, in 1957, led to the federal Civil Rights Commission, which had the power to investigate discriminatory conditions throughout the country and to recommend corrective measures to the President. Northern and Western states outlawed discrimination in employment, housing, and public accommodations, while the NAACP, in successive court victories, ended racially restrictive covenants in housing, segregation in interstate transportation, and discrimination in publicly-owned recreational facilities. The NAACP helped register voters, and in 1954,

Brown v. *Board of Education* became the triumphant climax to the NAACP's campaign against educational segregation in the public schools of the South.

CORE, demonstrating in the Border States, its major focus on public accommodations, began experimenting with direct-action techniques to open employment opportunities. In 1947, in conjunction with the Fellowshp of Reconciliation, CORE conducted a "Journey of Reconciliation"—what would later be called a "Freedom Ride"—in the states of the Upper South to test compliance with the Supreme Court decision outlawing segregation on interstate buses. The resistance met by riders in some areas, the sentencing of two to 30 days on a North Carolina road gang, dramatized the gap between American democratic theory and practice.

But what captured the imagination of the nation and of the Negro community in particular, and what was chiefly reponsible for the growing use of direct-action techniques, was the Montgomery, Alabama, bus boycott of 1955–1956, which catapulted into national prominence the Reverend Martin Luther King, Jr. Like the founders of CORE, King held to a Gandhian belief in the principles of pacifism.

Even before a court decision obtained by NAACP attorneys in November 1956 desegregated the Montgomery buses, a similar movement had started in Tallahassee, Florida. Afterward another one developed in Birmingham, Alabama. In 1957, the Tuskegee Negroes undertook a three-year boycott of local merchants after the state legislature gerrymandered nearly all of the Negro voters outside of the town's boundaries. In response to a lawsuit filed by the NAACP, the Supreme Court ruled the Tuskegee gerrymander illegal.

These events were widely heralded. A "new negro" had emerged in the South—militant, no longer fearful of white hoodlums or mobs, and ready to use his collective weight to achieve his ends. In this mood, King established the Southern Christian Leadership Conference in 1957 to coordinate direct-action activities in Southern cities.

Negro protest had now moved in a vigorous fashion into the South, and like similar activities in the North, it was concentrated in the urban ghettos.

THE PERSISTENCE OF DISCRIMINATION

Nonviolent direct action attained popularity not only because of the effectiveness of King's leadership but because the older techniques of legal and legislative action had had limited success. Impressive as the advances in the 15 years after World War II were, in spite of state laws and Supreme Court decisions, something was still clearly wrong. Negroes were disfranchised in most of the South, though in the 12 years following the outlawing of the white primary in 1944, the number of Negroes registered in Southern states had risen from about 250,000 to nearly a million and a quarter. Supreme Court decisions desegregating transportation facilities were still being largely ignored in the South. Discrimination in employment and housing continued, not only in the South but also in Northern states with model civil rights laws. The Negro unemployment rate steadily moved upward after 1954. The South reacted to the Supreme Court's decision on school desegregation by attempting to outlaw the NAACP, intimidating civil rights leaders, bringing "massive resistance" to the Court's decision, curtailing Negro voter registration, and forming White Citizens' Councils.

REVOLUTION OF RISING EXPECTATIONS

At the same time, Negro attitudes were changing. In what has been described as a "revolution in expectations," Negroes were gaining a new sense of self-respect and a new self-image as a result of the civil rights movement and their own advancement. King and others were demonstrating that nonviolent direct action could succeed in the South. New laws and court decisions and increasing support of white public opinion gave American Negroes a new confidence in the future.

Negroes no longer felt that they had to accept the humiliations of second-class citizenship. Ironically, it was the very successes in the legislatures and the courts that, more perhaps than any other single factor, led to intensified Negro expectations and resulting dissatisfaction with the limitations of legal and legislative programs. Increasing Negro impatience accounted for the rising tempo of nonviolent direct action in the late 1950's, culminating in the student sit-ins of 1960 and the inauguration of what is popularly known as the "Civil Rights Revolution" or the "Negro Revolt."

Many believe that the Montgomery boycott ushered in this Negro Revolt, and there is no doubt that, in projecting the image of King and his techniques, it had great importance. But the decisive break with traditional techniques came with the college student sit-ins that swept the South in the winter and spring of 1960. In dozens of communities in the Upper South, the Atlantic coastal states, and Texas, student demonstrations secured the desegregation of lunch counters in drug and variety stores. Arrests were numbered in the thousands, and brutality was evident in scores of communities. In the Deep South the campaign ended in failure, even in instances where hundreds had been arrested, as in Montgomery; Orangeburg, South Carolina; and Baton Rouge. But the youth had captured the imagination of the Negro community and to a remarkable extent of the whole nation.

STUDENT INVOLVEMENT

The Negro protest movement would never be the same again. The Southern college students shook the power structure of the Negro community, made direct action temporarily pre-eminent as a civil rights tactic, speeded up the process of social change in race relations, and ultimately turned the Negro protest organizations toward a deep concern with the economic and social problems of the masses.

Involved in this was a gradual shift in both tactics and goals: from legal to direct action, from middle and upper class to mass action, from attempts to guarantee the Negro's constitutional rights to efforts to secure economic policies giving him equality of opportunity, from appeals to the sense of fair play of white Americans to demands based upon power in the black ghetto.

The successes of the student movement threatened existing Negro leadership and precipitated a spirited rivalry among civil rights organizations. The NAACP and SCLC associated themselves with the student movement. The organizing meeting of the Student Nonviolent Coordinating Committee (SNCC) at Raleigh, North Carolina, in April 1960 was called by Martin Luther King, but within a year the youth considered King too cautious and broke with him.

The NAACP now decided to make direct action a major part of its strategy and organized and reactivated college and youth chapters in Southern and Border states. CORE still unknown to the general public, installed James Farmer as national director in January 1961, and that spring joined the front rank of civil rights organizations with the famous Freedom Ride to Alabama and Mississippi that dramatized the persistence of segregated public transportation. A bus-burning resulted in Alabama, and hundreds of demonstrators spent a month or more in Mississippi prisons. Finally, a new order from the Interstate Commerce Commission desegregating all interstate transportation facilities received partial compliance.

ORGANIZATIONAL RIVALRIES

Disagreement over strategy and tactics inevitably became intertwined with personal and organizational rivalries. Each civil rights group felt the need for proper credit in order to obtain the prestige and financial contributions necessary to maintain and expand its own programs. The local and national, individual and organizational clashes only stimulated competition and activity that further accelerated the pace of social change.

Yet there were differences in style. CORE was the most interracial. SCLC appeared to be the most deliberate. SNCC staff workers lived on subsistence allowances and seemed to regard going to jail as a way of life. The NAACP continued the most varied programs, retaining a strong emphasis on court litigation, maintaining a highly effective lobby at the national capital, and engaging in direct-action campaigns. The National Urban League, under the leadership of Whitney M. Young Jr., appointed executive director in 1961, became more outspoken and talked more firmly to businessmen who had previously been treated with utmost tact and caution.

THE ROLE OF WHITES

The role of whites in the protest movement gradually changed. Instead of occupying positions of leadership, they found themselves relegated to the role of followers. Whites were likely to be suspect in the activist organizations. Negroes had come to feel less dependent on whites, more confident of their own power, and they demanded that their leaders be black. The NAACP had long since acquired Negro leadership but continued to welcome white liberal support. SCLC and SNCC were from the start Negro-led and Negro-dominated. CORE became predominantly Negro as it expanded in 1962 and 1963; today all executives are Negro, and a constitutional amendment adopted in 1965 officially limited white leadership in the chapters.

THE BLACK MUSLIMS

A major factor intensifying the civil rights movement was widespread Negro unemployment and poverty; an important force in awakening Negro protest was the meteoric rise to national prominence of the Black Muslims, established around 1930. The organization reached the peak of its influence when more progress toward equal rights was being made than ever before in American history while at the same time economic opportunity for the poorest groups in the urban ghettos was stagnating.

Increasing unemployment among Negroes, combined with the revolution in expectations, created a climate in which the Black Muslims thrived. They preached a vision of the doom of the white "devils" and the coming dominance of the black man, promised a utopian paradise of a separate territory within the United States for a Negro state, and offered a practical program of building Negro business through hard work, thrift, and racial unity. To those willing to submit to the rigid discipline of the movement, the Black Muslims organization gave a sense of purpose and dignity.

"FREEDOM NOW!"

As the direct-action tactics took more dramatic form, as the civil rights groups began to articulate the needs of the masses and draw some of them to their demonstrations, the protest movement in 1963 assumed a new note of urgency, a demand for complete "Freedom Now!" Direct action returned to the Northern cities, taking the form of massive protests against economic, housing and educational inequities, and a fresh wave of demonstrations swept the South from Cambridge, Maryland, to Birmingham, Alabama. Northern Negroes launched street demonstrations against discrimination in the building trade unions and, the following winter, school boycotts against de facto segregation.

In the North, 1963 and 1964 brought the beginning of the waves of civil disorders in Northern urban centers. In the South, incidents occurred of brutal white resistance to the civil rights movement, beginning with the murder of Mississippi Negro leader Medgar Evers and four Negro schoolgirls in a church in Birmingham. These disorders and the events in the South are detailed in the introduction to Chapter 1, the *Profiles of Disorder.*

The massive anti-negro actions in Birmingham and numerous other Southern cities during the spring of 1963, compelled the nation to face the problem of race prejudice in the South. President Kennedy affirmed that racial discrimination was a moral issue and asked Congress for a major civil rights bill. But a major impetus for what was to be the Civil Rights Act of 1964 was the March on Washington in August 1963.

Early in the year, A. Philip Randolph issued a call for a March on Washington to dramatize the need for jobs and to press for a federal commitment to job action. At about the same time, Protestant, Jewish, and Catholic churches sought and obtained representation on the March committee. Although the AFL-CIO national council refused to endorse the March, a number of labor leaders and international unions participated.

Reversing an earlier stand, President Kennedy approved the March. A quarter of a million people, about 20 percent of them white, participated. It was more than a summation of the past years of struggle and aspiration. It symbolized certain new directions: a deeper concern for the economic problems of the masses; more involvement of white moderates and new demands from the most militant, who implied that only a revolutionary change in American institutions would permit Negroes to achieve the dignity of citizens.

President Kennedy had set the stage for the Civil Rights Act of 1964. After his death President Johnson took forceful and effective action to secure its enactment. The law settled the public accommodations issue in the South's major cities. Its voting section, however, promised more than it could accomplish. Martin Luther King and SCLC dramatized the issue locally with demonstrations at Selma, Alabama, in the spring of 1965. Again the national government was forced to intervene, and a new and more effective voting law was passed.

FAILURES OF DIRECT ACTION

Birmingham had made direct action respectable, but Selma which drew thousands of white moderates from the North made direct action fashionable. Yet as early as 1964, it was becoming evident that, like legal action, direct action has limited usefulness.

In deep South states like Mississippi and Alabama, direct action had failed to desegregate public accommodations with the sit-ins of 1960–1961. A major reason was that Negroes lacked the leverage of the vote. The demonstrations of the early 1960's had been successful principally in places like Atlanta, Nashville, Durham, Winston-Salem, Louisville, Savannah, New Orleans, Charleston, and Dallas—where Negroes voted and could swing elections. Beginning in 1961 Robert Moses of SNCC, with the cooperation of CORE and NAACP, established voter registration projects in the cities and county seats of Mississippi. He succeeded in registering only a handful of Negroes, but by 1964, he had generated enough support throughout the country to enable the Mississippi Freedom Democratic Party, which he had created, to challenge dramatically the seating of the official white delegates from the state at the Democratic National Convention.

In the black ghettos of the North direct action also largely failed. Street demonstrations did compel employers, from supermarkets to banks, to add Negroes to their work force in Northern and Western cities, and even in some Southern cities where the Negroes had considerable buying power. However, separate and inferior schools, slum housing, and police hostility proved invulnerable to direct attack.

NEW DIRECTIONS

But while Negroes were being hired in increasing numbers, mass unemployment and underemployment remained. As economist Vivian Henderson pointed out in his testimony before the Commission:

> No one can deny that all Negroes have benefited from civil rights laws and desegregation in public life in one way or another. The fact is, however, that the masses of Negroes have not experienced tangible benefits in a significant way. This is so in education and housing. It is critically so in the area of jobs and economic security. Expectations of Negro masses for equal job opportunity programs have fallen far short of fulfillment.

Negroes have made gains. . . . There have been important gains. But . . . the masses of Negroes have been virtually untouched by those gains.

Faced with the intransigence of the deep South and the inadequacy of direct action to solve the problems of the slum dwellers, Negro protest organizations began to diverge. The momentum toward unity, apparent in 1963, was lost. At the very time that white support for the protest movement was rising markedly, militant Negroes felt increasingly isolated from the American scene. On two things, however, all segments of the protest movement agreed: (1) future civil rights activity would have to focus on the economic and social discrimination in the urban ghettos and (2) while demonstrations would still have a place, the major weapon would have to be the political potential of the black masses.

By the middle of the decade, many militant Negro members of SNCC and CORE began to turn away from American society and the "middle-class way of life." Cynical about the liberals and the leaders of organized labor, they regarded compromise, even as a temporary tactical device, as anathema. They talked more of "revolutionary" changes in the social structure, of retaliatory violence, and increasingly rejected white assistance. They insisted that Negro power alone could compel the white "ruling class" to make concessions. Yet they also spoke of an alliance of Negroes and unorganized lower-class whites to overthrow the "power structure" of capitalists, politicians and bureaucratic labor leaders who exploited the poor of both races by dividing them through an appeal to race prejudice.

At the same time that their activities declined, other issues, particularly Vietnam, diverted the attention of the country, including some Negro leaders, from the issue of equality. Reduced financing made it increasingly difficult to support staff personnel, even on a subsistence basis. Most important was the increasing frustration of expectations that affected the direct-action advocates of the early 1960's—the sense of futility growing out of the feeling that progress had turned out to be "tokenism," that the compromises of the white community were sedatives rather than solutions and that the current methods of Negro protest were doing little for the masses of the race.

As frustration grew, the ideology and rhetoric of a number of civil rights activists became angrier. One man more than any other—a black man who grew up believing whites had murdered his father—became the spokesman for this anger: Malcolm X, who perhaps best embodied the belief that racism was so deeply ingrained in white America that appeals to conscience would bring no fundamental change.

"BLACK POWER"

In this setting the rhetoric of "Black Power" developed. The precipitating occasion was the Meredith March from Memphis to Jackson in June 1966, but the slogan expressed tendencies that had been present for a long time and had been gaining strength in the Negro community.

Black Power first articulated a mood rather than a program—disillusionment and alienation from white America and independence, race pride, and self-respect, or "black consciousness." Having become a household phrase, the term generated intense discussion of its real meaning, and a broad spectrum of ideologies and programmatic proposals emerged.

In politics, Black Power meant independent action—Negro control of the political power of the black ghettos and its conscious use to better slum dwellers' conditions. It could take the form of organizing a black political party or controlling the political machinery within the ghetto without the guidance or support of white politicians. Where predominantly Negro areas lacked Negroes in elective office, whether in the rural Black Belt of the South or in the urban centers, Black Power advocates sought the election of Negroes by voter registration campaigns, by getting out the vote, and by working for redrawing electoral districts. The basic belief was that only a well-organized and cohesive bloc of Negro voters could provide for the needs of the black masses. Even some Negro politicians allied to the major political parties adopted the term "Black Power" to describe their interest in the Negro vote.

In economic terms, Black Power meant creating independent, self-sufficient Negro business enterprise, not only by encouraging Negro entrepreneurs but also by forming Negro cooperatives in the ghettos and in the predominantly black rural counties of the South. In the area of education, Black Power called for local community control of the public schools in the black ghettos.

Throughout, the emphasis was on self-help, racial unity, and, among the most militant, retaliatory violence, the latter ranging from the legal right of self-defense to attempts to justify looting and arson in ghetto riots, guerrilla warfare and armed rebellion.

Phrases like "Black Power," "Black Consciousness," and "Black is Beautiful," enjoyed an extensive currency in the Negro community, even within the NAACP and among relatively conservative politicians, but particularly among young intellectuals and Afro-American student groups on predominantly white college campuses. Expressed in its most extreme form by small, often local, fringe groups, the Black Power ideology became associated with SNCC and CORE.

Generally regarded as the most militant among the important Negro protest organizations, they have different interpretations of the Black Power doctrine. SNCC calls for totally independent political action outside the established political parties, as with the Black Panther Party in Lowndes County, Alabama; questions the value of political alliances with other groups until Negroes have themselves built a substantial base of independent political power; applauds the idea of guerrilla warfare and regards riots as rebellions.

CORE has been more flexible. Approving the SNCC strategy, it also advocates working within the Democratic Party; forming alliances with other groups and, while seeking to justify riots as the natural explosion of an oppressed people against intolerable conditions, advocates violence only in self-defense. Both groups favor cooperatives, but CORE has seemed more inclined toward job-training programs and developing a Negro entrepreneurial class, based upon the market within the black ghettos.

OLD WINE IN NEW BOTTLES

What is new about "Black Power" is phraseology rather than substance. Black Consciousness has roots in the organization of Negro churches and mutual benefit societies in the early days of the republic, the antebellum Negro convention movement, the Negro colonization schemes of the 19th century, Du Bois' concept of Pan-Africanism, Booker T. Washington's advocacy of race pride, self-help, and racial solidarity, the Harlem Renaissance, and the Garvey movement. The decade after World War I—which saw the militant, race-proud "new Negro," the relatively widespread theory of retaliatory violence, and the high tide of the Negro-support-of-Negro-business ideology—exhibits striking parallels with the 1960's.

The theme of retaliatory violence is hardly new for American Negroes. Most racial disorders in American history until recent years, were characterized by white attacks on Negroes. But Negroes retaliated violently in the past.

Black Power rhetoric and ideology actually express a lack of power. The slogan emerged when the Negro protest movement was slowing down, when it was finding increasing resistance to its changing goals, when it discovered that nonviolent direct action was no more a panacea than legal action, when CORE and SNCC were declining in terms of activity, membership, and financial support. This combination of circumstances provoked anger deepened by impotence. Powerless to make any fundamental changes in the life of the masses—powerless, that is, to compel white America to make those changes—many advocates of Black Power have retreated into an unreal world, where they see an outnumbered and poverty-stricken minority organizing itself separately from whites and creating sufficient power to force white America to grant its demands. To date, the evidence suggests that the situation is much like that of the 1840's, when a small group of intellectuals advocated slave insurrections, but stopped short of organizing them.

The Black Power advocates of today consciously feel that they are the most militant group in the Negro protest movement. Yet they have retreated from a direct confrontation with American society on the issue of integration and, by preaching separatism, unconsciously function as an accommodation to white racism. Much of their economic program, as well as their interest in Negro history, self-help, racial solidarity and separation, is reminiscent of Booker T. Washington. The rhetoric is different, but the ideas are remarkably similar.

THE MEANING

By 1967, whites could point to the demise of slavery, the decline of illiteracy among Negroes, the legal protection provided by the constitutional amendments and civil rights legislation, and the growing size of the Negro middle class. Whites would call it Negro progress from slavery to freedom toward equality.

Negroes could point to the doctrine of white supremacy, its widespread acceptance, its persistence after emancipation, and its influence on the definition of the place of Negroes in American life. They could point to their long fight for full citizenship, when they had active opposition from most of the white population and little or no support from the government. They could see progress toward equality accompanied by bitter resistance. Perhaps most of all, they could feel the persistent, pervasive racism that kept them in inferior segregated schools, restricted them to ghettos, barred them from fair employment, provided double standards in courts of justice, inflicted bodily harm on their children, and blighted their lives with a sense of hopelessness and despair.

In all of this and in the context of professed ideals, Negroes would find more retrogression than progress, more rejection than acceptance.

Until the middle of the 20th century, the course of Negro protest movements in the United States, except for slave revolts, was based in the cities of the North, where Negroes enjoyed sufficient freedom to mount a sustained protest. It was in the cities, North and South, that Negroes had their greatest independence and mobility. It was natural, therefore, for black protest movements to be urban-based—and, until the last dozen years or so, limited to the North. As Negroes migrated from the South, the mounting strength of their votes in Northern cities became a vital element in drawing the federal government into the defense of the civil rights of Southern Negroes. White rural Negroes today face great racial problems, the major unsolved questions that touch the core of Negro life stem from discrimination embedded in urban housing, employment, and education.

Over the years the character of Negro protest has changed. Originally it was a white liberal and Negro upper class movement aimed at securing the constitutional rights of Negroes through propaganda, lawsuits, and legislation. In recent years the emphasis in tactics shifted first to direct action and then—among the most militant—to the rhetoric of "Black Power." The role of white liberals declined as Negroes came to direct the struggle. At the same time the Negro protest movement became more of a mass movement, with increasing participation from the working classes. As these changes were occurring, and while substantial progress was being made to secure constitutional rights for the Negroes, the goals of the movement were broadened. Protest groups now demand special efforts to overcome the Negro's poverty and cultural deprivation—conditions that cannot be erased simply by ensuring constitutional rights.

The central thrust of Negro protest in the current period has aimed at the inclusion of Negroes in American society on a basis of full equality rather than at a fundamental transformation of American institutions. There have been elements calling for a revolutionary overthrow of the American social system or for a complete withdrawal of Negroes from American society. But these solutions have had little popular support. Negro protest, for the most part, has been firmly rooted in the basic values of American society, seeking not their destruction but their fulfillment.

^aLetter from Birmingham Jail*

Martin Luther King, Jr.

April 16, 1963

MY DEAR FELLOW CLERGYMEN:

While confined here in the Birmingham city jail, I came across your recent statement calling my present activities "unwise and untimely." Seldom do I pause to answer criticism of my work and ideas. If I sought to answer all the criticisms that cross my desk, my secretaries would have little time for anything other than such correspondence in the course of the day, and I would have no time for constructive work. But since I feel that you are men of genuine good will and that your criticisms are sincerely set forth, I want to try to answer your statement in what I hope will be patient and reasonable terms.

I think I should indicate why I am here in Birmingham, since you have been influenced by the view which argues against "outsiders coming in." I have the honor of serving as president of the Southern Christian Leadership Conference, an organization operating in every southern state, with headquarters in Atlanta, Georgia. We have some eighty-five affiliated organizations across the South, and one of them is the Alabama Christian Movement for Human Rights. Frequently we share staff, educational and financial resources with our affiliates. Several months ago the affiliate here in Birmingham asked us to be on call to engage in a nonviolent direct-action program if such were deemed necessary. We readily consented, and when the hour came we lived up to our promise. So I, along with several members of my staff, am here because I was invited here. I am here because I have organizational ties here.

ᵃ AUTHOR'S NOTE: This response to a published statement by eight fellow clergymen from Alabama (Bishop C. C. J. Carpenter, Bishop Joseph A. Durick, Rabbi Hilton L. Grafman, Bishop Paul Hardin, Bishop Holan B. Harmon, the Reverend George M. Murray, the Reverend Edward V. Ramage and the Reverend Earl Stallings) was composed under somewhat constricting circumstances. Begun on the margins of the newspaper in which the statement appeared while I was in jail, the letter was continued on scraps of writing paper supplied by a friendly Negro trusty, and concluded on a pad my attorneys were eventually permitted to leave me. Although the text remains in substance unaltered, I have indulged in the author's prerogative of polishing it for publication.

* From Martin Luther King, Jr., "Letter from Birmingham Jail, April 16, 1963," in *Why We Can't Wait* (New York: Harper & Row, Publishers, Inc., 1964), pp. 77–100. Copyright © 1963 by Martin Luther King, Jr. Reprinted by permission of Harper & Row, Publishers, Inc.

But more basically, I am in Birmingham because injustice is here. Just as the prophets of the eighth century B.C. left their villages and carried their "thus saith the Lord" far beyond the boundaries of their home towns, and just as the Apostle Paul left his village of Tarsus and carried the gospel of Jesus Christ to the far corners of the Greco-Roman world, so am I compelled to carry the gospel of freedom beyond my own home town. Like Paul, I must constantly respond to the Macedonian call for aid.

Moreover, I am cognizant of the interrelatedness of all communities and states. I cannot sit idly by in Atlanta and not be concerned about what happens in Birmingham. Injustice anywhere is a threat to justice everywhere. We are caught in an inescapable network of mutuality, tied in a single garment of destiny. Whatever affects one directly, affects all indirectly. Never again can we afford to live with the narrow, provincial "outside agitator" idea. Anyone who lives inside the United States can never be considered an outsider anywhere within its bounds.

You deplore the demonstrations taking place in Birmingham. But your statement, I am sorry to say, fails to express a similar concern for the conditions that brought about the demonstrations. I am sure that none of you would want to rest content with the superficial kind of social analysis that deals merely with effects and does not grapple with underlying causes. It is unfortunate that demonstrations are taking place in Birmingham, but it is even more unfortunate that the city's white power structure left the Negro community with no alternative.

In any nonviolent campaign there are four basic steps: collection of the facts to determine whether injustices exist; negotiation; self-purification; and direct action. We have gone through all these steps in Birmingham. There can be no gainsaying the fact that racial injustice engulfs this community. Birmingham is probably the most thoroughly segregated city in the United States. Its ugly record of brutality is widely known. Negroes have experienced grossly unjust treatment in the courts. There have been more unsolved bombings of Negro homes and churches in Birmingham than in any other city in the nation. These are the hard, brutal facts of the case. On the basis of these conditions, Negro leaders sought to negotiate with the city fathers. But the latter consistently refused to engage in good-faith negotiation.

Then, last September, came the opportunity to talk with leaders of Birmingham's economic community. In the course of the negotiations, certain promises were made by the merchants—for example, to remove the stores' humiliating racial signs. On the basis of these promises, the Reverend Fred Shuttlesworth and the leaders of the Alabama Christian Movement for Human Rights agreed to a moratorium on all demonstrations. As the weeks and months went by, we realized that we were the victims of a broken promise. A few signs, briefly removed, returned; the others remained.

As in so many past experiences, our hopes had been blasted, and the shadow of deep disappointment settled upon us. We had no alternative except to prepare for direct action, whereby we would present our very bodies as a means of laying our case before the conscience of the local and the national community. Mindful of the difficulties involved, we decided to undertake a process of self-purification. We began a series of workshops on nonviolence, and we repeatedly asked ourselves: "Are you able to accept blows without retaliating?" "Are you able to endure the ordeal of jail?" We decided to schedule our direct-action program for the Easter season, realizing that except for Christmas, this is the main shopping period of the year. Knowing that a strong economic-withdrawal program would be the by-product of direct action, we felt that this would be the best time to bring pressure to bear on the merchants for the needed change.

Then it occurred to us that Birmingham's mayoralty election was coming up in March, and we speedily decided to postpone action until after election day. When we discovered that the Commissioner of Public Safety, Eugene "Bull" Connor, had piled up enough votes to be in the run-off, we decided again to postpone action until the day after the run-off so that the demonstrations could not be used to cloud the issues. Like many others, we waited to see Mr. Connor defeated, and to this end we endured postponement after postponement. Having aided in this community need, we felt that our direct-action program could be delayed no longer.

You may well ask: "Why direct action? Why sit-ins, marches and so forth? Isn't negotiation a better path?" You are quite right in calling for negotiation. Indeed, this is the very purpose of direct action. Nonviolent direct action seeks to create such a crisis and foster such a tension that a community which has constantly refused to negotiate is forced to confront the issue. It seeks so to dramatize the issue that it can no longer be ignored. My citing the creation of tension as part of the work of the nonviolent-resister may sound rather shocking. But I must confess that I am not afraid of the word "tension." I have earnestly opposed violent tension, but there is a type of constructive, nonviolent tension which is necessary for growth. Just as Socrates felt that it was necessary to create a tension in the mind so that individuals could rise from the bondage of myths and half-truths to the unfettered realm of creative analysis and objective appraisal, so must we see the need for nonviolent gadflies to create the kind of tension in society that will help men rise from the dark depths of prejudice and racism to the majestic heights of understanding and brotherhood.

The purpose of our direct-action program is to create a situation so crisis-packed that it will inevitably open the door to negotiation. I therefore concur with you in your call for negotiation. Too long has our beloved Southland been bogged down in a tragic effort to live in monologue rather than dialogue.

One of the basic points in your statement is that the action that I and my associates have taken in Birmingham is untimely. Some have asked: "Why didn't you give the new city administration time to act?" The only answer that I can give to this query is that the new Birmingham administration must be prodded about as much as the outgoing one, before it will act. We are sadly mistaken if we feel that the election of Albert Boutwell as mayor will bring the millennium to Birmingham. While Mr. Boutwell is a much more gentle person than Mr. Connor, they are both segregationists, dedicated to maintenance of the status quo. I have hope that Mr. Boutwell will be reasonable enough to see the futility of massive resistance to desegregation. But he will not see this without pressure from devotees of civil rights. My friends, I must say to you that we have not made a single gain in civil rights without determined legal and nonviolent pressure. Lamentably, it is an historical fact that privileged groups seldom give up their privileges voluntarily. Individuals may see the moral light and voluntarily give up their unjust posture; but, as Reinhold Niebuhr has reminded us, groups tend to be more immoral than individuals.

We know through painful experience that freedom is never voluntarily given by the oppressor; it must be demanded by the oppressed. Frankly, I have yet to engage in a direct-action campaign that was "well timed" in the view of those who have not suffered unduly from the disease of segregation. For years now I have heard the word "Wait!" It rings in the ear of every Negro with piercing familiarity. This "Wait" has almost always meant "Never." We must come to see, with one of our distinguished jurists, that "justice too long delayed is justice denied."

We have waited for more than 340 years for our constitutional and God-given rights. The nations of Asia and Africa are moving with jetlike speed toward gaining political independence, but we still creep at horse-and-buggy pace toward gaining a cup of coffee at a lunch counter. Perhaps it is easy for those who have never felt the stinging darts of segregation to say, "Wait." But when you have seen vicious mobs lynch your mothers and fathers at will and drown your sisters and brothers at whim; when you have seen hate-filled policemen curse, kick and even kill your black brothers and sisters; when you see the vast majority of your twenty million Negro brothers smothering in an airtight cage of poverty in the midst of an affluent society; when you suddenly find your tongue twisted and your speech stammering as you seek to explain to your six-year-old daughter why she can't go to the public amusement park that has just been advertised on television, and see tears welling up in her eyes when she is told that Funtown is closed to colored children, and see ominous clouds of inferiority beginning to form in her little mental sky, and see her beginning to distort her personality by developing an unconscious bitterness toward white people; when you have to concoct an answer for a five-year-old son who is asking: "Daddy, why do white people treat colored people so mean?"; when you take a cross-country drive and find it necessary to sleep night after night in the uncomfortable corners of your automobile because no motel will accept you; when you are humiliated day in and day out by nagging signs reading "white" and "Colored"; when your first name becomes "nigger," your middle name becomes "boy" (however old you are) and your last name becomes "John," and your wife and mother are never given the respected title "Mrs."; when you are harried by day and haunted by night by the fact that you are a Negro, living constantly at tiptoe stance, never quite knowing what to expect next, and are plagued with inner fears and outer resentments; when you are forever fighting a degenerating sense of "nobodiness"—then you will understand why we find it difficult to wait. There comes a time when the cup of endurance runs over, and men are no longer willing to be plunged into the abyss of despair. I hope, sirs, you can understand our legitimate and unavoidable impatience.

You express a great deal of anxiety over our willingness to break laws. This is certainly a legitimate concern. Since we so diligently urge people to obey the Supreme Court's decision of 1954 outlawing segregation in the public schools, at first glance it may seem rather paradoxical for us consciously to break laws. One may well ask: "How can you advocate breaking some laws and obeying others?" The answer lies in the fact that there are two types of laws: just and unjust. I would be the first to advocate obeying just laws. One has not only a legal but a moral responsibility to obey just laws. Conversely, one has a moral responsibility to disobey unjust laws. I would agree with St. Augustine that "an unjust law is no law at all."

Now, what is the difference between the two? How does one determine whether a law is just or unjust? A just law is a man-made code that squares with the moral law or the law of God. An unjust law is a code that is out of harmony with the moral law. To put it in the terms of St. Thomas Aquinas: An unjust law is a human law that is not rooted in eternal law and natural law. Any law that uplifts human personality is just. Any law that degrades human personality is unjust. All segregation statutes are unjust because segregation distorts the soul and damages the personality. It gives the segregator a false sense of superiority and the segregated a false sense of inferiority. Segregation, to use the terminology of the Jewish philosopher Martin Buber, substitutes an "I-it" relationship for an "I-thou" relationship and ends up relegating persons to the status of things. Hence segregation is not only politically, economically and sociologically unsound, it is morally wrong and sinful. Paul Tillich has said that sin is separation. Is not segregation an existential expression of man's tragic separation, his awful estrangement, his terrible sinfulness? Thus it is that I can urge men to obey the 1954 decision of the Supreme Court, for it is morally right; and I can urge them to disobey segregation ordinances, for they are morally wrong.

Let us consider a more concrete example of just and unjust laws. An unjust law is a code that a numerical or power majority group compels a minority group to obey but does not make binding on itself. This is *difference* made legal. By the same token, a just law is a code that a majority compels a minority to follow and that it is willing to follow itself. This is *sameness* made legal.

Let me give another explanation. A law is unjust if it is inflicted on a minority that, as a result of being denied the right to vote, had no part in enacting or devising the law. Who can say that the legislature of Alabama which set up that state's segregation laws was democratically elected? Throughout Alabama all sorts of devious methods are used to prevent Negroes from becoming registered voters, and there are some counties in which, even though Negroes constitute a majority of the population, not a single Negro is registered. Can any law enacted under such circumstances be considered democratically structured?

Sometimes a law is just on its face and unjust in its application. For instance, I have been arrested on a charge of parading without a permit. Now, there is nothing wrong in having an ordinance which requires a permit for a parade. But such an ordinance becomes unjust when it is used to maintain segregation and to deny citizens the First-Amendment privilege of peaceful assembly and protest.

I hope you are able to see the distinction I am trying to point out. In no sense do I advocate evading or defying the law, as would the rabid segregationist. That would lead to anarchy. One who breaks an unjust law must do so openly, lovingly, and with a willingness to accept the penalty. I submit that an individual who breaks a law that conscience tells him is unjust, and who willingly accepts the penalty of imprisonment in order to arouse the conscience of the community over its injustice, is in reality expressing the highest respect for law.

Of course, there is nothing new about this kind of civil disobedience. It was evidenced sublimely in the refusal of Shadrach, Meshach and Abednego to obey the laws of Nebuchadnezzar, on the ground that a higher moral law was at stake. It was practiced superby by the early Christians, who were willing to face hungry lions and the excruciating pain of chopping blocks rather than submit to certain unjust laws of the Roman Empire. To a degree, academic freedom is a reality today because Socrates practiced civil disobedience. In our own nation, the Boston Tea Party represented a massive act of civil disobedience.

We should never forget that everything Adolf Hitler did in Germany was "legal" and everything the Hungarian freedom fighters did in Hungary was "illegal." It was "illegal" to aid and comfort a Jew in Hitler's Germany. Even so, I am sure that, had I lived in Germany at the time, I would have aided and comforted my Jewish brothers. If today I lived in a Communist country where certain principles dear to the Christian faith are suppressed, I would openly advocate disobeying that country's antireligious laws.

I must make two honest confessions to you, my Christian and Jewish brothers. First, I must confess that over the past few years I have been gravely disappointed with the white moderate. I have almost reached the regrettable conclusion that the Negro's great stumbling block in his stride toward freedom is not the White Citizen's Counciler or the Ku Klux Klanner, but the white moderate, who is more devoted to "order" than to justice; who prefers a negative peace which is the absence of tension to a positive peace which is the presence of justice; who constantly says: "I agree with you in the goal you seek, but I cannot agree with your methods of direct action"; who paternalistically believes he can set the timetable for another man's freedom; who lives by a mythical concept of time and who constantly advises the Negro to wait for a "more convenient season." Shallow understanding from people of good will is more frustrating than absolute misunderstanding from people of ill will. Lukewarm acceptance is much more bewildering than outright rejection.

I had hoped that the white moderate would understand that law and order exist for the purpose of establishing justice and that when they fail in this purpose they become the dangerously structured dams that block the flow of social progress. I had hoped that the white moderate would understand that the present tension in the South is a necessary phase of the transition from an obnoxious negative peace, in which the Negro passively accepted his unjust plight, to a substantive and positive peace, in which all men will respect the dignity and worth of human personality. Actually, we who engage in nonviolent direct action are not the creators of tension. We merely bring to the surface the hidden tension that is already alive. We bring it out in the open, where it can be seen and dealt with. Like a boil that can never be cured so long as it is covered up but must be opened with all its ugliness to the natural medicines of air and light, injustice must be exposed, with all the tension its exposure creates, to the light of human conscience and the air of national opinion before it can be cured.

In your statement you assert that our actions, even though peaceful, must be condemned because they precipitate violence. But is this a logical assertion? Isn't this like condemning a robbed man because his possession of money precipitated the evil act of robbery? Isn't this like condemning Socrates because his unswerving commitment to truth and his philosophical inquiries precipitated the act by the misguided populace in which they made him drink hemlock? Isn't this like condemning Jesus because his unique God-consciousness and never-ceasing devotion to God's will precipitated the evil act of crucifixion? We must come to see that, as the federal courts have consistently affirmed, it is wrong to urge an individual to cease his efforts to gain his basic constitutional rights because the quest may precipitate violence. Society must protect the robbed and punish the robber.

I had also hoped that the white moderate would reject the myth concerning time in relation to the struggle for freedom. I have just received a letter from a white brother in Texas. He writes: "All Christians know that the colored people will receive equal rights eventually, but it is possible that you are in too great a religious hurry. It has taken Christianity almost two thousand years to accomplish what it has. The teachings of Christ take time to come to earth." Such an attitude stems from a tragic misconception of time, from the strangely irrational notion that there is something in the very flow of time that will inevitably cure all ills. Actually, time itself is neutral; it can be used either destructively or constructively. More and more I feel that the people of ill will have used time much more effectively than have the people of good will. We will have to repent in this generation not merely for the hateful words and actions of the bad people but for the appalling silence of the good people. Human progress never rolls in on wheels of inevitability; it comes through the tireless efforts of men willing to be co-workers with God, and without this hard work, time itself becomes an ally of the forces of social stagnation. We must use time creatively, in the knowledge that the time is always ripe to do right. Now is the time to make real the promise of democracy and transform our pending national elegy into a creative psalm of brotherhood. Now is the time to lift our national policy from the quicksand of racial injustice to the solid rock of human dignity.

You speak of our activity in Birmingham as extreme. At first I was rather disappointed that fellow clergymen would see my nonviolent efforts as those of an extremist. I began thinking about the fact that I stand in the middle of two opposing forces in the Negro community. One is a force of complacency, made up in part of Negroes who, as a result of long years of oppression, are so drained of self-respect and a sense of "somebodiness" that they have adjusted to segregation; and in part of a few middle-class Negroes who, because of a degree of academic and economic security and because in some ways they profit by segregation, have become insensitive to the problems of the masses. The other force is one of bitterness and hatred, and it comes perilously close to advocating violence. It is expressed in the various black nationalist groups that are springing up across the nation, the largest and best-known being Elijah Muhammad's Muslim movement. Nourished by the Negro's frustration over the continued existence of racial discrimination, this movement is made up of people who have lost faith in America, who have absolutely repudiated Christianity, and who have concluded that the white man is an incorrigible "devil."

I have tried to stand between these two forces, saying that we need emulate neither the "do-nothingism" of the complacent nor the hatred and despair of the black nationalist. For there is the more excellent way of love and nonviolent protest. I am grateful to God that, through the influence of the Negro church, the way of nonviolence became an integral part of our struggle.

If this philosophy had not emerged, by now many streets of the South would, I am convinced, be flowing with blood. And I am further convinced that if our white brothers dismiss as "rabble-rousers" and "outside agitators" those of us who employ nonviolent direct action, and if they refuse to support our nonviolent efforts, millions of Negroes will, out of frustration and despair, seek solace and security in black-nationalist ideologies—a development that would inevitably lead to a frightening racial nightmare.

Oppressed people cannot remain oppressed forever. The yearning for freedom eventually manifests itself, and that is what has happened to the American Negro. Something within has reminded him of his birthright of freedom, and something without has reminded him that it can be gained. Consciously or unconsciously, he has been caught up by the *Zeitgeist,* and with his black brothers of Africa and his brown and yellow brothers of Asia, South America and the Caribbean, the United States Negro is moving with a sense of great urgency toward the promised land of racial justice. If one recognizes this vital urge that has engulfed the Negro community, one should readily understand why public demonstrations are taking place. The Negro has many pent-up resentments and latent frustrations, and he must release them. So let him march; let him make prayer pilgrimages to the city hall; let him go on freedom rides—and try to understand why he must do so. If his repressed emotions are not released in nonviolent ways, they will seek expression through violence; this is not a threat but a fact of history. So I have not said to my people: "Get rid of your discontent." Rather, I have tried to say that this normal and healthy discontent can be channeled into the creative outlet of nonviolent direct action. And now this approach is being termed extremist.

But though I was initially disappointed at being categorized as an extremist, as I continued to think about the matter I gradually gained a measure of satisfaction from the label. Was not Jesus an extremist for love: "Love your enemies, bless them that curse you, do good to them that hate you, and pray for them which despitefully use you, and persecute you." Was not Amos an extremist for justice: "Let justice roll down like waters and righteousness like an ever-flowing stream." Was not Paul an extremist for the Christian gospel: "I bear in my body the marks of the Lord Jesus." Was not Martin Luther an extremist: "Here I stand; I cannot do otherwise, so help me God." And John Bunyan: "I will stay in jail to the end of my days before I make a butchery of my conscience." And Abraham Lincoln: "This nation cannot survive half slave and half free." And Thomas Jefferson: "We hold these truths to be self-evident, that all men are created equal . . ." So the question is not whether we will be extremists, but what kind of extremists we will be. Will we be extremists for hate or for love? Will we be extremists for the preservation of injustice or for the extension of justice? In that dramatic scene on Calvary's hill three men were crucified. We must never forget that all three were crucified for the same crime—the crime of extremism. Two were extremists for immorality, and thus fell below their environment. The other, Jesus Christ, was an extremist for love, truth and goodness, and thereby rose above his environment. Perhaps the South, the nation and the world are in dire need of creative extremists.

I had hoped that the white moderate would see this need. Perhaps I was too optimistic; perhaps I expected too much. I suppose I should have realized that few members of the oppressor race can understand the deep groans and passionate yearnings of the oppressed race, and still fewer have the vision to see that injustice must be rooted out by strong, persistent and determined action. I am thankful, however, that some of our white brothers in the South have grasped the meaning of this social revolution and committed themselves to it. They are still all too few in quantity, but they are big in quality. Some—such as Ralph McGill, Lillian Smith, Harry Golden, James McBride Dabbs, Ann Braden and Sarah Patton Boyle—have written about our struggle in eloquent and prophetic terms. Others have marched with us down nameless streets of the South. They have languished in filthy, roach-infested jails, suffering the abuse and brutality of policemen who view them as "dirty nigger-lovers." Unlike so many of their moderate brothers and sisters, they have recognized the urgency of the moment and sensed the need for powerful "action" antidotes to combat the disease of segregation.

Let me take note of my other major disappointment. I have been so greatly disappointed with the white church and its leadership. Of course, there are some notable exceptions. I am not unmindful of the fact that each of you has taken some significant stands on this issue. I commend you, Reverend Stallings, for your Christian stand on this past Sunday, in welcoming Negroes to your worship service on a nonsegregated basis. I commend the Catholic leaders of this state for integrating Spring Hill College several years ago.

But despite these notable exceptions, I must honestly reiterate that I have been disappointed with the church. I do not say this as one of those negative critics who can always find something wrong with the church. I say this as a minister of the gospel, who loves the church; who was nurtured in its bosom; who has been sustained by its spiritual blessings and who will remain true to it as long as the cord of life shall lengthen.

When I was suddenly catapulted into the leadership of the bus protest in Montgomery, Alabama, a few years ago, I felt we would be supported by the white church. I felt that the white ministers, priests and rabbis of the South would be among our strongest allies. Instead, some have been outright opponents, refusing to understand the freedom movement and misrepresenting its leaders; all too many others have been more cautious than courageous and have remained silent behind the anesthetizing security of stained-glass windows.

In spite of my shattered dreams, I came to Birmingham with the hope that the white religious leadership of this community would see the justice of our cause and, with deep moral concern, would serve as the channel through which our just grievances could reach the power structure. I had hoped that each of you would understand. But again I have been disappointed.

I have heard numerous southern religious leaders admonish their worshipers to comply with a desegregation decision because it is the law, but I have longed to hear white ministers declare: "Follow this decree because integration is morally right and because the Negro is your brother." In the midst of blatant injustices inflicted upon the Negro, I have watched white churchmen stand on the sideline and mouth pious irrelevancies and sanctimonious trivialities. In the midst of a mighty struggle to rid our nation of racial and economic injustice, I have heard many ministers say: "Those are social issues, with which the gospel has no real concern." And I have watched many churches commit themselves to a completely other-worldly religion which makes a strange, un-Biblical distinction between body and soul, between the sacred and the secular.

I have traveled the length and breadth of Alabama, Mississippi and all the other southern states. On sweltering summer days and crisp autumn mornings I have looked at the South's beautiful churches with their lofty spires pointing heavenward. I have beheld the impressive outlines of her massive religious-education buildings. Over and over I have found myself asking: "What kind of people worship here? Who is their God? Where were their voices when the lips of Governor Barnett dripped with words of interposition and nullification? Where were they when Governor Wallace gave a clarion call for defiance and hatred? Where were their voices of support when bruised and weary Negro men and women decided to rise from the dark dungeons of complacency to the bright hills of creative protest?"

Yes, these questions are still in my mind. In deep disappointment I have wept over the laxity of the church. But be assured that my tears have been tears of love. There can be no deep disappointment where there is not deep love. Yes, I love the church. How could I do otherwise? I am in the rather unique position of being the son, the grandson and the great-grandson of preachers. Yes, I see the church as the body of Christ. But, oh! How we have blemished and scarred that body through social neglect and through fear of being nonconformists.

There was a time when the church was very powerful—in the time when the early Christians rejoiced at being deemed worthy to suffer for what they believed. In those days the church was not merely a thermometer that recorded the ideas and principles of popular opinion; it was a thermostat that transformed the mores of society. Whenever the early Christians entered a town, the people in power became disturbed and immediately sought to convict the Christians for being "disturbers of the peace" and "outside agitators." But the Christians pressed on, in the conviction that they were "a colony of heaven," called to obey God rather than man. Small in number, they were big in commitment. They were too God-intoxicated to be "astronomically intimidated." By their effort and example they brought an end to such ancient evils as infanticide and gladiatorial contests.

Things are different now. So often the contemporary church is a weak, ineffectual voice with an uncertain sound. So often it is an archdefender of the status quo. Far from being disturbed by the presence of the church, the power structure of the average community is consoled by the church's silent—and often even vocal—sanction of things as they are.

But the judgment of God is upon the church as never before. If today's church does not recapture the sacrificial spirit of the early church, it will lose its authenticity, forfeit the loyalty of millions, and be dismissed as an irrelevant social club with no meaning for the twentieth century. Every day I meet young people whose disappointment with the church has turned into outright disgust.

Perhaps I have once again been too optimistic. Is organized religion too inextricably bound to the status quo to save our nation and the world? Perhaps I must turn my faith to the inner spiritual church, the church within the church, as the true *ekklesia* and the hope of the world. But again I am thankful to God that some noble souls from the ranks of organized religion have broken loose from the paralyzing chains of conformity and joined us as active partners in the struggle for freedom. They have left their secure congregations and walked the streets of Albany, Georgia, with us. They have gone down the highways of the South on tortuous rides for freedom. Yes, they have gone to jail with us. Some have been dismissed from their churches, have lost the support of their bishops and fellow ministers. But they have acted in the faith that right defeated is stronger than evil triumphant. Their witness has been the spiritual salt that has preserved the true meaning of the gospel in these troubled times. They have carved a tunnel of hope through the dark mountain of disappointment.

I hope the church as a whole will meet the challenge of this decisive hour. But even if the church does not come to the aid of justice, I have no despair about the future. I have no fear about the outcome of our struggle in Birmingham, even if our motives are at present misunderstood. We will reach the goal of freedom in Birmingham and all over the nation, because the goal of America is freedom. Abused and scorned though we may be, our destiny is tied up with America's destiny. Before the pilgrims landed at Plymouth, we were here. Before the pen of Jefferson etched the majestic words of the Declaration of Independence across the pages of history, we were here. For more than two centuries our forebears labored in this country without wages; they made cotton king; they built the homes of their masters while suffering gross injustice and shameful humiliation—and yet out of a bottomless vitality they continued to thrive and develop. If the inexpressible cruelties of slavery could not stop us, the opposition we now face will surely fail. We will win our freedom because the sacred heritage of our nation and the eternal will of God are embodied in our echoing demands.

Before closing I feel impelled to mention one other point in your statement that has troubled me profoundly. You warmly commended the Birmingham police force for keeping "order" and "preventing violence." I doubt that you would have so warmly commended the police force if you had seen its dogs sinking their teeth into unarmed, nonviolent Negroes. I doubt that you would so quickly commend the policemen if you were to observe their ugly and inhumane treatment of Negroes here in the city jail; if you were to watch them push and curse old Negro women and young Negro girls; if you were to see them slap and kick old Negro men and young boys; if you were to observe them, as they did on two occasions, refuse to give us food because we wanted to sing our grace together. I cannot join you in your praise of the Birmingham police department.

It is true that the police have exercised a degree of discipline in handling the demonstrators. In this sense they have conducted themselves rather "nonviolently" in public. But for what purpose? To preserve the evil system of segregation. Over the past few years I have consistently preached that nonviolence demands that the means we use must be as pure as the ends we seek. I have tried to make clear that it is wrong to use immoral means to attain moral ends. But now I must affirm that it is just as wrong, or perhaps even more so, to use moral means to preserve immoral ends. Perhaps Mr. Connor and his policemen have been rather nonviolent in public, as was Chief Pritchett in Albany, Georgia, but they have used the moral means of nonviolence to maintain the immoral end of racial injustice. As T. S. Eliot has said: "The last temptation is the greatest treason: To do the right deed for the wrong reason."

I wish you had commended the Negro sit-inners and demonstrators of Birmingham for their sublime courage, their willingness to suffer and their amazing discipline in the midst of great provocation. One day the South will recognize its real heroes. They will be the James Merediths, with the noble sense of purpose that enables them to face jeering and hostile mobs, and with the agonizing loneliness that characterizes the life of the pioneer. They will be old, oppressed, battered Negro women, symbolized in a seventy-two-year-old woman in Montgomery, Alabama, who rose up with a sense of dignity and with her people decided not to ride segregated buses, and who responded with ungrammatical profundity to one who inquired about her weariness: "My feets is tired, but my soul is at rest." They will be the young high school and college students, the young ministers of the gospel and a host of their elders, courageously and nonviolently sitting in at lunch counters and willingly going to jail for conscience' sake. One day the South will know that when these disinherited children of God sat down at lunch counters, they were in reality standing up for what is best in the American dream and for the most sacred values in our Judaeo-Christian heritage, thereby bringing our nation back to those great wells of democracy which were dug deep by the founding fathers in their formulation of the Constitution and the Declaration of Independence.

Never before have I written so long a letter. I'm afraid it is much too long to take your precious time. I can assure you that it would have been much shorter if I had been writing from a comfortable desk, but what else can one do when he is alone in a narrow jail cell, other than write long letters, think long thoughts and pray long prayers?

If I have said anything in this letter that overstates the truth and indicates an unreasonable impatience, I beg you to forgive me. If I have said anything that understates the truth and indicates my having a patience that allows me to settle for anything less than brotherhood, I beg God to forgive me.

I hope this letter finds you strong in the faith. I also hope that circumstances will soon make it possible for me to meet each of you, not as an integrationist or a civil-rights leader but as a fellow clergyman and a Christian brother. Let us all hope that the dark clouds of racial prejudice will soon pass away and the deep fog of misunderstanding will be lifted from our fear-drenched communities, and in some not too distant tomorrow the radiant stars of love and brotherhood will shine over our great nation with all their scintillating beauty.

Yours for the cause of Peace and Brotherhood,

MARTIN LUTHER KING, JR.

The Fire Next Time*

James Baldwin

. . . White Americans have contented themselves with gestures that are now described as "tokenism." For hard example, white Americans congratulate themselves on the 1954 Supreme Court decision outlawing segregation in the schools; they suppose, in spite of the mountain of evidence that has since accumulated to the contrary, that this was proof of a change of heart—or, as they like to say, progress. Perhaps. It all depends on how one reads the word "progress." Most of the Negroes I know do not believe that this immense concession would ever have been made if it had not been for the competition of the Cold War, and the fact that Africa was clearly liberating herself and therefore had, for political reasons, to be wooed by the descendants of her former masters. Had it been a matter of love or justice, the 1954 decision would surely have occurred sooner; were it not for the realities of power in this difficult era, it might very well not have occurred yet. This seems an extremely harsh way of stating the case—ungrateful, as it were—but the evidence that supports this way of stating it is not easily refuted. I myself do not think that it can be refuted at all. In any event, the sloppy and fatuous nature of American good will can never be relied upon to deal with hard problems. These have been dealt with, when they have been dealt with at all, out of necessity—and in political terms, anyway, necessity means concessions made in order to stay on top. I think this is a fact, which it serves no purpose to deny, *but, whether it is a fact or not, this is what the black population of the world, including black Americans, really believe.* The word "independence" in Africa and the word "integration" here are almost equally meaningless; that is, Europe has not yet left Africa, and black men here are not yet free. And both of these last statements are undeniable facts, related facts, containing the gravest implications for us all. The Negroes of this country may never be able to rise to power, but they are very well placed indeed to precipitate chaos and ring down the curtain on the American dream.

This has everything to do, of course, with the nature of that dream and with the fact that we Americans, of whatever color, do not dare examine it and are far from hav-

* From James Baldwin, *The Fire Next Time* (New York: Dial, 1963), pp. 117–41. Copyright © 1963, 1962 by James Baldwin. Reprinted by permission of the publisher, The Dial Press.

ing made it a reality. There are too many things we do not wish to know about ourselves. People are not, for example, terribly anxious to be equal (equal, after all, to what and to whom?) but they love the idea of being superior. And this human truth has an especially grinding force here, where identity is almost impossible to achieve and people are perpetually attempting to find their feet on the shifting sands of status. (Consider the history of labor in a country in which, spiritually speaking, there are no workers, only candidates for the hand of the boss's daughter.) Furthermore, I have met only a very few people—and most of these were not Americans—who had any real desire to be free. Freedom is hard to bear. It can be objected that I am speaking of political freedom in spiritual terms, but the political institutions of any nation are always menaced and are ultimately controlled by the spiritual state of that nation. We are controlled here by our confusion, far more than we know, and the American dream has therefore become something much more closely resembling a nightmare, on the private, domestic, and international levels. Privately, we cannot stand our lives and dare not examine them; domestically, we take no responsibility for (and no pride in) what goes on in our country; and, internationally, for many millions of people, we are an unmitigated disaster. Whoever doubts this last statement has only to open his ears, his heart, his mind, to the testimony of—for example—any Cuban peasant or any Spanish poet, and ask himself what *he* would feel about us if *he* were the victim of our performance in pre-Castro Cuba or in Spain. We defend our curious role in Spain by referring to the Russian menace and the necessity of protecting the free world. It has not occurred to us that we have simply been mesmerized by Russia, and that the only real advantage Russia has in what we think of as a struggle between the East and the West is the moral history of the Western world. Russia's secret weapon is the bewilderment and despair and hunger of millions of people of whose existence we are scarcely aware. The Russian Communists are not in the least concerned about these people. But our ignorance and indecision have had the effect, if not of delivering them into Russian hands, of plunging them very deeply in the Russian shadow, for which effect—and it is hard to blame them—the most articulate among them, and the most oppressed as well, distrust us all the more. Our power and our fear of change help bind these people to their misery and bewilderment, and insofar as they find this state intolerable we are intolerably menaced. For if they find their state intolerable, but are too heavily oppressed to change it, they are simply pawns in the hands of larger powers, which, in such a context, are always unscrupulous, and when, eventually, they do change their situation—as in Cuba—we are menaced more than ever, by the vacuum that succeeds all violent upheavals. We should certainly know by now that it is one thing to overthrow a dictator or repel an invader and quite another thing really to achieve a revolution. Time and time and time again, the people discover that they have merely betrayed themselves into the hands of yet another Pharaoh, who, since he was necessary to put the broken country together, will not let them go. Perhaps, people being the conundrums that they are, and having so little desire to shoulder the burden of their lives, this is what will always happen. But at the bottom of my heart I do not believe this. I think that people can be better than that, and I know that people can be better than they are. We are capable of bearing a great burden, once we discover that the burden is reality and arrive where reality is. Anyway, the point here is that we are living in an age of revolution, whether we will or no, and that America is the only Western nation with both the power and, as I hope to suggest, the experience that may help to make these revolutions real and minimize the human damage. Any attempt we make to oppose these outbursts of energy is tantamount to signing our death warrant.

Behind what we think of as the Russian menace lies what we do not wish to face, and what white Americans do not face when they regard a Negro: reality—the fact that life is tragic. Life is tragic simply because the earth turns and the sun inexorably rises and sets, and one day, for each of us, the sun will go down for the last, last time. Perhaps the whole root of our trouble, the human trouble, is that we will sacrifice all the beauty of our lives, will imprison ourselves in totems, taboos, crosses, blood sacrifices, steeples, mosques, races, armies, flags, nations, in order to deny the fact of death, which is the only fact we have. It seems to me that one ought to rejoice in the *fact* of death—ought to decide, indeed, to *earn* one's death by confronting with passion the conundrum of life. One is responsible to life: It is the small beacon in that terrifying darkness from which we come and to which we shall return. One must negotiate this passage as nobly as possible, for the sake of those who are coming after us. But white Americans do not believe in death, and this is why the darkness of my skin so intimidates them. And this is also why the presence of the Negro in this country can bring about its destruction. It is the responsibility of free men to trust and to celebrate what is constant—birth, struggle, and death are constant, and so is love, though we may not always think so—and to apprehend the nature of change, to be able and willing to change. I speak of change not on the surface but in the depths—change in the sense of renewal. But renewal becomes impossible if one supposes things to be constant that are not—safety, for example, or money, or power. One clings then to chimeras, by which one can only be betrayed, and the entire hope—the entire possibility—of freedom disappears. And by destruction I mean precisely the abdication by Americans of any effort really to be free. The Negro can precipitate this abdication because white Americans have never, in all their long history, been able to look on him as a man like themselves. This point need not be labored; it is proved over and over again by the Negro's continuing position here, and his indescribable struggle to defeat the stratagems that white Americans have used, and use, to deny him his humanity. America could have used in other ways the energy that both groups have expended in this conflict. America, of all the Western nations, has been best placed to prove the uselessness and the obsolescence of the concept of color. But it has not dared to accept this opportunity, or even to conceive of it as an opportunity. White Americans have thought of it as their shame, and have envied those more civilized and elegant European nations that were untroubled by the presence of black men on their shores. This is because white Americans have supposed "Europe" and "civilization" to be synonyms—which they are not—and have been distrustful of other standards and other sources of vitality, especially those produced in America itself, and have attempted to behave in all matters as though what was east for Europe was also east for them. What it comes to is that if we, who can scarcely be considered a white nation, persist in thinking of ourselves as one, we condemn ourselves, with the truly white nations, to sterility and decay, whereas if we could accept ourselves *as we are,* we might bring new life to the Western achievements, and transform them. The price of this transformation is the unconditional freedom of the Negro; it is not too much to say that he, who has been so long rejected, must now be embraced, and at no matter what psychic or social risk. He is *the* key figure in his country, and the American future is precisely as bright or as dark as his. And the Negro recognizes this, in a negative way. Hence the question: Do I really *want* to be integrated into a burning house?

White Americans find it as difficult as white people elsewhere do to divest themselves of the notion that they are in possession of some intrinsic value that black people need, or want. And this assumption—which, for example, makes the solution to the Negro problem depend on the speed with which Negroes accept and adopt white standards—is revealed in all kinds of striking ways, from Bobby Kennedy's assurance that a Negro can become President in forty years to the unfortunate tone of warm congratulation with which so many liberals address their Negro equals. It is the Negro, of course, who is presumed to have become equal—an achievement that not only proves the comforting fact that perseverance has no color but also overwhelmingly corroborates the white man's sense of his own value. Alas, this value can scarcely be corroborated in any other way; there is certainly little enough in the white man's public or private life that one should desire to imitate. White men, at the bottom of their hearts, know this. Therefore, a vast amount of the energy that goes into what we call the Negro problem is produced by the white man's profound desire not to be judged by those who are not white, not to be seen as he is, and at the same time a vast amount of the white anguish is rooted in the white man's equally profound need to be seen as he is, to be released from the tyranny of his mirror. All of us know, whether or not we are able to admit it, that mirrors can only lie, that death by drowning is all that awaits one there. It is for this reason that love is so desperately sought and so cunningly avoided. Love takes off the masks that we fear we cannot live without and know we cannot live within. I use the word "love" here not merely in the personal sense but as a state of being, or a state of grace—not in the infantile American sense of being made happy but in the tough and universal sense of quest and daring and growth. And I submit, then, that the racial tensions that menace Americans today have little to do with real antipathy—on the contrary, indeed—and are involved only symbolically with color. These tensions are rooted in the very same depths as those from which love springs, or murder. The white man's unadmitted—and apparently, to him, unspeakable—private fears and longings are projected onto the Negro. The only way he can be released from the Negro's tyrannical power over him is to consent, in effect, to become black himself, to become a part of that suffering and dancing country that he now watches wistfully from the heights of his lonely power and, armed with spiritual traveller's checks, visits surreptitiously after dark. How can one respect, let alone adopt, the values of a people who do not, on any level whatever, live the way they say they do, or the way they say they should? I cannot accept the proposition that the four-hundred-year travail of the American Negro should result merely in his attainment of the present level of the American civilization. I am far from convinced that being released from the African witch doctor was worthwhile if I am now—in order to support the moral contradictions and the spiritual aridity of my life—expected to become dependent on the American psychiatrist. It is a bargain I refuse. The only thing white people have that black people need, or should want, is power—and no one holds power forever. White people cannot, in the generality, be taken as models of how to live. Rather, the white man is himself in sore need of new standards, which will release him from his confusion and place him once again in fruitful communion with the depths of his own being. And I repeat: The price of the liberation of the white people is the liberation of the blacks—the total liberation, in the cities, in the towns, before the law, and in the mind. Why, for example—especially knowing the family as I do—I should *want* to marry your sister is a great mystery to me. But your sister and I have every right to marry if we wish to, and no one has the right to stop us. If she cannot raise me to her level, perhaps I can raise her to mine.

In short, we, the black and the white, deeply need each other here if we are really to become a nation—if we are really, that is, to achieve our identity, our maturity, as men and women. To create one nation has proved to be a hideously difficult task; there is certainly no need now to create two, one black and one white. But white men with far more political power than that possessed by the Nation of Islam movement have been advocating exactly this, in effect, for generations. If this sentiment is honored when it falls from the lips of Senator Byrd, then there is no reason it should not be honored when it falls from the lips of Malcolm X. And any Congressional committee wishing to investigate the latter must also be willing to investigate the former. They are expressing exactly the same sentiments and represent exactly the same danger. There is absolutely no reason to suppose that white people are better equipped to frame the laws by which I am to be governed than I am. It is entirely unacceptable that I should have no voice in the political affairs of my own country, for I am not a ward of America; I am one of the first Americans to arrive on these shores.

This past, the Negro's past, of rope, fire, torture, castration, infanticide, rape; death and humiliation; fear by day and night, fear as deep as the marrow of the bone; doubt that he was worthy of life, since everyone around him denied it; sorrow for his women, for his kinfolk, for his children, who needed his protection, and whom he could not protect; rage, hatred, and murder, hatred for white men so deep that it often turned against him and his own, and made all love, all trust, all joy impossible—this past, this endless struggle to achieve and reveal and confirm a human identity, human authority, yet contains, for all its horror, something very beautiful. I do not mean to be sentimental about suffering—enough is certainly as good as a feast—but people who cannot suffer can never grow up, can never discover who they are. That man who is forced each day to snatch his manhood, his identity, out of the fire of human cruelty that rages to destroy it knows, if he survives his effort, and even if he does not survive it, something about himself and human life that no school on earth—and, indeed, no church—can teach. He achieves his own authority, and that is unshakable. This is because, in order to save his life, he is forced to look beneath appearances, to take nothing for granted, to hear the meaning behind the words. If one is continually surviving the worst that life can bring, one eventually ceases to be controlled by a fear of what life can bring, whatever it brings must be borne. And at this level of experience one's bitterness begins to be palatable, and hatred becomes too heavy a sack to carry. The apprehension of life here so briefly and inadequately sketched has been the experience of generations of Negroes, and it helps to explain how they have endured and how they have been able to produce children of kindergarten age who can walk through mobs to get to school. It demands great force and great cunning continually to assault the mighty and indifferent fortress of white supremacy, as Negroes in this country have done so long. It demands great spiritual resilience not to hate the hater whose foot is on your neck, and an even greater miracle of perception and charity not to teach your child to hate. The Negro boys and girls who are facing mobs today come out of a long line of improbable aristo-crats—the only genuine aristocrats this country has produced. I say "this country" be-cause their frame of reference was totally American. They were hewing out of the mountain of white supremacy the stone of their individuality. I have great respect for that unsung army of black men and women who trudged down back lanes and entered back doors, saying "Yes, sir" and "No, Ma'am" in order to acquire a new roof for the schoolhouse, new books, a new chemistry lab, more beds for the dormitories, more dor-mitories. They did not like saying "Yes, sir" and "No, Ma'am," but the country was in no hurry to educate Negroes, these black men and women knew that the job had to be done, and they put their pride in their pockets in order to do it. It is very hard to believe that they were in any way inferior to the white men and women who opened those back doors. It is very hard to believe that those men and women, raising their children, eat-ing their greens, crying their curses, weeping their tears, singing their songs, making their love, as the sun rose, as the sun set, were in any way inferior to the white men and women who crept over to share these splendors after the sun went down. But we must avoid the European error; we must not suppose that, because the situation, the ways, the perceptions of black people so radically differed from those of whites, they were ra-cially superior. I am proud of these people not because of their color but because of their intelligence and their spiritual force and their beauty. The country should be proud of them, too, but, alas, not many people in this country even know of their exist-ence. And the reason for this ignorance is that a knowledge of the role these people played—and play—in American life would reveal more about America to Americans than Americans wish to know.

The American Negro has the great advantage of having never believed that col-lection of myths to which white Americans cling: that their ancestors were all freedom-loving heroes, that they were born in the greatest country the world has ever seen, or that Americans are invincible in battle and wise in peace, that Americans have always dealt honorably with Mexicans and Indians and all other neighbors or inferiors, that American men are the world's most direct and virile, that American women are pure. Negroes know far more about white Americans than that; it can almost be said, in fact, that they know about white Americans what parents—or, anyway, mothers—know about their children, and that they very often regard white Americans that way. And perhaps this attitude, held in spite of what they know and have endured, helps to ex-plain why Negroes, on the whole, and until lately, have allowed themselves to feel so little hatred. The tendency has really been, insofar as this was possible, to dismiss white people as the slightly mad victims of their own brainwashing. One watched the lives they led. One could not be fooled about that; one watched the things they did and the excuses that they gave themselves, and if a white man was really in trouble, deep trouble, it was to the Negro's door that he came. And one felt that if one had had that white man's worldly advantages, one would never have become as bewildered and as joyless and as thoughtlessly cruel as he. The Negro came to the white man for a roof or for five dollars or for a letter to the judge; the white man came to the Negro for love. But he was not often able to give what he came seeking. The price was too high; he had too much to lose. And the Negro knew this, too. When one knows this about a man, it is impossible for one to hate him, but unless he becomes a man—becomes equal—it is also impossible for one to love him. Ultimately, one tends to avoid him, for the universal characteristic of children is to assume that they have a monopoly on trouble, and therefore a monopoly on *you.* (Ask any Negro what he knows about the white people with whom he works. And then ask the white people with whom he works what they know about *him.*)

How can the American Negro past be used? It is entirely possible that this dishonored past will rise up soon to smite all of us. There are some wars, for example (if anyone on the globe is still mad enough to go to war) that the American Negro will not support, however many of his people may be coerced—and there is a limit to the number of people any government can put in prison, and a rigid limit indeed to the practicality of such a course. A bill is coming in that I fear America is not prepared to pay. "The problem of the twentieth century," wrote W. E. B. Du Bois around sixty years ago, "is the problem of the color line." A fearful and delicate problem, which compromises, when it does not corrupt, all the American efforts to build a better world —here, there, or anywhere. It is for this reason that everything white Americans think they believe in must now be reëxamined. What one would not like to see again is the consolidation of peoples on the basis of their color. But as long as we in the West place on color the value that we do, we make it impossible for the great unwashed to consolidate themselves according to any other principle. Color is not a human or a personal reality; it is a political reality. But this is a distinction so extremely hard to make that the West has not been able to make it yet. And at the center of this dreadful storm, this vast confusion, stand the black people of this nation, who must now share the fate of a nation that has never accepted them, to which they were brought in chains. Well, if this is so, one has no choice but to do all in one's power to change that fate, and at no matter what risk—eviction, imprisonment, torture, death. For the sake of one's children, in order to minimize the bill that *they* must pay, one must be careful not to take refuge in any delusion—and the value placed on the color of the skin is always and everywhere and forever a delusion. I know that what I am asking is impossible. But in our time, as in every time, the impossible is the least that one can demand—and one is, after all, emboldened by the spectacle of human history in general, and American Negro history in particular, for it testifies to nothing less than the perpetual achievement of the impossible.

When I was very young, and was dealing with my buddies in those wine- and urine-stained hallways, something in me wondered, *What will happen to all that beauty?* For black people, though I am aware that some of us, black and white, do not know it yet, are very beautiful. And when I sat at Elijah's table and watched the baby, the women, and the men, and we talked about God's—or Allah's—vengeance, I wondered, when that vengeance was achieved, *What will happen to all that beauty then?* I could also see that the intransigence and ignorance of the white world might make that vengeance inevitable—a vengeance that does not really depend on, and cannot really be executed by, any person or organization, and that cannot be prevented by any police force or army: historical vengeance, a cosmic vengeance, based on the law that we recognize when we say, "Whatever goes up must come down." And here we are, at the center of the arc, trapped in the gaudiest, most valuable, and most improbable water wheel the world has ever seen. Everything now, we must assume, is in our hands; we have no right to assume otherwise. If we—and now I mean the relatively conscious whites and the relatively conscious blacks, who must, like lovers, insist on, or create, the consciousness of the others—do not falter in our duty now, we may be able, handful that we are, to end the racial nightmare, and achieve our country, and change the history of the world. If we do not now dare everything, the fulfillment of that prophecy, recreated from the Bible in song by a slave, is upon us: *God gave Noah the rainbow sign, No more water, the fire next time!*

Mission Accomplished*
Ben Caldwell

BLACK KING

TWO BLACK ACES (GUARDS)

PRIEST

INTERPRETER

TWO SINGING-DANCING NUNS

The hot heart of Africa. Late nineteenth century, by the white man's count. We see sunshine-bright blue sky. We see green-growth in almost architectural forms. Underneath this is a gold-fringed shade-canopy. Seated beneath this canopy is a regally dressed black man. His face is shielded by gold fringes that hang from his velvet fez-crown. Ancestral figures (statues) stand around. Beside him are two equally regal-looking black men. They almost seem burdened by their gold trimmed apparel. We hear a variety of tones from a variety of percussion instruments. A marimba. They seem like statues themselves, so still, so deep, are they in concentration-contemplation of the music and their surroundings. The peaceful mood is disrupted by the sounds of people approaching. They are singing (a white hymn). A group of whites come into view, led by a man in a tropical white suit, pith helmet. A PRIEST, *in long flowing black robes, with a big wooden cross dangling from his neck. A big Bible under his arm. He is followed by two nuns. The black men become alert and draw their sharp-looking steel swords.*

INTERPRETER. Wait! We come in peace! Waa mcome gpeace! Waa mcome gpeace!

PRIEST, *in a loud Billy Graham voice.* I bring the word of God! To this savage wilderness!

INTERPRETER. Mgoon mwan ngold nresources nland! Mgive ugoda!

KING. Mwha sisi mfool twa!

PRIEST. What did he say?

INTERPRETER. He said this is not a "savage wilderness"—this is the Kingdom of Baboza. A long-flourishing kingdom. A kingdom that existed when you were still just a gleam in Darwin's eye! He says he is a king and these are his two aces.

PRIEST. He said all that? *He affects a saintly pose, eyes heavenward.* I bring the word of God!

The gospel! The wisdom of the Bible to you and your humble people. I come to lead you away from this pagan primitive existence!

INTERPRETER. Mbrainwash ngood mcrap ntell!

KING. Mbullshit sisi nfool! ufool!

PRIEST. What?

INTERPRETER. He said his people are not humble, but proud—he said theirs is not a pagan existence—and he'll buy a dozen of your Bibles if you just get the hell out of here and go back to where you came from. He says they have their own gods!

PRIEST. Tell him my god is more powerful than all of his gods!

INTERPRETER. Ooboy! Ooboy nmassive olie B's!

KING. Mcanopul ncrap onme! noforme!

PRIEST. What did he say?

INTERPRETER. He said, "We'll let the gods settle that!"

KING. Umr mbada nfuc! Mwa nnopartu! *Ecstatic.* Ahsiwawamgantubasisi!

PRIEST. What in the hell was that?

INTERPRETER. He said his senses warn him that you are evil and your god must be evil. A man is as his god. If his god is strong and good and kind then the man of that god is by nature good and kind. If a god is evil that god's man is by nature evil, and he will be weak, because evil is weakness, and weakness is evil. The man of the strong, good, kind god is superior to the man of the evil god. The man of the good god does not lie, and steal, and kill for gain. All the universe is his provision, by his being a natural part of it! The evil god provokes the good god, and the good god is strong enough to destroy him, as he must keep the universe pure and peaceful. You are the man of an evil god! An accident!

PRIEST. He said all that with one word? My God! *Decides to try a different approach.* Gentle savage, let Christ be your salvation. Let Christ save your people from sins. Let Christ save your souls! Let Christ give you everlasting life and unlimited credit!

INTERPRETER. Mr mtry nulie nmor bs! Ugofor?

KING. Mno chump! Nmore bulshi fum sisi fool! *Ecstatic.* Ahsiwamaumbanti.

PRIEST. What did he say?

INTERPRETER. He said they are in need of no salvation. He said his people have visible, beautiful souls that do not need saving. He said no man, among his people, wants everlasting life! He said he is not gentle. He said he is not a savage! He said who the hell is Christ?

PRIEST. Who the hell is Christ? He died on the cross! He died for you and your people's sins!

INTERPRETER. Mwa mmnu bs ntell alshi ugofor ifi?

KING. Ahahwa mpa ngood elie!

PRIEST. Huh?

INTERPRETER. He said his people do not sin, but if they do sin *they die* for their own sins—they don't need Christ!

PRIEST. But Christ will heal your sick and raise your dead!

INTERPRETER. Nmuch nmore bs iff nugofor!

KING. Mjuju mcando.

PRIEST. What?

INTERPRETER. He said *he* can heal the sick and raise the dead.

PRIEST. Oh, hell! They're too filled with pagan beliefs. Maybe the girls can convince them. Take out your hymnbooks, girls.

The two NUNS *go into a burlesque-type song-dance, with the most vulgar, obscene bumps and grinds, in their habits.*

NUNS. Have you had any Christ lately? We've got Christ right here! Pray! And come and getsomechrist todaaaaaaaay!

Tossing their skirts, showing their legs—their asses—in an attempt at temptation. The KING *turns away, holding his nose, and has to pull his curious guards away. The* PRIEST *notices this weakness.*

KING. Mgeback! Mgeback!

PRIEST. That didn't work. Mmmm? How can you fail to put all your faith in HE who made the blind see! Who walked the waters of Galilee!

INTERPRETER, *exasperated.* Abu wabanshi abu ngo mnuli bsi?

KING. Waa ha hmfool msay!

PRIEST. What did he say this time?

INTERPRETER. He says he doesn't believe it. No one can walk on water.

PRIEST. Get the pictures, girls, quick! They're interested! We've got 'em!

The NUNS *run off—return with large picture of Christ in his act. The* KING *examines the pictures, held by the* INTERPRETER, *as the* NUNS *rush to the other two black men and passionately embrace them. Overwhelming them, pushing them to the ground.*

PRIEST. You see. Jesus walking the water. *He comes behind the* KING *and strikes him with the cross, knocking him senseless.* There! That oughta civilize him! Get the chains!

While the INTERPRETER *chains them, the* NUNS *remove all the valuables. The* PRIEST *removes the* KING'S *jewelry—stuffing his pockets full.*

PRIEST. Call the Pope. Tell him the gold is on the way to Rome—tell him we've spread Christianity to another dark corner of Africa. *He gets a small bowl with water and starts sprinkling the prostrate* KING.

PRIEST. When he wakes up, tell him the spirit hit him, and that he's saved. Hard as I hit him he won't remember a damned thing—but be sure to leave the chains on. I think it was Christ who said, "don't take any chances with a king and two aces, unless you can beat the king and cover the aces"—or was it the Pope who said that?

The baptism begins to revive the KING, *he looks around, bewildered at the changed scene. The* PRIEST *is mumbling incoherently about "Christ," "peace," "Salvation," "non-violence," "birth control." His voice sounds hypnotic. Lights gradually to black.*

A Black at the Gridiron Dinner*

Roger Wilkins

When it was all over, a number of men had tears in their eyes, even more had lifted hearts and spirits, but a few were so disspirited that they went upstairs to get drunk. We had just heard the President and Vice President of the United States in a unique piano duet—and to many old Gridiron Dinner veterans, it was a moving show-stopper. To a few others, it was a depressing display of gross insensitivity and both conscious and unconscious racism—further proof that they and their hopes for their country are becoming more and more isolated from those places where America's heart and power seem to be moving.

The annual dinner of the Gridiron Club is the time when men can put on white ties and tails and forget the anxiety and loneliness that are central to the human condition and look at other men in white ties and tails and know that they have arrived or are still there.

The guests are generally grateful and gracious. But the event's importance is beyond the structures of graciousness because it shows the most powerful elements of the nation's daily press and all elements of the nation's government locked in a symbiotic embrace. The rich and the powerful in jest tell many truths about themselves and about their country. I don't feel very gracious about what they told me.

Some weeks ago, to my surprise and delight, a friend—a sensitive man of honor —with a little half-apology about the required costume, invited me to attend the dinner.

The first impression was stunning: almost every passing face was a familiar one. Some had names that were household words. Some merely made up a montage of the familiar faces and bearings of our times. There were Richard Helms and Walter Mondale and Henry Kissinger and George McGovern and Joel Broyhill and Tom Wicker and William Westmoreland and John Mitchell and Tom Clark (ironically placed, by

* From Roger Wilkins, "A Black at the Gridiron Dinner," *Washington Post,* 26 March 1970. © The Washington Post. Reprinted by permission of author and publisher.

some pixie no doubt, next to each other on the dais) and Robert Finch and Ralph Nader, and of course, the President of the United States.

One thing quickly became clear about those faces. Apart from Walter Washington— who, I suppose, as Mayor had to be invited—mine was the only face in a crowd of some 500 that was not white. There were no Indians, there were no Asians, there were no Puerto Ricans, there were no Mexican-Americans. There were just the Mayor and me. Incredibly, I sensed that there were few in that room who thought that anything was missing.

There is something about an atmosphere like that that is hard to define, but excruciatingly easy for a black man to feel. It is the heavy, almost tangible, clearly visible, broad assumption that in places where it counts, America is a white country. I was an American citizen sitting in a banquet room in a hotel which I had visited many times. (My last occasion for a visit to that hotel was the farewell party for the white staff director and the black deputy staff director of the United States Commission on Civil Rights.) This night in that room, less than three miles from my home in the nation's capital, a 60 per cent black city, I felt out of place in America.

That is not to say that there were not kind men, good men, warm men in and around and about the party, nor is it to say that anyone was personally rude to me. There were some old friends and some new acquaintances whom I was genuinely glad to see. Ed Muskie who had given a very funny and exquisitely partisan speech (the Republicans have three problems: the war, inflation, and what to say on Lincoln's Birthday) was one of those. I was even warmly embraced by the Deputy Attorney General, Mr. Kleindienst, and had a long conversation with the associate director of the FBI, Mr. DeLoach.

But it was not the people so much who shaped the evening. It was the humor amidst that pervasive whiteness about what was going on in this country these days that gave the evening its form and substance. There were many jokes about the "Southern strategy." White people have funny senses of humor. Some of them found something to laugh about in the Southern strategy. Black people don't think it's funny at all. That strategy hits men where they live—in their hopes for themselves and their dreams for their children. We find it sinister and frightening. And let it not be said that the Gridiron Club and its guests are not discriminating about their humor. There was a real sensitivity about the inappropriateness of poking fun that night about an ailing former President, but none about laughing about policies which crush the aspirations of millions of citizens of this nation. An instructive distinction, I thought.

There was a joke about the amendments to the Constitution (so what if we rescind the First Amendment, there'll still be 25 left), and about repression (you stop bugging me, I'll stop bugging you), and there were warm, almost admiring jokes about the lady who despises "liberal Communists" and thinks something like the Russian Revolution occurred in Washington on November 15. There was applause—explosive and prolonged—for Judges Clement Haynsworth and Julius Hoffman (the largest hands of the evening by my reckoning.)

As I looked, listened and saw the faces of those judges and of the generals and of the admirals and of the old members of the oligarchies of the House and Senate, I thought of the soft, almost beatific smile of Cesar Chavez; the serious troubled face of Vine Deloria Jr., and the handsome, sensitive faces of Andy Young and Julian Bond of Georgia. All those men and more have fought with surely as much idealism as any general ever carried with him to Saigon, with as much courage as any senator ever took with him on a fact-finding trip to a Vietnam battlefield, or even as much hope, spirit and belief in the American dream as any Peace Corps kid ever took to the Andes in Peru. But the men I have named fought for American freedom on American soil. And they were not there. But Julius Hoffman was.

As the jokes about the "Southern strategy" continued, I thought about the one-room segregated schoolhouse where I began my education in Kansas City. That was my neighborhood school. When they closed it, I was bused—without an apparent second thought—as a 5-year-old kindergartener, across town to the black elementary school. It was called Crispus Attucks.

And I thought of the day I took my daughter when she was seven along the Freedom Trail, in Boston, and of telling her about the black man named Crispus Attucks who was the first American to die in our revolution. And I remember telling her that white America would try very hard in thousands of conscious and unconscious ways both to make her feel that her people had had no part in building America's greatness and to make her feel inferior. And I remember the profoundly moving and grateful look in her eyes and the wordless hug she gave me when I told her, "Don't you believe them because they are lies." And I felt white America in that room in the Statler Hilton telling me all those things that night, and I told myself, "Don't you believe them because they are lies."

And when it came to the end, the President and the Vice President of the United States, in an act which they had consciously worked up, put on a Mr. Bones routine about the Southern strategy with the biggest boffo coming as the Vice President affected a deep Southern accent. And then they played their duets—the President playing his sons, the Vice President playing "Dixie," the whole thing climaxed by "God Bless America" and "Auld Lang Syne." The crowd ate it up. They roared. As they roared I thought that after our black decade of imploring, suing, marching, lobbying, singing, rebelling, praying and dying we had come to this: a Vice Presidential Dixie with the President as his straight man. In the serious and frivolous places of power—at the end of that decade—America was still virtually lily white. And most of the people in that room were reveling in it. What, I wondered, would it take for them to understand that men also come in colors other than white. Seeing and feeling their blindness, I shuddered at the answers that came most readily to mind.

As we stood voluntarily, some more slowly than others, when the two men began to play God Bless America, I couldn't help remembering Judy Collins (who could not sing in Chicago) singing "Where Have All the Flowers Gone?"

So, later, I joined Nick Kotz, author of "Let Them Eat Promises" and we drank down our dreams.

I don't believe that I have been blanketed in and suffocated by such racism and insensitivity since I was a sophomore in college when I was the only black invited to a minstrel spoof put on at a white fraternity house.

But then, they were only fraternity brothers, weren't they?

Black Power
and Black History*
John Henrik Clarke

> It is not really a "Negro revolution" that is upsetting the country. What is upsetting the country is a sense of its own identity. If, for example, one managed to change the curriculum in all the schools so that Negroes learned more about themselves and their real contributions to this culture, you would be liberating not only Negroes, you'd be liberating white people who know nothing about their own history. And the reason is that if you are compelled to lie about one aspect of anybody's history, you must lie about it all. If you have to lie about my real role here, if you have to pretend that I hoed all that cotton just because I loved you, then you have done something to yourself. You are mad.
> —James Baldwin from "A Talk to Teachers," December 1963

Figuratively speaking, the concept of Black Power and Black History are twins that were fathered by the same historical experience. This concept was created to counteract another concept: that the people of African descent had no history worthy of respect. The Europeans who started the slave trade and the colonial system that followed needed to propagate this concept in order to justify their action.

The present-day young black militants are asking, in many ways, why the word *history* is so limited when it is applied to their people. They are beginning to learn (belatedly) that history, depending on how it is manipulated, can be either an instrument of oppression or of liberation. In most cases, what is called "African History" is only the history of Africa's contact with Europe, beginning with the slave trade. What is called "Negro History" is generally the history of American slavery and subsequent effects.

The Europeans who started the slave trade in the fifteen century had to forget—or pretend to forget—all they had previously known about Africa's contribution to the development of mankind.

* From John Henrik Clarke, "Black Power and Black History," *Negro Digest*, XVIII (Feb. 1969), 13–22, 83–85. Copyright © February 1969 by *Negro Digest*. Reprinted by permission of *Black World*.

The present-day Black Power and Black History advocates are trying to restore what the slave trade and the system of economic oppression took away. Their fight has long roots and it was not started by Stokely Carmichael or H. Rap Brown.

In a formal sense the concept of Black Power started in the nineteenth century, concurrent with the many attempts to restore Black men to an honorable place in history. The concept of Black Power confuses most people because they are looking for a complicated system. Black Power means no more or less than the right to determine your own destiny, starting with the control of your own communities. This is the same thing that every ethnic group in America has—or is trying to get. Black Power without a respect for Black History is meaningless. Until the essential manhood of a people is respected, no power in their hands is effective.

In a speech made in Cuba last year, Stokely Carmichael, while addressing himself to the subject "Black Power and The Third World," said this:

> Since 1966, the cry of the rebellions has been "Black Power." In this cry, there was an ideology implied which the masses understood instinctively. It is because we are powerless that we are oppressed and it is only with power that we can make the decisions governing our lives and our communities. . . . Black Power is more than a slogan; it is a way of looking at our problems and the beginning of a solution. Because our color has been used as a weapon to oppress us, we must use our color as a weapon of liberation. This is the same as other people using their nationality as a weapon for their liberation. . . . This coming together around our race was an inevitable part of our struggle. We recognize, however, that this is not the totality, only the necessary beginning.

Then, while emphasizing the need for the cultural restoration of a people he said:

> Black Power recognizes that while we are made to feel inferior, this is only that we can be easily exploited. Color and culture were and are key in our oppression, therefore our analysis of history and our economic analysis are rooted in these concepts. With power we will take our birthright, because it was with power that our birthright was taken from us. . . . Black Power not only addresses itself to exploitation, but to the problem of cultural integrity.

The nineteenth century black militants, and some before them, were saying essentially the same thing in different ways.

The fight against the distortion and suppression of the true history of the Africans and Afro-Americans was started long before the Civil War by "free Negroes" and escaped slaves who had learned to read and write.

The back-to-Africa idea has been a recurring theme in the lives of Black Americans for more than a hundred years. The thought was strong during the formative years of the Colonization Society and some of the most outstanding Black men of the eighteenth and nineteenth centuries came under its persuasion. In the middle of the nineteenth century, while the issue of slavery was being debated in most of the country, the feeling for Africa among American blacks was growing stronger. Publications like Freedoms' Journal and Douglass Monthly, edited by Frederick Douglass, called attention to the plight of the people of Africa as well as the Black Americans.

As far back as 1881, the renowned scholar and benefactor of West Africa, Dr. Edward Wilmot Blyden, speaking on the occasion of his inauguration as President of Liberia College, sounded the note for the organized teaching of the culture and civilization of Africa and decried the fact that the world's image of Africa was not in keeping with Africa's true status in world history. I quote from his address on this occasion:

> The people generally are not yet prepared to understand their own interests in the great work to be done for themselves and their children. We shall be obliged to work for some time to come not only without the popular sympathy we ought to have but with utterly inadequate resources.

> In all English-speaking countries the mind of the intelligent Negro child revolts against the descriptions of the Negro given in elementary books, geographies, travels, histories. . . .

> Having embraced or at least assented to these falsehoods about himself, he concludes that his only hope of rising in the scale of respectable manhood is to strive for what is most unlike himself and most alien to his peculiar tastes. And whatever his literary attainments or acquired ability, he fancies that he must grind at the mill which is provided for him, putting in material furnished by his hands, bringing no contribution from his own field; and of course nothing comes out but what is put in.

The great human drama now being called "The Black Revolution in the U.S.A." has long historical roots, and it cannot be fully understood until it is seen in this context. In his 1944 book, *Capitalism and Slavery*, Dr. Eric Williams places the origin of this Revolution in historical perspective and calls attention to its early development:

> When, in 1492, Columbus, representing the Spanish monarchy, discovered the New World, he set in train the long and bitter international rivalry over colonial possessions for which, after four and a half centuries, no solution has yet been found. Portugal, which had initiated the movement of international expansion, claimed the new territories on the ground that they fell within the scope of a papal bull of 1455 authorizing her to reduce to servitude all infidel people. The two powers (Spain and Portugal), to avoid controversy, sought arbitration and, as Catholics, turned to the Pope—a natural and logical step in an age when the universal claims of the Papacy were still unchallenged by individuals and governments. After carefully sifting the rival claims, the Pope issued, in 1493, a series of papal bulls which established a line of demarcation between the colonial possessions of the states: The East went to Portugal and the West went to Spain.

Though the announcement of the fact came much later, the European "scramble for Africa" and subsequently, Asia and North America, started with this act. The labor and raw materials of Africa, Asia, South America and the West Indies financed the European Industrial Revolution.

The Africans who were brought to the New World against their will were dehumanized, and in most cases, deculturalized. They were neither respected Africans nor accepted New World Americans. They were renamed, and became a marginal branch of the human family now referred to as Negroes. The Europeans needed a rationale for their actions and a rationale was created with supporting concepts. The cruelest concept ever devised by the mind of man was created to support the slave trade and the colonial system that followed—the concept of race and the assumption that there are superior and inferior races. The Africans were depicted as a people without a history who had never properly handled power and who, certainly, had made no contribution to the development of human cultures. And thus the seeds of the present-day conflict were planted.

The American Federation of Teachers' Conference on "Racism in Education" held in Washington, D. C. on December 8, 9, and 10, 1966, set in motion much of the present action and the debate about Black History and how it should be taught in the public schools.

The noted actor, Ossie Davis, addressed the conference on the first day. His opening remarks were: "Those of us who are concerned, who are caught up, who really want to be involved in the revolution, must be prepared at this conference to tear aside our most private thoughts and prejudices. . . ."

The tone for the conference had been set. For two days more than 1,500 teachers and educators examined and indicated the American educational system. They were told that a curtain of ignorance hangs over the school systems of this nation and that our children are not being educated to face the realities of this nation and this world. Cases of deliberate distortion of the role that the Black Americans have played in the making of this country were pointed out. And it was further stated that everyone from professional textbook writers to missionaries had participated in this distortion.

Ossie Davis cited the English language as a basic transmitter of prejudice. In his speech entitled, "The English Language is My Enemy," he said that he counted 120 synonyms for the term "blackness" in Roget's Thesaurus, half of which were grossly unfavorable.

Davis argued that right from the time a black child learns the English language he learns 60 ways to despise himself, and a white child learns 60 ways to aid and abet the crime.

Keith E. Baird, a New York school teacher, who followed Ossie Davis, talked about the importance of ethnic identification for Afro-Americans. Mr. Baird, who is a teacher of languages, spoke of the respected place in history, as celebrated in the Jewish holiday of Hanukkah of the Maccabees of Biblical times. He also pointed out that in the process of ethnic identification, not only a person's individual attributes are considered, but the "cultural identification of this group."

Baird presented to the conference a resolution that he urged it to adopt, the wording of which was:

To say that the slavery-connected word "Negro" should be abandoned, and in its place the words "Afro" or "African-American" be applied to persons of African descent in the United States in all places where such reference to ethnic descent is appropriate.

At a later conference session concerning resolutions, this one was unanimously adopted.

In his presentation, Mr. Baird had defined what the cry for Black History is about—it is about the search for a people's identity and their need for a new image of themselves. The Black Americans are trying to locate themselves on the map of human geography. This explains the growing preference for the words "Black African" and "Afro-American". These words show how the Black Americans relate to a land, a history and a culture.

In a number of other conferences sponsored by the local branches of the American Federation of Teachers and the UFT, the teachers agreed on plans to implement courses in Black History. The main conferences were held in Detroit (May 11–13, 1967) and in Chicago (March 22–24, 1968), and conferences in Denver and St. Louis followed. While many of the white teachers clearly admitted that racism is rampant in the American educational system, very few of them had any basic plan concerning what to do about it. Their reluctance to commit themselves to the correction of this racism caused a lot of black teachers to form separate organizations, some within the framework of the American Federation of Teachers and the UFT. The Chicago Black Teachers' Caucus was one. In New York City the Afro-American Teachers' Association was another.

Still another organization, the Conference of Afro-American Educators, which met in Chicago in June 1968, shows the best potential of becoming a nation-wide force to affect change in the educational system. At this conference Donald Freeman, who renamed himself Baba Lamumba, defined education as it relates to black people:

What we understand by education is the application of all one's knowledge for the benefit of the collective which in turn will benefit each individual within the collective. To this end what must constitute a basic part of one's education is the understanding of people rather than things. We realize that once people understand themselves, their knowledge of things is facilitated, that the exclusive knowledge of things does not guarantee knowledge of people and in fact contributes to the erosion, disintegration, and destruction of the creativity of man.

Therefore, education must (1) teach Black people who they are, (2) teach Black people what they are fighting for, (3) teach Black people who they must identify with, (4) teach Black people where their loyalty must lie, (5) teach Black people what must be done, (6) teach Black people how to do it, and (7) teach Black people that the destinies of all Black people are inseparably linked whether we are in North, Central, or South America, the West Indies, Europe, Asia, or Africa.

Broadening his explanation, Mr. Freeman continued:

Now, there must be a complete unity of all aspects of one's life and in particular education must be indelibly linked with one's life processes for the benefit of each Black man and woman and all Black people. Those who have knowledge primarily from books must be linked with those who have knowledge from the streets and vice versa to confront and solve all the problems of Black people. Education must assure that all of what one learns can be and will be applied to concrete practical problems and their solutions. If our people can throw molotov cocktails in white stores, we can certainly throw molotov cocktails in our minds. Mathematics, physics, electronics, sociology, religion and other sciences must not be viewed as abstractions, but comprehended as the concentrated experiences of man's inter-relationships with man, nature, and the universe to mold and control his own destiny.

It is obvious that the American educational establishment is not ready to correct itself and implement these suggestions that it would consider extreme. This would not only be tantamount to correcting itself, it would also be tantamount to repudiating itself. At the base of the grievance of the Black teachers and growing numbers of black people is the fact that they have been educated or miseducated in a system that has yet to acknowledge that they are an integral part of American or Western Civilization. Both the clamor for Black Power and Black History are the clamor of people to enter the mainstream of a society and to institute dynamic social reform—or to replace that society. The most far-reaching reforms will be in the field of education. Control is the key word in the school situation because it implies power to act in one's best interest at a time and a place of one's choosing. The educational establishment could digest or tolerate decentralization because the school system would still be run in the main by the educational establishment, which is a force operating outside of the local community. When community control is added to decentralization, a whole new area of power is defined. This means that the community will have the right to hire and fire teachers and to control the massive budget of the school system that is now a major American industry.

In an address in Ann Arbor, Michigan on May 25, 1968, Dr. Grace Boggs said in effect that the question of Black control of the schools has now become a question of survival for all black people. Urban school systems are disintegrating before their eyes to the point where their actual physical and mental safety are at stake. Black children and their parents have lost the traditional respect for the teachers and principals of their schools because of the growing alienation between the school and the community. The mass media, principally television, have taught these children to become suspicious of most large establishments, especially police forces and governmental agencies that make promises which they do not keep.

Many of the white teachers in the large educational systems in cities like New York, Detroit, Philadelphia, Chicago, and Los Angeles, come to the system with preconceived notions about the ability of the Black child to learn. Instead of teaching him they spend a lot of time convincing themselves that the children are unteachable. They do not bring their best teaching ability to these communities because they do not respect the children or the community well enough to do so. In addition to being poor teachers for the Black community, these teachers are not even good baby-sitters. In a lot of cases they are arrogant, unfulfilled and insecure people, long overdue for analysis. Very often the Black child and the Black community become whipping-boys for their neuroses. Community control would mean that these teachers can be transferred or fired, once their lack of qualifications have been proven.

There is no attempt to drive all white teachers out of any Black community. However, teachers who fall within the above description will not be secure under any form of community control.

Keith E. Baird, director of the Afro-American History and Cultural Unit of the Board of Education, gave the following explanation of decentralization and community control at the Summer Forum at Columbia University in August of 1968 on the Black Experience.

I am going to talk about decentralization in the public schools and its implications. I use the term "decentralization" largely because it is the one that is generally used. Now, most words that begin with this prefix "de-" suggest a kind of fall from grace, and I think that discussion about the changes that are being sought in the school system suffer somewhat from this semantic difficulty. I rejoice, however, to see that in this booklet the "Decentralization" means re-forming the present school system in New York City into largely autonomous school districts, joined with the central education agency into a city-wide federation.

Now this is a fairly decent and workable definition, but what does it actually mean in terms of the "Black Experience," the context in which we have come together to discuss this matter? We seem to have two separate questions before us: "decentralization" and "community control." Of course, the two are not necessarily mutually exclusive: you can have decentralization without having community control and you can have community control without having decentralization.

Now there is no problem about white people controlling the schools, because that, of course, is what has always happened. The schools are run by white people: the majority of the teachers are white, and the people who administer the schools are in great part white. Thus we have what are essentially white schools, reflecting white interests, a white self-concept, and white culture. The question of community control comes in because certain enclaves, certain new ethnic enclaves, will now be having greater control, or at any rate be in a better position to exercise control over the schools their children go to—provided, of course, that the rules and regulations of the New York City Board of Education actually permit this to happen.

Thus we come to what is really the crux of the situation, namely, the control of schools in Afro-American and Puerto Rican areas by the Afro-American and Puerto Rican communities, particularly because these communities have not been significantly represented until now at the policy-making level in educational affairs. What community control boils down to is simply this: are we or are we not going to let Black people and Puerto Rican people really tell teachers what to do? Especially, tell white teachers what to do? And so on. That is really what this whole thing boils down to, and we may as well face up to it.

Because most of the decentralization and community control talk in New York City is centered around I. S. 201 in Harlem and Ocean Hill Brownsville in Brooklyn, it would be well to show the essence of the background of this conflict.

The crucial issue of the I. S. 201 controversy is the poor quality of education in ghettos such as Harlem.

From the first through the twelfth grade, an increasingly larger proportion of ghetto youth perform below their grade level in reading and math. Eighty-seven percent of the pupils in the Harlem school district are below grade level. Better than two-thirds of the pupils drop out before graduation from high school. Daniel Schreiber, the former assistant superintendent of District 4, in which I. S. 201 is located, verified these figures.

The parents of school district 4 were willing to accept the promise of the Board of Education that integration would help solve the problem of poor education for their children.

When 201 was proposed as a junior high school as far back as 1958, parents objected on the grounds that construction of a school at the proposed site would create another segregated school. As late as 1965, Dr. Bernard Donavan maintained that 201 would be an integrated school. He even alluded to having the school related to a University, accompanied by special programs. By February of 1966, Daniel Schreiber maintained that 201 would be integrated, but by this time, "integrated" had come to mean representative groups of black and Puerto Rican children.

As early as March 28, community representatives were demanding the establishment of a community group to which teachers would be responsible in addition to the demand for an integrated school. Parents' opposition to the Board of Education's response (or lack of response) to these demands canceled the scheduled opening of 201 for the spring term of 1966. The school district was gerrymandered without the consultation of the community to create a student body of Puerto Ricans and Negroes.

"Integration" gives way to "quality education." By the end of the summer, the Board of Education had to admit that it had no plan for truly integrating I. S. 201. The parents, realizing that the Board of Education had no intention of integrating the schools of Harlem, focused attention on the basic problem of improving the quality of education in Harlem with the realization that it would in reality have to be segregated.

There is agreement between the parents and the Board of Education that the Board has failed to integrate the Harlem schools. There is also agreement between the parents and the Board that the quality of education in Harlem is low. The disagreement lies in the means used to improve the quality of education. The parents place the full responsibility of poor education in Harlem upon the Board of Education whose present structure they feel is incapable of providing or administering a quality educational system to meet the needs of the ghetto community. The composition of the board, how its members are selected and its source of power indicate the distance that exists between the body that makes educational policy and the community for whom the policy is made.

The Ocean Hill-Brownsville decentralization experiment in Brooklyn, New York was spoiled by success. The Local School Board, consisting mainly of parents from the community, took their jobs seriously and asked that a number of teachers who they deemed incompetent be transferred. This move seemed to have shocked and angered both the Board of Education and the head of the United Federation of Teachers. This abrupt exercising of power by the Local School Board and their Unit Administrator came unexpectedly.

The two large black ghettos of Brooklyn merge at Ocean Hill. Its inhabitants include a growing number of Puerto Ricans. Nothing of a dynamic nature was expected of these slumdwellers.

In September 1966, the controversy around I. S. 201 in Harlem had a profound effect on the Ocean Hill-Brownsville school district. That month a group of parents in Harlem demanded that the Board of Education respect their right to select the principal for I. S. 201. These parents were asking, for the first time, to have a voice in the administration of the schools in their community. The contagious cry for community control was now spreading beyond Harlem. It did not bypass the Ocean Hill-Brownsville School District in Brooklyn.

After some protracted agitation, the Board of Education allowed the people of Ocean Hill to form an administrative unit, with the understanding that the Board would relinquish some of its authority to this unit. The Administrative Unit and the local Governing Board succeeded and began to exercise the authority that the Board of Education never thought it would use. This is the basis of their trouble with the Board of Education and the United Federation of Teachers.

The dispute between the people of Ocean Hill-Brownsville on one side and the Board of Education and United Federation of Teachers on the other side might well be a sad indication of what will soon be a national crisis in education. The cry for Black Power and Black History has rekindled a long smoldering fire that will, no doubt, affect major changes in the educational, political and economic structure of the United States.

Black Muslims*

Malcolm X

. . . I would come to the microphone, specifically to condition the audience to hear Mr. Muhammad who had flown from Chicago to teach us all in person.

I would raise up my hand, *"As-Salaikum-Salaam—"*

"Wa-Alaikum-Salaam!" It was a roared response from the great audience's Muslim seating section.

There was a general pattern that I would follow on these occasions:

"My black brothers and sisters—of all religious beliefs, or of no religious beliefs —we all have in common the greatest binding tie we could have . . . we all are *black* people!

"I'm not going to take all day telling you some of the greatnesses of The Honorable Elijah Muhammad. I'm just going to tell you now his *greatest* greatness! He is the *first,* the *only* black leader to identify, to you and me, *who* is our enemy!

"The Honorable Elijah Muhammad is the first black leader among us with the *courage* to tell us—out here in public—something which when you begin to think of it back in your homes, you will realize we black people have been *living* with, we have been *seeing,* we have been *suffering,* all of our lives!

"Our *enemy* is the *white man!*

"And why is Mr. Muhammad's teaching us this such a great thing? Because when you know *who* your enemy is, he can no longer keep you divided, and fighting, one brother against the other! Because when you *recognize* who your enemy is, he can no longer use trickery, promises, lies, hypocrisy, and his evil acts to keep you deaf, dumb, and blinded!

"When you recognize *who* your enemy is, he can no longer brainwash you, he can no longer pull wool over your eyes so that you never stop to see that you are living in pure *hell* on this earth, while *he* lives in pure *heaven* right on this same earth!—This enemy who tells you that you are both supposed to be worshiping the same white Christian God that—you are told—stands for the *same* things for *all* men!

* From Malcolm X, with the assistance of Alex Haley, *The Autobiography of Malcolm X* (New York: Grove Press, Inc., 1965), pp. 251–65. Copyright © 1964 by Alex Haley and Malcolm X. Copyright © 1965 by Alex Haley and Betty Shabazz. Reprinted by permission of Grove Press, Inc.

"Oh, *yes,* that devil is our enemy. I'll *prove* it! Pick up any daily newspaper! Read the false charges leveled against our beloved religious leader. It only points up the fact that the Caucasian race never wants any black man who is not their puppet or parrot to speak for our people. This Caucasian devil slavemaster does not want or trust us to leave him—yet when we stay here among him, he continues to keep us at the very *lowest level* of his society!

"The white man has always *loved* it when he could keep us black men tucked away somewhere, always out of sight, around the corner! The white man has always *loved* the kind of black leaders whom he could ask, 'Well, how's things with your people up there?' But because Mr. Elijah Muhammad takes an uncompromising stand with the white man, the white man *hates* him! When you hear the *white man* hate him, you, too, because you don't understand Biblical prophecy, wrongly label Mr. Muhammad—as a racist, a hate-teacher, or of being anti-white and teaching black supremacy—"

The audience suddenly would begin a rustling of turning. . . .

Mr. Muhammad would be rapidly moving along up a center aisle from the rear—as once he had entered our humble little mosques—this man whom we regarded as Islam's gentle, meek, brown-skinned Lamb. Stalwart, striding, close-cropped, handpicked Fruit of Islam guards were a circle surrounding him. He carried his Holy Bible, his holy Quran. The small, dark pillbox atop his head was gold-embroidered with Islam's flag, the sun, moon, and stars. The Muslims were crying out their adoration and their welcome. "Little Lamb!" "As-Salaikum-Salaam!" "Praise be to Allah!"

Tears would be in more eyes than mine. He had rescued me when I was a convict; Mr. Muhammad had trained me in his home, as if I was his son. I think that my life's peaks of emotion, until recently, at least, were when, suddenly, the Fruit of Islam guards would stop stiffly at attention, and the platform's several steps would be mounted alone by Mr. Muhammad, and his ministers, including me, sprang around him, embracing him, wringing both his hands. . . .

I would turn right back to the microphone, not to keep waiting those world's biggest black audiences who had come to hear him.

"My black brothers and sisters—*no* one will know *who* we are . . . until *we* know who we are! We never will be able to *go* anywhere until we know *where* we are! The Honorable Elijah Muhammad is giving us a true identity, and a true position—the first time they have ever been *known* to the American black man!

"You can be around this man and never *dream* from his actions the power and the authority he has—" (Behind me, believe me when I tell you, I could *feel* Mr. Muhammad's *power.*)

"He does not *display,* and *parade,* his *power!* But no other black leader in America has followers who will lay down their lives if he says so! And I don't mean all of this non-violent, begging-the-white-man kind of dying . . . all of this sitting-in, sliding-in, wading-in, eating-in, diving-in, and all the rest—

"My black brothers and sisters, you have come from your homes to hear—now you are *going* to hear—America's *wisest* black man! America's *boldest* black man! America's most *fearless* black man! This wilderness of North America's most *powerful* black man!"

Mr. Muhammad would come quickly to the stand, looking out over the vacuum-quiet audience, his gentle-looking face set, for just a fleeting moment. Then, "As-Salai-kum-Salaam—"

"WA-ALAIKUM-SALAAM!"

The Muslims roared it, as they settled to listen. From experience, they knew that for the next two hours Mr. Muhammad would wield his two-edged sword of truth. In fact, every Muslim worried that he overtaxed himself in the length of his speeches, considering his bronchial asthmatic condition.

"I don't have a degree like many of you out there before me have. But history don't care anything about your degrees.

"The white man, he has filled you with a fear of him from ever since you were little black babies. So over you is the greatest enemy a man can have—and that is fear. I know some of you are afraid to listen to the truth—you have been raised on fear and lies. But I am going to preach to you the truth until you are free of that fear. . . .

"Your slavemaster, he brought you over here, and of your past everything was destroyed. Today, you do not know your true language. What tribe are you from? You would not recognize your tribe's name if you heard it. You don't know nothing about your true culture. You don't even know your family's real name. You are wearing a *white man's* name! The white slavemaster, who *hates* you!

"You are a people who think you know all about the Bible, and all about Christianity. You even are foolish enough to believe that nothing is *right* but Christianity!

"You are the planet Earth's only group of people ignorant of yourself, ignorant of your own kind, of your true history, ignorant of your enemy! You know nothing at *all* but what your white slavemaster has chosen to tell you. And he has told you only that which will benefit himself, and his own kind. He has taught you, for *his* benefit, that you are a neutral, shiftless, helpless so-called 'Negro.'

"I say *'so-called'* because you are *not* a 'Negro.' There is no such thing as a race of *'Negroes.'* You are members of the Asiatic nation, from the tribe of *Shabazz!* 'Negro' is a false label forced on you by your slavemaster! He has been pushing things onto you and me and our kind ever since he brought the first slave shipload of us black people here—"

When Mr. Muhammad paused, the Muslims before him cried out, "Little Lamb!" . . . "All praise is due to Allah!" . . . *"Teach,* Messenger!" He would continue.

"The *ignorance* we of the black race here in America have, and the *self-hatred* we have, they are fine examples of what the white slavemaster has seen fit to teach to us. Do we show the plain common sense, like every other people on this planet Earth, to unite among ourselves? No! We are humbling ourselves, sitting-in, and begging-in, trying to *unite* with the slavemaster! I don't seem able to imagine any more ridiculous sight. A thousand ways every day, the white man is telling you 'You can't live here, you can't enter here, you can't eat here, drink here, walk here, work here, you can't ride here, you can't play here, you can't study here.' Haven't we yet seen enough to see that he has no plan to *unite* with you?

"You have tilled his fields! Cooked his food! Washed his clothes! You have cared for his wife and children when he was away. In many cases, you have even suckled him at your *breast!* You have been far and away better Christians than this slavemaster who *taught* you his Christianity!

"You have sweated blood to help him build a country so rich that he can today afford to give away millions—even to his *enemies!* And when those enemies have gotten enough from him to then be able to attack him, you have been his brave soldiers, *dying* for him. And you have been always his most faithful servant during the so-called 'peaceful' times—

"And, *still,* this Christian American white man has not got it in him to find the human *decency,* and enough sense of *justice,* to recognize us, and accept us, the black people who have done so much for him, as fellow human beings!"

"YAH, Man!" . . . *"Um-huh!"* *"Teach,* Messenger!" . . . *"Yah!"* . . . *"Tell 'em!"* . . . "You *right!"* . . . "Take your *time* up there, little Messenger!" . . . "Oh, *yes!"*

Others besides the Muslims would be shouting now. We Muslims were less extroverted than Christian Negroes. It would sound now like an old-fashioned camp meeting.

"So let us, the black people, *separate* ourselves from this white man slavemaster, who despises us so much! You are out here begging him for some so-called *'integration!'* But what is this slavemaster white, *rapist,* going about saying! He is saying *he* won't integrate because black blood will *mongrelize* his race! *He* says that—and look at *us!* Turn around in your seats and look at each other! This slavemaster white man already has *'integrated'* us until you can hardly find among us today any more than a very few who are the black color of our foreparents!"

"God-a-mighty, the man's right!" . . . *"Teach,* Messenger—" "Hear him! *Hear* him!"

"He has left such a little black in us," Mr. Muhammad would go on, "that now he despises us so bad—meaning he despises *himself,* for what he has *done* to us—that he tells us that *legally* if we have got *one drop* of black blood in us, that means you are all-black as far as his laws are concerned! Well, if that's all we've got left, we want to *reclaim* that one drop!"

Mr. Muhammad's frail strength could be seen to be waning. But he would teach on:

"So let us *separate* from this white man, and for the same reason *he* says—in time to save ourselves from any more *'integration!'*

"Why *shouldn't* this white man who likes to think and call himself so good, and so generous, this white man who finances even his enemies—why *shouldn't* he subsidize a separate state, a separate territory, for we black people who have been such faithful slaves and servants? A separate territory on which we can lift *ourselves* out of these white man's *slums* for us, and his *breadlines* for us. And even for *those* he is complaining that we cost him too much! We can do something for *ourselves!* We never have done what we *could*—because we have been brainwashed so well by the slavemaster white man that we must come to him, begging him, for everything we want, and need—"

After perhaps ninety minutes, behind Mr. Muhammad, every minister would have to restrain himself from bolting up to his side, to urge him that it was enough. He would be pressing his hands tightly against the edges of the speaker's stand, to support himself.

"We black people don't *know* what we can do. You never can know what *any-thing* can do—until it is set *free*, to act by itself! If you have a cat in your house that you pamper and pet, you have to free that cat, set it on its *own*, in the woods, before you can see that the cat had it *in* him to shelter and feed itself!

"We, the black people here in America, we never have been *free* to find *out* what we really can *do!* We have knowledge and experience to pool to do for ourselves! All of our lives we have farmed—we can grow our own food. We can set up factories to manu-facture our own necessities! We can build other kinds of businesses, to establish trade, and commerce—and become independent, as other civilized people are—

"We can *throw off* our brainwashing, and our self-hate, and live as *brothers* to-gether . . .

". . . some land of our *own!* . . . Something for *ourselves!* . . . leave this white slavemaster to *himself*. . . ."

Mr. Muhammad always stopped abruptly when he was unable to speak any longer.

The standing ovation, a solid wall of sound, would go on unabating.

Standing up there, flailing my arms, finally I could quiet the audiences as Fruit of Islam ushers began to pass along the seating rows the large, waxed paper buckets we used to take up the collection. I would speak.

"You *know*, from what you have just heard, that no white money finances The Honorable Elijah Muhammad and his program—to 'advise' him and 'contain' him! Mr. Muhammad's program, and his followers, are not 'integrated.' Mr. Muhammad's pro-gram and organization are *all*-black!

"We are the *only* black organization that *only* black people support! These so-called 'Negro progress' organizations—Why, they insult your intelligence, claiming they are fighting in your behalf, to get you the equal rights you are asking for . . . claiming they are *fighting* the white man who refuses to give you your rights. Why, the white man *supports* those organizations! If you belong, you pay your two, or three, or five dollars a year—but *who* gives those organizations those two, and three, and five *thousand* dollar donations? The *white* man! He *feeds* those organizations! So he controls those organizations! He *advises* them—so he *contains* them! Use your common sense—aren't you going to advise and control and contain anyone that you support, like your child?

"The white man would love to support Mr. Elijah Muhammad. Because if Mr. Muhammad had to rely on his support, he could *advise* Mr. Muhammad. My black brothers and sisters, it is *only* because *your* money, *black* money, supports Mr. Muham-mad, that he can hold these all-black meetings from city to city, telling us black men the *truth!* That's why we are asking for your all-black *support!*"

Nearly all bills—and far from all one-dollar bills, either, filled the waxed buckets.

The buckets were swiftly emptied, then refilled, as the Fruit of Islam ushers covered the entire audience.

The audience atmosphere was almost as if the people had gone limp. The collections always covered the rally expenses, and anything beyond that helped to continue building the Nation of Islam.

After several big rallies, Mr. Muhammad directed that we would admit the white press. Fruit of Islam men thoroughly searched them, as everyone else was searched—their notebooks, their cameras, camera cases, and whatever else they carried. Later, Mr. Muhammad said that *any* whites who wanted to hear the truth could attend our public rallies, until a small separate section for whites was filled.

Most whites who came were students and scholars. I would watch their congealed and reddened faces staring up at Mr. Muhammad. "The white man *knows* that his acts have been those of a devil!" I would watch also the faces of the professional black men, the so-called intellectuals who attacked us. They possessed the academic know-how, they possessed the technical and the scientific skills that could help to lead their mass of poor, black brothers out of our condition. But all these intellectual and professional black men could seem to think of was humbling themselves, and begging, trying to "integrate" with the so-called "liberal" white man who was telling them, "In time . . . everything's going to work out one day . . . just wait and have patience." These intellectual and professional Negroes couldn't use what they knew for the benefit of their own black kind simply because even among themselves they were disunited. United among themselves, united with their own kind, they could have benefited black people all over the world!

I would watch the faces of those intellectual and professional Negroes growing grave, and set—as the truth hit home to them.

We were watched. Our telephones were tapped. Still right today, on my home telephone, if I said, "I'm going to bomb the Empire State Building," I guarantee you in five minutes it would be surrounded. When I was speaking publicly sometimes I'd guess which were F.B.I. faces in the audience, or other types of agents. Both the police and the F.B.I. intently and persistently visited and questioned us. "I do not fear them," Mr. Muhammad said. "I have all that I need—the truth."

Many a night, I drifted off to sleep, filled with wonder at how the two-edged-sword teachings so hurt, confused, concerned, and upset the government full of men trained highly in all of the modern sciences. I felt that it never could have been unless The Most Learned One, Allah Himself, had given the little fourth-grade-trained Messenger something.

Black agents were sent to infiltrate us. But the white man's "secret" spy often proved, first of all, a black man. I can't say *all* of them, of course, there's no way to know—but some of them, after joining us, and hearing, seeing and *feeling* the truth for every black man, revealed their roles to us. Some resigned from the white man's agencies and came to work in the Nation of Islam. A few kept their jobs to counterspy, telling us the white man's statements and plans about our Nation. This was how we learned that after wanting to know what happened within our Temples, the white law agencies' second major concern was the thing that I believe still ranks today as a big worry among America's penologists: the steadily increasing rate at which black convicts embrace Islam.

Generally, while still in prison, our convict-converts preconditioned themselves to meet our Nation's moral laws. As it had happened with me, when they left prison, they entered a Temple fully qualified to become registered Muslims. In fact, convict-converts usually were better prepared than were numerous prospective Muslims who never had been inside a prison.

We were not nearly so easy to enter as a Christian church. One did not merely declare himself a follower of Mr. Muhammad, then continue leading the same old, sinful, immoral life. The Muslim first had to change his physical and moral self to meet our strict rules. To remain a Muslim he had to maintain those rules.

Few temple meetings were held, for instance, without the minister looking down upon some freshly shaved bald domes of new Muslim brothers in the audience. They had just banished from their lives forever that phony, lye-conked, metallic-looking hair, or "the process," as some call it these days. It grieves me that I don't care where you go, you see this symbol of ignorance and self-hate on so many Negroes' heads. I know it's bound to hurt the feelings of some of my good conked non-Muslim friends—but if you study closely any conked or "processed" Negro, you usually find he is an ignorant Negro. Whatever "show" or "front" he affects, his hair lye-cooked to be "white-looking" fairly shouts to everyone who looks at his head, "I'm ashamed to be a Negro." He will discover, just as I did, that he will be much-improved mentally whenever he discovers enough black self-pride to have that mess clipped off, and then wear the natural hair that God gives black men to wear.

No Muslim smokes—that was another of our rules. Some prospective Muslims found it more difficult to quit tobacco than others found quitting the dope habit. But black men and women quit more easily when we got them to consider seriously how the white man's government cared less about the public's health than about continuing the tobacco industry's *billions* in tax revenue. "What does a serviceman pay for a carton of cigarettes?" a prospective Muslim convert would be asked. It helped him to see that every regularly priced carton he bought meant that the white man's government took around two dollars of a black man's hard-earned money for taxes, not for tobacco.

You may have read somewhere—a lot has been written concerning it—about the Nation of Islam's phenomenal record of dope-addiction cures of longtime junkies. In fact, the *New York Times* carried a story about how some of the social agencies have asked representatives of the Muslim program for clinical suggestions.

The Muslim program began with recognizing that color and addiction have a distinct connection. It is no accident that in the entire Western Hemisphere, the greatest localized concentration of addicts is in *Harlem.*

Our cure program's first major ingredient was the painfully patient work of Muslims who previously were junkies themselves.

In the ghetto's dope jungle, the Muslim ex-junkies would fish out addicts who knew them back in those days. Then with an agonizing patience that might span anywhere from a few months to a year, our ex-junky Muslims would conduct the addicts through the Muslim six-point therapeutic process.

The addict first was brought to admit to himself that he was an addict. Secondly, he was taught *why* he used narcotics. Third, he was shown that there was a *way* to stop addiction. Fourth, the addict's shattered self-image, and ego, were built up until the addict realized that he had, *within,* the self-power to end his addiction. Fifth, the addict voluntarily underwent a cold turkey break with drugs. Sixth, finally cured, now an ex-addict completes the cycle by "fishing" up other addicts whom he knows, and supervising their salvaging.

This sixth stage always instantly eliminated what so often defeats the average social agencies—the characteristic addict's hostility and suspicion. The addict who is "fished" up knew personally that the Muslim approaching him very recently had the same fifteen to thirty dollar a day habit. The Muslim may be this addict's buddy; they had plied the same dope jungle. They even may have been thieves together. The addict had *seen* the Muslim drifting off to sleep leaning against a building, or stepping as high over a matchstick as if it were a dog. And the Muslim, approaching the addict, uses the same old junkie jungle language.

Like the alcoholic, the junkie can never start to cure himself until he recognizes and accepts his true condition. The Muslim sticks like a leech, drumming at his old junkie buddy, "You're hooked, man!" It might take months before the addict comes to grips with this. The curative program is never really underway until this happens.

The next cure-phase is the addict's realization of *why* he takes dope. Still working on his man, right in the old jungle locale, in dives that you wouldn't believe existed, the Muslim often collects audiences of a dozen junkies. They listen only because they know the clean-cut proud Muslim had earlier been like them.

Every addict takes junk to escape something, the Muslim explains. He explains that most black junkies really are trying to narcotize themselves against being a black man in the white man's America. But, actually, the Muslim says, the black man taking dope is only helping the white man to "prove" that the black man is nothing.

The Muslim talks confidentially, and straight. "Daddy, you know I know how you feel. Wasn't I right out here with you? Scratching like a monkey, smelling all bad, living mad, hungry, stealing and running and hiding from Whitey. Man, what's a black man buying Whitey's dope for but to make Whitey richer—killing yourself!"

The Muslim can tell when his quarry is ready to be shown that the way for him to quit dope is through joining the Nation of Islam. The addict is brought into the local Muslim restaurant, he may occasionally be exposed to some other social situations —among proud, clean Muslims who show each other mutual affection and respect instead of the familiar hostility of the ghetto streets. For the first time in years, the addict hears himself called, genuinely, "Brother," "Sir" and "Mr." No one cares about his past. His addiction may casually be mentioned, but if so, it is spoken of as merely an especially tough challenge that he must face. Everyone whom this addict meets is confident that he will kick his habit.

As the addict's new image of himself builds, inevitably he begins thinking that he can break the habit. For the first time he is feeling the effects of black self-pride.

That's a powerful combination for a man who has been existing in the mud of society. In fact, once he is motivated no one can change more completely than the man who has been at the bottom. I call myself the best example of that.

Finally, vitally, this addict will decide for himself that he wants to go on cold turkey. This means to endure the physical agonies of abruptly quitting dope.

When this time comes, ex-addict Muslims will arrange to spend the necessary days in around-the-clock shifts, attending the addict who intends to purge himself, on the way to becoming a Muslim.

When the addict's withdrawal sets in, and he is screaming, cursing, and begging, "Just one shot, man!" the Muslims are right there talking junkie jargon to him. "Baby, knock that monkey off your back! Kick that habit! Kick Whitey off your back!" The addict, writhing in pain, his nose and eyes running, is pouring sweat from head to foot. He's trying to knock his head against the wall, flailing his arms, trying to fight his attendants, he is vomiting, suffering diarrhea. "Don't hold nothing back! Let Whitey go, baby! You're going to stand tall, man! I can see you now in the Fruit of Islam!"

When the awful ordeal is ended, when the grip of dope is broken, the Muslims comfort the weak ex-addict, feeding him soups and broths, to get him on his feet again. He will never forget these brothers who stood by him during this time. He will never forget that it was the Nation of Islam's program which rescued him from the special hell of dope. And that black brother (or the sister, whom Muslim sisters attend) rarely ever will return to the use of narcotics. Instead, the ex-addict when he is proud, clean, renewed, can scarcely wait to hit the same junkie jungle he was in, to "fish" out some buddy and salvage *him!*

If some white man, or "approved" black man, created a narcotics cure program as successful as the one conducted under the aegis of the Muslims, why, there would be government subsidy, and praise and spotlights, and headlines. But we were attacked instead. Why shouldn't the Muslims be subsidized to save millions of dollars a year for the government and the cities? I don't know what addicts' crimes cost nationally, but it is said to be *billions* a year in New York City. An estimated $12 million a year is lost to thieves in Harlem alone.

An addict doesn't work to supply his habit, which may cost anywhere from ten to fifty dollars a day. How could he earn that much? No! The addict steals, he hustles in other ways; he preys upon other human beings like a hawk or a vulture—as I did. Very likely, he is a school drop-out, the same as I was, an Army reject, psychologically unsuited to a job even if he was offered one, the same as I was.

Women addicts "boost" (shoplift), or they prostitute themselves. Muslim sisters talk hard to black prostitutes who are struggling to quit using dope in order to qualify morally to become registered Muslims. "You are helping the white man to regard your body as a garbage can—"

Numerous "exposés" of the Nation of Islam have implied that Mr. Muhammad's followers were chiefly ex-cons and junkies. In the early years, yes, the converts from society's lowest levels were a sizable part of the Nation's broad base of membership. Always Mr. Muhammad instructed us, "Go after the black man in the mud." Often, he said, those converted made the best Muslims.

But gradually we recruited other black people—the "good Christians" whom we "fished" from their churches. Then, an increase began in the membership percentage of educated and trained Negroes. For each rally attracted to the local temple a few more of that particular city's so-called "middle-class" Negroes, the type who previously had scoffed at us "Black Muslims" as "demagogues," and "hate-teachers," "black racists" and all the rest of the names. The Muslim truths—listened to, thought about—reaped for us a growing quota of young black men and women. For those with training and talents, the Nation of Islam had plenty of positions where those abilities were needed.

There were some registered Muslims who would never reveal their membership, except to other Muslims, because of their positions in the white man's world. There were, I know, a few, who because of their positions were known only to their ministers and to Mr. Elijah Muhammad.

In 1961, our Nation flourished. Our newspaper *Muhammad Speaks'* full back page carried an architect's drawing of a $20 million Islamic Center proposed to be built in Chicago. Every Muslim was making personal financial contribution toward the Center. It would include a beautiful mosque, school, library, and hospital, and a museum documenting the black man's glorious history.

Mr. Muhammad visited the Muslim countries, and upon his return he directed that we would begin calling our temples "mosques."

There was a sharp climb now, too, in the number of Muslim-owned small businesses. Our businesses sought to demonstrate to the black people what black people could do for themselves—if they would only unify, trade with each other—exclusively where possible—and hire each other, and in so doing, keep black money within the black communities, just as other minorities did.

Recordings of Mr. Muhammad's speeches were now regularly being broadcast across America over small radio stations. In Detroit and Chicago, school-age Muslim children attended our two Universities of Islam—through high school in Chicago, and through junior high in Detroit. Starting from kindergarten, they learned of the black man's glorious history and from the third grade they studied the black man's original language, Arabic.

Mr. Muhammad's eight children now were all deeply involved in key capacities in the Nation of Islam. I took a deep personal pride in having had something to do with that—at least in some cases, years before. When Mr. Muhammad had sent me out in his service as a minister, I began to feel it was a shame that his children worked as some of them then did for the white man, in factories, construction work, driving taxis, things like that. I felt that I should work for Mr. Muhammad's family as sincerely as I worked for him. I urged Mr. Muhammad to let me put on a special drive within our few small mosques, to raise funds which would enable those of his children working for the white man to be instead employed within our Nation. Mr. Muhammad agreed, the special fund drive did prove successful, and his children gradually did begin working for the Nation. Emanuel, the oldest, today runs the dry-cleaning plant. Sister Ethel (Muhammad) Sharrieff is the Muslim Sisters' Supreme Instructor. (Her husband, Raymond Sharrieff, is Supreme Captain of the Fruit of Islam.) Sister Lottie Muhammad supervises the two Universities of Islam. Nathaniel Muhammad assists Emanuel in the dry-cleaning plant. Herbert Muhammad now publishes *Muhammad Speaks*, the Nation's newspaper that I began. Elijah Muhammad, Jr., is the Fruit of Islam Assistant Supreme Captain. Wallace Muhammad was the Philadelphia Mosque Minister, until finally he was suspended from the Nation along with me—for reasons I will go into. The youngest child, Akbar Muhammad, the family student, attends the University of Cairo at El-Azhar. Akbar also has broken with his father.

I believe that it was too strenuous a marathon of long speeches that Mr. Muhammad made at our big rallies which, abruptly, badly aggravated his long-bothersome bronchial asthmatic condition.

Just in conversation, Mr. Muhammad would suddenly begin coughing, and the coughing tempo would increase until it racked his slight body.

Mr. Muhammad almost doubled up sometimes. Soon, he had to take to his bed. As hard as he tried not to, as deeply as it grieved him, he had to cancel several long-scheduled appearances at big-city rallies. Thousands were disappointed to have to hear me instead, or other poor substitutes for Mr. Muhammad in person.

Members of the Nation were deeply concerned. Doctors recommended a dry climate. The Nation bought Mr. Muhammad a home in Phoenix, Arizona. One of the first times I visited Mr. Muhammad there, I stepped off a plane into flashing and whirring cameras until I wondered who was behind me. Then I saw the cameramen's guns; they were from the Arizona Intelligence Division.

The wire of our Nation of Islam brought all Muslims the joyful news that the Arizona climate did vastly relieve the Messenger's suffering. Since then he has spent most of each year in Phoenix.

Despite the fact that Mr. Muhammad, convalescing, could no longer work the daily long hours he had previously worked in Chicago, he was now more than ever burdened with heavy decision-making and administrative duties. In every respect, the Nation was expanded both internally and externally. Mr. Muhammad simply could no longer allot as much time as previously to considering and deciding which public-speaking, radio, and television requests he felt I should accept—as well as to some organizational matters which I had always brought to him for advice or decision.

Mr. Muhammad evidenced the depth of his trust in me. In those areas I've described, he told me to make the decisions myself. He said that my guideline should be whatever I felt was wise—whatever was in the general good interests of our Nation of Islam.

"Brother Malcolm, I want you to become well known," Mr. Muhammad told me one day. "Because if you are well known, it will make *me* better known," he went on.

"But, Brother Malcolm, there is something you need to know. You will grow to be hated when you become well known. Because usually people get jealous of public figures."

Nothing that Mr. Muhammad ever said to me was more prophetic.

Domestic Law and International Order*

Eldridge Cleaver

The police department and the armed forces are the two arms of the power structure, the muscles of control and enforcement. They have deadly weapons with which to inflict pain on the human body. They know how to bring about horrible deaths. They have clubs with which to beat the body and the head. They have bullets and guns with which to tear holes in the flesh, to smash bones, to disable and kill. They use force, to make you do what the deciders have decided you must do.

Every country on earth has these agencies of force. The people everywhere fear this terror and force. To them it is like a snarling wild beast which can put an end to one's dreams. They punish. They have cells and prisons to lock you up in. They pass out sentences. They won't let you go when you want to. You have to stay put until they give the word. If your mother is dying, you can't go to her bedside to say goodbye or to her graveside to see her lowered into the earth, to see her, for the last time, swallowed up by that black hole.

The techniques of the enforcers are many: firing squads, gas chambers, electric chairs, torture chambers, the garrote, the guillotine, the tightening rope around your throat. It has been found that the death penalty is necessary to back up the law, to make it easier to enforce, to deter transgressions against the penal code. That everybody doesn't believe in the same laws is beside the point.

Which laws get enforced depends on who is in power. If the capitalists are in power, they enforce laws designed to protect their system, their way of life. They have a particular abhorrence for crimes against property, but are prepared to be liberal and show a modicum of compassion for crimes against the person—unless, of course, an instance of the latter is combined with an instance of the former. In such cases, nothing can stop them from throwing the whole book at the offender. For instance, armed rob-

* From Eldridge Cleaver, *Soul on Ice* (New York: McGraw-Hill Book Company, 1968), pp. 128–37. Copyright © 1968 by Eldridge Cleaver. Used with permission of McGraw-Hill Book Company.

bery with violence, to a capitalist, is the very epitome of evil. Ask any banker what he thinks of it.

If Communists are in power, they enforce laws designed to protect their system, their way of life. To them, the horror of horrors is the speculator, that man of magic who has mastered the art of getting something with nothing and who in America would be a member in good standing of his local Chamber of Commerce.

"The people," however, are nowhere consulted, although everywhere everything is done always in their name and ostensibly for their betterment, while their real-life problems go unsolved. "The people" are a rubber stamp for the crafty and sly. And no problem can be solved without taking the police department and the armed forces into account. Both kings and bookies understand this, as do first ladies and common prostitutes.

The police do on the domestic level what the armed forces do on the international level: protect the way of life of those in power. The police patrol the city, cordon off communities, blockade neighborhoods, invade homes, search for that which is hidden. The armed forces patrol the world, invade countries and continents, cordon off nations, blockade islands and whole peoples; they will also overrun villages, neighborhoods, enter homes, huts, caves, searching for that which is hidden. The policeman and the soldier will violate your person, smoke you out with various gases. Each will shoot you, beat your head and body with sticks and clubs, with rifle butts, run you through with bayonets, shoot holes in your flesh, kill you. They each have unlimited firepower. They will use all that is necessary to bring you to your knees. They won't take no for an answer. If you resist their sticks, they draw their guns. If you resist their guns, they call for reinforcements with bigger guns. Eventually they will come in tanks, in jets, in ships. They will not rest until you surrender or are killed. The policeman and the soldier will have the last word.

Both police and the armed forces follow orders. Orders. Orders flow from the top down. Up there, behind closed doors, in antechambers, in conference rooms, gavels bang on the tables, the tinkling of silver decanters can be heard as icewater is poured by well-fed, conservatively dressed men in hornrimmed glasses, fashionably dressed American widows with rejuvenated faces and tinted hair, the air permeated with the square humor of Bob Hope jokes. Here all the talking is done, all the thinking, all the deciding. Gray rabbits of men scurry forth from the conference room to spread the decisions throughout the city, as News. Carrying out orders is a job, a way of meeting the payments on the house, a way of providing for one's kiddies. In the armed forces it is also a duty, patriotism. Not to do so is treason.

Every city has its police department. No city would be complete without one. It would be sheer madness to try operating an American city without the heat, the fuzz, the man. Americans are too far gone, or else they haven't arrived yet; the center does not exist, only the extremes. Take away the cops and Americans would have a coast-to-coast free-for-all. There are, of course, a few citizens who carry their own private cops around with them, built into their souls. But there is robbery in the land, and larceny, murder, rape, burglary, theft, swindles, all brands of crime, profit, rent, interest—and these blasé descendants of Pilgrims are at each other's throats. To complicate matters, there are also rich people and poor people in America. There are Negroes and whites, Indians, Puerto Ricans, Mexicans, Jews, Chinese, Arabs, Japanese—all with equal rights but unequal possessions. Some are haves and some are have-nots. All have been taught to worship at the shrine of General Motors. The whites are on top in America and they want to stay there, up there. They are also on top in the world, on the international level, and they want to stay up there, too. Everywhere there are those who want to smash this precious toy clock of a system, they want ever so much to change it, to rearrange things, to pull the whites down off their high horse and make them equal. Everywhere the whites are fighting to prolong their status, to retard the erosion of their position. In America, when everything else fails, they call out the police. On the international level, when everything else fails, they call out the armed forces.

A strange thing happened in Watts, in 1965, August. The blacks, who in this land of private property have all private and no property, got excited into an uproar because they noticed a cop before he had a chance to wash the blood off his hands. Usually the police department can handle such flare-ups. But this time it was different. Things got out of hand. The blacks were running amok, burning, shooting, breaking. The police department was powerless to control them; the chief called for reinforcements. Out came the National Guard, that ambiguous hybrid from the twilight zone where the domestic army merges with the international; that hypocritical force poised within America and capable of action on either level, capable of backing up either the police or the armed forces. Unleashing their formidable firepower, they crushed the blacks. But things will never be the same again. Too many people saw that those who turned the other cheek in Watts got their whole head blown off. At the same time, heads were being blown off in Vietnam. America was embarrassed, not by the quality of her deeds but by the surplus of publicity focused upon her negative selling points, and a little frightened because of what all those dead bodies, on two fronts, implied. Those corpses spoke eloquently of potential allies and alliances. A community of interest began to emerge, dripping with blood, out of the ashes of Watts. The blacks in Watts and all over America could now see the Viet Cong's point: both were on the receiving end of what the armed forces were dishing out.

So now the blacks, stung by the new knowledge they have unearthed, cry out: "POLICE BRUTALITY!" From one end of the country to the other, the new war cry is raised. The youth, those nodes of compulsive energy who are all fuel and muscle, race their motors, itch to do something. The Uncle Toms, no longer willing to get down on their knees to lick boots, do so from a squatting position. The black bourgeoisie call for Citizens' Review Boards, to assert civilian control over the activity of the police. In back rooms, in dark stinking corners of the ghettos, self-conscious black men curse their own cowardice and stare at their rifles and pistols and shotguns laid out on tables before them, trembling as they wish for a manly impulse to course through their bodies and send them screaming mad into the streets shooting from the hip. Black women look at their men as if they are bugs, curious growths of flesh playing an inscrutable waiting game. Violence becomes a homing pigeon floating through the ghettos seeking a black brain in which to roost for a season.

In their rage against the police, against police brutality, the blacks lose sight of the fundamental reality: that the police are only an instrument for the implementation of the policies of those who make the decisions. Police brutality is only one facet of the crystal of terror and oppression. Behind police brutality there is social brutality, economic brutality, and political brutality. From the perspective of the ghetto, this is not easy to discern: the TV newscaster and the radio announcer and the editorialists of the newspapers are wizards of the smoke screen and the snow job.

What is true on the international level is true also at home; except that the ace up the sleeve is easier to detect in the international arena. Who would maintain that American soldiers are in Vietnam on their own motion? They were conscripted into the armed forces and taught the wisdom of obeying orders. They were sent to Vietnam by orders of the generals in the Pentagon, who receive them from the Secretary of Defense, who receives them from the President, who is shrouded in mystery. The soldier in the field in Vietnam, the man who lies in the grass and squeezes the trigger when a little half-starved, trembling Vietnamese peasant crosses his sights, is only following orders, carrying out a policy and a plan. He hardly knows what it is all about. They have him wired-up tight with the slogans of TV and the World Series. All he knows is that he has been assigned to carry out a certain ritual of duties. He is well trained and does the best he can. He does a good job. He may want to please those above him with the quality of his performance. He may want to make sergeant, or better. This man is from some hicky farm in Shit Creek, Georgia. He only knew whom to kill after passing through boot camp. He could just as well come out ready to kill Swedes. He will kill a Swede dead, if he is ordered to do so.

Same for the policeman in Watts. He is not there on his own. They have all been assigned. They have been told what to do and what not to do. They have also been told what they better not do. So when they continually do something, in every filthy ghetto in this shitty land, it means only that they are following orders.

It's no secret that in America the blacks are in total rebellion against the System. They want to get their nuts out of the sand. They don't like the way America is run, from top to bottom. In America, everything is owned. Everything is held as private property. Someone has a brand on everything. There is nothing left over. Until recently, the blacks themselves were counted as part of somebody's private property, along with the chickens and goats. The blacks have not forgotten this, principally because they are still treated as if they are part of someone's inventory of assets—or perhaps, in this day of rage against the costs of welfare, blacks are listed among the nation's liabilities. On any account, however, blacks are in no position to respect or help maintain the institution of private property. What they want is to figure out a way to get some of that property for themselves, to divert it to their own needs. This is what it is all about, and this is the real brutality involved. This is the source of all brutality.

The police are the armed guardians of the social order. The blacks are the chief domestic victims of the American social order. A conflict of interest exists, therefore, between the blacks and the police. It is not solely a matter of trigger-happy cops, of brutal cops who love to crack black heads. Mostly it's a job to them. It pays good. And there are numerous fringe benefits. The real problem is a trigger-happy social order.

The Utopians speak of a day when there will be no police. There will be nothing for them to do. Every man will do his duty, will respect the rights of his neighbor, will not disturb the peace. The needs of all will be taken care of. Everyone will have sympathy for his fellow man. There will be no such thing as crime. There will be, of course, no prisons. No electric chairs, no gas chambers. The hangman's rope will be the thing of the past. The entire earth will be a land of plenty. There will be no crimes against property, no speculation.

It is easy to see that we are not on the verge of entering Utopia: there are cops everywhere. North and South, the Negroes are the have-nots. They see property all around them, property that is owned by whites. In this regard, the black bourgeoisie has become nothing but a ridiculous nuisance. Having waged a battle for entrance into the American mainstream continually for fifty years, all of the black bourgeoisie's defenses are directed outward, against the whites. They have no defenses against the blacks and no time to erect any. The black masses can handle them any time they choose, with one mighty blow. But the white bourgeoisie presents a bigger problem, those whites who own everything. With many shackled by unemployment, hatred in black hearts for this system of private property increases daily. The sanctity surrounding property is being called into question. The mystique of the deed of ownership is melting away. In other parts of the world, peasants rise up and expropriate the land from the former owners. Blacks in America see that the deed is not eternal, that it is not signed by God, and that new deeds, making blacks the owners, can be drawn up.

The Black Muslims raised the cry, *"WE MUST HAVE SOME LAND!" "SOME LAND OF OUR OWN OR ELSE!"* Blacks in America shrink from the colossus of General Motors. They can't see how to wade through that thicket of common stocks, preferred stocks, bonds and debentures. They only know that General Motors is huge, that it has billions of dollars under its control, that it owns land, that its subsidiaries are legion, that it is a repository of vast powers. The blacks want to crack the nut of General Motors. They are meditating on it. Meanwhile, they must learn that the police take orders from General Motors. And that the Bank of America has something to do with them even though they don't have a righteous penny in the bank. They have no bank accounts, only bills to pay. The only way they know of making withdrawals from the bank is at the point of a gun. The shiny fronts of skyscrapers intimidate them. They do not own them. They feel alienated from the very sidewalks on which they walk. This white man's country, this white man's world. Overflowing with men of color. An economy consecrated to the succor of the whites. Blacks are incidental. The war on poverty, that monstrous insult to the rippling muscles in a black man's arms, is an index of how men actually sit down and plot each other's deaths, actually sit down with slide rules and calculate how to hide bread from the hungry. And the black bourgeoisie greedily sopping up what crumbs are tossed into their dark corner.

There are 20,000,000 of these blacks in America, probably more. Today they repeat, in awe, this magic number to themselves: there are 20,000,000 of us! They shout this to each other in humiliated astonishment. No one need tell them that there is vast power latent in their mass. They know that 20,000,000 of anything is enough to get some recognition and consideration. They know also that they must harness their number and hone it into a sword with a sharp cutting edge. White General Motors also knows that the unity of these 20,000,000 ragamuffins will spell the death of the system of its being. At all costs, then, they will seek to keep these blacks from uniting, from becoming bold and revolutionary. These white property owners know that they must keep the blacks cowardly and intimidated. By a complex communications system of hints and signals, certain orders are given to the chief of police and the sheriff, who pass them on to their men, the footsoldiers in the trenches of the ghetto.

We experience this system of control as madness. So that Leonard Deadwyler, one of these 20,000,000 blacks, is rushing his pregnant wife to the hospital and is shot dead by a policeman. An accident. That the sun rises in the east and sets in the west is also an accident, by design. The blacks are up in arms. From one end of America to the other, blacks are outraged at this accident, this latest evidence of what an accident-prone people they are, of the cruelty and pain of their lives, these blacks at the mercy of trigger-happy Yankees and Rebs in coalition against their skin. They want the policeman's blood as a sign that the Viet Cong is not the only answer. A sign to save them from the deaths they must die, and inflict. The power structure, without so much as blinking an eye, wouldn't mind tossing Bova to the mob, to restore law and order, but it knows in the vaults of its strength that at all cost the blacks must be kept at bay, that it must uphold the police department, its Guardian. Nothing must be allowed to threaten the set-up. Justice is secondary. Security is the byword.

Meanwhile, blacks are looking on and asking tactical questions. They are asked to die for the System in Vietnam. In Watts they are killed by it. Now—*NOW!*—they are asking each other, in dead earnest: Why not die right here in Babylon fighting for a better life, like the Viet Cong? If those little cats can do it, what's wrong with big studs like us?

A mood sets in, spreads across America, across the face of Babylon, jells in black hearts everywhere.